THE VIKIN

E

EDMUND BURKE (1729–97) was born in Dublin, and educated at Abraham Shackleton's Quaker school in Balitore and Trinity College, Dublin. In 1730 he entered the Middle Temple in London, but soon left law for literature and, later, politics. His first publication, the parodic *A Vindication of Natural Society* (1756), was followed in 1757 by *A Philosophical Inquiry into the Origin of Our Ideas of the Sublime and the Beautiful,* a text that was to influence the writers of the Romantic period. His political career began in 1765 when, having become secretary to the then Prime Minister the Marquis of Rockingham, he was made member of Parliament for Wendover. His oratory gained him influence in the Whig party, although he was not to hold office until the downfall of the Tories under Lord North in 1783. Burke became M.P. for Bristol in 1774, but his support for the then unpopular causes of Catholic Emancipation and the relaxation of the Irish Trade laws cost him the seat in 1780. Subsequently elected M.P. for Malton in 1781, he became paymaster of the forces in 1782, resigned with Fox and returned to the same office under the coalition government in 1783. He retired in 1794 and received a large pension from the ministry.

A large part of Burke's political career was dedicated to the problem of India (he took part in the investigation of the East India Company affair) and he wrote widely on the subject. Throughout his career he wrote and spoke on many of the major governmental and constitutional issues of his day: the troubles in America resulted in his *Thoughts on Present Discontents* (1770) and *Letter to the Sheriffs of Bristol* (1777), and the French Revolution produced one of his most famous works, *Reflections on the Revolution in France* (1790). This latter work explained at some length his opposition to the doctrines of the revolution and it was this subject that was to be the last great political theme of his public life.

ISAAC KRAMNICK was born in 1938 and educated at Harvard University, where he received a B.A. degree in 1959 and a Ph.D. in 1965, and at Peterhouse, Cambridge. He has taught at Harvard, Brandeis, Yale, and Cornell, where he is now professor of government. He is married to Miriam Brody and lives in Ithaca, New York. Among his publications are *Bolingbroke and His Circle*, *The Rage of Edmund Burke*, and numerous articles on eighteenth-century topics. He has edited *The Federalist Papers*, William Godwin's *Enquiry Concerning Political Justice*, Thomas Paine's *Common Sense*, and the *Thomas Paine Reader* for Penguin Classics. Most recently he is the author, with Barry Sheerman, M.P., of *Laski: A Life on the Left*, and, with R. Laurence Moore, of *The Godless Constitution*.

Each volume in the Viking Portable Library either presents a representative selection from the works of a single outstanding writer or offers a comprehensive anthology on a special subject. Averaging 700 pages in length and designed for compactness and readability, these books fill a need not met by other compilations. All are edited by distinguished authorities who have written introductory essays and included other helpful material.

The Portable
EDMUND BURKE

Edited with an Introduction by

Isaac Kramnick

PENGUIN BOOKS

PENGUIN BOOKS
Published by the Penguin Group
Penguin Group (USA) Inc., 375 Hudson Street, New York, New York 10014, U.S.A.
Penguin Group (Canada), 90 Eglinton Avenue East, Suite 700, Toronto,
Ontario, Canada M4P 2Y3 (a division of Pearson Penguin Canada Inc.)
Penguin Books Ltd, 80 Strand, London WC2R 0RL, England
Penguin Ireland, 25 St Stephen's Green, Dublin 2, Ireland (a division of Penguin Books Ltd)
Penguin Group (Australia), 250 Camberwell Road, Camberwell,
Victoria 3124, Australia (a division of Pearson Australia Group Pty Ltd)
Penguin Books India Pvt Ltd, 11 Community Centre, Panchsheel Park, New Delhi – 110 017, India
Penguin Group (NZ), cnr Airborne and Rosedale Roads,
Albany, Auckland 1310, New Zealand (a division of Pearson New Zealand Ltd)
Penguin Books (South Africa) (Pty) Ltd, 24 Sturdee Avenue,
Rosebank, Johannesburg 2196, South Africa

Penguin Books Ltd, Registered Offices: 80 Strand, London WC2R 0RL, England

First published in Penguin Books 1999

10

LIBRARY OF CONGRESS CATALOGING IN PUBLICATION DATA
Burke, Edmund, 1729–1797.
[Selections. 1999]
The portable Edmund Burke / edited with an introduction
by Isaac Kramnick.
p. cm.—(The Viking portable library)
Includes bibliographical references.
ISBN 0 14 02.6760 3
1. Political science—Early works to 1800. 2. Conservatism.
3. Great Britain—Politics and government—18th century.
I. Kramnick, Isaac. II. Title. III. Series.
JC176.B826 1999
320′.092—dc21 98-41476

Printed in the United States of America
Set in Bembo

CONTENTS

III. AMERICA AND REVOLUTION

IV. IRELAND AND CATHOLICISM

V. INDIA AND COLONIALISM

VI. THE FRENCH REVOLUTION

VII. SELECTED LETTERS

INTRODUCTION

I.

EDMUND BURKE played a central role in the political history of England during the first forty years of George III's long reign. In the House of Commons he defended the cause of the American colonies, championed the rights of persecuted Catholics in England and Ireland, criticized the parliamentary meddling of the Hanoverian monarchy, and decried the rape of the Indian subcontinent by English adventurers. In that same house he also rejected pleas for the reform of the archaic English Constitution, ridiculed efforts to lift the civil restrictions on Unitarian and other Protestant dissenters, and, most famously, called down the wrath of God and right-thinking Englishmen on the French revolutionaries and their Jacobin sympathizers in England. Burke's historical and intellectual importance rests, however, on more than this fascinating and controversial career; he stands, after all, as the intellectual source of one of the modern world's most influential political visions—conservatism. His writings and speeches are the bible, and he the prophet of that ideology, in much the same way that *The Second Treatise of Government* and *The Communist Manifesto* and John Locke and Karl Marx are the bibles and prophets of liberalism and communism respectively. In reviewing and assessing the historical person, role, and impact of Burke one must, thus, confront both the statesman of Georgian England and the philosopher of conservatism.

Even had Burke not become the philosopher of conservatism and been only the Whig statesman, his parliamentary role would have itself been worthy of posterity's notice. His was a great success story: an outsider of no great means rises by dint of his own wits, skills, and energy to the inner circles of power in a closed aristocratic political community. To be sure, he never quite made it to the real pinnacles of power; instead he became the articulate defender of a class that refused to accept him as one of its own. Still, his career is linked closely with much of consequence that transpired in the public life of England in the second half of the eighteenth century.

This prophetic voice of Anglo-American conservatism was Irish, born in Dublin in 1729 to a Protestant father and a Catholic mother. He was raised in the faith of his solicitor father and schooled at Dublin's famous Trinity College, an Anglican institution. In the 1750s Burke moved to London to study law, though he eventually turned to literary and intellectual pursuits in a circle that included Samuel Johnson and Oliver Goldsmith. After writing two well-received essays on society and aesthetics, he turned his attention to politics. He entered public life in the middle 1760s as private secretary to the great Whig magnate the marquis of Rockingham, which led to his election in 1765 to the House of Commons, where he would sit until 1794. In the 1770s, as part of Lord Rockingham's "political connection," he defended the American colonies in their developing clash with English commercial and imperial policy.

By 1780 he had also emerged as the principal critic of what was considered George III's corrupt interference with the independence of the House of Commons. Although Burke saw the power of the Crown as a threat to the ancient English Constitution and its sacred principles of mixed government and the separation of power, in the 1780s he also spoke out strongly against the radical agitation associated with the Yorkshire movement and the reform effort of the Younger Pitt. Democratic enlargement of the suffrage was, he argued, also a threat to the perfectly balanced English Constitution; it would admit the people to too great a share of power.

In the late 1780s Burke turned much of his parliamentary energy to two causes, the impeachment proceedings against Warren Hastings, the former governor-general of the East India Company, and legislative efforts to improve the status of Catholics in both England and Ireland. These efforts paled in significance, however, as the French Revolution dominated the last years of his life. More than any other figure in English public life, Burke mobilized sentiment against the Jacobin cause at home and abroad. In the course of this, he split the Whig party, denouncing his former colleagues for their continued sympathy with the French experiment.

Few of his contemporaries had neutral views on this amazing public career. Burke was passionately worshiped and with equal passion hated. With puffy cheeks, fiery red hair, and excessive emotion, he held forth in the senate forum that was the unreformed House of Commons until three years before his death, in 1797. Some would be moved by the fount of republican wisdom, and others would rush for the exits. Perhaps this lay behind his ultimate failure to achieve the heights of political success: his intensity and passionate involvement were not the style appropriate for the pragmatic world of political management and leadership. But this is Burke the statesman; there is also Burke the enduring philosopher of conservatism.

II.

Burke's conservatism is grounded in skepticism. He stands in revolt against the eighteenth century and, as he saw it, the "smugness of adulterated metaphysics." The "faith in the dogmatism of philosophers" had led Enlightenment thinkers to place faith in reason and abstract ideas, in speculation and a priori principles of natural right, freedom, and equality, as the basis on which to reform existing government. The English had no such illusions, he argued; they understood the complexity and fragility of human nature and human institutions; they were not "the converts of Rousseau . . . the disciples of Voltaire; Helvetius [had] made no progress amongst [them]." The English, according to Burke, regarded the rampant rationalism of the French philosophers and their quest for an ideal and perfect political order with sluggish skepticism. They understood that since the nature of man was intricate and society complex, "simple governments are fundamentally defective."[1]

Burke's political skepticism was, however, by no means simply a reaction to the trauma of the French Revolution. His opposition to abstract reasoning in philosophy and social matters appeared as early as his undergraduate years at Trinity College, Dublin, during the late 1740s. It also appeared in the religious and philosophical essays he produced between his graduation and the publication, in 1756, of his attack on Lord Bolingbroke's religious rationalism as politically extrapolated. We know, for example, that in these years Burke attacked "great subtleties and refinements of reasoning," which, he felt, produced disorders of the brain. "Custom is to be regarded with great deference" as "a more sure guide than our theories."[2] The conservative thrust of the skepticism found in the *Reflections on the Revolution in France* is also seen writ large in Burke's response to radical demands in England for democratic reform of Parliament in the early 1780s. The agitation, he declared, approached the Constitution totally oblivious to the fact that the "House of Commons is a legislative body, corporate by prescription, not made upon any given theory." The English radicals assumed that legislators could remake governments when all wise men knew that "a prescriptive government never was made upon any foregone theory." How ridiculous, then, to put governments on procrustean beds and make them fit "the theories which learned and speculative men have made."[3] Such speculators, with their ideal blueprints, were political magicians cutting up the Constitution into pieces "in order to boil it, with the puddle of their compounds, into youth and vigor."[4]

But this is by no means the full measure of Burke's skepticism. It can be seen even more completely in his conception of the art of governing, and in his views on the limited rational capacity of mankind. The conservative skeptic like Burke is deeply interested in the character and style of those who govern. He is convinced that pursuit of policies, of preconceived speculative plans—in short, of what we might today call ideology—is inappropriate behavior for political leadership. The major function of a magistrate is seen as prudential manager. Stable government must eschew ideology. What matters most is not the pursuit of policy but the quality of leadership. In Burke's writings, this theme of the importance of wise management is carefully developed.

Government for Burke was not a science with exact and precise methods and conclusions; it was an art, practiced by artists skilled in prudence. Governors had to approach political issues according to their peculiar circumstances, not in light of abstract ideas or general theories of government. In his speeches on America and the taxation issue, Burke repeatedly insisted that "metaphysical distinctions" of abstract right be kept out of the deliberation and that prudence and virtuous discretion rule the day. Good political leadership was informed by principle, not ruled by it; and, more importantly, it was guided by circumstances. The wise magistrate, Burke argued, ought to respect the temper and opinions of a particular people, the spirit of their age; and, particularly, ought to respect and not tamper with the manners of the people, which in many ways formed the basis of their laws.

However distinguished his own public career in Parliament was, Burke knew that the likes of himself were not those rightly destined to be in the front ranks of England's rulers. No matter how much he might proclaim himself not a friend to aristocracy, the overwhelming thrust of his writings insists that only men of breeding possess this quality of prudence so fundamental to the art of governing. This, after all, was the ultimate sin of the French: their failure to recognize the prescriptive role of aristocracy and its production of qualified governors. Governors ought "to see nothing low and sordid from one's infancy," ought to stand upon "elevated ground," "to have leisure to read, to reflect, to converse."[5] Before the great families, Burke humbly denies his capacity to possess the quality of character and skills of learning required to make a prudential magistrate; thus he writes to the duke of Richmond:

> Persons in your station of life ought to have long views. You people of great families in hereditary trusts and fortunes, are not like such as I am, who, whatever we may be, by the rapidity of our growth, and even by the fruit we bear, and flatter ourselves that while we creep on the ground, we belly into melons that are exquisite for size and flavor, yet still are but annual plants, that perish without season, and leave no sort of traces behind us. You, if you are what you ought to be, are in my eye the great oaks that shade a country, and perpetuate your benefits from generation to generation.[6]

No greater threat existed to the likes of the duke of Richmond than the French Revolution and its ideals, in Burke's estimation. His monumental achievement was in denouncing the Revolution while all about him political and intellectual sentiment in Britain celebrated it.

For Burke's contemporaries the Revolution was testimony to the imminence of the millennium. It was, as Shelley saw it, "the master theme of the epoch in which we live."[7] On this master theme Blake, the young Coleridge, Wordsworth, and Southey wrote poems of revolution. Looking back on those years, Southey, by then respectable and Tory, wrote that "few persons but those who have lived [through the 1790s] can conceive or comprehend . . . what a visionary world seemed to open upon those who were just entering it. Old things seemed passing away and nothing was dreamt of but the regeneration of the human race."[8] All the poets echoed these sentiments. For Wordsworth, "bliss was it in that dawn to be alive." For Blake, the friend of Mary Wollstonecraft and Thomas Paine, "the times are ended . . . the morning 'gins to break."[9] For William Hazlitt it was "that glad dawn of the day-star of liberty; that spring-time of the world, in which the hopes and expectations of the human race seemed opening in the same gay career with our own."[10]

The radical Protestant minister Richard Price preached sermons on the imminent arrival of the kingdom of heaven. He informed his prosperous bourgeois audience that a heavenly city would be realized in this world. They were witness to "a progressive improvement in human affairs which will terminate in greater degrees of light and virtue and happiness than have yet been known." There was no doubt, he noted, that the "present day world is unspeakably different from what it was." Superstition was giving ground, "the world outgrowing its evils . . . anti-Christ falling and the millennium hastening."[11] Price echoed what Hazlitt called "the spirit of the age." "We live in happier times than our forefathers." The "shades of night are departing," Price noted characteristically; "the day dawns."[12]

Joseph Priestley, the great scientist and also radical Protestant minister, was ecstatic about the prospects for millennial regeneration. The French and American Revolutions were, according to Priestley, "unparalleled in all history." They opened a new and wonderful era in the history of mankind. They moved the world "from darkness to light, from superstition to sound knowledge and from a most debasing servitude to a state of the most exalted freedom."[13]

It was against this vision of secular perfection, of the absolute elimination of evil and misery that Burke reacted in the late eighteenth century. It is because he rejected this optimism and, in turn, insisted on the inevitability of sin, suffering, and imperfection, and did it in a prose style of compelling grandeur, that he has attracted to his name the legions of disciples who spread his teachings to this day.

The principal source of these teachings is Burke's *Reflections on the Revolution in France.* In it his basic tactic is to contrast the virtuous English and the radical French, which at the same time is to contrast virtuous English and radical millenarian English. Priestley and Price had abandoned the English past, and this disrespect led ultimately to the crimes of the Jacobins. The English in 1688 had no "idea of the fabrication of a new government." Even in 1790, Burke suggests, such thoughts "fill us with disgust and horror."

Inferior men governed France and pushed their claims in England. "Are all orders, ranks, and distinctions to be confounded?" Burke asks. This would "pervert" the natural order of things, would "set up on high in the air what is required to be on the ground." The radicals (French and English) are guilty of "selfish and mischievous ambition," an ambition that is undermining the age of chivalry and its corporate-feudal worldview. Ambitious man would not find his self-fulfillment outside himself in guild, church, city, or in the secure knowledge that he kept to God's assigned place. Ambitious man is the individualist of liberal ideology who would experience his individual dignity not as an expression of some ascribed role but as a personal achievement reflecting his own intrinsic talent and merit. Before such ambitious men the corporate medieval world would fall, and from it would grow the individualism of the new age. Burke sees all of this, and he rejects the ideology of these sinful radicals. To be virtuous for Burke is "to be attached to the subdivision, to love the little platoon we belong to in society."[14] As the old order crumbles, the acceptance of one's place in it is transformed by Burke into the love for the particular link in the chain of being that one occupies.

Burke takes the very vocabulary of the radicals and translates it back into the preliberal ethos of chivalry. Equality and happiness are transposed. They exist only in the old order where each one knows his place. Many twentieth-century disciples of Burke have drunk deep at this particular Burkean fountain.

> You would have had a protected, satisfied, laborious, and obedient people, taught to seek and to recognise the happiness that is to be found by virtue in all conditions; in which consists the true moral equality of mankind, and not in that monstrous fiction, which by inspiring false ideas and vain expectations into men destined to travel in the obscure walk of laborious life, serves only to aggravate and embitter that real inequality which it never can remove; and which the order of civil life establishes as much for the benefit of those whom it must leave in an humble state, as those whom it is able to exalt to a condition more splendid but not more happy.[15]

Having rejected the Lockean liberal ideal of equality, the elimination of ascribed distinctions, Burke moves on to Locke's theory of government. In the liberal scheme of things government is a neutral arbiter, an umpire over the race for wealth. It is a necessary evil because autonomous self-directed individuals occasionally bump into each other. Usually well-meaning and rational, individuals sometimes forget themselves and interfere with one another's natural rights. On these occasions government is called in to protect the right of the aggrieved party. But liberal government is out to do no more, neither to dictate beliefs nor to lead citizens to a just or virtuous life. Government for Burke, however, has much more to do than this passive policing function. It is a positive tool of repressing, in the real sense of the term. Burke rejects, as have generations of conservatives after him, the optimism and rationalism of the liberal theory of human nature. Deep reservoirs of evil and sin lurk in human nature, according to Burke, and government is necessary not as an occasional umpire but as an indispensable external authority to thwart and repress the antisocial inclinations of individuals. To govern is to restrain man.

The source of Burke's ideal is, of course, religion. As the liberal optimism of the Enlightenment had been premised on the denial of original sin (about the only thing all the philosophes, including Rousseau, agreed upon), so Burke revives the staple of the chivalric worldview. Government's function, he writes, is not to protect natural rights but to provide authority, constraint, and domination.

> Society requires not only that the passions of individuals should be subjected, but that even in the mass and body, as well as in the individual, the inclinations of men should frequently be thwarted, their will be controlled, and their passions brought into subjection. This can only be done *by a power out of themselves.*[16]

That power is government. The focus has shifted away from the liberal's preoccupation with freedom from government and his voluntaristic manipulation, based on the power within him, of his social environment and institutions.

Since government is not a mechanical umpire merely called upon when rights need protection, but a positive agency constraining the evil tendencies inherent in human nature, it follows that government is much more than the simple, efficient, and cheap policeman envisioned by radical theorists. Its proper functioning requires a deep understanding of human nature, rare skills acquired only with long experience. Governing, according to Burke, is "a matter of the most delicate and complicated skill." One can't simply renovate it, or reform it from some preconceived idea. To govern requires "more experience than any person can gain in his whole life." Cheap, simple, limited government is illusory, as is the notion of simple, swift, and radical social surgery.

> The nature of man is intricate; the objects of society are of the greatest complexity: and therefore no simple disposition or direction of power can be suited either to man's nature or to the quality of his affairs. When I hear the simplicity of contrivance aimed at and boasted of in any new political constitutions, I am at no loss to decide that the artificers are grossly ignorant of their trade or totally negligent of their duty. The simple governments are fundamentally defective, to say no worse of them.[17]

Radical man knows no limits, no boundaries to his excesses, which is well illustrated by the Jacobin attack on, and humiliation of, the queen of France on October 6, 1789. Burke's *Reflections* reach their literary, emotional, and theoretical crescendo in the passages he devotes to the queen. All his literary genius, all the frenzy of his fury, is in the service of his consummate artistry as he manipulates the reader with this poignant and unforgettable tale of radical savagery. Roused from her peaceful sleep, this gentle soul, "glittering like the morning-star, full of life and splendor and joy," is forced to flee her palace "almost naked." Her guards are butchered, and her rooms in that "most splendid palace in the world" are left "swimming in blood, polluted by massacre, and strewed with scattered limbs and mutilated carcasses." The queen and her husband flee Versailles, and have their subjects avenged this humiliation? They have not. It is this which prompts Burke to lament the demise of the ancien régime, its institutions and its values.

> Little did I dream that I should have lived to see such disasters fallen upon her in a nation of gallant men, in a nation of men of honor, and of cavaliers. I thought ten thousand swords must have leaped from their scabbards to avenge even a look that

> threatened her with insult. But the age of chivalry is gone. That of sophisters, economists, and calculators has succeeded; and the glory of Europe is extinguished for ever.[18]

Burke moves immediately from this condemnation of the failure to respect the exalted rank of the queen to a basic repudiation of the liberal notion of freedom. What he had begun by giving government a positive role in repressing the evil inclinations of unbridled individualism, he completes now by a redefinition of freedom. In liberal theory, freedom is the simple and empirical experience of the lack of constraint. It consists in the independence and autonomy of the self-willing ego. Burke sees this very freedom as the death blow to the old order, and rightly so. It is this new notion of freedom that accounts for no one rising to champion the queen. What it has replaced is what freedom means for Burke, whose definition differs profoundly.

> Never, never more shall we behold that generous loyalty to rank and sex, that proud submission, that dignified obedience, that subordination of the heart, which kept alive even in servitude itself, the spirit of an exalted freedom![19]

The corporate-feudal world of hierarchy where everyone knows and loves his "little platoon" is thus revived in Burke's assault on the new age of sophistry, economists, and calculators. Burke's notion of freedom denies the very basis of the new liberal ideal. The exalted freedom of a hierarchical social structure is in reality the absence of "selfish and mischievous ambition." Man is free in his little platoon, subordinate and obedient to those above him, in the sense that he is free of striving, free from ambition, free from the restless anxiety associated with ambition. Man is free from competition. His exalted freedom is the serenity and peace of mind that comes from knowing and loving his place. Man is free who has ambition neither to lift himself above his platoon nor to topple and replace those set above him like the queen.

What has passed is a social order characterized by what Burke calls "a noble equality"—a far cry from liberal notions of equality. Noble equality recognizes rank and "the gradations of social life." It is the principle of "love, veneration, admiration, or attachment" to persons. It is the "old feudal and chivalrous spirit of fealty." The mechanistic and abstract philosophy of the rights of man, of individual freedom, has no respect for this nobler equality that unites in personal bonds people who are fundamentally unequal. Radical man levels all such noble distinctions; he dissolves all that softened private society with "the new conquering empire of light and reason."

> All the decent drapery of life is to be rudely torn off. All the superadded ideas, furnished from the wardrobe of a moral imagination, which the heart owns and the understanding ratifies, as necessary to cover the defects of our naked, shivering nature, and to raise it to dignity in our own estimation, are to be exploded, as ridiculous, absurd, and antiquated fashion.[20]

The theme of man's inadequacy, his basic limitation, is here reintroduced. In his essence man is defective and imperfect. He requires "the pleasing illusions," the myths and superstitions that make life livable and tolerable. The radical who seeks to free man from the past, from tradition, myth, and religion, and who sets him to live by his own light and reason, is unaware of man's intrinsic weakness and fallibility. The rationalism and utopianism of the radicals is rejected here, as is the basic Enlightenment assumption of the unbounded horizons of the empire of reason. It is the eighteenth century itself that Burke repudiates in his proud admission that

> we are generally men of untaught feelings: that, instead of casting away all our old prejudices, we cherish them to a very considerable degree; and, to take more shame to ourselves, we cherish them because they are prejudices; and the longer they have lasted, and the more generally they have prevailed, the more we cherish them. We are afraid to put men to live and trade each on his own private stock of reason; because we suspect that this stock in each man is small, and that the individuals would do better to avail themselves of the general bank and capital of nations and of ages. Many of our men of speculation, instead of exploding general prejudices, employ their sagacity to discover the latent wisdom which prevails in them. If they find what they seek, (and they seldom fail,) they think it more wise to continue the prejudice, with the reason involved, than to cast away the coat of prejudice, and to leave nothing but the naked reason.[21]

It is all here, the cornerstone of Burke's counterrevolution, and with it a great deal of the future conservative creed. The most basic Enlightenment assumptions are written off with the stroke of a pen. Man is not only ruled by evil passions; but his rational capacity is severely limited as well. Without the warm cloak of custom, tradition, experience, history, religion, and social hierarchy—all of which radical man would rip off—man is shivering and naked. Free man from all mystery, demystify his institutions and his intellectual world, and you leave him alone in a universe of insignificance, incapacity, and inadequacy. But he is free, as the radicals construe freedom. This is indeed where their freedom leads, and why virtuous men pull about them their cloaks of unfreedom. In this wardrobe there are, according to Burke, two basic outfits: the "spirit of a gentleman" and the "spirit of religion," of "nobility and the clergy."[22] It is the prescription of aristocracy—the ancient and received institutions of hierarchy—and the prejudice of religion—the ancient and received ideas of God and his mercy—that rescue man from his shivering fearful self. They ennoble life; they rescue the individual by submerging his individuality in the "general bank and capital of nations and of ages." Who is man, then, to question his social institutions, to envy his betters, to seek perfection in this world? He is puny and ineffectual, Burke answers, meaningless and irrelevant on his own. He is someone only when guided by "ancient opinions and rules of life." Freed from the wisdom and experience of the ages, ungoverned by prescription and prejudice, men are no more than a "swinish multitude," or "little, shrivelled, meagre, hopping, though loud and troublesome insects of the hour."[23]

The liberal sees the state as a mere contractual arrangement, a voluntaristic creation of self-seeking and autonomous individuals concerned primarily with the secure enjoyment of their property rights. But the state is more to Burke, much more than the joint stock company arrangement of liberal theory, which he ridicules as the paltry vision of "sophisters, economists, and calculators." The state is, he wrote, "better than a partnership agreement in a trade of pepper and coffee, calico or tobacco, or some other such low concern, to be taken up for a little temporary interest, and to be dissolved by the fancy of the parties."[24] Men ought to look to the state with more reverence than to the East India Company. Political and social life involves more than the scramble of mortal individuals for wealth and profit, for self-fulfillment, oblivious to those who have lived before or who will live hereafter. Whatever the liberal touches becomes, in Burke's mind, a matter of economics and commercial calculation. "Let us not," he pleaded in the House of Commons, "turn our everything, the love of our country, our honour, our virtue, our religion, and our security to traffic—and estimate them by the scale of pecuniary or commercial reckoning. The nation that goes to that calculation destroys itself."[25]

Calculating and reckoning man is irrevocably and misguidedly mired in the present. Focused on the individual and his rights, he has no sense of continuity, of roots in the past, or of obligations to the future. Burke and conservatives after him turned to a partnership of generations that transcended individual egos. The state involves a contract serving nobler ends. It is a partnership between the living, the dead, and the yet unborn in all of life's dimensions: art, sciences, virtue, and perfection. Individuals, then, can never be free and autonomous for yet another reason. They always bear with them the constraints of the past. They have duties and responsibilities to the past as well as to the future.

Rationalists, the skeptic Burke holds, have too exalted a view of man and of his rational capacities. The restlessness of mind that has produced the tumult of ideological politics is seen as symptomatic of a general malady that besets modern man: his prideful belief in his own superiority. Burke's is the most developed and articulate of all indictments of ideology and of what the skeptic perceives as the prideful quest for perfect schemes and ideal politics. Burke saw the stock of reason in man as small. Despite this, men still fled their basic limitations in flights of ideological fancy. They recognized no barrier to their powers and sought in politics to make reality match their speculative visions. Burke devotedly wished that men would appreciate the weakness of their own minds, what he called in the *Vindication of Natural Society* their "subordinate rank in the creation." The cosmology embodied in the medieval concept of the chain of being was revived in all its glory by Burke to remind man of his lowly place in God's divine scheme; for Burke "assumes that the awful Author of our being is the Author of our place in the order of existence." In doing this, God has "subjected us to act the part which belongs to the place assigned to us." And that place is to know the limits of one's rational and speculative faculties.[26]

III.

Woodrow Wilson, writing just before the centenary of Burke's death, noted that Burke's every sentence was "stamped in the colors of his extraordinary imagination. The movement takes your breath and quickens your pulses. The glow and power of the matter rejuvenates your faculties."[27] Wilson was right. For generations, pulses have been quickened and breath taken away by Burke's words; more often than not, the pulses and breath belonged to conservatives.

People have even learned to write good English by reading Burke. In the late nineteenth century his *Speech on Conciliation with the Colonies* was made a part of the basic school English curriculum. Generations of Americans deep into the twentieth century learned how to construct topic sentences and write extended outlines of prose on the model of Edmund Burke's works. It was no accident, of course, that of the master's works this particular piece was chosen. Until the cold war of the 1950s it was as an opponent of the "American War" that Burke was primarily known in America. And this older identification still lingers. The week of March 22, 1975, found the *Christian Science Monitor* and the *Philadelphia Bulletin* using Burke in their editorials on the bicentenary of his great speech. On the twenty-second itself the CBS television network chose Ronald Reagan (a subtle and all too clever choice) to read Burke's words on its nightly "200 Years Ago Today."

Burke's contemporaries on the left were generally enraged by the *Reflections on the Revolution in France.* Their reactions capture what would be the dominant response from liberals and radicals to this day. The radical novelist Robert Bage mocked the very passage in the *Reflections* that so moved Burke and many of his readers. The knight-errant becomes modern man striking blows at the chains of chivalry and at such as Burke who glory in that servitude:

> Ten thousand pens must start from their inkstands, to punish the man who dares attempt to restore the empire of prejudice and passion. The age of chivalry, heaven be praised, is gone. The age of truth and reason is commenced, and will advance to maturity in spite of cant and bishops. Law—active, invincible, avenging law, is here the knight-errant that redresses wrongs, protects damsels, and punishes the base miscreants who oppress them. . . . All this is happily changed. Philosophy and commerce

> have transformed that *generous loyalty to rank,* into attachment to peace, to law, to the general happiness of mankind; that *proud submission* and *dignified obedience* into an unassuming consciousness of natural equality; and that *subordination of the heart* into an honest veneration of superior talents, conjoined with superior benevolence.[28]

Joseph Priestley, in responding to the *Reflections*, dealt metaphor for metaphor. His concern was Burke's discussion of the clothes and the drapery of life that cover naked, shivering man. Priestley replied with the characteristic radical metaphor of a new day dawning:

> Cherish them [prejudices], then, sir, as much as you please. Prejudice and error is only a mist, which the sun, which has now risen, will effectively disperse. Keep them about you as tight as the countryman in the fable did his cloak; the same sun without any more violence than the warmth of his beams, will compel you to throw it aside, unless you chose to sweat under it, and bear the ridicule of all your cooler and less encumbered companions.[29]

Among the radicals who had self-consciously put aside all cloaks of mist and mystery was Jeremy Bentham, who was not above using, against the *Reflections*, the same exaggerated near-hysterical rhetoric that was Burke's trademark. Bentham described Burke as "blinded by his rage, in this his frantic exclamation, wrung from him by the unquenched thirst for lucre—this mad man, than whom none perhaps was ever more mischievous—this incendiary."[30]

Two of the most famous radical replies to Burke's *Reflections* emphasized the same theme—Burke's disregard for the age-old suffering of the common people in his preoccupation with the brutality of revolutionary justice. Thomas Paine, in his *Rights of Man*, saw Burke venerating power and "all the governments in the world, while the victims who suffer under them, whether sold into slavery, or tortured out of existence, are wholly forgotten."[31] But it was the feminist Mary Wollstonecraft who best captured this common radical response to Burke.

> Misery to reach your heart I perceive, must have its caps and bells; your tears are reserved, very naturally considering your

> character, for the declamation of the theater, or for the downfall of queens, whose rank throws a graceful veil over vices that degrade humanity; but the distress of many industrious mothers whose helpmates have been torn from them, and the hungry cry of the helpless babes, were vulgar sorrows that could not move your commiseration, though they might extort an alms.[32]

Burke was, of course, soundly praised by members of the belles-lettres circles in which he moved after his literary and political debut in London. He was feted by the likes of Samuel Johnson, David Garrick, and Oliver Goldsmith, on the one hand, and by bluestockings like Mrs. Montagu, Mrs. Carter, and Mrs. Veysey, on the other. James Boswell, Horace Walpole, Arthur Young, and Fanny Burney sang his praises. They all were dazzled primarily by his reputation for spellbinding oratory in the Commons. It would be the French Revolution, however, and his response to it that made him a legendary figure. In seventeen days after its publication on November 1, 1790, 5,500 copies of his *Reflections* were sold. By November 29 the sales had reached twelve thousand, according to Burke's account. Within a year some nineteen thousand copies had been sold in England.

The establishment loved *Reflections*, and with its response began the myth of Burke as heroic Tory defender of the faith. Conservatives rallied to what they had long sought—a resounding defense of their privileges and a clarion call for resistance to Jacobinism, to democracy and leveling in both France and England. William Windham, fast becoming a leader in the House of Commons, wrote that "never was there, I suppose, a work so valuable in its kind, or that displayed powers of so extraordinary a nature." It was a work, he wrote, quite "capable of . . . turning the stream of opinion throughout Europe."[33] George III is quoted as having said, "Burke's *Reflections* is a good book, a very good book; every gentleman ought to read it."[34] At Oxford there was talk of awarding Burke an LL.D. "in consideration of his very able Representation of the True Principles of our Constitution Ecclesiastical and Civil."[35] The *Times* of London saw it as a welcome antidote to "all those dark insidious minds who would wish to level it in a similar manner with the French for the sake of their own selfish purposes."[36] The great historian Edward Gibbon agreed. *Reflections* was "a most admirable medicine against the French disease," which was making too much headway in England. He admired Burke's eloquence and "adored his chivalry." He even forgave him his superstition.[37]

The mythic figure of Burke was fast taking form even in the last years of the eighteenth century. Two people crucial in helping to give Burke to history were poets who came to Burke guilt-ridden over their own early enthusiasm for Jacobinism. The young Coleridge, for example, had attacked in an ode of 1794 Burke's "wizard spell" in rallying Europe against Jacobinism. Years later he wrote of Burke as "a great man," a man of "transcendent greatness" and "of measureless superiority to those about him." He could not conceive "of a time or a state of things in which the writings of Burke will not have the highest value." He saw in Burke's writings "the germs of almost all political truths."[38] Wordsworth in 1799 wrote of "that great stage, where Senators, tongue-favoured men, perform." One senator he remembers above all. And so the legend of Burke who said "no" took shape.

Genius of Burke! forgive the pen reduced
By specious wonders, and too slow to tell
Of what the ingenuous, what bewildered men,
Beginning to mistrust their boastful guides,
And wise men, willing to grow wiser, caught
Rapt auditors! from they most eloquent tongue—
Now mute, for ever mute in the cold grave
I see him,—old, but vigorous in age,—
Stand like an oak whose stag-horn branches start
Out of its leafy brow, the more to awe
The younger brethren of the grove. But some—
While he forewarns, denounces, launches forth,
Against all systems built on abstract rights,
Keen ridicule; the majesty proclaims
Of Institutes and Laws, hallowed by time;
Declares the vital power of social ties
Endeared by custom; and with high disdain,
Exploding against Theory, insists
Upon the allegiance to which men are born.[39]

In the nineteenth century, however, Burke the heroic and legendary figure, the conservative prophet, lay dormant. He was remembered more as the model of the prudent statesman whose teaching contained the essence of political wisdom. Even more than this, he was eulogized as a great master of the English language. William Hazlitt, Thomas De Quincey, and Matthew Arnold praised Burke's prose. According to Macaulay he was the greatest Englishman of letters since Milton. Nineteenth-century biographers MacKnight and Prior went even further, the latter noting, for example, that it took "two thousand years to produce one Cicero and one Burke."[40]

One nineteenth-century biographer, however, did keep alive the myth of heroic Tory Burke, and in doing so was an early example of a tendency in Burkeana that would flower in the twentieth century—the latter-day partisan use of Burke. George Croly was an Anglican minister actively opposed to the Chartist movement. It was a time, he felt, much like the last decade of the eighteenth century. His purpose in writing on and editing Burke in 1840, he informed his readers, was to compile "an anti-revolutionary manual of the wisdom of the wisest of men." Burke had been the genius behind "the forces that preserved society as it was," and his words could do that again against the new menace. Croly may well have been the first to refer to Burke's "renown as a prophet," as well as to use him as a weapon in counterrevolutionary politics. Until our own day few have written of Burke as the Reverend Croly did.

> The politician was elevated into the philosopher, and in that loftier atmosphere from which he looked down on the cloudy and turbulent contests of the time, he soared upward calmly in the light of truth and became more splendid at every wave of his wing.[41]

Croly was an exception, however. The nineteenth century in general had little of Burke as prophet of reaction. He was percieved, on the contrary, as an exemplar of the school that dominated Victorian thought, utilitarian liberalism. This was in no small part due to the efforts of Burke's great nineteenth-century biographer, John Morley. Morley was a liberal and a positivist, schooled like John Stuart Mill in the writings of Auguste Comte. His two biographies of Burke rooted him in the liberal cause, emphasizing his years of opposition to the Crown and especially his role in the American Revolution, "that part of his history about the majestic and noble wisdom of which there can be least dispute." On the French Revolution there was indeed dispute. Morley avoided the problem by leaving the verdict to history, "to our grandchildren."[42] What attracted Morley to Burke was his conviction that Burke's political philosophy was at bottom Benthamite utilitarianism. It seemed this way to Morley because Burke had rejected natural rights and other abstract and absolute principles. His every utterance praised expediency and prudence at the expense of rigid adherence to ultimate values. Henry Buckle, Leslie Stephen, and William Lecky agreed; Burke was a utilitarian liberal.

These Victorian liberals who wrote of Burke as in their camp were no less outspoken in their praise for him. It was in fact partly because of his alleged utilitarian affinities that they were so effusive. They considered utility, expediency, and prudential calculation to be the heart of politics, and so it was that they saw in Burke a kindred spirit. While they had little taste for the gorgeous excesses of his prose, he was for them the theorist par excellence of political wisdom. Lecky wrote of Burke's writings that "the time may come when they will no longer be read. The time will never come in which men would not grow wiser by reading them."[43] Buckle described Burke as "one of the greatest men, and, Bacon alone excepted, the greatest thinker who ever devoted himself to English politics."[44]

What happened to Burke at the hands of the Victorian liberals is of crucial importance. It represents the first and most important step in his capture by the middle class and his enlistment to save their cause and their interests. His aristocratic biases as displayed in his writings on France and India were pushed to the side, and his writings on America are pushed front and center. More important than this, however, was the realization that his empiricism—and his skepticism, when severed from his "unfortunate" predilection for aristocracy—could serve the new status quo in which the middle class dominates. The age of chivalry was indeed dead and buried. The powers that be were now the triumphant middle class, which had already turned its back on the French Revolution and the politics of upheaval. The romance of Jacobinism was appropriate only for the assertive and struggling bourgeoisie seeking to find its place in the sun. It might not even be necessary then to overlook Burke's writings on the Revolution. For it would come to pass that middle-class liberals could find wisdom in this very tirade against their earlier struggle. It was after all, a plea for order, for stability, for submissive obedience to the powers that be.

One sees this deep conservative strain in the nineteenth-century liberal embrace of Burke at work in Woodrow Wilson. It is not surprising that Wilson, the professor of government enamored of English parliamentary politics, would gravitate so naturally to the pull of this House of Commons man. But it is the passion of Wilson's attraction that is so striking, and which seems to bespeak some deeper response that Burke struck in the repressed conservative Presbyterian within the liberal Wilson. For the soon-to-be president, Burke was the embodiment of racial wisdom, the instinctive common sense and practical soul of the Anglo-Saxon. An interaction with Burke was emotionally and physically stimulating. To read him was to hasten the pulse, quicken the breath. "Does not your blood stir at these passages?" Wilson asks the reader. Like his contemporaries, the liberal scholars who were writing on Burke in England, Wilson was struck by Burke's "concrete mind." Burke's disdain for "abstract speculation" and for "system" appealed to him, as did his "practical" approach and his preference for "expediency." Wilson, however, unlike his contemporaries, was not afraid to meet the French Revolution head on, and to shout amen to Burke's crusade against Jacobinism. "The things he hated are truly hateful," Wilson wrote of Burke. "He hated the French Revolutionary philosophy and deemed it unfit for free men, and that philosophy is in fact radically evil and corrupting."[45] That this liberal president could be so taken by Burke is additional evidence of the general historical process by which Burke was possessed and used by the middle class, a process of course intensified in the United States, where that class lacked even an aristocratic enemy to overthrow. They were no longer frightened off by Burke; indeed, some of their spokesmen were quite taken by his conservatism and how it could now serve their interests.

All would not be praise of Burke in the twentieth century, however. To be sure, Arthur Bauman could sing his praises in 1929 as the "founder of Conservatism," and in 1931 the Reverend Robert Murray could write that Soviet Russia needed a strong dose of Burkean wisdom to cure it of its miseries.[46] And those years also saw Alfred Cobban's brilliant and sympathetic characterization of Burke as gravedigger for the eighteenth-century Enlightenment.[47] But in those very same years a marked departure in the history of Edmund Burke occurred. Beginning in 1929 and 1930, Burke's reputation was subjected to the most serious assault on it since the radical crew of Wollstonecraft, Priestley, Paine, William Godwin, and others had finished with it one hundred and thirty-five years earlier. His principal critic was the distinguished historian Sir Lewis Namier.

The burden of Namierite scholarship has been "to correct" the Whig conception of eighteenth-century history, with its scenario of the villain George III set against the virtuous House of Commons. Standing very much in the way, then, of Namierite revisionism is Burke and the picture of George III he had circulated from the late 1760s in the Wilkes crisis, through the American crisis in the 1770s, into the 1780s with his economic reforms, and finally with his outspoken views on the king's insanity during the Regency crisis. Wrote Namier:

> What I have never been able to find, is the man [George III] arrogating power to himself, the ambitious schemer out to dominate, the intriguer dealing in an underhand fashion with his ministers; in short, any evidence for the stories circulated about him by very clever and eloquent contemporaries.[48]

Namier had one particular clever contemporary in mind, Edmund Burke, as the author of the legend that George III was out to destroy the Constitution. Burke's vision of George's double cabinet was a fiction, according to Namier. Equally misguided was his notion of the "king's friends" and the "ascendency" of the earl of Bute. These were the products solely of Burke's "fertile, disordered, and malignant imagination," Namier argued.[49] But the Namierite attack on Burke is even more fundamental than this, for at bottom it insists that he was guilty of hypocrisy and cant. Namierism is itself a profoundly positivist indictment of the role of ideas and ideals in eighteenth-century politics. To understand the structure of politics, one looks not at what Bolingbroke or Burke wrote, not at party pamphlets and manifestos, but at connections and configurations of interests. Men were not moved by ideas or ideals but by interests. Politics was a game played by shifting connections of "ins" and "outs" who wove idea structures around this basic fact of political life. The ideas were meaningless, mere rationalizations for the position then held. What the Namierites are saying, then, is that Burke's writings and ideas are mere cant, high-sounding principles that were laid over the base opposition of the "outs."

It is this much broader and more basic assumption about politics that informs the Namierite indictment of Burke as a weaver of legends. His ideals are seen as hypocritical cloaks thrown over the material and personal interests of faction and connection. According to Namier, then, Burke was consumed with "blatant egocentricity." He was "self-righteous," "hardly a reliable witness," and a "party politician with a minority mind." His political writings are filled with "arrant nonsense written with much self-assurance," informed and distorted by a "blinding rage."[50] The Namierites cavalierly brush aside the writings of Burke, so treasured by the generations.

> Burke's writings, admired beyond measure and most copiously quoted for nearly two hundred years, stand as a magnificent facade between the man and his readers. . . . When the trend of his perceptions is examined, he is frequently found to be a poor observer, only in distant touch with reality, and apt to substitute for it figments of his own imagination, which grow and harden and finish by dominating both him and widening rings of men whom he influenced.[51]

One might think Burke would never recover from the viciousness of the Namierite attack. But just when he seemed to be down and out, Burke was rescued by American friends, who revived his reputation to heights never before experienced. The history of Burke since the Second World War is thus of two Burkes, an English version and an American version. In neither case is he regarded with scholarly detachment. His name evokes passion and polemics; one is for him or against him. He is despised by one school in England, and beatified by another in America.

The tremendous renewal of interest in Burke in America is wrapped up with the here-and-now dynamics of American politics. As one American Burkean aptly put it in 1967:

> As everyone knows, an enormous revival of interest in Edmund Burke has taken place during the past twenty years or so, the period roughly, since the end of the Second World War. Scholars, to be sure, have always been interested in him, and he was widely admired for his style, and by some for his "practical wisdom," during the nineteenth century. But the point is that in our time he has come to be read not merely as one among a large number of other important figures in the history of political thought, but as a thinker of intense, of special, contemporary relevance. Burke is our contemporary, he is an issue, in a way that Locke is not, and Leibniz is not, and even Mill is not.[52]

This evolution of Burke as himself an issue, the defining of one's own politics through coming to terms with his ideas, occurred in two separate stages in postwar America: the "cold war conservatism" of the 1950s and 1960s, and the more recent neoconservatism of the 1970s and 1980s.

Nothing less than the defense of Christian civilization is the mission that American conservatives gave to Burke in the first blush of their love affair with him. The wooers, who included Russell Kirk, Ross J. S. Hoffman, Francis Canavan, Louis Bredvold, Peter J. Stanlis, and C. P. Ives, had uppermost in their minds the threat of world communism. "The rise of the doctrines of Karl Marx and Communism" is comparable in scale only "to the ascending movement of the doctrines of Rousseau and the kind of democracy that was called Jacobinism." As Burke saved Christendom then, so his words could do it now. "He had become relevant again."[53] For Russell Kirk the impact of *The Communist Manifesto* was to efface "in much of the world . . . that order governed by what Burke described as the spirit of religion and the spirit of a gentleman." For Kirk, Burke is our mentor in puncturing "the overweening self-confidence of modern man." His wisdom and his example are a mighty bulwark "against the fanatic ideologue and the armed doctrine, the great plagues of our time." Because we are attacked by the same enemy, fanaticism, "the resonance of Burke's voice still is heard amidst the howl of our winds of abstract doctrine." Burke was the inspiration America needed in the cold war, according to Kirk.

> Burke's ideas did more than establish islands in the sea of radical thought; they provided the defenses of conservatism, on a grand scale, that still stand and are not liable to fall in our time. . . . Our age . . . seems to be groping for certain of the ideas which Burke's inspiration formed into a system of social preservation.[54]

At the hands of Burke's cold war disciples the French Revolution becomes a totalitarian forerunner of the modern bolshevist state. As then, so now, free men must choose, as Burke put it, between "the fanatics of popular arbitrary power" and "a manly, moral regulated liberty." In this struggle men "will have their faith in liberty renewed by turning to the political writings of Edmund Burke."[55] What Americans had to combat, according to P. J. Stanlis, was what Burke had opposed throughout his life, the pride and self-confidence of the Enlightenment. Nothing short, then, of repudiating the basic American mentality is what Burke requires of America in the cold war. "Unbounded confidence in logical reason, science, and progress pointed toward the reign of Terror and political despotism." Naive optimism and scheming social projects are equally dangerous. America must repudiate her twentieth-century sophists, economists, and calculators and acknowledge the dual constraints of sin and history. When all is said and done, however, there is one reason above all for mass conversion to Burke:

> His reply to the totalitarian challenge of the French Revolution has a special significance to twentieth century man. We, too, are confronted with Jacobin types of popular collectivism which would make society and the State everything and the individual nothing. We have witnessed the rise of impersonal leviathan states, claiming the sanction of the popular will, in which every local corporate interest and every personal human right is extinguished or exists solely at the discretion of a centralized Sovereign power. If the Commonwealth of Christian Europe is to survive and form the ethical norms of civilization throughout the world, all men, but particularly Americans, will have to learn the great lessons in Burke's philosophy.[56]

Historically, then, American cold war conservatism was based on the reaction against the threat of international communism. Intellectually, the Burke revival was also a reaction against the nineteenth-century liberal and utilitarian reading of Burke. The two are, of course, related. Burke had to be rescued from Morley, Buckle, and others because the very expediency, relativism, and prudential quest for utility which they attributed to and praised in him is part of the modern menace of bolshevism, whose most grievous barbarity is its renunciation of absolute moral values, at least those of the Christian, now capitalist, West. Enter Burke the theorist of natural law. Based upon the meager evidence of Burke's Indian speeches and the towering intellectual influence in the conservative intellectual community of Leo Strauss, who was much more cautious in seeing Burke as classical natural-law thinker than they were, the cold war conservatives packaged a Burke foursquare in the tradition of Aristotle, Cicero, and Aquinas. Kirk, Canavan, and especially Stanlis see Burke as turning upon the apostasy of the liberal Hobbes and Locke, who had betrayed the true classical and Christian concept of natural law in their philosophies of egocentric natural and individual rights. Far from the philosopher of expediency, Burke emerges now as the philosopher of fixed eternal principles, of the moral laws of God that enjoin certain actions and require others.

Another intellectual movement for which Burke is of central importance is neoconservatism. He is of use to it not in a crusade against world revolution but in a more pragmatic response to the politics of domestic American liberalism. Whereas the cold war Burkeans were by nature or creed conservatives to the core, many neoconservatives were formerly liberals or radicals who have moved to the right in reaction to the militancy of blacks, students, women, and war protestors in the 1960s, or those who have come to conservatism after disillusionment with the Great Society's efforts to eliminate poverty and prejudice from the American scene. From their ivy-covered campuses, their prestigious think tanks, and the pages of *Commentary* and *The Public Interest*, the neoconservatives may not always refer to Burke or invoke his name and principles, but their reflexes are Burkean, and as the new conservative mood spreads and deepens, conscious credit is increasingly being given to Burke as the inspirational source of what is basically a politics of skepticism.

Echoes of Burke are clearly discernible in the new conservatism's cult of complexity, for example. Nathan Glazer writes that what he learned from a stint of government service was that there were no simple solutions and that society was complex:

> It was a big country and it contained more kinds of people than were dreamed of on the shores of the Hudson. I learned in quite strictly conservative fashion, to develop a certain respect for what was; in a world of infinite complexity some things had emerged and survived.

Radical social programs, he writes, are misguided because their naive authors have no sense of "the lineaments of modern society." In the face of this impenetrable complexity their simplistic solutions are the heights of presumption and arrogance. They assume that they "understand the causes of our ills," and that they know "how to get them right."[57] It may well be that we know neither, replies the deradicalized realist Glazer.

Burkean wisdom lives on in the writings of Irving Kristol as well. Burke had argued that radicals often cause more harm by efforts to remake society than existed in the evil they were reacting against. Kristol agrees. "I have observed over the years that the unanticipated consequences of social action are always more important, and usually less agreeable, than the intended consequences." Behind radicalism, Kristol, like Burke, sees both a conspiracy of critical, naysaying "men of letters" and the decline of religious faith, fueled in part by a self-proclaimed cultural and intellectual elite. Like Burke, Kristol faults these "men of letters" for their naive utopianism, their simplistic conviction that the world can be made right:

> I also regard the exaggerated hopes we attach to politics as the curse of our age. . . . To think we have it in our power to change people so as to make the human estate wonderfully better than it is, remarkably different from what it is, and in very short order, is to assume that this generation of Americans can do what no other generation in all of human history could accomplish.[58]

Kristol acknowledges his agreement with Burke on how fortunate it is that most people refuse to question their society and merely accept it as given.

In the context of American politics, the neoconservative rejects the role of government as problem solver or perfection planner because he knows that in a complex world some problems cannot be solved and in a sinful world perfection is an illusory goal. The political scientist Edward Banfield cautions against governmental intervention, suggesting that if you do not know what you are doing, do not do it at all. The problems of the inner city cannot be solved, so leave them be.[59] Daniel Patrick Moynihan argues, similarly, to get government out of race relations. By raising expectations unrealistically more evil is done than good. The problem is unsolvable, or will conceivably fix itself; what is needed is benign neglect.

But there is one area in which neoconservatives plead for more government action—crime control—and this is because of their very sense of man's inherent baseness. It is evident in the writings of James Q. Wilson, for example, and his insistence on a stronger governmental role in curbing crime. Such a view revives the classic conservative model of the state as represser of evil passions. The liberal is naive in his belief that good men are rendered criminal solely by environment and society. The modern conservative appreciates that some men are by nature evil or sinful and that the law-and-order state must actively punish them, less as a deterrent than as external just deserts for their internal failure to curb themselves.[60]

But even today Burke's most enduring legacy is his skepticism. His conservative disciples envision government as primarily an act of management and administration. Burke's theory of "prudential management" as the true art of government has been stated most succinctly in the contemporary age by Michael Oakeshott, the late English political philosopher. Oakeshott calls upon political leaders to take the ship of state to no particular port of call, no abstract or ideological ideal. Their task is to manage wisely the crises that arise out of day-to-day developments—to keep the ship afloat: "in political activity, then, men sail a boundless and bottomless sea; there is neither harbor for shelter, nor floor for anchorage, neither starting place nor appointed destination. The enterprise is to keep afloat on an even keel."[61] Such skills, of course, require men of a high quality and character not found among the democratic citizenry.

Skepticism also involves a specific orientation to change. Change and development are inevitable in any body, and the body politic is no exception. What the Burkean skeptic fears today, however, is planned change, change that is informed by some ideal, some abstract a priori blueprint. Self-consciously tampering and tinkering with the given structure out of a concern for efficiency, justice, or economy is fraught with danger. Better to suffer apparent inequity and imperfection than tempt the possible disorder and unpredictability of planned change. Any attempt to rationalize social or political life raises this specter of chaos for the conservative skeptic. The social order is complex and fragile; who knows what hell will break loose should people set about to structure it according to their abstract notions. This seemed tragically borne out for Burke when he reflected on the French having unleashed a monstrous nightmare on all Europe in their misguided zeal to change the apparently few defects and corruptions of their constitution. The skeptic Burke, then, cautions against zealous efforts to remedy evil, lest these very efforts create even greater unintended evil. The position is echoed once again by the American conservative skeptic Edward Banfield. In an essay criticizing plans to rationalize and reorganize the American party system, he argues with pure Burkean skepticism:

> A political system is an accident. It is an accumulation of habits, customs, prejudices and principles that have survived a long process of trial and error and of ceaseless response to changing circumstance. If the system works well on the whole, it is a lucky accident—the luckiest, indeed, that can befall a society. . . . To meddle with the structure and operation of a successful political system is therefore the greatest foolishness that men are capable of. Because the system is intricate beyond comprehension, the chance of improving it in the ways intended is slight, whereas the danger of disturbing its working and of setting off a succession of unwanted effects that will extend throughout the whole society is great.[62]

It is the same plea heard from some American liberal skeptics. There is, for example, the law school professor Alex Bickel, who suggested in the 1970s in the widely read *New Republic* that

> Our problem, as much as Burke's, is that we cannot govern, and should not, in submission to the dictates of abstract theories, and that we cannot live, much less govern, without some "uniform rule and scheme of life," without principles, however provisionally and skeptically held. Burke's conservatism, if that is what it was, which at any rate belongs to the liberal tradition properly understood and translated to our time, is the way.[63]

It was his skepticism, so praised in our day, that drove the Whig Burke from his alliance with liberals like Charles James Fox and that defined his unique vision of conservatism. So is it this same skepticism that appeals to neoconservatives and chastened liberals today and drives them in conservative flight from the reformer's zeal. The legitimacy and ethical justification of such skeptical naysaying is not our concern here. All that needs be insisted upon here is the remarkable legacy of Burke's ideas.[64]

NOTES

1. Edmund Burke, *Reflections on the Revolution in France.* See below, pp. 417, 443, 451.
2. H. W. F. Somerset, ed., *A Notebook of Edmund Burke* (Cambridge, England, 1957), pp. 90–91.

3. Edmund Burke, *Speech on the State of Representation of the Commons in Parliament.* See below, p. 178.
4. Ibid. See below, p. 182.
5. Edmund Burke, *An Appeal from the New to the Old Whigs.* See below, p. 495.
6. Edmund Burke, Letter to the duke of Richmond. See below, p. 533.
7. Quoted in M. H. Abrams, *Natural Supernaturalism* (New York, 1971), p. 328.
8. Edward Dowdeen, ed., *The Correspondence of Robert Southey with Caroline Bowles* (Dublin, 1881), p. 52.
9. William Blake, "The French Revolution," in *The Poetry and Prose of William Blake*, David Erdman, ed. (New York, 1970), pp. 11–12.
10. Quoted in Abrams, *Natural Supernaturalism*, p. 331.
11. Richard Price, *Evidence for a Future Period of Improvement in the State of Mankind with the Means and Duty of Promoting It: An Address to Supporters of New Academical Institutions Among Protestant Dissenters* (London, 1787), pp. 5, 22, 25.
12. Ibid., p. 53.
13. Joseph Priestley, *Letters to the Right Honourable Edmund Burke* (Birmingham, 1791), letter 14, p. 25.
14. Burke, *Reflections.* See below, p. 437.
15. Ibid. See below, p. 431, and Burke's *Works* (London, 1882), p. 310.
16. Ibid. See below, p. 442.
17. Ibid. See below, p. 443.
18. Ibid. See below, p. 446.
19. Ibid. See below, p. 446.
20. Ibid. See below, p. 447.
21. Ibid. See below, pp. 451–52.
22. Ibid. See below, p. 448.
23. Ibid. See below, p. 448, 450.
24. Ibid. See below, pp. 457–58.
25. *Parliamentary History* 30 (1792–94), p. 646.
26. Burke, *An Appeal*. See below, p. 491.
27. Woodrow Wilson, *Mere Literature and Other Essays* (Boston, 1896), p. 160.
28. Robert Bage, *Man As He Is* (London, 1792), vol. 4, pp. 72–73.
29. Priestley, *Letters to the Right Honourable Edmund Burke*, p. 112.
30. Cited in Mary Mack, *Jeremy Bentham* (London, 1962), p. 347.
31. Tom Paine, *The Rights of Man*, H. Collins, ed. (Harmondsworth, England: Penguin, 1969), p. 71.
32. Mary Wollstonecraft, *A Reply to Mr. Burke's Invective* (London, 1792), pp. 98–99.
33. Mrs. Henry Baring, ed., *The Diary of the Right Honourable William Windham 1784–1810* (London: 1866), pp. 212–13.
34. Quoted in Sir Philip Magnus, *Edmund Burke* (London, 1939), p. 195.

35. Quoted in Boulton, *The Language of Politics in the Age of Wilkes and Burke* (London, 1963), p. 80.
36. *The Times* (London) November 30, 1790.
37. R. E. Prothero, ed., *The Private Letters of Edward Gibbon* (London, 1897), vol. 2, pp. 237, 251.
38. Samuel Taylor Coleridge, *Religious Musings* (1794), *Table Talk* (London, 1835), vol. 5, p. 18; vol. 2, p. 147.
39. William Wordsworth, *The Prelude*, Book 7, lines 512–30.
40. James Prior, *Memoirs of the Life and Character of the Right Honourable Edmund Burke* (London, 1824), vol. 1, pp. 364, 564.
41. George Croly, *A Memoir of the Political Life of the Right Honourable Edmund Burke: With Extracts From His Writings* (London, 1840), vol. 1, pp. 145–46, viii, 24, 3.
42. John Morley, *A Historical Study* (London, 1867), p. 123; *Burke* (London, 1888), p. 210.
43. William Lecky, *A History of England in the Eighteenth Century* (New York, 1891), vol. 5, p. 476; vol. 3, p. 197.
44. Cited in T. W. Copeland, "The Reputation of Edmund Burke," *Journal of British Studies* (no. 2, 1962), p. 83.
45. Woodrow Wilson, *Mere Literature*, pp. 107, 128, 141, 158, 155.
46. Arthur Baumann, *Burke the Founder of Conservatism* (London, 1929), pp. 37, 46; Robert Murray, *Edmund Burke: A Biography* (London, 1931), p. 407.
47. Alfred Cobban, *Edmund Burke and the Revolt Against the Eighteenth Century* (New York: 1929), p. 12.
48. Sir Lewis Namier, "King George III: A Study of Personality" in *Crossroads of Power* (New York, 1962), p. 140. The major works of Namier were *The Structure of Politics at the Accession of George III* (London, 1929) and *England in the Age of the American Revolution* (London, 1930).
49. Namier, "Monarchy and the Party System" in *Personalities and Powers* (London, 1955), p. 143.
50. Namier, "The Character of Burke," *The Spectator*, December 19, 1958.
51. Namier, "King George III," p. 140.
52. Jeffrey Hart, "Burke and Radical Freedom," *The Review of Politics* 29 (April 1967), p. 221.
53. R. J. S. Hoffman and P. Levack, eds., *Burke's Politics* (New York, 1959), pp. xiii, xii.
54. Russell Kirk, "Edmund Burke and National Rights," *The Review of Politics* 13, no. 4 (October 1951), pp. 16, 21, 209, 211; *The Conservative Mind* (New York, 1953), p. 123.
55. P. J. Stanlis, "Edmund Burke in the Twentieth Century," in *The Relevance of Edmund Burke*, ed. P. J. Stanlis (New York, 1964), p. 53.
56. Stanlis, *Edmund Burke and the Natural Law* (Ann Arbor, 1958), pp. 247–49.

57. Nathan Glazer, "On Being Deradicalized," *Commentary* 50, no. 4 (October 1970), p. 75.
58. Irving Kristol, *On the Democratic Idea in America* (New York, 1972), pp. ix, 69, 149, 144.
59. See E. C. Banfield, *The Unheavenly City* (Boston, 1970).
60. See, for example, James Q. Wilson, *Thinking About Crime* (New York, 1975), as well as his numerous articles in *The New York Times Magazine* and *Commentary.*
61. M. Oakeshott, *Rationalism in Politics* (London, 1962), p. 127.
62. Edward Banfield, "In Defense of the American Party System," in *Political Parties U.S.A.*, ed. E. Goldwin (Chicago, 1964), pp. 37–38.
63. Alex Bickel, "Reconsideration: Edmund Burke," in *New Republic,* March 17, 1973.
64. The editor thanks Michael Busch, yet again, for his invaluable assistance on this project.

SUGGESTIONS FOR FURTHER READING

Ayling, S. *Edmund Burke: His Life and Opinions* (1988)

Blakemore, S. *Burke and the Fall of Language* (1988)

Bryant, D. C. *Edmund Burke and His Literary Friends* (1939)

Canavan, F. *Edmund Burke: Prescription and Providence* (1987)

Chapman, G. *Edmund Burke: The Practical Imagination* (1967)

Cobban, A. *Edmund Burke and the Revolt Against the Eighteenth Century* (1929)

Conniff, J. *The Useful Cobbler: Edmund Burke and The Politics of Progress* (1994)

Crowe, I., ed. *Edmund Burke: His Life and Legacy* (1997)

Freeman, M. *Edmund Burke and the Critique of Political Radicalism* (1980)

Kirk, R. *Edmund Burke: A Genius Reconsidered* (1967)

Kramnick, I. *The Rage of Edmund Burke* (1977)

Macpherson, C. B. *Burke* (1980)

O'Brien, C. C. *The Great Melody: A Thematic Biography of Edmund Burke* (1992)

Ritchie, D. *Edmund Burke: Appraisals and Appreciations* (1990)

Stanlis, P. *Edmund Burke and the Natural Law* (1958)

Whelan, F. *Edmund Burke and India* (1997)

White, S. K. *Edmund Burke: Modernity, Politics, and Aesthetics* (1994)

Wilkins, B. T. *The Problem of Burke's Political Philosophy* (1969)

A NOTE ON THE SELECTIONS

WITH THE EXCEPTION of the pieces from *The Reformer, A Notebook of Edmund Burke*, and *The Annual Register*, all the selections in this collection, including the letters, can be found in any standard edition of Burke's collected works. I have used the 1851 London edition in eight volumes of *The Works and Correspondence of the Right Honourable Edmund Burke.*

The Portable
EDMUND BURKE

PART I

CULTURE AND HISTORY

The Reformer

While a student at Trinity College, Dublin, Burke wrote, edited, and published his own weekly periodical, The Reformer. *Patterned after London's* Spectator, *it ran for thirteen issues from January 28 to April 21, 1748. In these, his first published works, the nineteen-year-old Burke brashly and presumptuously criticized the pretensions—cultural, intellectual, social, and political—of his elders. Particularly interesting, given Burke's late career, is Number 7, in which he lashes out at the privilege and splendor of the well-to-do while lamenting the misery of the Irish poor.*

NO. 4

WE LAID IT DOWN as a Certainty in our First Paper, that Taste and Virtue had a close Connection; in Consequence to which, before we attempted to reform the Morals of the People, we began with their Taste; and the Encouragement we have met with makes up hope, that our Industry may at last prove effectual to the Amendment of both: Several perhaps might have been alarmed, and attributed that to particular Prejudice, which was meant for the public Emolument: The Ladies might have feared this Paper was design'd to destroy their Pleasures, when its Aim was but to refine, and render them worthy their Attention.

When we set up for Reformers, we expected a violent Opposition, therefore we enter'd boldly on our Design, and threw the Odium where we thought it due; we excus'd none thro' Partiality, nor attacked any thro' Prejudice, but in warring with Ignorance, we could not let those escape who publickly countenanced it, nor could we in endeavouring to overthrow Vice pass by so great an Obstacle as the *Theatre*, for which Reason we exposed the ill Choice of some Plays, and recommended those which we thought at once instructive and entertaining. We are very easy about those who for this Reason brand us with the Name of *Party*, and equally despise the Appellation, and those who give it, unless they mean, that by their Dulness they have made all Persons of Taste a Party against them, and then we Glory in the Title. But 'twas no Hatred to particular Persons, but a Love of the *Publick* that gave life to this Design; and we would endeavour as much as in us lies, to infuse the same Spirit into our Readers.

Hospitality and *Public-Spirit* have the same Source, namely, the Love of Mankind; yet 'tis no less certain than surprising, that we who are remarkable for the former, discover very little of the latter, tho' it seems more strongly enforced by Nature, yet thro' an odd Perverseness, all People are welcome to our Favour, but those whom Nature and their own Merits make worthy of it; while several of the Nobility and Gentry, in whose power alone it is to prevent this Evil, are not only passive, but Assistants to it, as if conscious of the Poverty and Infamy their Behaviour raises to their Country, they fly it and bestow their Riches, where, as they are less wanted, the People are less thankful for them.

Men of Virtue will require no other Incentive to doing Good than Virtue itself; but as if that was not sufficient, Providence often joins Honour and Interest in rewarding it, but to no Virtue more than this of *Publick-Spirit*: What can the ambitious Man hope for more, than to live where all Men honour him as a Friend or Benefactor, to meet none but those who have been made happy by his Influence, and whom his Goodness hath tied in a Relation nearer and dearer than that of Blood? such are not only Rewards for what is done, but Incentives to proceed in so honourable a Course; and surely no Country has more need of the Exertion of such a Virtue, whose Men of Fortune are not satisfied with impoverishing, but also despise it. The Complaint of our Manufactures is so generally known, we need not instance it, but let us beg leave to mention that those Gentlemen who are the most violent Decryers of them are the most easily deceived, not chusing goods from their own Knowledge, but the Shop-keeper's Testimony of their being Foreign; what an unaccountable Temper is this, that Men must be cheated to do good! But even if our Manufactures were inferior to other Nations, (which we will by no Means allow) what is the greatest Hindrance to their Improvement, is Want of Encouragement; the Trader meeting no Reward adequate to his Labour contracts a Poverty of Spirit that restrains him from contending with Foreigners, who he knows will gain more Credit from their Name, than he from Years of Labour; whereas were our People properly zealous for their Honour, in bearing indifferent Things at first, they would shortly have Goods of equal excellence with any in *Europe:* And who would think his Expence ill bestow'd, because not he but his Children were to have the Reward.

If in so few years the DUBLIN SOCIETY could be of such signal service to our Country, what might we not expect from the joint Endeavours of Nobility, Gentry, and People?

It seems very odd that a civilized Country should labour to deserve the Name of *the only Nation whose People entirely neglected their own Interest*, yet such it is, that had not a few risen up for the publick Good, even the manual Arts would have wanted a Support, and all the Industry of the Trader had never made this Country emerge from Scandal or Poverty. But besides Riches there are many Things necessary to the Prosperity of a Nation, and bad as the State of Trade is, that of Science is still worse, which as the noblest may be made the most profitable Acquisition of Man. Not to mention how few Patrons of it there are, Learning is fallen into such Disrepute that an Author is generally hated or contemn'd.

The first Reflection a good and wise Man has, after his Studies is, how to make them useful to Mankind; but he generally meets so many Obstacles from the Pride or Dulness of many that he must sit down content with the Appellation of Learned; or, if he does write, comply with the capricious Multitude, and follow the Road their vitiated Taste points out, rendring those Talents designed for their Instruction, the Debauchers both of their Taste and Manners.

With many it is a Fault to be above the common Level in Knowledge, and to have Wit odious, because unfashionable or unintelligible;—from such Science can have no hopes; but 'tis hard that those who owe much of their own Fortune to their Parts, should be so slow in rewarding them in others, and be so diligent in raising Funds for Folly, but none for Science. We before discover'd, that it was not what was truly valuable in our Plays that met with Applause, let us now also shew that those very Plays which the Publick esteem are less encouraged than Dancers or Singers; so that proportionably as those things decrease in real Value, they grow higher in Esteem: I have seen what they call a polite Assembly, sit in Rapture a full half hour at the Gestures of a foreign Dancer, and after reward him with the loudest Applauses, while an endeavouring Native who has racked his Lungs in their Service met with Inattention, or had his Words drowned in their Clamours. This might perhaps have proceeded from the Politeness of the Audience, who would not dishonour their Country, by ill-treating a Foreigner; but let them consider that this Complaisance is a Detriment, not to say Disgrace to our Nation; Politeness we grant in itself very laudable, but when, by Misapplication, it opposes that greater Virtue *Publick-Spirit* it is liable to the severest Reproach.

We shall perhaps enlarge more another time on this Head, tho' we are sure that the living Examples of some excellent Men will have much more Force than any thing we can say. We shall however be happy, if we can by our Writings assist in carrying on this great End, and persuade Men of Fortune to promote useful Arts, and prove their Worth consists more in the just Uses, than the bare Possession of Estates.

NO. 6

O let not those, of whom the Muse is scorn'd,
Alive nor dead, be of the Muse adorn'd.

Spenser.

My friend *Asper*, tho' sometimes too severe in his Judgment, is yet a Man of good Sense, and a Sincere Lover of his Country. In a Discourse we had the other Day on the Advancement of polite Literature in this Kingdom, he gave it as his opinion, that the Thing was impracticable: "In what Country (says he) have you heard, that the fine Arts flourished when the leading Men did not countenance them? Stop the Lifeblood at the Source, and the depending Members must necessarily perish. And what Attention can those give to Things of this Nature, who are constantly employed in the Study of accumulating Wealth, or idly spending it? I say, the Study of spending Money; for as if the old were not sufficient, they are daily finding out new Methods of Extravagance, yet never happen in all their searches on applying it to Merit. In those Pursuits, they lose the Taste of True Glory, and naturally hate these Arts, which as they are the Ornaments of good, are often the Scourges of bad Men. Yet, tho' sunk to the lowest Pitch, they retain Ambition enough to hinder them from consorting with those whose Understanding is a Reproach to their Ignorance. But if any should happen through the extraordinary Blessing of Nature, or otherwise, to have a juster taste, he must relinquish it, or be kept in perpetual Uneasiness, by the clashing of his Sentiments with those whom he consorts with. No Man can stand out as it were from the rest of the World; for when Fools become so numerous as to over-bear the thinking part of Mankind, they get the Laugh on their Side. By these Means our Gentry become only externally distinguishable from the Vulgar; and being inured to Vice and Folly, are pleas'd with nothing that does not Savour of them: How many good Things have been the Objects of the publick Censure? How many of the vilest have met general Approbation? Else sure *Fustian* playing would never be term'd *Genius; Faction, Spirit*; nor a Set of leaden-headed Fellows, the lowest of Mankind, set up for Men of Taste; nor books the vilest in their nature" (here he mentioned *Clarissa* and some other of our modern Pieces) "be accepted and universally read. These Things show the Flood of Barbarism to be at the highest, and 'tis vain to oppose it. There is a Fatality in all Things, some Ages shine with the Light of Science and Virtue, while others are buried in the grossest Darkness: These mutually and naturally succeed each other as Night does Day; and when it comes to any Nation's Turn to fall into Ignorance, Experience shews it can no more be avoided than the Change of the Seasons. Men may see it, and complain of it, but it serves only to disquiet themselves, not prevent the Evil."

Notwithstanding the Warmth he pronounced this with, I perceived he spoke with the Air of one who prophesies what he fears, and wishes his Predictions may prove false.

I answered with my usual calmness, "That the Encouragement of bad Things was not the peculiar Fault of this Age, as in all Times Blockheads at their first Appearance had the best Reception; and as to what he said of our great People having shewn themselves such able Politicians; that to have a Taste beside for the polite Arts, was perhaps more than human Nature would allow; and as they could not give their Attention to them, they might be easily deceived and take bad Writers for good ones for fear of which, they encourage none at all, and so are sure not to be mistaken."

This Discourse threw me into a serious Reflection on the State of Learning, and the more I considered it, the more Reason I had to fear the Truth of my Friend's Assertions.

The *Desire of Lucre* is become almost the general Spring of Action, and it has never produced any but mean ones; besides the Taste for irrational Pleasures has made the Souls of many so callous, as not to be sensible of any thing delicate. These two Passions naturally destroy the Love of Glory, which is the only Soil proper for producing generous Patrons as well as good Writers. If any one is known to expend something on the encouragement of Genius, the People stare, shake their Heads, and wish it may hold out with him; but no one wonders or blames him who expends his whole Time and Fortune on Trifles, empty if not vicious; or if he appears by the whole Tenor of his Life to be actuated by the desire of Gain, (a Passion much more unworthy a Gentleman) he passes for a sober and wise Man. Indeed the young Gentlemen of this Age, partly from Nature, partly from Education, have got a low kind of Prudence, and are taught to think every Thing that does not gratify the Senses, unsubstantial and trifling, and fit only for romantick Heads. And as for Praise, as they do nothing to deserve it, they are indifferent about it. *Don't wonder then* (says *Petronius* talking of Painting) *if these Arts have failed, when in the Eyes of Gods and Men, a Mass of Gold is more beautiful than all the Works of those foolish Greeklings*, PHIDIAS, APELLES, &c. This would be a melancholy Prospect, did not the many Societies we see formed for the Support of useful Trades and Charities, make us hope better Things. Nothing comes to its height at first, and the Spirit of encouraging Trade, may at length rise to Science. What has been done hitherto has been by Bodies of Men, few have had the courage singly to venture any Thing, tho' private Men have always been the Support of Works of Politeness.

No one can with any Colour of Reason pretend they love their Country, and affect to despise these Things; as they often contribute to, and are always the sign of its Prosperity, for as *Roscommon* says,

By secret influence of indulgent Skies,
Empire and Poesy together rise,
True Poets are the Guardians of a State,
And when they fail, portend approaching Fate;
For that which Rome to Conquest did inspire,
Was not the Vestal, but the Muses Fire;
Heav'n joins the Blessings, no declining Age,
E'er felt the Raptures of Poetick Rage.

Poetry should be esteemed, if not for its own Sake, on account of the good Company it appears in; as Swallows are held sacred, not because they Bring, but because they accompany the Summer.

NO. 7

Take Physic, Pomp!
Expose thyself to feel, what Wretches feel;
That thou mayst shake the Superflux to them,
And shew the Heavens more just.

Shakespear.

The Riches of a Nation are not to be estimated by the splendid Appearance or luxurious Lives of its Gentry; it is the uniform Plenty diffused through a People, of which the meanest as well as greatest partake, that makes them happy, and the Nation powerful. When this is wanting, the Splendour of the Great is rather a Reproach than Honour to them: As Mr *Addison* justly censures an *Italian* Prince, whose Subjects liv'd in the greatest Poverty, and were exposed to continual Dangers for want of a Bridge over a rapid River, whilst he lived in the utmost Magnificence. It is the Care of every wise Government to secure the lives and Properties of those who live under it: Why should it be less worth Consideration, to make those Lives comfortable, and these Properties worth preserving? Whoever travels through this Kingdom will see such Poverty, as few Nations in *Europe* can equal. In this City Things have the best Face; but still, as you leave the Town, the Scene grows worse, and presents you with the utmost Penury in the Midst of a rich Soil. Nothing perhaps shews it more clearly, than that though the People have but one small tax of Two Shillings a Year, yet when the Collector comes, for Default of Payment, he is obliged to carry off such of their poor Utensils, as their being forced to use denotes the utmost Misery; those he keeps, until by begging, or other Shifts more hard, they can redeem them. Indeed Money is a Stranger to them; and were they as near the *Golden Age* in some other Respects, as they are in this, they would be the happiest People in the World. As for their Food, it is notorious they seldom taste Bread or Meat; their Diet, in Summer, is Potatoes and sour Milk; in Winter, when something is required comfortable, they are still worse, living on the same Root, made palatable only by a little Salt, and accompanied with Water: Their Cloaths so ragged, that they rather publish than conceal the Wretchedness it was meant to hide; nay, it is no uncommon Sight to see half a dozen Children run quite naked out of a Cabin, scarcely distinguishable from a Dunghill, to the great Disgrace of our Country with Foreigners, who would doubtless report them Savages, imputing that to choice which only proceeds from their irremediable Poverty. Let any one take a Survey of their Cabins, and then say, whether such a Residence be worthy any thing that challenges the Title of a human Creature. You enter, or rather creep in, at a Door of Hurdles plaistered with Dirt, of which the Inhabitant is generally the Fabricator; within-side you see (if the Smoke will permit you) the Men, Women, Children, Dogs, and Swine lying promiscuously; for their Opulence is such that they cannot have a separate House for their Cattle, as it would take too much from the Garden, whose produce is their only Support. Their Furniture is much fitter to be lamented than described, such as a Pot, a Stool, a few wooden Vessels, and a broken bottle: In this manner all the Peasantry, to a Man, live: and I Appeal to any one, who knows the Country, for the Justness of the Picture. Who, after having seen this, comes to Town and beholds their sumptuous and expensive Equipages, their Treats and Diversions, can contain the highest Indignation? Such Follies considered in themselves, are but ridiculous; but when we see the bitter consequences of them, 'twere Inhumanity to laugh. BOCCALINI, to create a Distaste for false Glory, introduces SFORZA Duke of *Milan*, making his triumphal entry into *Parnassus*, attended, by Order of *Apollo*, by all whom his Victories had made miserable. *Never* (says the Writer) *was seen so sad a Spectacle, the Eyes of the most obdurate were melted into Tears, to see such an infinite Number of Creatures; some starved in loathsome Hospitals, some mangled and hewed to pieces by horrid Wounds, some trampled to Death under Horses Feet; and others begging their Bread on the Road; their Prince's Service, in which they had lost their Blood, and exposed their Lives to a thousand Dangers, not having furnished them with enough to carry them to their Homes, which, to their Misfortune, they had so foolishly abandoned. As he passed, a thousand curses were thrown on him, on the Art of War, and that false Love of Glory, which renders Mankind miserable.* I fancy, many of our fine Gentlemen's Pageantry would be greatly tarnished, were their gilt coaches to be preceded and followed by the miserable Wretches, whose Labour supports them. That some should live in a more sumptuous manner than others, is very allowable; but sure it is hard, that those who cultivate the Soil, should have so small a Part of its Fruits; and that among Creatures of the same Kind there should be such a Disproportion in their manner of living; it is a kind of Blasphemy on Providence, and seems to shew, as our Motto finely expresses it, "the Heavens unjust." Our modern Systems hold, that the Riches and Power of Kings are by no means their Property, but a Depositum in their Hands, for the Use of the People: And if we consider the natural Equality of Mankind, we shall believe the same of the Estates of Gentlemen, bestowed on them at the first distribution of Properties, for promoting the Public Good: And when, by the use they make of their Fortunes, they thwart that End, they are liable to the same or a greater Reproach than a Prince who abuses his Power. Is it not natural for a Man, who rides in his Coach on a bitter Day, or lies on his Velvet Couch, secured from all the Inclemencies of the Weather, to reflect with Pity on those who suffer Calamities equal to his Enjoyments?

But there are some People who shut their Hearts to Charity, and to excuse their want of Compassion, throw all the Fault as well as Misfortune on the unhappy Poor. Their Sloth, say those, is the cause of their Misery. 'Tis pleasant to observe, that this Objection frequently comes from those who in all their lives have not been as serviceable to their Country, as the idlest of these poor Creatures in one Day; but the Falsity of the Thing shews evidently the Ignorance of the Assertors. We shall examine into their Means, and thence judge, how much the greatest Industry does or can better them. There are three kinds of people in the country besides the Gentlemen of Fortune; we shall begin with the lowest and most numerous, the *Labourers*; they have an Acre of Land at a very high Rent, to pay which they must work for their Master a great part of the Year, the rest is employed in cultivating their own Garden for an immediate Support; then judge what Time they have to procure Cloaths and other Necessaries for themselves and their Families: Thus they must labour, and that without Intermission, for the lowest Livelyhood: yet there are few whom hard Seasons or other Calamities have not sometime in their Lives sent to beg. The poorer kind of Farmers called in some parts of the Kingdom *Cottiers*, live nigh as miserably as the former, though they hold larger Quantities of Land, but at such a Rent as both hurts them and the Landlord. Gentlemen perceiving that in *England* Farmers pay heavy Rent, and yet live comfortably, without considering the Disproportion of Markets and every Thing else, raise their Rent high, and extort it heavily. Thus none will hold from them but those desperate Creatures who ruin the Land (in vain) to make their Rent; they fly; the Landlord seizes, and to avoid the like Mischance, takes all into his own hands; which being unable to manage, he turns to grazing; thus one part of the Nation is starved, and the other deserted. The rich Farmers or *Graziers*, the third Sort, hold vast Quantities of Land, and as they live like estated Men, equally contribute to the Poverty of the rest.

The Evil is easier seen than remedied; but perhaps the Example of a Gentleman of Fortune, whom I knew, may be useful. He came early to the Possession of an Estate valued 2000*l. per Ann.* but set to a vast Number of Tenants at a very high rent: As usual in such cases, nothing could be in a worse Condition than his Estate: his Rents ill paid, the Land out of Heart, and not a Bush, not a tolerable Enclosure, much less Habitation, to be seen. He found his Leases out, but he did not study, with the Greediness of a young Heir, how to raise the price nor Value of his Lands, nor turn out all his poor Tenants to make room for two or three rich. He retained all those to whose honest Industry he had been Witness, and lowered his Rents very considerably: he bound them to plant certain Quantities of Trees, and make other Improvements. Thus in a few years Things had another Face, his Rent was well paid, his Tenants grew rich, and his Estate increased daily in Beauty and Value: There was a Village on it, which was equally ruinous with the rest; when he designed the Improvement of this, he did not take the ordinary Method of establishing *Horse-races* and *Assemblies*, which do but encourage Drinking and Idleness but at a much smaller Expence he introduced a *Manufacture* which, though not very considerable, employed the whole Town, and in Time made it opulent. Notwithstanding all this, no Person lives more hospitably in the Country, in the Town more genteel. I have often heard him discourse on this Subject. "I have lowered my Rents (says he) but how much am I the poorer? What Gratification do I want? 'Tis true, I have not every Month some new invented Carriage coming from *England* to make the Town amazed at my Folly: I keep no *French* Cook, I wear my own Country manufactures; by which means I save, I believe, more than I lose by the lowness of my Rent: At the same time I am satisfied I am making Numbers happy, without Expence to myself, doing my Country Service without Ostentation, and leaving my son a better Estate without oppressing any one."

Had many of our Gentlemen the same just Way of thinking, we should no doubt see this Nation in a short time in the most flourishing Condition, notwithstanding all the Disadvantages we labour under. But while they proceed on a quite Opposite Plan, it can never emerge, though we were possess'd of many more Advantages than we are able to boast of.

NO. II

Our Papers are sometimes employed on Subjects which we think useful, tho' no present Occasion should suggest them, at other Times, the posture of Affairs affords us Matter of Speculation, and now the Season presents one, which it were equally blameable in us and all good Men to neglect.

Pythagoras recommends to his Disciples, to pass the Close of each Day in Retirement, to revolve their past Actions, to contemplate useful Matters, and lay in proper Resolutions for their future Conduct; nor is it less wisely ordained in the Christian Polity, that certain Times recurring annually, should be devoted to Religion, lest the Mind too much softened by Pleasures, or overgrown with the Rust of worldly Cares, should forget its high Destination. I have read of Persons whom some Misfortune threw among barbarous People, where being habituated to their Company, they grew in Love with their Manners and never remembered or never desired to see their native Country. A small Time properly applied to Reflection, would prevent such a scandalous Degeneracy; and there is none who cannot spare it, cannot spare the smallest Part of their Time to provide for the longest of their Existence, where their Happiness, or Misery is not Precarious, or by Fits, but to endure without Interruption thro' all Eternity.

There are a Set of Men not infrequent in this City, who tho' they allow of Morality, cry down reveal'd Religion, yet in their Practice, they make them equal, neglecting both; how weak an Obligation, Morality consider'd in itself would be, may be seen, by supposing Laws imposed on a Nation, without Rewards for those who kept, or Punishments for those who broke them. They are not true friends to Virtue, who would deprive it of any thing which serves to enforce or strengthen it; they are like the Wolves in the Fable, who enter'd into a Treaty with the Sheep, wherein it was stipulated, that they should dismiss the Dogs; and then they tore the flock to Pieces. These Men have so far interwoven their darling Appetites with every Thought, that their most refined Judgments on Things become but Gratifications to a favourite Passion, and all the Actions resulting from thence, tho' agreeable to their System of Morality, are not less opposite to Religion than right Reason, for herein they coincide, as those two only produce Actions which are called good and wise. Formerly an affectation of Singularity caused such Opinions; but now, to have no Taint of them, is almost as Singular, they have since got a Reason more substantial, they form a Set of Rules at one to indulge their Passions and lull their Conscience. Thus they sometimes deceive Men of Sense thro' the hardiness of their Notions, and the Vulgar very often, from an Ability to talk more against Religion, than they can for it, and flush'd with this Appearance of Success, attribute that to a Defect in the Cause, which was merely in the Defender.

The two greatest Enemies of Religion are the above-mentioned *Infidelity* and *Blind Zeal*, the former attacks it like an open Enemy, and the latter like an indiscreet Friend, does it more Harm than Good; the first gives rise to the Free-Thinkers, the latter to our Sectaries, a truly religious Life has the same Efficacy to the prevention of both. This would soon convince Unbelievers of the superior Power of Religion towards a Moral Life, and shew at the same time how much it exceeds all Systems of Philosophy, in supporting us under Misfortunes as that teaches us only to bear; but this to rejoice in them, by fastening our Thoughts on something indeed past our Comprehension, but not our Hopes: And even this Appearance of Religion would hinder many from throwing themselves into the Arms of the first false Teacher that offers, who with the Advantage of a Shew of Zeal, promises that Comfort they could not find before.

The Practice of Virtue and Religion is indispensible at all Times; but never more than at this, when we commemorate the Time our Creator became our Redeemer, and for our sake manifested in the highest manner the highest Attributes of his Divinity, his *Love* and his *Power*, the one in dying for us, and the other in conquering Death, by giving that glorious Proof of our Immortality, and being himself the first Fruits of the Resurrection.

A Notebook of Edmund Burke

Only in the middle of the twentieth century was a notebook of early Burke writings found in Burke's papers belonging to Earl Fitzwilliam and deposited in the public library of Sheffield, England. The notebook sheds important light on Burke's thinking in his first years in England, since the essays in it are assumed to have been written between 1750 and 1756. Included here are two short pieces in which Burke describes his ideal of a "gentleman" and of a "wise man." In a third sketch from the notebook he offers his "idea of a woman," which is assumed to be a sketch of Mrs. Burke. Finally, there are some interesting early observations on religion.

THE CHARACTER OF A FINE GENTLEMAN

SOME OF THE LEARNED have quarrelled with the vulgar notions of a fine Gentleman; and because they thought this a Character highly esteemable, were displeased to see it so often applied to a sort of men they could by no means approve. They therefore wholly excluded from this denomination all whose morals were dissolute, though their manners were none so agreeable; and they concluded that the man of compleat vertue was alone the fine Gentleman.

We must trust the world to give names to Characters; to change and transpose the distinctions Custom has settled, would not be an improvement of knowledge, but an abuse of words. Let us see then, what sort of men they are, who are generally termed fine Gentlemen, and endeavour to settle with ourselves a notion of this Character. But a Character is too complete a thing to be drawn into a Definition. We may acquire a much better Idea of it from viewing it in as great a variety of Lights as the Subject will bear.

This Character is not denominated from excellence in any sort of Business or employment; it belongs solely to conversation, and the habitudes of pleasant Society; its Basis is politeness, whose essence is Ease: and hence it is that there is no Character more rarely found; for easy behaviour, easy conversation, and easy writing are the hardest things in the world. At your first Entrance into any company, the fine Gentleman is not the person who strikes you most, and you may possibly converse with him several times before you discover what his excellence is, and where it lies.

He is no Scholar; every accomplishment he has seems to be derived immediately from his nature; there must be no appearance of any thing borrowed; to think justly, costs him no more trouble than to breathe freely. Yet he is not ignorant; he seems rather to slight books, than not to know them.

There is very little of Wit in his conversation; this is a quality that draws the admiration of company, but often at the expense of their esteem. It very soon tires; and there is such an immense distance between the heights of that, and the plainness of common discourse, that it breaks the even tenor of conversation that can alone take in the whole company and make it agreeable in all its parts.

Neither is his discourse of the humorous kind; it never raises a laugh; but yet it is not wholly averse from that Strain. There is a sort of concealed Irony that tinges his whole conversation. He entertains no extremes of opinion; he scarcely ever disputes; he is sceptical in his notions; and not fond of deep disquisitions; there is some one point in all Topics that seems to determine his judgement about them without much enquiries into other particulars. He seldom contradicts your opinions, and you will gain very little by contradicting his.

To make a man perfectly agreeable to his company he ought not to exert such Talents as may raise the envy, and consequently the uneasiness, of anybody in it. 'Tis on this principle, that the Character of a fine gentleman is not a brilliant one. There is no part of his discourse you prefer to another; and he is never the man whose bons mots are retailed in every company. His expressions are well chosen and easy, but they are not strong. There is no Glare; but there is a universal Effect produced by an infinity of fine Touches, which are imperceptible and inimitable. You may observe in lower Life, that a speaker of wise Sentences, a strenuous disputant, or one ostentatious of knowledge, never want[s] abundance of admirers; but in an higher Sphere such persons are in no great request. People of rank can brook a superiority, especially an avowed superiority, much less than others; there is a principle of politeness that forms an apparent level of their understanding. And hence I believe it is that politeness is apt sometimes to flatten into the Insipid.

The Vulgar are apt to judge of politeness by a number of ceremonious observances; but this notion is a good deal exploded amongst people of good sense and breeding. You distinguish nothing in the address of the fine Gentleman other than that it is free and unconstrained; there is a sort of openness and candour in his demeanor that invite you to that same openness and freedom; his Civilities and compliments are few, for there is something in professions that confound[s] a man; and a complement has not always a very pleasing Effect when it cannot be answered with Spirit.

Nothing is more disengaged than the language, the behaviour and the very looks of a perfect Gentleman; for which reason it can seldom be reached by men of Business, or professions, or those who are given to a close attention to any thing. This part grows almost spontaneously out of a plentiful fortune, the smiles of the world, and acquaintance with Courts.

Indolence is a predominant ingredient in this Character; Diligence, economy, prudence, and a consideration of the future are the virtues of men of business; and give an air of closeness and reserve, inconsistent with the perpetual Gaiety and ease that shine with such a constant Lustre in the fine Gentleman.

To be libertine in his practices and opinions is another part of his Character; but he is not a debauchee; 'tis only so much as may make him entirely a man of the world. In point of Gallantry he is no way scrupulous. The greatest liberty in his actions, and the greatest decency in his discourse are his Character in that point. Drunkenness is a Vice he abhors; but Luxury in point of eating he is not ashamed of. He may be accused of excess in Gaming; but the great Temper he preserves under his Losses, is one of his remarkable excellencies.

You see no Tincture of Vanity in his conversation; and it is a nice Eye that under that air of Affability and complaisance can discern a great deal of pride.

The fine Gentleman is never a warm friend;—it is but too true, that a Close attachment to particulars makes a man less easy and pleasing in general Society; and it is there and not in the relations of a friend, a father, a husband, or a relation, or any close connexions that a fine Gentleman shines. France is a great polisher of manners; for there they pursue publick assemblies, and neglect the satisfactions of privacy and retirement. The fine Gentleman has but little of Tenderness or what is called Good nature; a frequent feeling for others, a mixing with the unfortunate, and interesting oneself in their concerns, tends to throw a gloom on a man's Character and make it splenetick and uneven.

It is almost impossible for any man to be a fine Gentleman, who has not courage. But as such a Character is not ostentatious or affected, it is equally Essential to it to conceal this Quality. It is only to appear in a composure, formed by a confidence a man finds in himself, that he is able to prevent being disturbed in his own Course by the insolence or brutality of others. The whole Circle of Taste must be open to him; but the affected parts, the Cant of a dealer in pictures, or the Chimeras of a Virtuoso never make their appearance. Such a Character goes through Life with great Smoothness. He is praised by everybody; respected, esteemed, courted, and everything but really Loved.

I am not sure as to this last point; for he receives all the marks of Love, except the disagreeable one[s] that arise in Close intimacies, when men are undisguised and unrestrained, and give their Tempers a loose in all humours.

Perhaps this Character in all its points is not to be met. I have sometimes seen something not very far from it. To be consistent and perfect, I fancy it must be nearly as this is described. I do not mean a perfect man, for this Character has many faults; but none that do not in a good measure contribute to what we find most beautiful and pleasing in it.

THE CHARACTER OF A WISE MAN

The person I intend to describe is not the wise man of the Stoics, much less is he one of those whom the scripture calls wise unto Salvation; but a mere wise man of this world; one who chooses some desirable end in life and disposes the means of it judiciously and with efficacy. Having given this definition, any further character may seem useless and idle; as to give a Character of prudence and industry in the abstract. But to me it seems otherwise. Those things which appear to depend wholly on reason and prudence have always some inferior supports in our passions; even reason and prudence themselves depend, if not for their substance, yet certainly for their colour and bent on our native constitution and complexions. A certain adjustment of passions, and a certain mode of understanding, are as requisite to form a wise man as a certain degree of reason and good sense.

A wise man may properly be said to have but two passions, avarice and ambition; the rest are absorbed in these. And if they appear, it is in a subordinate way and to serve the purposes of the two principal.

When he has any end in view, he never looses sight of it; he never suffers it to be sacrificed to intermediate and triffling gratifications. Weak minds cannot fix their eyes steadily on one object. They are soon weary of the pursuit. At the same time that they are unwilling wholly to relinquishing the principal Design, they cannot avoid taking up with some temporary Reliefs, every one of which, however, puts them further and further from their Object.

They waste their whole life without the enjoyment of their pleasures or the establishment of their interest; and drop into their Graves fatigued, restless, anxious, unsatisfied, unsuccessful beings. But the whole life of a wise man is one uniform plot;—everything lends the main design. He knows he cannot enjoy all things, and therefore he drives at some one secure and permanent enjoyment. He leaves nothing to chance; and you might as well take away his Life as make him live extempore. He considers each day only as it does something for the next, and every Year he lives only as it promises a greater interest or grandeur for the future. Yet he is not without the enjoyment of his grandeur or fortune; but this enjoyment only whets him for new ones; and the chief satisfaction he has in them is that they are the certain pledges of more.

He is courageous in an high degree; and knowing that Life without its ends is nothing, he will always venture his life for his ends; and the ends themselves sometimes to extend them. But this never without reason; for his courage is rather of the steady than adventurous kind. He will not move one foot untill he has fixed the other. Yet as he has always a principle of Vigour within him; when he has done so, no frivolous fears shall hinder him from moving both. His pace is not rapid but firm and even. If he does not gain ground as fast as they who move by starts, he never looses any; and is always gaining something. He is called fortunate, and he is so; there happen chances nearly equal to all men; but only those who are ever attentive to their Design, see all the accidents that may tend to it. And it is not that more of these adventures happen to him than to other men; but he knows them when they do happen and knows too how to make use of them. His understanding is strong without being very extensive; and the stronger for being confined. His imagination is neither warm nor bright; so that all his actions are rather to be approved than admired. Vanity is a little passion gratified with little things; and always pernicious to the owner of it. It never gains much, because it lays by nothing, and works always for present pay; it has an appetite early many [may be] satisfied but [which] must be fed often. A wise design has been disconcerted because the vain contriver must needs have his wisdom appear as well as his design executed: but the wise man is far above that triffling gratification which puts him in the power of every fool; yet he knows his own value to a scruple; he is even proud to the last degree; a passion which never yet brought any man into contempt but one extremely weak,—a sort of people who are seldom proud. But as he carefully avoids contempt he is not passionate for admiration; he gains a solid esteem attended with solid advantage; he admires no man, esteems very few, and those he esteems he always fears. Those whom he holds in the lowest contempt are good natured men of no great abilities and men of fine parts who are imprudent and unsuccessful in the World. He knows that patient suffering one injury is sure to draw on another; his pride makes him feel all injuries deeply, and his constancy enables him to keep any resolution he has formed. So that his revenge is deep, slow, certain, implaccable and ruinous. On the other hand his friendship is sure; oblige him and he never forgets it. He understands the Value of a good Office; and that is a great deal. He knows likewise the use of a friend in any design. In choosing his friends he has little regard to the heart or moral character; and once he has chosen a friend, no vice of his can alianate [*sic*] him. He expects them in men. It is not vice but folly he objects to;

and as he never much esteems his friends, even something of that he may forgive. But if he should chang[e] his friendship, the object is not neglected but ruined.

In his discourse he is not eloquent, yet he is always very well heard; because no man has ever heard him say a light undigested thing. He seems to say more than he expresses; he has a slowness to determine; he draws all his ideas from experience rather than Speculation; and chooses to appear not so much an agreeable man as a Man of good contrivance and sagacity; and of Action rather than Elocution. He is extremely slow in trusting or believing; and he is confirmed in this disposition every day he lives. When he sees any man perfidious, he grows more cautious. And when he sees another faithful, he does not change his mind; because he believes he has an interest in his fidelity. This belief of men acting more according to their interest than they really do, is what prejudices him more than anything else. He trusts much to himself; this sometimes hurts him too.

He has nothing of that milky quality of good nature which, as it softens, generally something enfeebles the mind. He is in his nature stern, severe, and inflexible. The life of a man is nothing in his eyes if his dying should be anything more conducive to the management of his business than his living. Yet he cannot be said to be cruel or fond of blood, because he never chooses to do anything unnecessary. And he is seldom in the passion of anger.

It is hardness in his Character I take to be the cause why he has no Religion. His passions are not easily moved; and he is incredulous in his nature. He is, besides, proud; apt to reject anything which has a mean aspect in any sense, or is much venerated by mean people. He estimates things merely as they are estimated in the world; and he is always ready to suspect everything of policy and contrivance. In that light he looks upon Religion; which he esteems and despises at once. But he never seeks an empty and foolish reputation from running it down. You cannot discover his Sentiments any otherwise than by his indifference in it and the discoveries which being too cautious of a discovery sometimes makes.

His conversation is not without an agreeable pleasantry; but his mirth is usually dry and sarcastical. His way of loving mankind is but an intercourse of business; not of affection. For he neither loves nor hates anybody. When he marries he makes a good choice because he chooses without passion. Family and fortune he secures; and does not neglect those qualities that may make his Wife an useful and agreeable companion. He makes to her a good husband; but she has not a great deal of his attention; and when she dies, he has a loss of which he is not insensible; but not to that degree which may hinder him of reflecting that his eldest Son may have a better match by the removal of her jointure.

His Children are well educated, and well kept; and in general well instructed to make a figure in the World. Far from being a burden to him, they may be considered as instruments of his Ambition. By advancing them he makes them useful to him; advancing thereby his own importance and grandeur in publick life.

He is steady to his party, and useful to it; and seeks preferment without being servile. In an Office of trust he does not betray it by dishonesty, nor degrade it by inability; but it acquires no dignity under him; and passes to his successor just as he found it. He neglects no usual profit, and scruples no usual action of whatever nature; but to innovate is dangerous and uncertain; so that, wronging no man in triffles, nor exasperating any by petty injuries; standing no man's rival in inferior accomplishments or pleasures, and serving many for his own ends; ruining those who endeavour to disserve him; being a man to be depended on in business, and adhering to justice whilst it is consistent with sound policy, (and it is not often otherwise), he passes thro affairs with reputation; not being capricious and splenetick; advancing his Children by all means; and not exasperating one set of his neighbours by being of party with the other, he passes for no ill natured Man. Having lived successfully, respected, feared, courted, and something envied; hated but by few, and that secretly; with a Character defended by all the common maxims of Life to which he has always carefully adjusted his conduct, he dies, is emboweld, embalmed, and buried, with a Monument expressing his family, his places, and his Alliances.

THE CHARACTER OF— [MRS EDMUND BURKE]

I intend to give my Idea of a woman. If it at all answers any Original I shall be pleased; for if such a person really exists as I would describe, she must be far Superior to any Description, and such as I must love too well to be able to paint as I ought.

She is handsome; but it is a Beauty not arising from features, from Complexion and Shape. She has all these in an high degree; but whoever looks at her never perceives them, nor makes them the Topic of his Praise. 'Tis all the sweetness of Temper, Benevolence, Innocence and Sensibility which a face can express, that forms her beauty.

She has a face that just raises your attention at first sight; it grows on you every moment, and you wonder it did no more than raise your Attention at first.

Her Eyes have a mild light, but they awe you when she pleases; they command like a good man out of office, not by Authority but virtue.

Her features are not perfectly regular; this Sort of Exactness is more to be praised than loved; it is never animated.

Her stature is not tall. She is not to be the admiration of everybody, but the happiness of one.

She has all the Delicacy that does not Exclude firmness.

She has all the Softness that does not imply weakness.

There is often more of the Coquet shewn in an Effected plainness, than a Tawdry finery; she is always clean without preciseness or affectation.

Her Gravity is a gentle thoughtfulness that Softens the features without discomposing them. She is usually grave.

Her Smiles are . . . inexpressible—

Her Voice is a low, Soft musick; not formed to rule in publick Assemblies, but to charm those who can distinguish a Company from a Croud. It has this advantage, you must come Close to her to hear it.

To describe her body, describes her mind; one is the Transcript of the other.

Her understanding is not shewn in the Variety of matters it exerts itself on, but the goodness of the Choice she makes.

She does not Shew it so much in doing or Saying striking things, as in avoiding such as she ought not to say or do.

She discovers the right from the wrong in things not by reasoning, but Sagacity.

Most women, and many good ones, have a Closeness and something Selfish in their Disposition:—She has a true generosity of Temper. The most extravagant cannot be more willing to give; the most Covetous not more cautious to whom they give.

No person of so few years can know the world better: no person was ever less corrupted by that knowledge. Her politeness seems to flow rather from a natural disposition to oblige, than from any rules on that subject; and therefore never fails to Strike those who understand good breeding, and those who do not.

She does not run with a Girlish eagerness into new friendships; which as they have no foundation in reason, only tend to multiply and imbitter disputes. 'Tis long before she chuses; but then it is fixid forever; and the first hours of romantick friendships are not more warm than hers after years.

As she never disgraces her good nature by severe reflections on any body, so she never degrades her Judgement by immoderate or ill-placed praises; for everything violent is contrary to the Gentleness of her disposition, and the evenness of her virtue. She has a steady and firm mind, which takes no more from the female Character than the Solidity of marble does from its Polish and Lustre.

She has such virtues as make us value the truely great of our own Sex. She has all the winning Graces that make us love even the faults we see in the weak and Beautiful of hers.

Who can see and know such a Creature and not love to Distraction? Who can know her, and himself, and entertain much hope?

RELIGION OF NO EFFICACY

Nothing can operate but from its own principles. The Principle of Religion is that God attends to our actions to reward and punish them. This Principle has an independent Operation, and Influences our Actions much to the Benefit of civil Society. But then the Influence on civil Society is only an oblique Influence. The Direct Influence is the civil Law itself, its own Principles and its own Sanctions. If you attempt to make the end of Religion to be its Utility to human Society, to make it only a sort of supplement to the Law, and insist principally upon this Topic, as is very common to do, you then change its principle of Operation, which consists on Views beyond this Life, to a consideration of another kind, and of an inferiour kind; and thus, by forcing it against its Nature to become a Political Engine, You make it an Engine of no efficacy at all. It can never operate for the Benefit of human Society but when we think it is directed quite another way: because it then only operates from its own principle. Will any Man believe that eternal rewards and Punishments are the Sanctions of Momentary things of no Concern? Will he not think it a strange Machine that employs so vast, so immense a force, such a grand Apparatus to move so insignificant a weight? Is it not much more natural, much more in the order of things, to suppose that if a reasonable Creature is to determine of his own Destiny so as to determine him for Bliss or for Misery everlastingly, that the Trial is made subservient to a great End of the last Importance, and that Trial the *Means* of Attaining that End, rather than that all Eternity should be subservient to the purposes of a moment? When we are told this, we cool immediately. The Springs are seen; we value ourselves on the Discovery; we cast Religion to the Vulgar and lose all restraint. For as we confine the Ends of Religion to this world, we naturally annihilate its Operation, which must wholly depend upon the Consideration of another. Men never gain anything, by forcing Nature to conform to their Politicks. I know the Clergy, shamed and frightend at the Imputation of Enthusiasm, endeavour to cover Religion under the Shield of Reason, which will have some force with their Adversaries. But God has been pleased to give Mankind an Enthusiasm to supply the want of Reason; and truely, Enthusiasm comes nearer the great and comprehensive Reason in its effects, though not in the Manner of Operation, than the Common Reason does; which works on confined, narrow, common, and therefore plausible, Topics. The former is the lot of very few. The latter is common; and fit enough for common affairs—to buy and sell, to teach Grammar and the like; but is utterly unfit to meddle with Politics, Divinity and Philosophy. But Enthusiasm is a sort of Instinct, in those who possess it, that operates, like all Instincts, better than a mean Species of Reason.

It is true indeed that enthusiasm often misleads us. So does reason too. Such is the Condition of our Nature; and we can't help it. But I believe that we act most when we act with all the Powers of our Soul; when we use our Enthusiasm to elevate and expand our Reasoning; and our Reasoning to check the Roving of our Enthusiasm.

As God has made all his Creatures active, He has made Man principally so. Many of our actions that compose our principal Duties are difficult, attended with trouble, and often with Danger. But action is influenced by Opinion—and our Notion of things; and nothing but strong and confirmed Opinion can lead to resolute Action. Therefore doubt and Scepticism were no more made for Man than Pride and Positiveness; for no Action, or but feeble and imperfect essays towards action, can arise from dubious Notions and fluctuating Principles.

RELIGION

If there be a God such as we conceive, He must be our Maker.

If he is our Maker, there is a Relation between us.

If there be a Relation between us, some Duty must arise from that Relation, since [we] cannot conceive that a reasonable Creature can be placed in any Relation that does not give rise to some Duty.

This Relation betwixt God and Man, is that Man has received several Benefits but can return none. That he may suffer all Manner of Mischief, but can return none, or by himself avert none.

Therefore by no *act* can he perform this Duty; but he can by the Sentiments of his Mind.

Where we have received good, 'tis natural to Praise.

Where we hope good, it is natural to pray.

Where we fear Evil, 'tis natural to deprecate it.

This is the foundation of Religion.

We have a Relation to other Men.

We want many things compassable only by the help of other beings like ourselves.

They want things compassable within our Help.

We love these beings and have a Sympathy with them.

If we require help, 'tis reasonable we should give help.

If we love, 'tis natural to do good to those whom we love.

Henee one Branch of our Duties to our fellow Creatures is active—Hence Benevolence.

This is the foundation of Morality.

Morality does not necessarily include Religion, since it concerns only our Relation with Men.

But Religion necessarily includes Morality, because the Relation of God as a Creator is the same to other Men as to us.

If God has placed us in a Relation attended with Duties, it must be agreeable to him that we perform those Duties.

Hence Moral Duties are included in Religion, and enforced by it.

If God has provided fatally for all things, we may honour him but we can neither love him, fear him, nor hope in Him. For there is no object for those Passions.

This would reduce all worship to praise only, and Gratitude.

Gratitude is an inert Principal, because it concerns only things done.

Hope and fear are the Springs of everything in us, because they look to the future about which, only, Mankind can be sollicitous. To take away Providence would therefore be to take away Religion.

The Arguments against Providence are from our *Reasonings*, observing a certain order in the works of God. There is nothing at all in our natural feelings against it.

There is a great deal in our natural feelings for it.

All Dependant Beings that have a Sense of their Dependence naturally cry out to their Superiour for assistance.

No man can act uniformly as if a fatality governed everything.

Men do not naturally conceive that, when they are strongly actuated to call upon a Superior, that [*sic*] they cannot be heard; they do not conceive that they have Passions which have no Purpose.

They naturally measure their Duties to the Divinity by their own wants and their feelings, and not by abstract Speculations.

In the one they cannot be deceived, in the other they may.

One is taken from the Nature of God which we do not understand, the other from our own which we understand better.

Metaphysical or Physical Speculations neither are, or ought to be, the Grounds of our Duties; because we can arrive at no certainty in them. They have a weight when they concur with our own natural feelings; very little when against them.

The Ends of a transitory Animal may be answered without any knowledge of a God. They are so answered in Beasts.

Men have some knowledge of God.

Hence we presume other Ends are to be answered.

Man has Ideas of Immortality, and wishes for it; he does not think he has Ideas and Wishes, for no End.

Hence he presumes he may be Immortal.

Man is sensible he has Duties; that the Performance of these Duties must be agreeable to God; That being agreeable to God is the way to be happy.

Experience shows him that the Performance of these Duties does not give him happiness in Life;—therefore He concludes that they must make him happy after Death; and that for that Reason, something in him must survive.

He sees that this Notion is favourable to the performance of all his Duties, and that the Contrary notion is unfavourable to it.

He observes that this Notion tends to perfect his Nature; that the contrary tends to sink him to a level of Inferiour Natures.

In disputed Questions those Notions that tend to make him better and happier, to bind him to his fellow Creatures, and to his Creator and to make him a more excellent Creature, are true rather than the Contrary. These Arguments are taken from within; the others are foreign.

If his Soul survives after Death; it does not appear why it should not live for ever.

If the Soul lives for ever, the Space of time spent in this Life is inconsiderable. It is therefore reasonable that it should take up but the smallest part of our Attention.

We do not know how far our relation to other Men shall continue after Death.

We know that our Relation to God must continue the same after Death.

We know therefore that our Duty to God is of more Moment than our Attention to ourselves or others.

It is natural to suppose that what goes first in the order of Nature should produce what follows it.

It is therefore reasonable to conclude that our Performance of our Duty here must make our fate afterwards.

It is reasonable that the smallest part of anything should be destined for the Uses of the whole, rather than that the whole should be employed for the purposes of a part.

It is therefore reasonable to suppose that our Actions here are made the *Causes* of our future happiness or Misery, and not that our future Misery and Happiness are designed as the Sanctions of our Duties here.

Hence it is that this Life is a Preparation for the next.

Hence it is that we ought not to emmerse ourselves too much in the things which make us consider this Life as our all.

Hence it is that for this Purpose we ought to deny ourselves; since an Indulgence in Pleasures here removes our Attention from further Objects, and weakens our Desire for them.

We may have observed that the Passions which arise from self love frequently clash with those Duties which arise from our Relation to other Men.

But less mischief arises from a restraint on our desires, than from indulging them to the prejudice of others.

Thus self-Denial becomes the second of the Pillars of Morality.

This is the more austere part of our Duty, and the most difficult.

If we depend upon a Superior being, it is but just that we should pray to him; because we have no other means of sufficiently expressing our Dependence; though he should already be sufficiently apprised of our wants, and willing to supply them.

If we depend upon any Superior being, it is reasonable that we should trust in him, though we do not see the Motives and tendencies of his Actions. Good Will even among Men could not be supported otherwise.

If we have Reason to suppose that he has proposed any thing, we ought to believe it firmly, though we should not thoroughly comprehend the Nature of the things proposed; otherwise we break off our Dependence as much as we should our Connexion with Men if we refused them all Credit.

God has given us a knowledge of himself, and we believe that knowledge to be of some Importance to us.

We therefore ought not to imagine it impossible that he may be willing to give us some further knowledge of his Nature or his Will.

Neither is it reasonable that we should judge it impossible for him to find fit Means of communicating this knowledge.

If he intends to communicate such knowledge, the best Proofs of such a Design are such acts of Power as can leave us no Doubt of their coming from God; for thus it is we know that he exist[s] and that he is all powerful and all-wise.

God has for the most Parts made Men the Instruments of all the Good he does to Men.

Most of their strength is from mutual Assistance.

Most of their knowledge from mutual Instruction.

There is a principal of Credit, or faith, in Man to Man without which this Assistance and Instruction would be impracticable.

Therefore Human Testimony is the strongest Proof we can have of anything; and leaves no doubt when it is very strong.

That there is such a City as Rome, is a Proposition of which we can doubt less than that the Square of the Hypotenuse is equal to the Squares of the two Sides, even when the latter is demonstrated.

The highest Degree of testimony leaves less doubt than Demonstration.

Besides the force of it is more easily and generally comprehended.

If God has revealed anything by evident Proofs from his Power, and that these Proofs of Power are conveyed to us by as high a Degree of Testimony as the thing can bear, we ought to believe it.

If the thing[s] conveyed be intended to last in the world, there must be means taken to make them last; there must be Men appointed to teach them,—and Books written to record.

There should be some evident marks of the Designation of such Men; that all may know, who they are that teach this Doctrine.

These Men should be compellable to teach it; lest the knowledge of these truths might depend upon Caprice. There must therefore be a Society for this Purpose.

A Vindication of Natural Society

Burke's first major work, A Vindication, *was published in 1756, anonymously. It seems to be a root and branch assault on the traditional social order in the style of Lord Bolingbroke's radical deism and rationalism. In a second edition, Burke added a preface revealing that he was the "late noble writer" and describing his purpose as irony and satire. By applying Bolingbroke's ideas on natural religion to society, he explained, he had hoped to prove how ludicrous they were. Several recent students of Burke have suggested that he was himself less sure of his intention than this preface indicates.*

BEFORE the philosophical works of Lord Bolingbroke had appeared, great things were expected from the leisure of a man, who, from the splendid scene of action in which his talents had enabled him to make so conspicuous a figure, had retired to employ those talents in the investigation of truth. Philosophy began to congratulate herself upon such a proselyte from the world of business, and hoped to have extended her power under the auspices of such a leader. In the midst of these pleasing expectations, the works themselves at last appeared in *full body*, and with great pomp. Those who searched in them for new discoveries in the mysteries of nature; those who expected something which might explain or direct the operations of the mind; those who hoped to see morality illustrated and enforced; those who looked for new helps to society and government; those who desired to see the characters and passions of mankind delineated; in short, all who consider such things as philosophy, and require some of them at least in every philosophical work, all these were certainly disappointed; they found the landmarks of science precisely in their former places: and they thought they received but a poor recompense for this disappointment, in seeing every mode of religion attacked in a lively manner, and the foundation of every virtue, and of all government, sapped with great art and much ingenuity. What advantage do we derive from such writings? What delight can a man find in employing a capacity which might be usefully exerted for the noblest purposes, in a sort of sullen labor, in which, if the author could succeed, he is obliged to own, that nothing could be more fatal to mankind than his success?

I cannot conceive how this sort of writers propose to compass the designs they pretend to have in view, by the instruments which they employ. Do they pretend to exalt the mind of man, by proving him no better than a beast? Do they think to enforce the practice of virtue, by denying that vice and virtue are distinguished by good or ill fortune here, or by happiness or misery hereafter? Do they imagine they shall increase our piety, and our reliance on God, by exploding his providence, and insisting that he is neither just nor good? Such are the doctrines which, sometimes concealed, sometimes openly and fully avowed, are found to prevail throughout the writings of Lord Bolingbroke; and such are the reasonings which this noble writer and several others have been pleased to dignify with the name of philosophy. If these are delivered in a specious manner, and in a style above the common, they cannot want a number of admirers of as much docility as can be wished for in disciples. To these the editor of the following little piece has addressed it: there is no reason to conceal the design of it any longer.

The design was to show that, without the exertion of any considerable forces, the same engines which were employed for the destruction of religion, might be employed with equal success for the subversion of government; and that specious arguments might be used against those things which they, who doubt of everything else, will never permit to be questioned. It is an observation which I think Isocrates makes in one of his orations against the sophists, that it is far more easy to maintain a wrong cause, and to support paradoxical opinions to the satisfaction of a common auditory, than to establish a doubtful truth by solid and conclusive arguments. When men find that something can be said in favor of what, on the very proposal, they have thought utterly indefensible, they grow doubtful of their own reason; they are thrown into a sort of pleasing surprise; they run along with the speaker, charmed and captivated to find such a plentiful harvest of reasoning, where all seemed barren and unpromising. This is the fairy land of philosophy. And it very frequently happens, that those pleasing impressions on the imagination subsist and produce their effect, even after the understanding has been satisfied of their unsubstantial nature. There is a sort of gloss upon ingenious falsehoods that dazzles the imagination, but which neither belongs to, nor becomes the sober aspect of truth. I have met with a quotation in Lord Coke's Reports that pleased me very much, though I do not know from whence he has taken it; "*Interdum fucata falsitas* (says he), *in multis est probabilior, et sœpe rationibus vincit nudam veritatem.*" In such cases the writer has a certain fire and alacrity inspired into him by a consciousness, that, let it fare how it will with the subject, his ingenuity will be sure of applause; and this alacrity becomes much greater if he acts upon the offensive, by the impetuosity that always accompanies an attack, and the unfortunate propensity which mankind have to the finding and exaggerating faults. The editor is satisfied that a mind which has no restraint from a sense of its own weakness, of its subordinate rank in the creation, and of the extreme danger of letting the imagination loose upon some subjects, may very plausibly attack everything the most excellent and venerable; that it would not be difficult to criticise the creation itself; and that if we were to examine the divine fabrics by our ideas of reason and fitness, and to use the same method of attack by which some men have assaulted revealed religion, we might with as good color, and with the same success, make the wisdom and power of God in his creation appear to many no better than foolishness. There is an air of plausibility which accompanies vulgar reasonings and notions, taken from the beaten circle of ordinary experience, that is admirably suited to the narrow capacities of some, and to the laziness of others. But this advantage is in a great measure lost, when a painful, comprehensive survey of a very complicated matter, and which requires a great variety of considerations, is to be made; when we must seek in a profound subject, not only for arguments, but for new materials of argument, their measures and their method of arrangement; when we must go out of the sphere of our ordinary ideas, and when we can never walk surely, but by being sensible of our blindness. And this we must do, or we do nothing, whenever we examine the result of a reason which is not our own. Even in matters which are, as it were, just within our reach, what would become of the world, if the practice of all moral duties, and the foundations of society, rested upon having their reasons made clear and demonstrative to every individual?

The editor knows that the subject of this letter is not so fully handled as obviously it might; it was not his design to say all that could possibly be said. It had been inexcusable to fill a large volume with the abuse of reason; nor would such an abuse have been tolerable, even for a few pages, if some under-plot, of more consequence than the apparent design, had not been carried on.

Some persons have thought that the advantages of the state of nature ought to have been more fully displayed. This had undoubtedly been a very ample subject for declamation; but they do not consider the character of the piece. The writers against religion, whilst they oppose every system, are wisely careful never to set up any of their own. If some inaccuracies in calculation, in reasoning, or in method, be found, perhaps these will not be looked upon as faults by the admirers of Lord Bolingbroke; who will, the editor is afraid, observe much more of his lordship's character in such particulars of the following letter, than they are likely to find of that rapid torrent of an impetuous and overbearing eloquence, and the variety of rich imagery for which that writer is justly admired. . . .

Shall I venture to say, my lord, that in our late conversation, you were inclined to the party which you adopted rather by the feelings of your good nature, than by the conviction of your judgment? We laid open the foundations of society; and you feared that the curiosity of this search might endanger the ruin of the whole fabric. You would readily have allowed my principle, but you dreaded the consequences; you thought, that having once entered upon these reasonings, we might be carried insensibly and irresistibly farther than at first we could either have imagined or wished. But for my part, my lord, I then thought, and am still of the same opinion, that error, and not truth of any kind, is dangerous; that ill conclusions can only flow from false propositions; and that, to know whether any proposition be true or false, it is a preposterous method to examine it by its apparent consequences.

These were the reasons which induced me to go so far into that inquiry; and they are the reasons which direct me in all my inquiries. I had indeed often reflected on that subject before I could prevail on myself to communicate my reflections to anybody. They were generally melancholy enough; as those usually are which carry us beyond the mere surface of things; and which would undoubtedly make the lives of all thinking men extremely miserable, if the same philosophy which caused the grief, did not at the same time administer the comfort.

On considering political societies, their origin, their constitution, and their effects, I have sometimes been in a good deal more than doubt, whether the Creator did ever really intend man for a state of happiness. He has mixed in his cup a number of natural evils, (in spite of the boasts of stoicism they are evils,) and every endeavor which the art and policy of mankind has used from the beginning of the world to this day, in order to alleviate or cure them, has only served to introduce new mischiefs, or to aggravate and inflame the old. Besides this, the mind of man itself is too active and restless a principle ever to settle on the true point of quiet. It discovers every day some craving want in a body, which really wants but little. It every day invents some new artificial rule to guide that nature which, if left to itself, were the best and surest guide. It finds out imaginary beings prescribing imaginary laws; and then, it raises imaginary terrors to support a belief in the beings, and an obedience to the laws.—Many things have been said, and very well undoubtedly, on the subjection in which we should preserve our bodies to the government of our understanding; but enough has not been said upon the restraint which our bodily necessities ought to lay on the extravagant sublimities and eccentric rovings of our minds. The body, or as some love to call it, our inferior nature, is wiser in its own plain way, and attends its own business more directly than the mind with all its boasted subtlety.

In the state of nature, without question, mankind was subjected to many and great inconveniences. Want of union, want of mutual assistance, want of a common arbitrator to resort to in their differences. These were evils which they could not but have felt pretty severely on many occasions. The original children of the earth lived with their brethren of the other kinds in much equality. Their diet must have been confined almost wholly to the vegetable kind; and the same tree, which in its flourishing state produced them berries, in its decay gave them an habitation. The mutual desires of the sexes uniting their bodies and affections, and the children which are the results of these intercourses, introduced first the notion of society, and taught its conveniences. This society, founded in natural appetites and instincts, and not in any positive institution, I shall call *natural society.* Thus far nature went and succeeded: but man would go farther. The great error of our nature is, not to know where to stop, not to be satisfied with any reasonable acquirement; not to compound with our condition; but to lose all we have gained by an insatiable pursuit after more. Man found a considerable advantage by this union of many persons to form one family; he therefore judged that he would find his account proportionably in an union of many families into one body politic. And as nature has formed no bond of union to hold them together, he supplied this defect by *laws.*

This is *political society.* And hence the sources of what are usually called states, civil societies, or governments; into some form of which, more extended or restrained, all mankind have gradually fallen. And since it has so happened, and that we owe an implicit reverence to all the institutions of our ancestors, we shall consider these institutions with all that modesty with which we ought to conduct ourselves in examining a received opinion; but with all that freedom and candor which we owe to truth wherever we find it, or however it may contradict our own notions, or oppose our own interests. There is a most absurd and audacious method of reasoning avowed by some bigots and enthusiasts, and through fear assented to by some wiser and better men; it is this: they argue against a fair discussion of popular prejudices, because, say they, though they would be found without any reasonable support, yet the discovery might be productive of the most dangerous consequences. Absurd and blasphemous notion! as if all happiness was not connected with the practice of virtue, which necessarily depends upon the knowledge of truth; that is, upon the knowledge of those unalterable relations which Providence has ordained that every thing should bear to every other. These relations, which are truth itself, the foundation of virtue, and consequently the only measures of happiness, should be likewise the only measures by which we should direct our reasoning. To these we should conform in good earnest; and not think to force nature, and the whole order of her system, by a compliance with our pride and folly, to conform to our artificial regulations. It is by a conformity to this method we owe the discovery of the few truths we know, and the little liberty and rational happiness we enjoy. We have something fairer play than a reasoner could have expected formerly; and we derive advantages from it which are very visible.

The fabric of superstition has in this our age and nation received much ruder shocks than it had ever felt before; and through the chinks and breaches of our prison, we see such glimmerings of light, and feel such refreshing airs of liberty, as daily raise our ardor for more. The miseries derived to mankind from superstition under the name of religion, and of ecclesiastical tyranny under the name of church government, have been clearly and usefully exposed. We begin to think and to act from reason and from nature alone. This is true of several, but by far the majority is still in the same old state of blindness and slavery; and much is it to be feared that we shall perpetually relapse, whilst the real productive cause of all this superstitious folly, enthusiastical nonsense, and holy tyranny, holds a reverend place in the estimation even of those who are otherwise enlightened.

Civil government borrows a strength from ecclesiastical; and artificial laws receive a sanction from artificial revelations. The ideas of religion and government are closely connected; and whilst we receive government as a thing necessary, or even useful to our well-being, we shall in spite of us draw in, as a necessary, though undesirable consequence, an artificial religion of some kind or other. To this the vulgar will always be voluntary slaves; and even those of a rank of understanding superior, will now and then involuntarily feel its influence. It is therefore of the deepest concernment to us to be set right in this point; and to be well satisfied whether civil government be such a protector from natural evils, and such a nurse and increaser of blessings, as those of warm imaginations promise. In such a discussion, far am I from proposing in the least to reflect on our most wise form of government; no more than I would, in the freer parts of my philosophical writings, mean to object to the piety, truth, and perfection of our most excellent Church. Both, I am sensible, have their foundations on a rock. No discovery of truth can prejudice them. On the contrary, the more closely the origin of religion and government is examined, the more clearly their excellences must appear. They come purified from the fire. My business is not with them. Having entered a protest against all objections from these quarters, I may the more freely inquire, from history and experience, how far policy has contributed in all times to alleviate those evils which Providence, that perhaps has designed us for a state of imperfection, has imposed; how far our physical skill has cured our constitutional disorders; and whether it may not have introduced new ones, curable perhaps by no skill.

In looking over any state to form a judgment on it, it presents itself in two lights; the external, and the internal. The first, that relation which it bears in point of friendship or enmity to other states. The second, that relation which its component parts, the governing and the governed, bear to each other. The first part of the external view of all states, their relation as friends, makes so trifling a figure in history, that I am very sorry to say, it affords me but little matter on which to expatiate. The good offices done by one nation to its neighbor; the support given in public distress; the relief afforded in general calamity; the protection granted in emergent danger; the mutual return of kindness and civility, would afford a very ample and very pleasing subject for history. But, alas! all the history of all times, concerning all nations, does not afford matter enough to fill ten pages, though it should be spun out by the wire-drawing amplification of a Guicciardini himself. The glaring side is that of enmity. War is the matter which fills all history, and consequently the only or almost the only view in which we can see the external of political society is in a hostile shape; and the only actions to which we have always seen, and still see all of them intent, are such as tend to the destruction of one another. "War," says Machiavel, "ought to be the only study of a prince"; and by a prince, he means every sort of state, however constituted. "He ought," says this great political doctor, "to consider peace only as a breathing-time, which gives him leisure to contrive, and furnishes ability to execute military plans." A meditation on the conduct of political societies made old Hobbes imagine, that war was the state of nature; and truly, if a man judged of the individuals of our race by their conduct when united and packed into nations and kingdoms, he might imagine that every sort of virtue was unnatural and foreign to the mind of man.

The first accounts we have of mankind are but so many accounts of their butcheries. All empires have been cemented in blood; and, in those early periods, when the race of mankind began first to form themselves into parties and combinations, the first effect of the combination, and indeed the end for which it seems purposely formed, and best calculated, was their mutual destruction. All ancient history is dark and uncertain. One thing, however, is clear,—there were conquerors, and conquests in those days; and, consequently, all that devastation by which they are formed, and all that oppression by which they are maintained. . . .

Instances of this sort compose the uniform of history. But there have been periods when no less than universal destruction to the race of mankind seems to have been threatened. Such was that when the Goths, the Vandals, and the Huns, poured into Gaul, Italy, Spain, Greece, and Africa, carrying destruction before them as they advanced, and leaving horrid deserts every way behind them. *Vastum ubique silentium, secreti colles; fumantia procul testa; nemo exploratoribus obvius,* is what Tacitus calls *facies victoriæ*. It is always so; but was here emphatically so. From the north proceeded the swarms of Goths, Vandals, Huns, Ostrogoths, who ran towards the south, into Africa itself, which suffered as all to the north had done. About this time, another torrent of barbarians, animated by the same fury, and encouraged by the same success, poured out of the south, and ravaged all to the northeast and west, to the remotest parts of Persia on one hand, and to the banks of the Loire or farther on the other; destroying all the proud and curious monuments of human art, that not even the memory might seem to survive of the former inhabitants. What has been done since, and what will continue to be done while the same inducements to war continue, I shall not dwell upon. I shall only in one word mention the horrid effects of bigotry and avarice, in the conquest of Spanish America; a conquest, on a low estimation, effected by the murder of ten millions of the species. I shall draw to a conclusion of this part, by making a general calculation of the whole. I think I have actually mentioned above thirty-six millions. I have not particularized any more. I don't pretend to exactness; therefore, for the sake of a general view, I shall lay together all those actually slain in battles, or who have perished in a no less miserable manner by the other destructive consequences of war from the beginning of the world to this day, in the four parts of it, at a thousand times as much; no exaggerated calculation, allowing for time and extent. We have not perhaps spoke of the five-hundredth part; I am sure I have not of what is actually ascertained in history; but how much of these butcheries are only expressed in generals, what part of time history has never reached, and what vast spaces of the habitable globe it has not embraced, I need not mention to your lordship. I need not enlarge on those torrents of silent and inglorious blood which have glutted the thirsty sands of Afric, or discolored the polar snow, or fed the savage forests of America for so many ages of continual war. Shall I, to justify my calculations from the charge of extravagance, add to the account those skirmishes which happen in all wars, without being singly of sufficient dignity in mischief, to merit a place in history, but which by their frequency compensate for this comparative innocence? shall I inflame the account by those general massacres which have devoured whole cities and nations; those wasting pestilences, those consuming famines, and all those furies that follow in the train of war? I have no need to exaggerate; and I have purposely avoided a parade of eloquence on this occasion. I should despise it upon any occasion; else in mentioning these slaughters, it is obvious how much the whole might be heightened, by an affecting description of the horrors that attend the wasting of kingdoms, and sacking of cities. But I do not write to the vulgar, nor to that which only governs the vulgar, their passions. I go upon a naked and moderate calculation, just enough, without a pedantical exactness, to give your lordship some feeling of the effects of political society. I charge the whole of these effects on political society. I avow the charge, and I shall presently make it good to your lordship's satisfaction. The numbers I particularized are about thirty-six millions. Besides those killed in battles I have said something, not half what the matter would have justified, but something I have said concerning the consequences of war even more dreadful than that monstrous carnage itself which shocks our humanity, and almost staggers our belief. So that, allowing me in my exuberance one way for my deficiencies in the other, you will find me not unreasonable. I think the numbers of men now upon earth are computed at five hundred millions at the most. Here the slaughter of mankind, on what you will call a small calculation, amounts to upwards of seventy times the number of souls this day on the globe: a point which may furnish matter of reflection to one less inclined to draw consequences than your lordship.

I now come to show that political society is justly chargeable with much the greatest part of this destruction of the species. To give the fairest play to every side of the question, I will own that there is a haughtiness and fierceness in human nature, which will cause innumerable broils, place men in what situation you please; but owning this, I still insist in charging it to political regulations, that these broils are so frequent, so cruel, and attended with consequences so deplorable. In a state of nature, it had been impossible to find a number of men, sufficient for such slaughters, agreed in the same bloody purpose; or allowing that they might have come to such an agreement (an impossible supposition), yet the means that simple nature has supplied them with, are by no means adequate to such an end; many scratches, many bruises undoubtedly would be received upon all hands; but only a few, a very few deaths. Society and politics, which have given us these destructive views, have given us also the means of satisfying them. From the earliest dawnings of policy to this day, the invention of men has been sharpening and improving the mystery of murder, from the first rude essays of clubs and stones, to the present perfection of gunnery, cannoneering, bombarding, mining, and all those species of artificial, learned, and refined cruelty, in which we are now so expert, and which make a principal part of what politicians have taught us to believe is our principal glory.

How far mere nature would have carried us, we may judge by the example of those animals who still follow her laws, and even of those to whom she has given dispositions more fierce, and arms more terrible than ever she intended we should use. It is an incontestable truth that there is more havoc made in one year by men of men, than has been made by all the lions, tigers, panthers, ounces, leopards, hyenas, rhinoceroses, elephants, bears and wolves, upon their several species, since the beginning of the world; though these agree ill enough with each other, and have a much greater proportion of rage and fury in their composition than we have. But with respect to you, ye legislators, ye civilizers of mankind! ye Orpheuses, Moseses, Minoses, Solons, Theseuses, Lycurguses, Numas! with respect to you be it spoken, your regulations have done more mischief in cold blood, than all the rage of the fiercest animals in their greatest terrors, or furies, has ever done, or ever could do!

These evils are not accidental. Whoever will take the pains to consider the nature of society will find that they result directly from its constitution. For as *subordination*, or, in other words, the reciprocation of tyranny and slavery, is requisite to support these societies; the interest, the ambition, the malice, or the revenge, nay, even the whim and caprice of one ruling man among them, is enough to arm all the rest, without any private views of their own, to the worst and blackest purposes: and what is at once lamentable, and ridiculous, these wretches engage under those banners with a fury greater than if they were animated by revenge for their own proper wrongs.

It is no less worth observing, that this artificial division of mankind into separate societies is a perpetual source in itself of hatred and dissension among them. The names which distinguish them are enough to blow up hatred and rage. Examine history; consult present experience; and you will find that far the greater part of the quarrels between several nations had scarce any other occasion than that these nations were different combinations of people, and called by different names: to an Englishman, the name of a Frenchman, a Spaniard, an Italian, much more a Turk, or a Tartar, raises of course ideas of hatred and contempt. If you would inspire this compatriot of ours with pity or regard for one of these, would you not hide that distinction? You would not pray him to compassionate the poor Frenchman, or the unhappy German. Far from it; you would speak of him as a *foreigner*, an accident to which all are liable. You would represent him as a *man*; one partaking with us of the same common nature, and subject to the same law. There is something so averse from our nature in these artificial political distinctions, that we need no other trumpet to kindle us to war and destruction. But there is something so benign and healing in the general voice of humanity that, maugre all our regulations to prevent it, the simple name of man applied properly, never fails to work a salutary effect.

This natural unpremeditated effect of policy on the unpossessed passions of mankind appears on other occasions. The very name of a politician, a statesman, is sure to cause terror and hatred; it has always connected with it the ideas of treachery, cruelty, fraud, and tyranny; and those writers who have faithfully unveiled the mysteries of state-freemasonry, have ever been held in general detestation, for even knowing so perfectly a theory so detestable. The case of Machiavel seems at first sight something hard in that respect. He is obliged to bear the iniquities of those whose maxims and rules of government he published. His speculation is more abhorred than their practice.

But if there were no other arguments against artificial society than this I am going to mention, methinks it ought to fall by this one only. All writers on the science of policy are agreed, and they agree with experience, that all governments must frequently infringe the rules of justice to support themselves; that truth must give way to dissimulation; honesty to convenience; and humanity itself to the reigning interest. The whole of this mystery of iniquity is called the reason of state. It is a reason which I own I cannot penetrate. What sort of a protection is this of the general right, that is maintained by infringing the rights of particulars? What sort of justice is this, which is enforced by breaches of its own laws? These paradoxes I leave to be solved by the able heads of legislators and politicians. For my part, I say what a plain man would say on such an occasion. I can never believe that any institution, agreeable to nature, and proper for mankind, could find it necessary, or even expedient, in any case whatsoever, to do what the best and worthiest instincts of mankind warn us to avoid. But no wonder, that what is set up in opposition to the state of nature should preserve itself by trampling upon the law of nature.

To prove that these sorts of policed societies are a violation offered to nature, and a constraint upon the human mind, it needs only to look upon the sanguinary measures, and instruments of violence, which are everywhere used to support them. Let us take a review of the dungeons, whips, chains, racks, gibbets, with which every society is abundantly stored; by which hundreds of victims are annually offered up to support a dozen or two in pride and madness, and millions in an abject servitude and dependence. There was a time when I looked with a reverential awe on these mysteries of policy; but age, experience, and philosophy, have rent the veil; and I view this *sanctum sanctorum*, at least, without any enthusiastic admiration. I acknowledge, indeed, the necessity of such a proceeding in such institutions; but I must have a very mean opinion of institutions where such proceedings are necessary.

It is a misfortune that in no part of the globe natural liberty and natural religion are to be found pure, and free from the mixture of political adulterations. Yet we have implanted in us by Providence, ideas, axioms, rules, of what is pious, just, fair, honest, which no political craft, nor learned sophistry can entirely expel from our breasts. By these we judge, and we cannot otherwise judge, of the several artificial modes of religion and society, and determine of them as they approach to or recede from this standard.

The simplest form of government is *despotism*, where all the inferior orbs of power are moved merely by the will of the Supreme, and all that are subjected to them directed in the same manner, merely by the occasional will of the magistrate. This form, as it is the most simple, so it is infinitely the most general. Scarcely any part of the world is exempted from its power. And in those few places where men enjoy what they call liberty, it is continually in a tottering situation, and makes greater and greater strides to that gulf of despotism which at last swallows up every species of government. The manner of ruling being directed merely by the will of the weakest, and generally the worst man in the society, becomes the most foolish and capricious thing, at the same time that it is the most terrible and destructive that well can be conceived. In a despotism, the principal person finds that, let the want, misery, and indigence of his subjects be what they will, he can yet possess abundantly of everything to gratify his most insatiable wishes. He does more. He finds that these gratifications increase in proportion to the wretchedness and slavery of his subjects. Thus encouraged both by passion and interest to trample on the public welfare, and by his station placed above both shame and fear, he proceeds to the most horrid and shocking outrages upon mankind. Their persons become victims of his suspicions. The slightest displeasure is death; and a disagreeable aspect is often as great a crime as high treason. In the court of Nero, a person of learning, of unquestioned merit, and of unsuspected loyalty, was put to death for no other reason, than that he had a pedantic countenance which displeased the emperor. This very monster of mankind appeared in the beginning of his reign to be a person of virtue. Many of the greatest tyrants on the records of history have begun their reigns in the fairest manner. But the truth is, this unnatural power corrupts both the heart and the understanding. And to prevent the least hope of amendment, a king is ever surrounded by a crowd of infamous flatterers, who find their account in keeping him from the least light of reason, till all ideas of rectitude and justice are utterly erased from his mind. When Alexander had in his fury inhumanly butchered one of his best friends and bravest captains; on the return of reason he began to conceive an horror suitable to the guilt of such a murder. In this juncture his council came to his assistance. But what did his council? They found him out a philosopher who gave him comfort. And in what manner did this philosopher comfort him for the loss of such a man, and heal his conscience, flagrant with the smart of such a crime? You have the matter at length in Plutarch. He told him, *"that let a sovereign do what he will, all his actions are just and lawful, because they are his."* The palaces of all princes abound with such courtly philosophers. The consequence was such as might be expected. He grew every day a monster more abandoned to unnatural lust, to debauchery, to drunkenness, and to murder. And yet this was originally a great man, of uncommon capacity, and a strong propensity to virtue. But unbounded power proceeds step by step, until it has eradicated every laudable principle. It has been remarked, that there is no prince so bad, whose favorites and ministers are not worse. There is hardly any prince without a favorite, by whom he is governed in as arbitrary a manner as he governs the wretches subjected to him. Here the tyranny is doubled. There are two courts, and two interests; both very different from the interests of the people. The favorite knows that the regard of a tyrant is as unconstant and capricious as that of a woman; and concluding his time to be short, he makes haste to fill up the measure of his iniquity, in rapine, in luxury, and in revenge. Every avenue to the throne is shut up. He oppresses and ruins the people, whilst he persuades the prince that those murmurs raised by his own oppression are the effects of disaffection to the prince's government. Then is the natural violence of despotism inflamed and aggravated by hatred and revenge. To deserve well of the state is a crime against the prince. To be popular, and to be a traitor, are considered as synonymous terms. Even virtue is dangerous, as an aspiring quality, that claims an esteem by itself, and independent of the countenance of the court. What has been said of the chief, is true of the inferior officers of this species of government; each in his province exercising the same tyranny, and grinding the people by an oppression, the more severely felt, as it is near them, and exercised by base and subordinate persons. For the gross of the people, they are considered as a mere herd of cattle; and really in a little time become no better; all principle of honest pride, all sense of the dignity of their nature, is lost in their slavery. The day, says Homer, which makes a man a slave, takes away half his worth; and, in fact, he loses every impulse to action, but that low and base one of fear. In this kind of government human nature is not only abused and insulted, but it is actually degraded and sunk into a species of brutality. The consideration of this made Mr. Locke say, with great justice, that a government of this kind was worse than anarchy: indeed it is so abhorred and detested by all who live under forms that have a milder appearance, that there is scarcely a rational man in Europe that would not prefer death to Asiatic despotism. Here then we have the acknowledgment of a great philosopher, that an irregular state of nature is preferable to such a government; we have the consent of all sensible and generous men, who carry it yet further, and avow that death itself is preferable; and yet this species of government, so justly condemned, and so generally detested, is what infinitely the greater part of mankind groan under, and have groaned under from the beginning. So that, by sure and uncontested principles, the greatest part of the governments on earth must be concluded tyrannies, impostures, violations of the natural rights of mankind, and worse than the most disorderly anarchies. How much other forms exceed this we shall consider immediately.

In all parts of the world, mankind, however debased, retains still the sense of *feeling*; the weight of tyranny at last becomes insupportable; but the remedy is not so easy: in general, the only remedy by which they attempt to cure the tyranny is to change the tyrant. This is, and always was, the case for the greater part. In some countries, however, were found men of more penetration, who discovered *"that to live by one man's will was the cause of all men's misery."* They therefore changed their former method, and assembling the men in their several societies the most respectable for their understanding and fortunes, they confided to them the charge of the public welfare. This originally formed what is called an *aristocracy.* They hoped it would be impossible that such a number could ever join in any design against the general good; and they promised themselves a great deal of security and happiness from the united counsels of so many able and experienced persons. But it is now found by abundant experience, that an *aristocracy*, and a *despotism*, differ but in name; and that a people who are in general excluded from any share of the legislative, are, to all intents and purposes, as much slaves, when twenty, independent of them, govern, as when but one domineers. The tyranny is even more felt, as every individual of the nobles has the haughtiness of a sultan; the people are more miserable, as they seem on the verge of liberty, from which they are forever debarred; this fallacious idea of liberty, whilst it presents a vain shadow of happiness to the subject, binds faster the chains of his subjection. What is left undone by the natural avarice and pride of those who are raised above the others, is completed by their suspicions, and their dread of losing an authority, which has no support in the common utility of the nation. A Genoese or a Venetian republic is a concealed *despotism*; where you find the same pride of the rulers, the same base subjection of the people, the same bloody maxims of a suspicious policy. In one respect the *aristocracy* is worse than the *despotism*. A body politic, whilst it retains its authority, never changes its maxims; a *despotism*, which is this day horrible to a supreme degree, by the caprice natural to the heart of man, may, by the same caprice otherwise exerted, be as lovely the next; in a succession, it is possible to meet with some good princes. If there have been Tiberiuses, Caligulas, Neros, there have been likewise the serener days of Vespasians, Tituses, Trajans, and Antonines; but a body politic is not influenced by caprice or whim, it proceeds in a regular manner, its succession is insensible; and every man as he enters it, either has, or soon attains, the spirit of the whole body. Never was it known that an *aristocracy*, which was haughty and tyrannical in one century, became easy and mild in the next. In effect, the yoke of this species of government is so galling, that whenever the people have got the least power, they have shaken it off with the utmost indignation, and established a popular form. And when they have not had strength enough to support themselves, they have thrown themselves into the arms of *despotism*, as the more eligible of the two evils. This latter was the case of Denmark, who sought a refuge from the oppression of its nobility, in the strong hold of arbitrary power. Poland has at present the name of republic, and it is one of the *aristocratic* form; but it is well known that the little finger of this government is heavier than the loins of arbitrary power in most nations. The people are not only politically, but personally slaves, and treated with the utmost indignity. The republic of Venice is somewhat more moderate; yet even here, so heavy is the *aristocratic* yoke, that the nobles have been obliged to enervate the spirit of their subjects by every sort of debauchery; they have denied them the liberty of reason, and they have made them amends by what a base soul will think a more valuable liberty, by not only allowing, but encouraging them to corrupt themselves in the most scandalous manner. They consider their subjects as the farmer does the hog he keeps to feast upon. He holds him fast in his sty, but allows him to wallow as much as he pleases in his beloved filth and gluttony. So scandalously debauched a people as that of Venice is to be met with nowhere else. High, low, men, women, clergy, and laity, are all alike. The ruling nobility are no less afraid of one another than they are of the people; and, for that reason, politically enervate their own body by the same effeminate luxury by which they corrupt their subjects. They are impoverished by every means which can be invented; and they are kept in a perpetual terror by the horrors of a state inquisition. Here you see a people deprived of all rational freedom, and tyrannized over by about two thousand men; and yet this body of two thousand are so far from enjoying any liberty by the subjection of the rest, that they are in an infinitely severer state of slavery; they make themselves the most degenerate and unhappy of mankind, for no other purpose than that they may the more effectually contribute to the misery of a whole nation. In short, the regular and methodical proceedings of an *aristocracy* are more intolerable than the very excesses of a *despotism*, and, in general, much further from any remedy.

Thus, my lord, we have pursued *aristocracy* through its whole progress; we have seen the seeds, the growth, and the fruit. It could boast none of the advantages of a *despotism*, miserable as those advantages were, and it was overloaded with an exuberance of mischiefs, unknown even to *despotism* itself. In effect, it is no more than a disorderly tyranny. This form, therefore, could be little approved, even in speculation, by those who were capable of thinking, and could be less borne in practice by any who were capable of feeling. However, the fruitful policy of man was not yet exhausted. He had yet another farthing candle to supply the deficiencies of the sun. This was the third form, known by political writers under the name of *democracy*. Here the people transacted all public business, or the greater part of it, in their own persons; their laws were made by themselves, and, upon any failure of duty, their officers were accountable to themselves, and to them only. In all appearance, they had secured by this method the advantages of order and good government, without paying their liberty for the purchase. Now, my lord, we are come to the masterpiece of Grecian refinement, and Roman solidity,—a popular government. The earliest and most celebrated republic of this model was that of Athens. It was constructed by no less an artist than the celebrated poet and philosopher, Solon. But no sooner was this political vessel launched from the stocks, than it overset, even in the lifetime of the builder. A tyranny immediately supervened; not by a foreign conquest, not by accident, but by the very nature and constitution of a *democracy*. An artful man became popular, the people had power in their hands, and they devolved a considerable share of their power upon their favorite; and the only use he made of this power was, to plunge those who gave it into slavery. Accident restored their liberty, and the same good fortune produced men of uncommon abilities and uncommon virtues amongst them. But these abilities were suffered to be of little service either to their possessors or to the state. Some of these men, for whose sakes alone we read their history, they banished; others they imprisoned, and all they treated with various circumstances of the most shameful ingratitude. Republics have many things in the spirit of absolute monarchy, but none more than this. A shining merit is ever hated or suspected in a popular assembly, as well as in a court; and all services done the state are looked upon as dangerous to the rulers, whether sultans or senators. The *ostracism* at Athens was built upon this principle. The giddy people whom we have now under consideration, being elated with some flashes of success, which they owed to nothing less than any merit of their own, began to tyrannize over their equals, who had associated with them for their common defence. With their prudence they renounced all appearance of justice. They entered into wars rashly and wantonly. If they were unsuccessful, instead of growing wiser by their misfortune, they threw the whole blame of their own misconduct on the ministers who had advised, and the generals who had conducted, those wars; until by degrees they had cut off all who could serve them in their councils or their battles. If at any time these wars had a happier issue, it was no less difficult to deal with them on account of their pride and insolence. Furious in their adversity, tyrannical in their successes, a commander had more trouble to concert his defence before the people, than to plan the operations of the campaign. It was not uncommon for a general, under the horrid *despotism* of the Roman emperors, to be ill received in proportion to the greatness of his services. Agricola is a strong instance of this. No man had done greater things, nor with more honest ambition. Yet, on his return to court, he was obliged to enter Rome with all the secrecy of a criminal. He went to the palace, not like a victorious commander who had merited and might demand the greatest rewards, but like an offender who had come to supplicate a pardon for his crimes. His reception was answerable; *"Exceptusque brevi osculo et nullo sermone, turbœ servientium immixtus est."* Yet in that worst season of this worst of monarchical tyrannies, modesty, discretion, and a coolness of temper, formed some kind of security, even for the highest merit. But at Athens, the nicest and best studied behavior was not a sufficient guard for a man of great capacity. Some of their bravest commanders were obliged to fly their country, some to enter into the service of its enemies, rather than abide a popular determination on their conduct, lest, as one of them said, their giddiness might make the people condemn where they meant to acquit; to throw in a black bean even when they intended a white one.

The Athenians made a very rapid progress to the most enormous excesses. The people, under no restraint, soon grew dissolute, luxurious, and idle. They renounced all labor, and began to subsist themselves from the public revenues. They lost all concern for their common honor or safety, and could bear no advice that tended to reform them. At this time truth became offensive to those lords the people, and most highly dangerous to the speaker. The orators no longer ascended the *rostrum*, but to corrupt them further with the most fulsome adulation. These orators were all bribed by foreign princes on the one side or the other. And besides its own parties, in this city there were parties, and avowed ones too, for the Persians, Spartans, and Macedonians, supported each of them by one or more demagogues pensioned and bribed to this iniquitous service. The people, forgetful of all virtue and public spirit, and intoxicated with the flatteries of their orators (these courtiers of republics, and endowed with the distinguishing characteristics of all other courtiers), this people, I say, at last arrived at that pitch of madness, that they coolly and deliberately, by an express law, made it capital for any man to propose an application of the immense sums squandered in public shows, even to the most necessary purposes of the state. When you see the people of this republic banishing and murdering their best and ablest citizens, dissipating the public treasure with the most senseless extravagance, and spending their whole time, as spectators or actors, in playing, fiddling, dancing, and singing, does it not, my lord, strike your imagination with the image of a sort of complex Nero? And does it not strike you with the greater horror, when you observe, not one man only, but a whole city, grown drunk with pride and power, running with a rage of folly into the same mean and senseless debauchery and extravagance? But if this people resembled Nero in their extravagance, much more did they resemble and even exceed him in cruelty and injustice. In the time of Pericles, one of the most celebrated times in the history of that commonwealth, a king of Egypt sent them a donation of corn. This they were mean enough to accept. And had the Egyptian prince intended the ruin of this city of wicked Bedlamites, he could not have taken a more effectual method to do it than by such an ensnaring largess. The distribution of this bounty caused a quarrel; the majority set on foot an inquiry into the title of the citizens; and upon a vain pretence of illegitimacy, newly and occasionally set up, they deprived of their share of the royal donation no less than five thousand of their own body. They went further; they disfranchised them; and, having once begun with an act of injustice, they could set no bounds to it. Not content with cutting them off from the rights of citizens, they plundered these unfortunate wretches of all their substance; and, to crown this masterpiece of violence and tyranny, they actually sold every man of the five thousand as slaves in the public market. Observe, my lord, that the five thousand we here speak of were cut off from a body of no more than nineteen thousand; for the entire number of citizens was no greater at that time. Could the tyrant who wished the Roman people but one neck; could the tyrant Caligula himself have done, nay, he could scarcely wish for, a greater mischief than to have cut off, at one stroke, a fourth of his people? Or has the cruelty of that series of sanguine tyrants, the Caesars, ever presented such a piece of flagrant and extensive wickedness? The whole history of this celebrated republic is but one tissue of rashness, folly, ingratitude, injustice, tumult, violence, and tyranny, and, indeed, of every species of wickedness that can well be imagined. This was a city of wise men, in which a minister could not exercise his functions; a warlike people, amongst whom a general did not dare either to gain or lose a battle; a learned nation, in which a philosopher could not venture on a free inquiry. This was the city which banished Themistocles, starved Aristides, forced into exile Miltiades, drove out Anaxagoras, and poisoned Socrates. This was a city which changed the form of its government with the moon; eternal conspiracies, revolutions daily, nothing fixed and established. A republic, as an ancient philosopher has observed, is no one species of government, but a magazine of every species; here you find every sort of it, and that in the worst form. As there is a perpetual change, one rising and the other falling, you have all the violence and wicked policy by which a beginning power must always acquire its strength, and all the weakness by which falling states are brought to a complete destruction.

Rome has a more venerable aspect than Athens; and she conducted her affairs, so far as related to the ruin and oppression of the greatest part of the world, with greater wisdom and more uniformity. But the domestic economy of these two states was nearly or altogether the same. An internal dissension constantly tore to pieces the bowels of the Roman commonwealth. You find the same confusion, the same factions, which subsisted at Athens, the same tumults, the same revolutions, and, in fine, the same slavery; if, perhaps, their former condition did not deserve that name altogether as well. All other republics were of the same character. Florence was a transcript of Athens. And the modern republics, as they approach more or less to the democratic form, partake more or less of the nature of those which I have described.

We are now at the close of our review of the three simple forms of artificial society; and we have shown them, however they may differ in name, or in some slight circumstances, to be all alike in effect: in effect, to be all tyrannies. But suppose we were inclined to make the most ample concessions; let us concede Athens, Rome, Carthage, and two or three more of the ancient, and as many of the modern, commonwealths, to have been, or to be, free and happy, and to owe their freedom and happiness to their political constitution. Yet, allowing all this, what defence does this make for artificial society in general, that these inconsiderable spots of the globe have for some short space of time stood as exceptions to a charge so general? But when we call these governments free, or concede that their citizens were happier than those which lived under different forms, it is merely *ex abundanti*. For we should be greatly mistaken, if we really thought that the majority of the people which filled these cities enjoyed even that nominal political freedom of which I have spoken so much already. In reality, they had no part of it. In Athens there were usually from ten to thirty thousand freemen; this was the utmost. But the slaves usually amounted to four hundred thousand, and sometimes to a great many more. The freemen of Sparta and Rome were not more numerous in proportion to those whom they held in a slavery even more terrible than the Athenian. Therefore state the matter fairly: the free states never formed, though they were taken altogether, the thousandth part of the habitable globe; the freemen in these states were never the twentieth part of the people, and the time they subsisted is scarce anything in that immense ocean of duration in which time and slavery are so nearly commensurate. Therefore call these free states, or popular governments, or what you please; when we consider the majority of their inhabitants, and regard the natural rights of mankind, they must appear, in reality and truth, no better than pitiful and oppressive oligarchies.

After so fair an examen, wherein nothing has been exaggerated; no fact produced which cannot be proved, and none which has been produced in any wise forced or strained, while thousands have, for brevity, been omitted; after so candid a discussion in all respects; what slave so passive, what bigot so blind, what enthusiast so headlong, what politician so hardened, as to stand up in defence of a system calculated for a curse to mankind? a curse under which they smart and groan to this hour, without thoroughly knowing the nature of the disease, and wanting understanding or courage to supply the remedy.

I need not excuse myself to your lordship, nor, I think, to any honest man, for the zeal I have shown in this cause; for it is an honest zeal, and in a good cause. I have defended natural religion against a confederacy of atheists and divines. I now plead for natural society against politicians, and for natural reason against all three. When the world is in a fitter temper than it is at present to hear truth, or when I shall be more indifferent about its temper, my thoughts may become more public. In the mean time, let them repose in my own bosom, and in the bosoms of such men as are fit to be initiated in the sober mysteries of truth and reason. My antagonists have already done as much as I could desire. Parties in religion and politics make sufficient discoveries concerning each other, to give a sober man a proper caution against them all. The monarchic, and aristocratical, and popular partisans, have been jointly laying their axes to the root of all government, and have, in their turns, proved each other absurd and inconvenient. In vain you tell me that artificial government is good, but that I fall out only with the abuse. The thing! the thing itself is the abuse! Observe, my lord, I pray you, that grand error upon which all artificial legislative power is founded. It was observed, that men had ungovernable passions, which made it necessary to guard against the violence they might offer to each other. They appointed governors over them for this reason. But a worse and more perplexing difficulty arises, how to be defended against the governors? *Quis custodiet ipsos custodes?* In vain they change from a single person to a few. These few have the passions of the one; and they unite to strengthen themselves, and to secure the gratification of their lawless passions at the expense of the general good. In vain do we fly to the many. The case is worse; their passions are less under the government of reason, they are augmented by the contagion, and defended against all attacks by their multitude.

I have purposely avoided the mention of the mixed form of government, for reasons that will be very obvious to your lordship. But my caution can avail me but little. You will not fail to urge it against me in favor of political society. You will not fail to show how the errors of the several simple modes are corrected by a mixture of all of them, and a proper balance of the several powers in such a state. I confess, my lord, that this has been long a darling mistake of my own; and that of all the sacrifices I have made to truth, this has been by far the greatest. When I confess that I think this notion a mistake, I know to whom I am speaking, for I am satisfied that reasons are like liquors, and there are some of such a nature as none but strong heads can bear. There are few with whom I can communicate so freely as with Pope. But Pope cannot bear every truth. He has a timidity which hinders the full exertion of his faculties, almost as effectually as bigotry cramps those of the general herd of mankind. But whoever is a genuine follower of truth keeps his eye steady upon his guide, indifferent whither he is led, provided that she is the leader. And, my lord, if it be properly considered, it were infinitely better to remain possessed by the whole legion of vulgar mistakes, than to reject some, and at the same time to retain a fondness for others altogether as absurb and irrational. The first has at least a consistency, that makes a man, however erroneously, uniform at least; but the latter way of proceeding is such an inconsistent chimera and jumble of philosophy and vulgar prejudice, that hardly anything more ridiculous can be conceived. Let us therefore freely, and without fear or prejudice, examine this last contrivance of policy. And, without considering how near the quick our instruments may come, let us search it to the bottom.

First, then, all men are agreed that this junction of regal, aristocratic, and popular power, must form a very complex, nice, and intricate machine, which being composed of such a variety of parts, with such opposite tendencies and movements, it must be liable on every accident to be disordered. To speak without metaphor, such a government must be liable to frequent cabals, tumults, and revolutions, from its very constitution. These are undoubtedly as ill effects as can happen in a society; for in such a case, the closeness acquired by community, instead of serving for mutual defence, serves only to increase the danger. Such a system is like a city, where trades that require constant fires are much exercised, where the houses are built of combustible materials, and where they stand extremely close.

In the second place, the several constituent parts having their distinct rights, and these many of them so necessary to be determined with exactness, are yet so indeterminate in their nature, that it becomes a new and constant source of debate and confusion. Hence it is, that whilst the business of government should be carrying on, the question is, Who has a right to exercise this or that function of it, or what men have power to keep their offices in any function? Whilst this contest continues, and whilst the balance in any sort continues, it has never any remission; all manner of abuses and villanies in officers remain unpunished; the greatest frauds and robberies in the public revenues are committed in defiance of justice; and abuses grow, by time and impunity, into customs; until they prescribe against the laws, and grow too inveterate often to admit a cure, unless such as may be as bad as the disease.

Thirdly, the several parts of this species of government, though united, preserve the spirit which each form has separately. Kings are ambitious; the nobility haughty; and the populace tumultuous and ungovernable. Each party, however in appearance peaceable, carries on a design upon the others; and it is owing to this, that in all questions, whether concerning foreign or domestic affairs, the whole generally turns more upon some party-matter than upon the nature of the thing itself; whether such a step will diminish or augment the power of the crown, or how far the privileges of the subject are likely to be extended or restricted by it. And these questions are constantly resolved, without any consideration of the merits of the cause, merely as the parties who uphold these jarring interests may chance to prevail; and as they prevail, the balance is overset, now upon one side, now upon the other. The government is, one day, arbitrary power in a single person; another, a juggling confederacy of a few to cheat the prince and enslave the people; and the third, a frantic and unmanageable democracy. The great instrument of all these changes, and what infuses a peculiar venom into all of them, is party. It is of no consequence what the principles of any party, or what their pretensions are; the spirit which actuates all parties is the same; the spirit of ambition, of self-interest, of oppression and treachery.

This spirit entirely reverses all the principles which a benevolent nature has erected within us; all honesty, all equal justice, and even the ties of natural society, the natural affections. In a word, my lord, we have all *seen*, and, if any outward considerations were worthy the lasting concern of a wise man, we have some of us *felt*, such oppression from party government as no other tyranny can parallel. We behold daily the most important rights, rights upon which all the others depend, we behold these rights determined in the last resort, without the least attention even to the appearance or color of justice; we behold this without emotion, because we have grown up in the constant view of such practices; and we are not surprised to hear a man requested to be a knave and a traitor, with as much indifference as if the most ordinary favor were asked; and we hear this request refused, not because it is a most unjust and unreasonable desire, but because this worthy has already engaged his injustice to another. These and many more points I am far from spreading to their full extent. You are sensible that I do not put forth half my strength; and you cannot be at a loss for the reason. A man is allowed sufficient freedom of thought, provided he knows how to choose his subject properly. You may criticise freely upon the Chinese constitution, and observe with as much severity as you please upon the absurd tricks, or destructive bigotry of the bonzees. But the scene is changed as you come homeward, and atheism or treason may be the names given in Britain, to what would be reason and truth if asserted of China. I submit to the condition, and though I have a notorious advantage before me, I waive the pursuit. For else, my lord, it is very obvious what a picture might be drawn of the excesses of party even in our own nation. I could show, that the same faction has, in one reign, promoted popular seditions, and, in the next, been a patron of tyranny: I could show that they have all of them betrayed the public safety at all times, and have very frequently with equal perfidy made a market of their own cause and their own associates. I could show how vehemently they have contended for names, and how silently they have passed over things of the last importance. And I could demonstrate that they have had the opportunity of doing all this mischief, nay, that they themselves had their origin and growth from that complex form of government, which we are wisely taught to look upon as so great a blessing. Revolve, my lord, our history from the Conquest. We scarcely ever had a prince, who, by fraud or violence, had not made some infringement on the constitution. We scarcely ever had a Parliament which knew, when it attempted to set limits to the royal authority, how to set limits to its own. Evils we have had continually calling for reformation, and reformations more grievous than any evils. Our boasted liberty sometimes trodden down, sometimes giddily set up, and ever precariously fluctuating and unsettled; it has only been kept alive by the blasts of continual feuds, wars, and conspiracies. In no country in Europe has the scaffold so often blushed with the blood of its nobility. Confiscations, banishments, attainders, executions, make a large part of the history of such of our families as are not utterly extinguished by them. Formerly, indeed, things had a more ferocious appearance than they have at this day. In these early and unrefined ages, the jarring part of a certain chaotic constitution supported their several pretensions by the sword. Experience and policy have since taught other methods.

> *At nunc res agitur tenui pulmone rubetæ.*

But how far corruption, venality, the contempt of honor, the oblivion of all duty to our country, and the most abandoned public prostitution, are preferable to the more glaring and violent effects of faction, I will not presume to determine. Sure I am that they are very great evils.

I have done with the forms of government. During the course of my inquiry you may have observed a very material difference between my manner of reasoning and that which is in use amongst the abettors of artificial society. They form their plans upon what seems most eligible to their imaginations, for the ordering of mankind. I discover the mistakes in those plans, from the real known consequences which have resulted from them. They have enlisted reason to fight against itself, and employ its whole force to prove that it is an insufficient guide to them in the conduct of their lives. But unhappily for us, in proportion as we have deviated from the plain rule of our nature, and turned our reason against itself, in that proportion have we increased the follies and miseries of mankind. The more deeply we penetrate into the labyrinth of art, the further we find ourselves from those ends for which we entered it. This has happened in almost every species of artificial society, and in all times. We found, or we thought we found, an inconvenience in having every man the judge of his own cause. Therefore judges were set up, at first, with discretionary powers. But it was soon found a miserable slavery to have our lives and properties precarious, and hanging upon the arbitrary determination of any one man, or set of men. We fled to laws as a remedy for this evil. By these we persuaded ourselves we might know with some certainty upon what ground we stood. But lo! differences arose upon the sense and interpretation of these laws. Thus we were brought back to our old incertitude. New laws were made to expound the old; and new difficulties arose upon the new laws; as words multiplied, opportunities of cavilling upon them multiplied also. Then recourse was had to notes, comments, glosses, reports, *responsa prudentum*, learned readings: eagle stood against eagle: authority was set up against authority. Some were allured by the modern, others reverenced the ancient. The new were more enlightened, the old were more venerable. Some adopted the comment, others stuck to the text. The confusion increased, the mist thickened, until it could be discovered no longer what was allowed or forbidden, what things were in property, and what common. In this uncertainty, (uncertain even to the professors, an Egyptian darkness to the rest of mankind), the contending parties felt themselves more effectually ruined by the delay, than they could have been by the injustice of any decision. Our inheritances are become a prize for disputation; and disputes and litigations are become an inheritance.

The professors of artificial law have always walked hand in hand with the professors of artificial theology. As their end, in confounding the reason of man, and abridging his natural freedom, is exactly the same, they have adjusted the means to that end in a way entirely similar. The divine thunders out his *anathemas* with more noise and terror against the breach of one of his positive institutions, or the neglect of some of his trivial forms, than against the neglect or breach of those duties and commandments of natural religion, which by these forms and institutions he pretends to enforce. The lawyer has his forms, and his positive institutions too, and he adheres to them with a veneration altogether as religious. The worst cause cannot be so prejudicial to the litigant, as his advocate's or attorney's ignorance or neglect of these forms. A lawsuit is like an ill-managed dispute, in which the first object is soon out of sight, and the parties end upon a matter wholly foreign to that on which they began. In a lawsuit the question is, who has a right to a certain house or farm? And this question is daily determined, not upon the evidence of the right, but upon the observance or neglect of some forms of words in use with the gentlemen of the robe, about which there is even amongst themselves such a disagreement, that the most experienced veterans in the profession can never be positively assured that they are not mistaken.

Let us expostulate with these learned sages, these priests of the sacred temple of justice. Are we judges of our own property? By no means.

You then, who are initiated into the mysteries of the blindfold goddess, inform me whether I have a right to eat the bread I have earned by the hazard of my life or the sweat of my brow? The grave doctor answers me in the affirmative; the reverend serjeant replies in the negative; the learned barrister reasons upon one side and upon the other, and concludes nothing. What shall I do? An antagonist starts up and presses me hard. I enter the field, and retain these three persons to defend my cause. My cause, which two farmers from the plough could have decided in half an hour, takes the court twenty years. I am however at the end of my labor, and have in reward for all my toil and vexation a judgment in my favor. But hold—a sagacious commander, in the adversary's army, has found a flaw in the proceeding. My triumph is turned into mourning. I have used *or*, instead of *and*, or some mistake, small in appearance, but dreadful in its consequences; and have the whole of my success quashed in a writ of error. I remove my suit; I shift from court to court; I fly from equity to law, and from law to equity; equal uncertainty attends me everywhere; and a mistake in which I had no share, decides at once upon my liberty and property, sending me from the court to a prison, and adjudging my family to beggary and famine. I am innocent, gentlemen, of the darkness and uncertainty of your science. I never darkened it with absurd and contradictory notions, nor confounded it with chicane and sophistry. You have excluded me from any share in the conduct of my own cause; the science was too deep for me; I acknowledged it; but it was too deep even for yourselves: you have made the way so intricate, that you are yourselves lost in it; you err, and you punish me for your errors.

The delay of the law is, your lordship will tell me, a trite topic, and which of its abuses have not been too severely felt not to be complained of? A man's property is to serve for the purposes of his support; and therefore, to delay a determination concerning that, is the worst injustice, because it cuts off the very end and purpose for which I applied to the judicature for relief. Quite contrary in the case of a man's life; there the determination can hardly be too much protracted. Mistakes in this case are as often fallen into as many other; and if the judgment is sudden, the mistakes are the most irretrievable of all others. Of this the gentlemen of the robe are themselves sensible, and they have brought it into a maxim. *De morte hominis nulla est cunctatio longa*. But what could have induced them to reverse the rules, and to contradict that reason which dictated them, I am utterly unable to guess. A point concerning property, which ought, for the reasons I have just mentioned, to be most speedily decided, frequently exercises the wit of successions of lawyers, for many generations. *Multa virûm volvens durando sæcula vincit.* But the question concerning a man's life, that great question in which no delay ought to be counted tedious, is commonly determined in twenty-four hours at the utmost. It is not to be wondered at, that injustice and absurdity should be inseparable companions.

Ask of politicians the end for which laws were originally designed; and they will answer, that the laws were designed as a protection for the poor and weak, against the oppression of the rich and powerful. But surely no pretence can be so ridiculous; a man might as well tell me he has taken off my load, because he has changed the burden. If the poor man is not able to support his suit, according to the vexatious and expensive manner established in civilized countries, has not the rich as great an advantage over him as the strong has over the weak in a state of nature? But we will not place the state of nature, which is the reign of God, in competition with political society, which is the absurd usurpation of man. In a state of nature, it is true that a man of superior force may beat or rob me; but then it is true, that I am at full liberty to defend myself, or make reprisal by surprise or by cunning, or by any other way in which I may be superior to him. But in political society, a rich man may rob me in another way. I cannot defend myself; for money is the only weapon with which we are allowed to fight. And if I attempt to avenge myself the whole force of that society is ready to complete my ruin.

A good parson once said, that where mystery begins, religion ends. Cannot I say, as truly at least, of human laws, that where mystery begins, justice ends? It is hard to say, whether the doctors of law or divinity have made the greater advances in the lucrative business of mystery. The lawyers, as well as the theologians, have erected another reason besides natural reason; and the result has been, another justice besides natural justice. They have so bewildered the world and themselves in unmeaning forms and ceremonies, and so perplexed the plainest matters with metaphysical jargon, that it carries the highest danger to a man out of that profession, to make the least step without their advice and assistance. Thus, by confining to themselves the knowledge of the foundation of all men's lives and properties, they have reduced all mankind into the most abject and servile dependence. We are tenants at the will of these gentlemen for everything; and a metaphysical quibble is to decide whether the greatest villain breathing shall meet his deserts, or escape with impunity, or whether the best man in the society shall not be reduced to the lowest and most despicable condition it affords. In a word, my lord, the injustice, delay, puerility, false refinement, and affected mystery of the law are such, that many who live under it come to admire and envy the expedition, simplicity, and equality of arbitrary judgments. I need insist the less on this article to your lordship, as you have frequently lamented the miseries derived to us from artificial law, and your candor is the more to be admired and applauded in this, as your lordship's noble house has derived its wealth and its honors from that profession.

Before we finish our examination of artificial society, I shall lead your lordship into a closer consideration of the relations which it gives birth to, and the benefits, if such they are, which result from these relations. The most obvious division of society is into rich and poor; and it is no less obvious, that the number of the former bear a great disproportion to those of the latter. The whole business of the poor is to administer to the idleness, folly, and luxury of the rich; and that of the rich, in return, is to find the best methods of confirming the slavery and increasing the burdens of the poor. In a state of nature, it is an invariable law, that a man's acquisitions are in proportion to his labors. In a state of artificial society, it is a law as constant and as invariable, that those who labor most enjoy the fewest things; and that those who labor not at all have the greatest number of enjoyments. A constitution of things this, strange and ridiculous beyond expression! We scarce believe a thing when we are told it, which we actually see before our eyes every day without being in the least surprised. I suppose that there are in Great Britain upwards of a hundred thousand people employed in lead, tin, iron, copper, and coal mines; these unhappy wretches scarce ever see the light of the sun; they are buried in the bowels of the earth; there they work at a severe and dismal task, without the least prospect of being delivered from it; they subsist upon the coarsest and worst sort of fare; they have their health miserably impaired, and their lives cut short, by being perpetually confined in the close vapor of these malignant minerals. A hundred thousand more at least are tortured without remission by the suffocating smoke, intense fires, and constant drudgery necessary in refining and managing the products of those mines. If any man informed us that two hundred thousand innocent persons were condemned to so intolerable slavery, how should we pity the unhappy sufferers, and how great would be our just indignation against those who inflicted so cruel and ignominious a punishment! This is an instance—I could not wish a stronger—of the numberless things which we pass by in their common dress, yet which shock us when they are nakedly represented. But this number, considerable as it is, and the slavery, with all its baseness and horror, which we have at home, is nothing to what the rest of the world affords of the same nature. Millions daily bathed in the poisonous damps and destructive effluvia of lead, silver, copper, and arsenic. To say nothing of those other employments, those stations of wretchedness and contempt, in which civil society has placed the numerous *enfans perdus* of her army. Would any rational man submit to one of the most tolerable of these drudgeries, for all the artificial enjoyments which policy has made to result from them? By no means. And yet need I suggest to your lordship, that those who find the means, and those who arrive at the end, are not at all the same persons? On considering the strange and unaccountable fancies and contrivances of artificial reason, I have somewhere called this earth the Bedlam of our system. Looking now upon the effects of some of those fancies, may we not with equal reason call it likewise the Newgate and the Bridewell of the universe? Indeed the blindness of one part of mankind co-operating with the frenzy and villany of the other, has been the real builder of this respectable fabric of political society: and as the blindness of mankind has caused their slavery, in return their state of slavery is made a pretence for continuing them in a state of blindness; for the politician will tell you gravely, that their life of servitude disqualifies the greater part of the race of man for a search of truth, and supplies them with no other than mean and insufficient ideas. This is but too true; and this is one of the reasons for which I blame such institutions.

In a misery of this sort, admitting some few lenitives, and those too but a few, nine parts in ten of the whole race of mankind drudge through life. It may be urged perhaps, in palliation of this, that at least the rich few find a considerable and real benefit from the wretchedness of the many. But is this so in fact? Let us examine the point with a little more attention. For this purpose the rich in all societies may be thrown into two classes. The first is of those who are powerful as well as rich, and conduct the operations of the vast political machine. The other is of those who employ their riches wholly in the acquisition of pleasure. As to the first sort, their continual care and anxiety, their toilsome days, and sleepless nights, are next to proverbial. These circumstances are sufficient almost to level their condition to that of the unhappy majority; but there are other circumstances which place them in a far lower condition. Not only their understandings labor continually, which is the severest labor, but their hearts are torn by the worst, most troublesome, and insatiable of all passions, by avarice, by ambition, by fear and jealousy. No part of the mind has rest. Power gradually extirpates from the mind every humane and gentle virtue. Pity, benevolence, friendship, are things almost unknown in high stations. *Veræ amicitiæ rarissime inveniuntur in iis qui in honoribus reque publica versantur*, says Cicero. And indeed courts are the schools where cruelty, pride, dissimulation, and treachery are studied and taught in the most vicious perfection. This is a point so clear and acknowledged, that if it did not make a necessary part of my subject, I should pass it by entirely. And this has hindered me from drawing at full length, and in the most striking colors, this shocking picture of the degeneracy and wretchedness of human nature, in that part which is vulgarly thought its happiest and most amiable state. You know from what originals I could copy such pictures. Happy are they who know enough of them to know the little value of the possessors of such things, and of all that they possess; and happy they who have been snatched from that post of danger which they occupy, with the remains of their virtue; loss of honors, wealth, titles, and even the loss of one's country, is nothing in balance with so great an advantage.

Let us now view the other species of the rich, those who devote their time and fortunes to idleness and pleasure. How much happier are they? The pleasures which are agreeable to nature are within the reach of all, and therefore can form no distinction in favor of the rich. The pleasures which art forces up are seldom sincere, and never satisfying. What is worse, this constant application to pleasure takes away from the enjoyment, or rather turns it into the nature of a very burdensome and laborious business. It has consequences much more fatal. It produces a weak valetudinary state of body, attended by all those horrid disorders, and yet more horrid methods of cure, which are the result of luxury on the one hand, and the weak and ridiculous efforts of human art on the other. The pleasures of such men are scarcely felt as pleasures; at the same time that they bring on pains and diseases, which are felt but too severely. The mind has its share of the misfortune; it grows lazy and enervate, unwilling and unable to search for truth, and utterly uncapable of knowing, much less of relishing, real happiness. The poor by their excessive labor, and the rich by their enormous luxury, are set upon a level, and rendered equally ignorant of any knowledge which might conduce to their happiness. A dismal view of the interior of all civil society! The lower part broken and ground down by the most cruel oppression; and the rich by their artificial method of life bringing worse evils on themselves than their tyranny could possibly inflict on those below them. Very different is the prospect of the natural state. Here there are no wants which nature gives, and in this state men can be sensible of no other wants, which are not to be supplied by a very moderate degree of labor; therefore there is no slavery. Neither is there any luxury, because no single man can supply the materials of it. Life is simple, and therefore it is happy.

I am conscious, my lord, that your politician will urge in his defence, that this unequal state is highly useful. That without dooming some part of mankind to extraordinary toil, the arts which cultivate life could not be exercised. But I demand of this politician, how such arts came to be necessary? He answers, that civil society could not well exist without them. So that these arts are necessary to civil society, and civil society necessary again to these arts. Thus are we running in a circle, without modesty, and without end, and making one error and extravagance an excuse for the other. My sentiments about these arts and their cause, I have often discoursed with my friends at large. Pope has expressed them in good verse, where he talks with so much force of reason and elegance of language, in praise of the state of nature:

> *"Then was not pride, nor arts that pride to aid,*
> *Man walked with beast, joint tenant of the shade."*

On the whole, my lord, if political society, in whatever form, has still made the many the property of the few; if it has introduced labors unnecessary, vices and diseases unknown, and pleasures incompatible with nature; if in all countries it abridges the lives of millions, and renders those of millions more utterly abject and miserable, shall we still worship so destructive an idol, and daily sacrifice to it our health, our liberty, and our peace? Or shall we pass by this monstrous heap of absurd notions, and abominable practices, thinking we have sufficiently discharged our duty in exposing the trifling cheats, and ridiculous juggles of a few mad, designing, or ambitious priests? Alas! my lord, we labor under a mortal consumption, whilst we are so anxious about the cure of a sore finger. For has not this leviathan of civil power overflowed the earth with a deluge of blood, as if he were made to disport and play therein? We have shown that political society, on a moderate calculation, has been the means of murdering several times the number of inhabitants now upon the earth, during its short existence, not upwards of four thousand years in any accounts to be depended on. But we have said nothing of the other, and perhaps as bad, consequence of these wars, which have spilled such seas of blood, and reduced so many millions to a merciless slavery. But these are only the ceremonies performed in the porch of the political temple. Much more horrid ones are seen as you enter it. The several species of government vie with each other in the absurdity of their constitutions, and the oppression which they make their subjects endure. Take them under what form you please, they are in effect but a despotism, and they fall, both in effect and appearance too, after a very short period, into that cruel and detestable species of tyranny: which I rather call it, because we have been educated under another form, than that this is of worse consequences to mankind. For the free governments, for the point of their space, and the moment of their duration, have felt more confusion, and committed more flagrant acts of tyranny, than the most perfect despotic governments which we have ever known. Turn your eye next to the labyrinth of the law, and the iniquity conceived in its intricate recesses. Consider the ravages committed in the bowels of all commonwealths by ambition, by avarice, envy, fraud, open injustice, and pretended friendship; vices which could draw little support from a state of nature, but which blossom and flourish in the rankness of political society. Revolve our whole discourse; add to it all those reflections which your own good understanding shall suggest, and make a strenuous effort beyond the reach of vulgar philosophy, to confess that the cause of artificial society is more defenceless even than that of artificial religion; that it is as derogatory from the honor of the Creator, as subversive of human reason, and productive of infinitely more mischief to the human race.

If pretended revelations have caused wars where they were opposed, and slavery where they were received, the pretended wise inventions of politicians have done the same. But the slavery has been much heavier, the wars far more bloody, and both more universal by many degrees. Show me any mischief produced by the madness or wickedness of theologians, and I will show you a hundred resulting from the ambition and villany of conquerors and statesmen. Show me an absurdity in religion, and I will undertake to show you a hundred for one in political laws and institutions. If you say that natural religion is a sufficient guide without the foreign aid of revelation, on what principle should political laws become necessary? Is not the same reason available in theology and in politics? If the laws of nature are the laws of God, is it consistent with the Divine wisdom to prescribe rules to us, and leave the enforcement of them to the folly of human institutions? Will you follow truth but to a certain point?

We are indebted for all our miseries to our distrust of that guide which Providence thought sufficient for our condition, our own natural reason, which rejecting both in human and divine things, we have given our necks to the yoke of political and theological slavery. We have renounced the prerogative of man, and it is no wonder that we should be treated like beasts. But our misery is much greater than theirs, as the crime we commit in rejecting the lawful dominion of our reason is greater than any which they can commit. If, after all, you should confess all these things, yet plead the necessity of political institutions, weak and wicked as they are, I can argue with equal, perhaps superior, force, concerning the necessity of artificial religion; and every step you advance in your argument, you add a strength to mine. So that if we are resolved to submit our reason and our liberty to civil usurpation, we have nothing to do but to conform as quietly as we can to the vulgar notions which are connected with this, and take up the theology of the vulgar as well as their politics. But if we think this necessity rather imaginary than real, we should renounce their dreams of society, together with their visions of religion, and vindicate ourselves into perfect liberty. . . .

A Philosophical Inquiry into the Origins of Our Ideas of the Sublime and the Beautiful

Burke's essay on aesthetics, published in 1757, has long been regarded as a critical document in the emergence of the romantic spirit, repudiating as it does the Enlightenment's classical ideal of moderation, harmony, and distaste for change and variety. The essay, with its depiction of the sublime as involving pain, terror, and danger, and beauty involving pleasure, love, and tenderness, has been praised by a long list of distinguished writers that includes Johnson, Wordsworth, Blake, Thomas Hardy, Gotthold Lessing, Denis Diderot, and Immanuel Kant. Its appeal endures, for it has become by now a canonical text in the history of aesthetic theory.

THE PASSION CAUSED by the great and sublime in *nature*, when those causes operate most powerfully, is astonishment; and astonishment is that state of the soul, in which all its motions are suspended, with some degree of horror. In this case the mind is so entirely filled with its object, that it cannot entertain any other, nor by consequence reason on that object which employs it. Hence arises the great power of the sublime, that, far from being produced by them, it anticipates our reasonings, and hurries us on by an irresistible force. Astonishment, as I have said, is the effect of the sublime in its highest degree; the inferior effects are admiration, reverence, and respect. . . .

No passion so effectually robs the mind of all its powers of acting and reasoning as *fear.* For fear being an apprehension of pain or death, it operates in a manner that resembles actual pain. Whatever therefore is terrible, with regard to sight, is sublime too, whether this cause of terror be endued with greatness of dimensions or not; for it is impossible to look on anything as trifling, or contemptible, that may be dangerous. There are many animals, who though far from being large, are yet capable of raising ideas of the sublime, because they are considered as objects of terror. As serpents and poisonous animals of almost all kinds. And to things of great dimensions, if we annex an adventitious idea of terror, they become without comparison greater. A level plain of a vast extent on land, is certainly no mean idea; the prospect of such a plain may be as extensive as a prospect of the ocean: but can it ever fill the mind with anything so great as the ocean itself? This is owing to several causes; but it is owing to none more than this, that the ocean is an object of no small terror. Indeed, terror is in all cases whatsoever, either more openly or latently, the ruling principle of the sublime. Several languages bear a strong testimony to the affinity of these ideas. They frequently use the same word, to signify indifferently the modes of astonishment or admiration, and those of terror. θάμβος is in Greek, either fear or wonder; δεινὸς is terrible or respectable; αἰδέω, to reverence or to fear. *Vereor* in Latin, is what αἰδέω is in Greek. The Romans used the verb *stupeo*, a term which strongly marks the state of an astonished mind, to express the effect either of simple fear or of astonishment; the word *attonitus* (thunderstruck) is equally expressive of the alliance of these ideas; and do not the French *etonnement*, and the English *astonishment* and *amazement*, point out as clearly the kindred emotions which attend fear and wonder? They who have a more general knowledge of languages, could produce, I make no doubt, many other and equally striking examples. . . .

To make anything very terrible, obscurity seems in general to be necessary. When we know the full extent of any danger, when we can accustom our eyes to it, a great deal of the apprehension vanishes. Every one will be sensible of this, who considers how greatly night adds to our dread, in all cases of danger, and how much the notions of ghosts and goblins, of which none can form clear ideas, affect minds which give credit to the popular tales concerning such sorts of beings. Those despotic governments, which are founded on the passions of men, and principally upon the passion of fear, keep their chief as much as may be from the public eye. The policy has been the same in many cases of religion. Almost all the heathen temples were dark. Even in the barbarous temples of the Americans at this day, they keep their idol in a dark part of the hut, which is consecrated to his worship. For this purpose too the Druids performed all their ceremonies in the bosom of the darkest woods, and in the shade of the oldest and most spreading oaks. No person seems better to have understood the secret of heightening, or of setting terrible things, if I may use the expression, in their strongest light, by the force of a judicious obscurity, than Milton. His description of Death in the second book is admirably studied; it is astonishing with what a gloomy pomp, with what a significant and expressive uncertainty of strokes and colouring, he has finished the portrait of the king of terrors:

—The other shape,
If shape it might be called that shape had none
Distinguishable, in member, joint, or limb;
Or substance might be called that shadow seemed;
For each seemed either; black he stood as night;
Fierce as ten furies; terrible as hell;
And shook a deadly dart. What seemed his head
The likeness of a kingly crown had on.

In this description all is dark, uncertain, confused, terrible, and sublime to the last degree. . . .

It is one thing to make an idea clear, and another to make it *affecting* to the imagination. If I make a drawing of a palace, or a temple, or a landscape, I present a very clear idea of those objects; but then (allowing for the effect of imitation, which is something) my picture can at most affect only as the palace, temple, or landscape would have affected in the reality. On the other hand, the most lively and spirited verbal description I can give raises a very obscure and imperfect *idea* of such objects; but then it is in my power to raise a stronger *emotion* by the description than I could do by the best painting. This experience constantly evinces. The proper manner of conveying the *affections* of the mind from one to another, is by words; there is a great insufficiency in all other methods of communication; and so far is a clearness of imagery from being absolutely necessary to an influence upon the passions, that they may be considerably operated upon, without presenting any image at all, by certain sounds adapted to that purpose; of which we have a sufficient proof in the acknowledged and powerful effects of instrumental music. In reality, a great clearness helps but little towards affecting the passions, as it is in some sort an enemy to all enthusiasms whatsoever. . . .

There are two verses in Horace's Art of Poetry, that seem to contradict this opinion; for which reason I shall take a little more pains in clearing it up. The verses are,

> *Segnius irritant animos demissa per aures,*
> *Quaæ quæ sunt oculis subjecta fidelibus.*

On this the Abbé du Bos founds a criticism, wherein he gives painting the preference to poetry in the article of moving the passions; principally on account of the greater *clearness* of the ideas it represents. I believe this excellent judge was led into this mistake (if it be a mistake) by his system; to which he found it more conformable than I imagine it will be found by experience. I know several who admire and love painting, and yet who regard the objects of their admiration in that art with coolness enough in comparison of that warmth with which they are animated by affecting pieces of poetry or rhetoric. Among the common sort of people, I never could perceive that painting had much influence on their passions. It is true, that the best sorts of painting, as well as the best sorts of poetry, are not much understood in that sphere. But it is most certain, that their passions are very strongly roused by a fanatic preacher, or by the ballads of Chevy-chace, or the Children in the Wood, and by other little popular poems and tales that are current in that rank of life. I do not know of any paintings, bad or good, that produce the same effect. So that poetry, with all its obscurity, has a more general, as well as a more powerful, dominion over the passions, than the other art. And I think there are reasons in nature, why the obscure idea, when properly conveyed, should be more affecting than the clear. It is our ignorance of things that causes all our admiration, and chiefly excites our passions. Knowledge and acquaintance make the most striking causes affect but little. It is thus with the vulgar; and all men are as the vulgar in what they do not understand. The ideas of eternity and infinity are among the most affecting we have; and yet perhaps there is nothing of which we really understand so little, as of infinity and eternity. We do not anywhere meet a more sublime description than this justly celebrated one of Milton, wherein he gives the portrait of Satan with a dignity so suitable to the subject:

—He above the rest
In shape and gesture proudly eminent
Stood like a tower; his form had yet not lost
All her original brightness, nor appeared
Less than archangel ruined, and th' excess
Of glory obscured: as when the sun new risen
Looks through the horizontal misty air
Shorn of his beams; or from behind the moon
In dim eclipse disastrous twilight sheds
On half the nations; and with fear of change
Perplexes monarchs.—

Here is a very noble picture; and in what does this poetical picture consist? In images of a tower, an archangel, the sun rising through mists, or in an eclipse, the ruin of monarchs, and the revolutions of kingdoms. The mind is hurried out of itself, by a crowd of great and confused images; which affect because they are crowded and confused. For, separate them, and you lose much of the greatness; and join them, and you infallibly lose the clearness. The images raised by poetry are always of this obscure kind; though in general the effects of poetry are by no means to be attributed to the images it raises; which point we shall examine more at large hereafter. But painting, when we have allowed for the pleasure of imitation, can only affect simply by the images it presents; and even in painting, a judicious obscurity in some things contributes to the effect of the picture; because the images in painting are exactly similar to those in nature; and in nature, dark, confused, uncertain images have a greater power on the fancy to form the grander passions, than those have which are more clear and determinate. But where and when this observation may be applied to practice, and how far it shall be extended, will be better deduced from the nature of the subject, and from the occasion, than from any rules that can be given.

I am sensible that this idea has met with opposimon, and is likely still to be rejected by several. But let it be considered, that hardly anything can strike the mind with its greatness, which does not make some sort of approach towards infinity; which nothing can do whilst we are able to perceive its bounds; but to see an object distinctly, and to perceive its bounds, is one and the same thing. A clear idea is therefore another name for a little idea. There is a passage in the book of Job amazingly sublime, and this sublimity is principally due to the terrible uncertainty of the thing described: *In thoughts from the visions of the night, when deep sleep falleth upon men, fear came upon me, and trembling, which made all my bones to shake. Then a spirit passed before my face; the hair of my flesh stood up. It stood still*, but I could not discern the form thereof: *an image was before mine eyes, there was silence, and I heard a voice,—Shall mortal man be more just than God?* We are first prepared with the utmost solemnity for the vision; we are first terrified, before we are let even into the obscure cause of our emotion: but when this grand cause of terror makes its appearance, what is it? Is it not wrapt up in the shades of its own incomprehensible darkness, more awful, more striking, more terrible, than the liveliest description, than the clearest painting, could possibly represent it? When painters have attempted to give us clear representations of these very fanciful and terrible ideas, they have, I think, almost always failed; insomuch that I have been at a loss, in all the pictures I have seen of hell, to determine whether the painter did not intend something ludicrous. Several painters have handled a subject of this kind, with a view of assembling as many horrid phantoms as their imagination could suggest; but all the designs I have chanced to meet of the temptation of St. Anthony were rather a sort of odd, wild grotesques, than anything capable of producing a serious passion. In all these subjects poetry is very happy. Its apparitions, its chimeras, its harpies, its allegorical figures, are grand and affecting; and though Virgil's Fame and Homer's Discord are obscure, they are magnificent figures. These figures in painting would be clear enough, but I fear they might become ridiculous. . . .

Besides those things which *directly* suggest the idea of danger, and those which produce a similar effect from a mechanical cause, I know of nothing sublime, which is not some modification of power. And this branch rises, as naturally as the other two branches, from terror, the common stock of everything that is sublime. The idea of power, at first view, seems of the class of those indifferent ones, which may equally belong to pain or to pleasure. But in reality, the affection, arising from the idea of vast power, is extremely remote from that neutral character. For first, we must remember, that the idea of pain, in its highest degree, is much stronger than the highest degree of pleasure; and that it preserves the same superiority through all the subordinate gradations. From hence it is, that where the chances for equal degrees of suffering or enjoyment are in any sort equal, the idea of the suffering must always be prevalent. And indeed the ideas of pain, and, above all, of death, are so very affecting, that whilst we remain in the presence of whatever is supposed to have the power of inflicting either, it is impossible to be perfectly free from terror. Again, we know by experience, that, for the enjoyment of pleasure, no great efforts of power are at all necessary; nay, we know, that such efforts would go a great way towards destroying our satisfaction: for pleasure must be stolen, and not forced upon us; pleasure follows the will; and therefore we are generally affected with it by many things of a force greatly inferior to our own. But pain is always inflicted by a power in some way superior, because we never submit to pain willingly. So that strength, violence, pain, and terror, are ideas that rush in upon the mind together. Look at a man, or any other animal of prodigious strength, and what is your idea before reflection? Is it that this strength will be subservient to you, to your ease, to your pleasure, to your interest in any sense? No; the emotion you feel is, lest this enormous strength should be employed to the purposes of rapine and destruction. That power derives all its sublimity from the terror with which it is generally accompanied, will appear evidently from its effect in the very few cases, in which it may be possible to strip a considerable degree of strength of its ability to hurt. When you do this, you spoil it of everything sublime, and it immediately becomes contemptible. An ox is a creature of vast strength; but he is an innocent creature, extremely serviceable, and not at all dangerous; for which reason the idea of an ox is by no means grand. A bull is strong too: but his strength is of another kind; often very destructive, seldom (at least amongst us) of any use in our business; the idea of a bull is therefore great, and it has frequently a place in sublime descriptions, and elevating comparisons. Let us look at another strong animal, in the two distinct lights in which we may consider him. The horse in the light of a useful beast, fit for the plough, the road, the draft; in every social, useful light, the horse has nothing sublime: but is it thus that we are affected with him, *whose neck is clothed with thunder, the glory of whose nostrils is terrible, who swalloweth the ground with fierceness and rage, neither believeth that it is the sound of the trumpet?* In this description, the useful character of the horse entirely disappears, and the terrible and sublime blaze out together. We have continually about us animals of a strength that is considerable, but not pernicious. Amongst these we never look for the sublime; it comes upon us in the gloomy forest, and in the howling wilderness, in the form of the lion, the tiger, the panther, or rhinoceros. Whenever strength is only useful, and employed for our benefit or our pleasure, then it is never sublime: for nothing can act agreeably to us, that does not act in conformity to our will; but to act agreeably to our will, it must be subject to us, and therefore can never be the cause of a grand and commanding conception. The description of the wild ass, in Job, is worked up into no small sublimity, merely by insisting on his freedom, and his setting mankind at defiance; otherwise the description of such an animal could have had nothing noble in it. *Who hath loosed* (says he) *the bands of the wild ass? whose house I have made the wilderness, and the barren land his dwellings. He scorneth the multitude of the city, neither regardeth he the voice of the driver. The range of the mountains is his pasture.* The magnificent description of the unicorn and of leviathan, in the same book, is full of the same heightening circumstances: *Will the unicorn be willing to serve thee? canst thou bind the unicorn with his band in the furrow? wilt thou trust him because his strength is great?—Canst thou draw out leviathan with an hook?—will he make a covenant with thee? wilt thou take him for a servant for ever? shall not one be cast down even at the sight of him?* In short, wheresoever we find strength, and in what light soever we look upon power we shall all along observe the sublime the concomitant of terror, and contempt the attendant on a strength that is subservient and innoxious. The race of dogs, in many of their kinds, have generally a competent degree of strength and swiftness; and they exert these and other valuable qualities which they possess, greatly to our convenience and pleasure. Dogs are indeed the most social, affectionate, and amiable animals of the whole brute creation; but love approaches much nearer to contempt than is commonly imagined; and accordingly, though we caress dogs, we borrow from them an appellation of the most despicable kind, when we employ terms of reproach; and this appellation is the common mark of the last vileness and contempt in every language. Wolves have not more strength than several species of dogs; but, on account of their unmanageable fierceness, the idea of a wolf is not despicable; it is not excluded from grand descriptions and similitudes. Thus we are affected by strength, which is *natural* power. The power which arises from institution in kings and commanders, has the same connexion with terror. Sovereigns are frequently addressed with the title of *dread majesty.* And it may be observed, that young persons, little acquainted with the world, and who have not been used to approach men in power, are commonly struck with an awe which takes away the free use of their faculties. *When I prepared my seat in the street,* (says Job,) *the young men saw me, and hid themselves.* Indeed, so natural is this timidity with regard to power, and so strongly does it inhere in our constitution, that very few are able to conquer it, but by mixing much in the business of the great world, or by using no small violence to their natural dispositions. I know some people are of opinion, that no awe, no degree of terror, accompanies the idea of power; and have hazarded to affirm, that we can contemplate the idea of God himself without any such emotion. I purposely avoided, when I first considered this subject, to introduce the idea of that great and tremendous Being, as an example in an argument so light as this; though it frequently occurred to me, not as an objection to, but as a strong confirmation of, my notions in this matter. I hope, in what I am going to say, I shall avoid presumption, where it is almost impossible for any mortal to speak with strict propriety. I say then, that whilst we consider the Godhead merely as he is an object of the understanding, which forms a complex idea of power, wisdom, justice, goodness, all stretched to a degree far exceeding the bounds of our comprehension, whilst we consider the Divinity in this refined and abstracted light, the imagination and passions are little or nothing affected. But because we are bound, by the condition of our nature, to ascend to these pure and intellectual ideas, through the medium of sensible images, and to judge of these divine qualities by their evident acts and exertions, it becomes extremely hard to disentangle our idea of the cause from the effect by which we are led to know it. Thus when we contemplate the Deity, his attributes and their operation, coming united on the mind, form a sort of sensible image, and as such are capable of affecting the imagination. Now, though in a just idea of the Deity perhaps none of his attributes are predominant, yet, to our imagination, his power is by far the most striking. Some reflection, some comparing, is necessary to satisfy us of his wisdom, his justice, and his goodness. To be struck with his power, it is only necessary that we should open our eyes. But whilst we contemplate so vast an object, under the arm, as it were, of almighty power, and invested upon every side with omnipresence, we shrink into the minuteness of our own nature, and are, in a manner, annihilated before him. And though a consideration of his other attributes may relieve, in some measure, our apprehensions; yet no conviction of the justice with which it is exercised, nor the mercy with which it is tempered, can wholly remove the terror that naturally arises from a force which nothing can withstand. If we rejoice, we rejoice with trembling: and even whilst we are receiving benefits, we cannot but shudder at a power which can confer benefits of such mighty importance. When the prophet David contemplated the wonders of wisdom and power which are displayed in the economy of man, he seems to be struck with a sort of divine horror, and cries out, *Fearfully and wonderfully am I made!* An heathen poet has a sentiment of a similar nature; Horace looks upon it as the last effort of philosophical fortitude, to behold without terror and amazement, this immense and glorious fabric of the universe.

Hunc solem, et stellas, et decedentia certis
Tempora momentis, sunt qui formidine nulla
Imbuti spectent.

Lucretius is a poet not to be suspected of giving way to superstitious terrors; yet when he supposes the whole mechanism of nature laid open by the master of his philosophy, his transport on this magnificent view, which he has represented in the colours of such bold and lively poetry, is overcast with a shade of secret dread and horror:

His ibi me rebus quœdam divina voluptas
Percipit, atque horror; quod sic Natura, tua vi
Tam manifesta patens, ex omni parte retecta est.

But the Scripture alone can supply ideas answerable to the majesty of this subject. In the Scripture, wherever God is represented as appearing or speaking, everything terrible in nature is called up to heigten the awe and solemnity of the Divine presence. The Psalms, and the prophetical books, are crowded with instances of this kind. *The earth shook*, (says the psalmist,) *the heavens also dropped at the presence of the Lord*. And, what is remarkable, the painting preserves the same character, not only when he is supposed descending to take vengeance upon the wicked, but even when he exerts the like plenitude of power in acts of beneficence to mankind. *Tremble, thou earth! at the presence of the Lord; at the presence of the God of Jacob; which turned the rock into standing water, the flint into a fountain of waters!* It were endless to enumerate all the passages, both in the sacred and profane writers, which establish the general sentiment of mankind, concerning the inseparable union of a sacred and reverential awe, with our ideas of the Divinity. Hence the common maxim, *Primus in orbe deos fecit timor.* This maxim may be, as I believe it is, false with regard to the origin of religion. The maker of the maxim saw how inseparable these ideas were, without considering that the notion of some great power must be always precedent to our dread of it. But this dread must necessarily follow the idea of such a power, when it is once excited in the mind. It is on this principle that true religion has, and must have, so large a mixture of salutary fear; and that false religions have generally nothing else but fear to support them. Before the Christian religion had, as it were, humanized the idea of the Divinity, and brought it somewhat nearer to us, there was very little said of the love of God. The followers of Plato have something of it, and only something; the other writers of pagan antiquity, whether poets or philosophers, nothing at all. And they who consider with what infinite attention, by what a disregard of every perishable object, through what long habits of piety and contemplation, it is that any man is able to attain an entire love and devotion to the Deity, will easily perceive, that it is not the first, the most natural and the most striking, effect which proceeds from that idea. Thus we have traced power through its several gradations unto the highest of all, where our imagination is finally lost; and we find terror, quite throughout the progress, its inseparable companion, and growing along with it, as far as we can possibly trace them. Now as power is undoubtedly a capital source of the sublime, this will point out evidently from whence its energy is derived, and to what class of ideas we ought to unite it. . . .

All *general* privations are great, because they are all terrible; *Vacuity*, *Darkness*, *Solitude*, and *Silence*. With what a fire of imagination, yet with what severity of judgment, has Virgil amassed all these circumstances, where he knows that all the images of a tremendous dignity ought to be united, at the mouth of hell! where, before he unlocks the secrets of the great deep, he seems to be seized with a religious horror, and to retire astonished at the boldness of his own design:

Dii, quibus imperium est animarum, umbrœque—silentes!
Et Chaos, et Phlegethon, loca nocte silentia *late,*
Sit mihi fas audita loqui; sit, numine vestro,
Pandere res alta terra et caligine *mersas.*
Ibant obscuri, sola *sub* nocte, *per* umbram,
Perque domos Ditis vacuas, *et* inania *regna.*

Ye subterraneous gods, whose awful sway
The gliding ghosts and silent shades obey;
O Chaos hoar! and Phlegethon profound!
Whose solemn empire stretches wide around;
Give me, ye great, tremendous powers, to tell
Of scenes and wonders in the depth of hell:
Give me your mighty secrets to display
From those black *realms of darkness to the day.*

PITT.

Obscure *they went through dreary* shades *that led*
Along the waste *dominions of the* dead.

DRYDEN.

Greatness of dimension is a powerful cause of the sublime. This is too evident, and the observation too common, to need any illustration: it is not so common to consider in what ways greatness of dimension, vastness of extent or quantity, has the most striking effect. For certainly, there are ways and modes, wherein the same quantity of extension shall produce greater effects than it is found to do in others. Extension is either in length, height, or depth. Of these the length strikes least; an hundred yards of even ground will never work such an effect as a tower an hundred yards high, or a rock or mountain of that altitude. I am apt to imagine likewise, that height is less grand than depth; and that we are more struck at looking down from a precipice, than looking up at an object of equal height; but of that I am not very positive. A perpendicular has more force in forming the sublime, than an inclined plane; and the effects of a rugged and broken surface seem stronger than where it is smooth and polished. It would carry us out of our way to enter in this place into the cause of these appearances; but certain it is they afford a large and fruitful field of speculation. However, it may not be amiss to add to these remarks upon magnitude, that, as the great extreme of dimension is sublime, so the last extreme of littleness is in some measure sublime likewise: when we attend to the infinite divisibility of matter, when we pursue animal life into these excessively small, and yet organized beings, that escape the nicest inquisition of the sense; when we push our discoveries yet downward, and consider those creatures so many degrees yet smaller, and the still diminishing scale of existence, in tracing which the imagination is lost as well as the sense; we become amazed and confounded at the wonders of minuteness; nor can we distinguish in its effects this extreme of littleness from the vast itself. For division must be infinite as well as addition; because the idea of a perfect unity can no more be arrived at, than that of a complete whole, to which nothing may be added. . . .

Another source of the sublime is *infinity*; if it does not rather belong to the last. Infinity has a tendency to fill the mind with that sort of delightful horror, which is the most genuine effect and truest test of the sublime. There are scarce any things which can become the objects of our senses, that are really and in their own nature infinite. But the eye not being able to perceive the bounds of many things, they seem to be infinite, and they produce the same effects as if they were really so. We are deceived in the like manner, if the parts of some large object are so continued to any indefinite number, that the imagination meets no check which may hinder its extending them at pleasure. . . .

It is my design to consider beauty as distinguished from the sublime; and, in the course of the inquiry, to examine how far it is consistent with it. But previous to this, we must take a short review of the opinions already entertained of this quality; which I think are hardly to be reduced to any fixed principles; because men are used to talk of beauty in a figurative manner, that is to say, in a manner extremely uncertain, and indeterminate. By beauty I mean that quality or those qualities in bodies, by which they cause love, or some passion similar to it. I confine this definition to the merely sensible qualities of things, for the sake of preserving the utmost simplicity in a subject, which must always distract us whenever we take in those various causes of sympathy which attach us to any persons or things from secondary considerations, and not from the direct force which they have merely on being viewed. I likewise distinguish love (by which I mean that satisfaction which arises to the mind upon contemplating anything beautiful, of whatsoever nature it may be) from desire or lust; which is an energy of the mind, that hurries us on to the possession of certain objects, that do not affect us as they are beautiful, but by means altogether different. We shall have a strong desire for a woman of no remarkable beauty; whilst the greatest beauty in men, or in other animals, though it causes love, yet excites nothing at all of desire. Which shows that beauty, and the passion caused by beauty, which I call love, is different from desire, though desire may sometimes operate along with it; but it is to this latter that we must attribute those violent and tempestuous passions, and the consequent emotions of the body, which attend what is called love in some of its ordinary acceptations, and not to the effects of beauty merely as it is such. . . .

On the whole; if such parts in human bodies as are found proportioned, were likewise constantly found beautiful, as they certainly are not; or if they were so situated, as that a pleasure might flow from the comparison, which they seldom are; or if any assignable proportions were found, either in plants or animals, which were always attended with beauty, which never was the case; or if, where parts were well adapted to their purposes, they were constantly beautiful, and when no use appeared, there was no beauty, which is contrary to all experience; we might conclude, that beauty consisted in proportion or utility. But since, in all respects, the case is quite otherwise; we may be satisfied that beauty does not depend on these, let it owe its origin to what else it will. . . .

There is another notion current, pretty closely allied to the former; that *Perfection* is the constituent cause of beauty. This opinion has been made to extend much further than to sensible objects. But in these, so far is perfection, considered as such, from being the cause of beauty, that this quality, where it is highest, in the female sex, almost always carries with it an idea of weakness and imperfection. Women are very sensible of this; for which reason, they learn to lisp, to totter in their walk, to counterfeit weakness, and even sickness. In all they are guided by nature. Beauty in distress is much the most affecting beauty. Blushing has little less power; and modesty in general, which is a tacit allowance of imperfection, is itself considered as an amiable quality, and certainly heightens every other that is so. I know it is in everybody's mouth, that we ought to love perfection. This is to me a sufficient proof, that it is not the proper object of love. Who ever said we *ought* to love a fine woman, or even any of these beautiful animals which please us? Here to be affected, there is no need of the concurrence of our will. . . .

Nor is this remark in general less applicable to the qualities of the mind. Those virtues which cause admiration, and are of the sublimer kind, produce terror rather than love; such as fortitude, justice, wisdom, and the like. Never was any man amiable by force of these qualities. Those which engage our hearts, which impress us with a sense of loveliness, are the softer virtues; easiness of temper, compassion, kindness, and liberality; though certainly those latter are of less immediate and momentous concern to society, and of less dignity. But it is for that reason that they are so amiable. The great virtues turn principally on dangers, punishments, and troubles, and are exercised rather in preventing the worst mischiefs, than in dispensing favours; and are therefore not lovely though highly venerable. The subordinate turn on reliefs, gratifications, and indulgences; and are therefore more lovely, though inferior in dignity. Those persons who creep into the hearts of most people, who are chosen as the companions of their softer hours, and their reliefs from care and anxiety, are never persons of shining qualities or strong virtues. It is rather the soft green of the soul on which we rest our eyes, that are fatigued with beholding more glaring objects. It is worth observing how we feel ourselves affected in reading the characters of Cæsar and Cato, as they are so finely drawn and contrasted in Sallust. In one the *ignoscendo largiundo*; in the other, *nil largiundo.* In one, the *miseris perfugium*; in the other, *malis perniciem*. In the latter we have much to admire, much to reverence, and perhaps something to fear; we respect him, but we respect him at a distance. The former makes us familiar with him; we love him, and he leads us whither he pleases. To draw things closer to our first and most natural feelings, I will add a remark made upon reading this section by an ingenious friend. The authority of a father, so useful to our well-being, and so justly venerable upon all accounts, hinders us from having that entire love for him that we have for our mothers, where the parental authority is almost melted down into the mother's fondness and indulgence. But we generally have a great love for our grandfathers, in whom this authority is removed a degree from us, and where the weakness of age mellows it into something of a feminine partiality. . . .

From what has been said in the foregoing section, we may easily see how far the application of beauty to virtue may be made with propriety. The general application of this quality to virtue, has a strong tendency to confound our ideas of things; and it has given rise to an infinite deal of whimsical theory; as the affixing the name of beauty to proportion, congruity, and perfection, as well as to qualities of things yet more remote from our natural ideas of it, and from one another, has tended to confound our ideas of beauty, and left us no standard or rule to judge by, that was not even more uncertain and fallacious than our own fancies. This loose and inaccurate manner of speaking has therefore misled us both in the theory of taste and of morals; and induced us to remove the science of our duties from their proper basis, (our reason, our relations, and our necessities,) to rest it upon foundations altogether visionary and unsubstantial. . . .

Having endeavoured to show what beauty is not, it remains that we should examine, at least with equal attention, in what it really consists. Beauty is a thing much too affecting not to depend upon some positive qualities. And, since it is no creature of our reason, since it strikes us without any reference to use, and even where no use at all can be discerned, since the order and method of nature is generally very different from our measures and proportions, we must conclude that beauty is, for the greater part, some quality in bodies acting mechanically upon the human mind by the intervention of the senses. We ought therefore to consider attentively in what manner those sensible qualities are disposed, in such things as by experience we find beautiful, or which excite in us the passion of love, or some correspondent affection. . . .

The most obvious point that presents itself to us in examining any object, is its extent or quantity. And what degree of extent prevails in bodies that are held beautiful, may be gathered from the usual manner of expression concerning it. I am told that, in most languages, the objects of love are spoken of under diminutive epithets. It is so in all the languages of which I have any knowledge. In Greek the *ιων* and other diminutive terms are almost always the terms of affection and tenderness. These diminutives were commonly added by the Greeks to the names of persons with whom they conversed on terms of friendship and familiarity. Though the Romans were a people of less quick and delicate feelings, yet they naturally slid into the lessening termination upon the same occasions. Anciently in the English language the diminishing *ling* was added to the names of persons and things that were the objects of love. Some we retain still, as *darling*, (or little dear,) and a few others. But, to this day, in ordinary conversation, it is usual to add the endearing name of *little* to everything we love: the French and Italians make use of these affectionate diminutives even more than we. In the animal creation, out of our own species, it is the small we are inclined to be fond of; little birds, and some of the smaller kinds of beasts. A great beautiful thing is a manner of expression scarcely ever used; but that of a great ugly thing is very common. There is a wide difference between admiration and love. The sublime, which is the cause of the former, always dwells on great objects, and terrible; the latter on small ones, and pleasing; we submit to what we admire, but we love what submits to us; in one case we are forced, in the other we are flattered, into compliance. In short, the ideas of the sublime and the beautiful stand on foundations so different, that it is hard, I had almost said impossible, to think of reconciling them in the same subject, without considerably lessening the effect of the one or the other upon the passions. So that, attending to their quantity, beautiful objects are comparatively small. . . .

The next property constantly observable in such objects is *smoothness:* a quality so essential to beauty, that I do not now recollect anything beautiful that is not smooth. In trees and flowers, smooth leaves are beautiful; smooth slopes of earth in gardens; smooth streams in the landscape; smooth coats of birds and beasts in animal beauties; in fine women, smooth skins; and in several sorts of ornamental furniture, smooth and polished surfaces. A very considerable part of the effect of beauty is owing to this quality; indeed the most considerable. For take any beautiful object, and give it a broken and rugged surface; and however well formed it may be in other respects, it pleases no longer. Whereas, let it want ever so many of the other constituents, if it wants not this, it becomes more pleasing than almost all the others without it. This seems to me so evident, that I am a good deal surprised, that none who have handled the subject have made any mention of the quality of smoothness, in the enumeration of those that go to the forming of beauty. For indeed any ruggedness, any sudden projection, any sharp angle, is in the highest degree contrary to that idea. . . .

But as perfectly beautiful bodies are not composed of angular parts, so their parts never continue long in the same right line. They vary their direction every moment, and they change under the eye by a deviation continually carrying on, but for whose beginning or end you will find it difficult to ascertain a point. The view of a beautiful bird will illustrate this observation. Here we see the head increasing insensibly to the middle, from whence it lessens gradually until it mixes with the neck; the neck loses itself in a larger swell, which continues to the middle of the body, when the whole decreases again to the tail; the tail takes a new direction; but it soon varies its new course: it blends again with the other parts; and the line is perpetually changing, above, below, upon every side.

In this description I have before me the idea of a dove; it agrees very well with most of the conditions of beauty. It is smooth and downy; its parts are (to use that expression) melted into one another; you are presented with no sudden protuberance through the whole, and yet the whole is continually changing. Observe that part of a beautiful woman where she is perhaps the most beautiful, about the neck and breasts; the smoothness; the softness; the easy and insensible swell; the variety of the surface, which is never for the smallest space the same; the deceitful maze, through which the unsteady eye slides giddily, without knowing where to fix or whither it is carried. Is not this a demonstration of that change of surface, continual, and yet hardly perceptible at any point, which forms one of the great constituents of beauty? It gives me no small pleasure to find that I can strengthen my theory in this point, by the opinion of the very ingenious Mr. Hogarth; whose idea of the line of beauty I take in general to be extremely just. But the idea of variation, without attending so accurately to the *manner* of the variation, has led him to consider angular figures as beautiful: these figures, it is true, vary greatly; yet they vary in a sudden and broken manner; and I do not find any natural object which is angular, and at the same time beautiful. Indeed few natural objects are entirely angular. But I think those which approach the most nearly to it are the ugliest. I must add too, that, so far as I could observe of nature, though the varied line is that alone in which complete beauty is found, yet there is no particular line which is always found in the most completely beautiful, and which is therefore beautiful in preference to all other lines. At least I never could observe it. . . .

An air of robustness and strength is very prejudicial to beauty. An appearance of *delicacy*, and even of fragility, is almost essential to it. Whoever examines the vegetable or animal creation will find this observation to be founded in nature. It is not the oak, the ash, or the elm, or any of the robust trees of the forest, which we consider as beautiful: they are awful and majestic; they inspire a sort of reverence. It is the delicate myrtle, it is the orange, it is the almond, it is the jasmine, it is the vine, which we look on as vegetable beauties. It is the flowery species, so remarkable for its weakness and momentary duration, that gives us the liveliest idea of beauty and elegance. Among animals, the greyhound is more beautiful than the mastiff; and the delicacy of a gennet, a barb, or an Arabian horse, is much more amiable than the strength and stability of some horses of war or carriage. I need here say little of the fair sex, where I believe the point will be easily allowed me. The beauty of women is considerably owing to their weakness or delicacy, and is even enhanced by their timidity, a quality of mind analogous to it. I would not here be understood to say, that weakness betraying very bad health has any share in beauty; but the ill effect of this is not because it is weakness, but because the ill state of health, which produces such weakness, alters the other conditions of beauty; the parts in such a case collapse; the bright colour, the *lumen purpureum juventæ*, is gone; and the fine variation is lost in wrinkles, sudden breaks, and right lines. . . .

As to the colours usually found in beautiful bodies, it may be somewhat difficult to ascertain them, because, in the several parts of nature, there is an infinite variety. However, even in this variety, we may mark out something on which to settle. First, the colours of beautiful bodies must not be dusky or muddy, but clean and fair. Secondly, they must not be of the strongest kind. Those which seem most appropriated to beauty, are the milder of every sort; light greens; soft blues; weak whites; pink reds; and violets. Thirdly, if the colours be strong and vivid, they are always diversified, and the object is never of one strong colour; there are almost always such a number of them, (as in variegated flowers,) that the strength and glare of each is considerably abated. In a fine complexion, there is not only some variety in the colouring, but the colours: neither the red nor the white are strong and glaring. Besides, they are mixed in such a manner, and with such gradations, that it is impossible to fix the bounds. On the same principle it is, that the dubious colour in the necks and tails of peacocks, and about the heads of drakes, is so very agreeable. In reality, the beauty both of shape and colouring are as nearly related, as we can well suppose it possible for things of such different natures to be. . . .

On the whole, the qualities of beauty, as they are merely sensible qualities, are the following: First, to be comparatively small. Secondly, to be smooth. Thirdly, to have a variety in the direction of the parts; but, fourthly, to have those parts not angular, but melted as it were into each other. Fifthly, to be of a delicate frame, without any remarkable appearance of strength. Sixthly, to have its colours clear and bright, but not very strong and glaring. Seventhly, or if it should have any glaring colour, to have it diversified with others. These are, I believe, the properties on which beauty depends; properties that operate by nature, and are less liable to be altered by caprice, or confounded by a diversity of tastes, than any other. . . .

Fragment—An Essay Towards an History of the Laws of England

In the late 1750s Burke set about writing a one-volume history of England. He abandoned the project after taking it through the reign of King John. Some fifty pages of the history were published while Burke was alive, and in 1811 over three hundred pages were published with the title Essays Toward an Abridgement of the English History. *The last chapter of the posthumously published essay, reproduced here, is entitled "Fragment—An Essay Towards an History of the Laws of England."*

THERE IS SCARCE any object of curiosity more rational than the origin, the progress, and the various revolutions of human laws. Political and military relations are for the greater part accounts of the ambition and violence of mankind: this is an history of their justice. And surely there cannot be a more pleasing speculation than to trace the advances of men in an attempt to imitate the Supreme Ruler in one of the most glorious of His attributes, and to attend them in the exercise of a prerogative which it is wonderful to find intrusted to the management of so weak a being. In such an inquiry we shall, indeed, frequently see great instances of this frailty; but at the same time we shall behold such noble efforts of wisdom and equity as seem fully to justify the reasonableness of that extraordinary disposition by which men, in one form or other, have been always put under the dominion of creatures like themselves. For what can be more instructive than to search out the first obscure and scanty fountains of that jurisprudence which now waters and enriches whole nations with so abundant and copious a flood,—to observe the first principles of RIGHT springing up, involved in superstition and polluted with violence, until by length of time and favorable circumstances it has worked itself into clearness: the laws sometimes lost and trodden down in the confusion of wars and tumults, and sometimes overruled by the hand of power; then, victorious over tyranny, growing stronger, clearer, and more decisive by the violence they had suffered; enriched even by those foreign conquests which threatened their entire destruction; softened and mellowed by peace and religion; improved and exalted by commerce, by social intercourse, and that great opener of the mind, ingenuous science?

These certainly were great encouragements to the study of historical jurisprudence, particularly of our own. Nor was there a want of materials or help for such an undertaking. Yet we have had few attempts in that province. Lord Chief Justice Hale's History of the Common Law is, I think, the only one, good or bad, which we have. But with all the deference justly due to so great a name, we may venture to assert that this performance, though not without merit, is wholly unworthy of the high reputation of its author. The sources of our English law are not well, nor indeed fairly, laid open; the ancient judicial proceedings are touched in a very slight and transient manner; and the great changes and remarkable revolutions in the law, together with their causes, down to his time, are scarcely mentioned.

Of this defect I think there were two principal causes. The first, a persuasion, hardly to be eradicated from the minds of our lawyers, that the English law has continued very much in the same state from an antiquity to which they will allow hardly any sort of bounds. The second is, that it was formed and grew up among ourselves; that it is in every respect peculiar to this island; and that, if the Roman or any foreign laws attempted to intrude into its composition, it has always had vigor enough to shake them off, and return to the purity of its primitive constitution.

These opinions are flattering to national vanity and professional narrowness; and though they involved those that supported them in the most glaring contradictions, and some absurdities even too ridiculous to mention, we have always been, and in a great measure still are, extremely tenacious of them. If these principles are admitted, the history of the law must in a great measure be deemed superfluous. For to what purpose is a history of a law of which it is impossible to trace the beginning, and which during its continuance has admitted no essential changes? Or why should we search foreign laws or histories for explanation or ornament of that which is wholly our own, and by which we are effectually distinguished from all other countries? Thus the law has been confined and drawn up into a narrow and inglorious study, and that which should be the leading science in every well-ordered commonwealth remained in all the barbarism of the rudest times, whilst every other advanced by rapid steps to the highest improvement both in solidity and elegance; insomuch that the study of our jurisprudence presented to liberal and well-educated minds, even in the best authors, hardly anything but barbarous terms, ill explained, a coarse, but not a plain expression, an indigested method, and a species of reasoning the very refuse of the schools, which deduced the spirit of the law, not from original justice or legal conformity, but from causes foreign to it and altogether whimsical. Young men were sent away with an incurable, and, if we regard the manner of handling rather than the substance, a very well-founded disgust. The famous antiquary, Spelman, though no man was better formed for the most laborious pursuits, in the beginning deserted the study of the law in despair, though he returned to it again when a more confirmed age and a strong desire of knowledge enabled him to wrestle with every difficulty.

The opinions which have drawn the law into such narrowness, as they are weakly founded, so they are very easily refuted. With regard to that species of eternity which they attribute to the English law, to say nothing of the manifest contradictions in which those involve themselves who praise it for the frequent improvements it has received, and at the same time value it for having remained without any change in all the revolutions of government, it is obvious, on the very first view of the Saxon laws, that we have entirely altered the whole frame of our jurisprudence since the Conquest. Hardly can we find in these old collections a single title which is law at this day; and one may venture to assert, without much hazard, that, if there were at present a nation governed by the Saxon laws, we should find it difficult to point out another so entirely different from everything we now see established in England.

This is a truth which requires less sagacity than candor to discover. The spirit of party, which has misled us in so many other particulars, has tended greatly to perplex us in this matter. For as the advocates for prerogative would, by a very absurd consequence drawn from the Norman Conquest, have made all our national rights and liberties to have arisen from the grants, and therefore to be revocable at the will of the sovereign, so, on the other hand, those who maintained the cause of liberty did not support it upon more solid principles. They would hear of no beginning to any of our privileges, orders, or laws, and, in order to gain them a reverence, would prove that they were as old as the nation; and to support that opinion, they put to the torture all the ancient monuments. Others, pushing things further, have offered a still greater violence to them. N. Bacon, in order to establish his republican system, has so distorted all the evidence he has produced, concealed so many things of consequence, and thrown such false colors upon the whole argument, that I know no book so likely to mislead the reader in our antiquities, if yet it retains any authority. In reality, that ancient Constitution and those Saxon laws make little or nothing for any of our modern parties, and, when fairly laid open, will be found to compose such a system as none, I believe, would think it either practicable or desirable to establish. I am sensible that nothing has been a larger theme of panegyric with all our writers on politics and history than the Anglo-Saxon government; and it is impossible not to conceive an high opinion of its laws, if we rather consider what is said of them than what they visibly are. These monuments of our pristine rudeness still subsist; and they stand out of themselves indisputable evidence to confute the popular declamations of those writers who would persuade us that the crude institutions of an unlettered people had reached a perfection which the united efforts of inquiry, experience, learning, and necessity have not been able to attain in many ages.

But the truth is, the present system of our laws, like our language and our learning, is a very mixed and heterogeneous mass: in some respects our own; in more borrowed from the policy of foreign nations, and compounded, altered, and variously modified, according to the various necessities which the manners, the religion, and the commerce of the people have at different times imposed. It is our business, in some measure, to follow and point out these changes and improvements: a task we undertake, not from any ability for the greatness of such a work, but purely to give some short and plain account of these matters to the very ignorant.

The Law of the Romans seems utterly to have expired in this island together with their empire, and that, too, before the Saxon establishment. The Anglo-Saxons came into England as conquerors. They brought their own customs with them, and doubtless did not take laws from, but imposed theirs upon, the people they had vanquished. These customs of the conquering nation were without question the same, for the greater part, they had observed before their migration from Germany. The best image we have of them is to be found in Tacitus. But there is reason to believe that some changes were made suitable to the circumstances of their new settlement, and to the change their constitution must have undergone by adopting a kingly government, not indeed with unlimited sway, but certainly with greater powers than their leaders possessed whilst they continued in Germany. However, we know very little of what was done in these respects until their conversion to Christianity, a revolution which made still more essential changes in their manners and government. For immediately after the conversion of Ethelbert, King of Kent, the missionaries, who had introduced the use of letters, and came from Rome full of the ideas of the Roman civil establishment, must have observed the gross defect arising from a want of written and permanent laws. The king, from their report of the Roman method, and in imitation of it, first digested the most material customs of this kingdom into writing, without having adopted anything from the Roman law, and only adding some regulations for the support and encouragement of the new religion. These laws still exist, and strongly mark the extreme simplicity of manners and poverty of conception of the legislators. They are written in the English of that time; and, indeed, all the laws of the Anglo-Saxons continued in that language down to the Norman Conquest. This was different from the method of the other Northern nations, who made use only of the Latin language in all their codes. And I take the difference to have arisen from this. At the time when the Visigoths, the Lombards, the Franks, and the other Northern nations on the continent compiled their laws, the provincial Romans were very numerous amongst them, or, indeed, composed the body of the people. The Latin language was yet far from extinguished; so that, as the greatest part of those who could write were Romans, they found it difficult to adapt their characters to these rough Northern tongues, and therefore chose to write in Latin, which, though not the language of the legislator, could not be very incommodious, as they could never fail of interpreters; and for this reason, not only their laws, but all their ordinary transactions, were written in that language. But in England, the Roman name and language having entirely vanished in the seventh century, the missionary monks were obliged to contend with the difficulty, and to adapt foreign characters to the English language; else none but a very few could possibly have drawn any advantage from the things they meant to record. And to this it was owing that many, even the ecclesiastical constitutions, and not a few of the ordinary evidences of the land, were written in the language of the country.

This example of written laws being given by Ethelbert, it was followed by his successors, Edric and Lothaire. The next legislator amongst the English was Ina, King of the West Saxons, a prince famous in his time for his wisdom and his piety. His laws, as well as those of the abovementioned princes, still subsist. But we must always remember that very few of these laws contained any new regulation, but were rather designed to affirm their ancient customs, and to preserve and fix them; and accordingly they are all extremely rude and imperfect. We read of a collection of laws by Offa, King of the Mercians; but they have been long since lost.

The Anglo-Saxon laws, by universal consent of all writers, owe more to the care and sagacity of Alfred than of any of the ancient kings. In the midst of a cruel war, of which he did not see the beginning nor live to see the end, he did more for the establishment of order and justice than any other prince has been known to do in the profoundest peace. Many of the institutions attributed to him undoubtedly were not of his establishment: this shall be shown, when we come to treat more minutely of the institutions. But it is clear that he raised, as it were, from the ashes, and put new life and vigor into the whole body of the law, almost lost and forgotten in the ravages of the Danish war; so that, having revived, and in all likelihood improved, several ancient national regulations, he has passed for their author, with a reputation perhaps more just than if he had invented them. In the prologue which he wrote to his own code, he informs us that he collected there whatever appeared to him most valuable in the laws of Ina and Offa and others of his progenitors, omitting what he thought wrong in itself or not adapted to the time; and he seems to have done this with no small judgment.

The princes who succeeded him, having by his labors enjoyed more repose, turned their minds to the improvement of the law; and there are few of them who have not left us some collection more or less complete.

When the Danes had established their empire, they showed themselves no less solicitous than the English to collect and enforce the laws: seeming desirous to repair all the injuries they had formerly committed against them. The code of Canute the Great is one of the most moderate, equitable, and full, of any of the old collections. There was no material change, if any at all, made in their general system by the Danish conquest. They were of the original country of the Saxons, and could not have differed from them in the groundwork of their policy. It appears by the league between Alfred and Guthrum, that the Danes took their laws from the English, and accepted them as a favor. They were more newly come out of the Northern barbarism, and wanted the regulations necessary to a civil society. But under Canute the English law received considerable improvement. Many of the old English customs, which, as that monarch justly observes, were truly odious, were abrogated; and, indeed, that code is the last we have that belongs to the period before the Conquest. That monument called the Laws of Edward the Confessor is certainly of a much later date; and what is extraordinary, though the historians after the Conquest continually speak of the Laws of King Edward, it does not appear that he ever made a collection, or that any such laws existed at that time. It appears by the preface to the Laws of St. Edward, that these written constitutions were continually falling into disuse. Although these laws had undoubtedly their authority, it was, notwithstanding, by traditionary customs that the people were for the most part governed, which, as they varied somewhat in different provinces, were distinguished accordingly by the names of the West Saxon, the Mercian, and the Danish Law; but this produced no very remarkable inconvenience, as those customs seemed to differ from each other, and from the written laws, rather in the quantity and nature of their pecuniary mulcts than in anything essential.

If we take a review of these ancient constitutions, we shall observe that their sanctions are mostly confined to the following objects.

1st. The preservation of the peace. This is one of the largest titles; and it shows the ancient Saxons to have been a people extremely prone to quarrelling and violence. In some cases the law ventures only to put this disposition under regulations: prescribing that no man shall fight with another until he has first called him to justice in a legal way; and then lays down the terms under which he may proceed to hostilities. The other less premediated quarrels, in meetings for drinking or business, were considered as more or less heinous, according to the rank of the person in whose house the dispute happened, or, to speak the language of that time, whose peace they had violated.

2d. In proportioning the pecuniary mulcts imposed by them for all, even the highest crimes, according to the dignity of the person injured, and to the quantity of the offence. For this purpose they classed the people with great regularity and exactness, both in the ecclesiastic and the secular lines, adjusting with great care the ecclesiastical to the secular dignities; and they not only estimated each man's life according to his quality, but they set a value upon every limb and member, down even to teeth, hair, and nails; and these are the particulars in which their laws are most accurate and best defined.

3d. In settling the rules and ceremonies of their oaths, their purgations, and the whole order and process of their superstitious justice: for by these methods they seem to have decided all controversies.

4th. In regulating the several fraternities of Frank-pledges, by which all the people were naturally bound to their good behavior to one another and to their superiors; in all which they were excessively strict, in order to supply by the severity of this police the extreme laxity and imperfection of their laws, and the weak and precarious authority of their kings and magistrates.

These, with some regulations for payment of tithes and Church dues, and for the discovery and pursuit of stealers of cattle, comprise almost all the titles deserving notice in the Saxon laws. In those laws there are frequently to be observed particular institutions, well and prudently framed; but there is no appearance of a regular, consistent, and stable jurisprudence. However, it is pleasing to observe something of equity and distinction gradually insinuating itself into these unformed materials, and some transient flashes of light striking across the gloom which prepared for the full day that shone out afterwards. The clergy, who kept up a constant communication with Rome, and were in effect the Saxon legislators, could not avoid gathering some informations from a law which never was perfectly extinguished in that part of the world. Accordingly we find one of its principles had strayed hither so early as the time of Edric and Lothaire. There are two maxims of civil law in their proper terms in the code of Canute the Great, who made and authorized that collection after his pilgrimage to Rome; and at this time, it is remarkable, we find the institutions of other nations imitated. In the same collection there is an express reference to the laws of the Werini. From hence it is plain that the resemblance between the polity of the several Northern nations did not only arise from their common original, but also from their adopting, in some cases, the constitutions of those amongst them who were most remarkable for their wisdom.

In this state the law continued until the Norman Conquest. But we see that even before that period the English law began to be improved by taking in foreign learning; we see the canons of several councils mixed indiscriminately with the civil constitutions; and, indeed, the greatest part of the reasoning and equity to be found in them seems to be derived from that source.

Hitherto we have observed the progress of the Saxon laws, which, conformably to their manners, were rude and simple,—agreeably to their confined situation, very narrow,—and though in some degree, yet not very considerably, improved by foreign communication. However, we can plainly discern its three capital sources. First, the ancient traditionary customs of the North, which, coming upon this and the other civilized parts of Europe with the impetuosity of a conquest, bore down all the ancient establishments, and, by being suited to the genius of the people, formed, as it were, the great body and main stream of the Saxon laws. The second source was the canons of the Church. As yet, indeed, they were not reduced into system and a regular form of jurisprudence; but they were the law of the clergy, and consequently influenced considerably a people over whom that order had an almost unbounded authority. They corrected, mitigated, and enriched those rough Northern institutions; and the clergy having once bent the stubborn necks of that people to the yoke of religion, they were the more easily susceptible of other changes introduced under the same sanction. These formed the third source,—namely, some parts of the Roman civil law, and the customs of other German nations. But this source appears to have been much the smallest of the three, and was yet inconsiderable.

The Norman Conquest is the great era of our laws. At this time the English jurisprudence, which had hitherto continued a poor stream, fed from some few, and those scanty sources, was all at once, as from a mighty flood, replenished with a vast body of foreign learning, by which, indeed, it might be said rather to have been increased than much improved: for this foreign law, being imposed, not adopted, for a long time bore strong appearances of that violence by which it had been first introduced. All our monuments bear a strong evidence to this change. New courts of justice, new names and powers of officers, in a word, a new tenure of land as well as new possessors of it, took place. Even the language of public proceedings was in a great measure changed.

Book Reviews in the *Annual Register*

Between 1759 and 1761 Burke wrote book reviews for the extremely popular Annual Register. *Included here are reviews of three important eighteenth-century writers: Rousseau, Adam Smith, and Hume. Of particular interest is the generally favorable tone of his two Rousseau reviews, given his later, post–French Revolution opinions on Rousseau.*

A LETTER FROM *M. Rousseau of Geneva, to M. d'Alembert, of Paris, concerning the effects of theatrical entertainments on the manners of mankind.* None of the present writers have a greater share of talents and learning than Rousseau; yet it has been his misfortune and that of the world, that those of his works which have made the greatest noise, and acquired to their author the highest reputation, have been of little real use or emolument to mankind. A tendency to paradox, which is always the bane of solid learning, and threatens now to destroy it, a splenetic disposition carried to misanthropy, and an austere virtue pursued to an unsociable fierceness, have prevented a great deal of the good effects which might be expected from such a genius. A satire upon civilized society, a satire upon learning, may make a tolerable sport for an ingenious fancy; but if carried farther it can do no more (and that in such a way is surely too much) than to unsettle our notions of right and wrong, and lead by degrees to universal scepticism. His having before attempted two such subjects, must make his attack upon the stage far less formidable than otherwise it would have been. This last subject has been often discussed before him; more good pieces have been written against the stage than in its favour; but this is by far the most ingenious, spirited, and philosophical performance that ever appeared on theatrical entertainments. The author has placed the matter in a light almost wholly new. So far as his remarks relate to small and indigent states in general, and to that of Geneva in particular, they are as just as they are ingenious; but with regard to the stage writers and performers in nations not so circumstanced, he seems to have pushed his objections much too far. There are certainly plays which show, that the stage may at least be made as innocent as any other public entertainments; as innocent as his favourite entertainment of dancing; and there are actors of both sexes, who (though it must be admitted their situation is a little dangerous) have proved by their conduct the injustice of his assertion, which makes vice inseparable from their profession, and its infamy not created, but only declared by the laws. . . .

Emilius and Sophia: or, A new System of Education. Translated from the French of J. J. Rousseau, Citizen of Geneva. The fault most generally observed in discourses upon education, is a tendency to commonplace. Nothing, in fact, can be more trite, than the greatest part of the observations, which have been retailed upon that subject from Quintilian down to Monsieur Rollin. This is however the fault, into which the ingenious author of Emilius is, of all others, in the least danger of falling. To know what the received notions are upon any subject, is to know with certainty what those of Rousseau are not. In his treatise on the inequality amongst mankind, he has shown his man in a natural state; in his Emilius he undertakes to educate him. In the prosecution of this design he begins early, and carefully attends his pupil from his cradle to his marriage-bed. He forms him to morals, to science, to knowledge of men, and to natural labour, and at length gives him a wife, whom he has previously educated for him according to ideas a little different from that model which he has formed in his Eloise.

In this system of education there are some very considerable parts that are impracticable, others that are chimerical; and not a few highly blameable, and dangerous both to piety and morals. It is easy to discern how it has happened, that this book should be censured as well at Geneva as in Paris. However, with those faults in the design, with the whimsies into which his paradoxical genius continually hurries him, there are a thousand noble hints relative to his subject, grounded on a profound knowledge of the human mind, and the order of its operations. There are many others, which, though they have little relation to the subject, are admirable on their own account; and even, in his wildest sallies, we now and then discover strokes of the most solid sense, and instructions of the most useful nature. Indeed he very seldom thinks himself bound to adhere to any settled order or design, but is borne away by every object started by his vivid imagination, and hurries continually from system to system, in the career of an animated, glowing, exuberant style, which paints everything with great minuteness, yet with infinite spirit.

There is, it must be acknowledged, one considerable defect in his judgment, which infects both his matter and his style. He never knows where to stop. He seldom can discover that precise point in which excellence consists, where to exceed is almost as bad as to fall short, and which every step you go beyond, you grow worse and worse. He is therefore frequently tiresome and disgusting by pushing his notions to excess; and by repeating the same thing in a thousand different ways. Poverty can hardly be more vicious than such an abundance. . . .

The Theory of Moral Sentiments, by Adam Smith. It is very difficult, if not impossible, consistently with the brevity of our design, to give the reader a proper idea of this excellent work. A dry abstract of the system would convey no juster idea of it, than the skeleton of a departed beauty would of her form when she was alive; at the same time the work is so well methodized, the parts grow so naturally and gracefully out of each other, that it would be doing it equal injustice to show it by broken and detached pieces. . . .

There have been of late many books written on our moral duties, and our moral sensations. One would have thought the matter had been exhausted. But this author has struck out a new, and at the same time a perfectly natural road of speculation on this subject. Had it been only an ingenious novelty on any other subject, it might have been praised; but with regard to morals, nothing could be more dangerous. We conceive, that here the theory is in all its essential parts just, and founded on truth and nature. The author seeks for the foundation of the just, the fit, the proper, the decent, in our most common and most allowed passions; and making approbation and disapprobation the tests of virtue and vice, and showing that those are founded on sympathy, he raises from this simple truth, one of the most beautiful fabrics of moral theory, that has perhaps ever appeared. The illustrations are numerous and happy, and show the author to be a man of uncommon observation. His language is easy and spirited, and puts things before you in the fullest light; it is rather painting than writing. . . .

The History of England, from the Invasion of Julius Caesar to the Accession of Henry VII . . . By David Hume. Our writers had commonly so ill succeeded in history, the Italians and even the French had so long continued our acknowledged superiors, that it was almost feared that the British genius, which had so happily displayed itself in every other kind of writing, and had gained the prize in most, yet could not enter the lists in this. The historical work Mr. Hume first published, discharged our country from this opprobrium.

This very ingenious and elegant writer is certainly a very profound thinker. The idea of the growth, as I may call it, of our present constitution seems to be the principle of the whole work completed by the part now published, which is written in the same bold masterly manner as the two formerly published; and though in point of time it precedes them, is possibly, in reason, but a consequence of the other two; and the three parts, we imagine, may with propriety enough be read in the order the ingenious author has chosen to publish them.

It is natural that the line, which is always kept to its utmost length, must break at last; and probably in its recoil hurt them who endeavour to keep it at full stretch; and so it fared with the Stuarts, who, we imagine with this ingenious author, erred not so much in extending the prerogative, as in not having had sagacity enough to see that they had fallen in the times, when, from the opinions and fashions of the age, it behoved them to slacken and remit of the authority exercised by their predecessors.

The second work, which appeared, certainly showed that the Tudors had not left it in the power of any other family to carry the prerogative higher than they had done. They left it to their successors, adorned and supported with every sanction, which custom, and which, in many cases, legal institution, could give it.

The third part seems to evince, that this pitch, which the prerogative had attained, was not the effect of the abilities, or the violence, of this or that family, so much as the natural course of things.

If the periods of the history first published interested our passions more, the curiosity of the learned will be more gratified in that now before us. It will be curious to observe from what a strange chaos of liberty and tyranny, of anarchy and order, the constitution, we are now blessed with, has at length arisen. . . .

No man perhaps has come nearer to that so requisite and so rare a quality in an historian of unprejudiced partiality. . . .

Speech on the Repeal of the Marriage Act

In 1781 Burke spoke during an important parliamentary debate concerned with changes in the marriage laws, specifically the age when marriage could occur without parental consent. His comments provide interesting glimpses of Burke's attitudes to these two most important traditional institutions, marriage and family.

THIS ACT [*the Marriage Act*] stands upon *two* principles: one, that the power of marrying without consent of parents should not take place till twenty-one years of age; the other, that all marriages should be *public.*

The proposition of the honorable mover goes to the first; and undoubtedly his motives are fair and honorable; and even in that measure by which he would take away paternal power, he is influenced to it by filial piety; and he is led into it by a natural, and to him inevitable, but real mistake,—that the ordinary race of mankind advance as fast towards maturity of judgment and understanding as he does.

The question is not now, whether the law ought to acknowledge and protect such a state of life as minority, nor whether the continuance which is fixed for that state be not improperly prolonged in the law of England. Neither of these in general are questioned. The only question is, whether matrimony is to be taken out of the general rule, and whether the minors of both sexes, without the consent of their parents, ought to have a capacity of contracting the matrimonial, whilst they have not the capacity of contracting any other engagement. Now it appears to me very clear that they ought not. It is a great mistake to think that mere *animal* propagation is the sole end of matrimony. Matrimony is instituted not only for the propagation of men, but for their nutrition, their education, their establishment, and for the answering of all the purposes of a rational and moral being; and it is not the duty of the community to consider alone of how many, but how useful citizens it shall be composed.

It is most certain that men are well qualified for propagation long before they are sufficiently qualified even by bodily strength, much less by mental prudence, and by acquired skill in trades and professions, for the maintenance of a family. Therefore to enable and authorize any man to introduce citizens into the commonwealth, before a rational security can be given that he may provide for them and educate them as citizens ought to be provided for and educated, is totally incongruous with the whole order of society. Nay, it is fundamentally unjust; for a man that breeds a family without competent means of maintenance incumbers other men with his children, and disables them so far from maintaining their own. The improvident marriage of one man becomes a tax upon the orderly and regular marriage of all the rest. Therefore those laws are wisely constituted that give a man the use of all his faculties at one time, that they may be mutually subservient, aiding and assisting to each other: that the time of his completing his bodily strength, the time of mental discretion, the time of his having learned his trade, and the time at which he has the disposition of his fortune, should be likewise the time in which he is permitted to introduce citizens into the state, and to charge the community with their maintenance. To give a man a family during his apprenticeship, whilst his very labor belongs to another,—to give him a family, when you do not give him a fortune to maintain it,—to give him a family before he can contract any one of those engagements without which no business can be carried on, would be to burden the state with families without any security for their maintenance. When parents themselves marry their children, they become in some sort security to prevent the ill consequences. You have this security in parental consent; the state takes its security in the knowledge of human nature. Parents ordinarily consider little the passion of their children and their present gratification. Don't fear the power of a father: it is kind to passion to give it time to cool. But their censures sometimes make me smile,—sometimes, for I am very infirm, make me angry: *sæpe bilem, sæpe jocum movent.*

It gives me pain to differ on this occasion from many, if not most, of those whom I honor and esteem. To suffer the grave animadversion and censorial rebuke of the honorable gentleman who made the motion, of him whose good-nature and good sense the House look upon with a particular partiality, whose approbation would have been one of the highest objects of my ambition,—this hurts me. It is said the Marriage Act is aristocratic. I am accused, I am told abroad, of being a man of aristocratic principles. If by aristocracy they mean the peers, I have no vulgar admiration, nor any vulgar antipathy towards them; I hold their order in cold and decent respect. I hold them to be of an absolute necessity in the Constitution; but I think they are only good when kept within their proper bounds. I trust, whenever there has been a dispute between these Houses, the part I have taken has not been equivocal. If by the aristocracy (which, indeed, comes nearer to the point) they mean an adherence to the rich and powerful against the poor and weak, this would, indeed, be a very extraordinary part. I have incurred the odium of gentlemen in this House for not paying sufficient regard to men of ample property. When, indeed, the smallest rights of the poorest people in the kingdom are in question, I would set my face against any act of pride and power countenanced by the highest that are in it; and if it should come to the last extremity, and to a contest of blood,—God forbid! God forbid!—my part is taken: I would take my fate with the poor and low and feeble. But if these people came to turn their liberty into a cloak for maliciousness, and to seek a privilege of exemption, not from power, but from the rules of morality and virtuous discipline, then I would join my hand to make them feel the force which a few united in a good cause have over a multitude of the profligate and ferocious.

I wish the nature of the ground of repeal were considered with a little attention. It is said the act tends to accumulate, to keep up the power of great families, and to add wealth to wealth. It may be that it does so. It is impossible that any principle of law or government useful to the community should be established without an advantage to those who have the greatest stake in the country. Even some vices arise from it. The same laws which secure property encourage avarice; and the fences made about honest acquisition are the strong bars which secure the hoards of the miser. The dignities of magistracy are encouragements to ambition, with all the black train of villanies which attend that wicked passion. But still we must have laws to secure property, and still we must have ranks and distinctions and magistracy in the state, notwithstanding their manifest tendency to encourage avarice and ambition.

By affirming the parental authority throughout the state, parents in high rank will generally aim at, and will sometimes have the means, too, of preserving their minor children from any but wealthy or splendid matches. But this authority preserves from a thousand misfortunes which embitter every part of every man's domestic life, and tear to pieces the dearest ties in human society.

I am no peer, nor like to be,—but am in middle life, in the mass of citizens; yet I should feel for a son who married a prostituted woman, or a daughter who married a dishonorable and prostituted man, as much as any peer in the realm.

You are afraid of the avaricious principle of fathers. But observe that the avaricious principle is here mitigated very considerably. It is avarice by proxy; it is avarice not working by itself or for itself, but through the medium of parental affection, meaning to procure good to its offspring. But the contest is not between love and avarice.

While you would guard against the possible operation of this species of benevolent avarice, the avarice of the father, you let loose another species of avarice,—that of the fortune-hunter, unmitigated, unqualified. To show the motives, who has heard of a man running away with a woman not worth six-pence? Do not call this by the name of the sweet and best passion,—love. It is robbery,—not a jot better than any other.

Would you suffer the sworn enemy of his family, his life, and his honor, possibly the shame and scandal and blot of human society, to debauch from his care and protection the dearest pledge that he has on earth, the sole comfort of his declining years, almost in infantine imbecility,—and with it to carry into the hands of his enemy, and the disgrace of

Nature, the dear-earned substance of a careful and laborious life? Think of the daughter of an honest, virtuous parent allied to vice and infamy. Think of the hopeful son tied for life by the meretricious arts of the refuse of mercenary and promiscuous lewdness. Have mercy on the youth of both sexes; protect them from their ignorance and inexperience; protect one part of life by the wisdom of another; protect them by the wisdom of laws and the care of Nature.

Speeches on Religious Establishment and Toleration

During Burke's parliamentary career, Catholics and Protestant Dissenters (non-Anglicans like Unitarians, Quakers, Congregationalists, Baptists, and Presbyterians) were prohibited by the Religious Test Acts from holding an appointed governmental office in England and from attending Oxford and Cambridge. Repeated efforts were made during the last three decades of the eighteenth century to remedy these disabilities, and frequently Burke spoke in these debates. They were often difficult occasions, for he was forced to weigh his sympathy for Catholics with his growing fear of the Dissenters' political radicalism. The three speeches on church-state relations included here are from 1772, 1773, and 1792.

SPEECH ON THE ACTS OF UNIFORMITY

MR. SPEAKER,—I should not trouble the House upon this question, if I could at all acquiesce in many of the arguments, or justify the vote I shall give upon several of the reasons which have been urged in favor of it. I should, indeed, be very much concerned, if I were thought to be influenced to that vote by those arguments.

In particular, I do most exceedingly condemn all such arguments as involve any kind of reflection on the personal character of the gentlemen who have brought in a petition so decent in the style of it, and so constitutional in the mode. Besides the unimpeachable integrity and piety of many of the promoters of this petition, which render those aspersions as idle as they are unjust, such a way of treating the subject can have no other effect than to turn the attention of the House from the merits of the petition, the only thing properly before us, and which we are sufficiently competent to decide upon, to the motives of the petitioners, which belong exclusively to the Great Searcher of Hearts.

We all know that those who loll at their ease in high dignities, whether of the Church or of the State, are commonly averse to all reformation. It is hard to persuade them that there can be anything amiss in establishments which by feeling experience they find to be so very comfortable. It is as true, that, from the same selfish motives, those who are struggling upwards are apt to find everything wrong and out of order. These are truths upon one side and on the other; and neither on the one side or the other in argument are they worth a single farthing. I wish, therefore, so much had not been said upon these ill-chosen, and worse than ill-chosen, these very invidious topics.

I wish still more that the dissensions and animosities which had slept for a century had not been just now most unseasonably revived. But if we must be driven, whether we will or not, to recollect these unhappy transactions, let our memory be complete and equitable, let us recollect the whole of them together. If the Dissenters, as an honorable gentleman has described them, have formerly risen from a "whining, canting, snivelling generation," to be a body dreadful and ruinous to all our establishments, let him call to mind the follies, the violences, the outrages, and persecutions, that conjured up, very blamably, but very naturally, that same spirit of retaliation. Let him recollect, along with the injuries, the services which Dissenters have done to our Church and to our State. If they have once destroyed, more than once they have saved them. This is but common justice, which they and all mankind have a right to.

There are, Mr. Speaker, besides these prejudices and animosities, which I would have wholly removed from the debate, things more regularly and argumentatively urged against the petition, which, however, do not at all appear to me conclusive.

First, two honorable gentlemen, one near me, the other, I think, on the other side of the House, assert, that, if you alter her symbols, you destroy the being of the Church of England. This, for the sake of the liberty of that Church, I must absolutely deny. The Church, like every body corporate, may alter her laws without changing her identity. As an independent church, professing fallibility, she has claimed a right of acting without the consent of any other; as a church, she claims, and has always exercised, a right of reforming whatever appeared amiss in her doctrine, her discipline, or her rites. She did so, when she shook off the Papal supremacy in the reign of Henry the Eighth, which was an act of the body of the English Church, as well as of the State (I don't inquire how obtained). She did so, when she twice changed the Liturgy in the reign of King Edward, when she then established Articles, which were themselves a variation from former professions. She did so, when she cut off three articles from her original forty-two, and reduced them to the present thirty-nine; and she certainly would not lose her corporate identity, nor subvert her fundamental principles, though she were to leave ten of the thirty-nine which remain out of any future confession of her faith. She would limit her corporate powers, on the contrary, and she would oppose her fundamental principles, if she were to deny herself the prudential exercise of such capacity of reformation. This, therefore, can be no objection to your receiving the petition.

In the next place, Sir, I am clear, that the Act of Union, reciting and ratifying one Scotch and one English act of Parliament, has not rendered any change whatsoever in our Church impossible, but by a dissolution of the union between the two kingdoms.

The honorable gentleman who has last touched upon that point has not gone quite so far as the gentlemen who first insisted upon it. However, as none of them wholly abandon that post, it will not be safe to leave it behind me unattacked. I believe no one will wish their interpretation of that act to be considered as authentic. What shall we think of the wisdom (to say nothing of the competence) of that legislature which should ordain to itself such a fundamental law, at its outset, as to disable itself from executing its own functions,—which should prevent it from making any further laws, however wanted, and that, too, on the most interesting subject that belongs to human society, and where she most frequently wants its interposition,—which should fix those fundamental laws that are forever to prevent it from adapting itself to its opinions, however clear, or to its own necessities, however urgent? Such an act, Mr. Speaker, would forever put the Church out of its own power; it certainly would put it far above the State, and erect it into that species of independency which it has been the great principle of our policy to prevent.

The act never meant, I am sure, any such unnatural restraint on the joint legislature it was then forming. History shows us what it meant, and all that it could mean with any degree of common sense.

In the reign of Charles the First a violent and ill-considered attempt was made unjustly to establish the platform of the government and the rites of the Church of England in Scotland, contrary to the genius and desires of far the majority of that nation. This usurpation excited a most mutinous spirit in that country. It produced that shocking fanatical Covenant (I mean the Covenant of '36) for forcing their ideas of religion on England, and indeed on all mankind. This became the occasion, at length, of other covenants, and of a Scotch army marching into England to fulfil them; and the Parliament of England (for its own purposes) adopted their scheme, took their last covenant, and destroyed the Church of England. The Parliament, in their ordinance of 1643, expressly assign their desire of conforming to the Church of Scotland as a motive for their alteration.

To prevent such violent enterprises on the one side or on the other, since each Church was going to be disarmed of a legislature wholly and peculiarly affected to it, and lest this new uniformity in the State should be urged as a reason and ground of ecclesiastical uniformity, the Act of Union provided that presbytery should continue the Scoth, as episcopacy the English establishment, and that this separate and mutually independent Church-government was to be considered as a part of the Union, without aiming at putting the regulation within each Church out of its own power, without putting both Churches out of the power of the State. It could not mean to forbid us to set anything ecclesiastical in order, but at the expense of tearing up all foundations, and forfeiting the inestimable benefits (for inestimable they are) which we derive from the happy union of the two kingdoms. To suppose otherwise is to suppose that the act intended we could not meddle at all with the Church, but we must as a preliminary destroy the State.

Well, then, Sir, this is, I hope, satisfactory. The Act of Union does not stand in our way. But, Sir, gentlemen think we are not competent to the reformation desired, chiefly from our want of theological learning. If we were the legal assembly. . . .

If ever there was anything to which, from reason, nature, habit, and principle, I am totally averse, it is persecution for conscientious difference in opinion. If these gentlemen complained justly of any compulsion upon them on that article, I would hardly wait for their petitions; as soon as I knew the evil, I would haste to the cure; I would even run before their complaints.

I will not enter into the abstract merits of our Articles and Liturgy. Perhaps there are some things in them which one would wish had not been there. They are not without the marks and characters of human frailty.

But it is not human frailty and imperfection, and even a considerable degree of them, that becomes a ground for your alteration; for by no alteration will you get rid of those errors, however you may delight yourselves in varying to infinity the fashion of them. But the ground for a legislative alteration of a legal establishment is this, and this only,—that you find the inclinations of the majority of the people, concurring with your own sense of the intolerable nature of the abuse, are in favor of a change.

If this be the case in the present instance, certainly you ought to make the alteration that is proposed, to satisfy your own consciences, and to give content to your people. But if you have no evidence of this nature, it ill becomes your gravity, on the petition of a few gentlemen, to listen to anything that tends to shake one of the capital pillars of the state, and alarm the body of your people upon that one ground, in which every hope and fear, every interest, passion, prejudice, everything which can affect the human breast, are all involved together. If you make this a season for religious alterations, depend upon it, you will soon find it a season of religious tumults and religious wars.

These gentlemen complain of hardship. No considerable number shows discontent; but, in order to give satisfaction to any number of respectable men, who come in so decent and constitutional a mode before us, let us examine a little what that hardship is. They want to be preferred clergymen in the Church of England as by law established; but their consciences will not suffer them to conform to the doctrines and practices of that Church: that is, they want to be teachers in a church to which they do not belong; and it is an odd sort of hardship. They want to receive the emoluments appropriated for teaching one set of doctrines, whilst they are teaching another. A church, in any legal sense, is only a certain system of religious doctrines and practices fixed and ascertained by some law,—by the difference of which laws different churches (as different commonwealths) are made in various parts of the world; and the establishment is a tax laid by the same sovereign authority for payment of those who so teach and so practise: for no legislature was ever so absurd as to tax its people to support men for teaching and acting as they please, but by some prescribed rule.

The hardship amounts to this,—that the people of England are not taxed two shillings in the pound to pay them for teaching, as divine truths, their own particular fancies. For the state has so taxed the people; and by way of relieving these gentlemen, it would be a cruel hardship on the people to be compelled to pay, from the sweat of their brow, the most heavy of all taxes to men, to condemn as heretical the doctrines which they repute to be orthodox, and to reprobate as superstitious the practices which they use as pious and holy. If a man leaves by will an establishment for preaching, such as Boyle's Lectures, or for charity sermons, or funeral sermons, shall any one complain of an hardship, because he has an excellent sermon upon matrimony, or on the martyrdom of King Charles, or on the Restoration, which I, the trustee of the establishment, will not pay him for preaching?—S. Jenyns, Origin of Evil.—Such is the hardship which they complain of under the present Church establishment, that they have not the power of taxing the people of England for the maintenance of their private opinions.

The laws of toleration provide for every real grievance that these gentlemen can rationally complain of. Are they hindered from professing their belief of what they think to be truth? If they do not like the Establishment, there are an hundred different modes of Dissent in which they may teach. But even if they are so unfortunately circumstanced that of all that variety none will please them, they have free liberty to assemble a congregation of their own; and if any persons think their fancies (they may be brilliant imaginations) worth paying for, they are at liberty to maintain them as their clergy: nothing hinders it. But if they cannot get an hundred people together who will pay for their reading a liturgy after their form, with what face can they insist upon the nation's conforming to their ideas, for no other visible purpose than the enabling them to receive with a good conscience the tenth part of the produce of your lands?

Therefore, beforehand, the Constitution has thought proper to take a security that the tax raised on the people shall be applied only to those who profess such doctrines and follow such a mode of worship as the legislature, representing the people, has thought most agreeable to their general sense,—binding, as usual, the minority, not to an assent to the doctrines, but to a payment of the tax.

But how do you ease and relieve? How do you know, that, in making a new door into the Church for these gentlemen, you do not drive ten times their number out of it? Supposing the contents and not-contents strictly equal in numbers and consequence, the possession, to avoid disturbance, ought to carry it. You displease all the clergy of England now actually in office, for the chance of obliging a score or two, perhaps, of gentlemen, who are, or want to be, beneficed clergymen: and do you oblige? Alter your Liturgy,—will it please all even of those who wish an alteration? will they agree in what ought to be altered? And after it is altered to the mind of every one, you are no further advanced than if you had not taken a single step; because a large body of men will then say you ought to have no liturgy at all: and then these men, who now complain so bitterly that they are shut out, will themselves bar the door against thousands of others. Dissent, not satisfied with toleration, is not conscience, but ambition.

You altered the Liturgy for the Directory. This was settled by a set of most learned divines and learned laymen: Selden sat amongst them. Did this please? It was considered upon both sides as a most unchristian imposition. Well, at the Restoration they rejected the Directory, and reformed the Common Prayer,—which, by the way, had been three times reformed before. Were they then contented? Two thousand (or some great number) of clergy resigned their livings in one day rather than read it: and truly, rather than raise that second idol, I should have adhered to the Directory, as I now adhere to the Common Prayer. Nor can you content other men's conscience, real or pretended, by any concessions: follow your own; seek peace and ensue it. You have no symptoms of discontent in the people to their Establishment. The churches are too small for their congregations. The livings are too few for their candidates. The spirit of religious controversy has slackened by the nature of things: by act you may revive it. I will not enter into the question, how much truth is preferable to peace. Perhaps truth may be far better. But as we have scarcely ever the same certainty in the one that we have in the other, I would, unless the truth were evident indeed, hold fast to peace, which has in her company charity, the highest of the virtues.

This business appears in two points of view: 1st, Whether it is a matter of grievance; 2nd, Whether it is within our province to redress it with propriety and prudence. Whether it comes properly before us on a petition upon matter of grievance I would not inquire too curiously. I know, technically speaking, that nothing agreeable to law can be considered as a grievance. But an over-attention to the rules of any act does sometimes defeat the ends of it; and I think it does so in this Parliamentary act, as much at least as in any other. I know many gentlemen think that the very essence of liberty consists in being governed according to law, as if grievances had nothing real and intrinsic; but I cannot be of that opinion. Grievances may subsist by law. Nay, I do not know whether any grievance can be considered as intolerable, until it is established and sanctified by law. If the Act of Toleration were not perfect, if there were a complaint of it, I would gladly consent to amend it. But when I heard a complaint of a pressure on religious liberty, to my astonishment I find that there was no complaint whatsoever of the insufficiency of the act of King William, nor any attempt to make it more sufficient. The matter, therefore, does not concern toleration, but establishment; and it is not the rights of private conscience that are in question, but the propriety of the terms which are proposed by law as a title to public emoluments: so that the complaint is not, that there is not toleration of diversity in opinion, but that diversity in opinion is not rewarded by bishoprics, rectories, and collegiate stalls. When gentlemen complain of the subscription as matter of grievance, the complaint arises from confounding private judgment, whose rights are anterior to law, and the qualifications which the law creates for its own magistracies, whether civil or religious. To take away from men their lives, their liberty, or their property, those things for the protection of which society was introduced, is great hardship and intolerable tyranny; but to annex any condition you please to benefits artificially created is the most just, natural, and proper thing in the world. When *e novo* you form an arbitrary benefit, an advantage, preëminence, or emolument, not by Nature, but institution, you order and modify it with all the power of a creator over his creature. Such benefits of institution are royalty, nobility, priesthood, all of which you may limit to birth: you might prescribe even shape and stature. The Jewish priesthood was hereditary. Founders' kinsmen have a preference in the election of fellows in many colleges of our universities: the qualifications at All Souls are, that they should be *optime nati, bene vestiti, mediocriter docti.*

By contending for liberty in the candidate for orders, you take away the liberty of the elector, which is the people, that is, the state. If they can choose, they may assign a reason for their choice; if they can assign a reason, they may do it in writing, and prescribe it as a condition; they may transfer their authority to their representatives, and enable them to exercise the same. In all human institutions, a great part, almost all regulations, are made from the mere necessity of the case, let the theoretical merits of the question be what they will. For nothing happened at the Reformation but what will happen in all such revolutions. When tyranny is extreme, and abuses of government intolerable, men resort to the rights of Nature to shake it off. When they have done so, the very same principle of necessity of human affairs to establish some other authority, which shall preserve the order of this new institution, must be obeyed, until they grow intolerable; and you shall not be suffered to plead original liberty against such an institution. See Holland, Switzerland.

If you will have religion publicly practised and publicly taught, you must have a power to say what that religion will be which you will protect and encourage, and to distinguish it by such marks and characteristics as you in your wisdom shall think fit. As I said before, your determination may be unwise in this as in other matters; but it cannot be unjust, hard, or oppressive, or contrary to the liberty of any man, or in the least degree exceeding your province. It is, therefore, as a grievance, fairly none at all,—nothing but what is essential, not only to the order, but to the liberty, of the whole community.

The petitioners are so sensible of the force of these arguments, that they do admit of one subscription,—that is, to the Scripture. I shall not consider how forcibly this argument militates with their whole principle against subscription as an usurpation on the rights of Providence: I content myself with submitting to the consideration of the House, that, if that rule were once established, it must have some authority to enforce the obedience; because, you well know, a law without a sanction will be ridiculous. Somebody must sit in judgment on his conformity; he must judge on the charge; if he judges, he must ordain execution. These things are necessary consequences one of the other; and then this judgment is an equal and a superior violation of private judgment; the right of private judgment is violated in a much greater degree than it can be by any previous subscription. You come round again to subscription, as the best and easiest method; men must judge of his doctrine, and judge definitively: so that either his test is nugatory, or men must first or last prescribe his public interpretation of it.

If the Church be, as Mr. Locke defines it, *a voluntary society*, &c., then it is essential to this voluntary society to exclude from her voluntary society any member she thinks fit, or to oppose the entrance of any upon such conditions as she thinks proper. For, otherwise, it would be a voluntary society acting contrary to her will, which is a contradiction in terms. And this is Mr. Locke's opinion, the advocate for the largest scheme of ecclesiastical and civil toleration to Protestants (for to Papists he allows no toleration at all).

They dispute only the extent of the subscription; they therefore tacitly admit the equity of the principle itself. Here they do not resort to the original rights of Nature, because it is manifest that those rights give as large a power of controverting every part of Scripture, or even the authority of the whole, as they do to the controverting any articles whatsoever. When a man requires you to sign an assent to Scripture, he requires you to assent to a doctrine as contrary to your natural understanding, and to your rights of free inquiry, as those who require your conformity to any one article whatsoever.

The subscription to Scripture is the most astonishing idea I ever heard, and will amount to just nothing at all. Gentlemen so acute have not, that I have heard, ever thought of answering a plain, obvious question: What is that Scripture to which they are content to subscribe? They do not think that a book becomes of divine authority because it is bound in blue morocco, and is printed by John Baskett and his assigns. The Bible is a vast collection of different treatises: a man who holds the divine authority of one may consider the other as merely human. What is his Canon? The Jewish? St. Jerome's? that of the Thirty-Nine Articles? Luther's? There are some who reject the Canticles; others, six of the Epistles; the Apocalypse has been suspected even as heretical, and was doubted of for many ages, and by many great men. As these narrow the Canon, others have enlarged it by admitting St. Barnabas's Epistles, the Apostolic Constitutions, to say nothing of many other Gospels. Therefore, to ascertain Scripture, you must have one article more; and you must define what that Scripture is which you mean to teach. There are, I believe, very few who, when Scripture is so ascertained, do not see the absolute necessity of knowing what general doctrine a man draws from it, before he is sent down authorized by the state to teach it as pure doctrine, and receive a tenth of the produce of our lands.

The Scripture is no one summary of doctrines regularly digested, in which a man could not mistake his way. It is a most venerable, but most multifarious, collection of the records of the divine economy: a collection of an infinite variety,—of cosmogony, theology, history, prophecy, psalmody, morality, apologue, allegory, legislation, ethics, carried through different books, by different authors, at different ages, for different ends and purposes. It is necessary to sort out what is intended for example, what only as narrative,—what to be understood literally, what figuratively,—where one precept is to be controlled and modified by another,—what is used directly, and what only as an argument *ad hominem*,—what is temporary, and what of perpetual obligation,—what appropriated to one state and to one set of men, and what the general duty of all Christians. If we do not get some security for this, we not only permit, but we actually pay for, all the dangerous fanaticism which can be produced to corrupt our people, and to derange the public worship of the country. We owe the best we can (not infallibility, but prudence) to the subject,—first sound doctrine, then ability to use it.

SPEECH ON THE RELIEF OF PROTESTANT DISSENTERS

I assure you, Sir, that the honorable gentleman who spoke last but one need not be in the least fear that I should make a war of particles upon his opinion, whether the Church of England *should*, *would*, or *ought* to be alarmed. I am very clear that this House has no one reason in the world to think she is alarmed by the bill brought before you. It is something extraordinary that the only symptom of alarm in the Church of England should appear in the petition of some Dissenters, with whom, I believe, very few in this House are yet acquainted, and of whom you know no more than that you are assured by the honorable gentleman that they are not Mahometans. Of the Church we know they are not, by the name that they assume. They are, then, Dissenters. The first symptom of an alarm comes from some Dissenters assembled round the lines of Chatham: these lines become the security of the Church of England! The honorable gentleman, in speaking of the lines of Chatham, tells us that they serve not only for the security of the wooden walls of England, but for the defence of the Church of England. I suspect the wooden walls of England secure the lines of Chatham, rather than the lines of Chatham secure the wooden walls of England.

Sir, the Church of England, if only defended by this miserable petition upon your table, must, I am afraid, upon the principles of true fortification, be soon destroyed. But, fortunately, her walls, bulwarks, and bastions are constructed of other materials than of stubble and straw,—are built up with the strong and stable matter of the gospel of liberty, and founded on a true, constitutional, legal establishment. But, Sir, she has other securities: she has the security of her own doctrines; she has the security of the piety, the sanctity, of her own professors,—their learning is a bulwark to defend her; she has the security of the two universities, not shook in any single battlement, in any single pinnacle.

But the honorable gentleman has mentioned, indeed, principles which astonish me rather more than ever. The honorable gentleman thinks that the Dissenters enjoy a large share of liberty under a connivance; and he thinks that the establishing toleration by law is an attack upon Christianity.

The first of these is a contradiction in terms. Liberty under a connivance! Connivance is a relaxation from slavery, not a definition of liberty. What is connivance, but a state under which all slaves live? If I was to describe slavery, I would say, with those who *hate* it, it is living under will, not under law; if as it is stated by its advocates, I would say, that, like earthquakes, like thunder, or other wars the elements make upon mankind, it happens rarely, it occasionally comes now and then upon people, who, upon ordinary occasions, enjoy the same legal government of liberty. Take it under the description of those who would soften those features, the state of slavery and connivance is the same thing. If the liberty enjoyed be a liberty not of toleration, but of connivance, the only question is, whether establishing such by law is an attack upon Christianity. Toleration an attack upon Christianity! What, then! are we come to this pass, to suppose that nothing can support Christianity but the principles of persecution? Is that, then, the idea of establishment? Is it, then, the idea of Christianity itself, that it ought to have establishments, that it ought to have laws against Dissenters, but the breach of which laws is to be connived at? What a picture of toleration! what a picture of laws, of establishments! what a picture of religious and civil liberty! I am persuaded the honorable gentleman does not see it in this light. But these very terms become the strongest reasons for my support of the bill: for I am persuaded that toleration, so far from being an attack upon Christianity, becomes the best and surest support that possibly can be given to it. The Christian religion itself arose without establishment,—it arose even without toleration; and whilst its own principles were not tolerated, it conquered all the powers of darkness, it conquered all the powers of the world. The moment it began to depart from these principles, it converted the establishment into tyranny; it subverted its foundations from that very hour. Zealous as I am for the principle of an establishment, so just an abhorrence do I conceive against whatever may shake it. I know nothing but the supposed necessity of persecution that can make an establishment disgusting. I would have toleration a part of establishment, as a principle favorable to Christianity, and as a part of Christianity.

All seem agreed that the law, as it stands, inflicting penalties on all religious teachers and on school-masters who do not sign the Thirty-Nine Articles of Religion, ought not to be executed. We are all agreed that *the law is not good:* for that, I presume, is undoubtedly the idea of a law that ought not to be executed. The question, therefore, is, whether in a well-constituted commonwealth, which we desire ours to be thought, and I trust intend that it should be, whether in such a commonwealth it is wise to retain those laws which it is not proper to execute. A penal law not ordinarily put in execution seems to me to be a very absurd and a very dangerous thing. For if its principle be right, if the object of its prohibitions and penalties be a real evil, then you do in effect permit that very evil, which not only the reason of the thing, but your very law, declares ought not to be permitted; and thus it reflects exceedingly on the wisdom, and consequently derogates not a little from the authority, of a legislature who can at once forbid and suffer, and in the same breath promulgate penalty and indemnity to the same persons and for the very same actions. But if the object of the law be no moral or political evil, then you ought not to hold even a terror to those whom you ought certainly not to punish: for if it is not right to hurt, it is neither right nor wise to menace. Such laws, therefore, as they must be defective either in justice or wisdom or both, so they cannot exist without a considerable degree of danger. Take them which way you will, they are pressed with ugly alternatives.

1st. All penal laws are either upon popular prosecution, or on the part of the crown. Now if they may be roused from their sleep, whenever a minister thinks proper, as instruments of oppression, then they put vast bodies of men into a state of slavery and court dependence; since their liberty of conscience and their power of executing their functions depend entirely on his will. I would have no man derive his means of continuing any function, or his being restrained from it, but from the laws only: they should be his only superior and sovereign lords.

2nd. They put statesmen and magistrates into an habit of playing fast and loose with the laws, straining or relaxing them as may best suit their political purposes,—and in that light tend to corrupt the executive power through all its offices.

3rd. If they are taken up on popular actions, their operation in that light also is exceedingly evil. They become the instruments of private malice, private avarice, and not of public regulation; they nourish the worst of men to the prejudice of the best, punishing tender consciences, and rewarding informers.

Shall we, as the honorable gentleman tells us we may with perfect security, trust to the manners of the age? I am well pleased with the general manners of the times; but the desultory execution of penal laws, the thing I condemn, does not depend on the manners of the times. I would, however, have the laws tuned in unison with the manners. Very dissonant are a gentle country and cruel laws; very dissonant, that your reason is furious, but your passions moderate, and that you are always equitable except in your courts of justice.

I will beg leave to state to the House one argument which has been much relied upon: that the Dissenters are not unanimous upon this business; that many persons are alarmed; that it will create a disunion among the Dissenters.

When any Dissenters, or any body of people, come here with a petition, it is not the number of people, but the reasonableness of the request, that should weigh with the House. A body of Dissenters come to this House, and say, "Tolerate us: we desire neither the parochial advantage of tithes, nor dignities, nor the stalls of your cathedrals: no! let the venerable orders of the hierarchy exist with all their advantages." And shall I tell them, "I reject your just and reasonable petition, not because it shakes the Church, but because there are others, while you lie grovelling upon the earth, that will kick and bite you"? Judge which of these descriptions of men comes with a fair request: that which says, "Sir, I desire liberty for my own, because I trespass on no man's conscience,"—or the other, which says, "I desire that these men should not be suffered to act according to their consciences, though I am tolerated to act according to mine. But I sign a body of Articles, which is my title to toleration; I sign no more, because more are against my conscience. But I desire that you will not tolerate these men, because they will not go so far as I, though I desire to be tolerated, who will not go as far as you. No, imprison them, if they come within five miles of a corporate town, because they do not believe what I do in point of doctrines." Shall I not say to these men, *Arrangez-vous, canaille?* You, who are not the predominant power, will not give to others the relaxation under which you are yourself suffered to live. I have as high an opinion of the doctrines of the Church as you. I receive them implicitly, or I put my own explanation on them, or take that which seems to me to come best recommended by authority. There are those of the Dissenters who think more rigidly of the doctrine of the Articles relative to Predestination than others do. They sign the Article relative to it *ex animo*, and literally. Others allow a latitude of construction. These two parties are in the Church, as well as among the Dissenters; yet in the Church we live quietly under the same roof. I do not see why, as long as Providence gives us no further light into this great mystery, we should not leave things as the Divine Wisdom has left them. But suppose all these things to me to be clear, (which Providence, however, seems to have left obscure,) yet, whilst Dissenters claim a toleration in things which, seeming clear to me, are obscure to them, without entering into the merit of the Articles, with what face can these men say, "Tolerate us, but do not tolerate them"? Toleration is good for all, or it is good for none.

The discussion this day is not between establishment on one hand and toleration on the other, but between those who, being tolerated themselves, refuse toleration to others. That power should be puffed up with pride, that authority should degenerate into rigor, if not laudable, is but too natural. But this proceeding of theirs is much beyond the usual allowance to human weakness: it not only is shocking to our reason, but it provokes our indignation. *Quid domini facient, audent cum talia fures?* It is not the proud prelate thundering in his Commission Court, but a pack of manumitted slaves, with the lash of the beadle flagrant on their backs, and their legs still galled with their fetters, that would drive their brethren into that prison-house from whence they have just been permitted to escape. If, instead of puzzling themselves in the depths of the Divine counsels, they would turn to the mild morality of the Gospel, they would read their own condemnation:—"O thou wicked servant, I forgave thee all that debt because thou desiredst me: shouldest not thou also have compassion on thy fellow-servant, even as I had pity on thee?"

In my opinion, Sir, a magistrate, whenever he goes to put any restraint upon religious freedom, can only do it upon this ground,—that the person dissenting does not dissent from the scruples of ill-informed conscience, but from a party ground of dissension, in order to raise a faction in the state. We give, with regard to rites and ceremonies, an indulgence to tender consciences. But if dissent is at all punished in any country, if at all it can be punished upon any pretence, it is upon a presumption, not that a man is supposed to differ conscientiously from the establishment, but that he resists truth for the sake of faction,—that he abets diversity of opinions in religion to distract the state, and to destroy the peace of his country. This is the only plausible,—for there is no true ground of persecution. As the laws stand, therefore, let us see how we have thought fit to act.

If there is any one thing within the competency of a magistrate with regard to religion, it is this: that he has a right to direct the exterior ceremonies of religion; that, whilst interior religion is within the jurisdiction of God alone, the external part, bodily action, is within the province of the chief governor. Hooker, and all the great lights of the Church, have constantly argued this to be a part within the province of the civil magistrate. But look at the Act of Toleration of William and Mary: there you will see the civil magistrate has not only dispensed with those things which are more particularly within his province, with those things which faction might be supposed to take up for the sake of making visible and external divisions and raising a standard of revolt, but has also from sound politic considerations relaxed on those points which are confessedly without his province.

The honorable gentleman, speaking of the heathens, certainly could not mean to recommend anything that is derived from that impure source. But he has praised the tolerating spirit of the heathens. Well! but the honorable gentleman will recollect that heathens, that polytheists, must permit a number of divinities. It is the very essence of its constitution. But was it ever heard that polytheism tolerated a dissent from a polytheistic establishment,—the belief of one God only? Never! never! Sir, they constantly carried on persecution against that doctrine. I will not give heathens the glory of a doctrine which I consider the best part of Christianity. The honorable gentleman must recollect the Roman law, that was clearly against the introduction of any foreign rites in matters of religion. You have it at large in Livy, how they persecuted in the first introduction the rites of Bacchus; and even before Christ, to say nothing of their subsequent persecutions, they persecuted the Druids and others. Heathenism, therefore, as in other respects erroneous, was erroneous in point of persecution. I do not say every heathen who persecuted was therefore an impious man: I only say he was mistaken, as such a man is now. But, says the honorable gentleman, they did not persecute Epicureans. No: the Epicureans had no quarrel with their religious establishment, nor desired any religion for themselves. It would have been very extraordinary, if irreligious heathens had desired either a religious establishment or toleration. But, says the honorable gentleman, the Epicureans entered, as others, into the temples. They did so; they defied all subscription; they defied all sorts of conformity; there was no subscription to which they were not ready to set their hands, no ceremonies they refused to practise; they made it a principle of their irreligion outwardly to conform to any religion. These atheists eluded all that you could do: so will all freethinkers forever. Then you suffer, or the weakness of your law has suffered, those great dangerous animals to escape notice, whilst you have nets that entangle the poor fluttering silken wings of a tender conscience.

The honorable gentleman insists much upon this circumstance of objection,—namely, the division amongst the Dissenters. Why, Sir, the Dissenters, by the nature of the term, are open to have a division among themselves. They are Dissenters because they differ from the Church of England: not that they agree among themselves. There are Presbyterians, there are Independents,—some that do not agree to infant baptism, others that do not agree to the baptism of adults, or any baptism. All these are, however, tolerated under the acts of King William, and subsequent acts; and their diversity of sentiments with one another did not and could not furnish an argument against their toleration, when their difference with ourselves furnished none.

But, says the honorable gentleman, if you suffer them to go on, they will shake the fundamental principles of Christianity. Let it be considered, that this argument goes as strongly against connivance, which you allow, as against toleration, which you reject. The gentleman sets out with a principle of perfect liberty, or, as he describes it, connivance. But, for fear of dangerous opinions, you leave it in your power to vex a man who has not held any one dangerous opinion whatsoever. If one man is a professed atheist, another man the best Christian, but dissents from two of the Thirty-Nine Articles, I may let escape the atheist, because I know him to be an atheist, because I am, perhaps, so inclined myself, and because I may connive where I think proper; but the conscientious Dissenter, on account of his attachment to that general religion which perhaps I hate, I shall take care to punish, because I may punish when I think proper. Therefore, connivance being an engine of private malice or private favor, not of good government,—an engine which totally fails of suppressing atheism, but oppresses conscience,—I say that principle becomes, not serviceable, but dangerous to Christianity; that it is not toleration, but contrary to it, even contrary to peace; that the penal system to which it belongs is a dangerous principle in the economy either of religion or government.

The honorable gentleman (and in him I comprehend all those who oppose the bill) bestowed in support of their side of the question as much argument as it could bear, and much more of learning and decoration than it deserved. He thinks connivance consistent, but legal toleration inconsistent, with the interests of Christianity. Perhaps I would go as far as that honorable gentleman, if I thought toleration inconsistent with those interests. God forbid! I may be mistaken, but I take toleration to be a part of religion. I do not know which I would sacrifice: I would keep them both: it is not necessary I should sacrifice either. I do not like the idea of tolerating the doctrines of Epicurus: but nothing in the world propagates them so much as the oppression of the poor, of the honest and candid disciples of the religion we profess in common,—I mean revealed religion; nothing sooner makes them take a short cut out of the bondage of sectarian vexation into open and direct infidelity than tormenting men for every difference. My opinion is, that, in establishing the Christian religion wherever you find it, curiosity or research is its best security; and in this way a man is a great deal better justified in saying, Tolerate all kinds of consciences, than in imitating the heathens, whom the honorable gentleman quotes, in tolerating those who have none. I am not over-fond of calling for the secular arm upon these misguided or misguiding men; but if ever it ought to be raised, it ought surely to be raised against these very men, not against others, whose liberty of religion you make a pretext for proceedings which drive them into the bondage of impiety. What figure do I make in saying, I do not attack the works of these atheistical writers, but I will keep a rod hanging over the conscientious man, their bitterest enemy, because these atheists may take advantage of the liberty of their foes to introduce irreligion? The best book that ever, perhaps, has been written against these people is that in which the author has collected in a body the whole of the infidel code, and has brought the writers into one body to cut them all off together. This was done by a Dissenter, who never did subscribe the Thirty-Nine Articles,—Dr. Leland. But if, after all this, danger is to be apprehended, if you are really fearful that Christianity will indirectly suffer by this liberty, you have my free consent: go directly, and by the straight way, and not by a circuit in which in your road you may destroy your friends; point your arms against these men who do the mischief you fear promoting; point your arms against men who, not contented with endeavoring to turn your eyes from the blaze and effulgence of light by which life and immortality is so gloriously demonstrated by the Gospel, would even extinguish that faint glimmering of Nature, that only comfort supplied to ignorant man before this great illumination,—them who, by attacking even the possibility of all revelation, arraign all the dispensations of Providence to man. These are the wicked Dissenters you ought to fear; these are the people against whom you ought to aim the shaft of the law; these are the men to whom, arrayed in all the terrors of government, I would say, You shall not degrade us into brutes! These men, these factious men, as the honorable gentleman properly called them, are the just objects of vengeance, not the conscientious Dissenter,—these men, who would take away whatever ennobles the rank or consoles the misfortunes of human nature, by breaking off that connection of observances, of affections, of hopes and fears, which bind us to the Divinity, and constitute the glorious and distinguishing prerogative of humanity, that of being a religious creature: against these I would have the laws rise in all their majesty of terrors, to fulminate such vain and impious wretches, and to awe them into impotence by the only dread they can fear or believe, to learn that eternal lesson, *Discite justitiam moniti, et non temnere Divos!*

At the same time that I would cut up the very root of atheism, I would respect all conscience,—all conscience that is really such, and which perhaps its very tenderness proves to be sincere. I wish to see the Established Church of England great and powerful; I wish to see her foundations laid low and deep, that she may crush the giant powers of rebellious darkness; I would have her open wide her hospitable gates by a noble and liberal comprehension, but I would have no breaches in her wall; I would have her cherish all those who are within, and pity all those who are without; I would have her a common blessing to the world, an example, if not an instructor, to those who have not the happiness to belong to her; I would have her give a lesson of peace to mankind, that a vexed and wandering generation might be taught to seek for repose and toleration in the maternal bosom of Christian charity, and not in the harlot lap of infidelity and indifference. Nothing has driven people more into that house of seduction than the mutual hatred of Christian congregations. Long may we enjoy our church under a learned and edifying episcopacy! But episcopacy may fail, and religion exist. The most horrid and cruel blow that can be offered to civil society is through atheism. Do not promote diversity; when you have it, bear it; have as many sorts of religion as you find in your country; there is a reasonable worship in them all. The others, the infidels, are outlaws of the constitution, not of this country, but of the human race. They are never, never to be supported, never to be tolerated. Under the systematic attacks of these people, I see some of the props of good government already begin to fail; I see propagated principles which will not leave to religion even a toleration. I see myself sinking every day under the attacks of these wretched people. How shall I arm myself against them? By uniting all those in affection, who are united in the belief of the great principles of the Godhead that made and sustains the world. They who hold revelation give double assurance to their country. Even the man who does not hold revelation, yet who wishes that it were proved to him, who observes a pious silence with regard to it, such a man, though not a Christian, is governed by religious principles. Let him be tolerated in this country. Let it be but a serious religion, natural or revealed, take what you can get. Cherish, blow up the slightest spark: one day it may be a pure and holy flame. By this proceeding you form an alliance offensive and defensive against those great ministers of darkness in the world who are endeavoring to shake all the works of God established in order and beauty. . . .

SPEECH ON THE PETITION OF THE UNITARIAN SOCIETY

I never govern myself, no rational man ever did govern himself, by abstractions and universals. I do not put abstract ideas wholly out of any question; because I well know that under that name I should dismiss principles, and that without the guide and light of sound, well-understood principles, all reasonings in politics, as in everything else, would be only a confused jumble of particular facts and details, without the means of drawing out any sort of theoretical or practical conclusion. A statesman differs from a professor in an university: the latter has only the general view of society; the former, the statesman, has a number of circumstances to combine with those general ideas, and to take into his consideration. Circumstances are infinite, are infinitely combined, are variable and transient: he who does not take them into consideration is not erroneous, but stark mad; *dat operam ut cum ratione insaniat;* he is metaphysically mad. A statesman, never losing sight of principles, is to be guided by circumstances; and judging contrary to the exigencies of the moment, he may ruin his country forever.

I go on this ground,—that government, representing the society, has a general superintending control over all the actions and over all the publicly propagated doctrines of men, without which it never could provide adequately for all the wants of society: but then it is to use this power with an equitable discretion, the only bond of sovereign authority. For it is not, perhaps, so much by the assumption of unlawful powers as by the unwise or unwarrantable use of those which are most legal, that governments oppose their true end and object: for there is such a thing as tyranny, as well as usurpation. You can hardly state to me a case to which legislature is the most confessedly competent, in which, if the rules of benignity and prudence are not observed, the most mischievous and oppressive things may not be done. So that, after all, it is a moral and virtuous discretion, and not any abstract theory of right, which keeps governments faithful to their ends. Crude, unconnected truths are in the world of practice what falsehoods are in theory. A reasonable, prudent, provident, and moderate coercion may be a means of preventing acts of extreme ferocity and rigor: for by propagating excessive and extravagant doctrines, such extravagant disorders take place as require the most perilous and fierce corrections to oppose them.

It is not morally true that we are bound to establish in every country that form of religion which in *our* minds is most agreeable to truth, and conduces most to the eternal happiness of mankind. In the same manner, it is not true that we are, against the conviction of our own judgment, to establish a system of opinions and practices directly contrary to those ends, only because some majority of the people, told by the head, may prefer it. No conscientious man would willingly establish what he knew to be false and mischievous in religion, or in anything else. No wise man, on the contrary, would tyrannically set up his own sense so as to reprobate that of the great prevailing body of the community, and pay no regard to the established opinions and prejudices of mankind, or refuse to them the means of securing a religious instruction suitable to these prejudices. A great deal depends on the state in which you find men. . . .

An alliance between Church and State in a Christian commonwealth is, in my opinion, an idle and a fanciful speculation. An alliance is between two things that are in their nature distinct and independent, such as between two sovereign states. But in a Christian commonwealth the Church and the State are one and the same thing, being different integral parts of the same whole. For the Church has been always divided into two parts, the clergy and the laity,—of which the laity is as much an essential integral part, and has as much its duties and privileges, as the clerical member, and in the rule, order, and government of the Church has its share. Religion is so far, in my opinion, from being out of the province or the duty of a Christian magistrate, that it is, and it ought to be, not only his care, but the principal thing in his care; because it is one of the great bonds of human society, and its object the supreme good, the ultimate end and object of man himself. The magistrate, who is a man, and charged with the concerns of men, and to whom very specially nothing human is remote and indifferent, has a right and a duty to watch over it with an unceasing vigilance, to protect, to promote, to forward it by every rational, just, and prudent means. It is principally his duty to prevent the abuses which grow out of every strong and efficient principle that actuates the human mind. As religion is one of the bonds of society, he ought not to suffer it to be made the pretext of destroying its peace, order, liberty, and its security. Above all, he ought strictly to look to it, when men begin to form new combinations, to be distinguished by new names, and especially when they mingle a political system with their religious opinions, true or false, plausible or implausible.

It is the interest, and it is the duty, and because it is the interest and the duty, it is the right of government to attend much to opinions; because, as opinions soon combine with passions, even when they do not produce them, they have much influence on actions. Factions are formed upon opinions, which factions become in effect bodies corporate in the state; nay, factions generate opinions, in order to become a centre of union, and to furnish watchwords to parties; and this may make it expedient for government to forbid things in themselves innocent and neutral. I am not fond of defining with precision what the ultimate rights of the sovereign supreme power, in providing for the safety of the commonwealth, may be, or may not extend to. It will signify very little what my notions or what their own notions on the subject may be; because, according to the exigence, they will take, in fact, the steps which seem to them necessary for the preservation of the whole: for as self-preservation in individuals is the first law of Nature, the same will prevail in societies, who will, right or wrong, make that an object paramount to all other rights whatsoever. There are ways and means by which a good man would not even save the commonwealth. . . . All things founded on the idea of danger ought in a great degree to be temporary. All policy is very suspicious that sacrifices any part to the ideal good of the whole. The object of the state is (as far as may be) the happiness of the whole. Whatever makes multitudes of men utterly miserable can never answer that object; indeed, it contradicts it wholly and entirely; and the happiness or misery of mankind, estimated by their feelings and sentiments, and not by any theories of their rights, is, and ought to be, the standard for the conduct of legislators towards the people. This naturally and necessarily conducts us to the peculiar and characteristic situation of a people, and to a knowledge of their opinions, prejudices, habits, and all the circumstances that diversify and color life. The first question a good statesman would ask himself, therefore, would be, How and in what circumstances do you find the society? and to act upon them.

To the other laws relating to other sects I have nothing to say: I only look to the petition which has given rise to this proceeding. I confine myself to that, because in my opinion its merits have little or no relation to that of the other laws which the right honorable gentleman has with so much ability blended with it. With the Catholics, with the Presbyterians, with the Anabaptists, with the Independents, with the Quakers, I have nothing at all to do. They are in *possession*,—a great title in all human affairs. The tenor and spirit of our laws, whether they were restraining or whether they were relaxing, have hitherto taken another course. The spirit of our laws has applied their penalty or their relief to the supposed abuse to be repressed or the grievance to be relieved; and the provision for a Catholic and a Quaker has been totally different, according to his exigence: you did not give a Catholic liberty to be freed from an oath, or a Quaker power of saying mass with impunity. You have done this, because you never have laid it down as an universal proposition, as a maxim, that nothing relative to religion was your concern, but the direct contrary; and therefore you have always examined whether there was a grievance. It has been so at all times: the legislature, whether right or wrong, went no other way to work but by circumstances, times, and necessities. My mind marches the same road; my school is the practice and usage of Parliament.

Old religious factions are volcanoes burnt out; on the lava and ashes and squalid scoriæ of old eruptions grow the peaceful olive, the cheering vine, and the sustaining corn. Such was the first, such the second condition of Vesuvius. But when a new fire bursts out, a face of desolations comes on, not to be rectified in ages. Therefore, when men come before us, and rise up like an exhalation from the ground, they come in a questionable shape, and we must *exorcise* them, and try whether their intents be wicked or charitable, whether they bring airs from heaven or blasts from hell. This is the first time that our records of Parliament have heard, or our experience or history given us an account of any religious congregation or association known by the name which these petitioners have assumed. We are now to see by what people, of what character, and under what temporary circumstances, this business is brought before you. We are to see whether there be any and what mixture of political dogmas and political practices with their religious tenets, of what nature they are, and how far they are at present practically separable from them. This faction (the authors of the petition) are not confined to a *theological* sect, but are also a *political* faction. 1st, As theological, we are to show that they do not aim at the quiet enjoyment of their own liberty, but are *associated* for the express purpose of proselytism. In proof of this first proposition, read their primary association. 2nd, That their purpose of proselytism is to collect a multitude sufficient by force and violence to overturn the Church. In proof of the second proposition, see the letter of Priestley to Mr. Pitt, and extracts from his works. 3rd, That the designs against the Church are concurrent with a design to subvert the State. In proof of the third proposition, read the advertisement of the Unitarian Society for celebrating the 14th of July. 4th, On what *model* they intend to build,—that it is the *French.* In proof of the fourth proposition, read the correspondence of the Revolution Society with the clubs of France, read Priestley's adherence to their opinions. 5th, What the *French* is with regard to religious toleration, and with regard to, 1. Religion,—2. Civil happiness,—3. Virtue, order, and real liberty,—4. Commercial opulence,—5. National defence. In proof of the fifth proposition, read the representation of the French minister of the Home Department, and the report of the committee upon it.

Formerly, when the superiority of two parties contending for dogmas and an establishment was the question, we knew in such a contest the whole of the evil. We knew, for instance, that Calvinism would prevail according to the Westminster Catechism with regard to *tenets.* We knew that Presbytery would prevail in *church government.* But we do not know what opinions would prevail, if the present Dissenters should become masters. They will not tell us their present opinions; and one principle of modern Dissent is, not to discover them. Next, as their religion is in a continual fluctuation, and is so by principle and in profession, it is impossible for us to know what it will be. If religion only related to the individual, and was a question between God and the conscience, it would not be wise, nor in my opinion equitable, for human authority to step in. But when religion is embodied into faction, and factions have objects to pursue, it will and must, more or less, become a question of power between them. If even, when embodied into congregations, they limited their principle to their own congregations, and were satisfied themselves to abstain from what they thought unlawful, it would be cruel, in my opinion, to molest them in that tenet, and a consequent practice. But we know that they not only entertain these opinions, but entertain them with a zeal for propagating them by force, and employing the power of law and place to destroy establishments, if ever they should come to power sufficient to effect their purpose: that is, in other words, they declare they would persecute the heads of our Church; and the question is, whether you should keep them within the bounds of toleration, or subject yourself to their persecution.

A bad and very censurable practice it is to warp doubtful and ambiguous expressions to a perverted sense, which makes the charge not the crime of others, but the construction of your own malice; nor is it allowed to draw conclusions from allowed premises, which those who lay down the premises utterly deny, and disown as their conclusions. For this, though it may possibly be good logic, cannot by any possibility whatsoever be a fair or charitable representation of any man or any set of men. It may show the erroneous nature of principles, but it argues nothing as to dispositions and intentions. Far be such a mode from me! A mean and unworthy jealousy it would be to do anything upon the mere speculative apprehension of what men will do. But let us pass by *our* opinions concerning the danger of the Church. What do the gentlemen themselves think of that danger? They from whom the danger is apprehended, what do they declare to be their own designs? What do they conceive to be their own forces? And what do they proclaim to be their means? Their designs they declare to be to destroy the Established Church, and not to set up a new one of their own. See Priestley. If they should find the State stick to the Church, the question is, whether they love the constitution in *State* so well as that they would not destroy the constitution of the State in order to destroy that of the Church. Most certainly they do not.

The foundations on which obedience to governments is founded are not to be constantly discussed. That we are here supposes the discussion already made and the dispute settled. We must assume the rights of what represents the public to control the individual, to make his will and his acts to submit to their will, until some intolerable grievance shall make us know that it does not answer its end, and will submit neither to reformation nor restraint. Otherwise we should dispute all the points of morality, before we can punish a murderer, robber, and adulterer; we should analyze all society. Dangers by being despised grow great; so they do by absurd provision against them. *Stulti est dixisse, Non putâram.* Whether an early discovery of evil designs, an early declaration, and an early precaution against them be more wise than to stifle all inquiry about them, for fear they should declare themselves more early than otherwise they would, and therefore precipitate the evil,—all this depends on the reality of the danger. Is it only an unbookish jealousy, as Shakespeare calls it? It is a question of fact. Does a design against the Constitution of this country exist? If it does, and if it is carried on with increasing vigor and activity by a restless faction, and if it receives countenance by the most ardent and enthusiastic applauses of its object in the great council of this kingdom, by men of the first parts which this kingdom produces, perhaps by the first it has ever produced, can I think that there is no danger? If there be danger, must there be no precaution at all against it? If you ask whether I think the danger urgent and immediate, I answer, Thank God, I do not. The body of the people is yet sound, the Constitution is in their hearts, while wicked men are endeavoring to put another into their heads. But if I see the very same beginnings which have commonly ended in great calamities, I ought to act as if they might produce the very same effects. Early and provident fear is the mother of safety; because in that state of things the mind is firm and collected, and the judgment unembarrassed. But when the fear and the evil feared come on together, and press at once upon us, deliberation itself is ruinous, which saves upon all other occasions; because, when perils are instant, it delays decision: the man is in a flutter, and in a hurry, and his judgment is gone,—as the judgment of the deposed King of France and his ministers was gone, if the latter did not premeditately betray him. He was just come from his usual amusement of hunting, when the head of the column of treason and assassination was arrived at his house. Let not the king, let not the Prince of Wales, be surprised in this manner. Let not both Houses of Parliament be led in triumph along with him, and have law dictated to them by the Constitutional, the Revolution, and the Unitarian Societies. These insect reptiles, whilst they go on only caballing and toasting, only fill us with disgust; if they get above their natural size, and increase the quantity whilst they keep the quality of their venom, they become objects of the greatest terror. A spider in his natural size is only a spider, ugly and loathsome; and his flimsy net is only fit for catching flies. But, good God! suppose a spider as large as an ox, and that he spread cables about us, all the wilds of Africa would not produce anything so dreadful:—

> *Quale portentum neque militaris*
> *Daunia in latis alit esculetis,*
> *Nec Jubæ tellus generat, leonum*
> *Arida nutrix.*

Think of them who dare menace in the way they do in their present state, what would they do, if they had power commensurate to their malice? God forbid I ever should have a despotic master!—but if I must, my choice is made. I will have Louis the Sixteenth rather than Monsieur Bailly, or Brissot, or Chabot,—rather George the Third, or George the Fourth, than Dr. Priestley, or Dr. Kippis,—persons who would not load a tyrannous power by the poisoned taunts of a vulgar, low-bred insolence. I hope we have still spirit enough to keep us from the one or the other. The contumelies of tyranny are the worst parts of it.

But if the danger be existing in reality, and silently maturing itself to our destruction, what! is it not better to take *treason* unprepared than that *treason* should come by surprise upon us and take us unprepared? If we must have a conflict, let us have it with all our forces fresh about us, with our government in full function and full strength, our troops uncorrupted, our revenues in the legal hands, our arsenals filled and possessed by government,—and not wait till the conspirators met to commemorate the 14th of July shall seize on the Tower of London and the magazines it contains, murder the governor, and the mayor of London, seize upon the king's person, drive out the House of Lords, occupy your gallery, and thence, as from an high tribunal, dictate to you. The degree of danger is not only from the circumstances which threaten, but from the value of the objects which are threatened. A small danger menacing an inestimable object is of more importance than the greatest perils which regard one that is indifferent to us. The whole question of the danger depends upon facts. The first fact is, whether those who sway in France at present confine themselves to the regulation of their internal affairs,—or whether upon system they nourish cabals in all other countries, to extend their power by producing revolutions similar to their own. 2. The next is, whether we have any cabals formed or forming within these kingdoms, to coöperate with them for the destruction of our Constitution. On the solution of these two questions, joined with our opinion of the value of the object to be affected by their machinations, the justness of our alarm and the necessity of our vigilance must depend. Every private conspiracy, every open attack upon the laws, is dangerous. One robbery is an alarm to all property; else I am sure we exceed measure in our punishment. As robberies increase in number and audacity, the alarm increases. These wretches are at war with us upon principle. They hold this government to be an usurpation. See the language of the Department.

The whole question is on the *reality* of the danger. Is it such a danger as would justify that fear *qui cadere potest in hominem constantem et non metuentem*? This is the fear which the principles of jurisprudence declare to be a lawful and justifiable fear. When a man threatens my life openly and publicly, I may demand from him securities of the peace. When every act of a man's life manifests such a design stronger than by words, even though he does not make such a declaration, I am justified in being on my guard. They are of opinion that they are already one fifth of the kingdom. If so, their force is naturally not contemptible. To say that in all contests the decision will of course be in favor of the greater number is by no means true in fact. For, first, the greater number is generally composed of men of sluggish tempers, slow to act, and unwilling to attempt, and, by being in possession, are so disposed to peace that they are unwilling to take early and vigorous measures for their defence, and they are almost always caught unprepared:—

> *Nec coïere pares: alter vergentibus annis*
> *In senium, longoque togæ tranquillior usu.*
> *Dedidicit jam pace ducem; . . .*
> *Nec reparare novas vires, multumque priori*
> *Credere fortunæ: stat magni nominis umbra.*

A smaller number, more expedite, awakened, active, vigorous, and courageous, who make amends for what they want in weight by their superabundance of velocity, will create an acting power of the greatest possible strength. When men are furiously and fanatically fond of an object, they will prefer it, as is well known, to their own peace, to their own property, and to their own lives: and can there be a doubt, in such a case, that they would prefer it to the peace of their country? Is it to be doubted, that, if they have not strength enough at home, they will call in foreign force to aid them?

Would you deny them *what is reasonable*, for fear they should? Certainly not. It would be barbarous to pretend to look into the minds of men. I would go further: it would not be just even to trace consequences from principles which, though evident to me, were denied by them. Let them disband as a faction, and let them act as individuals, and when I see them with no other views than to enjoy their own conscience in peace, I, for one, shall most cheerfully vote for their relief.

A tender conscience, of all things, ought to be tenderly handled; for if you do not, you injure not only the conscience, but the whole moral frame and constitution is injured, recurring at times to remorse, and seeking refuge only in making the conscience callous. But the conscience of faction,—the conscience of sedition,—the conscience of conspiracy, war, and confusion. . . .

Whether anything be proper to be denied, which is right in itself, because it may lead to the demand of others which it is improper to grant? Abstractedly speaking, there can be no doubt that this question ought to be decided in the negative. But as no moral questions are ever abstract questions, this, before I judge upon any abstract proposition, must be embodied in circumstances; for, since things are right or wrong, morally speaking, only by their relation and connection with other things, this very question of what it is politically right to grant depends upon this relation to its effects. It is the direct office of wisdom to look to the consequences of the acts we do: if it be not this, it is worth nothing, it is out of place and of function, and a downright fool is as capable of government as Charles Fox. A man desires a sword: why should he be refused? A sword is a means of defence, and defence is the natural right of man,—nay, the first of all his rights, and which comprehends them all. But if I know that the sword desired is to be employed to cut my own throat, common sense, and my own self-defence, dictate to me to keep out of his hands this natural right of the sword. But whether this denial be wise or foolish, just or unjust, prudent or cowardly, depends entirely on the state of the man's means. A man may have very ill dispositions, and yet be so very weak as to make all precaution foolish. See whether this be the case of these Dissenters, as to their designs, as to their means, numbers, activity, zeal, foreign assistance.

The first question to be decided, when we talk of the Church's being in danger from any particular measure, is, whether the danger to the

Church is a public evil: for to those who think that the national Church Establishment is itself a national grievance, to desire them to forward or to resist any measure, upon account of its conducing to the safety of the Church or averting its danger, would be to the last degree absurd. If you have reason to think thus of it, take the reformation instantly into your own hands, whilst you are yet cool, and can do it in measure and proportion, and not under the influence of election tests and popular fury. But here I assume that by far the greater number of those who compose the House are of opinion that this national Church Establishment is a great national benefit, a great public blessing, and that its existence or its non-existence of course is a thing by no means indifferent to the public welfare: then to them its danger or its safety must enter deeply into every question which has a relation to it. It is not because ungrounded alarms have been given that there never can exist a real danger: perhaps the worst effect of an ungrounded alarm is to make people insensible to the approach of a real peril. Quakerism is strict, methodical, in its nature highly aristocratical, and so regular that it has brought the whole community to the condition of one family; but it does not actually interfere with the government. The principle of your petitioners is no passive conscientious dissent, on account of an over-scrupulous habit of mind: the dissent on their part is fundamental, goes to the very root; and it is at issue not upon this rite or that ceremony, on this or that school opinion, but upon this one question of an Establishment, as unchristian, unlawful, contrary to the Gospel and to natural right, Popish and idolatrous. These are the principles violently and fanatically held and pursued,—taught to their children, who are sworn at the altar like Hannibal. The war is with the Establishment itself,—no quarter, no compromise. As a party, they are infinitely mischievous: see the declarations of Priestley and Price,—declarations, you will say, of *hot* men. Likely enough: but who are the *cool* men who have disclaimed them? Not one,—no, not one. Which of them has ever told you that they do not mean to *destroy the Church*, if ever it should be in their power? Which of them has told you that this would not be the first and favorite use of any power they should get? Not one,—no, not one. Declarations of hot men! The danger is thence, that they are under the *conduct* of hot men: *falsos in amore odia non fingere.*

They say they are well affected to the State, and mean only to destroy the Church. If this be the utmost of their meaning, you must first consider whether you wish your Church Establishment to be destroyed. If you do, you had much better do it now in temper, in a grave, moderate, and parliamentary way. But if you think otherwise, and that you think it to be an invaluable blessing, a way fully sufficient to nourish a manly, rational, solid, and at the same time humble piety,—if you find it well fitted to the frame and pattern of your civil constitution,—if you find it a barrier against fanaticism, infidelity, and atheism,—if you find that it furnishes support to the human mind in the afflictions and distresses of the world, consolation in sickness, pain, poverty, and death,—if it dignifies our nature with the hope of immortality, leaves inquiry free, whilst it preserves an authority to teach, where authority only can teach, *communia altaria, æque ac patriam, diligite, colite, fovete.*

PART II

POLITICS AND SOCIETY

Thoughts on the Present Discontents

It was in the service of the great Whig magnate Lord Rockingham that Burke entered Parliament in 1765. In this pamphlet, written in 1770, Burke makes the case for the Rockingham Whigs against the Whig factions led by Bedford, Temple, and William Pitt, the Elder, just as much as he attacks George III and his ministers. It is here we find Burke making his famous case for party government, government by men "bound together by common opinions . . . united for promoting by their joint endeavors the national interest."

IN SPEAKING OF THIS BODY, I have my eye chiefly on the House of Commons. I hope I shall be indulged in a few observations on the nature and character of that assembly; not with regard to its *legal form and power*, but to its *spirit*, and to the purposes it is meant to answer in the constitution.

The House of Commons was supposed originally to be *no part of the standing government of this country*. It was considered as a *control*, issuing *immediately* from the people, and speedily to be resolved into the mass from whence it arose. In this respect it was in the higher part of government what juries are in the lower. The capacity of magistrate being transitory, and that of a citizen permanent, the latter capacity it was hoped would of course preponderate in all discussions, not only between the people and the standing authority of the crown, but between the people and the fleeting authority of the House of Commons itself. It was hoped that, being of a middle nature between subject and government, they would feel with a more tender and a nearer interest everything that concerned the people, than the other remoter and more permanent parts of legislature.

Whatever the alterations time and the necessary accommodation of business may have introduced, this character can never be sustained, unless the House of Commons shall be made to bear some stamp of the actual disposition of the people at large. It would (among public misfortunes) be an evil more natural and tolerable, that the House of Commons should be infected with every epidemical frenzy of the people, as this would indicate some consanguinity, some sympathy of nature with their constituents, than that they should in all cases be wholly untouched by the opinions and feelings of the people out of doors. By this want of sympathy they would cease to be a House of Commons. For it is not the derivation of the power of that House from the people, which makes it in a distinct sense their representative. The king is the representative of the people; so are the lords; so are the judges. They all are trustees for the people, as well as the commons; because no power is given for the sole sake of the holder; and although government certainly is an institution of divine authority, yet its forms, and the persons who administer it, all originate from the people.

A popular origin cannot therefore be the characteristical distinction of a popular representative. This belongs equally to all parts of government and in all forms. The virtue, spirit, and essence of a House of Commons consists in its being the express image of the feelings of the nation. It was not instituted to be a control *upon* the people, as of late it has been taught, by a doctrine of the most pernicious tendency. It was designed as a control *for* the people. Other institutions have been formed for the purpose of checking popular excesses; and they are, I apprehend, fully adequate to their object. If not, they ought to be made so. The House of Commons, as it was never intended for the support of peace and subordination, is miserably appointed for that service; having no stronger weapon than its mace, and no better officer than its serjeant-at-arms, which it can command of its own proper authority. A vigilant and jealous eye over executory and judicial magistracy; an anxious care of public money; an openness, approaching towards facility, to public complaint: these seem to be the true characteristics of a House of Commons. But an addressing House of Commons, and a petitioning nation; a House of Commons full of confidence, when the nation is plunged in despair; in the utmost harmony with ministers, whom the people regard with the utmost abhorrence; who vote thanks, when the public opinion calls upon them for impeachments; who are eager to grant, when the general voice demands account; who, in all disputes between the people and administration, presume against the people; who punish their disorders, but refuse even to inquire into the provocations to them; this is an unnatural, a monstrous state of things in this constitution. Such an assembly may be a great, wise, awful senate; but it is not, to any popular purpose, a House of Commons. This change from an immediate state of procuration and delegation to a course of acting as from original power, is the way in which all the popular magistracies in the world have been perverted from their purposes. It is indeed their greatest and sometimes their incurable corruption. For there is a material distinction between that corruption by which particular points are carried against reason, (this is a thing which cannot be prevented by human wisdom, and is of less consequence,) and the corruption of the principle itself. For then the evil is not accidental, but settled. The distemper becomes the natural habit.

For my part, I shall be compelled to conclude the principle of Parliament to be totally corrupted, and therefore its ends entirely defeated, when I see two symptoms: first, a rule of indiscriminate support to all ministers; because this destroys the very end of Parliament as a control, and is a general, previous sanction to misgovernment: and secondly, the setting up any claims adverse to the right of free election; for this tends to subvert the legal authority by which the House of Commons sits.

I know that, since the Revolution, along with many dangerous, many useful powers of government have been weakened. It is absolutely necessary to have frequent recourse to the legislature. Parliaments must therefore sit every year, and for great part of the year. The dreadful disorders of frequent elections have also necessitated a septennial instead of a triennial duration. . . . The constant habit of authority, and the unfrequency of elections, have tended very much to draw the House of Commons towards the character of a standing senate. It is a disorder which has arisen from the cure of greater disorders; it has arisen from the extreme difficulty of reconciling liberty under a monarchical government, with external strength and with internal tranquility.

It is very clear that we cannot free ourselves entirely from this great inconvenience; but I would not increase an evil, because I was not able to remove it; and because it was not in my power to keep the House of Commons religiously true to its first principles, I would not argue for carrying it to a total oblivion of them. This has been the great scheme of power in our time. They, who will not conform their conduct to the public good, and cannot support it by the prerogative of the crown, have adopted a new plan. They have totally abandoned the shattered and old-fashioned fortress of prerogative, and made a lodgment in the stronghold of Parliament itself. If they have any evil design to which there is no ordinary legal power commensurate, they bring it into Parliament. In Parliament the whole is executed from the beginning to the end. In Parliament the power of obtaining their object is absolute; and the safety in the proceeding perfect: no rules to confine, no after-reckonings to terrify. Parliament cannot, with any great propriety, punish others for things in which they themselves have been accomplices. Thus the control of Parliament upon the executory power is lost; because Parliament is made to partake in every considerable act of government. *Impeachment, that great guardian of the purity of the constitution, is in danger of being lost, even to the idea of it.*

By this plan several important ends are answered to the cabal. If the authority of Parliament supports itself, the credit of every act of government, which they contrive, is saved; but if the act be so very odious that the whole strength of Parliament is insufficient to recommend it, then Parliament is itself discredited; and this discredit increases more and more that indifference to the constitution, which it is the constant aim of its enemies, by their abuse of Parliamentary powers, to render general among the people. Whenever Parliament is persuaded to assume the offices of executive government, it will lose all the confidence, love, and veneration, which it has ever enjoyed whilst it was supposed the *corrective and control* of the acting powers of the state. This would be the event, though its conduct in such a perversion of its functions should be tolerably just and moderate; but if it should be iniquitous, violent, full of passion, and full of faction, it would be considered as the most intolerable of all the modes of tyranny.

For a considerable time this separation of the representatives from their constituents went on with a silent progress; and had those, who conducted the plan for their total separation, been persons of temper and abilities any way equal to the magnitude of their design, the success would have been infallible: but by their precipitancy they have laid it open in all its nakedness; the nation is alarmed at it: and the event may not be pleasant to the contrivers of the scheme. In the last session, the corps called the *kings's friends* made a hardy attempt, all at once, *to alter the right of election itself*; to put it into the power of the House of Commons to disable any person disagreeable to them from sitting in Parliament, without any other rule than their own pleasure; to make incapacities, either general for descriptions of men, or particular for individuals; and to take into their body, persons who avowedly had never been chosen by the majority of legal electors, nor agreeably to any known rule of law. . . .

A violent rage for the punishment of Mr. Wilkes was the pretence of the whole. This gentleman, by setting himself strongly in opposition to the court cabal, had become at once an object of their persecution, and of the popular favor. The hatred of the court party pursuing, and the countenance of the people protecting him, it very soon became not at all a question on the man, but a trial of strength between the two parties. The advantage of the victory in this particular contest was the present, but not the only, nor by any means the principal object. Its operation upon the character of the House of Commons was the great point in view. The point to be gained by the cabal was this; that a precedent should be established, tending to show, *That the favor of the people was not so sure a road as the favor of the court even to popular honors and popular trusts.* A strenuous resistance to every appearance of lawless power; a spirit of independence carried to some degree of enthusiasm; an inquisitive character to discover, and a bold one to display, every corruption and every error of government; these are the qualities which recommend a man to a seat in the House of Commons, in open and merely popular elections. An indolent and submissive disposition; a disposition to think charitably of all the actions of men in power, and to live in a mutual intercourse of favors with them; an inclination rather to countenance a strong use of authority, than to bear any sort of licentiousness on the part of the people; these are unfavorable qualities in an open election for members of Parliament.

The instinct which carries the people towards the choice of the former, is justified by reason; because, a man of such a character, even in its exorbitances, does not directly contradict the purposes of a trust, the end of which is a control on power. The latter character, even when it is not in its extreme, will execute this trust but very imperfectly; and, if deviating to the least excess, will certainly frustrate instead of forwarding the purposes of a control on government. But when the House of Commons was to be new modelled, this principle was not only to be changed but reversed. Whilst any errors committed in support of power were left to the law, with every advantage of favorable construction, of mitigation, and finally of pardon; all excesses on the side of liberty, or in pursuit of popular favor, or in defence of popular rights and privileges, were not only to be punished by the rigor of the known law, but by a *discretionary* proceeding, which brought on *the loss of the popular object itself.* Popularity was to be rendered, if not directly penal, at least highly dangerous. The favor of the people might lead even to a disqualification of representing them. . . . Until this time, the opinion of the people, through the power of an assembly, still in some sort popular, led to the greatest honors and emoluments in the gift of the crown. Now the principle is reversed; and the favor of the court is the only sure way of obtaining and holding those honors which ought to be in the disposal of the people. . . .

I will not believe, what no other man living believes, that Mr. Wilkes was punished for the indecency of his publications, or the impiety of his ransacked closet. If he had fallen in a common slaughter of libellers and blasphemers, I could well believe that nothing more was meant than was pretended. But when I see, that, for years together full as impious, and perhaps more dangerous writings to religion, and virtue, and order, have not been punished, nor their authors discountenanced; that the most audacious libels on royal majesty have passed without notice; that the most treasonable invectives against the laws, liberties, and constitution of the country, have not met with the slightest animadversion; I must consider this as a shocking and shameful pretence. . . .

When therefore I reflect upon this method pursued by the cabal in distributing rewards and punishments, I must conclude that Mr. Wilkes is the object of persecution, not on account of what he has done in common with others who are the objects of reward, but for that in which he differs from many of them: that he is pursued for the spirited dispositions which are blended with his vices; for his unconquerable firmness, for his resolute, indefatigable, strenuous resistance against oppression. . . .

It behooves the people of England to consider how the House of Commons, under the operation of these examples, must of necessity be constituted. On the side of the court will be, all honors, offices, emoluments; every sort of personal gratification to avarice or vanity; and, what is of more moment to most gentlemen, the means of growing, by innumerable petty services to individuals, into a spreading interest in their country. On the other hand, let us suppose a person unconnected with the court, and in opposition to its system. For his own person, no office, or emolument, or title; no promotion, ecclesiastical, or civil, or military, or naval, for children, or brothers, or kindred. In vain an expiring interest in a borough calls for offices, or small livings, for the children of mayors, and aldermen, and capital burgesses. His court rival has them all. He can do an infinite number of acts of generosity and kindness, and even of public spirit. He can procure indemnity from quarters. He can procure advantages in trade. He can get pardons for offences. He can obtain a thousand favors, and avert a thousand evils. He may, while he betrays every valuable interest of the kingdom, be a benefactor, a patron, a father, a guardian angel to his borough. The unfortunate independent member has nothing to offer, but harsh refusal, or pitiful excuse, or despondent representation of a hopeless interest. Except from his private fortune, in which he may be equalled, perhaps exceeded, by his court competitor, he has no way of showing any one good quality, or of making a single friend. In the House, he votes forever in a dispirited minority. If he speaks, the doors are locked. A body of loquacious placemen go out to tell the world that all he aims at is to get into office. . . . Can we conceive a more discouraging post of duty than this? Strip it of the poor reward of popularity; suffer even the excesses committed in defence of the popular interest to become a ground for the majority of that House to form a disqualification out of the line of the law, and at their pleasure, attended not only with the loss of the franchise, but with every kind of personal disgrace:—If this shall happen, the people of this kingdom may be assured that they cannot be firmly or faithfully served by any man. It is out of the nature of men and things that they should; and their presumption will be equal to their folly if they expect it. The power of the people, within the laws, must show itself sufficient to protect every representative in animated performance of his duty, or that duty cannot be performed. The House of Commons can never be a control on other parts of government, unless they are controlled themselves by their constituents; and unless these constituents possess some right in the choice of that House, which it is not in the power of that House to take away. If they suffer this power of arbitrary incapacitation to stand, they have utterly perverted every other power of the House of Commons. . . .

The people indeed have been told, that this power of discretionary disqualification is vested in hands that they may trust, and who will be sure not to abuse it to their prejudice. Until I find something in this argument differing from that on which every mode of despotism has been defended, I shall not be inclined to pay it any great compliment. The people are satisfied to trust themselves with the exercise of their own privileges, and do not desire this kind of intervention of the House of Commons to free them from the burden. They are certainly in the right. They ought not to trust the House of Commons with a power over their franchises; because the constitution, which placed two other co-ordinate powers to control it, reposed no such confidence in that body. . . .

When the House of Commons, in an endeavor to obtain new advantages at the expense of the other orders of the state, for the benefit of the *commons at large,* have pursued strong measures; if it were not just, it was at least natural, that the constituents should connive at all their proceedings; because we were ourselves ultimately to profit. But when this submission is urged to us, in a contest between the representatives and ourselves, and where nothing can be put into their scale which is not taken from ours, they fancy us to be children when they tell us they are our representatives, our own flesh and blood, and that all the stripes they give us are for our good. The very desire of that body to have such a trust contrary to law reposed in them, shows that they are not worthy of it. They certainly will abuse it; because all men possessed of an uncontrolled discretionary power leading to the aggrandizement and profit of their own body have always abused it: and I see no particular sanctity in our times, that is at all likely, by a miraculous operation, to overrule the course of nature.

But we must purposely shut our eyes, if we consider this matter merely as a contest between the House of Commons and the electors. The true contest is between the electors of the kingdom and the crown; the crown acting by an instrumental House of Commons. . . .

If once members of Parliament can be practically convinced that they do not depend on the affection or opinion of the people for their political being, they will give themselves over, without even an appearance of reserve, to the influence of the court.

Indeed a Parliament unconnected with the people is essential to a ministry unconnected with the people; and therefore those who saw through what mighty difficulties the interior ministry waded, and the exterior were dragged, in this business, will conceive of what prodigious importance, the new corps of *king's men* held this principle of occasional and personal incapacitation, to the whole body of their design.

When the House of Commons was thus made to consider itself as the master of its constituents, there wanted but one thing to secure that House against all possible future deviation towards popularity: an *unlimited* fund of money to be laid out according to the pleasure of the court.

To complete the scheme of bringing our court to a resemblance to the neighboring monarchies, it was necessary, in effect, to destroy those appropriations of revenue, which seem to limit the property, as the other laws had done the powers, of the crown. An opportunity for this purpose was taken, upon an application to Parliament for payment of the debts of the civil list; which in 1769 had amounted to 513,000*l.* Such application had been made upon former occasions; but to do it in the former manner would by no means answer the present purpose. . . .

A deficiency of the civil list duties for several years before was stated as the principal, if not the sole ground on which an application to Parliament could be justified. . . .

To have exceeded the sum given for the civil list, and to have incurred a debt without special authority of Parliament, was *prima facie,* a criminal act. . . .

But, in order firmly to establish the precedent of *payment previous to account,* and to form it into a settled rule of the House, the god in the machine was brought down, nothing less than the wonder-working *law of Parliament.* It was alleged, that it is the law of Parliament, when any demand comes from the crown, that the House must go immediately into the committee of supply; in which committee it was allowed, that the production and examination of accounts would be quite proper and regular. It was therefore carried, that they should go into the committee without delay, and accounts, in order to examine with great order and regularity things that could not possibly come before them. After this stroke of orderly and Parliamentary wit and humor, they went into the committee; and very generously voted the payment. . . .

Five hundred thousand pounds is a serious sum. But it is nothing to the prolific principle upon which the sum was voted: a principle that may be well called, *the fruitful mother of an hundred more.* . . . The power of discretionary disqualification by one law of Parliament, and the necessity of paying every debt of the civil list by another law of Parliament, if suffered to pass unnoticed, must establish such a fund of rewards and terrors as will make Parliament the best appendage and support of arbitrary power that ever was invented by the wit of man. . . .

I know the diligence with which my observations on our public disorders have been made; I am very sure of the integrity of the motives on which they are published: I cannot be equally confident in any plan for the absolute cure of those disorders, or for their certain future prevention. . . .

The first ideas which generally suggest themselves, for the cure of Parliamentary disorders, are, to shorten the duration of Parliaments; and to disqualify all, or a great number of placemen, from a seat in the House of Commons. Whatever efficacy there may be in those remedies, I am sure in the present state of things it is impossible to apply them. A restoration of the right of free election is a preliminary indispensable to every other reformation. What alterations ought afterwards to be made in the constitution, is a matter of deep and difficult research.

If I wrote merely to please the popular palate, it would indeed be as little troublesome to me as to another, to extol these remedies, so famous in speculation, but to which their greatest admirers have never attempted seriously to resort in practice. I confess then, that I have no sort of reliance upon either a triennial Parliament, or a place-bill. With regard to the former, perhaps it might rather serve to counteract, than to promote the ends that are proposed by it. To say nothing of the horrible disorders among the people attending frequent elections, I should be fearful of committing, every three years, the independent gentlemen of the country into a contest with the treasury. It is easy to see which of the contending parties would be ruined first. Whoever has taken a careful view of public proceedings, so as to endeavor to ground his speculations on his experience, must have observed how prodigiously greater the power of ministry is in the first and last session of a Parliament, than it is in the intermediate period, when members sit a little firm on their seats. The persons of the greatest Parliamentary experience, with whom I have conversed, did constantly, in canvassing the fate of questions, allow something to the court side, upon account of the elections depending or imminent. The evil complained of, if it exists in the present state of things, would hardly be removed by a triennial Parliament: for unless the influence of government in elections can be entirely taken away, the more frequently they return, the more they will harass private independence; the more generally men will be compelled to fly to the settled systematic interest of government, and to the resources of a boundless civil list. Certainly something may be done, and ought to be done, towards lessening that influence in elections; and this will be necessary upon a plan either of longer or shorter duration of Parliament. . . .

The next favorite remedy is a place-bill. The same principle guides in both; I mean, the opinion which is entertained by many, of the infallibility of laws and regulations, in the cure of public distempers. Without being as unreasonably doubtful as many are unwisely confident, I will only say, that this also is a matter very well worthy of serious and mature reflection. It is not easy to foresee, what the effect would be, of disconnecting with Parliament the greatest part of those who hold civil employments, and of such mighty and important bodies as the military and naval establishments. It were better, perhaps, that they should have a corrupt interest in the forms of the constitution, than that they should have none at all. This is a question altogether different from the disqualification of a particular description of revenue-officers from seats in Parliament; or, perhaps, of all the lower sorts of them from votes in elections. In the former case, only the few are affected; in the latter, only the inconsiderable. But a great official, a great professional, a great military and naval interest, all necessarily comprehending many people of the first weight, ability, wealth, and spirit, has been gradually formed in the kingdom. These new interests must be let into a share of representation, else possibly they may be inclined to destroy those institutions of which they are not permitted to partake. This is not a thing to be trifled with; nor is it every well-meaning man that is fit to put his hands to it. Many other serious considerations occur. I do not open them here, because they are not directly to my purpose; proposing only to give the reader some taste of the difficulties that attend all capital changes in the constitution; just to hint the uncertainty, to say no worse, of being able to prevent the court, as long as it has the means of influence abundantly in its power, of applying that influence to Parliament; and perhaps, if the public method were precluded, of doing it in some worse and more dangerous method. Underhand and oblique ways would be studied. The science of evasion, already tolerably understood, would then be brought to the greatest perfection. It is no inconsiderable part of wisdom, to know how much of an evil ought to be tolerated; lest, by attempting a degree of purity impracticable in degenerate times and manners, instead of cutting off the subsisting ill-practices, new corruptions might be produced for the concealment and security of the old. It were better, undoubtedly, that no influence at all could affect the mind of a member of Parliament. But of all modes of influence, in my opinion, a place under the government is the least disgraceful to the man who holds it, and by far the most safe to the country. I would not shut out that sort of influence which is open and visible, which is connected with the dignity and the service of the state, when it is not in my power to prevent the influence of contracts, of subscriptions, of direct bribery, and those innumerable methods of clandestine corruption, which are abundantly in the hands of the court, and which will be applied as long as these means of corruption, and the disposition to be corrupted, have existence amongst us. Our constitution stands on a nice equipoise, with steep precipices and deep waters upon all sides of it. In removing it from a dangerous leaning towards one side, there may be a risk of oversetting it on the other. Every project of a material change in a government so complicated as ours, combined at the same time with external circumstances still more complicated, is a matter full of difficulties: in which a considerate man will not be too ready to decide; a prudent man too ready to undertake; or an honest man too ready to promise. They do not respect the public nor themselves, who engage for more than they are sure that they ought to attempt, or that they are able to perform. . . .

Indeed, in the situation in which we stand, with an immense revenue, an enormous debt, mighty establishments, government itself a great banker and a great merchant, I see no other way for the preservation of a decent attention to public interest in the representatives, but *the interposition of the body of the people itself,* whenever it shall appear, by some flagrant and notorious act, by some capital innovation, that these representatives are going to overlap the fences of the law, and to introduce an arbitrary power. This interposition is a most unpleasant remedy. But, if it be a legal remedy, it is intended on some occasion to be used; to be used then only, when it is evident that nothing else can hold the constitution to its true principles.

The distempers of monarchy were the greatest subjects of apprehension and redress, in the last century; in this the distemper of Parliament. It is not in Parliament alone that the remedy for Parliamentary disorders can be completed; hardly indeed can it begin there. Until a confidence in government is re-established, the people ought to be excited to a more strict and detailed attention to the conduct of their representatives. Standards for judging more systematically upon their conduct ought to be settled in the meetings of counties and corporations. Frequent and correct lists of the voters in all important questions ought to be procured.

By such means something may be done. By such means it may appear who those are, that, by an indiscriminate support of all administrations, have totally banished all integrity and confidence out of public proceedings; have confounded the best men with the worst; and weakened and dissolved, instead of strengthening and compacting, the general frame of government. If any person is more concerned for government and order, than for the liberties of his country; even he is equally concerned to put an end to this course of indiscriminate support. It is this blind and undistinguishing support, that feeds the spring of those very disorders, by which he is frightened into the arms of the faction which contains in itself the source of all disorders, by enfeebling all the visible and regular authority of the state. . . .

Let us learn from our experience. It is not support that is wanting to government, but reformation. When ministry rests upon public opinion, it is not indeed built upon a rock of adamant; it has, however, some stability. But when it stands upon private humor, its structure is of stubble, and its foundation is on quicksand. I repeat it again—He that supports every administration subverts all government. The reason is this: The whole business in which a court usually takes an interest goes on at present equally well, in whatever hands, whether high or low, wise or foolish, scandalous or reputable; there is nothing therefore to hold it firm to any one body of men, or to any one consistent scheme of politics. Nothing interposes, to prevent the full operation of all the caprices and all the passions of a court upon the servants of the public. The system of administration is open to continual shocks and changes, upon the principles of the meanest cabal, and the most contemptible intrigue. . . .

Such are the consequences of the division of court from the administration; and of the division of public men among themselves. By the former of these, lawful government is undone; by the latter, all opposition to lawless power is rendered impotent. Government may in a great measure be restored, if any considerable bodies of men have honesty and resolution enough never to accept administration, unless this garrison of *king's men,* which is stationed, as in a citadel, to control and enslave it, be entirely broken and disbanded, and every work they have thrown up be levelled with the ground. The disposition of public men to keep this corps together, and to act under it, or to co-operate with it, is a touchstone by which every administration ought in future to be tried. There has not been one which has not sufficiently experienced the utter incompatibility of that faction with the public peace, and with all the ends of good government: since, if they opposed it, they soon lost every power of serving the crown; if they submitted to it, they lost all the esteem of their country. . . . In this particular, it ought to be the electors' business to look to their representatives. The electors ought to esteem it no less culpable in their member to give a single vote in Parliament to such an administration, than to take an office under it; to endure it, than to act in it. The notorious infidelity and versatility of members of Parliament, in their opinions of men and things, ought in a particular manner to be considered by the electors in the inquiry which is recommended to them. This is one of the principal holdings of that destructive system, which has endeavored to unhinge all the virtuous, honorable, and useful connections in this kingdom.

This cabal has, with great success, propagated a doctrine which serves for a color to those acts of treachery; and whilst it receives any degree of countenance it will be utterly senseless to look for a vigorous opposition to the court party. The doctrine is this: That all political connections are in their nature factious, and as such ought to be dissipated and destroyed; and that the rule for forming administrations is mere personal ability, rated by the judgment of this cabal upon it, and taken by draughts from every division and denomination of public men. This decree was solemnly promulgated by the head of the court corps, the Earl of Bute himself, in a speech which he made, in the year 1766, against the then administration, the only administration which he has ever been known directly and publicly to oppose.

It is indeed in no way wonderful, that such persons should make such declarations. That connection and faction are equivalent terms, is an opinion which has been carefully inculcated at all times by unconstitutional statesmen. The reason is evident. Whilst men are linked together, they easily and speedily communicate the alarm of any evil design. They are enabled to fathom it with common counsel, and to oppose it with united strength. Whereas, when they lie dispersed, without concert, order, or discipline, communication is uncertain, counsel difficult, and resistance impracticable. Where men are not acquainted with each other's principles, nor experienced in each other's talents, nor at all practised in their mutual habitudes and dispositions by joint efforts in business; no personal confidence, no friendship, no common interest, subsisting among them; it is evidently impossible that they can act a public part with uniformity, perseverance, or efficacy. In a connection, the most inconsiderable man, by adding to the weight of the whole, has his value, and his use; out of it, the greatest talents are wholly unserviceable to the public. No man, who is not inflamed by vainglory into enthusiasm, can flatter himself that his single, unsupported, desultory, unsystematic endeavors are of power to defeat the subtle designs and united cabals of ambitious citizens. When bad men combine, the good must associate; else they will fall, one by one, an unpitied sacrifice in a contemptible struggle.

It is not enough in a situation of trust in the commonwealth, that a man means well to his country; it is not enough that in his single person he never did an evil act, but always voted according to his conscience, and even harangued against every design which he apprehended to be prejudicial to the interests of his country. This innoxious and ineffectual character, that seems formed upon a plan of apology and disculpation, falls miserably short of the mark of public duty. That duty demands and requires, that what is right should not only be made known, but made prevalent; that what is evil should not only be detected, but defeated. When the public man omits to put himself in a situation of doing his duty with effect, it is an omission that frustrates the purposes of his trust almost as much as if he had formally betrayed it. It is surely no very rational account of a man's life, that he has always acted right; but has taken special care, to act in such a manner that his endeavors could not possibly be productive of any consequence.

I do not wonder that the behavior of many parties should have made persons of tender and scrupulous virtue somewhat out of humor with all sorts of connection in politics. I admit that people frequently acquire in such confederacies a narrow, bigoted, and proscriptive spirit; that they are apt to sink the idea of the general good in this circumscribed and partial interest. But, where duty renders a critical situation a necessary one, it is our business to keep free from the evils attendant upon it; and not to fly from the situation itself. If a fortress is seated in an unwholesome air, an officer of the garrison is obliged to be attentive to his health, but he must not desert his station. Every profession, not excepting the glorious one of a soldier, or the sacred one of a priest, is liable to its own particular vices; which, however, form no argument against those ways of life; nor are the vices themselves inevitable to every individual in those professions. Of such a nature are connections in politics; essentially necessary for the full performance of our public duty, accidentally liable to degenerate into faction. Commonwealths are made of families, free commonwealths of parties also; and we may as well affirm, that our natural regards and ties of blood tend inevitably to make men bad citizens, as that the bonds of our party weaken those by which we are held to our country. . . .

Certain it is, the best patriots in the greatest commonwealths have always commended and promoted such connections. . . . The Romans carried this principle a great way. Even the holding of offices together, the disposition of which arose from chance, not selection, gave rise to a relation which continued for life. . . . Breaches of any of these kinds of civil relation were considered as acts of the most distinguished turpitude. The whole people was distributed into political societies, in which they acted in support of such interests in the state as they severally affected. For it was then thought no crime to endeavor by every honest means to advance to superiority and power those of your own sentiments and opinions. This wise people was far from imagining that those connections had no tie, and obliged to no duty; but that men might quit them without shame, upon every call of interest. They believed private honor to be the great foundation of public trust; that friendship was no mean step towards patriotism; that he who, in the common intercourse of life, showed he regarded somebody besides himself, when he came to act in a public situation, might probably consult some other interest than his own. . . . In one of the most fortunate periods of our history this country was governed by a *connection*; I mean, the great connection of Whigs in the reign of Queen Anne. . . .

The Whigs of those days believed that the only proper method of rising into power was through hard essays of practised friendship and experimented fidelity. At that time it was not imagined, that patriotism was a bloody idol, which required the sacrifice of children and parents, or dearest connections in private life, and of all the virtues that rise from those relations. They were not of that ingenious paradoxical morality, to imagine that a spirit of moderation was properly shown in patiently bearing the sufferings of your friends; or that disinterestedness was clearly manifested at the expense of other people's fortune. They believed that no men could act in concert, who did not act with confidence, who were not bound together by common opinions, common affections, and common interests. . . .

Party is a body of men united for promoting by their joint endeavors the national interest upon some particular principle in which they are all agreed. For my part, I find it impossible to conceive, that any one believes in his own politics, or thinks them to be of any weight, who refuses to adopt the means of having them reduced into practice. It is the business of the speculative philosopher to mark the proper ends of government. It is the business of the politician, who is the philosopher in action, to find out proper means towards those ends, and to employ them with effect. Therefore every honorable connection will avow it is their first purpose, to pursue every just method to put the men who hold their opinions into such a condition as may enable them to carry their common plans into execution, with all the power and authority of the state. As this power is attached to certain situations, it is their duty to contend for these situations. Without a proscription of others, they are bound to give to their own party the preference in all things; and by no means, for private considerations, to accept any offers of power in which the whole body is not included; nor to suffer themselves to be led, or to be controlled, or to be overbalanced, in office or in council, by those who contradict the very fundamental principles on which their party is formed, and even those upon which every fair connection must stand. Such a generous contention for power, on such manly and honorable maxims, will easily be distinguished from the mean and interested struggle for place and emolument. . . .

It is an advantage to all narrow wisdom and narrow morals, that their maxims have a plausible air: and, on a cursory view, appear equal to first principles. They are light and portable. They are as current as copper coin; and about as valuable. They serve equally the first capacities and the lowest; and they are, at least, as useful to the worst men as to the best. Of this stamp is the cant of *Not men, but measures*; a sort of charm by which many people get loose from every honorable engagement. When I see a man acting this desultory and disconnected part, with as much detriment to his own fortune as prejudice to the cause of any party, I am not persuaded that he is right; but I am ready to believe he is in earnest. I respect virtue in all its situations; even when it is found in the unsuitable company of weakness. I lament to see qualities, rare and valuable, squandered away without any public utility. But when a gentleman with great visible emoluments abandons the party in which he has long acted, and tells you, it is because he proceeds upon his own judgment; that he acts on the merits of the several measures as they arise; and that he is obliged to follow his own conscience, and not that of others; he gives reasons which it is impossible to controvert, and discovers a character which it is impossible to mistake. What shall we think of him who never differed from a certain set of men until the moment they lost their power, and who never agreed with them in a single instance afterwards? Would not such a coincidence of interest and opinion be rather fortunate? . . . Whether a *measure* of government be right or wrong, is *no matter of fact*, but a mere affair of opinion, on which men may, as they do, dispute and wrangle without end. But whether the individual *thinks* the measure right or wrong, is a point at still a greater distance from the reach of all human decision. It is therefore very convenient to politicians, not to put the judgment of their conduct on overt acts, cognizable in any ordinary court, but upon such matter as can be triable only in that secret tribunal, where they are sure of being heard with favor, or where at worst the sentence will be only private whipping. . . .

In order to throw an odium on political connection, these politicians suppose it a necessary incident to it, that you are blindly to follow the opinions of your party, when in direct opposition to your own clear ideas; a degree of servitude that no worthy man could bear the thought of submitting to; and such as, I believe, no connections (except some court factions) ever could be so senselessly tyrannical as to impose. Men thinking freely, will, in particular instances, think differently. But still as the greater part of the measures which arise in the course of public business are related to, or dependent on, some great, *leading, general principles in government*, a man must be peculiarly unfortunate in the choice of his political company, if he does not agree with them at least nine times in ten. If he does not concur in these general principles upon which the party is founded, and which necessarily draw on a concurrence in their application, he ought from the beginning to have chosen some other, more conformable to his opinions. When the question is in its nature doubtful, or not very material, the modesty which becomes an individual, and, (in spite of our court moralists) that partiality which becomes a well-chosen friendship, will frequently bring on an acquiescence in the general sentiment. Thus the disagreement will naturally be rare; it will be only enough to indulge freedom, without violating concord, or disturbing arrangement. And this is all that ever was required for a character of the greatest uniformity and steadiness in connection. How men can proceed without any connection at all, is to me utterly incomprehensible. . . .

I remember an old scholastic aphorism, which says, "that the man who lives wholly detached from others, must be either an angel or a devil." When I see in any of these detached gentlemen of our times the angelic purity, power, and beneficence, I shall admit them to be angels. In the mean time we are born only to be men. We shall do enough if we form ourselves to be good ones. It is therefore our business carefully to cultivate in our minds, to rear to the most perfect vigor and maturity, every sort of generous and honest feeling, that belongs to our nature. To bring the dispositions that are lovely in private life into the service and conduct of the commonwealth; so to be patriots, as not to forget we are gentlemen. To cultivate friendships, and to incur enmities. To have both strong, but both selected: in the one, to be placable; in the other immovable. To model our principles to our duties and our situation. To be fully persuaded, that all virtue which is impracticable is spurious; and rather to run the risk of falling into faults in a course which leads us to act with effect and energy, than to loiter out our days without blame, and without use. Public life is a situation of power and energy; he trespasses against his duty who sleeps upon his watch, as well as he that goes over to the enemy.

There is, however, a time for all things. It is not every conjuncture which calls with equal force upon the activity of honest men; but critical exigencies now and then arise; and I am mistaken, if this be not one of them. Men will see the necessity of honest combination; but they may see it when it is too late. They may embody, when it will be ruinous to themselves, and of no advantage to the country; when, for want of such a timely union as may enable them to oppose in favor of the laws, with the laws on their side, they may at length find themselves under the necessity of conspiring, instead of consulting. The law, for which they stand, may become a weapon in the hands of its bitterest enemies; and they will be cast, at length, into that miserable alternative between slavery and civil confusion, which no good man can look upon without horror; an alternative in which it is impossible he should take either part, with a conscience perfectly at repose. To keep that situation of guilt and remorse at the utmost distance is, therefore, our first obligation. Early activity may prevent late and fruitless violence. As yet we work in the light. The scheme of the enemies of public tranquility has disarranged, it has not destroyed us.

If the reader believes that there really exists such a faction as I have described; a faction ruling by the private inclinations of a court, against the general sense of the people; and that this faction, whilst it pursues a scheme for undermining all the foundations of our freedom, weakens (for the present at least) all the powers of executory government, rendering us abroad contemptible, and at home distracted; he will believe also, that nothing but a firm combination of public men against this body, and that, too, supported by the hearty concurrence of the people at large, can possibly get the better of it. The people will see the necessity of restoring public men to an attention to the public opinion, and of restoring the constitution to its original principles. Above all, they will endeavor to keep the House of Commons from assuming a character which does not belong to it. They will endeavor to keep that House, for its existence, for its powers, and its privileges, as independent of every other, and as dependent upon themselves, as possible. . . . When, through the medium of this just connection with their constituents, the genuine dignity of the House of Commons is restored, it will begin to think of casting from it, with scorn, as badges of servility, all the false ornaments of illegal power, with which it has been, for some time, disgraced. It will begin to think of its old office of CONTROL. It will not suffer that last of evils to predominate in the country: men without popular confidence, public opinion, natural connection, or mutual trust, invested with all the powers of government.

When they have learned this lesson themselves, they will be willing and able to teach the court, that it is the true interest of the prince to have but one administration; and that one composed of those who recommend themselves to their sovereign through the opinion of their country, and not by their obsequiousness to a favorite. Such men will serve their sovereign with affection and fidelity; because his choice of them, upon such principles, is a compliment to their virtue. They will be able to serve him effectually; because they will add the weight of the country to the force of the executory power. They will be able to serve their king with dignity; because they will never abuse his name to the gratification of their private spleen or avarice. This, with allowances for human frailty, may probably be the general character of a ministry, which thinks itself accountable to the House of Commons; when the House of Commons thinks itself accountable to its constituents. If other ideas should prevail, things must remain in their present confusion, until they are hurried into all the rage of civil violence, or until they sink into the dead repose of despotism.

Speech on the Middlesex Elections

John Wilkes, a radical member of Parliament from London, was expelled from the House of Commons in 1764 for libeling the king in the press as well as for publishing an obscene poem. He was reelected to the House several times, and each time was prevented by the body from taking his seat. On the fourth such occasion, in 1771, Burke spoke in defense of Wilkes's right to be seated.

In every complicated constitution (and every free constitution is complicated) cases will arise when the several orders of the state will clash with one another, and disputes will arise about the limits of their several rights and privileges. It may be almost impossible to reconcile them. . . .

Carry the principle on by which you expelled Mr. Wilkes, there is not a man in the House, hardly a man in the nation, who may not be disqualified. That this House should have no power of expulsion is an hard saying: that this House should have a general discretionary power of disqualification is a dangerous saying. That the people should not choose their own representative is a saying that shakes the Constitution: that this House should name the representative is a saying which, followed by practice, subverts the Constitution. They have the right of electing; you have a right of expelling: they of choosing; you of judging, and only of judging, of the choice. What bounds shall be set to the freedom of that choice? Their right is prior to ours: we all originate there. They are the mortal enemies of the House of Commons who would persuade them to think or to act as if they were a self-originated magistracy, independent of the people, and unconnected with their opinions and feelings. Under a pretence of exalting the dignity, they undermine the very foundations of this House. When the question is asked *here*, What disturbs the people? whence all this clamor? we apply to the Treasury bench, and they tell us it is from the efforts of libellers, and the wickedness of the people: a worn-out ministerial pretence. If abroad the people are deceived by popular, within we are deluded by ministerial cant.

The question amounts to this: Whether you mean to be a legal tribunal, or an arbitrary and despotic assembly? I see and I feel the delicacy and difficulty of the ground upon which we stand in this question. I could wish, indeed, that they who advise the crown had not left Parliament in this very ungraceful distress, in which they can neither retract with dignity nor persist with justice. Another Parliament might have satisfied the people without lowering themselves. But our situation is not in our own choice: our conduct in that situation is all that is in our own option. The substance of the question is, to put bounds to your own power by the rules and principles of law. This is, I am sensible, a difficult thing to the corrupt, grasping, and ambitious part of human nature. But the very difficulty argues and enforces the necessity of it. First, because the greater the power, the more dangerous the abuse. Since the Revolution, at least, the power of the nation has all flowed with a full tide into the House of Commons. Secondly, because the House of Commons, as it is the most powerful, is the most corruptible part of the whole Constitution. Our public wounds cannot be concealed; to be cured, they must be laid open. The public does think we are a corrupt body. In our *legislative capacity*, we are, in most instances, esteemed a very wise body; in our judicial, we have no credit, no character at all. Our judgments stink in the nostrils of the people. They think us to be not only without virtue, but without shame. Therefore the greatness of our power, and the great and just opinion of our corruptibility and our corruption, render it necessary to fix some bound, to plant some landmark, which we are never to exceed. This is what the bill proposes.

First, on this head, I lay it down as a fundamental rule in the law and Constitution of this country, that this House has not by itself alone a legislative authority in any case whatsoever. I know that the contrary was the doctrine of the usurping House of Commons, which threw down the fences and bulwarks of law, which annihilated first the lords, then the crown, then its constituents. But the first thing that was done on the restoration of the Constitution was to settle this point. Secondly, I lay it down as a rule, that the power of occasional incapacitation, on discretionary grounds, is a legislative power. In order to establish this principle, if it should not be sufficiently proved by being stated, tell me what are the criteria, the characteristics, by which you distinguish between a legislative and a juridical act. It will be necessary to state, shortly, the difference between a legislative and a juridical act.

A legislative act has no reference to any rule but these two,—original justice, and discretionary application. Therefore it can give rights,—rights where no rights existed before; and it can take away rights where they were before established. For the law, which binds all others, does not and cannot bind the law-maker: he, and he alone, is above the law. But a judge, a person exercising a judicial capacity, is neither to apply to original justice nor to a discretionary application of it. He goes to justice and discretion only at second hand, and through the medium of some superiors. He is to work neither upon his opinion of the one nor of the other, but upon a fixed rule, of which he has not the making, but singly and solely the *application* to the case.

The power assumed by the House neither is nor can be judicial power exercised according to known law. The properties of law are, first, that it should be known; secondly, that it should be fixed, and not occasional. First, this power cannot be according to the first property of law; because no man does or can know it, nor do you yourselves know upon what grounds you will vote the incapacity of any man. No man in Westminster Hall, or in any court upon earth, will say that is law, upon which, if a man going to his counsel should say to him, "What is my tenure in law of this estate?" he would answer, "Truly, Sir, I know not; the court has no rule but its own discretion; they will determine." It is not a fixed law; because you profess you vary it according to the occasion, exercise it according to your discretion, no man can call for it as a right. It is argued, that the incapacity is not originally voted, but a consequence of a power of expulsion. But if you expel, not upon legal, but upon arbitrary, that is, upon discretionary grounds, and the incapacity is *ex vi termini* and inclusively comprehended in the expulsion, is not the incapacity voted in the expulsion? Are they not convertible terms? And if incapacity is voted to be inherent in expulsion, if expulsion be arbitrary, incapacity is arbitrary also. I have therefore shown that the power of incapacitation is a legislative power; I have shown that legislative power does not belong to the House of Commons; and therefore it follows that the House of Commons has not a power of incapacitation.

I know not the origin of the House of Commons, but am very sure that it did not create itself; the electors were prior to the elected, whose rights originated either from the people at large, or from some other form of legislature, which never could intend for the chosen a power of superseding the choosers.

If you have not a power of declaring an incapacity simply by the mere act of declaring it, it is evident to the most ordinary reason you cannot have a right of expulsion, inferring, or rather including, an incapacity. For as the law, when it gives any direct right, gives also as necessary incidents all the means of acquiring the possession of that right, so, where it does not give a right directly, it refuses all the means by which such a right may by any mediums be exercised, or in effect be indirectly acquired. Else it is very obvious that the intention of the law in refusing that right might be entirely frustrated, and the whole power of the legislature baffled. If there be no certain, invariable rule of eligibility, it were better to get simplicity, if certainty is not to be had, and to resolve all the franchises of the subject into this one short proposition,—the will and pleasure of the House of Commons.

The argument drawn from the courts of law applying the principles of law to new cases as they emerge is altogether frivolous, inapplicable, and arises from a total ignorance of the bounds between civil and criminal jurisdiction, and of the separate maxims that govern these two provinces of law, that are eternally separate. Undoubtedly the courts of law, where a new case comes before them, as they do every hour, then, that there may be no defect in justice, call in similar principles, and the example of the nearest determination, and do everything to draw the law to as near a conformity to general equity and right reason as they can bring it with its being a fixed principle. *Boni judicis est ampliare justitiam,*—that is, to make open and liberal justice. But in criminal matters this parity of reason and these analogies ever have been and ever ought to be shunned.

Whatever is incident to a court of judicature is necessary to the House of Commons as judging in elections. But a power of making incapacities is not necessary to a court of judicature: therefore a power of making incapacities is not necessary to the House of Commons.

Incapacity, declared by whatever authority, stands upon two principles: first, an incapacity arising from the supposed incongruity of two duties in the commonwealth; secondly, an incapacity arising from unfitness by infirmity of nature or the criminality of conduct. As to the first class of incapacities, they have no *hardship* annexed to them. The persons so incapacitated are paid by one dignity for what they abandon in another, and for the most part the situation arises from their own choice. But as to the second, arising from an unfitness not fixed by Nature, but superinduced by some positive acts, or arising from honorable motives, such as an occasional personal disability, of all things it ought to be defined by the fixed rule of law, what Lord Coke calls the golden metwand of the law, and not by the crooked cord of discretion. Whatever is general is better borne. We take our common lot with men of the same description. But to be selected and marked out by a particular brand of unworthiness among our fellow-citizens is a lot of all others the hardest to be borne, and consequently is of all others that act which ought only to be trusted to the legislature, as not only *legislative* in its nature, but of all parts of legislature the most odious. The question is over, if this is shown not to be a legislative act.

But what is very usual and natural is, to corrupt judicature into legislature. On this point it is proper to inquire whether a court of judicature which decides without appeal has it as a necessary incident of such judicature, that whatever it decides is *de jure* law. Nobody will, I hope, assert this; because the direct consequence would be the entire extinction of the difference between true and false judgments. For if the judgment makes the law, and not the law directs the judgment, it is impossible there should be such a thing as an illegal judgment given.

But instead of standing upon this ground, they introduce another question wholly foreign to it: Whether it ought not to be submitted to as if it were law? And then the question is,—By the Constitution of this country, what degree of submission is due to the authoritative acts of a limited power? This question of submission, determine it how you please, has nothing to do in this discussion and in this House. Here it is not, how long the people are bound to tolerate the illegality of our judgments, but whether we have a right to substitute our occasional opinion in the place of law, so as to deprive the citizen of his franchise. . . .

Speech at Mr. Burke's Arrival in Bristol

Burke was elected to the House in 1774 by the city of Bristol. In his election speech Burke made clear to his constituents that he did not intend to be simply their delegate, representing directly their views and interests in the Commons, a vision of the legislator's role quite widespread then in radical circles. In his now famous description of the representative's role, Burke announced that the legislator was not an agent for local constituents, but the unbiased and disinterested advocate of the general good.

I AM SORRY I cannot conclude without saying a word on a topic touched upon by my worthy colleague. I wish that topic had been passed by at a time when I have so little leisure to discuss it. But since he has thought proper to throw it out, I owe you a clear explanation of my poor sentiments on that subject.

He tells you that "the topic of instructions has occasioned much altercation and uneasiness in this city"; and he expresses himself (if I understand him rightly) in favor of the coercive authority of such instructions.

Certainly, Gentlemen, it ought to be the happiness and glory of a representative to live in the strictest union, the closest correspondence, and the most unreserved communication with his constituents. Their wishes ought to have great weight with him; their opinions high respect; their business unremitted attention. It is his duty to sacrifice his repose, his pleasure, his satisfactions, to theirs,—and above all, ever, and in all cases, to prefer their interest to his own.

But his unbiased opinion, his mature judgment, his enlightened conscience, he ought not to sacrifice to you, to any man, or to any set of men living. These he does not derive from your pleasure,—no, nor from the law and the Constitution. They are a trust from Providence, for the abuse of which he is deeply answerable. Your representative owes you, not his industry only, but his judgment; and he betrays, instead of serving you, if he sacrifices it to your opinion.

My worthy colleague says, his will ought to be subservient to yours. If that be all, the thing is innocent. If government were a matter of will upon any side, yours, without question, ought to be superior. But government and legislation are matters of reason and judgment, and not of inclination; and what sort of reason is that in which the determination precedes the discussion, in which one set of men deliberate and another decide, and where those who form the conclusion are perhaps three hundred miles distant from those who hear the arguments?

To deliver an opinion is the right of all men; that of constituents is a weighty and respectable opinion, which a representative ought always to rejoice to hear, and which he ought always most seriously to consider. But *authoritative* instructions, *mandates* issued, which the member is bound blindly and implicitly to obey, to vote, and to argue for, though contrary to the clearest conviction of his judgment and conscience,—these are things utterly unknown to the laws of this land, and which arise from a fundamental mistake of the whole order and tenor of our Constitution.

Parliament is not a *congress* of ambassadors from different and hostile interests, which interests each must maintain, as an agent and advocate, against other agents and advocates; but Parliament is a *deliberative* assembly of *one* nation, with *one* interest, that of the whole—where not local purposes, not local prejudices, ought to guide, but the general good, resulting from the general reason of the whole. You choose a member, indeed; but when you have chosen him, he is not member of Bristol, but he is a member of *Parliament*. If the local constituent should have an interest or should form an hasty opinion evidently opposite to the real good of the rest of the community, the member for that place ought to be as far as any other from any endeavor to give it effect. I beg pardon for saying so much on this subject; I have been unwillingly drawn into it; but I shall ever use a respectful frankness of communication with you. Your faithful friend, your devoted servant, I shall be to the end of my life: a flatterer you do not wish for. On this point of instructions, however, I think it scarcely possible we ever can have any sort of difference. Perhaps I may give you too much, rather than too little trouble.

From the first hour I was encouraged to court your favor, to this happy day of obtaining it, I have never promised you anything but humble and persevering endeavors to do my duty. The weight of that duty, I confess, makes me tremble; and whoever well considers what it is, of all things in the world, will fly from what has the least likeness to a positive and precipitate engagement. To be a good member of Parliament is, let me tell you, no easy task,—especially at this time, when there is so strong a disposition to run into the perilous extremes of servile compliance or wild popularity. To unite circumspection with vigor is absolutely necessary, but it is extremely difficult. We are now members for a rich commercial *city*; this city, however, is but a part of a rich commercial *nation*, the interests of which are various, multiform, and intricate. We are members for that great nation, which, however, is itself but part of a great *empire,* extended by our virtue and our fortune to the farthest limits of the East and of the West. All these wide-spread interests must be considered,—must be compared,—must be reconciled, if possible. We are members for a *free* country; and surely we all know that the machine of a free constitution is no simple thing, but as intricate and as delicate as it is valuable. We are members in a great and ancient *monarchy;* and we must preserve religiously the true, legal rights of the sovereign, which form the keystone that binds together the noble and well-constructed arch of our empire and our Constitution. A constitution made up of balanced powers must ever be a critical thing. As such I mean to touch that part of it which comes within my reach. I know my inability, and I wish for support from every quarter. In particular I shall aim at the friendship, and shall cultivate the best correspondence, of the worthy colleague you have given me.

I trouble you no farther than once more to thank you all: you, Gentlemen, for your favors; the candidates, for their temperate and polite behavior; and the sheriffs, for a conduct which may give a model for all who are in public stations.

Speech on Economical Reform

Throughout the eighteenth century the British monarchy used its vast financial resources to purchase support in the House of Commons through the distribution of patronage, pensions, sinecures, and public jobs. One aspect of the call for political reform that swept through England in the late 1770s and early 1780s was the effort to remove the Crown's excessive influence over Parliament by reducing royal corruption. Burke shared this concern with the reformers, and on February 11, 1780, he attacked the antiquated and wasteful structure of the royal household and demanded public frugality. A financially restrained monarch would better secure the independence of Parliament.

MR. SPEAKER—I rise, in acquittal of my engagement to the House, in obedience to the strong and just requisition of my constituents, and, I am persuaded, in conformity to the unanimous wishes of the whole nation, to submit to the wisdom of Parliament "A Plan of Reform in the Constitution of Several Parts of the Public Economy."

I have endeavored that this plan should include, in its execution, a considerable reduction of improper expense; that it should effect a conversion of unprofitable titles into a productive estate; that it should lead to, and indeed almost compel, a provident administration of such sums of public money as must remain under discretionary trusts; that it should render the incurring debts on the civil establishment (which must ultimately affect national strength and national credit) so very difficult as to become next to impracticable.

But what, I confess, was uppermost with me, what I bent the whole force of my mind to, was the reduction of that corrupt influence which is itself the perennial spring of all prodigality and of all disorder; which loads us more than millions of debt; which takes away vigor from our arms, wisdom from our councils, and every shadow of authority and credit from the most venerable parts of our constitution. . . .

To the last kind of necessity, the desires of the people, I have but a very few words to say. The ministers seem to contest this point, and affect to doubt whether the people do really desire a plan of economy in the civil government. Sir, this is too ridiculous. It is impossible that they should not desire it. It is impossible that a prodigality which draws its resources from their indigence should be pleasing to them. Little factions of pensioners, and their dependants, may talk another language. But the voice of nature is against them, and it will be heard. The people of England will not, they cannot, take it kindly that representatives should refuse to their constituents what an absolute sovereign voluntarily offers to his subjects. The expression of the petitions is that, *"before any new burdens are laid upon this country, effectual measures be taken by this House to inquire into and correct the gross abuses in the expenditure of public money."* . . .

These desires of the people of England, which come far short of the voluntary concessions of the King of France, are moderate indeed. They only contend that we should interweave some economy with the taxes with which we have chosen to begin the war. They request, not that you should rely upon economy exclusively, but that you should give it rank and precedence, in the order of the ways and means of this single session.

But if it were possible that the desires of our constituents, desires which are at once so natural and so very much tempered and subdued, should have no weight with a House of Commons which has its eye elsewhere, I would turn my eyes to the very quarter to which theirs are directed. I would reason this matter with the House on the mere policy of the question; and I would undertake to prove that an early dereliction of abuse is the direct interest of government—of government taken abstractedly from its duties, and considered merely as a system intending its own conservation.

If there is any one eminent criterion which above all the rest distinguishes a wise government from an administration weak and improvident, it is this: "well to know the best time and manner of yielding what it is impossible to keep." There have been, Sir, and there are, many who choose to chicane with their situation rather than be instructed by it. Those gentlemen argue against every desire of reformation upon the principles of a criminal prosecution. It is enough for them to justify their adherence to a pernicious system that it is not of their contrivance—that it is an inheritance of absurdity, derived to them from their ancestors—that they can make out a long and unbroken pedigree of mismanagers that have gone before them. They are proud of the antiquity of their house; and they defend their errors as if they were defending their inheritance, afraid of derogating from their nobility, and carefully avoiding a sort of blot in their scutcheon, which they think would degrade them forever.

It was thus that the unfortunate Charles the First defended himself on the practice of the Stuart who went before him, and of all the Tudors.

His partisans might have gone to the Plantagenets. They might have found bad examples enough, both abroad and at home, that could have shown an ancient and illustrious descent. But there is a time when men will not suffer bad things because their ancestors have suffered worse. . . .

I do most seriously put it to administration to consider the wisdom of a timely reform. Early reformations are amicable arrangements with a friend in power; late reformations are terms imposed upon a conquered enemy. Early reformations are made in cool blood; late reformations are made under a state of inflammation. In that state of things the people behold in government nothing that is respectable. They see the abuse, and they will see nothing else. They fall into the temper of a furious populace provoked at the disorder of a house of ill-fame; they never attempt to correct or regulate; they go to work by the shortest way: they abate the nuisance, they pull down the house.

This is my opinion with regard to the true interest of government. But as it is the interest of government that reformation should be early, it is the interest of the people that it should be temperate. It is their interest because a temperate reform is permanent, and because it has a principle of growth. Whenever we improve, it is right to leave room for a further improvement. It is right to consider, to look about us, to examine the effect of what we have done. Then we can proceed with confidence, because we can proceed with intelligence. Whereas in hot reformations, in what men more zealous than considerate call *making clear work*, the whole is generally so crude, so harsh, so indigested, mixed with so much imprudence and so much injustice, so contrary to the whole course of human nature and human institutions, that the very people who are most eager for it are among the first to grow disgusted at what they have done. Then some part of the abdicated grievance is recalled from its exile in order to become a corrective of the correction. Then the abuse assumes all the credit and popularity of a reform. The very idea of purity and disinterestedness in politics falls into disrepute, and is considered as a vision of hot and inexperienced men; and thus disorders become incurable, not by the virulence of their own quality, but by the unapt and violent nature of the remedies. A great part, therefore, of my idea of reform is meant to operate gradually: some benefits will come at a nearer, some at a more remote period. We must no more make haste to be rich by parsimony than by intemperate acquisition.

In my opinion, it is our duty, when we have the desires of the people before us, to pursue them, not in the spirit of literal obedience, which may militate with their very principle—much less to treat them with a peevish and contentious litigation, as if we were adverse parties in a suit. It would, Sir, be most dishonorable for a faithful representative of the Commons to take advantage of any inartificial expression of the people's wishes in order to frustrate their attainment of what they have an undoubted right to expect. We are under infinite obligations to our constituents, who have raised us to so distinguished a trust, and have imparted such a degree of sanctity to common characters. We ought to walk before them with purity, plainness, and integrity of heart—with filial love, and not with slavish fear, which is always a low and tricking thing. For my own part, in what I have meditated upon that subject, I cannot, indeed, take upon me to say I have the honor *to follow* the sense of the people. The truth is, *I met it on the way*, while I was pursuing their interest according to my own ideas. I am happy beyond expression to find that my intentions have so far coincided with theirs that I have not had cause to be in the least scrupulous to sign their petition, conceiving it to express my own opinions, as nearly as general terms can express the object of particular arrangements.

I am therefore satisfied to act as a fair mediator between government and the people, endeavoring to form a plan which should have both an early and a temperate operation. I mean, that it should be substantial, that it should be systematic, that it should rather strike at the first cause of prodigality and corrupt influence than attempt to follow them in all their effects. . . .

I am quite clear that if we do not go to the very origin and first ruling cause of grievances, we do nothing. What does it signify to turn abuses out of one door if we are to let them in at another? What does it signify to promote economy upon a measure and to suffer it to be subverted in the principle? Our ministers are far from being wholly to blame for the present ill order which prevails. Whilst institutions directly repugnant to good management are suffered to remain, no effectual or lasting reform *can* be introduced.

I therefore thought it necessary, as soon as I conceived thoughts of submitting to you some plan of reform, to take a comprehensive view of the state of this country: to make a sort of survey of its jurisdictions, its estates, and its establishments. Something in every one of them seemed to me to stand in the way of all economy in their administration, and prevented every possibility of methodizing the system. But being, as I ought to be, doubtful of myself, I was resolved not to proceed in an *arbitrary* manner in any particular which tended to change the settled state of things, or in any degree to affect the fortune or situation, the interest or the importance, of any individual. By an arbitrary proceeding I mean one conducted by the private opinions, tastes, or feelings of the man who attempts to regulate. These private measures are not standards of the exchequer, nor balances of the sanctuary. General principles cannot be debauched or corrupted by interest or caprice; and by those principles I was resolved to work. . . .

I therefore lay down to myself seven fundamental rules; they might, indeed, be reduced to two or three simple maxims; but they would be too general, and their application to the several heads of the business before us would not be so distinct and visible. I conceive, then,

First, That all jurisdictions which furnish more matter of expense, more temptation to oppression, or more means and instruments of corrupt influence than advantage to justice or political administration, ought to be abolished.

Secondly, That all public estates which are more subservient to the purposes of vexing, overawing, and influencing those who hold under them, and to the expense of perception and management, than of benefit to the revenue, ought, upon every principle both of revenue and of freedom, to be disposed of.

Thirdly, That all offices which bring more charge than proportional advantage to the state, that all offices which may be engrafted on others, uniting and simplifying their duties, ought, in the first case, to be taken away, and, in the second, to be consolidated.

Fourthly, That all such offices ought to be abolished as obstruct the prospect of the general superintendent of finance, which destroy his superintendency, which disable him from foreseeing and providing for charges as they may occur, from preventing expense in its origin, checking it in its progress, or securing its application to its proper purposes. A minister under whom expenses can be made without his knowledge can never say what it is that he can spend, or what it is that he can save.

Fifthly, That it is proper to establish an invariable order in all payments which will prevent partiality, which will give preference to services, not according to the importunity of the demandant, but the rank and order of their utility or their justice.

Sixthly, That it is right to reduce every establishment and every part of an establishment (as nearly as possible) to certainty, the life of all order and good management.

Seventhly, That all subordinate treasuries, as the nurseries of mismanagement, and as naturally drawing to themselves as much money as they can, keeping it as long as they can, and accounting for it as late as they can, ought to be dissolved. They have a tendency to perplex and distract the public accounts, and to excite a suspicion of government even beyond the extent of their abuse.

Under the authority and with the guidance of those principles I proceed; wishing that nothing in any establishment may be changed where I am not able to make a strong, direct, and solid application of those principles, or of some one of them. . . .

Speech on a Bill for Shortening the Duration of Parliaments

One demand of the reformers in 1780 was to elect the House of Commons every three years instead of every seven years. Burke was strongly opposed to such a dramatic change. In his speech against the idea, on May 8, 1780, he introduced one of his recurring themes, what we would now call the principle of unintended consequences, or what he described as the tendency of actions seeking good ends to "inevitably lead into some inconvenience" that undermines the original valuable intention.

IT IS ALWAYS to be lamented, when men are driven to search into the foundations of the commonwealth. It is certainly necessary to resort to the theory of your government, whenever you propose any alteration in the frame of it,—whether that alteration means the revival of some former antiquated and forsaken constitution of state, or the introduction of some new improvement in the commonwealth. The object of our deliberation is, to promote the good purposes for which elections have been instituted, and to prevent their inconveniences. If we thought frequent elections attended with no inconvenience, or with but a trifling inconvenience, the strong overruling principle of the Constitution would sweep us like a torrent towards them. But your remedy is to be suited to your disease, your present disease, and to your whole disease. That man thinks much too highly, and therefore he thinks weakly and delusively, of any contrivance of human wisdom, who believes that it can make any sort of approach to perfection. There is not, there never was, a principle of government under heaven, that does not, in the very pursuit of the good it proposes, naturally and inevitably lead into some inconvenience which makes it absolutely necessary to counterwork and weaken the application of that first principle itself, and to abandon something of the extent of the advantage you proposed by it, in order to prevent also the inconveniences which have arisen from the instrument of all the good you had in view.

To govern according to the sense and agreeably to the interests of the people is a great and glorious object of government. This object cannot be obtained but through the medium of popular election; and popular election is a mighty evil. It is such and so great an evil, that, though there are few nations whose monarchs were not originally elective, very few are now elected. They are the distempers of elections that have destroyed all free states. To cure these distempers is difficult, if not impossible; the only thing, therefore, left to save the commonwealth is, to prevent their return too frequently. The objects in view are, to have Parliaments as frequent as they can be without distracting them in the prosecution of public business: on one hand, to secure their dependence upon the people; on the other, to give them that quiet in their minds and that ease in their fortunes as to enable them to perform the most arduous and most painful duty in the world with spirit, with efficiency, with independency, and with experience, as real public counsellors, not as the canvassers at a perpetual election. It is wise to compass as many good ends as possibly you can, and, seeing there are inconveniences on both sides, with benefits on both, to give up a part of the benefit to soften the inconvenience. The perfect cure is impracticable; because the disorder is dear to those from whom alone the cure can possibly be derived. The utmost to be done is to palliate, to mitigate, to respite, to put off the evil day of the Constitution to its latest possible hour,—and may it be a very late one!

This bill, I fear, would precipitate one of two consequences,—I know not which most likely, or which most dangerous: either that the crown, by its constant, stated power, influence, and revenue, would wear out all opposition in elections, or that a violent and furious popular spirit would arise. I must see, to satisfy me, the remedies; I must see, from their operation in the cure of the old evil, and in the cure of those new evils which are inseparable from all remedies, how they balance each other, and what is the total result. The excellence of mathematics and metaphysics is, to have but one thing before you; but he forms the best judgment in all moral disquisitions who has the greatest number and variety of considerations in one view before him, and can take them in with the best possible consideration of the middle results of all.

We of the opposition, who are not friends to the bill, give this pledge at least of our integrity and sincerity to the people,—that in our situation of systematic opposition to the present ministers, in which all our hope of rendering it effectual depends upon popular interest and favor, we will not flatter them by a surrender of our uninfluenced judgment and opinion; we give a security, that, if ever we should be in another situation, no flattery to any other sort of power and influence would induce us to act against the true interests of the people.

All are agreed that Parliaments should not be perpetual; the only question is, What is the most convenient time for their duration?—on which there are three opinions. We are agreed, too, that the term ought not to be chosen most likely in its operation to spread corruption, and to augment the already overgrown influence of the crown. On these principles I mean to debate the question. It is easy to pretend a zeal for liberty. Those who think themselves not likely to be incumbered with the performance of their promises, either from their known inability or total indifference about the performance, never fail to entertain the most lofty ideas. They are certainly the most specious; and they cost them neither reflection to frame, nor pains to modify, nor management to support. The task is of another nature to those who mean to promise nothing that it is not in their intention, or may possibly be in their power to perform,—to those who are bound and principled no more to delude the understandings than to violate the liberty of their fellow-subjects. Faithful watchmen we ought to be over the rights and privileges of the people. But our duty, if we are qualified for it as we ought, is to give them information, and not to receive it from them: we are not to go to school to them, to learn the principles of law and government. In doing so, we should not dutifully serve, but we should basely and scandalously betray the people, who are not capable of this service by nature, nor in any instance called to it by the Constitution. I reverentially look up to the opinion of the people, and with an awe that is almost superstitious. I should be ashamed to show my face before them, if I changed my ground as they cried up or cried down men or things or opinions,—if I wavered and shifted about with every change, and joined in it or opposed as best answered any low interest or passion,—if I held them up hopes which I knew I never intended, or promised what I well knew I could not perform. Of all these things they are perfect sovereign judges without appeal; but as to the detail of particular measures, or to any general schemes of policy, they have neither enough of speculation in the closet nor of experience in business to decide upon it. They can well see whether we are tools of a court or their honest servants. Of that they can well judge,—and I wish that they always exercised their judgment; but of the particular merits of a measure I have other standards. . . .

That the frequency of elections proposed by this bill has a tendency to increase the power and consideration of the electors, not lessen corruptibility, I do most readily allow: so far it is desirable. This is what it has: I will tell you now what it has not. 1st. It has no sort of tendency to increase their integrity and public spirit, unless an increase of power has an operation upon voters in elections, that it has in no other situation in the world, and upon no other part of mankind. 2nd. This bill has no tendency to limit the quantity of influence in the crown, to render its operation more difficult, or to counteract that operation which it cannot prevent in any way whatsoever. It has its full weight, its full range, and its uncontrolled operation on the electors exactly as it had before. 3rd. Nor, thirdly, does it abate the interest or inclination of ministers to apply that influence to the electors: on the contrary, it renders it much more necessary to them, if they seek to have a majority in Parliament, to increase the means of that influence, and redouble their diligence, and to sharpen dexterity in the application. The whole effect of the bill is, therefore, the removing the application of some part of the influence from the elected to the electors, and further to strengthen and extend a court interest already great and powerful in boroughs: here to fix their magazines and places of arms, and thus to make them the principal, not the secondary, theatre of their manoeuvres for securing a determined majority in Parliament.

I believe nobody will deny that the electors are corruptible. They are men,—it is saying nothing worse of them; many of them are but ill informed in their minds, many feeble in their circumstances, easily overreached, easily seduced. If they are many, the wages of corruption are the lower; and would to God it were not rather a contemptible and hypocritical adulation than a charitable sentiment, to say that there is already no debauchery, no corruption, no bribery, no perjury, no blind fury and interested faction among the electors in many parts of this kingdom!—nor is it surprising, or at all blamable, in that class of private men, when they see their neighbors aggrandized, and themselves poor and virtuous without that *éclat* or dignity which attends men in higher situations.

But admit it were true that the great mass of the electors were too vast an object for court influence to grasp or extend to, and that in despair they must abandon it; he must be very ignorant of the state of every popular interest, who does not know that in all the corporations, all the open boroughs, indeed in every district of the kingdom, there is some leading man, some agitator, some wealthy merchant or considerable manufacturer, some active attorney, some popular preacher, some money-lender, &c., &c., who is followed by the whole flock. This is the style of all free countries.

Multum in Fabiâ valet hic, valet ille Velinâ;
Cuilibet hic fasces dabit, eripietque curule.

These spirits, each of which informs and governs his own little orb, are neither so many, nor so little powerful, nor so incorruptible, but that a minister may, as he does frequently, find means of gaining them, and through them all their followers. To establish, therefore, a very general influence among electors will no more be found an impracticable project than to gain an undue influence over members of Parliament. Therefore I am apprehensive that this bill, though it shifts the place of the disorder, does by no means relieve the Constitution. I went through almost every contested election in the beginning of this Parliament, and acted as a manager in very many of them; by which, though as at a school of pretty severe and rugged discipline, I came to have some degree of instruction concerning the means by which Parliamentary interests are in general procured and supported.

Theory, I know, would suppose that every general election is to the representative a day of judgment, in which he appears before his constituents to account for the use of the talent with which they intrusted him, and for the improvement he has made of it for the public advantage. It would be so, if every corruptible representative were to find an enlightened and incorruptible constituent. But the practice and knowledge of the world will not suffer us to be ignorant that the Constitution on paper is one thing, and in fact and experience is another. We must know that the candidate, instead of trusting at his election to the testimony of his behavior in Parliament, must bring the testimony of a large sum of money, the capacity of liberal expense in entertainments, the power of serving and obliging the rulers of corporations, of winning over the popular leaders of political clubs, associations, and neighborhoods. It is ten thousand times more necessary to show himself a man of power than a man of integrity, in almost all the elections with which I have been acquainted. Elections, therefore, become a matter of heavy expense; and if contests are frequent, to many they will become a matter of an expense totally ruinous, which no fortunes can bear, but least of all the landed fortunes, incumbered as they often, indeed as they mostly are, with debts, with portions, with jointures, and tied up in the hands of the possessor by the limitations of settlement. It is a material, it is in my opinion a lasting consideration, in all the questions concerning election. Let no one think the charges of elections a trivial matter.

The charge, therefore, of elections ought never to be lost sight of in a question concerning their frequency; because the grand object you seek is independence. Independence of mind will ever be more or less influenced by independence of fortune; and if every three years the exhausting sluices of entertainments, drinkings, open houses, to say nothing of bribery, are to be periodically drawn up and renewed,—if government favors, for which now, in some shape or other, the whole race of men are candidates, are to be called for upon every occasion, I see that private fortunes will be washed away, and every, even to the least, trace of independence borne down by the torrent. I do not seriously think this Constitution, even to the wrecks of it, could survive five triennial elections. If you are to fight the battle, you must put on the armor of the ministry, you must call in the public to the aid of private money. The expense of the last election has been computed (and I am persuaded that it has not been overrated) at 1,500,000*l.*,—three shillings in the pound more in [than?] the land-tax. About the close of the last Parliament and the beginning of this, several agents for boroughs went about, and I remember well that it was in every one of their mouths, "Sir, your election will cost you three thousand pounds, if you are independent; but if the ministry supports you, it may be done for two, and perhaps for less." And, indeed, the thing spoke itself. Where a living was to be got for one, a commission in the army for another, a lift in the navy for a third, and custom-house offices scattered about without measure or number, who doubts but money may be saved? The Treasury may even add money: but, indeed, it is superfluous. A gentleman of two thousand a year, who meets another of the same fortune, fights with equal arms; but if to one of the candidates you add a thousand a year in places for himself, and a power of giving away as much among others, one must, or there is no truth in arithmetical demonstration, ruin his adversary, if he is to meet him and to fight with him every third year. It will be said I do not allow for the operation of character: but I do; and I know it will have its weight in most elections,—perhaps it may be decisive in some; but there are few in which it will prevent great expenses.

The destruction of independent fortunes will be the consequence on the part of the candidate. What will be the consequence of triennial corruption, triennial drunkenness, triennial idleness, triennial lawsuits, litigations, prosecutions, triennial frenzy,—of society dissolved, industry interrupted, ruined,—of those personal hatreds that will never be suffered to soften, those animosities and feuds which will be rendered immortal, those quarrels which are never to be appeased,—morals vitiated and gangrened to the vitals? I think no stable and useful advantages were ever made by the money got at elections by the voter, but all he gets is doubly lost to the public: it is money given to diminish the general stock of the community, which is in the industry of the subject. I am sure that it is a good while before he or his family settle again to their business. Their heads will never cool; the temptations of elections will be forever glittering before their eyes. They will all grow politicians; every one, quitting his business, will choose to enrich himself by his vote. They will all take the gauging-rod; new places will be made for them; they will run to the custom-house quay; their looms and ploughs will be deserted.

So was Rome destroyed by the disorders of continual elections, though those of Rome were sober disorders. They had nothing but faction, bribery, bread, and stage-plays, to debauch them: we have the inflammation of liquor superadded, a fury hotter than any of them. There the contest was only between citizen and citizen: here you have the contests of ambitious citizens of one side supported by the crown to oppose to the efforts (let it be so) of private and unsupported ambition on the other. Yet Rome was destroyed by the frequency and charge of elections, and the monstrous expense of an unremitted courtship to the people. I think, therefore, the independent candidate and elector may each be destroyed by it, the whole body of the community be an infinite sufferer, and a vicious ministry the only gainer.

Gentlemen, I know, feel the weight of this argument; they agree, that this would be the consequence of more frequent elections, if things were to continue as they are. But they think the greatness and frequency of the evil would itself be a remedy for it,—that, sitting but for a short time, the member would not find it worth while to make such vast expenses, while the fear of their constituents will hold them the more effectually to their duty.

To this I answer, that experience is full against them. This is no new thing; we have had triennial Parliaments; at no period of time were seats more eagerly contested. The expenses of elections ran higher, taking the state of all charges, than they do now. The expense of entertainments was such, that an act, equally severe and ineffectual, was made against it; every monument of the time bears witness of the expense, and most of the acts against corruption in elections were then made; all the writers talked of it and lamented it. Will any one think that a corporation will be contented with a bowl of punch or a piece of beef the less, because elections are every three, instead of every seven years? Will they change their wine for ale, because they are to get more ale three years hence? Don't think it. Will they make fewer demands for the advantages of patronage in favors and offices, because their member is brought more under their power? We have not only our own historical experience in England upon this subject, but we have the experience coexisting with us in Ireland, where, since their Parliament has been shortened, the expense of elections has been so far from being lowered, that it has been very near doubled. Formerly they sat for the king's life; the ordinary charge of a seat in Parliament was then fifteen hundred pounds. They now sit eight years, four sessions; it is now twenty-five hundred pounds, and upwards. The spirit of *emulation* has also been extremely increased, and all who are acquainted with the tone of that country have no doubt that the spirit is still growing, that new candidates will take the field, that the contests will be more violent, and the expenses of elections larger than ever.

It never can be otherwise. A seat in this House, for good purposes, for bad purposes, for no purposes at all, (except the mere consideration derived from being concerned in the public counsels,) will ever be a first-rate object of ambition in England. Ambition is no exact calculator. Avarice itself does not calculate strictly, when it games. One thing is certain,—that in this political game the great lottery of power is that into which men will purchase with millions of chances against them. In Turkey, where the place, where the fortune, where the head itself are so insecure that scarcely any have died in their beds for ages, so that the bowstring is the natural death of bashaws, yet in no country is power and distinction (precarious enough, God knows, in all) sought for with such boundless avidity,—as if the value of place was enhanced by the danger and insecurity of its tenure. Nothing will ever make a seat in this House not an object of desire to numbers by any means or at any charge, but the depriving it of all power and all dignity. This would do it. This is the true and only nostrum for that purpose. But an House of Commons without power and without dignity, either in itself or in its members, is no House of Commons for the purposes of this Constitution.

But they will be afraid to act ill, if they know that the day of their account is always near. I wish it were true; but it is not: here again we have experience, and experience is against us. The distemper of this age is a poverty of spirit and of genius: it is trifling, it is futile, worse than ignorant, superficially taught, with the politics and morals of girls at a boarding-school rather than of men and statesmen: but it is not yet desperately wicked, or so scandalously venal as in former times. Did not a triennial Parliament give up the national dignity, approve the peace of Utrecht, and almost give up everything else, in taking every step to defeat the Protestant succession? Was not the Constitution saved by those who had no election at all to go to, the Lords, because the court applied to electors, and by various means carried them from their true interests, so that the Tory ministry had a majority without an application to a single member? Now as to the conduct of the members, it was then far from pure and independent. Bribery was infinitely more flagrant. A predecessor of yours, Mr. Speaker, put the question of his own expulsion for bribery. Sir William Musgrave was a wise man, a grave man, an independent man, a man of good fortune and good family; however, he carried on, while in opposition, a traffic, a shameful traffic, with the ministry. Bishop Burnet knew of six thousand pounds which he had received at one payment. I believe the payment of sums in hard money, plain, naked bribery, is rare amongst us. It was then far from uncommon.

A triennial was near ruining, a septennial Parliament saved your Constitution; nor, perhaps, have you ever known a more flourishing period, for the union of national prosperity, dignity, and liberty, than the sixty years you have passed under that constitution of Parliament.

The shortness of time in which they are to reap the profits of iniquity is far from checking the avidity of corrupt men; it renders them infinitely more ravenous. They rush violently and precipitately on their object; they lose all regard to decorum. The moments of profits are precious; never are men so wicked as during a general mortality. It was so in the great plague at Athens, every symptom of which (and this its worse symptom amongst the rest) is so finely related by a great historian of antiquity. It was so in the plague of London in 1665. It appears in soldiers, sailors, &c. Whoever would contrive to render the life of man much shorter than it is would, I am satisfied, find the surest receipt for increasing the wickedness of our nature.

Thus, in my opinion, the shortness of a triennial sitting would have the following ill effects: It would make the member more shamelessly and shockingly corrupt; it would increase his dependence on those who could best support him at his election; it would wrack and tear to pieces the fortunes of those who stood upon their own fortunes and their private interest; it would make the electors infinitely more venal; and it would make the whole body of the people, who are, whether they have votes or not, concerned in elections, more lawless, more idle, more debauched; it would utterly destroy the sobriety, the industry, the integrity, the simplicity of all the people, and undermine, I am much afraid, the deepest and best-laid foundations of the commonwealth.

Those who have spoken and written upon this subject without doors do not so much deny the probable existence of these inconveniences in their measure as they trust for their prevention to remedies of various sorts which they propose. First, a place bill. But if this will not do, as they fear it will not, then, they say, We will have a rotation, and a certain number of you shall be rendered incapable of being elected for ten years. Then for the electors, they shall ballot. The members of Parliament also shall decide by ballot. A fifth project is the change of the present legal representation of the kingdom. On all this I shall observe, that it will be very unsuitable to your wisdom to adopt the project of a bill to which there are objections insuperable by anything in the bill itself, upon the hope that those objections may be removed by subsequent projects, every one of which is full of difficulties of its own, and which are all of them very essential alterations in the Constitution. This seems very irregular and unusual. If anything should make this a very doubtful measure, what can make it more so than that in the opinion of its advocates it would aggravate all our old inconveniences in such a manner as to require a total alteration in the Constitution of the kingdom? If the remedies are proper in triennial, they will not be less so in septennial elections. Let us try them first,—see how the House relishes them,—see how they will operate in the nation,—and then, having felt your way, and prepared against these inconveniences. . . .

The honorable gentleman sees that I respect the principle upon which he goes, as well as his intentions and his abilities. He will believe that I do not differ from him wantonly and on trivial grounds. He is very sure that it was not his embracing one way which determined me to take the other. *I* have not in newspapers, to derogate from his fair fame with the nation, printed the first rude sketch of his bill with ungenerous and invidious comments. *I* have not, in conversations industriously circulated about the town, and talked on the benches of this House, attributed his conduct to motives low and unworthy, and as groundless as they are injurious. *I* do not affect to be frightened with this proposition, as if some hideous spectre had started from hell, which was to be sent back again by every form of exorcism and every kind of incantation. *I* invoke no Acheron to overwhelm him in the whirlpools of its muddy gulf. *I* do not tell the respectable mover and seconder, by a perversion of their sense and expressions, that their proposition halts between the ridiculous and the dangerous. *I* am not one of those who start up, three at a time, and fall upon and strike at him with so much eagerness that our daggers hack one another in his sides. My honorable friend has not brought down a spirited imp of chivalry to win the first achievement and blazon of arms on his milk-white shield in a field listed against him,—nor brought out the generous offspring of lions, and said to them,—"Not against that side of the forest! beware of that!—here is the prey, where you are to fasten your paws!"—and seasoning his unpractised jaws with blood, tell him,—"This is the milk for which you are to thirst hereafter!" *We* furnish at his expense no holiday,—nor suspend hell, that a crafty Ixion may have rest from his wheel,—nor give the common adversary (if he be a common adversary) reason to say,—"I would have put in my word to oppose, but the eagerness of your allies in your social war was such that I could not break in upon you." I hope he sees and feels, and that every member sees and feels along with him, the difference between amicable dissent and civil discord.

Speech on a Committee to Inquire into the State of the Representation of the Commons in Parliament

In 1782 the young William Pitt joined the radical reformers outside Parliament in urging a reduction of rotten boroughs, an increase of representation for large industrial cities, and an extension of the suffrage. In Burke's speech of May 7, 1782, a full seven years before the French Revolution, he thundered against anyone who would change constitutional structures "upon any given theory." The unreformed system should be left alone because "it has existed time out of mind." This speech dramatically indicates that Burke's profound conservatism was in place long before what he saw as the horrific sins of the French revolutionaries.

MR. SPEAKER,—We have now discovered, at the close of the eighteenth century, that the Constitution of England, which for a series of ages had been the proud distinction of this country, always the admiration and sometimes the envy of the wise and learned in every other nation,—we have discovered that this boasted Constitution, in the most boasted part of it, is a gross imposition upon the understanding of mankind, an insult to their feelings, and acting by contrivances destructive to the best and most valuable interests of the people. Our political architects have taken a survey of the fabric of the British Constitution. It is singular that they report nothing against the crown, nothing against the lords: but in the House of Commons everything is unsound; it is ruinous in every part; it is infested by the dry rot, and ready to tumble about our ears without their immediate help. You know by the faults they find what are their ideas of the alteration. As all government stands upon opinion, they know that the way utterly to destroy it is to remove that opinion, to take away all reverence, all confidence from it; and then, at the first blast of public discontent and popular tumult, it tumbles to the ground.

In considering this question, they who oppose it oppose it on different grounds. One is in the nature of a previous question: that some alterations may be expedient, but that this is not the time for making them. The other is, that no essential alterations are at all wanting, and that neither *now* nor at *any* time is it prudent or safe to be meddling with the fundamental principles and ancient tried usages of our Constitution,—that our representation is as nearly perfect as the necessary imperfection of human affairs and of human creatures will suffer it to be,—and that it is a subject of prudent and honest use and thankful enjoyment, and not of captious criticism and rash experiment.

On the other side there are two parties, who proceed on two grounds, in my opinion, as they state them, utterly irreconcilable. The one is juridical, the other political. The one is in the nature of a claim of right, on the supposed rights of man as man: this party desire the decision of a suit. The other ground, as far as I can divine what it directly means, is, that the representation is not so politically framed as to answer the theory of its institution. As to the claim of *right*, the meanest petitioner, the most gross and ignorant, is as good as the best: in some respects his claim is more favorable, on account of his ignorance; his weakness, his poverty, and distress only add to his titles; he sues *in forma pauperis*; he ought to be a favorite of the court. But when the *other* ground is taken, when the question is political, when a new constitution is to be made on a sound theory of government, then the presumptuous pride of didactic ignorance is to be excluded from the counsel in this high and arduous matter, which often bids defiance to the experience of the wisest. The first claims a personal representation; the latter rejects it with scorn and fervor. The language of the first party is plain and intelligible; they who plead an absolute right cannot be satisfied with anything short of personal representation, because all *natural* rights must be the rights of individuals, as by *nature* there is no such thing as politic or corporate personality: all these ideas are mere fictions of law, they are creatures of voluntary institution; men as men are individuals, and nothing else. They, therefore, who reject the principle of natural and personal representation are essentially and eternally at variance with those who claim it. As to the first sort of reformers, it is ridiculous to talk to them of the British Constitution upon any or upon all of its bases: for they lay it down, that every man ought to govern, himself, and that, where he cannot go, himself, he must send his representative; that all other government is usurpation, and is so far from having a claim to our obedience, it is not only our right, but our duty, to resist it. Nine tenths of the reformers argue thus,—that is, on the natural right.

It is impossible not to make some reflection on the nature of this claim, or avoid a comparison between the extent of the principle and the present object of the demand. If this claim be founded, it is clear to what it goes. The House of Commons, in that light, undoubtedly, is no representative of the people, as a collection of individuals. Nobody pretends it, nobody can justify such an assertion. When you come to examine into this claim of right, founded on the right of self-government in each individual, you find the thing demanded infinitely short of the principle of the demand. What! *one third* only of the legislature, and of the government no share at all? What sort of treaty of partition is this for those who have an inherent right to the whole? Give them all they ask, and your grant is still a cheat: for how comes only a third to be their younger-children's fortune in this settlement? How came they neither to have the choice of kings, or lords, or judges, or generals, or admirals, or bishops, or priests, or ministers, or justices of peace? Why, what have you to answer in favor of the prior rights of the crown and peerage but this: Our Constitution is a prescriptive constitution; it is a constitution whose sole authority is, that it has existed time out of mind? It is settled in these *two* portions against one, legislatively,—and in the whole of the judicature, the whole of the federal capacity, of the executive, the prudential, and the financial administration, in one alone. Nor was your House of Lords and the prerogatives of the crown settled on any adjudication in favor of natural rights: for they could never be so partitioned. Your king, your lords, your judges, your juries, grand and little, all are prescriptive; and what proves it is the disputes, not yet concluded, and never near becoming so, when any of them first originated. Prescription is the most solid of all titles, not only to property, but, which is to secure that property, to government. They harmonize with each other, and give mutual aid to one another. It is accompanied with another ground of authority in the constitution of the human mind, presumption. It is a presumption in favor of any settled scheme of government against any untried project, that a nation has long existed and flourished under it. It is a better presumption even of the *choice* of a nation,—far better than any sudden and temporary arrangement by actual election. Because a nation is not an idea only of local extent and individual momentary aggregation, but it is an idea of continuity which extends in time as well as in numbers and in space. And this is a choice not of one day or one set of people, not a tumultuary and giddy choice; it is a deliberate election of ages and of generations; it is a constitution made by what is ten thousand times better than choice; it is made by the peculiar circumstances, occasions, tempers, dispositions, and moral, civil, and social habitudes of the people, which disclose themselves only in a long space of time. It is a vestment which accommodates itself to the body. Nor is prescription of government formed upon blind, unmeaning prejudices. For man is a most unwise and a most wise being. The individual is foolish; the multitude, for the moment, is foolish, when they act without deliberation; but the species is wise, and, when time is given to it, as a species, it almost always acts right.

The reason for the crown as it is, for the lords as they are, is my reason for the commons as they are, the electors as they are. Now if the crown, and the lords, and the judicatures are all prescriptive, so is the House of Commons of the very same origin, and of no other. We and our electors have their powers and privileges both made and circumscribed by prescription, as much to the full as the other parts; and as such we have always claimed them, and on no other title. The House of Commons is a legislative body corporate by prescription, not made upon any given theory, but existing prescriptively,—just like the rest. This prescription has made it essentially what it is, an aggregate collection of three parts, knights, citizens, burgesses. The question is, whether this has been always so, since the House of Commons has taken its present shape and circumstances, and has been an essential operative part of the Constitution,—which, I take it, it has been for at least five hundred years.

This I resolve to myself in the affirmative: and then another question arises:—Whether this House stands firm upon its ancient foundations, and is not, by time and accidents, so declined from its perpendicular as to want the hand of the wise and experienced architects of the day to set it upright again, and to prop and buttress it up for duration;—whether it continues true to the principles upon which it has hitherto stood;—whether this be *de facto* the constitution of the House of Commons, as it has been since the time that the House of Commons has without dispute become a necessary and an efficient part of the British Constitution. To ask whether a thing which has always been the same stands to its usual principle seems to me to be perfectly absurd: for how do you know the principles, but from the construction? and if that remains the same, the principles remain the same. It is true that to say your Constitution is what it has been is no sufficient defence for those who say it is a bad constitution. It is an answer to those who say that it is a degenerate constitution. To those who say it is a bad one, I answer, Look to its effects. In all moral machinery, the moral results are its test.

On what grounds do we go to restore our Constitution to what it has been at some given period, or to reform and reconstruct it upon principles more conformable to a sound theory of government? A prescriptive government, such as ours, never was the work of any legislator, never was made upon any foregone theory. It seems to me a preposterous way of reasoning, and a perfect confusion of ideas, to take the theories which learned and speculative men have made from that government, and then, supposing it made on those theories which were made from it, to accuse the government as not corresponding with them. I do not vilify theory and speculation: no, because that would be to vilify reason itself. *Neque decipitur ratio, neque decipit unquam*. No,—whenever I speak against theory, I mean always a weak, erroneous, fallacious, unfounded, or imperfect theory; and one of the ways of discovering that it is a false theory is by comparing it with practice. This is the true touchstone of all theories which regard man and the affairs of men,—Does it suit his nature in general?—does it suit his nature as modified by his habits?

The more frequently this affair is discussed, the stronger the case appears to the sense and the feelings of mankind. I have no more doubt than I entertain of my existence, that this very thing, which is stated as an horrible thing, is the means of the preservation of our Constitution whilst it lasts,—of curing it of many of the disorders which, attending every species of institution, would attend the principle of an exact local representation, or a representation on the principle of numbers. If you reject personal representation, you are pushed upon expedience; and then what they wish us to do is, to prefer their speculations on that subject to the happy experience of this country, of a growing liberty and a growing prosperity for five hundred years. Whatever respect I have for their talents, this, for one, I will not do. Then what is the standard of expedience? Expedience is that which is good for the community, and good for every individual in it. Now this expedience is the *desideratum*, to be sought either without the experience of means or with that experience. If without, as in case of the fabrication of a new commonwealth, I will hear the learned arguing what promises to be expedient; but if we are to judge of a commonwealth actually existing, the first thing I inquire is, What has been *found* expedient or inexpedient? And I will not take their *promise* rather than the *performance* of the Constitution.

. . . But no, this was not the cause of the discontents. I went through most of the northern parts,—the Yorkshire election was then raging; the year before, through most of the western countries,—Bath, Bristol,

Gloucester: not one word, either in the towns or country, on the subject of representation; much on the receipt tax, something on Mr. Fox's ambition; much greater apprehension of danger from thence than from want of representation. One would think that the ballast of the ship was shifted with us, and that our Constitution had the gunwale under water. But can you fairly and distinctly point out what one evil or grievance has happened which you can refer to the representative not following the opinion of his constituents? What one symptom do we find of this inequality? But it is not an arithmetical inequality with which we ought to trouble ourselves. If there be a moral, a political equality, this is the *desideratum* in our Constitution, and in every constitution in the world. Moral inequality is as between places and between classes. Now, I ask, what advantage do you find that the places which abound in representation possess over others in which it is more scanty, in security for freedom, in security for justice, or in any one of those means of procuring temporal prosperity and eternal happiness, the ends for which society was formed? Are the local interests of Cornwall and Wiltshire, for instance, their roads, canals, their prisons, their police, better than Yorkshire, Warwickshire, or Staffordshire? Warwick has members: is Warwick or Stafford more opulent, happy, or free than Newcastle, or than Birmingham? Is Wiltshire the pampered favorite, whilst Yorkshire, like the child of the bondwoman, is turned out to the desert? This is like the unhappy persons who live, if they can be said to live, in the statical chair,—who are ever feeling their pulse, and who do not judge of health by the aptitude of the body to perform its functions, but by their ideas of what ought to be the true balance between the several secretions. Is a committee of Cornwall, &c., thronged, and the others deserted? No. You have an equal representation, because you have men equally interested in the prosperity of the whole, who are involved in the general interest and the general sympathy; and, perhaps, these places furnishing a superfluity of public agents and administrators, (whether in strictness they are representatives or not I do not mean to inquire, but they are agents and administrators,) they will stand clearer of local interests, passions, prejudices, and cabals than the others, and therefore preserve the balance of the parts, and with a more general view and a more steady hand than the rest. . . .

In every political proposal we must not leave out of the question the political views and object of the proposer; and these we discover, not by what he says, but by the principles he lays down. "I mean," says he, "a moderate and temperate reform: that is, I mean to do as little good as possible." If the Constitution be what you represent it, and there be no danger in the change, you do wrong not to make the reform commensurate to the abuse. Fine reformer, indeed! generous donor! What is the cause of this parsimony of the liberty which you dole out to the people? Why all this limitation in giving blessings and benefits to mankind? You admit that there is an extreme in liberty, which may be infinitely noxious to those who are to receive it, and which in the end will leave them no liberty at all. I think so, too. They know it, and they feel it. The question is, then, What is the standard of that extreme? What that gentleman, and the associations, or some parts of their phalanxes, think proper? Then our liberties are in their pleasure; it depends on their arbitrary will how far I shall be free. I will have none of that freedom. If, therefore, the standard of moderation be sought for, I will seek for it. Where? Not in their fancies, nor in my own: I will seek for it where I know it is to be found,—in the Constitution I actually enjoy. Here it says to an encroaching prerogative,—"Your sceptre has its length; you cannot add an hair to your head, or a gem to your crown, but what an eternal law has given to it." Here it says to an overweening peerage,—"Your pride finds banks that it cannot overflow": here to a tumultuous and giddy people,—"There is a bound to the raging of the sea." Our Constitution is like our island, which uses and restrains its subject sea; in vain the waves roar. In that Constitution, I know, and exultingly I feel, both that I am free, and that I am not free dangerously to myself or to others. I know that no power on earth, acting as I ought to do, can touch my life, my liberty, or my property. I have that inward and dignified consciousness of my own security and independence, which constitutes, and is the only thing which does constitute, the proud and comfortable sentiment of freedom in the human breast. I know, too, and I bless God for, my safe mediocrity: I know, that, if I possessed all the talents of the gentlemen on the side of the House I sit, and on the other, I cannot, by royal favor, or by popular delusion, or by oligarchical cabal, elevate myself above a certain very limited point, so as to endanger my own fall, or the ruin of my country. I know there is an order that keeps things fast in their place: it is made to us, and we are made to it. Why not ask another wife, other children, another body, another mind?

The great object of most of these reformers is, to prepare the destruction of the Constitution, by disgracing and discrediting the House of Commons. For they think, (prudently, in my opinion,) that, if they can persuade the nation that the House of Commons is so constituted as not to secure the public liberty, not to have a proper connection with the public interests, so constituted as not either actually or virtually to be the representative of the people, it will be easy to prove that a government composed of a monarchy, an oligarchy chosen by the crown, and such a House of Commons, whatever good can be in such a system, can by no means be a system of free government.

The Constitution of England is never to have a quietus; it is to be continually vilified, attacked, reproached, resisted; instead of being the hope and sure anchor in all storms, instead of being the means of redress to all grievances, itself is the grand grievance of the nation, our shame instead of our glory. If the only specific plan proposed, individual personal representation, is directly rejected by the person who is looked on as the great support of this business, then the only way of considering it is a question of convenience. An honorable gentleman prefers the individual to the present. He therefore himself sees no middle term whatsoever, and therefore prefers, of what he sees, the individual: this is the only thing distinct and sensible that has been advocated. He has, then, a scheme, which is the individual representation,—he is not at a loss, not inconsistent,—which scheme the other right honorable gentleman reprobates. Now what does this go to, but to lead directly to anarchy? For to discredit the only government which he either possesses or can project, what is this but to destroy all government? and this is anarchy. My right honorable friend, in supporting this motion, disgraces his friends and justifies his enemies in order to blacken the Constitution of his country, even of that House of Commons which supported him. There is a difference between a moral or political exposure of a public evil relative to the administration of government, whether in men or systems, and a declaration of defects, real or supposed, in the fundamental constitution of your country. The first may be cured in the individual by the motives of religion, virtue, honor, fear, shame, or interest. Men may be made to abandon also false systems, by exposing their absurdity or mischievous tendency to their own better thoughts, or to the contempt or indignation of the public; and after all, if they should exist, and exist uncorrected, they only disgrace individuals as fugitive opinions. But it is quite otherwise with the frame and constitution of the state: if that is disgraced, patriotism is destroyed in its very source. No man has ever willingly obeyed, much less was desirous of defending with his blood, a mischievous and absurd scheme of government. Our first, our dearest, most comprehensive relation, our country, is gone.

It suggests melancholy reflections, in consequence of the strange course we have long held, that we are now no longer quarrelling about the character, or about the conduct of men, or the tenor of measures, but we are grown out of humor with the English Constitution itself: this is become the object of the animosity of Englishmen. This Constitution in former days used to be the admiration and the envy of the world: it was the pattern for politicians, the theme of the eloquent, the meditation of the philosopher, in every part of the world. As to Englishmen, it was their pride, their consolation. By it they lived, for it they were ready to die. Its defects, if it had any, were partly covered by partiality, and partly borne by prudence. Now all its excellencies are forgot, its faults are now forcibly dragged into day, exaggerated by every artifice of representation. It is despised and rejected of men, and every device and invention of ingenuity or idleness set up in opposition or in preference to it. It is to this humor, and it is to the measures growing out of it, that I set myself (I hope not alone) in the most determined opposition. Never before did we at any time in this country meet upon the theory of our frame of government, to sit in judgment on the Constitution of our country, to call it as a delinquent before us, and to accuse it of every defect and every vice,—to see whether it, an object of our veneration, even our adoration, did or did not accord with a preconceived scheme in the minds of certain gentlemen. Cast your eyes on the journals of Parliament. It is for fear of losing the inestimable treasure we have that I do not venture to game it out of my hands for the vain hope of improving it. I look with filial reverence on the Constitution of my country, and never will cut it in pieces, and put it into the kettle of any magician, in order to boil it, with the puddle of their compounds, into youth and vigor. On the contrary, I will drive away such pretenders; I will nurse its venerable age, and with lenient arts extend a parent's breath.

Sketch of a Negro Code

Burke opposed, on moral and religious grounds, the slave trade and slavery itself. In 1792 he drafted a code for Henry Dundas, one of the king's principal secretaries of state. It is striking in its humane sentiments and in its envisioning a gradual emancipation of West Indian slaves.

Dear Sir,

I should have been punctual in sending you the sketch I promised of my old African Code, if some friends from London had not come in upon me last Saturday, and engaged me till noon this day; I send this pacquet by one of them, who is still here. If what I send be, as under present circumstances it must be, imperfect, you will excuse it, as being done near twelve years ago. About four years since I made an abstract of it, upon which I cannot at present lay my hands; but I hope the marginal heads will in some measure supply it.

If the African trade could be considered with regard to itself only, and as a single object, I should think the utter abolition to be, on the whole, more advisable than any scheme of regulation and reform. Rather than suffer it to continue as it is, I heartily wish it at an end. What has been lately done has been done by a popular spirit, which seldom calls for, and indeed very rarely relishes, a system made up of a great variety of parts, and which is to operate its effect in a great length of time. The people like short methods; the consequences of which they sometimes have reason to repent of. Abolition is but a single act. To prove the nature of the trade, and to expose it properly, required, indeed, a vast collection of materials, which have been laboriously collected, and compiled with great judgment. It required also much perseverance and address to excite the spirit which has been excited without-doors, and which has carried it through. The greatest eloquence ever displayed in the House has been employed to second the efforts which have been made abroad. All this, however, leads but to one single resolve. When this was done, all was done. I speak of absolute and immediate abolition, the point which the first motions went to, and which is in effect still pressed; though in this session, according to order, it cannot take effect. A *remote* and a *gradual* abolition, though they may be connected, are not the same thing. The idea of the House seems to me, if I rightly comprehend it, that the two things are to be combined; that is to say, that the trade is gradually to decline, and to cease entirely at a determinate period. To make the abolition gradual, the regulations must operate as a strong discouragement. But it is much to be feared, that a trade continued and discouraged, and with a sentence of death passed upon it, will perpetuate much ill blood between those who struggle for the abolition, and those who contend for an effectual continuance.

At the time when I formed the plan which I have the honour to transmit to you, an abolition of the slave trade would have appeared a very chimerical project. My plan, therefore, supposes the continued existence of that commerce. Taking for my basis, that I had an incurable evil to deal with, I cast about how I should make it as small an evil as possible, and draw out of it some collateral good.

In turning the matter over in my mind at that time, and since, I never was able to consider the African trade upon a ground disconnected with the employment of negroes in the West Indies, and distinct from their condition in the plantations whereon they serve. I conceived that the true origin of the trade was not in the place it was begun at, but at the place of its final destination. I therefore was, and still am, of opinion, that the whole work ought to be taken up together; and that a gradual abolition of slavery in the West Indies ought to go hand in hand with anything which should be done with regard to its supply from the coast of Africa. I could not trust a cessation of the demand for this supply to the mere operation of any abstract principle, (such as, that if their supply was cut off, the planters would encourage and produce an effectual population,) knowing that nothing can be more uncertain than the operation of general principles, if they are not embodied in specific regulations. I am very apprehensive that so long as the slavery continues some means for its supply will be found. If so, I am persuaded that it is better to allow the evil, in order to correct it, than by endeavouring to forbid, what we cannot be able wholly to prevent, to leave it under an illegal, and therefore an unreformed, existence. It is not, that my plan does not lead to the extinction of the slave trade; but it is through a very slow progress, the chief effect of which is to be operated in our own plantations by rendering, in a length of time, all foreign supply unnecessary. It was my wish, whilst the slavery continued, and the consequent commerce, to take such measures as to civilize the coast of Africa by the trade, which now renders it more barbarous; and to lead by degrees to a more reputable, and, possibly, a more profitable, connexion with it, than we maintain at present.

I am sure that you will consider, as a mark of my confidence in yours and Mr. Pitt's honour and generosity, that I venture to put into your hands a scheme composed of many and intricate combinations, without a full explanatory preface, or any attendant notes, to point out the principles upon which I proceeded in every regulation, which I have proposed towards the civilization and gradual manumission of negroes in the two hemispheres. I confess, I trust infinitely more (according to the sound principles of those who ever have at any time meliorated the state of mankind) to the effect and influence of religion, than to all the rest of the regulations put together.

Whenever, in my proposed reformation, we take our *point of departure* from a state of slavery, we must precede the donation of freedom by disposing the minds of the objects to a disposition to receive it without danger to themselves or to us. The process of bringing *free* savages to order and civilization is very different. When a state of slavery is that upon which we are to work, the very means which lead to liberty must partake of compulsion. The minds of men being crippled with that restraint can do nothing for themselves; everything must be done for them. The regulations can owe little to consent. Everything must be the creature of power. Hence it is, that regulations must be multiplied; particularly as you have two parties to deal with. The planter you must at once restrain and support; and you must control, at the same time that you ease, the servant. This necessarily makes the work a matter of care, labour, and expense. It becomes in its nature complex. But I think neither the object impracticable nor the expense intolerable; and I am fully convinced that the cause of humanity would be far more benefited by the continuance of the trade and servitude, regulated and reformed, than by the total destruction of both or either. What I propose, however, is but a beginning of a course of measures, which an experience of the effects of the evil and the reform will enable the legislature hereafter to supply and correct. . . .

And whereas the condition of persons in a state of slavery is such, that they are utterly unable to take advantage of any remedy which the laws may provide for their protection, and the amendment of their condition, and have not the proper means of pursuing any process for the same, but are and must be under guardianship: and whereas it is not fitting that they should be under the sole guardianship of their masters, or their attorney and overseers, to whom their grievances, whenever they suffer any, must ordinarily be owing;

1. Be it therefore enacted, that his Majesty's attorney-general for the time being successively shall, by his office, exercise the trust and employment of protector of negroes within the island, in which he is or shall be attorney-general to his Majesty, his heirs and successors: and that the said attorney-general, protector of negroes, is hereby authorized to hear any complaint on the part of any negro or negroes, and inquire into the same, or to institute an inquiry *ex officio* into any abuses, and to call before him and examine witnesses upon oath, relative to the subject matter of the said official inquiry or complaint; and it is hereby enacted and declared, that the said attorney-general, protector of negroes, is hereby authorized and empowered, at his discretion, to file an information *ex officio* for any offences committed against the provisions of this act, or for any misdemeanours or wrongs against the said negroes, or any of them.

2. And it is further enacted, that in all trials of such informations the said protector of negroes may and is hereby authorized to challenge, peremptorily, a number not exceeding ——— of the jury, who shall be impanelled to try the charge in the said information contained.

3. And be it enacted, that the said attorney-general, protector of negroes, shall appoint inspectors, not exceeding the number of ———, at his discretion; and the said inspectors shall be placed in convenient districts in each island severally, or shall twice in the year make a circuit in the same, according to the direction which they shall receive from the protector of negroes aforesaid; and the inspectors shall, and they are hereby required, twice in the year, to report in writing to the protector aforesaid the state and condition of the negroes in their districts, or on their circuit severally, the number, sex, age, and occupation of the said negroes on each plantation; and the overseer, or chief manager on each plantation, is hereby required to furnish an account thereof, within [ten days] after the demand of the said inspectors, and to permit the inspector or inspectors aforesaid to examine into the same; and the said inspectors shall set forth, in the said report, the distempers to which the negroes are most liable in the several parts of the island.

4. And be it enacted, that the said protector of negroes, by and with the consent of the governor and chief judge of each island, shall form instructions, by which the said inspectors shall discharge their trust in the manner the least capable of exciting any unreasonable hopes in the said

negroes, or of weakening the proper authority of the overseer, and shall transmit them to one of his Majesty's principal secretaries of state; and when sent back with his approbation, the same shall become the rule for the conduct of the said inspectors.

5. And be it enacted, that the said attorney-general, protector of negroes, shall appoint an office for registering all proceedings relative to the duty of his place, as protector of negroes, and shall appoint his chief clerk to be registrar, with a salary not exceeding ———.

6. And be it enacted, that no negroes shall be landed for sale in any but the ports following; that is to say, ———; and the collector of each of the said ports severally shall, within ——— days after the arrival of any ship transporting negroes, report the same to the protector of negroes, or to one of his inspectors; and the said protector is hereby authorized and required to examine, or cause to be examined by one of his inspectors, with the assistance of the said collector, or his deputy, and a surgeon to be called in on the occasion, the state of the said ship and negroes; and upon what shall appear to them, the said protector of negroes and the said collector and surgeon, to be a sufficient proof, either as arising from their own inspection, or sufficient information on a summary process, of any contravention of this act, or cruelty to the negroes, or other malversation of the said captain, or any of his officers, the said protector shall impose a fine on him or them, not exceeding ———; which shall not, however, weaken or invalidate any penalty growing from the bond of the said master or his owners. And it is hereby provided, that if the said master, or any of his officers, shall find himself aggrieved by the said fine, he may, within ——— days, appeal to the chief judge, if the court shall be sitting, or to the governor, who shall and are required to hear the said parties, and on hearing are to annul or confirm the same.

7. And be it enacted, that no sale of negroes shall be made but in the presence of an inspector, and all negroes shall be sold severally, or in known and ascertained lots, and not otherwise; and a paper containing the state and description of each negro severally sold, and of each lot, shall be taken and registered in the office aforesaid; and if on inspection or information it shall be found that any negroes shall have, in the same ship, or any other at the same time examined, a wife, a husband, a brother, sister, or child,—the person or persons so related, shall not be sold separately at that or any future sale.

8. And be it enacted, that each and every of his Majesty's islands and plantations, in which negroes are used in cultivation, shall be, by the gov-

ernor and the protector of negroes for the time being, divided into districts, allowing as much as convenience will admit to the present division into parishes, and subdividing them, where necessary, into districts, according to the number of negroes. And the said governor and protector of negroes shall cause in each district a church to be built in a convenient place, and a cemetery annexed, and a house for the residence of a clergyman, with ——— acres of land annexed; and they are hereby authorized to treat for the necessary ground with the proprietor, who is hereby obliged to sell and dispose of the same to the said use; and in case of dispute concerning the value, the same to be settled by a jury as in like cases is accustomed.

9. And be it enacted, that in each of the said districts shall be established a presbyter of the Church of England, as by law established, who shall appoint under him one clerk, who shall be a free negro, when such properly qualified can be found, (otherwise a white man,) with a salary, in each case, of ———; and the said minister and clerk, both or one, shall instruct the said negroes in the Church catechism, or such other as shall be provided by the authority in this act named; and the said minister shall baptize, as he shall think fit, all negroes not baptized, and not belonging to the dissenters from the Church of England.

10. And the principal overseer of each plantation is hereby required to deliver annually unto the minister a list of all the negroes upon his plantation, distinguishing their sex and age, and shall, under a penalty of ———, cause all the negroes under his care, above the age of ——— years, to attend divine service once on every Sunday, except in case of sickness, infirmity, or other necessary cause, to be given at the time; and shall, by himself or one of those who are under him, provide for the orderly behaviour of the negroes under him, and cause them to return to his plantation when divine service, or administration of sacraments, or catechism, is ended.

11. And be it enacted, that the minister shall have power to punish any negro for disorderly conduct during divine service, by a punishment not exceeding [ten] blows, to be given in one day, and for one offence, which the overseer, or his under agent or agents, is hereby directed, according to the orders of the said ministers, effectually to inflict, whenever the same shall be ordered.

12. And be it enacted, that no spirituous liquors of any kind shall be sold, except in towns, within ——— miles distant of any church, nor

within any district during divine service, and an hour preceding, and an hour following, the same; and the minister of each parish shall and is hereby authorized to act as a justice of the peace in enforcing the said regulation.

13. And be it enacted, that every minister shall keep a register of births, burials, and marriages of all negroes and mulattoes in his district.

14. And be it enacted, that the ministers of the several districts shall meet annually, on the ——— day of ———, in a synod of the island, to which they belong; and the said synod shall have for its president such person as the bishop of London shall appoint for his commissary; and the said synod or general assembly is hereby authorized, by a majority of voices, to make regulations, which regulations shall be transmitted by the said president or commissary to the bishop of London; and when returned by the bishop of London approved of, then, and not before, the said regulations shall be held in force to bind the said clergy, their assistants, clerks, and schoolmasters only, and no other persons.

15. And be it enacted, that the said president shall collect matter in the said assembly, and shall make a report of the state of religion and morals in the several parishes from whence the synod is deputed, and shall transmit the same, once in the year, in duplicate, through the governor and protector of negroes, to the bishop of London.

16. And be it enacted and declared, that the bishop of London for the time being shall be patron to all and every the said cures in this act directed, and the said bishop is hereby required to provide for the due filling thereof, and is to receive from the fund in this act provided, for the due execution of this act, a sum not exceeding ——— for each of the said ministers, for his outfit and passage.

17. And be it enacted, that on misbehaviour and on complaint from the said synod, and on hearing the party accused in a plain and summary manner, it shall and may be lawful for the bishop of London to suspend or to remove any minister from his cure, as his said offences shall appear to merit.

18. And be it enacted, that for every two districts a school shall be established for young negroes to be taught three days in the week, and to be detained from their owner four hours in each day: the number not to be more or fewer than twenty males in each district, who shall be chosen, and vacancies filled, by the minister of the district; and the said minister shall pay to the owner of the said boy, and shall be allowed the same

in his accounts at the synod, to the age of twelve years old, threepence by the day; and for every boy, from twelve years old to fifteen, five-pence by the day.

19. And it is enacted, that if the president of the synod aforesaid shall certify to the protector of negroes, that any boys in the said schools (provided, that the number in no one year shall exceed one in the island of Jamaica, and one in two years in the islands of Barbadoes, Antigua, and Grenada, and one in four years in any of the other islands) do show a remarkable aptitude for learning, the said protector is hereby authorized and directed to purchase the said boy at the best rate, at which boys of that age and strength have been sold within the year; and the said negro so purchased shall be under the entire guardianship of the said protector of negroes, who shall send him to the bishop of London, for his further education in England, and may charge in his accounts for the expense of transporting him to England: and the bishop of London shall provide for the education of such of the said negroes as he shall think proper subjects, until the age of twenty-four years, and shall order those, who shall fall short of expectation after one year, to be bound apprentice to some handicraft trade; and when his apprenticeship is finished, the lord mayor of London is hereby authorized and directed to receive the said negro from his master, and to transmit him to the island from which he came in the West Indies, to be there as a free negro; subject, however, to the direction of the protector of negroes, relatively to his behaviour and employment.

20. And it is hereby enacted and provided, that any planter or owner of negroes, not being of the Church of England, and not choosing to send his negroes to attend divine service in manner by this act directed, shall give, jointly or severally, as the case shall require, security to the protector of negroes, that a competent minister of some Christian church or congregation shall be provided for the due instruction of the negroes, and for their performing divine service according to the description of the religion of the master or masters, in some church or house thereto allotted, in the manner and with the regulations in this act prescribed with regard to the exercise of religion according to the Church of England.

Provided always, that the marriages of the said negroes belonging to dissenters shall be celebrated only in the church of the said district, and that a register of the births shall be transmitted to the minister of the said district.

21. And whereas a state of matrimony, and the government of a

family, is a principal means of forming men to a fitness for freedom, and to become good citizens; Be it enacted, that all negro men and women, above eighteen years of age for the man, and sixteen for the woman, who have cohabited together for twelve months or upwards, or shall cohabit for the same time and have a child or children, shall be deemed to all intents and purposes to be married; and either of the parties is authorized to require of the ministers of the district to be married in the face of the church.

22. And be it enacted, that from and after the ——— of ——— all negro men in a healthy condition, and so reported to be, in case the same is denied, by a surgeon and by an inspector of negroes, and being twenty-one years old, or upwards, until fifty, and not being before married, shall, on requisition of the inspectors, be provided by their masters or overseers with a woman not having children living, and not exceeding the age of the man; nor in any case exceeding the age of twenty-five years; and such person shall be married publicly in the face of the church.

23. And be it enacted, that if any negro shall refuse a competent marriage tendered to him, and shall not demand another specifically, such as it may be in his master's power to provide, the master or overseer shall be authorized to constrain him by an increase of work, or a lessening of allowance.

24. And be it enacted, that the minister in each district shall have, with the assent of the inspector, full power and authority to punish all acts of adultery, unlawful concubinage, and fornication, amongst negroes, on hearing and a summary process, by ordering a number of blows, not exceeding ——— for each offence; and if any white person shall be proved, on information in the supreme court, to be exhibited by the protector of negroes, to have committed adultery with any negro woman, or to have corrupted any negro woman under sixteen years of age, he shall be fined in the sum of ———, and shall be for ever disabled from serving the office of overseer of negroes or being attorney to any plantation.

25. And be it enacted, that no slaves shall be compelled to do any work for their masters for [three] days after their marriage.

26. And be it enacted, that no woman shall be obliged to field-work, or any other laborious work, for one month before her delivery, or for six weeks afterwards.

27. And be it enacted, that no husband and wife shall be sold sepa-

rately if originally belonging to the same master, nor shall any children, under sixteen, be sold separately from their parents, or one parent, if one be living.

28. And be it enacted, that if a husband and wife, which before their intermarriage belonged to different owners, shall be sold, they shall not be sold at such a distance as to prevent mutual help and cohabitation; and of this distance the minister shall judge, and his certificate of the inconvenient distance shall be valid, so as to make such sale unlawful, and to render the same null and void.

29. And be it enacted, that no negro shall be compelled to work for his owner at field-work, or any service relative to a plantation, or to work at any handicraft trade, from eleven o'clock on Saturday forenoon until the usual working hour on Monday morning.

30. And whereas habits of industry and sobriety, and the means of acquiring and preserving property, are proper and reasonable preparatives to freedom, and will secure against the abuse of the same; Be it enacted, that every negro man, who shall have served ten years, and is thirty years of age, and is married, and has had two children born of any marriage, shall obtain the whole of Saturday for himself and his wife, and for his own benefit; and after thirty-seven years of age the whole of Friday for himself and his wife; provided, that in both cases the minister of the district, and the inspector of negroes, shall certify, that they know nothing against his peaceable, orderly, and industrious behaviour.

31. And be it enacted, that the master of every plantation shall provide the materials of a good and substantial hut for each married field negro; and if his plantation shall exceed ——— acres, he shall allot to the same a portion of land not less than ———: and the said hut and land shall remain and stand annexed to the said negro, for his natural life, or during his bondage; but the same shall not be alienated without the consent of the owners.

32. And be it enacted, that it shall not be lawful for the owner of any negro, by himself or any other, to take from him any land, house, cattle, goods, or money, acquired by the said negro, whether by purchase, donation, or testament, whether the same has been derived from the owner of the said negro, or any other.

33. And be it enacted, that if the said negro shall die possessed of any lands, goods, or chattels, and dies without leaving a wife or issue, it shall be lawful for the said negro to devise or bequeath the same by his

last will: but in case the said negro shall die intestate, and leave a wife and children, the same shall be distributed amongst them, according to the usage under the statute, commonly called the Statute of Distributions. But if the said negro shall die intestate without wife or children, then and in that case his estate shall go to the fund provided for the better execution of this act.

34. And be it enacted, that no negro, who is married, and hath resided upon any plantation for twelve months, shall be sold either privately, or by the decree of any court, but along with the plantation on which he hath resided, unless he should himself request to be separated therefrom.

35. And be it enacted, that no blows or stripes, exceeding thirteen, shall be inflicted for one offence upon any negro, without the order of one of his Majesty's justices of peace.

36. And it is enacted, that it shall be lawful for the protector of negroes, as often as on complaint and hearing he shall be of opinion that any negro hath been cruelly and inhumanly treated, or when it shall be made to appear to him that an overseer hath any particular malice, to order, at the desire of the suffering party, the said negro to be sold to another master.

37. And be it enacted, that, in all cases of injury to member or life, the offences against a negro shall be deemed and taken to all intents and purposes as if the same were perpetrated against any of his Majesty's subjects; and the protector of negroes, on complaint, or if he shall receive credible information thereof, shall cause an indictment to be presented for the same; and in case of suspicion of any murder of a negro, an inquest by the coroner, or officer acting as such, shall, if practicable, be held into the same.

38. And in order to a gradual manumission of slaves, as they shall seem fitted to fill the offices of freemen, Be it enacted, that every negro slave, being thirty years of age and upwards, and who has had three children born to him in lawful matrimony, and who hath received a certificate from the minister of his district, or any other Christian teacher, of his regularity in the duties of religion, and of his orderly and good behaviour, may purchase, at rates to be fixed by two justices of peace, the freedom of himself, or his wife or children, or of any of them separately, valuing the wife and children, if purchased into liberty by the father of the family, at half only of their marketable values; provided, that the said

father shall bind himself in a penalty of ——— for the good behaviour of his children.

39. And be it enacted, that it shall be lawful for the protector of negroes to purchase the freedom of any negro, who shall appear to him to excel in any mechanical art, or other knowledge or practice deemed liberal, and the value shall be settled by a jury.

40. And be it enacted, that the protector of negroes shall be and is authorized and required to act as a magistrate for the coercion of all idle, disobedient, or disorderly free negroes, and he shall by office prosecute them for the offences of idleness, drunkenness, quarrelling, gaming, or vagrancy, in the supreme court, or cause them to be prosecuted before one justice of peace, as the case may require.

41. And be it enacted, that if any free negro hath been twice convicted for any of the said misdemeanours, and is judged by the said protector of negroes, calling to his assistance two justices of the peace, to be incorrigibly idle, dissolute, and vicious, it shall be lawful, by the order of the said protector and two justices of the peace, to sell the said free negro into slavery; the purchase-money to be paid to the person so remanded into servitude, or kept in hand by the protector and governor for the benefit of his family.

42. And be it enacted, that the governor in each colony shall be assistant to the execution of this act, and shall receive the reports of the protector, and such other accounts, as he shall judge material, relative thereto, and shall transmit the same annually to one of his Majesty's principal secretaries of state.

Thoughts and Details on Scarcity

In this, his most important statement on economic principles, Burke dramatically identifies himself with the laissez-faire *ideals of Adam Smith. Famine and scarcity of foods had hit England in the 1790s as it waged war against France. Burke cautioned Pitt against using government relief to solve the crisis, for it would violate the natural laws of the market. Government intervention would, Burke writes, defy "the laws of commerce, which are the laws of nature, and consequently the laws of God."*

OF ALL THINGS, an indiscreet tampering with the trade of provisions is the most dangerous, and it is always worst in the time when men are most disposed to it; that is, in the time of scarcity. Because there is nothing on which the passions of men are so violent, and their judgment so weak, and on which there exists such a multitude of ill-founded popular prejudices.

The great use of government is as a restraint; and there is no restraint which it ought to put upon others, and upon itself too, rather than that which is imposed on the fury of speculating under circumstances of irritation. The number of idle tales, spread about by the industry of faction, and by the zeal of foolish good-intention, and greedily devoured by the malignant credulity of mankind, tends infinitely to aggravate prejudices, which, in themselves, are more than sufficiently strong. In that state of affairs, and of the public with relation to them, the first thing that government owes to us, the people, is *information*; the next is timely coercion:—the one to guide our judgment; the other to regulate our tempers.

To provide for us in our necessities is not in the power of government. It would be a vain presumption in statesmen to think they can do it. The people maintain them, and not they the people. It is in the power of government to prevent much evil; it can do very little positive good in this, or perhaps in anything else. It is not only so of the state and statesman, but of all the classes and descriptions of the rich—they are the pensioners of the poor, and are maintained by their superfluity. They are under an absolute, hereditary, and indefeasible dependence on those who labour, and are miscalled the poor.

The labouring people are only poor, because they are numerous. Numbers in their nature imply poverty. In a fair distribution among a vast multitude none can have much. That class of dependent pensioners called the rich is so extremely small, that if all their throats were cut, and a distribution made of all they consume in a year, it would not give a bit of bread and cheese for one night's supper to those who labour, and who in reality feed both the pensioners and themselves.

But the throats of the rich ought not to be cut, nor their magazines plundered; because in their persons they are trustees for those who labour, and their hoards are the banking houses of these latter. Whether they mean it or not, they do, in effect, execute their trust—some with more, some with less, fidelity and judgment. But, on the whole, the duty is performed, and everything returns, deducting some very trifling commission and discount, to the place from whence it arose. When the poor rise to destroy the rich, they act as wisely for their own purposes, as when they burn mills, and throw corn into the river, to make bread cheap.

When I say, that we of the people ought to be informed, inclusively I say, we ought not to be flattered; flattery is the reverse of instruction. The *poor* in that case would be rendered as improvident as the rich, which would not be at all good for them.

Nothing can be so base and so wicked as the political canting language, "The labouring *poor.*" Let compassion be shown in action, the more the better, according to every man's ability; but let there be no lamentation of their condition. It is no relief to their miserable circumstances; it is only an insult to their miserable understandings. It arises from a total want of charity, or a total want of thought. Want of one kind was never relieved by want of any other kind. Patience, labour, sobriety, frugality, and religion, should be recommended to them; all the rest is downright *fraud.* It is horrible to call them "The *once happy* labourer."

Whether what may be called the moral or philosophical happiness of the laborious classes is increased or not, I cannot say. The seat of that species of happiness is in the mind and there are few data to ascertain the comparative state of the mind at any two periods. Philosophical happiness is, to want little. Civil or vulgar happiness is, to want much, and to enjoy much.

If the happiness of the animal man (which certainly goes somewhere towards the happiness of the rational man) be the object of our estimate, then I assert without the least hesitation, that the condition of those who labour (in all descriptions of labour, and in all gradations of labour, from the highest to the lowest inclusively) is on the whole extremely meliorated, if more and better food is any standard of melioration. They work more, it is certain; but they have the advantage of their augmented labour; yet whether that increase of labour be on the whole a *good* or an *evil,* is a consideration that would lead us a great way, and is not for my present purpose. But as to the fact of the melioration of their diet, I shall enter into the detail of proof whenever I am called upon: in the mean time, the known difficulty of contenting them with anything but bread made of the finest flour, and meat of the first quality, is proof sufficient.

I further assert, that even under all the hardships of the last year, the labouring people did, either out of their direct gains, or from charity, (which it seems is now an insult to them,) in fact, fare better than they did in seasons of common plenty, fifty or sixty years ago; or even at the period of my English observation, which is about forty-four years. I even assert, that full as many in that class as ever were known to do it before continued to save money; and this I can prove, so far as my own information and experience extend.

It is not true that the rate of wages has not increased with the nominal price of provisions. I allow it has not fluctuated with that price, nor ought it; and the squires of Norfolk had dined, when they gave it as their opinion, that it might or it ought to rise and fall with the market of provisions. The rate of wages in truth has no *direct* relation to that price. Labour is a commodity like every other, and rises or falls according to the demand. This is in the nature of things; however, the nature of things has provided for their necessities. Wages have been twice raised in my time; and they bear a full proportion, or even a greater than formerly, to the medium of provision during the last bad cycle of twenty years. They bear a full proportion to the result of their labour. If we were wildly to attempt to force them beyond it, the stone which we had forced up the hill would only fall back upon them in a diminished demand, or, what indeed is the far lesser evil, an aggravated price, of all the provisions which are the result of their manual toil.

There is an implied contract, much stronger than any instrument or article of agreement between the labourer in any occupation and his employer—that the labour, so far as that labour is concerned, shall be sufficient to pay to the employer a profit on his capital, and a compensation for his risk; in a word, that the labour shall produce an advantage equal to the payment. Whatever is above that is a direct *tax;* and if the amount of that tax be left to the will and pleasure of another, it is an *arbitrary tax*.

If I understand it rightly, the tax proposed on the farming interest of this kingdom is to be levied at what is called the discretion of justices of peace.

The questions arising on this scheme of arbitrary taxation are these,—Whether it is better to leave all dealing, in which there is no force or fraud, collusion or combination, entirely to the persons mutually concerned in the matter contracted for; or to put the contract into the hands of those who can have none, or a very remote interest in it, and little or no knowledge of the subject.

It might be imagined that there would be very little difficulty in solving this question; for what man of any degree of reflection can think, that a want of interest in any subject closely connected with a want of skill in it, qualifies a person to intermeddle in any the least affair; much less in affairs that vitally concern the agriculture of the kingdom, the first of all its concerns, and the foundation of all its prosperity in every other matter by which that prosperity is produced.

The vulgar error on this subject arises from a total confusion in the very idea of things widely different in themselves;—those of convention, and those of judicature. When a contract is making, it is a matter of discretion and of interest between the parties. In that intercourse, and in what is to arise from it, the parties are the masters. If they are not completely so, they are not free, and therefore their contracts are void.

But this freedom has no further extent, when the contract is made; then their discretionary powers expire, and a new order of things takes its origin. Then, and not till then, and on a difference between the parties, the office of the judge commences. He cannot dictate the contract. It is his business to see that it be *enforced*; provided that it is not contrary to pre-existing laws, or obtained by force or fraud. If he is in any way a maker or regulator of the contract, in so much he is disqualified from being a judge. But this sort of confused distribution of administrative and judicial characters, (of which we have already as much as is sufficient, and a little more,) is not the only perplexity of notions and passions which trouble us in the present hour.

What is doing supposes, or pretends, that the farmer and the labourer have opposite interests; that the farmer oppresses the labourer; and that a gentleman, called a justice of peace, is the protector of the latter, and a control and restraint on the former; and this is a point I wish to examine in a manner a good deal different from that in which gentlemen proceed, who confide more in their abilities than is fit, and suppose them capable of more than any natural abilities, fed with no other than the provender furnished by their own private speculations, can accomplish. Legislative acts attempting to regulate this part of economy do, at least as much as any other, require the exactest detail of circumstances, guided by the surest general principles that are necessary to direct experiment and inquiry, in order again from those details to elicit principles, firm and luminous general principles, to direct a practical legislative proceeding.

First, then, I deny that it is in this case, as in any other of necessary implication, that contracting parties should originally have had different interests. By accident it may be so undoubtedly at the outset; but then the contract is of the nature of a compromise; and compromise is founded on circumstances that suppose it the interest of the parties to be reconciled in some medium. The principle of compromise adopted, of consequence the interests cease to be different.

But in the case of the farmer and the labourer, their interests are always the same, and it is absolutely impossible that their free contracts can be onerous to either party. It is the interest of the farmer, that his work should be done with effect and celerity; and that cannot be, unless the labourer is well fed, and otherwise found with such necessaries of animal life, according to his habitudes, as may keep the body in full force, and the mind gay and cheerful. For of all the instruments of his trade, the labour of man (what the ancient writers have called the *instrumentum vocale*) is that on which he is most to rely for the repayment of his capital. The other two, the *semivocale* in the ancient classification, that is, the working stock of cattle, and the *instrumentum mutum*, such as carts, ploughs, spades, and so forth, though not all inconsiderable in themselves, are very much inferior in utility or in expense; and, without a given portion of the first, are nothing at all. For in all things whatever, the mind is the most valuable and the most important; and in this scale the whole of agriculture is in a natural and just order; the beast is as an informing principle to the plough and cart; the labourer is as reason to the beast; and the farmer is as a thinking and presiding principle to the labourer. An attempt to break this chain of subordination in any part is equally absurd; but the absurdity is the most mischievous in practical operation, where it is the most easy, that is, where it is the most subject to an erroneous judgment.

It is plainly more the farmer's interest that his men should thrive, than that his horses should be well fed, sleek, plump, and fit for use, or than that his waggon and ploughs should be strong, in good repair, and fit for service.

On the other hand, if the farmer cease to profit of the labourer, and that his capital is not continually manured and fructified, it is impossible that he should continue that abundant nutriment, and clothing, and lodging, proper for the protection of the instruments he employs.

It is therefore the first and fundamental interest of the labourer, that the farmer should have a full incoming profit on the product of his labour. The proposition is self-evident, and nothing but the malignity, perverseness, and ill-governed passions of mankind, and particularly the envy they bear to each other's prosperity, could prevent their seeing and acknowledging it, with thankfulness to the benign and wise Disposer of all things, who obliges men, whether they will or not, in pursuing their own selfish interests, to connect the general good with their own individual success.

But who are to judge what that profit and advantage ought to be? Certainly no authority on earth. It is a matter of convention dictated by the reciprocal conveniences of the parties, and indeed by their reciprocal necessities.—But, if the farmer is excessively avaricious?—why so much the better—the more he desires to increase his gains, the more interested is he in the good condition of those, upon whose labour his gains must principally depend.

I shall be told by the zealots of the sect of regulation, that this may be true, and may be safely committed to the convention of the farmer and the labourer, when the latter is in the prime of his youth, and at the time of his health and vigour, and in ordinary times of abundance. But in calamitous seasons, under accidental illness, in declining life, and with the pressure of a numerous offspring, the future nourishers of the community, but the present drains and bloodsuckers of those who produce them, what is to be done? When a man cannot live and maintain his family by the natural hire of his labour, ought it not to be raised by authority?

On this head I must be allowed to submit, what my opinions have ever been; and somewhat at large.

And, first, I premise that labour is, as I have already intimated, a commodity, and, as such, an article of trade. If I am right in this notion, then labour must be subject to all the laws and principles of trade, and not to regulations foreign to them, and that may be totally inconsistent with those principles and those laws. When any commodity is carried to market, it is not the necessity of the vender, but the necessity of the purchaser, that raises the price. The extreme want of the seller has rather (by the nature of things with which we shall in vain contend) the direct contrary operation. If the goods at market are beyond the demand, they fall in their value; if below it, they rise. The impossibility of the subsistence of a man, who carries his labour to a market, is totally beside the question in this way of viewing it. The only question is, what is it worth to the buyer?

But if authority comes in and forces the buyer to a price, what is this in the case (say) of a farmer who buys the labour of ten or twelve labouring men, and three or four handy-crafts, what is it, but to make an arbitrary division of his property among them?

The whole of his gains, I say it with the most certain conviction, never do amount anything like in value to what he pays to his labourers and artificers; so that a very small advance upon what *one* man pays to *many* may absorb the whole of what he possesses, and amount to an actual partition of all his substance among them. A perfect equality will indeed be produced;—that is to say, equal want, equal wretchedness, equal beggary, and on the part of the petitioners, a woeful, helpless, and desperate disappointment. Such is the event of all compulsory equalisations. They pull down what is above. They never raise what is below: and they depress high and low together beneath the level of what was originally the lowest.

If a commodity is raised by authority above what it will yield with a profit to the buyer, that commodity will be the less dealt in. If a second blundering interposition be used to correct the blunder of the first, and an attempt is made to force the purchase of the commodity, (of labour for instance,) the one of these two things must happen, either that the forced buyer is ruined, or the price of the product of the labour, in that proportion, is raised. Then the wheel turns round, and the evil complained of falls with aggravated weight on the complainant. The price of corn, which is the result of the expense of all the operations of husbandry taken together, and for some time continued, will rise on the labourer, considered as a consumer. The very best will be, that he remains where he was. But if the price of the corn should not compensate the price of labour, what is far more to be feared, the most serious evil, the very destruction of agriculture itself, is to be apprehended.

Nothing is such an enemy to accuracy of judgment as a coarse discrimination; a want of such classification and distribution as the subject admits of. Increase the rate of wages to the labourer, say the regulators—as if labour was but one thing, and of one value. But this very broad, generic term, *labour,* admits, at least, of two or three specific descriptions: and these will suffice, at least, to let gentlemen discern a little the necessity of proceeding with caution in their coercive guidance of those, whose existence depends upon the observance of still nicer distinctions and sub-divisions, than commonly they resort to in forming their judgments on this very enlarged part of economy.

The labourers in husbandry may be divided: 1st, into those who are able to perform the full work of a man; that is, what can be done by a person from twenty-one years of age to fifty. I know no husbandry work (mowing hardly excepted) that is not equally within the power of all persons within those ages, the more advanced fully compensating by knack and habit what they lose in activity. Unquestionably, there is a good deal of difference between the value of one man's labour and that of another, from strength, dexterity, and honest application. But I am quite sure, from my best observation, that any given five men will, in their total, afford a proportion of labour equal to any other five within the periods of life I have stated; that is, that among such five men there will be one possessing all the qualifications of a good workman, one bad, and the other three middling, and approximating to the first and the last. So that in so small a platoon as that of even five, you will find the full complement of all that five men *can* earn. Taking five and five throughout the kingdom, they are equal: therefore, an error with regard to the equalisation of their wages by those who employ five, as farmers do at the very least, cannot be considerable.

2dly, Those who are able to work, but not the complete task of a day-labourer. This class is infinitely diversified, but will aptly enough fall into principal divisions. *Men*, from the decline, which after fifty becomes every year more sensible, to the period of debility and decrepitude, and the maladies that precede a final dissolution. *Women*, whose employment on husbandry is but occasional, and who differ more in effective labour one from another, than men do, on account of gestation, nursing, and domestic management, over and above the difference they have in common with men in advancing, in stationary, and in declining life. *Children*, who proceed on the reverse order, growing from less to greater utility, but with a still greater disproportion of nutriment to labour than is found in the second of these sub-divisions; as is visible to those who will give themselves the trouble of examining into the interior economy of a poor-house.

This inferior classification is introduced to show, that laws prescribing, or magistrates exercising, a very stiff and often inapplicable rule, or a blind and rash discretion, never can provide the just proportions between earning and salary on the one hand, and nutriment on the other: whereas interest, habit, and the tacit convention, that arise from a thousand nameless circumstances, produce a *tact* that regulates without difficulty, what laws and magistrates cannot regulate at all. The first class of labour wants nothing to equalise it; it equalises itself. The second and third are not capable of any equalisation.

But what if the rate of hire to the labourer comes far short of his necessary subsistence, and the calamity of the time is so great as to threaten actual famine? Is the poor labourer to be abandoned to the flinty heart and griping hand of base self-interest, supported by the sword of law, especially when there is reason to suppose that the very avarice of farmers themselves has concurred with the errors of government to bring famine on the land?

In that case, my opinion is this: Whenever it happens that a man can claim nothing according to the rules of commerce and the principles of justice, he passes out of that department, and comes within the jurisdiction of mercy. In that province the magistrate has nothing at all to do: his interference is a violation of the property which it is his office to protect. Without all doubt, charity to the poor is a direct and obligatory duty upon all Christians, next in order after the payment of debts, full as strong, and by nature made infinitely more delightful to us. Puffendorff, and other casuists, do not, I think, denominate it quite properly, when they call it a duty of imperfect obligation. But the manner, mode, time, choice of objects, and proportion, are left to private discretion; and, perhaps, for that very reason it is performed with the greater satisfaction, because the discharge of it has more the appearance of freedom; recommending us besides very specially to the Divine favour, as the exercise of a virtue most suitable to a being sensible of its own infirmity.

The cry of the people in cities and towns, though unfortunately (from a fear of their multitude and combination) the most regarded, ought, in *fact*, to be the *least* attended to upon this subject; for citizens are in a state of utter ignorance of the means by which they are to be fed, and they contribute little or nothing, except in an infinitely circuitous manner, to their own maintenance. They are truly, *"Fruges consumere nati."* They are to be heard with great respect and attention upon matters within their province, that is, on trades and manufactures; but on anything that relates to agriculture, they are to be listened to with the same *reverence* which we pay to the dogmas of other ignorant and presumptuous men.

If any one were to tell them, that they were to give in an account of all the stock in their shops; that attempts would be made to limit their profits, or raise the price of the labouring manufacturers upon them, or recommend to government, out of a capital from the public revenues, to set up a shop of the same commodities, in order to rival them, and keep them to reasonable dealing, they would very soon see the impudence, injustice, and oppression of such a course. They would not be mistaken; but they are of opinion, that agriculture is to be subject to other laws, and to be governed by other principles.

A greater and more ruinous mistake cannot be fallen into, than that the trades of agriculture and grazing can be conducted upon any other than the common principles of commerce; namely, that the producer should be permitted, and even expected, to look to all possible profit, which, without fraud or violence, he can make; to turn plenty or scarcity to the best advantage he can; to keep back or to bring forward his commodities at his pleasure; to account to no one for his stock or for his gain. On any other terms he is the slave of the consumer; and that he should be so is of no benefit to the consumer. No slave was ever so beneficial to the master, as a freeman that deals with him on an equal footing by convention, formed on the rules and principles of contending interests and compromised advantages. The consumer, if he were suffered, would in the end always be the dupe of his own tyranny and injustice. The landed gentleman is never to forget, that the farmer is his representative.

It is a perilous thing to try experiments on the farmer. The farmer's capital (except in a few persons, and in a very few places) is far more feeble than commonly is imagined. The trade is a very poor trade; it is subject to great risks and losses. The capital, such as it is, is turned but once in the year; in some branches it requires three years before the money is paid. I believe never less than three in the turnip and grass land course, which is the prevalent course on the more or less fertile, sandy and gravelly loams, and these compose the soil in the south and south-east of England, the best adapted, and perhaps the only ones that are adapted, to the turnip husbandry.

It is very rare that the most prosperous farmer, counting the value of his quick and dead stock, the interest of the money he turns, together with his own wages as a bailiff or overseer, ever does make 12 or 15 *per centum* by the year on his capital. I speak of the prosperous. In most of the parts of England which have fallen within my observation, I have rarely known a farmer who to his own trade has not added some other employment or traffic, that, after a course of the most unremitting parsimony and labour, (such for the greater part is theirs,) and persevering in his business for a long course of years, died worth more than paid his debts, leaving his posterity to continue in nearly the same equal conflict between industry and want, in which the last predecessor, and a long line of predecessors before him, lived and died.

Observe that I speak of the generality of farmers, who have not more than from one hundred and fifty to three or four hundred acres. There are few in this part of the country within the former, or much beyond the latter extent. Unquestionably in other places there are much larger. But, I am convinced, whatever part of England be the theatre of his operations, a farmer, who cultivates twelve hundred acres, which I consider as a large farm, though I know there are larger, cannot proceed, with any degree of safety and effect, with a smaller capital than ten thousand pounds: and that he cannot, in the ordinary course of culture, make more upon that great capital of ten thousand pounds, than twelve hundred year.

As to the weaker capitals, an easy judgment may be formed by what very small errors they may be further attenuated, enervated, rendered unproductive, and perhaps totally destroyed.

This constant precariousness, and ultimately moderate limits of a farmer's fortune, on the strongest capital, I press, not only on account of the hazardous speculations of the times, but because the excellent and most useful works of my friend, Mr. Arthur Young, tend to propagate that error, (such I am very certain it is,) of the largeness of a farmer's profits. It is not that his account of the produce does often greatly exceed, but he by no means makes the proper allowance for accidents and losses. I might enter into a convincing detail, if other more troublesome and more necessary details were not before me.

This proposed discretionary tax on labour militates with the recommendations of the board of agriculture: they recommend a general use of the drill culture. I agree with the board, that where the soil is not excessively heavy, or encumbered with large loose stones, (which however is the case with much otherwise good land,) that course is the best, and most productive; provided that the most accurate eye, the most vigilant superintendence, the most prompt activity, which has no such day as to-morrow in its calendar, the most steady foresight and pre-disposing order to have everybody and everything ready in its place, and prepared to take advantage of the fortunate, fugitive moment, in this coquetting climate of ours—provided, I say, all these combine to speed the plough, I admit its superiority over the old and general methods. But under procrastinating, improvident, ordinary husbandmen, who may neglect or let slip the few opportunities of sweetening and purifying their ground with perpetually renovated toil, and undissipated attention, nothing, when tried to any extent, can be worse, or more dangerous: the farm may be ruined, instead of having the soil enriched and sweetened by it.

But the excellence of the method on a proper soil, and conducted by husbandmen, of whom there are few, being readily granted, how, and on what conditions, is this culture obtained? Why, by a very great increase of labour; by an augmentation of the third part, at least, of the hand-labour, to say nothing of the horses and machinery employed in ordinary tillage. Now, every man must be sensible how little becoming the gravity of legislature it is to encourage a board which recommends to us, and upon very weighty reasons unquestionably, an enlargement of the capital we employ in the operations of the hand, and then to pass an act, which taxes that manual labour, already at a very high rate; thus compelling us to diminish the quantity of labour which in the vulgar course we actually employ.

What is true of the farmer is equally true of the middle man; whether the middle man acts as factor, jobber, salesman, or speculator, in the markets of grain. These traders are to be left to their free course; and the more they make, and the richer they are, and the more largely they deal, the better both for the farmer and consumer, between whom they form a natural and most useful link of connexion; though, by the machinations of the old evil counsellor, *Envy*, they are hated and maligned by both parties.

I hear that middle men are accused of monopoly. Without question, the monopoly of authority is, in every instance and in every degree, an evil; but the monopoly of capital is the contrary. It is a great benefit, and a benefit particularly to the poor. A tradesman who has but an hundred pounds capital, which (say) he can turn but once a year, cannot live upon a *profit* of 10 *per cent.* because he cannot live upon ten pounds a year; but a man of ten thousand pounds capital can live and thrive upon 5 *per cent.* profit in the year, because he has five hundred pounds a year. The same proportion holds in turning it twice or thrice. These principles are plain and simple; and it is not our ignorance, so much as the levity, the envy, and the malignity of our nature, that hinders us from perceiving and yielding to them: but we are not to suffer our vices to usurp the place of our judgment.

The balance between consumption and production makes price. The market settles, and alone can settle, that price. Market is the meeting and conference of the *consumer* and *producer*, when they mutually discover each other's wants. Nobody, I believe, has observed with any reflection what market is, without being astonished at the truth, the correctness, the celerity, the general equity, with which the balance of wants is settled. They, who wish the destruction of that balance, and would fain by arbitrary regulation decree, that defective production should not be compensated by increased price, directly lay their *axe* to the root of production itself.

They may, even in one year of such false policy, do mischiefs incalculable; because the trade of a farmer is, as I have before explained, one of the most precarious in its advantages, the most liable to losses, and the least profitable of any that is carried on. It requires ten times more labour, of vigilance, of attention, of skill, and, let me add, of good fortune also, to carry on the business of a farmer with success, than what belongs to any other trade. Seeing things in this light, I am far from presuming to censure the late circular instruction of council to lord-lieutenants—but I confess I do not clearly discern its object. I am greatly afraid that the inquiry will raise some alarm as a measure, leading to the French system of putting corn into requisition. For that was preceded by an inquisition somewhat similar in its principle, though, according to their mode, their principles are full of that violence, *which here* is not much to be feared. It goes on a principle directly opposite to mine: it presumes, that the market is no fair *test* of plenty or scarcity. It raises a suspicion, which may affect the tranquillity of the public mind, "that the farmer keeps back, and takes unfair advantages by delay;" on the part of the dealer, it gives rise obviously to a thousand nefarious speculations.

In case the return should on the whole prove favourable, is it meant to ground a measure for encouraging exportation and checking the import of corn? If it is not, what end can it answer? And, I believe, it is not.

This opinion may be fortified by a report gone abroad, that intentions are entertained of erecting public granaries, and that this inquiry is to give government an advantage in its purchases.

I hear that such a measure has been proposed, and is under deliberation; that is, for government to set up a granary in every market town, at the expense of the state, in order to extinguish the dealer, and to subject the farmer to the consumer, by securing corn to the latter at a certain and steady price.

If such a scheme is adopted, I should not like to answer for the safety of the granary, of the agents, or of the town itself, in which the granary was erected—the first storm of popular phrensy would fall upon that granary.

So far in a political light.

In an economical light, I must observe, that the construction of such granaries throughout the kingdom would be at an expense beyond all calculation. The keeping them up would be at a great charge. The management and attendance would require an army of agents, store-keepers, clerks, and servants. The capital to be employed in the purchase of grain would be enormous. The waste, decay, and corruption, would be a dreadful drawback on the whole dealing; and the dissatisfaction of the people, at having decayed, tainted, or corrupted corn sold to them, as must be the case, would be serious.

This climate (whatever others may be) is not favourable to granaries, where wheat is to be kept for any time. The best, and indeed the only good granary, is the rick yard of the farmer, where the corn is preserved in its own straw, sweet, clean, wholesome, free from vermin and from insects, and comparatively at a trifle of expense. This, and the barn, enjoying many of the same advantages, have been the sole granaries of England from the foundation of its agriculture to this day. All this is done at the expense of the undertaker, and at his sole risk. He contributes to government, he receives nothing from it but protection, and to this he has a *claim*.

The moment that government appears at market, all the principles of market will be subverted. I don't know whether the farmer will suffer by it as long as there is a tolerable market of competition; but I am sure that, in the first place, the trading government will speedily become a bankrupt, and the consumer in the end will suffer. If government makes all its purchases at once it will instantly raise the market upon itself. If it makes them by degrees, it must follow the course of the market. If it follows the course of the market, it will produce no effect, and the consumer may as well buy as he wants—therefore all the expense is incurred gratis.

But if the object of this scheme should be, what I suspect it is, to destroy the dealer, commonly called the middle man, and by incurring a voluntary loss to carry the baker to deal with government, I am to tell them that they must set up another trade, that of a miller or a mealman, attended with a new train of expenses and risks. If in both these trades they should succeed, so as to exclude those who trade on natural and private capitals, then they will have a monopoly in their hands, which, under the appearance of a monopoly of capital, will, in reality, be a monopoly of authority, and will ruin whatever it touches. The agriculture of the kingdom cannot stand before it.

A little place like Geneva, of not more than from twenty-five to thirty thousand inhabitants, which has no territory, or next to none; which depends for its existence on the good-will of three neighbouring powers, and is of course continually in a state of something like a *siege*, or in the speculation of it, might find some resource in state granaries, and some revenue from the monopoly of what was sold to the keepers of public-houses. This is a policy for a state too small for agriculture. It is not (for instance) fit for so great a country as the Pope possesses, where, however, it is adopted and pursued in a greater extent, and with more strictness. Certain of the Pope's territories, from whence the city of Rome is supplied, being obliged to furnish Rome and the granaries of his Holiness with corn at a certain price, that part of the papal territories is utterly ruined. That ruin may be traced with certainty to this sole cause, and it appears indubitably by a comparison of their state and condition with that of the other part of the ecclesiastical dominions not subjected to the same regulations, which are in circumstances highly flourishing.

The reformation of this evil system is in a manner impracticable; for, first, it does keep bread and all other provisions equally subject to the chamber of supply, at a pretty reasonable and regular price, in the city of Rome. This preserves quiet among the numerous poor, idle, and naturally mutinous people of a very great capital. But the quiet of the town is purchased by the ruin of the country, and the ultimate wretchedness of both. The next cause which renders this evil incurable, is, the jobs which have grown out of it, and which, in spite of all precautions, would grow out of such things, even under governments far more potent than the feeble authority of the Pope.

This example of Rome, which has been derived from the most ancient times, and the most flourishing period of the Roman empire, (but not of the Roman agriculture,) may serve as a great caution to all governments, not to attempt to feed the people out of the hands of the magistrates. If once they are habituated to it, though but for one half year, they will never be satisfied to have it otherwise. And having looked to government for bread, on the very first scarcity they will turn and bite the hand that fed them. To avoid that evil, government will redouble the causes of it; and then it will become inveterate and incurable.

I beseech the government (which I take in the largest sense of the word, comprehending the two Houses of parliament) seriously to consider that years of scarcity or plenty do not come alternately, or at short intervals, but in pretty long cycles and irregularly, and consequently that we cannot assure ourselves, if we take a wrong measure, from the temporary necessities of one season; but that the next, and probably more, will drive us to the continuance of it; so that, in my opinion, there is no way of preventing this evil, which goes to the destruction of all our agriculture, and of that part of our internal commerce which touches our agriculture the most nearly, as well as the safety and very being of government, but manfully to resist the very first idea, speculative or practical, that it is within the competence of government, taken as government, or even of the rich, as rich, to supply to the poor those necessaries which it has pleased the Divine Providence for a while to withhold from them. We, the people, ought to be made sensible, that it is not in breaking the laws of commerce, which are the laws of nature, and consequently the laws of God, that we are to place our hope of softening the Divine displeasure to remove any calamity under which we suffer, or which hangs over us. . . .

After all, have we not reason to be thankful to the Giver of all good? In our history, and when the "labourer of England is said to have been once happy," we find constantly, after certain intervals, a period of real famine; by which a melancholy havoc was made among the human race. The price of provisions fluctuated dreadfully, demonstrating a deficiency very different from the worst failures of the present moment. Never, since I have known England, have I known more than a comparative scarcity. The price of wheat, taking a number of years together, has had no very considerable fluctuation, nor has it risen exceedingly until within this twelvemonth. Even now, I do not know of one man, woman, or child, that has perished from famine; fewer, if any, I believe, than in years of plenty, when such a thing may happen by accident. This is owing to a care and superintendence of the poor, far greater than any I remember.

The consideration of this ought to bind us all, rich and poor together, against those wicked writers of the newspapers, who would inflame the poor against their friends, guardians, patrons, and protectors.

Not only very few (I have observed that I know of none, though I live in a place as poor as most) have actually died of want, but we have seen no traces of those dreadful exterminating epidemics, which, in consequence of scanty and unwholesome food, in former times, not unfrequently wasted whole nations. Let us be saved from too much wisdom of our own, and we shall do tolerably well.

It is one of the finest problems in legislation, and what has often engaged my thoughts whilst I followed that profession, "What the state ought to take upon itself to direct by the public wisdom, and what it ought to leave, with as little interference as possible, to individual discretion." Nothing, certainly, can be laid down on the subject that will not admit of exceptions, many permanent, some occasional. But the clearest line of distinction, which I could draw, whilst I had my chalk to draw any line, was this; that the state ought to confine itself to what regards the state, or the creatures of the state, namely, the exterior establishment of its religion; its magistracy; its revenue; its military force by sea and land; the corporations that owe their existence to its fiat; in a word, to everything that is *truly and properly* public, to the public peace, to the public safety, to the public order, to the public prosperity. In its preventive police it ought to be sparing of its efforts, and to employ means, rather few, unfrequent, and strong, than many, and frequent, and, of course, as they multiply their puny politic race, and dwindle, small and feeble. Statesmen who know themselves will, with the dignity which belongs to wisdom, proceed only in this the superior orb and first mover of their duty steadily, vigilantly, severely, courageously: whatever remains will, in a manner, provide for itself. But as they descend from the state to a province, from a province to a parish, and from a parish to a private house, they go on accelerated in their fall. They *cannot* do the lower duty; and, in proportion as they try it, they will certainly fail in the higher. They ought to know the different departments of things; what belongs to laws, and what manners alone can regulate. To these, great politicians may give a leaning, but they cannot give a law.

Our legislature has fallen into this fault as well as other governments; all have fallen into it more or less. The once mighty state, which was nearest to us locally, nearest to us in every way, and whose ruins threaten to fall upon our heads, is a strong instance of this error. I can never quote France without a foreboding sigh—ΕΣΕΤΑΙ 'ΗΜΑΡ! Scipio said it to his recording Greek friend amidst the flames of the great rival of his country. That state has fallen by the hands of the parricides of their country, called the revolutionists, and constitutionalists, of France, a species of traitors, of whose fury and atrocious wickedness nothing in the annals of the phrensy and depravation of mankind had before furnished an example, and of whom I can never think or speak without a mixed sensation of disgust, of horror, and of detestation, not easy to be expressed. These nefarious monsters destroyed their country for what was good in it: for much good there was in the constitution of that noble monarchy, which, in all kinds, formed and nourished great men, and great patterns of virtue to the world. But though its enemies were not enemies to its faults, its faults furnished them with means for its destruction. My dear departed friend, whose loss is even greater to the public than to me, had often remarked, that the leading vice of the French monarchy, (which he had well studied,) was in good intention ill-directed, and a restless desire of governing too much. The hand of authority was seen in everything, and in every place. All, therefore, that happened amiss in the course even of domestic affairs, was attributed to the government; and as it always happens in this kind of officious universal interference, what began in odious power, ended always, I may say without an exception, in contemptible imbecility. For this reason, as far as I can approve of any novelty, I thought well of the provincial administrations. Those, if the superior power had been severe, and vigilant, and vigorous, might have been of much use politically in removing government from many invidious details. But as everything is good or bad, as it is related or combined, government being relaxed above as it was relaxed below, and the brains of the people growing more and more addle with every sort of visionary speculation, the shiftings of the scene in the provincial theatres became only preparatives to a revolution in the kingdom, and the popular actings there only the rehearsals of the terrible drama of the republic.

Tyranny and cruelty may make men justly wish the downfal of abused powers, but I believe that no government ever yet perished from any other direct cause than its own weakness. My opinion is against an over-doing of any sort of administration, and more especially against this most momentous of all meddling on the part of authority; the meddling with the subsistence of the people.

A Letter to a Noble Lord

Upon his retirement from Parliament, Burke received a government pension that was attacked by several Whig leaders as hypocritical given his earlier criticism of corrupt patronage. In 1795 Burke answered this criticism, particularly from the duke of Bedford, with a slashing personal attack on Bedford and the aristocratic lineage of the Russell family. Through his bitter indictment of the duke's unmerited privileged life breathes a self-conscious justification of Burke's own career, his hard-won achievements based solely on industry, ability, and merit. In this plea for personal vindication Burke lashes out at not only the duke of Bedford but also at the Jacobins, who at the end of the letter receive one of his bitterest attacks. They experiment with men as with "mice in an air pump," and, like the Abbé Sieyes, they have "pigeon-holes full of Constitutions . . . suited to every season and every fancy."

MY LORD,

I could hardly flatter myself with the hope, that so very early in the season I should have to acknowledge obligations to the Duke of BEDFORD, and to the Earl of LAUDERDALE. These noble persons have lost no time in conferring upon me that sort of honour, which it is alone within their competence, and which it is certainly most congenial to their nature, and to their manners, to bestow.

To be ill spoken of, in whatever language they speak, by the zealots of the new sect in philosophy and politics, of which these noble persons think so charitably, and of which others think so justly, to me, is no matter of uneasiness or surprise. To have incurred the displeasure of the Duke of Orleans or the Duke of Bedford, to fall under the censure of citizen Brissot or of his friend the Earl of Lauderdale, I ought to consider as proofs, not the least satisfactory, that I have produced some part of the effect I proposed by my endeavours. I have laboured hard to earn, what the noble lords are generous enough to pay. Personal offence I have given them none. The part they take against me is from zeal to the cause. It is well! It is perfectly well! I have to do homage to their justice. I have to thank the Bedfords and the Lauderdales for having so faithfully and so fully acquitted towards me whatever arrear of debt was left undischarged by the Priestleys and the Paines.

Some, perhaps, may think them executors in their own wrong: I at least have nothing to complain of. They have gone beyond the demands of justice. They have been (a little perhaps beyond their intention) favourable to me. They have been the means of bringing out, by their invectives, the handsome things which Lord Grenville has had the goodness and condescension to say in my behalf. Retired as I am from the world, and from all its affairs and all its pleasures, I confess it does kindle, in my nearly extinguished feelings, a very vivid satisfaction to be so attacked and so commended. It is soothing to my wounded mind, to be commended by an able, vigorous, and well-informed statesman, and at the very moment when he stands forth with a manliness and resolution, worthy of himself and of his cause, for the preservation of the person and government of our sovereign, and therein for the security of the laws, the liberties, the morals, and the lives of his people. To be in any fair way connected with such things, is indeed a distinction. No philosophy can make me above it: no melancholy can depress me so low, as to make me wholly insensible to such an honour.

Why will they not let me remain in obscurity and inaction? Are they apprehensive, that if an atom of me remains, the sect has something to fear? Must I be annihilated, lest, like old *John Zisca's*, my skin might be made into a drum, to animate Europe to eternal battle, against a tyranny that threatens to overwhelm all Europe, and all the human race?

My Lord, it is a subject of awful meditation. Before this of France, the annals of all time have not furnished an instance of a *complete* revolution. That Revolution seems to have extended even to the constitution of the mind of man. It has this of wonderful in it, that it resembles what Lord Verulam says of the operations of nature. It was perfect, not only in its elements and principles, but in all its members and its organs from the very beginning. The moral scheme of France furnishes the only pattern ever known, which they who admire will *instantly* resemble. It is indeed an inexhaustible repertory of one kind of examples. In my wretched condition, though hardly to be classed with the living, I am not safe from them. They have tigers to fall upon animated strength. They have hyenas to prey upon carcasses. The national menagerie is collected by the first physiologists of the time; and it is defective in no description of savage nature. They pursue even such as me, into the obscurest retreats, and haul them before their revolutionary tribunals. Neither sex, nor age, nor the sanctuary of the tomb, is sacred to them. They have so determined a hatred to all privileged orders, that they deny even to the departed the sad immunities of the grave. They are not wholly without an object. Their turpitude purveys to their malice; and they unplumb the dead for bullets to assassinate the living. If all revolutionists were not proof against all caution, I should recommend it to their consideration, that no persons were ever known in history, either sacred or profane, to vex the sepulchre, and, by their sorceries, to call up the prophetic dead, with any other event, than the prediction of their own disastrous fate.—"Leave me, oh leave me to repose!"

In one thing I can excuse the Duke of Bedford for his attack upon me and my mortuary pension. He cannot readily comprehend the transaction he condemns. What I have obtained was the fruit of no bargain; the production of no intrigue; the result of no compromise; the effect of no solicitation. The first suggestion of it never came from me, mediately or immediately, to his Majesty or any of his ministers. It was long known that the instant my engagements would permit it, and before the heaviest of all calamities had for ever condemned me to obscurity and sorrow, I had resolved on a total retreat. I had executed that design. I was entirely out of the way of serving or of hurting any statesman, or any party, when the ministers so generously and so nobly carried into effect the spontaneous bounty of the crown. Both descriptions have acted as became them. When I could no longer serve them, the ministers have considered my situation. When I could no longer hurt them, the revolutionists have trampled on my infirmity. My gratitude, I trust, is equal to the manner in which the benefit was conferred. It came to me indeed, at a time of life, and in a state of mind and body, in which no circumstance of fortune could afford me any real pleasure. But this was no fault in the royal donor, or in his ministers, who were pleased, in acknowledging the merits of an invalid servant of the public, to assuage the sorrows of a desolate old man.

It would ill become me to boast of anything. It would as ill become me, thus called upon, to depreciate the value of a long life, spent with unexampled toil in the service of my country. Since the total body of my services, on account of the industry which was shown in them, and the fairness of my intentions, have obtained the acceptance of my sovereign, it would be absurd in me to range myself on the side of the Duke of Bedford and the corresponding society, or, as far as in me lies, to permit a dispute on the rate at which the authority appointed by *our* constitution to estimate such things has been pleased to set them.

Loose libels ought to be passed by in silence and contempt. By me they have been so always. I knew that as long as I remained in public, I should live down the calumnies of malice, and the judgments of ignorance. If I happened to be now and then in the wrong, (as who is not?) like all other men, I must bear the consequence of my faults and my mistakes. The libels of the present day are just of the same stuff as the libels of the past. But they derive an importance from the rank of the persons they come from, and the gravity of the place where they were uttered. In some way or other I ought to take some notice of them. To assert myself thus traduced is not vanity or arrogance. It is a demand of justice; it is a demonstration of gratitude. If I am unworthy, the ministers are worse than prodigal. On that hypothesis, I perfectly agree with the Duke of Bedford.

For whatever I have been (I am now no more) I put myself on my country. I ought to be allowed a reasonable freedom, because I stand upon my deliverance; and no culprit ought to plead in irons. Even in the utmost latitude of defensive liberty, I wish to preserve all possible decorum. Whatever it may be in the eyes of these noble persons themselves, to me their situation calls for the most profound respect. If I should happen to trespass a little, which I trust I shall not, let it always be supposed, that a confusion of characters may produce mistakes; that, in the masquerades of the grand carnival of our age, whimsical adventures happen; odd things are said and pass off. If I should fail a single point in the high respect I owe to those illustrious persons, I cannot be supposed to mean the Duke of Bedford and the Earl of Lauderdale of the House of Peers, but the Duke of Bedford and the Earl of Lauderdale of Palace-Yard!—The Dukes and Earls of Brentford. There they are on the pavement; there they seem to come nearer to my humble level; and, virtually at least, to have waived their high privilege.

Making this protestation, I refuse all revolutionary tribunals, where men have been put to death for no other reason, than that they had obtained favours from the Crown. I claim, not the letter, but the spirit, of the old English law, that is, to be tried by my peers. I decline his Grace's jurisdiction as a judge. I challenge the Duke of Bedford as a juror to pass upon the value of my services. Whatever his natural parts may be, I cannot recognise, in his few and idle years, the competence to judge of my long and laborious life. If I can help it, he shall not be on the inquest of my *quantum meruit*. Poor rich man! He can hardly know anything of public industry in its exertions, or can estimate its compensations when its work is done. I have no doubt of his Grace's readiness in all the calculations of vulgar arithmetic; but I shrewdly suspect, that he is little studied in the theory of moral proportions; and has never learned the rule of three in the arithmetic of policy and state.

His Grace thinks I have obtained too much. I answer, that my exertions, whatever they have been, were such as no hopes of pecuniary reward could possibly excite; and no pecuniary compensation can possibly reward them. Between money and such services, if done by abler men than I am, there is no common principle of comparison; they are quantities incommensurable. Money is made for the comfort and convenience of animal life. It cannot be a reward for what mere animal life must indeed sustain, but never can inspire. With submission to his Grace, I have not had more than sufficient. As to any noble use, I trust I know how to employ, as well as he, a much greater fortune than he possesses. In a more confined application, I certainly stand in need of every kind of relief and easement much more than he does. When I say I have not received more than I deserve, is this the language I hold to Majesty? No! Far, very far, from it! Before that presence, I claim no merit at all. Everything towards me is favour, and bounty. One style to a gracious benefactor; another to a proud and insulting foe.

His Grace is pleased to aggravate my guilt, by charging my acceptance of his Majesty's grant as a departure from my ideas, and the spirit of my conduct with regard to economy. If it be, my ideas of economy were false and ill-founded. But they are the Duke of Bedford's ideas of economy I have contradicted, and not my own. If he means to allude to certain bills brought in by me on a message from the throne in 1782, I tell him that there is nothing in my conduct that can contradict either the letter or the spirit of those acts. Does he mean the pay-office act? I take it for granted he does not. The act to which he alludes, is, I suppose, the establishment act. I greatly doubt whether his Grace has ever read the one or the other. The first of these systems cost me, with every assistance which my then situation gave me, pains incredible. I found an opinion common through all the offices, and general in the public at large, that it would prove impossible to reform and methodize the office of paymaster-general. I undertook it, however; and I succeeded in my undertaking. Whether the military service, or whether the general economy of our finances, have profited by that act, I leave to those who are acquainted with the army, and with the treasury, to judge. . . .

My economical reforms were not, as his Grace may think, the suppression of a paltry pension or employment, more or less. Economy in my plans was, as it ought to be, secondary, subordinate, instrumental. I acted on state principles. I found a great distemper in the commonwealth; and, according to the nature of the evil and of the object, I treated it. The malady was deep; it was complicated, in the causes and in the symptoms. Throughout it was full of contra-indicants. On one hand government, daily growing more invidious from an apparent increase of the means of strength, was every day growing more contemptible by real weakness. Nor was this dissolution confined to government commonly so called. It extended to parliament; which was losing not a little in its dignity and estimation, by an opinion of its not acting on worthy motives. On the other hand, the desires of the people (partly natural and partly infused into them by art) appeared in so wild and inconsiderate a manner, with regard to the economical object, (for I set aside for a moment the dreadful tampering with the body of the constitution itself,) that, if their petitions had literally been complied with, the state would have been convulsed; and a gate would have been opened, through which all property might be sacked and ravaged. Nothing could have saved the public from the mischiefs of the false reform but its absurdity; which would soon have brought itself, and with it all real reform, into discredit. This would have left a rankling wound in the hearts of the people, who would know they had failed in the accomplishment of their wishes, but who, like the rest of mankind in all ages, would impute the blame to anything rather than to their own proceedings. But there were then persons in the world, who nourished complaint; and would have been thoroughly disappointed if the people were ever satisfied. I was not of that humour. I wished that they *should* be satisfied. It was my aim to give to the people the substance of what I knew they desired, and what I thought was right, whether they desired it or not, before it had been modified for them into senseless petitions. I knew that there is a manifest, marked distinction, which ill men with ill designs, or weak men incapable of any design, will constantly be confounding, that is, a marked distinction between change and reformation. The former alters the substance of the objects themselves; and gets rid of all their essential good, as well as of all the accidental evil, annexed to them. Change is novelty; and whether it is to operate any one of the effects of reformation at all, or whether it may not contradict the very principle upon which reformation is desired, cannot be certainly known beforehand. Reform is, not a change in the substance, or in the primary modification, of the object, but, a direct application of a remedy to the grievance complained of. So far as that is removed, all is sure. It stops there; and, if it fails, the substance which underwent the operation, at the very worst, is but where it was.

All this, in effect, I think, but am not sure, I have said elsewhere. It cannot at this time be too often repeated; line upon line; precept upon precept; until it comes into the currency of a proverb, *to innovate is not to reform*. The French revolutionists complained of everything; they refused to reform anything; and they left nothing, no, nothing at all *unchanged*. The consequences are *before* us,—not in remote history; not in future prognostication: they are about us; they are upon us. They shake the public security; they menace private enjoyment. They dwarf the growth of the young; they break the quiet of the old. If we travel, they stop our way. They infest us in town; they pursue us to the country. Our business is interrupted; our repose is troubled; our pleasures are saddened; our very studies are poisoned and perverted, and knowledge is rendered worse than ignorance, by the enormous evils of this dreadful innovation. The revolution harpies of France, sprung from night and hell, or from that chaotic anarchy, which generates equivocally "all monstrous, all prodigious things," cuckoo-like, adulterously lay their eggs, and brood over, and hatch them in the nest of every neighbouring state. These obscene harpies, who deck themselves in I know not what divine attributes, but who in reality are foul and ravenous birds of prey, (both mothers and daughters,) flutter over our heads, and souse down upon our tables, and leave nothing unrent, unrifled, unravaged, or unpolluted with the slime of their filthy offal.

If his Grace can contemplate the result of this complete innovation, or, as some friends of his will call it, *reform*, in the whole body of its solidity and compounded mass, at which, as Hamlet says, the face of heaven glows with horror and indignation, and which, in truth, makes every reflecting mind, and every feeling heart, perfectly thought-sick, without a thorough abhorrence of everything they say, and everything they do, I am amazed at the morbid strength or the natural infirmity of his mind.

It was then not my love, but my hatred, to innovation, that produced my plan of reform. Without troubling myself with the exactness of the logical diagram, I considered them as things substantially opposite. It was to prevent that evil, that I proposed the measures, which his Grace is pleased, and I am not sorry he is pleased, to recall to my recollection. I had (what I hope that noble duke will remember in all its operations) a state to preserve, as well as a state to reform. I had a people to gratify, but not to inflame, or to mislead. I do not claim half the credit for what I did, as for what I prevented from being done. In that situation of the public mind, I did not undertake, as was then proposed, to new-model the House of Commons or the House of Lords; or to change the authority under which any officer of the Crown acted, who was suffered at all to exist. . . .

The Duke of Bedford conceives, that he is obliged to call the attention of the House of Peers to his Majesty's grant to me, which he considers as excessive, and out of all bounds.

I know not how it has happened, but it really seems, that, whilst his Grace was meditating his well-considered censure upon me, he fell into a sort of sleep. Homer nods; and the Duke of Bedford may dream; and as dreams (even his golden dreams) are apt to be ill-pieced and incongruously put together, his Grace preserved his idea of reproach to *me,* but took the subject-matter from the Crown grants *to his own family.* This is "the stuff of which his dreams are made." In that way of putting things together his Grace is perfectly in the right. The grants to the house of Russell were so enormous, as not only to outrage economy, but even to stagger credibility. The Duke of Bedford is the leviathan among all the creatures of the Crown. He tumbles about his unwieldy bulk; he plays and frolics in the ocean of the royal bounty. Huge as he is, and whilst "he lies floating many a rood," he is still a creature. His ribs, his fins, his whalebone, his blubber, the very spiracles through which he spouts a torrent of brine against his origin, and covers me all over with the spray,—everything of him and about him is from the throne. Is it for *him* to question the dispensation of the royal favour?

I really am at a loss to draw any sort of parallel between the public merits of his Grace, by which he justifies the grants he holds, and these services of mine, on the favourable construction of which I have obtained what his Grace so much disapproves. In private life, I have not at all the honour of acquaintance with the noble Duke. But I ought to presume, and it costs me nothing to do so, that he abundantly deserves the esteem and love of all who live with him. But as to public service, why truly it would not be more ridiculous for me to compare myself in rank, in fortune, in splendid descent, in youth, strength, or figure, with the Duke of Bedford, than to make a parallel between his services and my attempts to be useful to my country. It would not be gross adulation, but uncivil irony, to say, that he has any public merit of his own to keep alive the idea of the services, by which his vast landed pensions were obtained.

My merits, whatever they are, are original and personal; his are derivative. It is his ancestor, the original pensioner, that has laid up this inexhaustible fund of merit, which makes his Grace so very delicate and exceptious about the merit of all other grantees of the Crown. Had he permitted me to remain in quiet, I should have said, 'tis his estate; that's enough. It is his by law; what have I to do with it or its history? He would naturally have said on his side, 'tis this man's fortune.—He is as good now as my ancestor was two hundred and fifty years ago. I am a young man with very old pensions; he is an old man with very young pensions,—that's all.

Why will his Grace, by attacking me, force me reluctantly to compare my little merit with that which obtained from the Crown those prodigies of profuse donation, by which he tramples on the mediocrity of humble and laborious individuals? I would willingly leave him to the herald's college, which the philosophy of the sans culottes (prouder by far than all the Garters, and Norroys, and Clarencieux, and Rouge Dragons, that ever pranced in a procession of what his friends call aristocrats and despots) will abolish with contumely and scorn. These historians, recorders, and blazoners of virtues and arms, differ wholly from that other description of historians, who never assign any act of politicians to a good motive. These gentle historians, on the contrary, dip their pens in nothing but the milk of human kindness. They seek no further for merit than the preamble of a patent, or the inscription on a tomb. With them every man created a peer is first a hero ready made. They judge of every man's capacity for office by the offices he has filled; and the more offices the more ability. Every general officer with them is a Marlborough; every statesman a Burleigh; every judge a Murray or a Yorke. They who, alive, were laughed at or pitied by all their acquaintance, make as good a figure as the best of them in the pages of Guillim, Edmondson, and Collins.

To these recorders, so full of good nature to the great and prosperous, I would willingly leave the first Baron Russell, and Earl of Bedford, and the merits of his grants. But the aulnager, the weigher, the meter of grants, will not suffer us to acquiesce in the judgment of the prince reigning at the time when they were made. They are never good to those who earn them. Well then; since the new grantees have war made on them by the old, and that the word of the sovereign is not to be taken, let us turn our eyes to history, in which great men have always a pleasure in contemplating the heroic origin of their house.

The first peer of the name, the first purchaser of the grants, was a

Mr. Russell, a person of an ancient gentleman's family raised by being a minion of Henry the Eighth. As there generally is some resemblance of character to create these relations, the favourite was in all likelihood much such another as his master. The first of those immoderate grants was not taken from the ancient demesne of the Crown, but from the recent confiscation of the ancient nobility of the land. The lion having sucked the blood of his prey, threw the offal carcass to the jackal in waiting. Having tasted once the food of confiscation, the favourites became fierce and ravenous. This worthy favourite's first grant was from the lay nobility. The second, infinitely improving on the enormity of the first, was from the plunder of the church. In truth his Grace is somewhat excusable for his dislike to a grant like mine, not only in its quantity, but in its kind so different from his own.

Mine was from a mild and benevolent sovereign; his from Henry the Eighth.

Mine had not its fund in the murder of any innocent person of illustrious rank, or in the pillage of any body of unoffending men. His grants were from the aggregate and consolidated funds of judgments iniquitously legal, and from possessions voluntarily surrendered by the lawful proprietors, with the gibbet at their door.

The merit of the grantee whom he derives from was that of being a prompt and greedy instrument of a *levelling* tyrant, who oppressed all descriptions of his people, but who fell with particular fury on everything that was *great and noble.* Mine has been, in endeavouring to screen every man, in every class, from oppression, and particularly in defending the high and eminent, who in the bad times of confiscating princes, confiscating chief governors, or confiscating demagogues, are the most exposed to jealousy, avarice, and envy.

The merit of the original grantee of his Grace's pensions was in giving his hand to the work and partaking the spoil with a prince, who plundered a part of the national church of his time and country. Mine was in defending the whole of the national church of my own time and my own country, and the whole of the national churches of all countries, from the principles and the examples which lead to ecclesiastical pillage, thence to a contempt of *all* prescriptive titles, thence to the pillage of *all* property, and thence to universal desolation.

The merit of the origin of his Grace's fortune was in being a favourite and chief adviser to a prince, who left no liberty to their native country. My endeavour was to obtain liberty for the municipal country in which I was born, and for all descriptions and denominations in it. Mine was to support with unrelaxing vigilance every right, every privilege, every franchise, in this my adopted, my dearer, and more comprehensive country; and not only to preserve those rights in this chief seat of empire, but in every nation, in every land, in every climate, language, and religion, in the vast domain that is still under the protection, and the larger that was once under the protection, of the British Crown.

His founder's merits were, by arts in which he served his master and made his fortune, to bring poverty, wretchedness, and depopulation on his country. Mine were, under a benevolent prince, in promoting the commerce, manufactures, and agriculture of his kingdom; in which his Majesty shows an eminent example, who even in his amusements is a patriot, and in hours of leisure an improver of his native soil.

His founder's merit was the merit of a gentleman raised by the arts of a court, and the protection of a Wolsey, to the eminence of a great and potent lord. His merit in that eminence was, by instigating a tyrant to injustice, to provoke a people to rebellion. My merit was, to awaken the sober part of the country, that they might put themselves on their guard against any one potent lord, or any greater number of potent lords, or any combination of great leading men of any sort, if ever they should attempt to proceed in the same courses, but in the reverse order; that is, by instigating a corrupted populace to rebellion, and, through that rebellion, introducing a tyranny yet worse than the tyranny which his Grace's ancestor supported, and of which he profited in the manner we behold in the despotism of Henry the Eighth.

The political merit of the first pensioner of his Grace's house was that of being concerned as a counsellor of state in advising, and in his person executing, the conditions of a dishonourable peace with France; the surrendering the fortress of Boulogne, then our out-guard on the continent. By that surrender, Calais, the key of France, and the bridle in the mouth of that power, was, not many years afterwards, finally lost. My merit has been in resisting the power and pride of France, under any form of its rule; but in opposing it with the greatest zeal and earnestness, when that rule appeared in the worst form it could assume; the worst indeed which the prime cause and principle of all evil could possibly give it. It was my endeavour by every means to excite a spirit in the House where I had the honour of a seat, for carrying on, with early vigour and decision, the most clearly just and necessary war, that this or any nation ever carried on; in order to save my country from the iron yoke of its power, and from the more dreadful contagion of its principles; to preserve, while they can be preserved, pure and untainted, the ancient, inbred integrity, piety, good nature, and good humour of the people of England, from the dreadful pestilence, which, beginning in France, threatens to lay waste the whole moral, and in a great degree the whole physical, world, having done both in the focus of its most intense malignity.

The labours of his Grace's founder merited the curses, not loud but deep, of the Commons of England, on whom *he* and his master had effected a *complete parliamentary reform*, by making them, in their slavery and humiliation, the true and adequate representatives of a debased, degraded, and undone people. My merits were, in having had an active, though not always an ostentatious, share, in every one act, without exception, of undisputed constitutional utility in my time, and in having supported, on all occasions, the authority, the efficiency, and the privileges of the Commons of Great Britain. I ended my services by a recorded and fully reasoned assertion on their own journals of their constitutional rights, and a vindication of their constitutional conduct. I laboured in all things to merit their inward approbation, and (along with the assistance of the largest, the greatest, and best of my endeavours) I received their free, unbiassed, public, and solemn thanks.

Thus stands the account of the comparative merits of the Crown grants which compose the Duke of Bedford's fortune as balanced against mine. In the name of common sense, why should the Duke of Bedford think, that none but of the House of Russell are entitled to the favour of the Crown? Why should he imagine that no king of England has been capable of judging of merit but King Henry the Eighth? Indeed, he will pardon me; he is a little mistaken; all virtue did not end in the first Earl of Bedford. All discernment did not lose its vision when his Creator closed his eyes. Let him remit his rigour on the disproportion between merit and reward in others, and they will make no inquiry into the origin of his fortune. They will regard with much more satisfaction, as he will contemplate with infinitely more advantage, whatever in his pedigree has been dulcified by an exposure to the influence of heaven in a long flow of generations, from the hard, acidulous, metallic tincture of the spring. It is little to be doubted, that several of his forefathers in that long series have degenerated into honour and virtue. Let the Duke of Bedford (I am sure he will) reject with scorn and horror the counsels of the lecturers, those wicked panders to avarice and ambition, who would tempt him, in the troubles of his country, to seek another enormous fortune from the forfeitures of another nobility, and the plunder of another church. Let him (and I trust that yet he will) employ all the energy of his youth, and all the resources of his wealth, to crush rebellious principles which have no foundation in morals, and rebellious movements that have no *provocation in tyranny*. . . . I assure his Grace, that if I state to him the designs of his enemies, in a manner which may appear to him ludicrous and impossible, I tell him nothing that has not exactly happened, point by point, but twenty-four miles from our own shore. I assure him that the Frenchified faction, more encouraged, than others are warned, by what has happened in France, look at him and his landed possessions as an object at once of curiosity and rapacity. He is made for them in every part of their double character. As robbers, to them he is a noble booty; as speculatists, he is a glorious subject for their experimental philosophy. He affords matter for an extensive analysis, in all the branches of their science, geometrical, physical, civil, and political. These philosophers are fanatics; independent of any interest, which if it operated alone would make them much more tractable, they are carried with such a headlong rage towards every desperate trial, that they would sacrifice the whole human race to the slightest of their experiments. I am better able to enter into the character of this description of men than the noble Duke can be. I have lived long and variously in the world. Without any considerable pretensions to literature in myself, I have aspired to the love of letters. I have lived for a great many years in habitudes with those who professed them. I can form a tolerable estimate of what is likely to happen from a character, chiefly dependent for fame and fortune on knowledge and talent, as well in its morbid and perverted state, as in that which is sound and natural. Naturally men so formed and finished are the first gifts of Providence to the world. But when they have once thrown off the fear of God, which was in all ages too often the case, and the fear of man, which is now the case, and when in that state they come to understand one another, and to act in corps, a more dreadful calamity cannot arise out of hell to scourge mankind. Nothing can be conceived more hard than the heart of a thoroughbred metaphysician. It comes nearer to the cold malignity of a wicked spirit than to the frailty and passion of a man. It is like that of the principle of evil himself, incorporeal, pure, unmixed, dephlegmated, defecated evil. It is no easy operation to eradicate humanity from the human breast. What Shakspeare calls "the compunctious visitings of nature" will sometimes knock at their hearts, and protest against their murderous speculations. But they have a means of compounding with their nature. Their humanity is not dissolved. They only give it a long prorogation. They are ready to declare, that they do not think two thousand years too long a period for the good that they pursue. It is remarkable, that they never see any way to their projected good but by the road of some evil. Their imagination is not fatigued with the contemplation of human suffering through the wild waste of centuries added to centuries of misery and desolation. Their humanity is at their horizon—and, like the horizon, it always flies before them. The geometricians, and the chemists, bring, the one from the dry bones of their diagrams, and the other from the soot of their furnaces, dispositions that make them worse than indifferent about those feelings and habitudes, which are the support of the moral world. Ambition is come upon them suddenly; they are intoxicated with it, and it has rendered them fearless of the danger, which may from thence arise to others or to themselves. These philosophers consider men in their experiments, no more than they do mice in an air pump, or in a recipient of mephitic gas. Whatever his Grace may think of himself, they look upon him, and everything that belongs to him, with no more regard than they do upon the whiskers of that little long-tailed animal, that has been long the game of the grave, demure, insidious, spring-nailed, velvet-pawed, green-eyed philosophers, whether going upon two legs, or upon four.

His Grace's landed possessions are irresistibly inviting to an *agrarian* experiment. They are a downright insult upon the rights of man. They are more extensive than the territory of many of the Grecian republics; and they are without comparison more fertile than most of them. There are now republics in Italy, in Germany, and in Switzerland, which do not possess anything like so fair and ample a domain. There is scope for seven philosophers to proceed in their analytical experiments, upon Harrington's seven different forms of republics, in the acres of this one duke. Hitherto they have been wholly unproductive to speculation; fitted for nothing but to fatten bullocks, and to produce grain for beer, still more to stupify the dull English understanding. Abbé Sieyes has whole nests of pigeon-holes full of constitutions ready made, ticketed, sorted, and numbered; suited to every season and every fancy; some with the top of the pattern at the bottom, and some with the bottom at the top; some plain, some flowered; some distinguished for their simplicity, others for their complexity; some of blood colour; some of *boue de Paris*; some with directories, others without a direction; some with councils of elders, and councils of youngsters; some without any council at all. Some where the electors choose the representatives; others, where the representatives choose the electors. Some in long coats, and some in short cloaks; some with pantaloons; some without breeches. Some with five-shilling qualifications; some totally unqualified. So that no constitution-fancier may go unsuited from his shop, provided he loves a pattern of pillage, oppression, arbitrary imprisonment, confiscation, exile, revolutionary judgment, and legalized premeditated murder, in any shapes into which they can be put. What a pity it is, that the progress of experimental philosophy should be checked by his Grace's monopoly! Such are their sentiments, I assure him; such is their language, when they dare to speak; and such are their proceedings, when they have the means to act.

Their geographers and geometricians have been some time out of practice. It is some time since they have divided their own country into squares. That figure has lost the charms of its novelty. They want new lands for new trials. It is not only the geometricians of the republic that find him a good subject, the chemists have bespoken him after the geometricians have done with him. As the first set have an eye on his Grace's lands, the chemists are not less taken with his buildings. They consider mortar as a very anti-revolutionary invention in its present state; but properly employed, an admirable material for overturning all establishments. They have found that the gunpowder of *ruins* is far the fittest for making other *ruins,* and so *ad infinitum*. They have calculated what quantity of matter convertible into nitre is to be found in Bedford House, in Woburn Abbey, and in what his Grace and his trustees have still suffered to stand of that foolish royalist Inigo Jones, in Covent Garden. Churches, play-houses, coffee-houses, all alike are destined to be mingled, and equalized, and blended into one common rubbish; and, well sifted and lixiviated, to crystallize into true, democratic, explosive, insurrectionary nitre. Their academy del *Cimento* (per antiphrasin) with Morveau and Hassenfrats at its head, have computed that the brave sans culottes may make war on all the aristocracy of Europe for a twelve-month, out of the rubbish of the Duke of Bedford's buildings.

While the Morveaux and Priestleys are proceeding with these experiments upon the Duke of Bedford's houses, the Sieyes, and the rest of the analytical legislators, and constitution-venders, are quite as busy in their trade of decomposing organization, in forming his Grace's vassals into primary assemblies, national guards, first, second, and third requisitioners, committees of research, conductors of the travelling guillotine, judges of revolutionary tribunals, legislative hangmen, supervisors of domiciliary visitation, exactors of forced loans, and assessors of the maximum.

The din of all this smithery may some time or other possibly wake this noble Duke, and push him to an endeavour to save some little matter from their experimental philosophy. If he pleads his grants from the Crown, he is ruined at the outset. If he pleads he has received them from the pillage of superstitious corporations, this indeed will stagger them a little, because they are enemies to all corporations, and to all religion. However, they will soon recover themselves, and will tell his Grace, or his learned council, that all such property belongs to the *nation*; and that it would be more wise for him, if he wishes to live the natural term of a *citizen*, (that is, according to Condorcet's calculation, six months on an average,) not to pass for an usurper upon the national property. This is what the *serjeants* at law of the rights of man will say to the puny *apprentices* of the common law of England.

Is the genius of philosophy not yet known? You may as well think the garden of the Tuilleries was well protected with the cords of ribbon insultingly stretched by the National Assembly to keep the sovereign canaille from intruding on the retirement of the poor king of the French, as that such flimsy cobwebs will stand between the savages of the Revolution and their natural prey. Deep philosophers are no triflers; brave sans-culottes are no formalists. They will no more regard a Marquis of Tavistock than an Abbot of Tavistock; the Lord of Woburn will not be more respectable in their eyes than the Prior of Woburn; they will make no difference between the superior of a Covent Garden of nuns, and of a Covent Garden of another description. They will not care a rush whether his coat is long or short; whether the colour be purple or blue and buff. They will not trouble *their* heads, with what part of *his* head his hair is cut from; and they will look with equal respect on a tonsure and a crop. Their only question will be that of their *Legendre*, or some other of their legislative butchers, how he cuts up? how he tallows in the cawl, or on the kidneys?

Is it not a singular phenomenon, that whilst the sans-culotte carcass-butchers, and the philosophers of the shambles, are pricking their dotted lines upon his hide, and, like the print of the poor ox that we see in the shop-windows at Charing Cross, alive as he is, and thinking no harm in the world, he is divided into rumps, and sirloins, and briskets, and into all sorts of pieces for roasting, boiling, and stewing, that all the while they are measuring *him*, his Grace is measuring *me*; is invidiously comparing the bounty of the Crown with the deserts of the defender of his order, and in the same moment fawning on those who have the knife half out of the sheath—poor innocent!

PART III

AMERICA AND REVOLUTION

An Account of the European Settlements in America

In the late 1750s and early 1760s Burke worked on a detailed history of the colonization of America, probably with the assistance of his cousin William Burke. In it one sees early on Burke's knowledge of and interest in America. These excerpts are from Burke's discussion of West Indian slavery and of the origins of Puritan New England.

SINCE I HAVE INDULGED MYSELF so long in a speculation which appears to me very material to the welfare of these colonies, I shall venture to say something further concerning another part of the inhabitants, though it may perhaps meet no warm reception from those who are the most nearly concerned.

The negroes in our colonies endure a slavery more complete, and attended with far worse circumstances, than what any people in their condition suffer in any other part of the world, or have suffered in any other period of time. Proofs of this are not wanting. The prodigious waste which we experience in this unhappy part of our species, is a full and melancholy evidence of this truth. The island of Barbadoes (the negroes upon which do not amount to eighty thousand) notwithstanding all the means which they use to increase them by propagation, notwithstanding that the climate is in every respect, except that of being more wholesome, exactly resembling the climate from whence they come; notwithstanding all this, Barbadoes lives under a necessity of an annual recruit of five thousand slaves to keep up the stock at the number I have mentioned. This prodigious failure, which is at least in the same proportion in all our islands, shows demonstratively that some uncommon and insupportable hardship lies upon the negroes, which wears them down in such a surprising manner; and this, I imagine, is principally the excessive labor which they undergo. For previously, I suppose, that none of the inhabitants of the countries between the tropics are capable, even in their own climates, of near so much labor, without great prejudice to them, as our people are in ours. But in our plantations the blacks work severely for five days, without any relaxation or intermission, for the benefit of the master, and the other two days they are obliged to labor for their own subsistence, during the rest of the week; and this, I imagine, with the other circumstances of great severity which depress their spirits, naturally cuts off great numbers, as well as disqualifies those who remain from supplying this waste by natural propagation.

The planter will say, that, if he is to allow his negroes more recreation and to indulge them in more hours of absence from their work, he can never reimburse himself for the charge he has been at in the purchase of the slave, nor make the profits which induced him to go to that expense. But this, though it appears plausible enough at first, because the slaves are very dear, and because they do not yield above ten or twelve pounds a head annually clear profit by their labor, is notwithstanding very fallacious. For let it be considered, that, out of their stock of eighty thousand in Barbadoes, there die every year five thousand negroes more than are born in that island: in effect, this people is under a necessity of being entirely renewed every sixteen years; and what must we think of the management of a people, who, far from increasing greatly, as those who have no loss by wars ought to do, must, in so short a space of time as sixteen years, without foreign recruits, be entirely consumed to a man? Let us suppose that these slaves stand the Barbadians in no more than twenty pounds a head out of the ship; whereas, in reality, they cost a great deal more; this makes one hundred thousand pounds every year, and in sixteen years, one million six hundred thousand pounds. A sum really astonishing, and amounting to a fourth of the value of every thing they export.

Now suppose, that, by allowing a more moderate labor and some other indulgences, a great number of these deaths might be prevented (and many I think it is probable would so be prevented,) and that they could keep up within a thousand of their stock (and why they could not entirely keep it up by such means, I cannot possibly guess) they would save in this way eighty thousand pounds every year. But from thence we must deduct the time in which these slaves have been unemployed. I suppose that all reasonable indulgences might be given of every sort for the difference of forty thousand pounds, which is the labor of four thousand slaves. This will be far from a small allowance, especially as in this way less time will be lost by sickness, and the surgeon will have less employment. Then, after all deductions, by behaving like good men, good masters, and good Christians, the inhabitants of this one island would save forty thousand pounds a year; which if, instead of being saved, it were lost by such a proceeding, it ought to be considered as a necessary loss, and borne accordingly.

This matter, though not, I think, before shown in this same light, seems in itself extremely clear; but if it were yet clearer, there are several gentlemen of the West Indies who could not comprehend it; though a wagoner in England will comprehend very clearly, that, if he works his horse but moderately and feeds him well, he will draw more profit from him in the end, than if he never gave him an hour's respite in the day from his work, and at night turned him upon the common for his subsistence. I am far from contending in favor of an effeminate indulgence to these people. I know that they are stubborn and intractable for the most part, and that they must be ruled with the rod of iron. I would have them ruled, but not crushed with it. I would have a humanity exercised which is consistent with steadiness. And I think it clear from the whole course of history, that those nations which have behaved with the greatest humanity to their slaves were always best served, and ran the least hazard from their rebellions. And I am the more convinced of the necessity of these indulgencies, as slaves certainly cannot go through so much work as freemen. The mind goes a great way in every thing; and when a man knows that his labor is for himself, and that the more he labors, the more he is to acquire, this consciousness carries him through, and supports him beneath fatigues, under which he otherwise would have sunk.

The prejudice this saving would be to the African trade is, I know, an objection which to some would appear very plausible. But surely, one cannot hear without horror of a trade which must depend for its support upon the annual murder of several thousands of innocent men; and indeed nothing could excuse the slave trade at all, but the necessity we are under of peopling our colonies, and the consideration that the slaves we buy were in the same condition in Africa, either hereditary or taken in war. But, in fact, if the waste of these men should become less, the price would fall; then, if a due order were taken, the same demand might be kept, by extending our colonies, which is now produced by the havoc made of the people. This is the case on the continent, where, though the slaves increase, there is an annual call for seven thousand at least.

The principal time I would have reserved for the indulgence I propose to be granted to the slaves is Sunday, or the Lord's day; a day which is profaned in a manner altogether scandalous in our colonies. On this day, I would have them regularly attend at church; I would have them, particularly the children, carefully (full as carefully as any others) instructed in the principles of religion and virtue, and especially in the humility, submission, and honesty, which become their condition. The rest of the day might be devoted to innocent recreation; to these days of relaxation, and with the same exercises, should be added some days in the grand festivals of Christmas, Easter, and Whitsuntide, and perhaps, four or five days in the year besides. Such methods would by degrees habituate their masters, not to think them a sort of beasts, and without souls, as some of them do at present, who treat them accordingly; and the slaves would of course grow more honest, tractable, and less of eye-servants; unless the sanctions of religion, the precepts of morality, and all the habits of an early institution, be of no advantage to mankind. Indeed I have before me an author, if he may be so called, who treats the notion of bringing the negroes to Christianity with contempt, and talks of it at the best, as a thing of indifference. But, besides that, he appears to me a writer of very little judgment, I cannot conceive with what face any body, who pretends to inform the public, can set up as an advocate for irreligion, barbarism, and gross ignorance. . . .

It is said, that the law of England is favorable to liberty; and so far this observation is just, that, when we had men in a servile condition amongst us, the law took advantage even of neglects of the masters to enfranchise the villain: and seemed for that purpose even to subtilize a little; because our ancestors judged, that freemen were the real support of the kingdom. What if in our colonies we should go so far as to find out some medium between liberty and absolute slavery, in which we might place all mulattoes after a certain limited servitude to the owner of the mother; and such blacks, who being born in the islands, their masters for their good services should think proper in some degree to enfranchise? These might have land allotted them, or, where that could not be spared, some sort of fixed employment, from either of which they should be obliged to pay a certain moderate rent to the public. Whatever they should acquire above this, to be the reward of their industry. The necessity of paying the rent would keep them from idleness; and when men are once set to work through necessity, they will not stop there; but they will gradually strive for conveniences, and some even for superfluities. All this will add to the demand for our goods, and the colony will be strengthened by the addition of so many men, who will have an interest of their own to fight for.

There is, amongst others, a very bad custom in our colonies of multiplying their household slaves far beyond reason and necessity. It is not uncommon for families of no very great fortunes, to have twenty-five or thirty in the capacity of menial servants only. These are so many hands taken from planting, to be of no manner of use to the public; but they are infinitely the most dangerous of the slaves; for being at all times about our people, they come to abate of that great reverence which the field negroes have for the whites, without losing any thing of the resentment of their condition, which is common to both. And besides, in any insurrection, they have it more in their power to strike a sudden and fatal blow. Surely a sumptuary law might be contrived to restrain the number of the menial slaves, as there might and ought to be one strictly enjoining all who keep five servants, to have one white man and one white woman amongst them, without any power of being indulged in a contrary practice; as it ought to be a rule never to be broken through, to have not only the overseers, but even all the drivers, white men.

The alarms we are under at the news of any petty armament in the West Indies is a demonstrative proof of the weakness of our condition there; which is, however, so far from rousing us to seek any proper remedy, that there are not wanting of the people of that country, many who would use a thousand pretences to prevent our taking the only possible means of securing their own possessions from danger; as the majority of men will always be found ready to prefer some present gain to their future and more permanent interests. But the apparent and dangerous progress of the French ought, methinks, to arouse us from our long inaction, and to animate us to enterprise some regulations, in a strain of policy far superior to any thing I have ventured to hint for the interest of the commerce and the honor of the councils of the British nation.

We derive our rights in America from the discovery of Sebastian Cabot, who first made the northern continent in 1497. The fact is sufficiently certain to establish a right to our settlements in North America: but the particulars are not known distinctly enough to encourage me to enter into a detail of his voyage. The country was in general called Newfoundland, a name which is now appropriated solely to an island upon its coast. It was a long time before we made any attempt to settle this country; though in this point we were no more backward than our neighbors, who probably did not abstain so long out of respect to our prior discovery. Sir Walter Raleigh showed the way, by planting a colony in the southern part, which he called Virginia. However, the spirit of colonization was not yet fully raised. Men lived at ease in their own country, and the new settlement of Virginia, though dressed up in all the showy colors which eloquence could bestow upon it, gave adventurers but little encouragement. The affairs of North America were in the hands of an exclusive company, and they prospered accordingly.

Things remained in this condition until the latter end of the reign of James the First. From the commencement of the Reformation in England, two parties of Protestants subsisted amongst us; the first had chosen gradually and almost imperceptibly to recede from the church of Rome; softening the lines rather than erasing the figure, they made but very little alteration in the appearances of things. And the people, seeing the exterior so little altered, hardly perceived the great changes they had made in the doctrines of their religion. The other party, of a warmer temper, had more zeal and less policy. Several of them had fled from the persecution in Queen Mary's days; and they returned in those of Queen Elizabeth with minds sufficiently heated by resentment of their sufferings, and by the perpetual disputations which had exercised them all the while they were abroad. Abroad they learned an aversion to the episcopal order, and to religious ceremonies of every sort; they were impregnated with a high spirit of liberty, and had a strong tendency to the republican form of government. Queen Elizabeth had enough of the blood of Harry the Eighth to make her impatient of an opposition to her will, especially in matters of religion, in which she had a high opinion of her own knowledge. She advised with the party but very little in the alterations which she thought proper to make; and, disliking the notions which they seemed to entertain in politics, she kept them down during the whole course of her reign with a uniform and inflexible severity.

However, the party was far enough from being destroyed. The merit of their sufferings, the affected plainness of their dress, the gravity of their deportment, the use of scripture phrases upon the most ordinary occasions, and even their names, which had something striking and venerable, as being borrowed from the Old Testament, or having a sort of affected relation to religious matters, gained them a general esteem amongst sober people of ordinary understandings. This party was very numerous; and their zeal made them yet more considerable than their numbers. They were commonly called Puritans.

When King James came to the throne, he had a very fair opportunity of pacifying matters; or at worst he might have left them in the condition he found them; but it happened quite otherwise. The unkingly disputation at Hampton Court did more to encourage the Puritans to persevere in their opinions, by the notice which was taken of them, than all King James's logic as a scholar, backed with all his power as a king, could do to suppress that party. They were persecuted, but not destroyed; they were exasperated, and yet left powerful; and a severity was exercised towards them which at once exposed the weakness and the ill intentions of the government.

In this state things continued until the accession of Charles, when they were far from mending. This prince, endowed with many great virtues, had very few amiable qualities. As grave as the Puritans themselves, he could never engage the licentious part of the world in his favor; and that gravity being turned against the Puritans, made him but the more odious to them. He gave himself up entirely to the church and churchmen; and he finished his ill conduct in this respect, by conferring the first ecclesiastical dignity of the kingdom, and a great sway in temporal affairs, upon Dr. Laud. Hardly fit to direct a college, he was called to govern a kingdom. He was one of those indiscreet men of good intentions, who are the people in the world that make the worst figure in politics. This man thought he did good service to religion by a scrupulous inquiry into the manner in which the ministers everywhere conformed to the regulations of the former reigns. He deprived great numbers for nonconformity. Not satisfied with this, in which perhaps he was justifiable enough if he had managed prudently, he made new regulations, and introduced on a people already abhorrent of the most necessary ceremonies, ceremonies of a new kind, of a most useless nature, and such as were even ridiculous, if the serious consequences which attended them may not entitle them to be considered as matters of importance.

Several great men, disgusted at the proceedings of the court, and entertaining very reasonable apprehensions for the public liberty, to make themselves popular, attached themselves to the popular notions of religion, and affected to maintain them with great zeal. Others became Puritans through principle. And now their affairs put on a respectable appearance; in proportion as they became of consequence, their sufferings seemed to be more and more grievous; the severities of Laud raised not terror as formerly, but a sort of indignant hatred; and they became every day further and further from listening to the least terms of agreement with surplices, organs, commonprayer, or table at the east end of the church. As they who are serious about trifles are serious indeed, their lives began to grow miserable to several on account of these ceremonies;

and, rather than be obliged to submit to them, there was no part of the world to which they would not have fled with cheerfulness.

Early in the reign of King James a number of persons of this persuasion had sought refuge in Holland; in which, though a country of the greatest religious freedom in the world, they did not find themselves better satisfied than they had been in England. There they were tolerated indeed, but watched; their zeal began to have dangerous languors for want of opposition; and, being without power or consequence, they grew tired of the indolent security of their sanctuary; they chose to remove to a place where they should see no superior; and therefore they sent an agent to England, who agreed with the council of Plymouth, for a tract of land in America, within their jurisdiction, to settle in, after they had obtained from the king a privilege to do so. The Plymouth council was a company, who, by their charter, had not only all the coast of North America from Nova Scotia to the southern parts of Carolina (the whole country being then distinguished by the names of South and North Virginia) as a scene for their exclusive trade; but they had the entire property of the soil besides.

This colony established itself at a place which they called New Plymouth. They were but few in number; they landed in a bad season; and they were not at all supported but from their private funds. The winter was premature and terribly cold. The country was all covered with wood, and afforded very little for the refreshment of persons sickly with such a voyage, or for sustenance of an infant people. Near half of them perished by the scurvy, by want, and the severity of the climate; but they who survived, not dispirited with their losses nor with the hardships they were still to endure, supported by the vigor which was then the character of Englishmen, and by the satisfaction of finding themselves out of the reach of the spiritual arm, reduced this savage country to yield them a tolerable livelihood, and by degrees a comfortable subsistence.

This little establishment was made in the year 1621. Several of their brethren in England, laboring under the same difficulties, took the same methods of escaping from them. The colony of Puritans insensibly increased; but as yet they had not extended themselves much beyond New Plymouth. It was in the year 1629, that the colony began to flourish in such a manner, that they soon became a considerable people. By the close of the ensuing year they had built four towns, Salem, Dorchester, Charlestown, and Boston, which has since become the capital of New

England. That enthusiasm which was reversing every thing at home, and which is so dangerous in every settled community, proved of admirable service here. It became a principle of life and vigor, that enabled them to conquer all the difficulties of a savage country. Their exact and sober manners proved a substitute for a proper subordination and regular form of government, which they had for some time wanted, and the want of which in such a country had otherwise been felt very severely.

And now, not only they who found themselves uneasy at home upon a religious account, but several by reason of the then profitable trade of furs and skins, and for the sake of the fishery, were invited to settle in New England. But this colony received its principal assistance from the discontent of several great men of the puritan party, who were its protectors, and who entertained a design of settling amongst them in New England, if they should fail in the measures they were pursuing for establishing the liberty, and reforming the religion of their mother country. They solicited grants in New England, and were at a great expense in settling them. Amongst these patentees, we see the Lords Brook, Say and Seal, the Pelhams, the Hampdens, and the Pyms; the names which afterwards appeared with so much eclat upon a greater stage. It was said that Sir Matthew Boynton, Sir William Constable, Sir Arthur Haslerig, and Oliver Cromwell were actually upon the point of embarking for New England, when Archbishop Laud, unwilling that so many objects of his hatred should be removed out of the reach of his power, applied for, and obtained, an order from the court to put a stop to these transportations; and thus he kept forcibly from venting itself that virulent humor which he lived to see the destruction of himself, his order, his religion, his master, and the constitution of his country. However, he was not able to prevail so far as to hinder New England from receiving vast reinforcements, as well of the clergy who were deprived of their livings, or not admitted to them for noncomformity, as of such of the laity who adhered to their opinions. . . .

The part of New England called Massachusetts Bay had now settlements very thick all along the sea-shore. Some slips from these were planted in the province of Maine and New Hampshire, being torn from the original stock by the religious violence, which was the chief characteristic of the first settlers in New England. The patentees we last mentioned principally settled upon the river Connecticut, and established a separate and independent government there: some persons having before that fixed themselves upon the borders of this river, who fled from the tyranny arising from the religious differences which were moulded into the first principles of the Plymouth and Massachusetts colonies.

For a considerable time, the people of New England had hardly any that deserved the name of a regular form of government. The court took very little care of them. By their charter they were empowered to establish such an order, and to make such laws, as they pleased, provided they were not contrary to the laws of England. A point not easily settled, neither was there any means appointed for settling it. As they who composed the new colonies were generally persons of a contracted way of thinking and most violent enthusiasts, they imitated the Jewish polity in almost all respects; and adopted the books of Moses as the law of the land. The first laws which they made were grounded upon them, and were therefore very ill suited to the customs, genius or circumstances of that country and of those times; for which reason they have since fallen into disuse.

As to religion, it was, as I have said, the Puritan. In England, this could hardly be considered as a formed sect at the time of their emigration, since several who had received episcopal ordination were reckoned to belong to it. But as soon as they found themselves at liberty in America, they fell into a way very little different from the independent mode. Every parish was sovereign within itself. Synods indeed were occasionally called; but they served only to prepare and digest matters, which were to receive their sanction from the approbation of the several churches. The synods could exercise no branch of ecclesiastical jurisdiction, either as to doctrine or to discipline. They had no power of excommunication. They could only refuse to hold communion with those whose principles and practices they disliked. The magistrates assisted in those synods, not only to hear, but to deliberate and determine. From such a form as this, great religious freedom might, one would have imagined, be well expected. But the truth is, they had no idea at all of such a freedom. The very doctrine of any sort of toleration was so odious to the greater part, that one of the first persecutions set up here was against a small party which arose amongst themselves, who were hardy enough to maintain, that the civil magistrate had no lawful power to use compulsory measures in affairs of religion. After harrassing these people by all the vexatious ways imaginable, they obliged them to fly out of their jurisdiction. These emigrants settled themselves to the southward, near Cape Cod, where they formed a new government upon their own principles, and built a town, which they called Providence. This has since made the fourth and smallest, but not the worst inhabited, of the New England governments, called Rhode Island, from an island of that name which forms a part of it. As a persecution gave rise to the first settlement of New England, so a subsequent persecution in this colony gave rise to new colonies, and this facilitated the spreading of the people over the country.

If men, merely for the moderation of their sentiments, were exposed to such severe treatment, it was not to be expected that others should escape unpunished. The very first colony had hardly set its foot in America, when, discovering that some amongst them were false brethren and ventured to make use of the common prayer, they found means of making the country so uneasy to them, that they were glad to fly back to England.

As soon as they began to think of making laws, I find no less than five about matters of religion; all contrived, and not only contrived but executed in some respects, with so much rigor, that the persecution which drove the Puritans out of England might be considered as great lenity and indulgence in the comparison. For, in the first of these laws, they deprive every one, who does not communicate with their established church, of the right to his freedom, or a vote in the election of any of their magistrates. In the second, they sentence to banishment any who should oppose the fourth commandment, or deny the validity of infant baptism or the authority of magistrates. In the third, they condemn Quakers to banishment, and make it capital for them to return; and, not stopping at the offenders, they lay heavy fines upon all who should bring them into the province, or even harbor them for an hour. In the fourth, they provide banishment, and death in case of return, for Jesuits and Popish priests of every denomination. In the fifth, they decree death to any who shall worship images. After they had provided such a complete code of persecution, they were not long without opportunities of reading bloody lectures upon it. The Quakers, warmed with that spirit which animates the beginning of most sects, had spread their doctrines all over the British dominions in Europe, and began at last to spread them with equal zeal in America. The clergy and the magistrates in New England took the alarm; they seized upon some of those people, they set them in the stocks and in the pillory without effect; they scourged, they imprisoned, they banished them; they treated all those, who seemed to commiserate their sufferings, with great rigor; but their persecution had no other effect than to inflame their own cruelty and the zeal of the sufferers. The constancy of the Quakers under their sufferings begot a pity and esteem for their persons, and an approbation of their doctrines; their proselytes increased; the Quakers returned as fast as they were banished; and the fury of the ruling party was raised to such a height, that they proceeded to the most sanguinary extremities. Upon the law they had made, they seized at different times upon five of those who had returned from banishment, condemned, and hanged them. It is unknown how far their madness had extended, if an order from the king and council in England about the year 1661 had not interposed to restrain them.

It is a task not very agreeable to insist upon such matters; but, in reality, things of this nature form the greatest part of the history of New England, for a long time. They persecuted the Anabaptists, who were no inconsiderable body amongst them, with almost an equal severity. In short, this people, who in England could not bear being chastised with rods, had no sooner got free from their fetters than they scourged their fellow refugees with scorpions; though the absurdity, as well as the injustice of such a proceeding in them might stare them in the face!

One may observe that men of all persuasions confine the word persecution, and all the ill ideas of injustice and violence which belong to it, solely to those severities which are exercised upon themselves, or upon the party they are inclined to favor. Whatever is inflicted upon others, is a just punishment upon obstinate impiety, and not a restraint upon conscientious differences. The persecution we have ourselves suffered is a good ground for retaliation against an old enemy; and if one of our friends and fellow-sufferers should prove so wicked as to quit our cause, and weaken it by his dissension, he deserves to be punished yet more than the old enemy himself. Besides this, the zealous never fail to draw political inferences from religious tenets, by which they interest the magistrate in the dispute; and then to the heat of a religious fervor is added the fury of a party zeal. All intercourse is cut off between the parties. They lose all knowledge of each other, though countrymen and neighbors; and are therefore easily imposed upon with the most absurd stories concerning each other's opinions and practices. They judge of the hatred of the adverse side by their own. Then fear is added to their hatred; and preventive injuries arise from their fear. The remembrance of the past, the dread of the future, the present ill, will join together to urge them forward to the most violent courses.

Such is the manner of proceeding of religious parties towards each other; and in this respect the New England people are not worse than the rest of mankind, nor was their severity any just matter of reflection upon that mode of religion which they profess. No religion whatsoever, true or false, can excuse its own members, or accuse those of any other, upon the score of persecution. The principles which give rise to it are common to all mankind, and they influence them as they are men, and not as they belong to this or that persuasion. In all persuasions the bigots are persecutors; the men of a cool and reasonable piety are favorers of toleration; because the former sort of men, not taking the pains to be acquainted with the grounds of their adversaries' tenets, conceive them to be so absurd and monstrous, that no man of sense can give in to them in good earnest. For which reason they are convinced that some oblique bad motive induces them to pretend to the belief of such doctrines and to the maintaining of them with obstinacy. This is a very general principle in all religious differences, and it is the corner stone of all persecution.

Besides the disputes with those of another denomination, the Independents were for a long time harrassed with one in the bowels of their own churches. The stale disputes about grace and works, produced dissensions, riots, and almost a civil war in the colony. The famous Sir Henry Vane the younger, an enthusiastic, giddy, turbulent man, of a no very good disposition, came hither with some of the adventurers; and rather than remain idle, played at small games in New England, where the people had chosen him governor. It is not hard to conceive, how such a man, at the head of such a people and engaged in such controversy, could throw every thing into confusion. In the very height of this hopeful dispute, they had a war upon their hands with some of the Indian nations. Their country was terribly harrassed, and numbers were every day murdered, by the incursions of the enemy. All this time they had an army in readiness for action, which they would not suffer to march even to defend their own lives and possessions, because "many of the officers and soldiers were under a covenant of works."

Observations on a Late Publication Entitled "The Present State of the Nation"

Burke was convinced that it was the misguided policies of Great Britain that had brought about the tension between the British government and America in the 1760s. In 1769 he published a pamphlet naming the former prime minister George Grenville and his Stamp Act as the principal villains. Burke's patron, Rockingham, who succeeded Grenville in 1765, repealed the Stamp Act, only to see the next ministry, the duke of Grafton's, impose the equally onerous Townsend duties on the Americans.

On the resignation of the Earl of Bute, in 1763, our affairs had been delivered into the hands of three ministers of his recommendation: Mr. Grenville, the Earl of Egremont, and the Earl of Halifax. This arrangement, notwithstanding the retirement of Lord Bute, announced to the public a continuance of the same measures; nor was there more reason to expect a change from the death of the Earl of Egremont. The Earl of Sandwich supplied his place. The Duke of Bedford, and the gentlemen who act in that connection, and whose general character and politics were sufficiently understood, added to the strength of the ministry, without making any alteration in their plan of conduct. . . .

As to their politics, the principles of the peace of Paris governed in foreign affairs. In domestic, the same scheme prevailed, of contradicting the opinions and disgracing most of the persons who had been countenanced and employed in the late reign. The inclinations of the people were little attended to; and a disposition to the use of forcible methods ran through the whole tenor of administration. The nation in general was uneasy and dissatisfied. Sober men saw causes for it in the constitution of the ministry and the conduct of the ministers. The ministers, who have usually a short method on such occasions, attributed their unpopularity wholly to the efforts of faction.

. . . With regard to our domestic affairs, there was no want of industry; but there was a great deficiency of temper and judgment, and manly comprehension of the public interest. The nation certainly wanted relief, and government attempted to administer it. Two ways were principally chosen for this great purpose. The first by regulations; the second by new funds of revenue. Agreeably to this plan, a new naval establishment was formed at a good deal of expense, and to little effect, to aid in the collection of the customs. Regulation was added to regulation; and the strictest and most unreserved orders were given, for a prevention of all contraband trade here, and in every part of America. A teasing custom-house, and a multiplicity of perplexing regulations, ever have, and ever will appear, the masterpiece of finance to people of narrow views. . . .

The greatest part of these regulations were made for America; and they fell so indiscriminately on all sorts of contraband, or supposed contraband, that some of the most valuable branches of trade were driven violently from our ports; which caused a universal consternation throughout the colonies. Every part of the trade was infinitely distressed by them. Men-of-war now for the first time, armed with regular commissions of custom-house officers, invested the coasts, and gave to the collection of revenue the air of hostile contribution. About the same time that these regulations seemed to threaten the destruction of the only trade from whence the plantations derived any specie, an act was made putting a stop to the future emission of paper currency, which used to supply its place among them. Hand in hand with this went another act, for obliging the colonies to provide quarters for soldiers. Instantly followed another law, for levying throughout all America new port duties, upon a vast variety of commodities of their consumption, and some of which lay heavy upon objects necessary for their trade and fishery. Immediately upon the heels of these, and amidst the uneasiness and confusion produced by a crowd of new impositions and regulations, some good, some evil, some doubtful, all crude and ill-considered, came another act, for imposing a universal stamp-duty on the colonies; and this was declared to be little more than an experiment, and a foundation of future revenue. To render these proceedings the more irritating to the colonies, the principal argument used in favor of their ability to pay such duties was the liberality of the grants of their assemblies during the late war. Never could any argument be more insulting and mortifying to a people habituated to the granting of their own money.

Taxes for the purpose of raising revenue had hitherto been sparingly attempted in America. Without ever doubting the extent of its lawful power, Parliament always doubted the propriety of such impositions. And the Americans on their part never thought of contesting a right by which they were so little affected. Their assemblies in the main answered all the purposes necessary to the internal economy of a free people, and provided for all the exigencies of government which arose amongst themselves. In the midst of that happy enjoyment, they never thought of critically settling the exact limits of a power which was necessary to their union, their safety, their equality, and even their liberty. Thus the two very difficult points, superiority in the presiding state, and freedom in the subordinate, were on the whole sufficiently, that is, practically, reconciled; without agitating those vexatious questions which in truth rather belong to metaphysics than politics, and which can never be moved without shaking the foundations of the best governments that have ever been constituted by human wisdom. By this measure was let loose that dangerous spirit of disquisition, not in the coolness of philosophical inquiry, but inflamed with all the passions of a haughty, resentful people, who thought themselves deeply injured, and that they were contending for everything that was valuable in the world.

In England, our ministers went on without the least attention to these alarming dispositions, just as if they were doing the most common things in the most usual way, and among a people not only passive, but pleased. They took no one step to divert the dangerous spirit which began even then to appear in the colonies, to compromise with it, to mollify it, or to subdue it. No new arrangements were made in civil government; no new powers or instructions were given to governors; no augmentation was made, or new disposition, of forces. Never was so critical a measure pursued with so little provision against its necessary consequences. As if all common prudence had abandoned the ministers, and as if they meant to plunge themselves and us headlong into that gulf which stood gaping before them, by giving a year's notice of the project of their Stamp Act they allowed time for all the discontents of that country to fester and come to a head, and for all the arrangements which factious men could make towards an opposition to the law. At the same time they carefully concealed from the eye of Parliament those remonstrances which they had actually received, and which in the strongest manner indicated the discontent of some of the colonies, and the consequences which might be expected; they concealed them even in defiance of an order of council that they should be laid before Parliament. Thus, by concealing the true state of the case, they rendered the wisdom of the nation as improvident as their own temerity, either in preventing or guarding against the mischief. . . .

It was at this time, and in these circumstances, that a new administration was formed. Professing even industriously, in this public matter, to avoid anecdotes, I say nothing of those famous reconciliations and quarrels which weakened the body that should have been the natural support of this administration. I run no risk in affirming that, surrounded as they were with difficulties of every species, nothing but the strongest and most uncorrupt sense of their duty to the public could have prevailed upon some of the persons who composed it to undertake the king's business at such a time. Their preceding character, their measures while in power, and the subsequent conduct of many of them, I think, leave no room to charge this assertion to flattery. Having undertaken the commonwealth, what remained for them to do? to piece their conduct upon the broken chain of former measures? If they had been so inclined, the ruinous nature of those measures, which began instantly to appear, would not have permitted it. Scarcely had they entered into office when letters arrived from all parts of America, making loud complaints, backed by strong reasons, against several of the principal regulations of the late ministry, as threatening destruction to many valuable branches of commerce. These were attended with representations from many merchants and capital manufacturers at home, who had all their interests involved in the support of lawful trade, and in the suppression of every sort of contraband. Whilst these things were under consideration, that conflagration blazed out at once in North America: a universal disobedience, and open resistance to the Stamp Act; and, in consequence, a universal stop to the course of justice, and to trade and navigation, throughout that great important country; an interval during which the trading interest of England lay under the most dreadful anxiety which it ever felt.

The repeal of that act was proposed. It was much too serious a measure, and attended with too many difficulties upon every side, for the then ministry to have undertaken it, as some paltry writers have asserted, from envy and dislike to their predecessors in office. As little could it be owing to personal cowardice, and dread of consequences to themselves. Ministers timorous from their attachment to place and power will fear more from the consequences of one court intrigue than from a thousand difficulties to the commerce and credit of their country by disturbances at three thousand miles distance. From which of these the ministers had most to apprehend at that time is known, I presume, universally. Nor did they take that resolution from a want of the fullest sense of the inconveniences which must necessarily attend a measure of concession from the sovereign to the subject. That it must increase the insolence of the mutinous spirits in America was but too obvious. No great measure indeed, at a very difficult crisis, can be pursued which is not attended with some mischief; none but conceited pretenders in public business will hold any other language; and none but weak and unexperienced men will believe them if they should. . . .

The disobedience to this act was universal throughout America; nothing, it was evident, but the sending a very strong military, backed by a very strong naval force, would reduce the seditious to obedience. To send it to one town would not be sufficient; every province of America must be traversed, and must be subdued. I do not entertain the least doubt but this could be done. We might, I think, without much difficulty, have destroyed our colonies. This destruction might be effected probably in a year, or in two at the utmost. If the question was upon a foreign nation, where every successful stroke adds to your own power and takes from that of a rival, a just war with such a certain superiority would be undoubtedly an advisable measure. But *four million* of debt due to our merchants, the total cessation of a trade annually worth *four million* more, a large foreign traffic, much home manufacture, a very capital immediate revenue arising from colony imports, indeed the produce of every one of our revenues greatly depending on this trade, all these were very weighty accumulated considerations, at least well to be weighed, before that sword was drawn which even by its victories must produce all the evil effects of the greatest national defeat. How public credit must have suffered, I need not say. . . . Far from being able to have entered into new plans of economy, we must have launched into a new sea, I fear a boundless sea, of expense. . . .

Our trade felt this to its vitals; and our then ministers were not ashamed to say that they sympathized with the feelings of our merchants. The universal alarm of the whole trading body of England will never be laughed at by them as an ill-grounded or a pretended panic. . . . Nothing amongst us is more quickly or deeply affected by taxes of any kind than trade; and if an American tax was a real relief to England, no part of the community would be sooner or more materially relieved by it than our merchants. But they well know that the trade of England must be more burdened by one penny raised in America than by three in England; and if that penny be raised with the uneasiness, the discontent, and the confusion of America, more than by ten.

If the opinion and wish of the landed interest is a motive, and it is a fair and just one, for taking away a real and large revenue, the desire of the trading interest of England ought to be a just ground for taking away a tax of little better than speculation, which was to be collected by a war, which was to be kept up with the perpetual discontent of those who were to be affected by it, and the value of whose produce even after the *ordinary* charges of collection was very uncertain. . . .

These were some of the motives drawn from principles of convenience for that repeal. When the object came to be more narrowly inspected, every motive concurred. These colonies were evidently founded in subservience to the commerce of Great Britain. From this principle, the whole system of our laws concerning them became a system of restriction. A double monopoly was established on the part of the parent country: I. A monopoly of their whole import, which is to be altogether from Great Britain; 2. A monopoly of all their export, which is to be nowhere but to Great Britain, as far as it can serve any purpose here. On the same idea it was contrived that they should send all their products to us raw, and in their first state; and that they should take everything from us in the last stage of manufacture.

Were ever a people under such circumstances—that is, a people who were to export raw, and to receive manufactured, and this, not a few luxurious articles, but all articles, even to those of the grossest, most vulgar, and necessary consumption, a people who were in the hands of a general monopolist—were ever such a people suspected of a possibility of becoming a just object of revenue? All the ends of their foundation must be supposed utterly contradicted before they could become such an object. Every trade law we have made must have been eluded, and become useless, before they could be in such a condition.

. . . I shall be ready to admit that the colonies ought to be taxed to the revenues of this country when I know that they are out of debt to its commerce. . . .

Whoever goes about to reason on any part of the policy of this country with regard to America upon the mere abstract principles of government, or even upon those of our own ancient constitution, will be often misled. Those who resort for arguments to the most respectable authorities, ancient or modern, or rest upon the clearest maxims drawn from the experience of other states and empires, will be liable to the greatest errors imaginable. The object is wholly new in the world. It is singular; it is grown up to this magnitude and importance within the memory of man; nothing in history is parallel to it. All the reasonings about it that are likely to be at all solid must be drawn from its actual circumstances. In this new system a principle of commerce, of artificial commerce, must predominate. This commerce must be secured by a multitude of restraints very alien from the spirit of liberty; and a powerful authority must reside in the principal state, in order to enforce them. But the people who are to be the subjects of these restraints are descendants of Englishmen, and of a high and free spirit. To hold over them a government made up of nothing but restraints and penalties, and taxes in the granting of which they can have no share, will neither be wise nor long practicable. People must be governed in a manner agreeable to their temper and disposition; and men of free character and spirit must be ruled with, at least, some condescension to this spirit and this character. The British colonist must see something which will distinguish him from the colonists of other nations.

Those reasonings which infer from the many restraints under which we have already laid America to our right to lay it under still more, and indeed under all manner of restraints, are conclusive—conclusive as to right, but the very reverse as to policy and practice. We ought rather to infer from our having laid the colonies under many restraints that it is reasonable to compensate them by every indulgence that can by any means be reconciled to our interest. We have a great empire to rule, composed of a vast mass of heterogeneous governments, all more or less free and popular in their forms, all to be kept in peace, and kept out of conspiracy, with one another, all to be held in subordination to this country; while the spirit of an extensive and intricate and trading interest pervades the whole, always qualifying, and often controlling, every general idea of constitution and government. It is a great and difficult object; and I wish we may possess wisdom and temper enough to manage it as we ought. Its importance is infinite.

. . . This colony intercourse is a new world of commerce in a manner created; it stands upon principles of its own; principles hardly worth endangering for any little consideration of extorted revenue.

The reader sees that I do not enter so fully into this matter as obviously I might. . . . It is enough to say that before the ministers of 1765 had determined to propose the repeal of the Stamp Act in Parliament, they had the whole of the American constitution and commerce very fully before them. They considered maturely; they decided with wisdom: let me add, with firmness. For they resolved, as a preliminary to that repeal, to assert in the fullest and least equivocal terms the unlimited legislative right of this country over its colonies; and, having done this, to propose the repeal, on principles, not of constitutional right, but on those of expediency, of equity, of lenity, and of the true interests present and future of that great object for which alone the colonies were founded, navigation and commerce. This plan, I say, required an uncommon degree of firmness, when we consider that some of those persons who might be of the greatest use in promoting the repeal violently withstood the Declaratory Act, and they who agreed with administration in the principles of that law equally made, as well the reasons on which the Declaratory Act itself stood as those on which it was opposed, grounds for an opposition to the repeal.

If the then ministry resolved first to declare the right, it was not from any opinion they entertained of its future use in regular taxation. Their opinions were full and declared against the ordinary use of such a power. But it was plain that the general reasonings which were employed against that power went directly to our whole legislative right; and one part of it could not be yielded to such arguments without a virtual surrender of all the rest. Besides, if that very specific power of levying money in the colonies were not retained as a sacred trust in the hands of Great Britain (to be used, not in the first instance for supply, but in the last exigence for control), it is obvious that the presiding authority of Great Britain, as the head, the arbiter, and director of the whole empire, would vanish into an empty name, without operation or energy. With the habitual exercise of such a power in the ordinary course of supply, no trace of freedom could remain to America. If Great Britain were stripped of this right, every principle of unity and subordination in the empire was gone forever. Whether all this can be reconciled in legal speculation is a matter of no consequence. It is reconciled in policy: and politics ought to be adjusted, not to human reasonings, but to human nature; of which the reason is but a part, and by no means the greatest part. . . .

Upon these principles was the act repealed, and it produced all the good effect which was expected from it: quiet was restored; trade generally returned to its ancient channels; time and means were furnished for the better strengthening of government there, as well as for recovering, by judicious measures, the affections of the people, had that ministry continued, or had a ministry succeeded with dispositions to improve that opportunity.

Such an administration did not succeed. Instead of profiting of that season of tranquillity, in the very next year they chose to return to measures of the very same nature with those which had been so solemnly condemned, though upon a smaller scale. The effects have been correspondent. America is again in disorder; not indeed in the same degree as formerly, nor anything like it. Such good effects have attended the repeal of the Stamp Act that the colonies have actually paid the taxes; and they have sought their redress (upon however improper principles) not in their own violence, as formerly, but in the experienced benignity of Parliament. . . . Whether the return to the system of 1764 for raising a revenue in America, the discontents which have ensued in consequence of it, the general suspension of the assemblies in consequence of these discontents, the use of the military power, and the new and dangerous commissions which now hang over them will produce equally good effects is greatly to be doubted. Never, I fear, will this nation and the colonies fall back upon their true center of gravity, and natural point of repose, until the ideas of 1766 are resumed, and steadily pursued. . . .

Speech on American Taxation

The Townsend duties angered the Americans, who responded with boycotts and resistance to custom payments. British troops were sent to Boston, producing the Boston Massacre of 1770. While some duties were lifted by Lord North, who became George III's first minister in 1770, taxes were left on tea, which was resisted by the rebellious Boston Tea Party of 1773. Burke, himself since 1771 the Agent in Great Britain for the colony of New York, appealed to the House of Commons in April 1774 to return to the conciliatory policies of the Rockingham administration.

HOW WE HAVE FARED since then: what woeful variety of schemes have been adopted; what enforcing, and what repealing; what bullying, and what submitting; what doing, and undoing; what straining, and what relaxing; what assemblies dissolved for not obeying, and called again without obedience; what troops sent out to quell resistance, and, on meeting that resistance, recalled; what shiftings, and changes, and jumblings of all kinds of men at home, which left no possibility of order, consistency, vigor, or even so much as a decent unity of color in any one public measure—It is a tedious, irksome task. My duty may call me to open it out some other time . . . for the present I shall forbear.

After all these changes and agitations, your immediate situation upon the question on your paper is at length brought to this. You have an act of Parliament stating that "it is *expedient* to raise a revenue in America." By a partial repeal you annihilated the greatest part of that revenue which this preamble declares to be so expedient. You have substituted no other in the place of it. A Secretary of State has disclaimed, in the King's name, all thoughts of such a substitution in future. The principle of this disclaimer goes to what has been left, as well as what has been repealed. The tax which lingers after its companions (under a preamble declaring an American revenue expedient, and for the sole purpose of supporting the theory of that preamble) militates with the assurance authentically conveyed to the colonies, and is an exhaustless source of jealousy and animosity. On this state—which I take to be a fair one—not being able to discern any grounds of honor, advantage, peace, or power for adhering either to the act or to the preamble, I shall vote for the question which leads to the repeal of both.

If you do not fall in with this motion, then secure something to fight for, consistent in theory and valuable in practice. If you must employ your strength, employ it to uphold you in some honorable right or some profitable wrong. If you are apprehensive that the concession recommended to you, though proper, should be a means of drawing on you further, but unreasonable claims—why, then employ your force in supporting that reasonable concession against those unreasonable demands. You will employ it with more grace, with better effect, and with great probable concurrence of all the quiet and rational people in the provinces, who are now united with and hurried away by the violent—having, indeed, different dispositions, but a common interest. If you apprehend that on a concession you shall be pushed by metaphysical process to the extreme lines, and argued out of your whole authority, my advice is this: when you have recovered your old, your strong, your tenable position, then face about—stop short—do nothing more—reason not at all—oppose the ancient policy and practice of the empire as a rampart against the speculations of innovators on both sides of the question—and you will stand on great, manly, and sure ground. On this solid basis fix your machines, and they will draw worlds towards you.

Your ministers, in their own and his Majesty's name, have already adopted the American distinction of internal and external duties. It is a distinction, whatever merit it may have, that was originally moved by the Americans themselves; and I think they will acquiesce in it, if they are not pushed with too much logic and too little sense, in all the consequences: that is, if external taxation be understood, as they and you understand it, when you please, to be not a distinction of geography, but of policy; that it is a power for regulating trade, and not for supporting establishments. The distinction, which is as nothing with regard to right, is of most weighty consideration in practice. Recover your old ground, and your old tranquillity; try it; I am persuaded the Americans will compromise with you. When confidence is once restored, the odious and suspicious *summum jus* will perish of course. The spirit of practicability, of moderation, and mutual convenience will never call in geometrical exactness as the arbitrator of an amicable settlement. Consult and follow your experience. . . .

Again, and again, revert to your old principles—seek peace and ensure it—leave America, if she has taxable matter in her, to tax herself. I am not here going into the distinctions of rights, nor attempting to mark their boundaries. I do not enter into these metaphysical distinctions; I hate the very sound of them. Leave the Americans as they anciently stood, and these distinctions, born of our unhappy contest, will die along with it. They and we, and their and our ancestors, have been happy under that system. Let the memory of all actions in contradiction to that good old mode, on both sides, be extinguished forever. Be content to bind America by laws of trade; you have always done it. Let this be your reason for binding their trade. Do not burden them by taxes; you were not used to do so from the beginning. Let this be your reason for not taxing. These are the arguments of states and kingdoms. Leave the rest to the schools; for there only they may be discussed with safety. But if, intemperately, unwisely, fatally, you sophisticate and poison the very source of government, by urging subtle deductions, and consequences odious to those you govern, from the unlimited and illimitable nature of supreme sovereignty, you will teach them by these means to call that sovereignty itself in question. When you drive him hard, the boar will surely turn upon the hunters. If that sovereignty and their freedom cannot be reconciled, which will they take? They will cast your sovereignty in your face. Nobody will be argued into slavery. Sir, let the gentlemen on the other side call forth all their ability; let the best of them get up and tell me what one character of liberty the Americans have, and what one brand of slavery they are free from, if they are bound in their property and industry by all the restraints you can imagine on commerce, and at the same time are made pack-horses of every tax you choose to impose, without the least share in granting them. When they bear the burdens of unlimited monopoly, will you bring them to bear the burdens of unlimited revenue too? The Englishman in America will feel that this is slavery; that it is *legal* slavery will be no compensation either to his feelings or his understanding.

. . . Reflect how you are to govern a people who think they ought to be free, and think they are not. Your scheme yields no revenue; it yields nothing but discontent, disorder, disobedience; and such is the state of America that, after wading up to your eyes in blood, you could only end just where you begun—that is, to tax where no revenue is to be found, to— My voice fails me; my inclination, indeed, carries me no further; all is confusion beyond it.

Well, Sir, I have recovered a little, and before I sit down I must say something to another point with which gentlemen urge us. What is to become of the Declaratory Act, asserting the entireness of British legislative authority, if we abandon the practice of taxation?

For my part, I look upon the rights stated in that act exactly in the manner in which I viewed them on its very first proposition, and which I have often taken the liberty, with great humility, to lay before you. I look, I say, on the imperial rights of Great Britain, and the privileges which the colonists ought to enjoy under these rights, to be just the most reconcilable things in the world. The Parliament of Great Britain sits at the head of her extensive empire in two capacities. One as the local legislature of this island, providing for all things at home, immediately, and by no other instrument than the executive power. The other, and I think her nobler capacity, is what I call her *imperial character*; in which, as from the throne of heaven, she superintends all the several inferior legislatures, and guides and controls them all without annihilating any. As all these provincial legislatures are only co-ordinate to each other, they ought all to be subordinate to her; else they can neither preserve mutual peace, nor hope for mutual justice, nor effectually afford mutual assistance. It is necessary to coerce the negligent, to restrain the violent, and to aid the weak and deficient, by the overruling plenitude of her power. She is never to intrude into the place of the others whilst they are equal to the common ends of their institution. But in order to enable Parliament to answer all these ends of provident and beneficient superintendence, her powers must be boundless. The gentlemen who think the powers of Parliament limited may please themselves to talk of requisitions. But suppose the requisitions are not obeyed? What! shall there be no reserved power in the empire to supply a deficiency which may weaken, divide, and dissipate the whole? We are engaged in war—the Secretary of State calls upon the colonies to contribute—some would do it, I think most would cheerfully furnish whatever is demanded—one or two, suppose, hang back, and, easing themselves, let the stress of the draft lie on the others—surely it is proper that some authority might legally say, "Tax yourselves for the common supply, or Parliament will do it for you." This backwardness was, as I am told, actually the case of Pennsylvania for some short time towards the beginning of the last war, owing to some internal dissensions in the colony. But whether the fact were so or otherwise, the case is equally to be provided for by a competent sovereign power. But then this ought to be no ordinary power, nor ever used in the first instance. This is what I meant when I have said, at various times, that I consider the power of taxing in Parliament as an instrument of empire, and not as a means of supply.

Such, Sir, is my idea of the constitution of the British Empire, as distinguished from the constitution of Britain; and on these grounds I think subordination and liberty may be sufficiently reconciled through the whole—whether to serve a refining speculatist or a factious demagogue I know not, but enough surely for the ease and happiness of man.

Sir, whilst we held this happy course, we drew more from the colonies than all the impotent violence of despotism ever could extort from them. We did this abundantly in the last war; it has never been once denied; and what reason have we to imagine that the colonies would not have proceeded in supplying government as liberally if you had not stepped in and hindered them from contributing, by interrupting the channel in which their liberality flowed with so strong a course—by attempting to take, instead of being satisfied to receive? Sir William Temple says that Holland has loaded itself with ten times the impositions which it revolted from Spain rather than submit to. He says true. Tyranny is a poor provider. It knows neither how to accumulate not how to extract.

I charge, therefore, to this new and unfortunate system the loss not only of peace, of union, and of commerce, but even of revenue, which its friends are contending for. It is morally certain that we have lost at least a million of free grants since the peace. I think we have lost a great deal more; and that those who look for a revenue from the provinces never could have pursued, even in that light, a course more directly repugnant to their purposes. . . .

On this business of America, I confess I am serious, even to sadness. I have had but one opinion concerning it since I sat, and before I sat, in Parliament. . . . I have in all seasons adhered to the system of 1766 for no other reason than that I think it laid deep in your truest interests; and that, by limiting the exercise, it fixes on the firmest foundations a real, consistent, well-grounded authority in Parliament. Until you come back to that system, there will be no peace for England.

Speech on Conciliation with the Colonies

Barely a month before the battles of Lexington and Concord, Burke had appealed one last time for a reconciliation with the colonies. In a Commons speech of March 22, 1775 he offered, as a possible solution to the crisis, the inclusion of the colonies in the parliamentary politics of Britain. Arguing his case, Burke insisted that what the Americans sought was their traditional rights as Englishmen. While American radicals like Sam Adams based their arguments on abstract natural rights, Burke's defense of the colonists was grounded in custom and tradition—"the ancient, rustic, manly, home-bred sense of this country."

AMERICA, GENTLEMEN SAY, is a noble object—it is an object well worth fighting for. Certainly it is, if fighting a people be the best way of gaining them. Gentlemen in this respect will be led to their choice of means by their complexions and their habits. Those who understand the military art will of course have some predilection for it. Those who wield the thunder of the state may have more confidence in the efficacy of arms. But I confess, possibly for want of this knowledge, my opinion is much more in favor of prudent management than of force; considering force not as an odious, but a feeble instrument for preserving a people so numerous, so active, so growing, so spirited as this, in a profitable and subordinate connection with us.

First, Sir, permit me to observe, that the use of force alone is but *temporary*. It may subdue for a moment; but it does not remove the necessity of subduing again; and a nation is not governed which is perpetually to be conquered.

My next objection is its *uncertainty*. Terror is not always the effect of force, and an armament is not a victory. If you do not succeed, you are without resource: for, conciliation failing, force remains; but force failing, no further hope of reconciliation is left. Power and authority are sometimes bought by kindness; but they can never be begged as alms by an impoverished and defeated violence.

A further objection to force is that you *impair the object* by your very endeavors to preserve it. The thing you fought for is not the thing which you recover, but depreciated, sunk, wasted, and consumed in the contest. Nothing less will content me than *whole America*. I do not choose to consume its strength along with our own; because in all parts it is the British strength that I consume. I do not choose to be caught by a foreign enemy at the end of this exhausting conflict, and still less in the midst of it. I may escape, but I can make no insurance against such an event. Let me add that I do not choose wholly to break the American spirit; because it is the spirit that has made the country.

Lastly, we have no sort of *experience* in favor of force as an instrument in the rule of our colonies. Their growth and their utility has been owing to methods altogether different. Our ancient indulgence has been said to be pursued to a fault. It may be so; but we know, if feeling is evidence, that our fault was more tolerable than our attempt to mend it, and our sin far more salutary than our penitence.

These, Sir, are my reasons for not entertaining that high opinion of untried force by which many gentlemen, for whose sentiments in other particulars I have great respect, seem to be so greatly captivated. But there is still behind a third consideration concerning this object, which serves to determine my opinion on the sort of policy which ought to be pursued in the management of America, even more than its population and its commerce: I mean its *temper and character*.

In this character of the Americans a love of freedom is the predominating feature which marks and distinguishes the whole; and as an ardent is always a jealous affection, your colonies become suspicious, restive, and untractable whenever they see the least attempt to wrest from them by force, or shuffle from them by chicane, what they think the only advantage worth living for. This fierce spirit of liberty is stronger in the

English colonies, probably, than in any other people of the earth, and this from a great variety of powerful causes; which, to understand the true temper of their minds, and the direction which this spirit takes, it will not be amiss to lay open somewhat more largely.

First, the people of the colonies are descendants of Englishmen. England, Sir, is a nation which still, I hope, respects, and formerly adored, her freedom. The colonists emigrated from you when this part of your character was most predominant; and they took this bias and direction the moment they parted from your hands. They are therefore not only devoted to liberty, but to liberty according to English ideas and on English principles. Abstract liberty, like other mere abstractions, is not to be found. Liberty inheres in some sensible object; and every nation has formed to itself some favorite point, which by way of eminence becomes the criterion of their happiness. It happened, you know, Sir, that the great contests for freedom in this country were from the earliest times chiefly upon the question of taxing. Most of the contests in the ancient commonwealths turned primarily on the right of election of magistrates, or on the balance among the several orders of the state. The question of money was not with them so immediate. But in England it was otherwise. On this point of taxes the ablest pens and most eloquent tongues have been exercised, the greatest spirits have acted and suffered. In order to give the fullest satisfaction concerning the importance of this point, it was not only necessary for those who in argument defended the excellence of the English constitution to insist on this privilege of granting money as a dry point of fact, and to prove that the right had been acknowledged in ancient parchments and blind usages to reside in a certain body called a House of Commons. They went much further: they attempted to prove, and they succeeded, that in theory it ought to be so, from the particular nature of a House of Commons, as an immediate representative of the people, whether the old records had delivered this oracle or not. They took infinite pains to inculcate, as a fundamental principle, that in all monarchies the people must in effect themselves, mediately or immediately, possess the power of granting their own money, or no shadow of liberty could subsist. The colonies draw from you, as with their lifeblood, these ideas and principles. . . . I do not say whether they were right or wrong in applying your general arguments to their own case. It is not easy, indeed, to make a monopoly of theorems and corollaries. The fact is that they did thus apply those general arguments; and your mode of governing them, whether through lenity or indolence, through wisdom or mistake, confirmed them in the imagination that they, as well as you, had an interest in these common principles.

They were further confirmed in this pleasing error by the form of their provincial legislative assemblies. Their governments are popular in a high degree: some are merely popular; in all, the popular representative is the most weighty; and this share of the people in their ordinary government never fails to inspire them with lofty sentiments, and with a strong aversion from whatever tends to deprive them of their chief importance.

If anything were wanting to this necessary operation of the form of government, religion would have given it a complete effect. Religion, always a principle of energy, in this new people is no way worn out or impaired; and their mode of professing it is also one main cause of this free spirit. The people are Protestants, and of that kind which is the most adverse to all implicit submission of mind and opinion. This is a persuasion not only favorable to liberty, but built upon it. I do not think, Sir, that the reason of this averseness in the dissenting churches from all that looks like absolute government is so much to be sought in their religious tenets as in their history. Everyone knows that the Roman Catholic religion is at least coeval with most of the governments where it prevails, that it has generally gone hand in hand with them, and received great favor and every kind of support from authority. The Church of England, too, was formed from her cradle under the nursing care of regular government. But the dissenting interests have sprung up in direct opposition to all the ordinary powers of the world, and could justify that opposition only on a strong claim to natural liberty. Their very existence depended on the powerful and unremitted assertion of that claim. All Protestantism, even the most cold and passive, is a sort of dissent. But the religion most prevalent in our northern colonies is a refinement on the principle of resistance: it is the dissidence of dissent, and the protestantism of the Protestant religion. This religion, under a variety of denominations agreeing in nothing but in the communion of the spirit of liberty, is predominant in most of the northern provinces, where the Church of England, notwithstanding its legal rights, is in reality no more than a sort of private sect, not composing, most probably, the tenth of the people. The colonists left England when this spirit was high, and in the emigrants was the highest of all; and even that stream of foreigners which has been constantly flowing into these colonies has, for the greatest part, been composed of dissenters from the establishments of their several countries, and have brought with them a temper and character far from alien to that of the people with whom they mixed.

Sir, I can perceive, by their manner, that some gentlemen object to the latitude of this description, because in the southern colonies the Church of England forms a large body, and has a regular establishment. It is certainly true. There is, however, a circumstance attending these colonies which, in my opinion, fully counterbalances this difference and makes the spirit of liberty still more high and haughty than in those to the northward. It is that in Virginia and the Carolinas they have a vast multitude of slaves. Where this is the case in any part of the world, those who are free are by far the most proud and jealous of their freedom. Freedom is to them not only an enjoyment, but a kind of rank and privilege. Not seeing there that freedom, as in countries where it is a common blessing, and as broad and general as the air, may be united with much abject toil, with great misery, with all the exterior of servitude, liberty looks, amongst them, like something that is more noble and liberal. I do not mean, Sir, to commend the superior morality of this sentiment, which has at least as much pride as virtue in it; but I cannot alter the nature of man. The fact is so; and these people of the southern colonies are much more strongly, and with a higher and more stubborn spirit, attached to liberty, than those to the northward. Such were all the ancient commonwealths; such were our Gothic ancestors; such in our days were the Poles; and such will be all masters of slaves, who are not slaves themselves. . . .

Permit me, Sir, to add another circumstance in our colonies which contributes no mean part towards the growth and effect of this untractable spirit: I mean their education. In no country, perhaps, in the world is the law so general a study. The profession itself is numerous and powerful, and in most provinces it takes the lead. The greater number of the deputies sent to the Congress were lawyers. But all who read, and most do read, endeavor to obtain some smattering in that science. . . . This study renders men acute, inquisitive, dexterous, prompt in attack, ready in defense, full of resources. In other countries, the people, more simple, and of a less mercurial cast, judge of an ill principle in government only by an actual grievance; here they anticipate the evil, and judge of the pressure of the grievance by the badness of the principle. They augur misgovernment at a distance, and snuff the approach of tyranny in every tainted breeze.

The last cause of this disobedient spirit in the colonies is hardly less powerful than the rest, as it is not merely moral, but laid deep in the natural constitution of things. Three thousand miles of ocean lie between you and them. No contrivance can prevent the effect of this distance in weakening government. Seas roll, and months pass, between the order and the execution; and the want of a speedy explanation of a single point is enough to defeat a whole system. You have, indeed, winged ministers of vengeance, who carry your bolts in their pounces to the remotest verge of the sea; but there a power steps in that limits the arrogance of raging passions and furious elements, and says, "So far shalt thou go, and no farther." Who are you that should fret and rage, and bite the chains of nature? Nothing worse happens to you than does to all nations who have extensive empire; and it happens in all the forms into which empire can be thrown. In large bodies, the circulation of power must be less vigorous at the extremities. Nature has said it. The Turk cannot govern Egypt, and Arabia, and Kurdistan, as he governs Thrace; nor has he the same dominion in Crimea and Algiers which he has at Brusa and Smyrna. Despotism itself is obliged to truck and huckster. The Sultan gets such obedience as he can. He governs with a loose rein that he may govern at all; and the whole of the force and vigor of his authority in his center is derived from a prudent relaxation in all his borders. Spain, in her provinces, is perhaps not so well obeyed as you are in yours. She complies, too; she submits; she watches times. This is the immutable condition, the eternal law, of extensive and detached empire.

Then, Sir, from these six capital sources, of descent, of form of government, of religion in the northern provinces, of manners in the southern, of education, of the remoteness of situation from the first mover of government—from all these causes a fierce spirit of liberty has grown up. It has grown with the growth of the people in your colonies, and increased with the increase of their wealth: a spirit that, unhappily meeting with an exercise of power in England, which, however lawful, is not reconcilable to any ideas of liberty, much less with theirs, has kindled this flame that is ready to consume us. . . .

Sir, I think you must perceive that I am resolved this day to have nothing at all to do with the question of the right of taxation. Some gentlemen startle—but it is true: I put it totally out of the question. It is less than nothing in my consideration. . . . I do not examine whether the giving away a man's money be a power excepted and reserved out of the general trust of government, and how far all mankind, in all forms of polity, are entitled to an exercise of that right by the charter of Nature—or whether, on the contrary, a right of taxation is necessarily involved in the general principle of legislation, and inseparable from the ordinary supreme power. These are deep questions, where great names militate against each other, where reason is perplexed, and an appeal to authorities only thickens the confusion; for high and reverend authorities lift up their heads on both sides, and there is no sure footing in the middle. This point is the *great Serbonian bog, betwixt Damiata and Mount Casius old, where armies whole have sunk*. I do not intend to be overwhelmed in that bog, though in such respectable company. The question with me is, not whether you have a right to render your people miserable, but whether it is not your interest to make them happy. It is not what a lawyer tells me I *may* do, but what humanity, reason, and justice tell me I ought to do. Is a politic act the worse for being a generous one? Is no concession proper but that which is made from your want of right to keep what you grant? . . .

Such is steadfastly my opinion of the absolute necessity of keeping up the concord of this empire by a unity of spirit, though in a diversity of operations, that, if I were sure the colonists had, at their leaving this country, sealed a regular compact of servitude; that they had solemnly abjured all the rights of citizens; that they had made a vow to renounce all ideas of liberty for them and their posterity to all generations, yet I should hold myself obliged to conform to the temper I found universally prevalent in my own day, and to govern two million of men, impatient of servitude, on the principles of freedom. I am not determining a point of law; I am restoring tranquillity; and the general character and situation of a people must determine what sort of government is fitted for them. . . .

My idea, therefore, without considering whether we yield as matter of right or grant as matter of favor, is *to admit the people of our colonies into an interest in the constitution*; and, by recording that admission in the journals of Parliament, to give them as strong an assurance as the nature of the thing will admit that we mean forever to adhere to that solemn declaration of systematic indulgence. . . .

I have taken a very incorrect measure of the disposition of the House if this proposal in itself would be received with dislike. I think, Sir, we have few American financiers. But our misfortune is we are too acute, we are too exquisite in our conjectures of the future, for men oppressed with such great and present evils. The more moderate among the opposers of parliamentary concession freely confess that they hope no good from taxation; but they apprehend the colonists have further views, and if this point were conceded, they would instantly attack the trade laws. These gentlemen are convinced that this was the intention from the beginning, and the quarrel of the Americans with taxation was no more than a cloak and cover to this design. . . .

One fact is clear and indisputable: the public and avowed origin of this quarrel was on taxation. This quarrel has, indeed, brought on new disputes on new questions, but certainly the least bitter, and the fewest of all, on the trade laws. To judge which of the two be the real, radical cause of quarrel, we have to see whether the commercial dispute did, in order of time, precede the dispute on taxation. There is not a shadow of evidence for it. Next, to enable us to judge whether at this moment a dislike to the trade laws be the real cause of quarrel, it is absolutely necessary to put the taxes out of the question by a repeal. See how the Americans act in this position, and then you will be able to discern correctly what is the true object of the controversy, or whether any controversy at all will remain. Unless you consent to remove this cause of difference, it is impossible, with decency, to assert that the dispute is not upon what it is avowed to be. And I would, Sir, recommend to your serious consideration whether it be prudent to form a rule for punishing people, not on their own acts, but on your conjectures. . . . Alas! alas! when will this speculating against fact and reason end? What will quiet these panic fears which we entertain of the hostile effect of a conciliatory conduct? Is it true that no case can exist in which it is proper for the sovereign to accede to the desires of his discontented subjects? Is there anything peculiar in this case, to make a rule for itself? Is all authority of course lost when it is not pushed to the extreme? Is it a certain maxim that the fewer causes of dissatisfaction are left by government, the more the subject will be inclined to resist and rebel?

All these objections being in fact no more than suspicions, conjectures, divinations, formed in defiance of fact and experience, they did not, Sir, discourage me from entertaining the idea of a conciliatory concession, founded on the principles which I have just stated.

In forming a plan for this purpose, I endeavored to put myself in that frame of mind which was the most natural and the most reasonable, and which was certainly the most probable means of securing me from all error. I set out with a perfect distrust of my own abilities, a total renunciation of every speculation of my own, and with a profound reverence for the wisdom of our ancestors, who have left us the inheritance of so happy a constitution and so flourishing an empire, and, what is a thousand times more valuable, the treasury of the maxims and principles which formed the one and obtained the other.

. . . Sir, I am sure that I shall not be misled when, in a case of constitutional difficulty, I consult the genius of the English constitution. Consulting at that oracle (it was with all due humility and piety), I found four capital examples in a similar case before me: those of Ireland, Wales, Chester, and Durham.

Ireland, before the English conquest, though never governed by a despotic power, had no parliament. How far the English Parliament itself was at that time modeled according to the present form is disputed among antiquarians. But we have all the reason in the world to be assured that a form of Parliament, such as England then enjoyed, she instantly communicated to Ireland; and we are equally sure that almost every successive improvement in constitutional liberty, as fast as it was made here, was transmitted thither. . . . It was not English arms, but the English constitution, that conquered Ireland. . . .

My next example is Wales. This country was said to be reduced by Henry the Third. It was said more truly to be so by Edward the First. But though then conquered, it was not looked upon as any part of the realm of England. . . . The manners of the Welsh nation followed the genius of the government: the people were ferocious, restive, savage, and uncultivated—sometimes composed, never pacified. Wales, within itself, was in perpetual disorder; and it kept the frontier of England in perpetual alarm. Benefits from it to the state there were none. Wales was only known to England by incursion and invasion.

Sir, during that state of things, Parliament was not idle. They attempted to subdue the fierce spirit of the Welsh by all sorts of rigorous laws. They prohibited by statute the sending all sorts of arms into Wales, as you prohibit by proclamation (with something more of doubt on the legality) the sending arms to America. They disarmed the Welsh by statute, as you attempted (but still with more question on the legality) to disarm New England by an instruction. They made an act to drag offenders from Wales into England for trial, as you have done (but with more hardship) with regard to America. By another act, where one of the parties was an Englishman, they ordained that his trial should be always by English. They made acts to restrain trade, as you do; and they prevented the Welsh from the use of fairs and markets, as you do the Americans from fisheries and foreign ports. . . .

Here we rub our hands—a fine body of precedents for the authority of Parliament and the use of it! I admit it fully; and pray add likewise to these precedents that all the while Wales rid this kingdom like an *incubus;* that it was an unprofitable and oppressive burden; and that an Englishman traveling in that country could not go six yards from the highroad without being murdered.

The march of the human mind is slow. Sir, it was not until after two hundred years discovered, that, by an eternal law, Providence had decreed vexation to violence, and poverty to rapine. Your ancestors did, however, at length open their eyes to the ill husbandry of injustice. They found that the tyranny of a free people could of all tyrannies the least be endured, and that laws made against a whole nation were not the most effectual methods for securing its obedience. Accordingly, in the twenty-seventh year of Henry the Eighth the course was entirely altered. With a preamble stating the entire and perfect rights of the crown of England, it gave to the Welsh all the rights and privileges of English subjects. A political order was established; the military power gave way to the civil; the marches were turned into counties. . . .

The very same year the County Palatine of Chester received the same relief from its oppressions, and the same remedy to its disorders. . . . Chester, civilized as well as Wales, has demonstrated that freedom, and not servitude, is the cure of anarchy; as religion, and not atheism, is the true remedy for superstition. Sir, this pattern of Chester was followed in the reign of Charles the Second with regard to the County Palatine of Durham, which is my fourth example. This county had long lain out of the pale of free legislation. So scrupulously was the example of Chester followed that the style of the preamble is nearly the same with that of the Chester act; and, without affecting the abstract extent of the authority of Parliament, it recognizes the equity of not suffering any considerable district, in which the British subjects may act as a body, to be taxed without their own voice in the grant.

Now if the doctrines of policy contained in these preambles, and the force of these examples in the acts of Parliament, avail anything, what can be said against applying them with regard to America? . . . Is America in rebellion? Wales was hardly ever free from it. Have you attempted to govern America by penal statutes? You made fifteen for Wales. But your legislative authority is perfect with regard to America; was it less perfect in Wales, Chester, and Durham? But America is virtually represented. What! does the electric force of virtual representation more easily pass over the Atlantic than pervade Wales, which lies in your neighborhood? or than Chester and Durham, surrounded by abundance of representation that is actual and palpable? But, Sir, your ancestors thought this sort of virtual representation, however ample, to be totally insufficient for the freedom of the inhabitants of territories that are so near, and comparatively so inconsiderable. How, then, can I think it sufficient for those which are infinitely greater, and infinitely more remote?

You will now, Sir, perhaps imagine that I am on the point of proposing to you a scheme for a representation of the colonies in Parliament. Perhaps I might be inclined to entertain some such thought; but a great flood stops me in my course. *Opposuit natura.* I cannot remove the eternal barriers of the creation. The thing, in that mode, I do not know to be possible. As I meddle with no theory, I do not absolutely assert the impracticability of such a representation; but I do not see my way to it; and those who have been more confident have not been more successful. However, the arm of public benevolence is not shortened; and there are often several means to the same end. What nature has disjoined in one way wisdom may unite in another. When we cannot give the benefit as we would wish, let us not refuse it altogether. If we cannot give the principal, let us find a substitute. But how? where? what substitute?

Fortunately, I am not obliged, for the ways and means of this substitute, to tax my own unproductive invention. I am not even obliged to go to the rich treasury of the fertile framers of imaginary commonwealths: not to the Republic of Plato, not to the Utopia of More, not to the Oceana of Harrington. . . . I only wish you to recognize, for the theory, the ancient constitutional policy of this kingdom with regard to representation, as that policy has been declared in acts of Parliament—and as to the practice, to return to that mode which a uniform experience has marked out to you as best, and in which you walked with security, advantage, and honor until the year 1763.

My resolutions, therefore, mean to establish the equity and justice of a taxation of America by *grant,* and not by *imposition;* to mark the *legal competency* of the colony assemblies for the support of their government in peace, and for public aids in time of war; to acknowledge that this legal competency has had *a dutiful and beneficial exercise,* and that experience has shown *the benefit of their grants,* and *the futility of parliamentary taxation, as a method of supply.*

These solid truths compose six fundamental propositions. . . . I think these six massive pillars will be of strength sufficient to support the temple of British concord. I have no more doubt than I entertain of my existence that, if you admitted these, you would command an immediate peace, and, with but tolerable future management, a lasting obedience in America. . . .

The first is a resolution: "That the colonies and plantations of Great Britain in North America, consisting of fourteen separate governments, and containing two millions and upwards of free inhabitants, have not had the liberty and privilege of electing and sending any knights and burgesses, or others, to represent them in the high court of Parliament." This is a plain matter of fact, necessary to be laid down, and (excepting the description) it is laid down in the language of the constitution; it is taken nearly *verbatim* from acts of Parliament.

The second is like unto the first: "That the said colonies and plantations have been made liable to, and bounden by, several subsidies, payments, rates, and taxes, given and granted by Parliament, though the said colonies and plantations have not their knights and burgesses in the said high court of Parliament, of their own election, to represent the condition of their country; by lack whereof they have been oftentimes touched and grieved by subsidies, given, granted, and assented to, in the said court, in a manner prejudicial to the common wealth, quietness, rest, and peace of the subjects inhabiting within the same."

Is this description too hot or too cold, too strong or too weak? Does it arrogate too much to the supreme legislature? Does it lean too much to the claims of the people? If it runs into any of these errors, the fault is not mine. It is the language of your own ancient acts of Parliament. . . . It is the genuine produce of the ancient, rustic, manly, home-bred sense of this country. I did not dare to rub off a particle of the venerable rust that rather adorns and preserves than destroys the metal. It would be a profanation to touch with a tool the stones which construct the sacred altar of peace. I would not violate with modern polish the ingenuous and noble roughness of these truly constitutional materials. Above all things, I was resolved not to be guilty of tampering—the odious vice of restless and unstable minds. I put my foot in the tracks of our forefathers, where I can neither wander nor stumble. . . .

The next proposition is: "That, from the distance of the said colonies, and from other circumstances, no method hath hitherto been devised for procuring a representation in Parliament for the said colonies." This is an assertion of a fact. I go no further on the paper; though, in my private judgment, a useful representation is impossible; I am sure it is not desired by them, nor ought it, perhaps, by us; but I abstain from opinions.

The fourth resolution is: "That each of the said colonies hath within itself a body, chosen, in part or in the whole, by the freemen, freeholders, or other free inhabitants thereof, commonly called the General Assembly, or General Court, with powers legally to raise, levy, and assess, according to the several usages of such colonies, duties and taxes towards defraying all sorts of public services." This competence in the colony assemblies is certain. It is proved by the whole tenor of their acts of supply in all the assemblies, in which the constant style of granting is: "An aid to his Majesty"; and acts granting to the crown have regularly, for near a century, passed the public offices without dispute. . . .

The fifth resolution is also a resolution of fact: "That the said general assemblies, general courts, or other bodies legally qualified as aforesaid, have at sundry times freely granted several large subsidies and public aids for his Majesty's service, according to their abilities, when required thereto by letter from one of his Majesty's principal Secretaries of State; and that their right to grant the same, and their cheerfulness and sufficiency in the said grants, have been at sundry times acknowledged by Parliament."

To say nothing of their great expenses in the Indian wars, and not to take their exertion in foreign ones, so high as the supplies in the year 1695, not to go back to their public contributions in the year 1710, I shall begin to travel only where the journals give me light; resolving to deal in nothing but fact authenticated by Parliamentary record, and to build myself wholly on that solid basis.

On the 4th of April 1748, a committee of this House came to the following resolution: "*Resolved,* That it is the opinion of this committee, *that it is just and reasonable,* that the several provinces and colonies of Massachusetts Bay, New Hampshire, Connecticut, and Rhode Island be reimbursed the expenses they have been at in taking and securing to the crown of Great Britain the island of Cape Breton and its dependencies." . . .

On the 28th of January 1756, a message from the King came to us, to this effect: "His Majesty, being sensible of the zeal and vigor with which his faithful subjects of certain colonies in North America have exerted themselves in defense of his Majesty's just rights and possessions, recommends it to this House to take the same into their consideration, and to enable his Majesty to give them such assistance as may be a *proper reward and encouragement.*"

On the 3d of February 1756, the House came to a suitable resolution, expressed in words nearly the same as those of the message; but with the further addition that the money then voted was as an *encouragement* to the colonies to exert themselves with vigor. . . .

Sir, here is the repeated acknowledgment of Parliament that the colonies not only gave, but gave to satiety. This nation has formally acknowledged two things: first, that the colonies had gone beyond their abilities, Parliament having thought it necessary to reimburse them; secondly, that they had acted legally and laudably in their grants of money, and their maintenance of troops, since the compensation is expressly given as reward and encouragement. Reward is not bestowed for acts that are unlawful; and encouragement is not held out to things that deserve reprehension. My resolution, therefore, does nothing more than collect into one proposition what is scattered through your journals. I give you nothing but your own; and you cannot refuse in the gross what you have so often acknowledged in detail. . . .

I think, then, I am, from those journals, justified in the sixth and last resolution, which is: "That it hath been found by experience, that the manner of granting the said supplies and aids by the said general assemblies hath been more agreeable to the inhabitants of the said colonies, and more beneficial and conducive to the public service, than the mode of giving and granting aids and subsidies in Parliament, to be raised and paid in the said colonies."

This makes the whole of the fundamental part of the plan. The conclusion is irresistible. You cannot say that you were driven by any necessity to an exercise of the utmost rights of legislature. You cannot assert that you took on yourselves the task of imposing colony taxes from the want of another legal body that is competent to the purpose of supplying the exigencies of the state without wounding the prejudices of the people. Neither is it true that the body so qualified, and having that competence, had neglected the duty.

The question now, on all this accumulated matter, is whether you will choose to abide by a profitable experience or a mischievous theory?

whether you choose to build on imagination or fact? whether you prefer enjoyment or hope? satisfaction in your subjects, or discontent?

If these propositions are accepted, everything which has been made to enforce a contrary system must, I take it for granted, fall along with it. . . .

I do not know that the colonies have, in any general way, or in any cool hour, gone much beyond the demand of immunity in relation to taxes. It is not fair to judge of the temper or dispositions of any man or any set of men, when they are composed and at rest, from their conduct or their expressions in a state of disturbance and irritation. It is, besides, a very great mistake to imagine that mankind follow up practically any speculative principle, either of government or of freedom, as far as it will go in argument and logical illation. We Englishmen stop very short of the principles upon which we support any given part of our constitution, or even the whole of it together. . . . All government, indeed every human benefit and enjoyment, every virtue and every prudent act, is founded on compromise and barter. We balance inconveniences; we give and take; we remit some rights that we may enjoy others; and we choose rather to be happy citizens than subtle disputants. As we must give away some natural liberty to enjoy civil advantages, so we must sacrifice some civil liberties for the advantages to be derived from the communion and fellowship of a great empire. But, in all fair dealings, the thing bought must bear some proportion to the purchase paid. None will barter away the immediate jewel of his soul. . . . None of us who would not risk his life rather than fall under a government purely arbitrary. But although there are some amongst us who think our constitution wants many improvements to make it a complete system of liberty, perhaps none who are of that opinion would think it right to aim at such improvement by disturbing his country and risking everything that is dear to him. In every arduous enterprise we consider what we are to lose as well as what we are to gain; and the more and better stake of liberty every people possess, the less they will hazard in a vain attempt to make it more. These are *the cords of man.* Man acts from adequate motives relative to his interest, and not on metaphysical speculations. Aristotle, the great master of reasoning, cautions us, and with great weight and propriety, against this species of delusive geometrical accuracy in moral arguments, as the most fallacious of all sophistry.

Address to the British Colonists in North America

In deeply moving terms Burke tried in 1777 to convince the colonists that they should not sever their relationship with Britain and pursue their independence. There were many in the mother country who opposed Lord North's policies and the use of force to subdue colonial unrest. Most Britons, he argued, "persevere in the most perfect unity of sentiments, principles, and affections, with you."

THE VERY DANGEROUS CRISIS, into which the British empire is brought, as it accounts for, so it justifies, the unusual step we take in addressing ourselves to you.

The distempers of the state are grown to such a degree of violence and malignity as to render all ordinary remedies vain and frivolous. In such a deplorable situation, an adherence to the common forms of business appears to us rather as an apology to cover a supine neglect of duty, than the means of performing it in a manner adequate to the exigency that presses upon us. The common means we have already tried, and tried to no purpose. As our last resource, we turn ourselves to you. We address you merely in our private capacity; vested with no other authority than what will naturally attend those, in whose declarations of benevolence you have no reason to apprehend any mixture of dissimulation or design.

We have this title to your attention: we call upon it in a moment of the utmost importance to us all. We find, with infinite concern, that arguments are used to persuade you of the necessity of separating yourselves from your ancient connexion with your parent country, grounded on a supposition that a general principle of alienation and enmity to you had pervaded the whole of this kingdom; and that there does no longer subsist between you and us any common and kindred principles, upon which we can possibly unite consistently with those ideas of liberty in which you have justly placed your whole happiness.

If this fact were true, the inference drawn from it would be irresistible. But nothing is less founded. We admit, indeed, that violent addresses have been procured with uncommon pains by wicked and designing men, purporting to be the genuine voice of the whole people of England; that they have been published by authority here; and made known to you by proclamations; in order, by despair and resentment, incurably to poison your minds against the origin of your race, and to render all cordial reconciliation between us utterly impracticable. The same wicked men, for the same bad purposes, have so far surprised the justice of parliament, as to cut off all communication betwixt us, except what is to go in their own fallacious and hostile channel.

But we conjure you by the invaluable pledges, which have hitherto united, and which we trust will hereafter lastingly unite us, that you do not suffer yourselves to be persuaded, or provoked, into an opinion, that you are at war with this nation. Do not think, that the whole, or even the uninfluenced majority, of Englishmen in this island are enemies to their own blood on the American continent. Much delusion has been practised; much corrupt influence treacherously employed. But still a large, and we trust the largest and soundest, part of this kingdom perseveres in the most perfect unity of sentiments, principles, and affections, with you. It spreads out a large and liberal platform of common liberty, upon which we may all unite for ever. It abhors the hostilities which have been carried on against you, as much as you who feel the cruel effect of them. It has disclaimed, in the most solemn manner, at the foot of the throne itself, the addresses, which tended to irritate your sovereign against his colonies. We are persuaded that even many of those who unadvisedly have put their hands to such intemperate and inflammatory addresses, have not at all apprehended to what such proceedings naturally lead; and would sooner die, than afford them the least countenance, if they were sensible of their fatal effects on the union and liberty of the empire.

For ourselves, we faithfully assure you that we have ever considered you as rational creatures; as free agents; as men willing to pursue, and able to discern, your own true interest. We have wished to continue united with you, in order that a people of one origin and one character should be directed to the rational objects of government by joint counsels, and protected in them by a common force. Other subordination in you we require none. We have never pressed that argument of general union to the extinction of your local, natural, and just privileges. Sensible of what is due both to the dignity and weakness of man, we have never wished to place over you any government, over which, in great fundamental points, you should have no sort of check or control in your own hands, or which should be repugnant to your situation, principles, and character.

No circumstances of fortune, you may be assured, will ever induce us to form, or tolerate, any such design. If the disposition of Providence (which we deprecate) should even prostrate you at our feet, broken in power and in spirit, it would be our duty and inclination to revive, by every practical means, that free energy of mind, which a fortune unsuitable to your virtue had damped and dejected; and to put you voluntarily in possession of those very privileges which you had in vain attempted to assert by arms. For we solemnly declare, that although we should look upon a separation from you as a heavy calamity, (and the heavier, because we know you must have your full share in it,) yet we had much rather see you totally independent of this Crown and kingdom, than joined to it by so unnatural a conjunction as that of freedom with servitude:—a conjunction which, if it were at all practicable, could not fail in the end of being more mischievous to the peace, prosperity, greatness, and power of this nation, than beneficial, by an enlargement of the bounds of nominal empire.

But because, brethren, these professions are general, and such as even enemies may make, when they reserve to themselves the construction of what servitude and what liberty are, we inform you, that we adopt your own standard of the blessing of free government. We are of opinion that you ought to enjoy the sole and exclusive right of freely granting, and applying to the support of your administration, what God has freely granted as a reward to your industry. And we do not confine this immunity from exterior coercion in this great point solely to what regards your local establishment, but also to what may be thought proper for the maintenance of the whole empire. In this resource we cheerfully trust and acquiesce: satisfied by evident reason that no other expectation of revenue can possibly be given by free men; and knowing, from an experience uniform both on yours and on our side of the ocean, that such an expectation has never yet been disappointed. We know of no road to your coffers but through your affections.

To manifest our sentiments the more clearly to you and to the world on this subject; we declare our opinion, that if no revenue at all, which, however, we are far from supposing, were to be obtained from you to this kingdom, yet as long as it is our happiness to be joined with you in bonds of fraternal charity and freedom, with an open and flowing commerce between us, one principle of enmity and friendship pervading, and one right of war and peace directing, the strength of the whole empire, we are likely to be, at least, as powerful as any nation, or as any combination of nations, which in the course of human events may be formed against us. We are sensible that a very large proportion of the wealth and power of every empire must necessarily be thrown upon the presiding state. We are sensible that such a state ever has borne, and ever must bear, the greatest part, and sometimes the whole, of the public expenses: and we think her well indemnified for that (rather apparent than real) inequality of charge, in the dignity and pre-eminence she enjoys, and in the superior opulence which, after all charges defrayed, must necessarily remain at the centre of affairs. Of this principle we are not without evidence in our remembrance (not yet effaced) of the glorious and happy days of this empire. We are, therefore, incapable of that prevaricating style, by which, when taxes without your consent are to be extorted from you, this nation is represented as in the lowest state of impoverishment and public distress; but when we are called upon to oppress you by force of arms, it is painted as scarcely feeling its impositions, abounding with wealth, and inexhaustible in its resources.

We also reason and feel as you do on the invasion of your charters. Because the charters comprehend the essential forms by which you enjoy your liberties, we regard them as most sacred, and by no means to be taken away or altered without process, without examination, and without hearing, as they have lately been. We even think that they ought by no means to be altered at all but at the desire of the greater part of the people who live under them. We cannot look upon men as delinquents in the mass; much less are we desirous of lording over our brethren, insulting their honest pride, and wantonly overturning establishments judged to be just and convenient by the public wisdom of this nation at their institution; and which long and inveterate use has taught you to look up to with affection and reverence. As we disapproved of the proceedings with regard to the forms of your constitution, so we are equally tender of every leading principle of free government. We never could think with approbation of putting the military power out of the coercion of the civil justice in the country where it acts.

We disclaim also any sort of share in that other measure which has been used to alienate your affections from this country, namely, the introduction of foreign mercenaries. We saw their employment with shame and regret, especially in numbers so far exceeding the English forces as in effect to constitute vassals who have no sense of freedom, and strangers who have no common interest or feelings, as the arbiters of our unhappy domestic quarrel.

We likewise saw with shame the African slaves, who had been sold to you on public faith, and under the sanction of acts of parliament, to be your servants and your guards, employed to cut the throats of their masters.

You will not, we trust, believe that, born in a civilized country, formed to gentle manners, trained in a merciful religion, and living in enlightened and polished times where even foreign hostility is softened from its original sternness, we could have thought of letting loose upon you, our late beloved brethren, these fierce tribes of savages and cannibals, in whom the traces of human nature are effaced by ignorance and barbarity. We rather wished to have joined with you in bringing gradually that unhappy part of mankind into civility, order, piety, and virtuous discipline, than to have confirmed their evil habits, and increased their natural ferocity, by fleshing them in the slaughter of you, whom our wiser and better ancestors had sent into the wilderness, with the express view of introducing, along with our holy religion, its humane and charitable manners. We do not hold that all things are lawful in war. We should think that every barbarity, in fire, in wasting, in murders, in tortures, and other cruelties too horrible, and too full of turpitude, for Christian mouths to utter, or ears to hear, if done at our instigation by those who we know will make war thus if they make it at all, to be to all intents and purposes as if done by ourselves. We clear ourselves to you our brethren, to the present age, and to future generations, to our king and our country, and to Europe, which as a spectator beholds this tragic scene, of every part or share in adding this last and worst of evils to the inevitable mischiefs of a civil war.

We do not call you rebels and traitors. We do not call for the vengeance of the Crown against you. We do not know how to qualify millions of our countrymen, contending with one heart for an admission to privileges which we have ever thought our own happiness and honour, by odious and unworthy names. On the contrary, we highly revere the principles on which you act, though we lament some of their effects. Armed as you are, we embrace you as our friends, and as our brethren, by the best and dearest ties of relation.

We view the establishment of the English colonies on principles of liberty as that which is to render this kingdom venerable to future ages. In comparison of this we regard all the victories and conquests of our warlike ancestors, or of our own times, as barbarous, vulgar distinctions, in which many nations, whom we look upon with little respect or value, have equalled if not far exceeded us. This is the peculiar and appropriated glory of England. Those who *have and who hold* to that foundation of common liberty, whether on this or on your side of the ocean, we consider as the true, and the only true, Englishmen. Those who depart from it, whether there or here, are attainted, corrupted in blood, and wholly fallen from their original rank and value. They are the real rebels to the fair constitution and just supremacy of England.

We exhort you, therefore, to cleave for ever to those principles, as being the true bond of union in this empire; and to show, by a manly perseverance, that the sentiments of honour, and the rights of mankind, are not held by the uncertain events of war, as you have hitherto shown a glorious and affecting example to the world that they are not dependent on the ordinary conveniences and satisfactions of life.

Knowing no other arguments to be used to men of liberal minds, it is upon these very principles, and these alone, we hope and trust that no flattering and no alarming circumstances shall permit you to listen to the seductions of those, who would alienate you from your dependence on the Crown and parliament of this kingdom. That very liberty, which you so justly prize above all things, originated here: and it may be very doubtful whether, without being constantly fed from the original fountain, it can be at all perpetuated or preserved in its native purity and perfection. Untried forms of government may, to unstable minds, recommend themselves even by their novelty. But you will do well to remember that England has been great and happy under the present limited monarchy (subsisting in more or less vigour and purity) for several hundred years. None but England can communicate to you the benefits of such a constitution. We apprehend you are not now, nor for ages are likely to be, capable of that form of constitution in an independent state. Besides, let us suggest to you our apprehensions that your present union (in which we rejoice, and which we wish long to subsist) cannot always subsist without the authority and weight of this great and long-respected body, to equipoise, and to preserve you amongst yourselves in a just and fair equality. It may not even be impossible that a long course of war with the administration of this country may be but a prelude to a series of wars and contentions among yourselves, to end, at length, (as such scenes have too often ended,) in a species of humiliating repose, which nothing but the preceding calamities would reconcile to the dispirited few who survived them. We allow that even this evil is worth the risk to men of honour, when rational liberty is at stake, as in the present case we confess and lament that it is. But if ever a real security, by parliament, is given against the terror or the abuse of unlimited power, and after such security given you should persevere in resistance, we leave you to consider whether the risk is not incurred without an object; or incurred for an object infinitely diminished by such concessions in its importance and value.

As to other points of discussion, when these grand fundamentals of your grants and charters are once settled and ratified by clear parliamentary authority, as the ground for peace and forgiveness on our side, and for a manly and liberal obedience on yours, treaty, and a spirit of reconciliation, will easily and securely adjust whatever may remain. Of this we give you our word, that so far as we are at present concerned, and if by any event we should become more concerned hereafter, you may rest assured, upon the pledges of honour not forfeited, faith not violated, and uniformity of character and profession not yet broken, we at least, on these grounds, will never fail you.

Respecting your wisdom, and valuing your safety, we do not call upon you to trust your existence to your enemies. We do not advise you to an unconditional submission. With satisfaction we assure you that almost all in both Houses (however unhappily they have been deluded, so as not to give any immediate effect to their opinion) disclaim that idea. You can have no friends in whom you cannot rationally confide. But parliament is your friend from the moment in which, removing its confidence from those who have constantly deceived its good intentions, it adopts the sentiments of those who have made sacrifices, (inferior indeed to yours,) but have, however, sacrificed enough to demonstrate the sincerity of their regard and value for your liberty and prosperity.

Arguments may be used to weaken your confidence in that public security; because, from some unpleasant appearances, there is a suspicion that parliament itself is somewhat fallen from its independent spirit. How far this supposition may be founded in fact we are unwilling to determine. But we are well assured from experience, that even if all were true that is contended for, and in the extent, too, in which it is argued, yet as long as the solid and well-disposed forms of this constitution remain, there ever is within parliament itself a power of renovating its principles, and effecting a self-reformation, which no other plan of government has ever contained. This constitution has therefore admitted innumerable improvements, either for the correction of the original scheme, or for removing corruptions, or for bringing its principles better to suit those changes which have successively happened in the circumstances of the nation, or in the manners of the people.

We feel that the growth of the colonies is such a change of circumstances; and that our present dispute is an exigency as pressing as any which ever demanded a revision of our government. Public troubles have often called upon this country to look into its constitution. It has ever been bettered by such a revision. If our happy and luxuriant increase of dominion, and our diffused population, have outgrown the limits of a constitution made for a contracted object, we ought to bless God, who has furnished us with this noble occasion for displaying our skill and beneficence in enlarging the scale of rational happiness, and of making the politic generosity of this kingdom as extensive as its fortune. If we set about this great work, on both sides, with the same conciliatory turn of mind, we may now, as in former times, owe even to our mutual mistakes, contentions, and animosities, the lasting concord, freedom, happiness, and glory of this empire.

Gentlemen, the distance between us, with other obstructions, has caused much misrepresentation of our mutual sentiments. We, therefore, to obviate them as well as we are able, take this method of assuring you of our thorough detestation of the whole war; and particularly the mercenary and savage war carried on or attempted against you: our thorough abhorrence of all addresses adverse to you, whether public or private; our assurances of an invariable affection towards you; our constant regard to your privileges and liberties; and our opinion of the solid security you ought to enjoy for them, under the paternal care and nurture of a protecting parliament.

Though many of us have earnestly wished that the authority of that august and venerable body, so necessary in many respects to the union of the whole, should be rather limited by its own equity and discretion, than by any bounds described by positive laws and public compacts; and though we felt the extreme difficulty, by any theoretical limitations, of qualifying that authority so as to preserve one part and deny another; and though you (as we gratefully acknowledge) had acquiesced most cheerfully under that prudent reserve of the constitution, at that happy moment, when neither you nor we apprehended a further return of the exercise of invidious powers, we are now as fully persuaded as you can be, by the malice, inconstancy, and perverse inquietude of many men, and by the incessant endeavours of an arbitrary faction, now too powerful, that our common necessities do require a full explanation and ratified security for your liberties and our quiet.

Although his Majesty's condescension in committing the direction of his affairs into the hands of the known friends of his family, and of the liberties of all his people, would, we admit, be a great means of giving repose to your minds, as it must give infinite facility to reconciliation, yet we assure you, that we think, with such a security as we recommend, adopted from necessity, and not choice, even by the unhappy authors and instruments of the public misfortunes, that the terms of reconciliation, if once accepted by parliament, would not be broken. We also pledge ourselves to you, that we should give, even to those unhappy persons, a hearty support in effectuating the peace of the empire; and every opposition in an attempt to cast it again into disorder.

When that happy hour shall arrive, let us in all affection recommend to you the wisdom of continuing, as in former times, or even in a more ample measure, the support of your government, and even to give to your administration some degree of reciprocal interest in your freedom. We earnestly wish you not to furnish your enemies, here or elsewhere, with any sort of pretexts for reviving quarrels by too reserved and severe or penurious an exercise of those sacred rights, which no pretended abuse in the exercise ought to impair, nor, by overstraining the principles of freedom, to make them less compatible with those haughty sentiments in others, which the very same principles may be apt to breed in minds not tempered with the utmost equity and justice.

The well-wishers of the liberty and union of this empire salute you, and recommend you most heartily to the Divine protection.

A Letter to the Sheriffs of Bristol on the Affairs of America

Legislation enacted in 1777 partially suspended the Habeas Corpus Act in Britain, and Burke worried that Lord North's administration would abrogate the traditional rights of Englishmen at home as he had in America. In a letter to some of his constituents Burke linked these concerns to his criticism of the government's policies that had led to the war in America. Particularly interesting is Burke's characteristic indictment of abstract and theoretical speculation in political affairs, alongside his plea for prudence, restraint, and moderation.

I THINK I KNOW AMERICA—if I do not, my ignorance is incurable, for I have spared no pains to understand it—and I do most solemnly assure those of my constituents who put any sort of confidence in my industry and integrity, that everything that has been done there has arisen from a total misconception of the object: that our means of originally holding America, that our means of reconciling with it after quarrel, of recovering it after separation, of keeping it after victory, did depend, and must depend, in their several stages and periods, upon a total renunciation of that unconditional submission which has taken such possession of the minds of violent men. The whole of those maxims upon which we have made and continued this war must be abandoned. Nothing, indeed (for I would not deceive you), can place us in our former situation. That hope must be laid aside. But there is a difference between bad and the worst of all. Terms relative to the cause of the war ought to be offered by the authority of Parliament. An arrangement at home promising some security for them ought to be made. By doing this, without the least impairing of our strength, we add to the credit of our moderation, which, in itself, is always strength more or less.

I know many have been taught to think that moderation in a case like this is a sort of treason, and that all arguments for it are sufficiently answered by railing at rebels and rebellion, and by charging all the present or future miseries which we may suffer on the resistance of our brethren. But I would wish them, in this grave matter, and if peace is not wholly removed from their hearts, to consider seriously, first, that to criminate and recriminate never yet was the road to reconciliation, in any difference amongst men. In the next place, it would be right to reflect that the American English (whom they may abuse, if they think it honorable to revile the absent) can, as things now stand, neither be provoked at our railing or bettered by our instruction. All communication is cut off between us. But this we know with certainty, that, though we cannot reclaim them, we may reform ourselves. If measures of peace are necessary, they must begin somewhere; and a conciliatory temper must precede and prepare every plan of reconciliation. Nor do I conceive that we suffer anything by thus regulating our own minds. We are not disarmed by being disencumbered of our passions. Declaiming on rebellion never added a bayonet or a charge of powder to your military force; but I am afraid that it has been the means of taking up many muskets against you.

This outrageous language, which has been encouraged and kept alive by every art, has already done incredible mischief. For a long time, even amidst the desolations of war, and the insults of hostile laws daily accumulated on one another, the American leaders seem to have had the greatest difficulty in bringing up their people to a declaration of total independence. But the Court Gazette accomplished what the abettors of independence had attempted in vain. . . .

I know it is said that your kindness is only alienated on account of their resistance, and therefore, if the colonies surrender at discretion, all sort of regard, and even much indulgence, is meant towards them in future. But can those who are partisans for continuing a war to enforce such a surrender be responsible (after all that has passed) for such a future use of a power that is bound by no compacts and restrained by no terror? Will they tell us what they call indulgences? Do they not at this instant call the present war and all its horrors a lenient and merciful proceeding?

No conqueror that I ever heard of has *professed* to make a cruel, harsh, and insolent use of his conquest. No! The man of the most declared pride scarcely dares to trust his own heart with this dreadful secret of ambition. But it will appear in its time; and no man who professes to reduce another to the insolent mercy of a foreign arm ever had any sort of good-will towards him. The profession of kindness, with that sword in his hand, and that demand of surrender, is one of the most provoking acts of his hostility. . . .

I am charged with being an American. If warm affection towards those over whom I claim any share of authority be a crime, I am guilty of this charge. But I do assure you (and they who know me publicly and privately will bear witness to me) that if ever one man lived more zealous than another for the supremacy of Parliament and the rights of this imperial crown, it was myself. Many others, indeed, might be more knowing in the extent of the foundation of these rights. I do not pretend to be an antiquary, a lawyer, or qualified for the chair of professor in metaphysics. I never ventured to put your solid interests upon speculative grounds. My having constantly declined to do so has been attributed to my incapacity for such disquisitions; and I am inclined to believe it is partly the cause. I never shall be ashamed to confess that where I am ignorant, I am diffident. I am, indeed, not very solicitous to clear myself of this imputed incapacity; because men even less conversant than I am in this kind of subtleties, and placed in stations to which I ought not to aspire, have, by the mere force of civil discretion, often conducted the affairs of great nations with distinguished felicity and glory.

When I first came into a public trust, I found your Parliament in possession of an unlimited legislative power over the colonies. I could not open the statute-book without seeing the actual exercise of it, more or less, in all cases whatsoever. This possession passed with me for a title. It does so in all human affairs. No man examines into the defects of his title to his paternal estate or to his established government. Indeed, common sense taught me that a legislative authority not actually limited by the express terms of its foundation, or by its own subsequent acts, cannot have its powers parcelled out by argumentative distinctions, so as to enable us to say that here they can and there they cannot bind. . . .

I had, indeed, very earnest wishes to keep the whole body of this authority perfect and entire as I found it—and to keep it so, not for our advantage solely, but principally for the sake of those on whose account all just authority exists: I mean the people to be governed. For I thought I saw that many cases might well happen in which the exercise of every power comprehended in the broadest idea of legislature might become, in its time and circumstances, not a little expedient for the peace and union of the colonies amongst themselves, as well as for their perfect harmony with Great Britain. . . . I was at the same time very sure that the authority of which I was so jealous could not, under the actual circumstances of our plantations, be at all preserved in any of its members but by the greatest reserve in its application, particularly in those delicate points in which the feelings of mankind are the most irritable. They who thought otherwise have found a few more difficulties in their work than (I hope) they were thoroughly aware of when they undertook the present business. I must beg leave to observe that it is not only the invidious branch of taxation that will be resisted, but that no other given part of legislative rights can be exercised without regard to the general opinion of those who are to be governed. That general opinion is the vehicle and organ of legislative omnipotence. Without this it may be a theory to entertain the mind, but it is nothing in the direction of affairs. The completeness of the legislative authority of Parliament *over this kingdom* is not questioned; and yet many things indubitably included in the abstract idea of that power, and which carry no absolute injustice in themselves, yet being contrary to the opinions and feelings of the people, can as little be exercised as if Parliament in that case had been possessed of no right at all. I see no abstract reason which can be given why the same power which made and repealed the High Commission Court and the Star Chamber might not revive them again; and these courts, warned by their former fate, might possibly exercise their powers with some degree of justice. But the madness would be as unquestionable as the competence of that Parliament which should attempt such things. If anything can be supposed out of the power of human legislature, it is religion; I admit, however, that the established religion of this country has been three or four times altered by act of Parliament, and therefore that a statute binds even in that case. But we may very safely affirm that, notwithstanding this apparent omnipotence, it would be now found as impossible for King and Parliament to alter the established religion of this country as it was to King James alone, when he attempted to make such an alteration without a Parliament. In effect, to follow, not to force, the public inclination; to give a direction, a form, a technical dress, and a specific sanction to the general sense of the community is the true end of legislature.

It is so with regard to the exercise of all the powers which our constitution knows in any of its parts, and indeed to the substantial existence of any of the parts themselves. The king's negative to bills is one of the most indisputed of the royal prerogatives; and it extends to all cases whatsoever. I am far from certain that if several laws which I know had fallen under the stroke of that sceptre, that the public would have had a very heavy loss. But it is not the *propriety* of the exercise which is in question. The exercise itself is wisely forborne. Its repose may be the preservation of its existence; and its existence may be the means of saving the constitution itself, on an occasion worthy of bringing it forth. . . .

As the disputants whose accurate and logical reasonings have brought us into our present condition think it absurd that powers or members of any constitution should exist rarely, if ever, to be exercised, I hope I shall be excused in mentioning another instance that is material. We know that the Convocation of the Clergy had formerly been called, and sat with nearly as much regularity to business as Parliament itself. It is now called for form only. It sits for the purpose of making some polite ecclesiastical compliments to the king, and, when that grace is said, retires and is heard of no more. It is, however, *a part of the constitution*, and may be called out into act and energy whenever there is occasion, and whenever those who conjure up that spirit will choose to abide the consequences. It is wise to permit its legal existence: it is much wiser to continue it a legal existence only. So truly has prudence (constituted as the god of this lower world) the entire dominion over every exercise of power committed into its hands! And yet I have lived to see prudence and conformity to circumstances wholly set at nought in our late controversies, and treated as if they were the most contemptible and irrational of all things. I have heard it a hundred times very gravely alleged that, in order to keep power in wind, it was necessary, by preference, to exert it in those very points in which it was most likely to be resisted and the least likely to be productive of any advantage.

These were the considerations, Gentlemen, which led me early to think that, in the comprehensive dominion which the Divine Providence had put into our hands, instead of troubling our understandings with speculations concerning the unity of empire and the identity or distinction of legislative powers, and inflaming our passions with the heat and pride of controversy, it was our duty, in all soberness, to conform our government to the character and circumstances of the several people who composed this mighty and strangely diversified mass. I never was wild enough to conceive that one method would serve for the whole, that the natives of Hindostan and those of Virginia could be ordered in the same manner, or that the Cutchery court and the grand jury of Salem could be regulated on a similar plan. I was persuaded that government was a practical thing, made for the happiness of mankind, and not to furnish out a spectacle of uniformity to gratify the schemes of visionary politicians. Our business was to rule, not to wrangle; and it would have been a poor compensation that we had triumphed in a dispute whilst we lost an empire.

If there be one fact in the world perfectly clear, it is this: "that the disposition of the people of America is wholly averse to any other than a free government"; and this is indication enough to any honest statesman how he ought to adapt whatever power he finds in his hands to their case. If any ask me what a free government is, I answer that, for any practical purpose, it is what the people think so—and that they, and not I, are the natural, lawful, and competent judges of this matter. If they practically allow me a greater degree of authority over them than is consistent with any correct ideas of perfect freedom, I ought to thank them for so great a trust, and not to endeavor to prove from thence that they have reasoned amiss, and that, having gone so far, by analogy they must hereafter have no enjoyment but by my pleasure.

If we had seen this done by any others, we should have concluded them far gone in madness. It is melancholy, as well as ridiculous, to observe the kind of reasoning with which the public has been amused, in order to divert our minds from the common sense of our American policy. There are people who have split and anatomized the doctrine of free government, as if it were an abstract question concerning metaphysical liberty and necessity, and not a matter of moral prudence and natural feeling. They have disputed whether liberty be a positive or a negative idea; whether it does not consist in being governed by laws, without considering what are the laws, or who are the makers; whether man has any rights by nature; and whether all the property he enjoys be not the alms of his government, and his life itself their favor and indulgence. Others, corrupting religion as these have perverted philosophy, contend that Christians are redeemed into captivity, and the blood of the Saviour of mankind has been shed to make them the slaves of a few proud and insolent sinners. These shocking extremes provoking to extremes of another kind, speculations are let loose as destructive to all authority as the former are to all freedom; and every government is called tyranny and usurpation which is not formed on their fancies. In this manner the stirrers-up of this contention, not satisfied with distracting our dependencies and filling them with blood and slaughter, are corrupting our understandings: they are endeavoring to tear up, along with practical liberty, all the foundations of human society, all equity and justice, religion and order.

Civil freedom, Gentlemen, is not, as many have endeavored to persuade you, a thing that lies hid in the depth of abstruse science. It is a blessing and a benefit, not an abstract speculation; and all the just reasoning that can be upon it is of so coarse a texture as perfectly to suit the ordinary capacities of those who are to enjoy, and of those who are to defend it. Far from any resemblance to those propositions in geometry and metaphysics which admit no medium, but must be true or false in all their latitude, social and civil freedom, like all other things in common life, are variously mixed and modified, enjoyed in very different degrees, and shaped into an infinite diversity of forms, according to the temper and circumstances of every community. The *extreme* of liberty (which is its abstract perfection, but its real fault) obtains nowhere, nor ought to obtain anywhere; because extremes, as we all know, in every point which relates either to our duties or satisfactions in life, are destructive both to virtue and enjoyment. Liberty, too, must be limited in order to be possessed. The degree of restraint it is impossible in any case to settle precisely. But it ought to be the constant aim of every wise public counsel to find out by cautious experiments, and rational, cool endeavors, with how little, not how much, of this restraint the community can subsist: for liberty is a good to be improved, and not an evil to be lessened. It is not only a private blessing of the first order, but the vital spring and energy of the state itself, which has just so much life and vigor as there is liberty in it. But whether liberty be advantageous or not (for I know it is a fashion to decry the very principle), none will dispute that peace is a blessing; and peace must, in the course of human affairs, be frequently bought by some indulgence and toleration at least to liberty; for as the Sabbath (though of divine institution) was made for man, not man for the Sabbath, government, which can claim no higher origin or authority, in its exercise at least, ought to conform to the exigencies of the time, and the temper and character of the people with whom it is concerned, and not always to attempt violently to bend the people to their theories of subjection. The bulk of mankind, on their part, are not excessively curious concerning any theories whilst they are really happy; and one sure symptom of an ill-conducted state is the propensity of the people to resort to them.

But when subjects, by a long course of such ill conduct, are once thoroughly inflamed, and the state itself violently distempered, the people must have some satisfaction to their feelings more solid than a sophistical speculation on law and government. Such was our situation: and such a satisfaction was necessary to prevent recourse to arms; it was necessary towards laying them down; it will be necessary to prevent the taking them up again and again. Of what nature this satisfaction ought to be I wish it had been the disposition of Parliament seriously to consider. It was certainly a deliberation that called for the exertion of all their wisdom.

I am, and ever have been, deeply sensible of the difficulty of reconciling the strong presiding power that is so useful towards the conservation of a vast, disconnected, infinitely diversified empire with that liberty and safety of the provinces which they must enjoy (in opinion and practice at least) or they will not be provinces at all. I know, and have long felt, the difficulty of reconciling the unwieldy haughtiness of a great ruling nation, habituated to command, pampered by enormous wealth, and confident from a long course of prosperity and victory, to the high spirit of free dependencies, animated with the first glow and activity of juvenile heat, and assuming to themselves, as their birthright, some part of that very pride which oppresses them. They who perceive no difficulty in reconciling these tempers (which, however, to make peace, must some way or other be reconciled) are much above my capacity, or much below the magnitude of the business. Of one thing I am perfectly clear: that it is not by deciding the suit, but by compromising the difference, that peace can be restored or kept. They who would put an end to such quarrels by declaring roundly in favor of the whole demands of either party have mistaken, in my humble opinion, the office of a mediator.

The war is now of full two years' standing: the controversy of many more. In different periods of the dispute, different methods of reconciliation were to be pursued. I mean to trouble you with a short state of things at the most important of these periods, in order to give you a more distinct idea of our policy with regard to this most delicate of all objects. The colonies were from the beginning subject to the legislature of Great Britain on principles which they never examined; and we permitted to them many local privileges without asking how they agreed with that legislative authority. Modes of administration were formed in an insensible and very unsystematic manner. But they gradually adapted themselves to the varying condition of things. What was first a single kingdom stretched into an empire; and an imperial superintendency, of some kind or other, became necessary. Parliament, from a mere representative of the people, and a guardian of popular privileges for its own immediate constituents, grew into a mighty sovereign. Instead of being a control on the crown on its own behalf, it communicated a sort of strength to the royal authority, which was wanted for the conservation of a new object, but which could not be safely trusted to the crown alone. On the other hand, the colonies, advancing by equal steps, and governed by the same necessity, had formed within themselves, either by royal instruction or royal charter, assemblies so exceedingly resembling a parliament, in all their forms, functions, and powers, that it was impossible they should not imbibe some opinion of a similar authority.

At the first designation of these assemblies, they were probably not intended for anything more (nor perhaps did they think themselves much higher) than the municipal corporations within this island, to which some at present love to compare them. But nothing in progression can rest on its original plan. We may as well think of rocking a grown man in the cradle of an infant. Therefore, as the colonies prospered and increased to a numerous and mighty people, spreading over a very great tract of the globe, it was natural that they should attribute to assemblies so respectable in their formal constitution some part of the dignity of the great nations which they represented. No longer tied to by-laws, these assemblies made acts of all sorts and in all cases whatsoever. They levied money, not for parochial purposes, but upon regular grants to the crown, following all the rules and principles of a parliament, to which they approached every day more and more nearly. Those who think themselves wiser than Providence and stronger than the course of nature may complain of all this variation, on the one side or the other, as their several humors and prejudices may lead them. But things could not be otherwise; and English colonies must be had on these terms, or not had at all. In the meantime neither party felt any inconvenience from this double legislature, to which they had been formed by imperceptible habits, and old custom, the great support of all the governments in the world. Though these two legislatures were sometimes found perhaps performing the very same functions, they did not very grossly or systematically clash. In all likelihood this arose from mere neglect, possibly from the natural operation of things, which, left to themselves, generally fall into their proper order. But whatever was the cause, it is certain that a regular revenue, by the authority of Parliament, for the support of civil and military establishments, seems not to have been thought of until the colonies were too proud to submit, too strong to be forced, too enlightened not to see all the consequences which must arise from such a system.

If ever this scheme of taxation was to be pushed against the inclinations of the people, it was evident that discussions must arise which would let loose all the elements that composed this double constitution, would show how much each of their members had departed from its original principles, and would discover contradictions in each legislature, as well to its own first principles as to its relation to the other, very difficult, if not absolutely impossible, to be reconciled.

Therefore, at the first fatal opening of this contest, the wisest course seemed to be to put an end as soon as possible to the immediate causes of the dispute, and to quiet a discussion, not easily settled upon clear principles, and arising from claims which pride would permit neither party to abandon, by resorting as nearly as possible to the old, successful course. A mere repeal of the obnoxious tax, with a declaration of the legislative authority of this kingdom, was then fully sufficient to procure peace to *both sides.* Man is a creature of habit, and, the first breach being of very short continuance, the colonies fell back exactly into their ancient state. The Congress has used an expression with regard to this pacification which appears to me truly significant. After the repeal of the Stamp Act, "the colonies fell," says this assembly, "into their ancient state of *unsuspecting confidence in the mother country.*" This unsuspecting confidence is the true center of gravity amongst mankind, about which all the parts are at rest. It is this *unsuspecting confidence* that removes all difficulties, and reconciles all the contradictions which occur in the complexity of all ancient puzzled political establishments. Happy are the rulers which have the secret of preserving it!

PART IV

IRELAND AND CATHOLICISM

Tract on the Popery Laws

Burke was a consistent critic of the brutal Protestant domination of Ireland, which followed upon William of Orange's suppression of the great rebellion of Tyreconnel. Anti-Catholic penal laws, or "popery laws," denied Catholics the traditional rights and benefits of British subjects, excluding them from all professions as well. Burke denounced these discriminatory laws in 1765, and his critique led him to a general exploration of the nature and purpose of law and government.

THE SYSTEM which we have just reviewed, and the manner in which religious influence on the public is made to operate upon the laws concerning property in Ireland, is in its nature very singular, and differs, I apprehend, essentially, and perhaps to its disadvantage, from any scheme of religious persecution now existing in any other country in Europe, or which has prevailed in any time or nation with which history has made us acquainted. I believe it will not be difficult to show that it is unjust, impolitic, and inefficacious; that it has the most unhappy influence on the prosperity, the morals, and the safety of that country; that this influence is not accidental, but has flowed as the necessary and direct consequence of the laws themselves, first on account of the object which they affect, and next by the quality of the greatest part of the instruments they employ. . . .

The first and most capital consideration with regard to this, as to every object, is the extent of it. And here it is necessary to premise, this system of penalty and incapacity has for its object no small sect or obscure party, but a very numerous body of men—a body which comprehends at least two thirds of that whole nation: it amounts to 2,800,000 souls, a number sufficient for the materials constituent of a great people. . . .

This consideration of the magnitude of the object ought to attend us through the whole inquiry: if it does not always affect the reason, it is always decisive on the importance of the question. It not only makes in itself a more leading point, but complicates itself with every other part of the matter, giving every error, minute in itself, a character and significance from its application. . . .

In the making of a new law it is undoubtedly the duty of the legislator to see that no injustice be done even to an individual: for there is then nothing to be unsettled, and the matter is under his hands to mould it as he pleases; and if he finds it untractable in the working, he may abandon it without incurring any new inconvenience. But in the question concerning the repeal of an old one, the work is of more difficulty; because laws, like houses, lean on one another, and the operation is delicate, and should be necessary: the objection, in such a case, ought not to arise from the natural infirmity of human institutions, but from substantial faults which contradict the nature and end of law itself—faults not arising from the imperfection, but from the misapplication and abuse of our reason. As no legislators can regard the *minima* of equity, a law may in some instances be a just subject of censure without being at all an object of repeal. But if its transgressions against common right and the ends of just government should be considerable in their nature and spreading in their effects, as this objection goes to the root and principle of the law, it renders it void in its obligatory quality on the mind, and therefore determines it as the proper object of abrogation and repeal, so far as regards its civil existence. The objection here is, as we observed, by no means on account of the imperfection of the law; it is on account of its erroneous principle: for if this be fundamentally wrong, the more perfect the law is made, the worse it becomes. It cannot be said to have the properties of genuine law, even in its imperfections and defects. The true weakness and opprobrium of our best general constitutions is, that they cannot provide beneficially for every particular case, and thus fill, adequately to their intentions, the circle of universal justice. But where the principle is faulty, the erroneous part of the law is the beneficial, and justice only finds refuge in those holes and corners which had escaped the sagacity and inquisition of the legislator. The happiness or misery of multitudes can never be a thing indifferent. A law against the majority of the people is in substance a law against the people itself; its extent determines its invalidity; it even changes its character as it enlarges its operation: it is not particular injustice, but general oppression; and can no longer be considered as a private hardship, which might be borne, but spreads and grows up into the unfortunate importance of a national calamity.

Now as a law directed against the mass of the nation has not the nature of a reasonable institution, so neither has it the authority: for in all forms of government the people is the true legislator; and whether the immediate and instrumental cause of the law be a single person or many, the remote and efficient cause is the consent of the people, either actual or implied; and such consent is absolutely essential to its validity. To the solid establishment of every law two things are essentially requisite: first, a proper and sufficient human power to declare and modify the matter of the law; and next, such a fit and equitable constitution as they have a right to declare and render binding. With regard to the first requisite, the human authority, it is their judgment they give up, not their right. The people, indeed, are presumed to consent to whatever the legislature ordains for their benefit; and they are to acquiesce in it, though they do not clearly see into the propriety of the means by which they are conducted to that desirable end. This they owe as an act of homage and just deference to a reason which the necessity of government has made superior to their own. But though the means, and indeed the nature, of a public advantage may not always be evident to the understanding of the subject, no one is so gross and stupid as not to distinguish between a benefit and an injury. No one can imagine, then, an exclusion of a great body of men, not from favors, privileges, and trusts, but from the common advantages of society, can ever be a thing intended for their good, or can ever be ratified by any implied consent of theirs. If, therefore, at least an implied human consent is necessary to the existence of a law, such a constitution cannot in propriety be a law at all.

But if we could suppose that such a ratification was made, not virtually, but actually, by the people, not representatively, but even collectively, still it would be null and void. They have no right to make a law prejudicial to the whole community, even though the delinquents in making such an act should be themselves the chief sufferers by it; because it would be made against the principle of a superior law, which it is not in the power of any community, or of the whole race of man, to alter—I mean the will of Him who gave us our nature, and in giving impressed an invariable law upon it. It would be hard to point out any error more truly subversive of all the order and beauty, of all the peace and happiness of human society, than the position, that any body of men have a right to make what laws they please—or that laws can derive any authority from their institution merely, and independent of the quality of the subject-matter. No arguments of policy, reason of state, or preservation of the constitution can be pleaded in favor of such a practice. They may, indeed, impeach the frame of that constitution, but can never touch this immovable principle. This seems to be, indeed, the doctrine which Hobbes broached in the last century, and which was then so frequently and so ably refuted. Cicero exclaims with the utmost indignation and contempt against such a notion: he considers it not only as unworthy of a philosopher, but of an illiterate peasant; that of all things this was the most truly absurd, to fancy that the rule of justice was to be taken from the constitutions of commonwealths, or that laws derived their authority from the statutes of the people, the edicts of princes, or the decrees of judges. If it be admitted that it is not the black-letter and the king's arms that makes the law, we are to look for it elsewhere.

In reality there are two, and only two, foundations of law; and they are both of them conditions without which nothing can give it any force: I mean equity and utility. With respect to the former, it grows out of the great rule of equality, which is grounded upon our common nature, and which Philo, with propriety and beauty, calls the mother of justice. All human laws are, properly speaking, only declaratory; they may alter the mode and application, but have no power over the substance of original justice. The other foundation of law, which is utility, must be understood, not of partial or limited, but of general and public utility, connected in the same manner with, and derived directly from, our rational nature: for any other utility may be the utility of a robber, but cannot be that of a citizen—the interest of the domestic enemy, and not that of a member of the commonwealth. This present equality can never be the foundation of statutes which create an artificial difference between men, as the laws before us do, in order to induce a consequential inequality in the distribution of justice. Law is a mode of human action respecting society, and must be governed by the same rules of equity which govern every private action; and so Tully considers it in his Offices as the only utility agreeable to that nature. . . .

If any proposition can be clear in itself, it is this: that a law which shuts out from all secure and valuable property the bulk of the people cannot be made for the utility of the party so excluded. This, therefore, is not the utility which Tully mentions. But if it were true (as it is not) that the real interest of any part of the community could be separated from the happiness of the rest, still it would afford no just foundation for a statute providing exclusively for that interest at the expense of the other; because it would be repugnant to the essence of law, which requires that it be made as much as possible for the benefit of the whole. If this principle be denied or evaded, what ground have we left to reason on? We must at once make a total change in all our ideas, and look for a new definition of law. Where to find it I confess myself at a loss. If we resort to the fountains of jurisprudence, they will not supply us with any that is for our purpose. . . .

It would be far more easy to heap up authorities on this article than to excuse the prolixity and tediousness of producing any at all in proof of a point which, though too often practically denied, is in its theory almost self-evident. For Suarez, handling this very question . . . does not hesitate a moment, finding no ground in reason or authority to render the affirmative in the least degree disputable. . . .

Partiality and law are contradictory terms. Neither the merits nor the ill deserts, neither the wealth and importance nor the indigence and obscurity, of the one part or of the other, can make any alteration in this fundamental truth. On any other scheme, I defy any man living to settle a correct standard which may discriminate between equitable rule and the most direct tyranny. For if we can once prevail upon ourselves to depart from the strictness and integrity of this principle in favor even of a considerable party, the argument will hold for one that is less so; and thus we shall go on, narrowing the bottom of public right, until step by step we arrive, though after no very long or very forced deduction, at what one of our poets calls the *enormous faith*—the faith of the many, created for the advantage of a single person. I cannot see a glimmering of distinction to evade it; nor is it possible to allege any reason for the proscription of so large a part of the kingdom, which would not hold equally to support, under parallel circumstances, the proscription of the whole.

I am sensible that these principles, in their abstract light, will not be very strenuously opposed. Reason is never inconvenient, but when it comes to be applied. Mere general truths interfere very little with the passions. They can, until they are roused by a troublesome application, rest in great tranquility, side by side with tempers and proceedings the most directly opposite to them. Men want to be reminded, who do not want to be taught; because those original ideas of rectitude, to which the mind is compelled to assent when they are proposed, are not always as present to it as they ought to be. When people are gone, if not into a denial, at least into a sort of oblivion of those ideas, when they know them only as barren speculations, and not as practical motives for conduct, it will be proper to press, as well as to offer them to the understanding; and when one is attacked by prejudices which aim to intrude themselves into the place of law, what is left for us but to vouch and call to warranty those principles of original justice from whence alone our title to everything valuable in society is derived? Can it be thought to arise from a superfluous, vain parade of displaying general and uncontroverted maxims, that we should revert at this time to the first principles of law, when we have directly under our consideration a whole body of statutes, which, I say, are so many contradictions, which their advocates allow to be so many exceptions from those very principles? Take them in the most favorable light, every exception from the original and fixed rule of equality and justice ought surely to be very well authorized in the reason of their deviation, and very rare in their use. For, if they should grow to be frequent, in what would they differ from an abrogation of the rule itself? By becoming thus frequent, they might even go further, and, establishing themselves into a principle, convert the rule into the exception. It cannot be dissembled that this is not at all remote from the case before us, where the great body of the people are excluded from all valuable property—where the greatest and most ordinary benefits of society are conferred as privileges, and not enjoyed on the footing of common rights.

The clandestine manner in which those in power carry on such designs is a sufficient argument of the sense they inwardly entertain of the true nature of their proceedings. Seldom is the title or preamble of the law of the same import with the body and enacting part; but they generally place some other color uppermost, which differs from that which is afterwards to appear, or at least one that is several shades fainter. Thus, the penal laws in question are not called laws to oblige men baptized and educated in Popery to renounce their religion or their property, but are called laws to prevent the growth of Popery; as if their purpose was only to prevent conversions to that sect, and not to persecute a million of people already engaged in it. But of all the instances of this sort of legislative artifice, and of the principles that produced it, I never met with any which made a stronger impression on me than that of Louis the Fourteenth, in the revocation of the Edict of Nantes. That monarch had, when he made that revocation, as few measures to keep with public opinion as any man. In the exercise of the most unresisted authority at home, in a career of uninterrupted victory abroad, and in a course of flattery equal to the circumstances of his greatness in both these particulars, he might be supposed to have as little need as disposition to render any sort of account to the world of his procedure towards his subjects. But the persecution of so vast a body of men as the Huguenots was too strong a measure even for the law of pride and power. It was too glaring a contradiction even to those principles upon which persecution itself is supported. Shocked at the naked attempt, he had recourse, for a palliation of his conduct, to an unkingly denial of the fact which made against him.

In the preamble, therefore, to his Act of Revocation, he sets forth that the Edict of Nantes was no longer necessary, as the object of it (the Protestants of his kingdom) were then reduced to a very small number. The refugees in Holland cried out against this misrepresentation. They asserted, I believe with truth, that this revocation had driven two hundred thousand of them out of their country, and that they could readily demonstrate there still remained six hundred thousand Protestants in France. If this were the fact, (as it was undoubtedly,) no argument of policy could have been strong enough to excuse a measure by which eight hundred thousand men were despoiled, at one stroke, of so many of their rights and privileges. Louis the Fourteenth confessed, by this sort of apology, that, if the number had been large, the revocation had been unjust. But, after all, is it not most evident that this act of injustice, which let loose on that monarch such a torrent of invective and reproach, and which threw so dark a cloud over all the splendor of a most illustrious reign, falls far short of the case in Ireland? The privileges which the Protestants of that kingdom enjoyed antecedent to this revocation were far greater than the Roman Catholics of Ireland ever aspired to under a contrary establishment. The number of their sufferers, if considered absolutely, is not half of ours; if considered relatively to the body of each community, it is not perhaps a twentieth part. And then the penalties and incapacities which grew from that revocation are not so grievous in their nature, nor so certain in their execution, nor so ruinous by a great deal to the civil prosperity of the state, as those which we have established for a perpetual law in our unhappy country. . . .

In putting this parallel, I take it for granted that we can stand for this short time very clear of our party distinctions. . . . I flatter myself that not a few will be found who do not think that the names of Protestant and Papist can make any change in the nature of essential justice. Such men will not allow that to be proper treatment to the one of these denominations which would be cruelty to the other, and which converts its very crime into the instrument of its defence: they will hardly persuade themselves that what was bad policy in France can be good in Ireland, or that what was intolerable injustice in an arbitrary monarch becomes, only by being more extended and more violent, an equitable procedure in a country professing to be governed by law. It is, however, impossible not to observe with some concern, that there are many also of a different disposition—a number of persons whose minds are so formed that they find the communion of religion to be a close and an endearing tie, and their country to be no bond at all—to whom common altars are a better relation than common habitations and a common civil interest—whose hearts are touched with the distresses of foreigners, and are abundantly awake to all the tenderness of human feeling on such an occasion, even at the moment that they are inflicting the very same distresses, or worse, on their fellow-citizens, without the least sting of compassion or remorse. To commiserate the distresses of all men suffering innocently, perhaps meritoriously, is generous, and very agreeable to the better part of our nature—a disposition that ought by all means to be cherished. But to transfer humanity from its natural basis, our legitimate and home-bred connections—to lose all feeling for those who have grown up by our sides, in our eyes, the benefit of whose cares and labors we have partaken from our birth, and meretriciously to hunt abroad after foreign affections, is such a disarrangement of the whole system of our duties, that I do not know whether benevolence so displaced is not almost the same thing as destroyed, or what effect bigotry could have produced that is more fatal to society. This no one could help observing, who has seen our doors kindly and bountifully thrown open to foreign sufferers for conscience, whilst through the same ports were issuing fugitives of our own, driven from their country for a cause which to an indifferent person would seem to be exactly similar, whilst we stood by, without any sense of the impropriety of this extraordinary scene, accusing and practising injustice. . . . These observations, which are a digression, but hardly, I think, can be considered as a departure from the subject, have detained us some time: we will now come more directly to our purpose.

It has been shown, I hope with sufficient evidence, that a constitution against the interest of the many is rather of the nature of a grievance than of a law; that of all grievances it is the most weighty and important; that it is made without due authority, against all the acknowledged principles of jurisprudence, against the opinions of all the great lights in that science; and that such is the tacit sense even of those who act in the most contrary manner. These points are, indeed, so evident, that I apprehend the abettors of the penal system will ground their defence on an admission, and not on a denial of them. They will lay it down as a principle, that the Protestant religion is a thing beneficial for the whole community, as well in its civil interests as in those of a superior order. From thence they will argue, that, the end being essentially beneficial, the means become instrumentally so; that these penalties and incapacities are not final causes of the law, but only a discipline to bring over a deluded people to their real interest, and therefore, though they may be harsh in their operation, they will be pleasant in their effects; and be they what they will, they cannot be considered as a very extraordinary hardship, as it is in the power of the sufferer to free himself when he pleases, and that only by converting to a better religion. . . .

I shall be very short, without being, I think, the less satisfactory, in my answer to these topics, because they never can be urged from a conviction of their validity, and are, indeed, only the usual and impotent struggles of those who are unwilling to abandon a practice which they are unable to defend. First, then, I observe, that, if the principle of their final and beneficial intention be admitted as a just ground for such proceedings, there never was, in the blamable sense of the word, nor ever can be, such a thing as a religious persecution in the world. Such an intention is pretended by all men—who all not only insist that their religion has the sanction of Heaven, but is likewise, and for that reason, the best and most convenient to human society. All religious persecution, Mr. Bayle well observes, is grounded upon a miserable *petitio principii*. You are wrong, I am right; you must come over to me, or you must suffer. Let me add, that the great inlet by which a color for oppression has entered into the world is by one man's pretending to determine concerning the happiness of another, and by claiming a right to use what means he thinks proper in order to bring him to a sense of it. It is the ordinary and trite sophism of oppression. But there is not yet such a convenient ductility in the human understanding as to make us capable of being persuaded that men can possibly mean the ultimate good of the whole society by rendering miserable for a century together the greater part of it—or that any one has such a reversionary benevolence as seriously to intend the remote good of a late posterity, who can give up the present enjoyment which every honest man must have in the happiness of his contemporaries. Everybody is satisfied that a conservation and secure enjoyment of our natural rights is the great and ultimate purpose of civil society, and that therefore all forms whatsoever of government are only good as they are subservient to that purpose to which they are entirely subordinate. Now to aim at the establishment of any form of government by sacrificing what is the substance of it, to take away or at least to suspend the rights of Nature in order to an approved system for the protection of them, and for the sake of that about which men must dispute forever to postpone those things about which they have no controversy at all, and this not in minute and subordinate, but large and principal objects, is a procedure as preposterous and absurd in argument as it is oppressive and cruel in its effect. For the Protestant religion, nor (I speak it with reverence, I am sure) the truth of our common Christianity, is not so clear as this proposition—that all men, at least the majority of men in the society, ought to enjoy the common advantages of it. You fall, therefore, into a double error: first, you incur a certain mischief for an advantage which is comparatively problematical, even though you were sure of obtaining it; secondly, whatever the proposed advantage may be, were it of a certain nature, the attainment of it is by no means certain; and such deep gaming for stakes so valuable ought not to be admitted: the risk is of too much consequence to society. If no other country furnished examples of this risk, yet our laws and our country are enough fully to demonstrate the fact: Ireland, after almost a century of persecution, is at this hour full of penalties and full of Papists. . . .

Now as to the other point, that the objects of these laws suffer voluntarily: this seems to me to be an insult rather than an argument. For, besides that it totally annihilates every characteristic and therefore every faulty idea of persecution, just as the former does, it supposes, what is false in fact, that it is in a man's moral power to change his religion whenever his convenience requires it. If he be beforehand satisfied that your opinion is better than his, he will voluntarily come over to you, and without compulsion, and then your law would be unnecessary; but if he is not so convinced, he must know that it is his duty in this point to sacrifice his interest here to his opinion of his eternal happiness, else he could have in reality no religion at all. In the former case, therefore, as your law would be unnecessary, in the latter it would be persecuting: that is, it would put your penalty and his ideas of duty in the opposite scales; which is, or I know not what is, the precise idea of persecution. If, then, you require a renunciation of his conscience, as a preliminary to his admission to the rights of society, you annex, morally speaking, an impossible condition to it. In this case, in the language of reason and jurisprudence, the condition would be void, and the gift absolute; as the practice runs, it is to establish the condition, and to withhold the benefit. The suffering is, then, not voluntary. . . .

The second head upon which I propose to consider those statutes with regard to their object, and which is the next in importance to the magnitude, and of almost equal concern in the inquiry into the justice of these laws, is its possession. It is proper to recollect that this religion, which is so persecuted in its members, is the old religion of the country, and the once established religion of the state—the very same which had for centuries received the countenance and sanction of the laws, and from which it would at one time have been highly penal to have dissented. In proportion as mankind has become enlightened, the idea of religious persecution, under any circumstances, has been almost universally exploded by all good and thinking men. The only faint shadow of difficulty which remains is concerning the introduction of new opinions. Experience has shown, that, if it has been favorable to the cause of truth, it has not been always conducive to the peace of society. Though a new religious sect should even be totally free in itself from any tumultuous and disorderly zeal, which, however, is rarely the case, it has a tendency to create a resistance from the establishment in possession, productive of great disorders, and thus becomes, innocently indeed, but yet very certainly, the cause of the bitterest dissensions in the commonwealth. To a mind not thoroughly saturated with the tolerating maxims of the Gospel, a preventive persecution, on such principles, might come recommended by strong, and, apparently, no immoral motives of policy, whilst yet the contagion was recent, and had laid hold but on a few persons. The truth is, these politics are rotten and hollow at bottom, as all that are founded upon any however minute a degree of positive injustice must ever be. But they are specious, and sufficiently so to delude a man of sense and of integrity. But it is quite otherwise with the attempt to eradicate by violence a widespreading and established religious opinion. If the people are in an error, to inform them is not only fair, but charitable; to drive them is a strain of the most manifest injustice. If not the right, the presumption, at least, is ever on the side of possession. Are they mistaken? If it does not fully justify them, it is a great alleviation of guilt, which may be mingled with their misfortune, that the error is none of their forging—that they received it on as good a footing as they can receive your laws and your legislative authority, because it was handed down to them from their ancestors. The opinion may be erroneous, but the principle is undoubtedly right; and you punish them for acting upon a principle which of all others is perhaps the most necessary for preserving society, an implicit admiration and adherence to the establishments of their forefathers.

If, indeed, the legislative authority was on all hands admitted to be the ground of religious persuasion, I should readily allow that dissent would be rebellion. In this case it would make no difference whether the opinion was sucked in with the milk or imbibed yesterday; because the same legislative authority which had settled could destroy it with all the power of a creator over his creature. But this doctrine is universally disowned, and for a very plain reason. Religion, to have any force on men's understandings, indeed to exist at all, must be supposed paramount to laws, and independent for its substance upon any human institution—else it would be the absurdest thing in the world, an acknowledged cheat. Religion, therefore, is not believed because the laws have established it, but it is established because the leading part of the community have previously believed it to be true. . . .

However, we are warranted to go thus far. The people often actually do (and perhaps they cannot in general do better) take their religion, not on the coercive, which is impossible, but on the influencing authority of their governors, as wise and informed men. But if they once take a religion on the word of the state, they cannot in common sense do so a second time, unless they have some concurrent reason for it. The prejudice in favor of your wisdom is shook by your change. You confess that you have been wrong, and yet you would pretend to dictate by your sole authority; whereas you disengage the mind by embarrassing it. For why should I prefer your opinion of to-day to your persuasion of yesterday? If we must resort to prepossessions for the ground of opinion, it is in the nature of man rather to defer to the wisdom of times past, whose weakness is not before his eyes, than to the present, of whose imbecility he has daily experience. Veneration of antiquity is congenial to the human mind. When, therefore, an establishment would persecute an opinion in possession, it sets against it all the powerful prejudices of human nature. It even sets its own authority, when it is of most weight, against itself in that very circumstance in which it must necessarily have the least; and it opposes the stable prejudice of time against a new opinion founded on mutability: a consideration that must render compulsion in such a case the more grievous, as there is no security, that, when the mind is settled in the new opinion, it may not be obliged to give place to one that is still newer, or even to a return of the old. But when an ancient establishment begins early to persecute an innovation, it stands upon quite other grounds, and it has all the prejudices and presumptions on its side. It puts its own authority, not only of compulsion, but prepossession, the veneration of past age, as well as the activity of the present time, against the opinion only of a private man or set of men. If there be no reason, there is at least some consistency in its proceedings. Commanding to constancy, it does nothing but that of which it sets an example itself. But an opinion at once new and persecuting is a monster; because, in the very instant in which it takes a liberty of change, it does not leave to you even a liberty of perseverance.

Is, then, no improvement to be brought into society? Undoubtedly; but not by compulsion—but by encouragement—but by countenance, favor, privileges, which are powerful, and are lawful instruments. The coercive authority of the state is limited to what is necessary for its existence. . . .

But, say the abettors of our penal laws, this old possessed superstition is such in its principles, that society, on its general principles, cannot subsist along with it. Could a man think such an objection possible, if he had not actually heard it made—an objection contradicted, not by hypothetical reasonings, but the clear evidence of the most decisive facts? Society not only exists, but flourishes at this hour, with this superstition, in many countries, under every form of government—in some established, in some tolerated, in others upon an equal footing. And was there no civil society at all in these kingdoms before the Reformation? To say it was not as well constituted as it ought to be is saying nothing at all to the purpose; for that assertion evidently regards improvements, not existence. It certainly did then exist; and it as certainly then was at least as much to the advantage of a very great part of society as what we have brought in the place of it: which is, indeed, a great blessing to those who have profited of the change; but to all the rest, as we have wrought, that is, by blending general persecution with partial reformation, it is the very reverse. We found the people heretics and idolaters; we have, by way of improving their condition, rendered them slaves and beggars: they remain in all the misfortune of their old errors, and all the superadded misery of their recent punishment. They were happy enough, in their opinion at least, before the change; what benefits society then had, they partook of them all. They are now excluded from those benefits; and, so far as civil society comprehends them, and as we have managed the matter, our persecutions are so far from being necessary to its existence, that our very reformation is made in a degree noxious. If this be improvement, truly I know not what can be called a depravation of society. . . .

Even if these laws could be supposed agreeable to those of Nature . . . on another and almost as strong a principle they are yet unjust, as being contrary to positive compact, and the public faith most solemnly plighted. On the surrender of Limerick, and some other Irish garrisons, in the war of the Revolution, the Lords Justices of Ireland and the commander-in-chief of the king's forces signed a capitulation with the

Irish, which was afterwards ratified by the king himself . . . under the great seal of England. It contains some public articles relative to the whole body of the Roman Catholics in that kingdom. . . . The first is of this tenor:—"The Roman Catholics of this kingdom [Ireland] shall enjoy such privileges in the exercise of their religion as are consistent with the laws of Ireland, or as they did enjoy in the reign of King Charles the Second. And their Majesties, as soon as affairs will permit them to summon a Parliament in this kingdom, will endeavor to procure the said Roman Catholics such farther security in that particular as may preserve them from any disturbance upon the account of their said religion." The ninth article is to this effect:—"The oath to be administered to such Roman Catholics as submit to their Majesties' government shall be the oath abovesaid, and no other,"—viz., the oath of allegiance, made by act of Parliament in England, in the first year of their then Majesties; as required by the second of the Articles of Limerick. Compare this latter article with the penal laws, . . . and judge whether they seem to be the public acts of the same power, and observe whether other oaths are tendered to them, and under what penalties. Compare the former with the same laws, from the beginning to the end, and judge whether the Roman Catholics have been preserved, agreeably to the sense of the article, from any disturbance upon account of their religion—or rather, whether on that account there is a single right of Nature or benefit of society which has not been either totally taken away or considerably impaired. . . .

The great prop of this whole system is not pretended to be its justice or its utility, but the supposed danger to the state, which gave rise to it originally, and which, they apprehend, would return, if this system were overturned. Whilst, say they, the Papists of this kingdom were possessed of landed property, and of the influence consequent to such property, their allegiance to the crown of Great Britain was ever insecure, the public peace was ever liable to be broken, and Protestants never could be a moment secure either of their properties or of their lives. Indulgence only made them arrogant, and power daring; confidence only excited and enabled them to exert their inherent treachery; and the times which they generally selected for their most wicked and desperate rebellions were those in which they enjoyed the greatest ease and the most perfect tranquillity.

Such are the arguments that are used, both publicly and privately, in every discussion upon this point. They are generally full of passion and of error, and built upon facts which in themselves are most false. It cannot, I confess, be denied, that those miserable performances which go about under the names of Histories of Ireland do, indeed, represent those events after this manner; and they would persuade us, contrary to the known order of Nature, that indulgence and moderation in governors is the natural incitement in subjects to rebel. But there is an interior history of Ireland, the genuine voice of its records and monuments, which speaks a very different language from these histories, from Temple and from Clarendon: these restore Nature to its just rights, and policy to its proper order. For they even now show to those who have been at the pains to examine them, and they may show one day to all the world, that these rebellions were not produced by toleration, but by persecution—that they arose not from just and mild government, but from the most unparalleled oppression. These records will be far from giving the least countenance to a doctrine so repugnant to humanity and good sense as that the security of any establishment, civil or religious, can ever depend upon the misery of those who live under it, or that its danger can arise from their quiet and prosperity. God forbid that the history of this or any country should give such encouragement to the folly or vices of those who govern! If it can be shown that the great rebellions of Ireland have arisen from attempts to reduce the natives to the state to which they are now reduced, it will show that an attempt to continue them in that state will rather be disadvantageous to the public peace than any kind of security to it. These things have in some measure begun to appear already; and as far as regards the argument drawn from former rebellions, it will fall readily to the ground. But, for my part, I think the real danger to every state is, to render its subjects justly discontented; nor is there in politics or science any more effectual secret for their security than to establish in their people a firm opinion that no change can be for their advantage. It is true that bigotry and fanaticism may for a time draw great multitudes of people from a knowledge of their true and substantial interest. But upon this I have to remark three things. First, that such a temper can never become universal, or last for a long time. . . . The majority of men are in no persuasion bigots; they are not willing to sacrifice, on every vain imagination that superstition or enthusiasm holds forth, or that even zeal and piety recommend, the certain possession of their temporal happiness. And if such a spirit has been at any time roused in a society, after it has had its paroxysm it commonly subsides and is quiet, and is even the weaker for the violence of its first exertion: security and ease are its mortal enemies. But, secondly, if anything can tend to revive and keep it up, it is to keep alive the passions of men by ill usage. This is enough to irritate even those who have not a spark of bigotry in their constitution to the most desperate enterprises; it certainly will inflame, darken, and render more dangerous the spirit of bigotry in those who are possessed by it. Lastly, by rooting out any sect, you are never secure against the effects of fanaticism; it may arise on the side of the most favored opinions; and many are the instances wherein the established religion of a state has grown ferocious and turned upon its keeper, and has often torn to pieces the civil establishment that had cherished it, and which it was designed to support: France—England—Holland. . . .

Address at Bristol on the Gordon Riots and the Catholic Question

The Savile Act of 1778 provided the first small reform of the anti-Catholic penal laws in England. Catholics could more easily purchase and inherit land, and priests were no longer jailed merely for saying mass. Notwithstanding the minor nature of the concessions, a backlash of anti-popery sentiment spread through England, culminating in the bloody anti-Catholic riots led by Lord George Gordon in June 1780. Burke, a committed Anglican, was widely known to be sympathetic to the cause of Catholic rights and was himself a target of the rioters' anger. His constituents in Bristol were unhappy with his interests in Catholic rights, and in this address to them he candidly sets forth his positions on Catholic issues.

GENTLEMEN, I ought to apologize to you for seeming to think anything at all necessary to be said upon this matter. The calumny is fitter to be scrawled with the midnight chalk of incendiaries, with "No Popery," on walls and doors of devoted houses, than to be mentioned in any civilized company. I had heard that the spirit of discontent on that subject was very prevalent here. With pleasure I find that I have been grossly misinformed. . . . I find with satisfaction and pride that not above four or five in this city (and I dare say these misled by some gross misrepresentation) have signed that symbol of delusion and bond of sedition, that libel on the national religion and English character, the Protestant Association. It is, therefore, Gentlemen, not by way of cure, but of prevention, and lest the arts of wicked men may prevail over the integrity of anyone amongst us, that I think it necessary to open to you the merits of this transaction pretty much at large; and I beg your patience upon it; for although the reasonings that have been used to depreciate the act are of little force, and though the authority of the men concerned in this ill design is not very imposing, yet the audaciousness of these conspirators against the national honor, and the extensive wickedness of their attempts, have raised persons of little importance to a degree of evil eminence, and imparted a sort of sinister dignity to proceedings that had their origin in only the meanest and blindest malice. . . .

Gentlemen, the condition of our nature is such that we buy our blessings at a price. The Reformation, one of the greatest periods of human improvement, was a time of trouble and confusion. The vast structure of superstition and tyranny which had been for ages in rearing, and which was combined with the interest of the great and of the many, which was molded into the laws, the manners, and civil institutions of nations, and blended with the frame and policy of states, could not be brought to the ground without a fearful struggle; nor could it fall without a violent concussion of itself and all about it. When this great revolution was attempted in a more regular mode by government, it was opposed by plots and seditions of the people; when by popular efforts, it was repressed as rebellion by the hand of power; and bloody executions (often bloodily returned) marked the whole of its progress through all its stages. The affairs of religion, which are no longer heard of in the tumult of our present contentions, made a principal ingredient in the wars and politics of that time; the enthusiasm of religion threw a gloom over the politics; and political interests poisoned and perverted the spirit of religion upon all sides. The Protestant religion, in that violent struggle, infected, as the Popish had been before, by worldly interests and worldly passions, became a persecutor in its turn, sometimes of the new sects, which carried their own principles further than it was convenient to the original reformers, and always of the body from whom they parted; and this persecuting spirit arose, not only from the bitterness of retaliation, but from the merciless policy of fear.

It was long before the spirit of true piety and true wisdom, involved in the principles of the Reformation, could be depurated from the dregs and feculence of the contention with which it was carried through. However, until this be done, the Reformation is not complete; and those who think themselves good Protestants, from their animosity to others, are in that respect no Protestants at all. It was at first thought necessary, perhaps, to oppose to Popery another Popery, to get the better of it. Whatever was the cause, laws were made in many countries, and in this kingdom in particular, against Papists, which are as bloody as any of those which had been enacted by the Popish princes and states; and where those laws were not bloody, in my opinion, they were worse; as they were slow, cruel outrages on our nature, and kept men alive only to insult in their persons every one of the rights and feelings of humanity. I pass those statutes, because I would spare your pious ears the repetition of such shocking things; and I come to that particular law the repeal of which has produced so many unnatural and unexpected consequences.

A statute was fabricated in the year 1699 by which the saying Mass (a church service in the Latin tongue, not exactly the same as our liturgy, but very near it, and containing no offense whatsoever against the laws, or against good morals) was forged into a crime, punishable with perpetual imprisonment. The teaching school, a useful and virtuous occupation, even the teaching in a private family, was in every Catholic subjected to the same unproportioned punishment. Your industry, and the bread of your children, was taxed for a pecuniary reward to stimulate avarice to do what nature refused, to inform and prosecute on this law. Every Roman Catholic was, under the same act, to forfeit his estate to his nearest Protestant relation, until, through a profession of what he did not believe, he redeemed by his hypocrisy what the law had transferred to the kinsman as the recompense of his profligacy. When thus turned out of doors from his paternal estate, he was disabled from acquiring any other by any industry, donation, or charity; but was rendered a foreigner in his native land, only because he retained the religion, along with the property, handed down to him from those who had been the old inhabitants of that land before him.

Does anyone who hears me approve this scheme of things, or think there is common justice, common sense, or common honesty in any part of it? If any does, let him say it, and I am ready to discuss the point with temper and candor. But instead of approving, I perceive a virtuous indignation beginning to rise in your minds on the mere cold stating of the statute.

But what will you feel when you know from history how this statute passed, and what were the motives, and what the mode of making it? A party in this nation, enemies to the system of the Revolution, were in opposition to the government of King William. They knew that our glorious deliverer was an enemy to all persecution. They knew that he came to free us from slavery and Popery, out of a country where a third of the people are contented Catholics under a Protestant government. He came with a part of his army composed of those very Catholics, to overset the power of a Popish prince. Such is the effect of a tolerating spirit; and so much is liberty served in every way, and by all persons, by a manly adherence to its own principles. Whilst freedom is true to itself, everything becomes subject to it, and its very adversaries are an instrument in its hands.

The party I speak of (like some amongst us who would disparage the best friends of their country) resolved to make the King either violate his principles of toleration or incur the odium of protecting Papists. They therefore brought in this bill, and made it purposely wicked and absurd that it might be rejected. The then court party, discovering their game, turned the tables on them, and returned their bill to them stuffed with still greater absurdities, that its loss might lie upon its original authors. They, finding their own ball thrown back to them, kicked it back again to their adversaries. And thus this act, loaded with the double injustice of two parties, neither of whom intended to pass what they hoped the other would be persuaded to reject, went through the legislature, contrary to the real wish of all parts of it, and of all the parties that composed it. In this manner these insolent and profligate factions, as if they were playing with balls and counters, made a sport of the fortunes and the liberties of their fellow-creatures. . . .

The effects of the act have been as mischievous as its origin was ludicrous and shameful. From that time, every person of that communion, lay and ecclesiastic, has been obliged to fly from the face of day. The clergy, concealed in garrets of private houses, or obliged to take a shelter (hardly safe to themselves, but infinitely dangerous to their country) under the privileges of foreign ministers, officiated as their servants and under their protection. The whole body of the Catholics, condemned to beggary and to ignorance in their native land, have been obliged to learn the principles of letters, at the hazard of all their other principles, from the charity of your enemies. They have been taxed to their ruin at the pleasure of necessitous and profligate relations, and according to the measure of their necessity and profligacy. Examples of this are many and affecting. . . . It is but six or seven years since a clergyman, of the name of Malony, a man of morals, neither guilty nor accused of anything noxious to the state, was condemned to perpetual imprisonment for exercising the functions of his religion; and after lying in jail two or three years, was relieved by the mercy of government from perpetual imprisonment, on condition of perpetual banishment. A brother of the Earl of Shrewsbury, a Talbot, a name respectable in this country whilst its glory is any part of its concern, was hauled to the bar of the Old Bailey, among common felons, and only escaped the same doom either by some error in the process, or that the wretch who brought him there could not correctly describe his person—I now forget which. In short, the persecution would never have relented for a moment if the judges, superseding (though with an ambiguous example) the strict rule of their artificial duty by the higher obligation of their conscience, did not constantly throw every difficulty in the way of such informers. But so ineffectual is the power of legal evasion against legal iniquity that it was but the other day that a lady of condition, beyond the middle of life, was on the point of being stripped of her whole fortune by a near relation to whom she had been a friend and benefactor; and she must have been totally ruined, without a power of redress or mitigation from the courts of law, had not the legislature itself rushed in, and by a special act of Parliament rescued her from the injustice of its own statutes. One of the acts authorizing such things was that which we in part repealed, knowing what our duty was, and doing that duty as men of honor and virtue, as good Protestants, and as good citizens. . . .

Gentlemen, bad laws are the worst sort of tyranny. In such a country as this they are of all bad things the worst—worse by far than anywhere else; and they derive a particular malignity even from the wisdom and soundness of the rest of our institutions. For very obvious reasons you cannot trust the crown with a dispensing power over any of your laws. However, a government, be it as bad as it may, will, in the exercise of a discretionary power, discriminate times and persons, and will not ordinarily pursue any man when its own safety is not concerned. A mercenary informer knows no distinction. Under such a system, the obnoxious people are slaves not only to the government, but they live at the mercy of every individual; they are at once the slaves of the whole community and of every part of it; and the worst and most unmerciful men are those on whose goodness they most depend.

In this situation, men not only shrink from the frowns of a stern magistrate, but they are obliged to fly from their very species. The seeds of destruction are sown in civil intercourse, in social habitudes. The blood of wholesome kindred is infected. Their tables and beds are surrounded with snares. All the means given by Providence to make life safe and comfortable are perverted into instruments of terror and torment. This species of universal subserviency, that makes the very servant who waits behind your chair the arbiter of your life and fortune, has such a tendency to degrade and abase mankind, and to deprive them of that assured and liberal state of mind which alone can make us what we ought to be, that I vow to God I would sooner bring myself to put a man to immediate death for opinions I disliked, and so to get rid of the man and his opinions at once, than to fret him with a feverish being, tainted with the jail-distemper of a contagious servitude, to keep him above ground an animated mass of putrefaction, corrupted himself, and corrupting all about him.

The act repealed was of this direct tendency; and it was made in the manner which I have related to you. I will now tell you by whom the bill of repeal was brought into Parliament. I find it has been industriously given out in this city (from kindness to me, unquestionably) that I was the mover or the seconder. The fact is, I did not once open my lips on the subject during the whole progress of the bill. I do not say this as disclaiming my share in that measure. Very far from it. I inform you of this fact lest I should seem to arrogate to myself the merits which belong to others. . . . That great work was in hands in every respect far better qualified than mine. The mover of the bill was Sir George Savile.

. . . I will next lay before you . . . the political grounds and reasons for the repeal of that penal statute, and the motives to its repeal at that particular time.

Gentlemen, America—When the English nation seemed to be dangerously, if not irrecoverably divided—when one, and that the most growing branch, was torn from the parent stock, and ingrafted on the power of France, a great terror fell upon this kingdom. On a sudden we awakened from our dreams of conquest, and saw ourselves threatened with an immediate invasion, which we were at that time very ill prepared to resist. You remember the cloud that gloomed over us all. In that hour of our dismay, from the bottom of the hiding-places into which the indiscriminate rigor of our statutes had driven them, came out the body of the Roman Catholics. They appeared before the steps of a tottering throne, with one of the most sober, measured, steady, and dutiful addresses that was ever presented to the crown. It was no holiday ceremony, no anniversary compliment of parade and show. It was signed by almost every gentleman of that persuasion, of note or property, in England. At such a crisis, nothing but a decided resolution to stand or fall with their country could have dictated such an address, the direct tendency of which was to cut off all retreat, and to render them peculiarly obnoxious to an invader of their own communion. The address showed what I long languished to see, that all the subjects of England had cast off all foreign views and connections, and that every man looked for his relief from every grievance at the hands only of his own natural government.

It was necessary, on our part, that the natural government should show itself worthy of that name. It was necessary, at the crisis I speak of, that the supreme power of the state should meet the conciliatory dispositions of the subject. To delay protection would be to reject allegiance. And why should it be rejected, or even coldly and suspiciously received? If any independent Catholic state should choose to take part with this kingdom in a war with France and Spain, that bigot (if such a bigot could be found) would be heard with little respect who could dream of objecting his religion to an ally whom the nation would not only receive with its freest thanks, but purchase with the last remains of its exhausted treasure. To such an ally we should not dare to whisper a single syllable of those base and invidious topics upon which some unhappy men would persuade the state to reject the duty and allegiance of its own members. Is it, then, because foreigners are in a condition to set our malice at defiance, that with *them* we are willing to contract engagements of friendship, and to keep them with fidelity and honor, but that, because we conceive some descriptions of our countrymen are not powerful enough to punish our malignity, we will not permit them to support our common interest? . . .

What shadow of reason could be assigned why, at a time when the most Protestant part of this Protestant empire found it for its advantage to unite with the two principal Popish states, to unite itself in the closest bonds with France and Spain, for our destruction, that we should refuse to unite with our own Catholic countrymen for our own preservation?

Ought we, like madmen, to tear off the plasters that the lenient hand of prudence had spread over the wounds and gashes which in our delirium of ambition we had given to our own body? . . . For one, I was delighted with the proposal of internal peace. I accepted the blessing with thankfulness and transport. I was truly happy to find *one* good effect of our civil distractions: that they had put an end to all religious strife and heartburning in our own bowels. . . .

Important effects followed this act of wisdom. They appeared at home and abroad, to the great benefit of this kingdom, and, let me hope, to the advantage of mankind at large. It betokened union among ourselves. It showed soundness, even on the part of the persecuted, which generally is the weak side of every community. But its most essential operation was not in England. The act was immediately, though very imperfectly, copied in Ireland, and this imperfect transcript of an imperfect act, this first faint sketch of toleration, which did little more than disclose a principle and mark out a disposition, completed in a most wonderful manner the reunion to the state of all the Catholics of that country. It made us what we ought always to have been, one family, one body, one heart and soul, against the family combination and all other combinations of our enemies. . . .

Men of another sort, I mean the bigoted enemies to liberty, may, perhaps, in their politics, make no account of the good or ill affection of the Catholics of England, who are but a handful of people (enough to torment, but not enough to fear), perhaps not so many, of both sexes and of all ages, as fifty thousand. But, Gentlemen, it is possible you may not know that the people of that persuasion in Ireland amount at least to sixteen or seventeen hundred thousand souls. I do not at all exaggerate the number. A *nation* to be persecuted! Whilst we were masters of the sea, embodied with America, and in alliance with half the powers of the Continent, we might, perhaps, in that remote corner of Europe, afford to tyrannize with impunity. But there is a revolution in our affairs, which makes it prudent to be just. In our late awkward contest with Ireland about trade, had religion been thrown in, to ferment and embitter the mass of discontents, the consequences might have been truly dreadful. . . .

Even in England, where I admit the danger from the discontent of that persuasion to be less than in Ireland, yet even here, had we listened to the counsels of fanaticism and folly, we might have wounded ourselves very deeply, and wounded ourselves in a very tender part. You are apprised that the Catholics of England consist mostly of our best manufacturers. Had the legislature chosen, instead of returning their declarations of duty with correspondent good-will, to drive them to despair, there is a country at their very door to which they would be invited—a country in all respects as good as ours, and with the finest cities in the world ready built to receive them. And thus the bigotry of a free country, and in an enlightened age, would have repeopled the cities of Flanders, which, in the darkness of two hundred years ago, had been desolated by the superstition of a cruel tyrant. Our manufactures were the growth of the persecutions in the Low Countries. What a spectacle would it be to Europe to see us at this time of day balancing the account of tyranny with those very countries, and by our persecutions driving back trade and manufacture, as a sort of vagabonds, to their original settlement! But I trust we shall be saved this last of disgraces.

So far as to the effect of the act on the interests of this nation. With regard to the interests of mankind at large, I am sure the benefit was very considerable. Long before this act, indeed, the spirit of toleration began to gain ground in Europe. In Holland the third part of the people are Catholics; they live at ease, and are a sound part of the state. In many parts of Germany, Protestants and Papists partake the same cities, the same councils, and even the same churches. . . . Even the Lutheran obstinacy of Sweden has thawed at length, and opened a toleration to all religions. I know, myself, that in France the Protestants begin to be at rest. . . . Tarnished as the glory of this nation is, and far as it has waded into the shades of an eclipse, some beams of its former illumination still play upon its surface; and what is done in England is still looked to, as argument, and as example. It is certainly true that no law of this country ever met with such universal applause abroad, or was so likely to produce the perfection of that tolerating spirit which, as I observed, has been long gaining ground in Europe; for abroad it was universally thought that we had done what I am sorry to say we had not; they thought we had granted a full toleration. That opinion was, however, so far from hurting the Protestant cause that I declare, with the most serious solemnity, my firm belief that no one thing done for these fifty years past was so likely to prove deeply beneficial to our religion at large as Sir George Savile's act. . . .

I do not wish to go over the horrid scene that was afterwards acted. Would to God it could be expunged forever from the annals of this country! But since it must subsist for our shame, let it subsist for our instruction. In the year 1780 there were found in this nation men deluded enough (for I give the whole to their delusion) on pretenses of zeal and piety, without any sort of provocation whatsoever, real or pretended, to make a desperate attempt which would have consumed all the glory and power of this country in the flames of London, and buried all law, order, and religion under the ruins of the metropolis of the Protestant world. Whether all this mischief done, or in the direct train of doing, was in their original scheme, I cannot say; I hope it was not; but this would have been the unavoidable consequence of their proceedings, had not the flames they had lighted up in their fury been extinguished in their blood.

All the time that this horrid scene was acting, or avenging, as well as for some time before, and ever since, the wicked instigators of this unhappy multitude, guilty, with every aggravation, of all their crimes, and screened in a cowardly darkness from their punishment, continued, without interruption, pity, or remorse, to blow up the blind rage of the populace with a continued blast of pestilential libels, which infected and poisoned the very air we breathed in.

The main drift of all the libels and all the riots was to force Parliament (to persuade us was hopeless) into an act of national perfidy which has no example. For, Gentlemen, it is proper you should all know what infamy we escaped by refusing that repeal, for a refusal of which, it seems, I, among others, stand somewhere or other accused. When we took away, on the motives which I had the honor of stating to you, a few of the innumerable penalties upon an oppressed and injured people, the relief was not absolute, but given on a stipulation and compact between them and us: for we bound down the Roman Catholics with the most solemn oaths to bear true allegiance to this government, to abjure all sort of temporal power in any other, and to renounce, under the same solemn obligations, the doctrines of systematic perfidy with which they stood (I conceive very unjustly) charged. Now our modest petitioners came up to us, most humbly praying nothing more than that we should break our faith, without any one cause whatsoever of forfeiture assigned; and when the subjects of this kingdom had, on their part, fully performed their engagement, we should refuse, on our part, the benefit we had stipulated on the performance of those very conditions that were prescribed by our own authority, and taken on the sanction of our public faith: that is to say, when we had inveigled them with fair promises within our door, we were to shut it on them, and, adding mockery to outrage, to tell them—"Now we have got you fast: your consciences are bound to a power resolved on your destruction. We have made you swear that your religion obliges you to keep your faith—fools as you are! We will now let you see that our religion enjoins us to keep no faith with you." They who would advisedly call upon us to do such things must certainly have thought us not only a convention of treacherous tyrants, but a gang of the lowest and dirtiest wretches that ever disgraced humanity. Had we done this, we should have indeed proved that there were *some* in the world whom no faith could bind; and we should have *convicted* ourselves of that odious principle of which Papists stood *accused* by those very savages who wished us, on that accusation, to deliver them over to their fury.

In this audacious tumult, when our very name and character as gentlemen was to be canceled forever, along with the faith and honor of the nation, I, who had exerted myself very little on the quiet passing of the bill, thought it necessary then to come forward. I was not alone; but though some distinguished members on all sides, and particularly on ours, added much to their high reputation by the part they took on that day (a part which will be remembered as long as honor, spirit, and eloquence have estimation in the world), I may and will value myself so far that, yielding in abilities to many, I yielded in zeal to none. With warmth and with vigor, and animated with a just and natural indignation, I called forth every faculty that I possessed, and I directed it in every way in which I could possibly employ it. I labored night and day. I labored in Parliament; I labored out of Parliament. If, therefore, the resolution of the House of Commons, refusing to commit this act of unmatched turpitude, be a crime, I am guilty among the foremost. But, indeed, whatever the faults of that House may have been, no one member was found hardy enough to propose so infamous a thing; and on full debate we passed the resolution against the petitions with as much unanimity as we had formerly passed the law of which these petitions demanded the repeal.

There was a circumstance (justice will not suffer me to pass it over) which, if anything could enforce the reasons I have given, would fully justify the act of relief, and render a repeal, or anything like a repeal, unnatural, impossible. It was the behavior of the persecuted Roman Catholics under the acts of violence and brutal insolence which they suffered. I suppose there are not in London less than four or five thousand of that persuasion from my country, who do a great deal of the most laborious works in the metropolis; and they chiefly inhabit those quarters which were the principal theater of the fury of the bigoted multitude.

They are known to be men of strong arms and quick feelings, and more remarkable for a determined resolution than clear ideas or much foresight. But, though provoked by everything that can stir the blood of men, their houses and chapels in flames, and with the most atrocious profanations of everything which they hold sacred before their eyes, not a hand was moved to retaliate, or even to defend. Had a conflict once begun, the rage of their persecutors would have redoubled. Thus fury increasing by the reverberation of outrages, house being fired for house, and church for chapel, I am convinced that no power under heaven could have prevented a general conflagration, and at this day London would have been a tale. But I am well informed, and the thing speaks it, that their clergy exerted their whole influence to keep their people in such a state of forbearance and quiet as, when I look back, fills me with astonishment—but not with astonishment only. Their merits on that occasion ought not to be forgotten; nor will they, when Englishmen come to recollect themselves. I am sure it were far more proper to have called them forth, and given them the thanks of both Houses of Parliament, than to have suffered those worthy clergymen and excellent citizens to be hunted into holes and corners, whilst we are making low-minded inquisitions into the number of their people; as if a tolerating principle was never to prevail, unless we were very sure that only a few could possibly take advantage of it. But, indeed, we are not yet well recovered of our fright. Our reason, I trust, will return with our security, and this unfortunate temper will pass over like a cloud.

Gentlemen, I have now laid before you a few of the reasons for taking away the penalties of the act of 1699, and for refusing to establish them on the riotous requisition of 1780. Because I would not suffer anything which may be for your satisfaction to escape, permit me just to touch on the objections urged against our act and our resolves, and intended as a justification of the violence offered to both Houses. "Parliament," they assert, "was too hasty, and they ought, in so essential and alarming a change, to have proceeded with a far greater degree of deliberation." The direct contrary. Parliament was too slow. They took fourscore years to deliberate on the repeal of an act which ought not to have survived a second session. . . .

But they tell us that those our fellow-citizens whose chains we have a little relaxed are enemies to liberty and our free constitution—not enemies, I presume, to their *own* liberty. And as to the constitution, until we give them some share in it, I do not know on what pretense we can examine into their opinions about a business in which they have no interest or concern. But, after all, are we equally sure that they are adverse to our constitution as that our statutes are hostile and destructive to them? For my part, I have reason to believe their opinions and inclinations in that respect are various, exactly like those of other men; and if they lean more to the crown than I and than many of you think *we* ought, we must remember that he who aims at another's life is not to be surprised if he flies into any sanctuary that will receive him. The tenderness of the executive power is the natural asylum of those upon whom the laws have declared war; and to complain that men are inclined to favor the means of their own safety is so absurd that one forgets the injustice in the ridicule.

I must fairly tell you that so far as my principles are concerned (principles that I hope will only depart with my last breath), that I have no idea of a liberty unconnected with honesty and justice. Nor do I believe that any good constitutions of government, or of freedom, can find it necessary for their security to doom any part of the people to a permanent slavery. Such a constitution of freedom, if such can be, is in effect no more than another name for the tyranny of the strongest faction; and factions in republics have been, and are, full as capable as monarchs of the most cruel oppression and injustice. It is but too true that the love, and even the very idea, of genuine liberty is extremely rare. It is but too true that there are many whose whole scheme of freedom is made up of pride, perverseness, and insolence. They feel themselves in a state of thraldom, they imagine that their souls are cooped and cabined in, unless they have some man or some body of men dependent on their mercy. . . . This disposition is the true source of the passion which many men in very humble life have taken to the American war. *Our* subjects in America; *our* colonies; *our* dependants. This lust of party power is the liberty they hunger and thirst for; and this siren song of ambition has charmed ears that one would have thought were never organized to that sort of music.

This way of *proscribing the citizens by denominations and general descriptions*, dignified by the name of reason of state, and security for constitutions and commonwealths, is nothing better at bottom than the miserable invention of an ungenerous ambition which would fain hold the sacred trust of power without any of the virtues or any of the energies that give a title to it—a receipt of policy, made up of a detestable compound of malice, cowardice, and sloth. They would govern men against their will; but in that government they would be discharged from the exercise of vigilance, providence, and fortitude; and therefore, that they may sleep on their watch, they consent to take some one division of the society into partnership of the tyranny over the rest. But let government, in what form it may be, comprehend the whole in its justice, and restrain the suspicious by its vigilance; let it keep watch and ward; let it discover by its sagacity, and punish by its firmness, all delinquency against its power, whenever delinquency exists in the overt acts—and then it will be as safe as ever God and nature intended it should be. Crimes are the acts of individuals, and not of denominations; and therefore arbitrarily to class men under general descriptions, in order to proscribe and punish them in the lump for a presumed delinquency, of which perhaps but a part, perhaps none at all, are guilty, is indeed a compendious method, and saves a world of trouble about proof. But such a method, instead of being law, is an act of unnatural rebellion against the legal dominion of reason and justice; and this vice, in any constitution that entertains it, at one time or other will certainly bring on its ruin.

We are told that this is not a religious persecution; and its abettors are loud in disclaiming all severities on account of conscience. Very fine indeed! Then let it be so: they are not persecutors; they are only tyrants. With all my heart. I am perfectly indifferent concerning the pretexts upon which we torment one another, or whether it be for the constitution of the Church of England, or for the constitution of the State of England, that people choose to make their fellow-creatures wretched. . . .

Since you have suffered me to trouble you so much on this subject, permit me, Gentlemen, to detain you a little longer. I am, indeed, most solicitous to give you perfect satisfaction. I find there are some of a better and softer nature than the persons with whom I have supposed myself in debate, who neither think ill of the act of relief, nor by any means desire the repeal—yet who, not accusing, but lamenting what was done, on account of the consequences, have frequently expressed their wish that the late act had never been made. Some of this description, and persons of worth, I have met with in this city. They conceive that the prejudices, whatever they might be, of a large part of the people ought not to have been shocked—that their opinions ought to have been previously taken, and much attended to—and that thereby the late horrid scenes might have been prevented.

I confess, my notions are widely different; and I never was less sorry for any action of my life. I like the bill the better on account of the events of all kinds that followed it. It relieved the real sufferers; it strengthened the state; and, by the disorders that ensued, we had clear evidence that there lurked a temper somewhere which ought not to be fostered by the laws. No ill consequences whatever could be attributed to the act itself. We knew beforehand, or we were poorly instructed, that toleration is odious to the intolerant, freedom to oppressors, property to robbers, and all kinds and degrees of prosperity to the envious. We knew that all these kinds of men would gladly gratify their evil dispositions under the sanction of law and religion, if they could; if they could not, yet, to make way to their objects, they would do their utmost to subvert all religion and all law. This we certainly knew. But, knowing this, is there any reason, because thieves break in and steal, and thus bring detriment to you, and draw ruin on themselves, that I am to be sorry that you are in possession of shops, and of warehouses, and of wholesome laws to protect them? Are you to build no houses, because desperate men may pull them down upon their own heads? Or if a malignant wretch will cut his own throat because he sees you give alms to the necessitous and deserving, shall his destruction be attributed to your charity, and not to his own deplorable madness? If we repent of our good actions, what, I pray you, is left for our faults and follies? It is not the beneficence of the laws, it is the unnatural temper which beneficence can fret and sour, that is to be lamented. It is this temper which, by all rational means, ought to be sweetened and corrected. . . .

As to the opinion of the people, which some think, in such cases, is to be implicitly obeyed, near two years' tranquillity which followed the act, and its instant imitation in Ireland, proved abundantly that the late horrible spirit was in a great measure the effect of insidious art, and perverse industry, and gross misrepresentation. But suppose that the dislike had been much more deliberate and much more general than I am persuaded it was—when we know that the opinions of even the greatest multitudes are the standard of rectitude, I shall think myself obliged to make those opinions the masters of my conscience. . . . No man carries further than I do the policy of making government pleasing to the people. But the widest range of this politic complaisance is confined within the limits of justice. I would not only consult the interest of the people, but I would cheerfully gratify their humors. We are all a sort of children that must be soothed and managed. I think I am not austere or formal in my nature. I would bear, I would even myself play my part in, any innocent buffooneries, to divert them. But I never will act the tyrant for their amusement. If they will mix malice in their sports, I shall never consent to throw them any living, sentient creature whatsoever, no, not so much as a kitling, to torment.

"But if I profess all this impolitic stubbornness, I may chance never to be elected into Parliament." It is certainly not pleasing to be put out of the public service. But I wish to be a member of Parliament to have my share of doing good and resisting evil. It would therefore be absurd to renounce my objects in order to obtain my seat. I deceive myself, indeed, most grossly, if I had not much rather pass the remainder of my life hidden in the recesses of the deepest obscurity, feeding my mind even with the visions and imaginations of such things, than to be placed on the most splendid throne of the universe, tantalized with a denial of the practice of all which can make the greatest situation any other than the greatest curse. Gentlemen, I have had my day. I can never sufficiently express my gratitude to you for having set me in a place wherein I could lend the slightest help to great and laudable designs. If I have had my share in any measure giving quiet to private property and private conscience; if by my vote I have aided in securing to families the best possession, peace; if I have joined in reconciling kings to their subjects, and subjects to their prince; if I have assisted to loosen the foreign holdings of the citizen, and taught him to look for his protection to the laws of his country, and for his comfort to the good-will of his countrymen; if I have thus taken my part with the best of men in the best of their actions, I can shut the book. I might wish to read a page or two more, but this is enough for my measure. I have not lived in vain.

And now, Gentlemen, on this serious day, when I come, as it were, to make up my account with you, let me take to myself some degree of honest pride on the nature of the charges that are against me. I do not here stand before you accused of venality, or of neglect of duty. It is not said that, in the long period of my service, I have, in a single instance, sacrificed the slightest of your interests to my ambition or to my fortune. It is not alleged that, to gratify any anger or revenge of my own, or of my party, I have had a share in wronging or oppressing any description of men, or any one man in any description. No! the charges against me are all of one kind: that I have pushed the principles of general justice and benevolence too far—further than a cautious policy would warrant, and further than the opinions of many would go along with me. In every accident which may happen through life, in pain, in sorrow, in depression, and distress, I will call to mind this accusation, and be comforted. . . .

A Letter to a Peer of Ireland on the Penal Laws Against Irish Catholics

Laws providing for some relief from the harsh discrimination against Catholics were passed by the Protestant government of Ireland in 1778 and 1782 as part of a strategy to encourage loyalty to the United Kingdom from Irish Catholics even as Catholic France was helping America. However, numerous disabilities still weighed upon the Catholics. In this letter, written in 1782 and published in his lifetime, Burke argues that the new laws did not go far enough and that Catholics should enjoy the same rights as Protestants.

MY LORD—I am obliged to your Lordship for your communication of the heads of Mr. Gardiner's bill. . . . Your Lordship is too well acquainted with men, and with affairs, to imagine that any true judgment can be formed on the value of a great measure of policy from the perusal of a piece of paper. At present I am much in the dark with regard to the state of the country which the intended law is to be applied to. It is not easy for me to determine whether or no it was wise (for the sake of expunging the black letter of laws which, menacing as they were in the language, were every day fading into disuse) solemnly to reaffirm the principles and to re-enact the provisions of a code of statutes by which you are totally excluded from THE PRIVILEGES OF THE COMMONWEALTH, from the highest to the lowest, from the most material of the civil professions, from the army, and even from education, where alone education is to be had.

Whether this scheme of indulgence, grounded at once on contempt and jealousy, has a tendency gradually to produce something better and more liberal, I cannot tell, for want of having the actual map of the country. If this should be the case, it was right in you to accept it, such as it is. But if this should be one of the experiments which have sometimes been made before the temper of the nation was ripe for a real reformation, I think it may possibly have ill effects, by disposing the penal matter in a more systematic order, and thereby fixing a permanent bar against any relief that is truly substantial. The whole merit or demerit of the measure depends upon the plans and dispositions of those by whom the act was made, concurring with the general temper of the Protestants of Ireland, and their aptitude to admit in time of some part of that equality without which you never can be FELLOW-CITIZENS.

To look at the bill in the abstract, it is neither more nor less than a renewed act of UNIVERSAL, UNMITIGATED, INDISPENSABLE, EXCEPTIONLESS DISQUALIFICATION.

One would imagine that a bill inflicting such a multitude of incapacities had followed on the heels of a conquest made by a very fierce enemy, under the impression of recent animosity and resentment. No man, on reading that bill, could imagine he was reading an act of amnesty and indulgence, following a recital of the good behavior of those who are the objects of it—which recital stood at the head of the bill as it was first introduced, but, I suppose for its incongruity with the body of the piece, was afterwards omitted. This I say on memory. It, however, still recites the oath, and that Catholics ought to be considered as good and loyal subjects to his Majesty, his crown and government. Then follows a universal exclusion of those GOOD and LOYAL subjects from every (even the lowest) office of trust and profit—from any vote at an election—from any privilege in a town corporate—from being even a freeman of such a corporation—from serving on grand juries—from a vote at a vestry—from having a gun in his house—from being a barrister, attorney, or solicitor, &c., &c., &c.

This has surely much more the air of a table of proscription than an act of grace. What must we suppose the laws concerning those *good* subjects to have been of which this is a relaxation? I know well that there is a cant language current about the difference between an exclusion from employments, even to the most rigorous extent, and an exclusion from the natural benefits arising from a man's own industry. I allow that, under some circumstances, the difference is very material in point of justice, and that there are considerations which may render it advisable for a wise government to keep the leading parts of every branch of civil and military administration in hands of the best trust; but a total exclusion from the commonwealth is a very different thing. When a government subsists (as governments formerly did) on an estate of its own, with but few and inconsiderable revenues drawn from the subject, then the few officers which existed in such establishments were naturally at the disposal of that government, which paid the salaries out of its own coffers: there an exclusive preference could hardly merit the name of proscription. Almost the whole produce of a man's industry at that time remained in his own purse to maintain his family. But times alter, and the *whole* estate of government is from private contribution. When a very great portion of the labor of individuals goes to the state, and is by the state again refunded to individuals, through the medium of offices, and in this circuitous progress from the private to the public, and from the public again to the private fund, the families from whom the revenue is taken are indemnified, and an equitable balance between the government and the subject is established. But if a great body of the people who contribute to this state lottery are excluded from all the prizes, the stopping the circulation with regard to them may be a most cruel hardship, amounting in effect to being double and treble taxed; and it will be felt as such to the very quick, by all the families, high and low, of those hundreds of thousands who are denied their chance in the returned fruits of their own industry. This is the thing meant by those who look upon the public revenue only as a spoil, and will naturally wish to have as few as possible concerned in the division of the booty. If a state should be so unhappy as to think it cannot subsist without such a barbarous proscription, the persons so proscribed ought to be indemnified by the remission of a large part of their taxes, by an immunity from the offices of public burden, and by an exemption from being pressed into any military or naval service.

. . . This hardship is the more intolerable because the professions are shut up. The Church is so of course. Much is to be said on that subject, in regard to them, and to the Protestant Dissenters. But that is a chapter by itself. I am sure I wish well to that Church, and think its ministers among the very best citizens of your country. However, such as it is, a great walk in life is forbidden ground to seventeen hundred thousand of the inhabitants of Ireland. Why are they excluded from the law? Do not they expend money in their suits? Why may not they indemnify themselves, by profiting, in the persons of some, for the losses incurred by others? Why may not they have persons of confidence, whom they may, if they please, employ in the agency of their affairs? The exclusion from the law, from grand juries, from sheriffships and under-sheriffships, as well as from freedom in any corporation, may subject them to dreadful hardships, as it may exclude them wholly from all that is beneficial and expose them to all that is mischievous in a trial by jury. This was manifestly within my own observation, for I was three times in Ireland from the year 1760 to the year 1767, where I had sufficient means of information concerning the inhuman proceedings (among which were many cruel murders, besides an infinity of outrages and oppressions unknown before in a civilized age) which prevailed during that period, in consequence of a pretended conspiracy among *Roman Catholics* against the king's government. I could dilate upon the mischiefs that may happen, from those which have happened, upon this head of disqualification, if it were at all necessary.

The head of exclusion from votes for members of Parliament is closely connected with the former. When you cast your eye on the statute-book, you will see that no *Catholic*, even in the ferocious acts of Queen Anne, was disabled from voting on account of his religion. The only conditions required for that privilege were the oaths of allegiance and abjuration—both oaths relative to a civil concern. Parliament has since added another oath of the same kind; and yet a House of Commons, adding to the securities of government in proportion as its danger is confessedly lessened, and professing both confidence and indulgence, in effect takes away the privilege left by an act full of jealousy and professing persecution.

The taking away of a vote is the taking away the shield which the subject has, not only against the oppression of power, but that worst of all oppressions, the persecution of private society and private manners. No candidate for parliamentary influence is obliged to the least attention towards them, either in cities or counties. On the contrary, if they should become obnoxious to any bigoted or malignant people amongst whom they live, it will become the interest of those who court popular favor to use the numberless means which always reside in magistracy and influence to oppress them. . . . The Protestants of Ireland feel well and naturally on the hardship of being bound by laws in the enacting of which they do not directly or indirectly vote. The bounds of these matters are nice, and hard to be settled in theory, and perhaps they have been pushed too far. But how they can avoid the necessary application of the principles they use in their disputes with others to their disputes with their fellow-citizens, I know not. . . .

The laws against foreign education are clearly the very worst part of the old code. Besides your laity, you have the succession of about four thousand clergymen to provide for. These, having no lucrative objects in prospect, are taken very much out of the lower orders of the people. At home they have no means whatsoever provided for their attaining a clerical education, or indeed any education at all. . . .

It has been the custom of poor persons in Ireland to pick up such knowledge of the Latin tongue as, under the general discouragements, and occasional pursuits of magistracy, they were able to acquire; and receiving orders at home, were sent abroad to obtain a clerical education. By officiating in petty chaplainships, and performing now and then certain offices of religion for small gratuities, they received the means of maintaining themselves until they were able to complete their education. Through such difficulties and discouragements, many of them have arrived at a very considerable proficiency, so as to be marked and distinguished abroad. These persons afterwards, by being sunk in the most abject poverty, despised and ill-treated by the higher orders among Protestants, and not much better esteemed or treated even by the few persons of fortune of their own persuasion, and contracting the habits and ways of thinking of the poor and uneducated, among whom they were obliged to live, in a few years retained little or no traces of the talents and acquirements which distinguished them in the early periods of their lives. Can we with justice cut them off from the use of places of education founded for the greater part from the economy of poverty and exile, without providing something that is equivalent at home?

Whilst this restraint of foreign and domestic education was part of a horrible and impious system of servitude, the members were well fitted to the body. To render men patient under a deprivation of all the rights of human nature, everything which could give them a knowledge or feeling of those rights was rationally forbidden. To render humanity fit to be insulted, it was fit that it should be degraded. But when we profess to restore men to the capacity for property, it is equally irrational and unjust to deny them the power of improving their minds as well as their fortunes. Indeed, I have ever thought the prohibition of the means of improving our rational nature to be the worst species of tyranny that the insolence and perverseness of mankind ever dared to exercise. This goes to all men, in all situations, to whom education can be denied. . . .

Letter to Sir Hercules Langrishe

After the French Revolution, Burke's interest in the full emancipation of the Catholics in Ireland took on a new dimension. Added to the justice of their cause was Burke's concern that continued discrimination would drive Irish Catholics into the camp of revolutionary France. He makes this political case in a pamphlet-length letter written in January 1792 to a fellow member of Parliament.

IN MY PRESENT STATE of imperfect information, you will pardon the errors into which I may easily fall. The principles you lay down are, "that the Roman Catholics should enjoy everything *under* the state, but should not be *the state itself*." And you add, "that, when you exclude them from being *a part of the state*, you rather conform to the spirit of the age than to any abstract doctrine"; but you consider the Constitution as already established—that our state is Protestant. "It was declared so at the Revolution. It was so provided in the acts for settling the succession of the crown:—the king's coronation oath was enjoined in order to keep it so. The king, as first magistrate of the state, is obliged to take the oath of abjuration, and to subscribe the Declaration; and by laws subsequent, every other magistrate and member of the state, legislative and executive, are bound under the same obligation."

As to the plan to which these maxims are applied, I cannot speak, as I told you, positively about it: because neither from your letter, nor from any information I have been able to collect, do I find anything settled, either on the part of the Roman Catholics themselves, or on that of any persons who may wish to conduct their affairs in Parliament. But if I have leave to conjecture, something is in agitation towards admitting them, under *certain qualifications*, to have *some share* in the election of members of Parliament. This I understand is the scheme of those who are entitled to come within your description of persons of consideration, property, and character—and firmly attached to the king and Constitution, as by "law established, with a grateful sense of your former concessions, and a patient reliance on the benignity of Parliament for the further mitigation of the laws that still affect them."—As to the low, thoughtless, wild, and profligate, who have joined themselves with those of other professions, but of the same character, you are not to imagine that for a moment I can suppose them to be met with anything else than the manly and enlightened energy of a firm government, supported by the united efforts of all virtuous men, if ever their proceedings should become so considerable as to demand its notice. I really think that such associations should be crushed in their very commencement.

Setting, therefore, this case out of the question, it becomes an object of very serious consideration, whether, because wicked men of *various* descriptions are engaged in seditious courses, the rational, sober, and valuable part of *one* description should not be indulged in their sober and rational expectations. You, who have looked deeply into the spirit of the Popery laws, must be perfectly sensible that a great part of the present mischief which we abhor in common (if it at all exists) has arisen from them. Their declared object was, to reduce the Catholics of Ireland to a miserable populace, without property, without estimation, without education. The professed object was, to deprive the few men, who, in spite of those laws, might hold or obtain any property amongst them, of all sort of influence or authority over the rest. They divided the nation into two distinct bodies, without common interest, sympathy, or connection. One of these bodies was to possess *all* the franchises, *all* the property, *all* the education: the other was to be composed of drawers of water and cutters of turf for them. Are we to be astonished, when, by the efforts of so much violence in conquest, and so much policy in regulation, continued without intermission for near an hundred years, we had reduced them to a mob, that, whenever they came to act at all, many of them would act exactly like a mob, without temper, measure, or foresight? Surely it might be just now a matter of temperate discussion, whether you ought not to apply a remedy to the real cause of the evil. If the disorder you speak of be real and considerable, you ought to raise an aristocratic interest, that is, an interest of property and education, amongst them—and to strengthen, by every prudent means, the authority and influence of men of that description. . . .

If the absurd persons you mention find no way of providing for liberty, but by overturning this happy Constitution, and introducing a frantic democracy, let us take care how we prevent better people from any rational expectations of partaking in the benefits of that Constitution *as it stands*. The maxims you establish cut the matter short. . . .

You begin by asserting, that "the Catholics ought to enjoy all things *under* the state, but that they ought not to *be the state*": a position which, I believe, in the latter part of it, and in the latitude there expressed, no man of common sense has ever thought proper to dispute; because the contrary implies that the state ought to be in them *exclusively*. But before you have finished the line, you express yourself as if the other member of your proposition, namely, that "they ought not to be *a part* of the state," were necessarily included in the first—whereas I conceive it to be as different as a part is from the whole, that is, just as different as possible. I know, indeed, that it is common with those who talk very differently from you, that is, with heat and animosity, to confound those things, and to argue the admission of the Catholics into any, however minute and subordinate, parts of the state, as a surrender into their hands of the whole government of the kingdom. To them I have nothing at all to say.

Wishing to proceed with a deliberative spirit and temper in so very serious a question, I shall attempt to analyze, as well as I can, the principles you lay down, in order to fit them for the grasp of an understanding so little comprehensive as mine.—"State"—"Protestant"—"Revolution." These are terms which, if not well explained, may lead us into many errors. In the word *State* I conceive there is much ambiguity. The state is sometimes used to signify *the whole commonwealth*, comprehending all its orders, with the several privileges belonging to each. Sometimes it signifies only *the higher and ruling part* of the commonwealth, which we commonly call *the Government*. In the first sense, to be under the state, but not the state itself, *nor any part of it*, that is, to be nothing at all in the commonwealth, is a situation perfectly intelligible—but to those who fill that situation, not very pleasant, when it is understood. It is a state of *civil servitude*, by the very force of the definition. . . . This servitude, which makes men *subject* to a state without being *citizens*, may be more or less tolerable from many circumstances; but these circumstances, more or less favorable, do not alter the nature of the thing. The mildness by which absolute masters exercise their dominion leaves them masters still. . . .

In the other sense of the word *State*, by which is understood the *Supreme Government* only, I must observe this upon the question: that to exclude whole classes of men entirely from this *part* of government cannot be considered as *absolute slavery*. It only implies a lower and degraded state of citizenship: such is (with more or less strictness) the condition of all countries in which an hereditary nobility possess the exclusive rule. This may be no bad mode of government—provided that the personal authority of individual nobles be kept in due bounds, that their cabals and factions are guarded against with a severe vigilance, and that the people (who have no share in granting their own money) are subjected to but light impositions, and are otherwise treated with attention, and with indulgence to their humors and prejudices. . . .

Between the extreme of *a total exclusion*, to which your maxim goes, and *an universal unmodified capacity*, to which the fanatics pretend, there are many different degrees and stages, and a great variety of temperaments, upon which prudence may give full scope to its exertions. For you know that the decisions of prudence (contrary to the system of the insane reasoners) differ from those of judicature; and that almost all the former are determined on the more or the less, the earlier or the later, and on a balance of advantage and inconvenience, of good and evil.

In all considerations which turn upon the question of vesting or continuing the state solely and exclusively in some one description of citizens, prudent legislators will consider how far *the general form and principles of their commonwealth render it fit to be cast into an oligarchical shape, or to remain always in it.* We know that the government of Ireland (the same as the British) is not in its constitution *wholly* aristocratical; and as it is not such in its form, so neither is it in its spirit. If it had been inveterately aristocratical, exclusions might be more patiently submitted to. The lot of one plebeian would be the lot of all; and an habitual reverence and admiration of certain families might make the people content to see government wholly in hands to whom it seemed naturally to belong. But our Constitution has *a plebeian member*, which forms an essential integrant part of it. A plebeian oligarchy is a monster; and no people, not absolutely domestic or predial slaves, will long endure it. The Protestants of Ireland are not *alone* sufficiently the people to form a democracy; and they are *too numerous* to answer the ends and purposes of *an aristocracy.* Admiration, that first source of obedience, can be only the claim or the imposture of the few. I hold it to be absolutely impossible for two millions of plebeians, composing certainly a very clear and decided majority in that class, to become so far in love with six or seven hundred thousand of their fellow-citizens (to all outward appearance plebeians like themselves, and many of them tradesmen, servants, and otherwise inferior to some of them) as to see with satisfaction, or even with patience, an exclusive power vested in them, by which *constitutionally* they become the absolute masters, and by the *manners* derived from their circumstances, must be capable of exercising upon them, daily and hourly, an insulting and vexatious superiority. Neither are the majority of the Irish indemnified (as in some aristocracies) for this state of humiliating vassalage (often inverting the nature of things and relations) by having the lower walks of industry wholly abandoned to them. They are rivalled, to say the least of the matter, in every laborious and lucrative course of life; while every franchise, every honor, every trust, every place, down to the very lowest and least confidential, (besides whole professions,) is reserved for the master caste.

Our Constitution is not made for great, general, and proscriptive exclusions; sooner or later it will destroy them, or they will destroy the

Constitution. In our Constitution there has always been a difference between *a franchise* and *an office*, and between the capacity for the one and for the other. Franchises were supposed to belong to the *subject*, as *a subject*, and not *as a member of the governing part of the state*. The policy of government has considered them as things very different; for, whilst Parliament excluded by the test acts (and for a while these test acts were not a dead letter, as now they are in England) Protestant Dissenters from all civil and military employments, they *never touched their right of voting for members of Parliament or sitting in either House*: a point I state, not as approving or condemning, with regard to them, the measure of exclusion from employments, but to prove that the distinction has been admitted in legislature, as, in truth, it is founded in reason.

I will not here examine whether the principles of the British [the Irish] Constitution be wise or not. I must assume that they are, and that those who partake the franchises which make it partake of a benefit. They who are excluded from votes (under proper qualifications inherent in the Constitution that gives them) are excluded, not from *the state*, but from *the British Constitution*. They cannot by any possibility, whilst they hear its praises continually rung in their ears, and are present at the declaration which is so generally and so bravely made by those who possess the privilege, that the best blood in their veins ought to be shed to preserve their share in it—they, the disfranchised part, cannot, I say, think themselves in an *happy* state, to be utterly excluded from all its direct and all its consequential advantages. The popular part of the Constitution must be to them by far the most odious part of it. To them it is not an *actual*, and, if possible, still less a *virtual* representation. It is, indeed, the direct contrary. It is power unlimited placed in the hands of *an adverse* description *because it is an adverse description*. And if they who compose the privileged body have not an interest, they must but too frequently have motives of pride, passion, petulance, peevish jealousy, or tyrannic suspicion, to urge them to treat the excluded people with contempt and rigor.

This is not a mere theory; though, whilst men are men, it is a theory that cannot be false. . . .

This universal exclusion seems to me a serious evil—because many collateral oppressions . . . have arisen from it. . . .

I have said enough of the question of state, *as it affects the people merely as such*. But it is complicated with a political question relative to religion, to which it is very necessary I should say something—because the term *Protestant,* which you apply, is too general for the conclusions which one of your accurate understanding would wish to draw from it, and because a great deal of argument will depend on the use that is made of that term.

It is *not* a fundamental part of the settlement at the Revolution that the state should be Protestant *without any qualification of the term.* With a qualification it is unquestionably true; not in all its latitude. With the qualification, it was true before the Revolution. Our predecessors in legislation were not so irrational (not to say impious) as to form an operose ecclesiastical establishment, and even to render the state itself in some degree subservient to it, when their religion (if such it might be called) was nothing but a mere *negation* of some other—without any positive idea, either of doctrine, discipline, worship, or morals, in the scheme which they professed themselves, and which they imposed upon others, even under penalties and incapacities. No! No! This never could have been done, even by reasonable atheists. They who think religion of no importance to the state have abandoned it to the conscience or caprice of the individual . . . There never has been a religion of the state (the few years of the Parliament only excepted) but that of *the Episcopal Church of England*: the Episcopal Church of England, before the Reformation, connected with the see of Rome; since then, disconnected, and protesting against some of her doctrines, and against the whole of her authority, as binding in our national church: nor did the fundamental laws of this kingdom (in Ireland it has been the same) ever know, at any period, any other church *as an object of establishment*—or, in that light, any other Protestant religion. Nay, our Protestant *toleration* itself, at the Revolution, and until within a few years, required a signature of thirty-six, and a part of the thirty-seventh, out of the Thirty-Nine Articles. So little idea had they at the Revolution of *establishing* Protestantism indefinitely, that they did not indefinitely *tolerate* it under that name. I do not mean to praise that strictness, where nothing more than merely religious toleration is concerned. Toleration, being a part of moral and political prudence, ought to be tender and large. . . .

For reasons forcible enough at all times, but at this time particularly forcible with me, I dwell a little the longer upon this matter, and take the more pains, to put us both in mind that it was not settled at the Revolution that the state should be Protestant, in the latitude of the term, but in a defined and limited sense only, and that in that sense only the king is sworn to maintain it. To suppose that the king has sworn with his utmost power to maintain what it is wholly out of his power to discover, or which, if he could discover, he might discover to consist of things directly contradictory to each other, some of them perhaps impious, blasphemous, and seditious upon principle, would be not only a gross, but a most mischievous absurdity. If mere dissent from the Church of Rome be a merit, he that dissents the most perfectly is the most meritorious. In many points we hold strongly with that church. He that dissents throughout with that church will dissent with the Church of England, and then it will be a part of his merit that he dissents with ourselves: a whimsical species of merit for any set of men to establish. . . . A man is certainly the most perfect Protestant who protests against the whole Christian religion. Whether a person's having no Christian religion be a title to favor, in exclusion to the largest description of Christians, who hold all the doctrines of Christianity, though holding along with them some errors and some superfluities, is rather more than any man, who has not become recreant and apostate from his baptism, will, I believe, choose to affirm. The countenance given from a spirit of controversy to that negative religion may by degrees encourage light and unthinking people to a total indifference to everything positive in matters of doctrine, and, in the end, of practice too. If continued, it would play the game of that sort of active, proselytizing, and persecuting atheism which is the disgrace and calamity of our time. . . .

Now let us fairly see what course has been taken relative to those against whom, in part at least, the king has sworn to maintain a church, *positive in its doctrine and its discipline.* The first thing done, even when the oath was fresh in the mouth of the sovereigns, was to give a toleration to Protestant Dissenters *whose doctrines they ascertained.* As to the mere civil privileges which the Dissenters held as subjects before the Revolution, these were not touched at all. The laws have fully permitted, in a qualification for all offices, to such Dissenters, *an occasional conformity*: a thing I believe singular, where tests are admitted. The act, called the Test Act, itself, is, with regard to them, grown to be hardly anything more than a dead letter. Whenever the Dissenters cease by their conduct to give any alarm to the government, in Church and State, I think it very probable that even this matter, rather disgustful than inconvenient to them, may be removed, or at least so modified as to distinguish the qualification to those offices which really *guide the state* from those which are *merely instrumental*, or that some other and better tests may be put in their place.

So far as to England. In Ireland you have outran us. Without waiting for an English example, you have totally, and without any modification whatsoever, repealed the test as to Protestant Dissenters. . . .

By this unqualified repeal you certainly did not mean to deny that it was the duty of the crown to preserve the Church against Protestant Dissenters; or taking this to be the true sense of the two Revolution acts of King William, and of the previous and subsequent Union acts of Queen Anne, you did not declare by this most unqualified repeal, by which you broke down all the barriers, not invented, indeed, but carefully preserved, at the Revolution—you did not then and by that proceeding declare that you had advised the king to perjury towards God and perfidy towards the Church. No! far, very far from it! You never would have done it, if you did not think it could be done with perfect repose to the royal conscience, and perfect safety to the national established religion. You did this upon a full consideration of the circumstances of your country. Now, if circumstances required it, why should it be contrary to the king's oath, his Parliament judging on those circumstances, to restore to his Catholic people, in such measure and with such modifications as the public wisdom shall think proper to add, *some part* in these franchises which they formerly had held without any limitation at all, and which, upon no sort of urgent reason at the time, they were deprived of? If such means can with any probability be shown, from circumstances, rather to add strength to our mixed ecclesiastical and secular Constitution than to weaken it, surely they are means infinitely to be preferred to penalties, incapacities, and proscriptions, continued from generation to generation. They are perfectly consistent with the other parts of the coronation oath, in which the king swears to maintain "the laws of God and the true profession of the Gospel, and to govern the people according to the statutes in Parliament agreed upon, and the laws and customs of the realm." In consenting to such a statute, the crown would act at least as agreeable to the laws of God, and to the true profession of the Gospel, and to the laws and customs of the kingdom. . . .

I cannot conceive how anything worse can be said of the Protestant religion of the Church of England than this—that, wherever it is judged proper to give it a legal establishment, it becomes necessary to deprive the body of the people, if they adhere to their old opinions, of "their liberties and of all their free customs," and to reduce them to a state of *civil* servitude.

There is no man on earth, I believe, more willing than I am to lay it down as a fundamental of the Constitution, that the Church of England should be united and even identified with it; but, allowing this, I cannot allow that all *laws of regulation*, made from time to time, in support of that fundamental law, are of course equally fundamental and equally unchangeable. This would be to confound all the branches of legislation and of jurisprudence. The *crown* and the personal safety of the monarch are *fundamentals* in our Constitution: yet I hope that no man regrets that the rabble of statutes got together during the reign of Henry the Eighth, by which treasons are multiplied with so prolific an energy, have been all repealed in a body; although they were all, or most of them, made in support of things truly fundamental in our Constitution. So were several of the acts by which the crown exercised its supremacy: such as the act of Elizabeth for making the *high commission courts*, and the like; as well as things made treason in the time of Charles the Second. None of this species of *secondary and subsidiary laws* have been held fundamental. They have yielded to circumstances; particularly where they were thought, even in their consequences, or obliquely, to affect other fundamentals. How much more, certainly, ought they to give way, when, as in our case, they affect, not here and there, in some particular point, or in their consequence, but universally, collectively, and directly, the fundamental franchises of a people equal to the whole inhabitants of several respectable kingdoms and states. . . . This way of proscribing men by whole nations, as it were, from all the benefits of the Constitution to which they were born, I never can believe to be politic or expedient, much less necessary for the existence of any state or church in the world. . . .

Recollect, my dear friend, that it was a fundamental principle in the French monarchy, whilst it stood, that the state should be Catholic; yet the Edict of Nantes gave, not a full ecclesiastical, but a complete civil *establishment*, with places of which only they were capable, to the Calvinists of France—and there were very few employments, indeed, of which they were not capable. The world praised the Cardinal de Richelieu, who took the first opportunity to strip them of their fortified places and cautionary towns. The same world held and does hold in execration (so far as that business is concerned) the memory of Louis the Fourteenth, for the total repeal of that favorable edict; though the talk of "fundamental laws, established religion, religion of the prince, safety to the state," &c., &c., was then as largely held, and with as bitter a revival of the animosities of the civil confusions during the struggles between the parties, as now they can be in Ireland.

Perhaps there are persons who think that the same reason does not hold, when the religious relation of the sovereign and subject is changed; but they who have their shop full of false weights and measures, and who imagine that the adding or taking away the name of Protestant or Papist, Guelph or Ghibelline, alters all the principles of equity, policy, and prudence, leave us no common data upon which we can reason. I therefore pass by all this, which on you will make no impression, to come to what seems to be a serious consideration in your mind: I mean the dread you express of "reviewing, for the purpose of altering, the *principles of the Revolution.*" This is an interesting topic, on which I will, as fully as your leisure and mine permits, lay before you the ideas I have formed.

First, I cannot possibly confound in my mind all the things which were done at the Revolution with the *principles* of the Revolution. As in most great changes, many things were done from the necessities of the time, well or ill understood, from passion or from vengeance, which were not only not perfectly agreeable to its principles, but in the most direct contradiction to them. I shall not think that the *deprivation of some millions of people of all the rights of citizens, and all interest in the Constitution, in and to which they were born*, was a thing conformable to the *declared principles* of the Revolution. This I am sure is true relatively to England (where the operation of these *anti-principles* comparatively were of little extent); and some of our late laws, in repealing acts made immediately after the Revolution, admit that some things then done were not done in the true spirit of the Revolution. But the Revolution operated differently in England and Ireland, in many, and these essential particulars. . . . In England it was the struggle of the *great body* of the people for the establishment of their liberties, against the efforts of a very *small faction*, who would have oppressed them. In Ireland it was the establishment of the power of the smaller number, at the expense of the civil liberties and properties of the far greater part, and at the expense of the political liberties of the whole. It was, to say the truth, not a revolution, but a conquest: which is not to say a great deal in its favor. To insist on everything done in Ireland at the Revolution would be to insist on the severe and jealous policy of a conqueror, in the crude settlement of his new acquisition, as a *permanent* rule for its future government. This no power, in no country that ever I heard of, has done or professed to do—except in Ireland; where it is done, and possibly by some people will be professed. Time has, by degrees, in all other places and periods, blended and coalited the conquered with the conquerors. So, after some time, and after one of the most rigid conquests that we read of in history, the Normans softened into the English. . . .

For a much longer period . . . the Protestants settled in Ireland considered themselves in no other light than that of a sort of a colonial garrison, to keep the natives in subjection to the other state of Great Britain. The whole spirit of the Revolution in Ireland was that of not the mildest conqueror. In truth, the spirit of those proceedings did not commence at that era, nor was religion of any kind their primary object. What was done was not in the spirit of a contest between two religious factions, but between two adverse nations. The statutes of Kilkenny show that the spirit of the Popery laws, and some even of their actual provisions, as applied between Englishry and Irishry, had existed in that harassed country before the words *Protestant* and *Papist* were heard of in the world. If we read Baron Finglas, Spenser, and Sir John Davies, we cannot miss the true genius and policy of the English government there before the Revolution, as well as during the whole reign of Queen Elizabeth. Sir John Davies boasts the benefits received by the natives, by extending to them the English law, and turning the whole kingdom into shire ground. But the appearance of things alone was changed. The original scheme was never deviated from for a single hour. Unheard-of confiscations were made in the northern parts, upon grounds of plots and conspiracies, never proved upon their supposed authors. The war of chicane succeeded to the war of arms and of hostile statutes; and a regular series of operations was carried on, particularly from Chichester's time, in the ordinary courts of justice, and by special commissions and inquisitions—first under pretence of tenures, and then of titles in the crown, for the purpose of the total extirpation of the interest of the natives in their own soil—until this species of subtle ravage, being carried to the last excess of oppression and insolence under Lord Strafford, it kindled the flames of that rebellion which broke out in 1641. By the issue of that war, by the turn which the Earl of Clarendon gave to things at the Restoration, and by the total reduction of the kingdom of Ireland in 1691, the ruin of the native Irish, and, in a great measure, too, of the first races of the English, was completely accomplished. The new English interest was settled with as solid a stability as anything in human affairs can look for. All the penal laws of that unparalleled code of oppression, which were made after the last event, were manifestly the effects of national hatred and scorn towards a conquered people, whom the victors delighted to trample upon and were not at all afraid to provoke. They were not the effect of their fears, but of their security. They who carried on this system looked to the irresistible force of Great Britain for their support in their acts of power. They were quite certain that no complaints of the natives would be heard on this side of the water with any other sentiments than those of contempt and indignation. . . . Whilst that temper prevailed, (and it prevailed in all its force to a time within our memory,) every measure was pleasing and popular just in proportion as it tended to harass and ruin a set of people who were looked upon as enemies to God and man, and, indeed, as a race of bigoted savages who were a disgrace to human nature itself.

However, as the English in Ireland began to be domiciliated, they began also to recollect that they had a country. The *English interest*, at first by faint and almost insensible degrees, but at length openly and avowedly, became an *independent Irish interest*—full as independent as it could ever have been if it had continued in the persons of the native Irish; and it was maintained with more skill and more consistency than probably it would have been in theirs. With their views, the *Anglo-Irish* changed their maxims: it was necessary to demonstrate to the whole people that there was something, at least, of a common interest, combined with the independency, which was to become the object of common exertions. The mildness of government produced the first relaxation towards the Irish; the necessities, and, in part, too, the temper that predominated at this great change, produced the second and the most important of these relaxations. English government and Irish legislature felt jointly the propriety of this measure. The Irish Parliament and nation became independent.

The true revolution to you, that which most intrinsically and substantially resembled the English Revolution of 1688, was the Irish Revolution of 1782. . . .

Great Britain, finding the Anglo-Irish highly animated with a spirit which had indeed shown itself before, though with little energy and many interruptions, and therefore suffered a multitude of uniform precedents to be established against it, acted, in my opinion, with the greatest temperance and wisdom. She saw that the disposition of the *leading part* of the nation would not permit them to act any longer the part of a *garrison*. She saw that true policy did not require that they ever should have appeared in that character; or if it had done so formerly, the reasons had now ceased to operate. She saw that the Irish of her race were resolved to build their Constitution and their politics upon another bottom. With those things under her view, she instantly complied with the whole of your demands, without any reservation whatsoever. She surrendered that boundless superiority, for the preservation of which, and the acquisition, she had supported the English colonies in Ireland for so long a time, and at so vast an expense (according to the standard of those ages) of her blood and treasure.

When we bring before us the matter which history affords for our selection, it is not improper to examine the spirit of the several precedents which are candidates for our choice. Might it not be as well for your statesmen, on the other side of the water, to take an example from this latter and surely more conciliatory revolution, as a pattern for your conduct towards your own fellow-citizens, than from that of 1688, when a paramount sovereignty over both you and them was more loftily claimed and more sternly exerted than at any former or at any subsequent period? Great Britain in 1782 rose above the vulgar ideas of policy, the ordinary jealousies of state, and all the sentiments of national pride and national ambition. . . .

At that time, on your part, you were not afraid to review what was done at the Revolution of 1688, and what had been continued during the subsequent flourishing period of the British empire. The change then made was a great and fundamental alteration. In the execution, it was an operose business on both sides of the water. It required the repeal of several laws, the modification of many, and a new course to be given to an infinite number of legislative, judicial, and official practices and usages in both kingdoms. This did not frighten any of us. You are now asked to give, in some moderate measure, to your fellow-citizens, what Great Britain gave to you without any measure at all. Yet, notwithstanding all the difficulties at the time, and the apprehensions which some very well-meaning people entertained, through the admirable temper in which this revolution (or restoration in the nature of a revolution) was conducted in both kingdoms, it has hitherto produced no inconvenience to either; and I trust, with the continuance of the same temper, that it never will. I think that this small, inconsiderable change, (relative to an exclusive statute not made at the Revolution,) for restoring the people to the benefits from which the green soreness of a civil war had not excluded them, will be productive of no sort of mischief whatsoever. Compare what was done in 1782 with what is wished in 1792; consider the spirit of what has been done at the several periods of reformation; and weigh maturely whether it be exactly true that conciliatory concessions are of good policy only in discussions between nations, but that among descriptions in the same nation they must always be irrational and dangerous. . . .

I do not mean to trouble you with anything to remove the objections, I will not call them arguments, against this measure, taken from a ferocious hatred to all that numerous description of Christians. It would be to pay a poor compliment to your understanding or your heart. Neither *your* religion nor *your* politics consist "in odd, perverse antipathies." You are not resolved to persevere in proscribing from the Constitution so many millions of your countrymen, because, in contradiction to experience and to common sense, you think proper to imagine that their principles are subversive of common human society. . . .

As little shall I detain you with matters that can as little obtain admission into a mind like yours: such as the fear, or pretence of fear, that, in spite of your own power and the trifling power of Great Britain, you may be conquered by the Pope; or that this commodious bugbear (who is of infinitely more use to those who pretend to fear than to those who love him) will absolve his Majesty's subjects from their allegiance, and send over the Cardinal of York to rule you as his viceroy; or that, by the plenitude of his power, he will take that fierce tyrant, the king of the French, out of his jail, and arm that nation (which on all occasions treats his Holiness so very politely) with his bulls and pardons, to invade poor old Ireland, to reduce you to Popery and slavery, and to force the free-born, naked feet of your people into the wooden shoes of that arbitrary monarch. I do not believe that discourses of this kind are held, or that anything like them will be held, by any who walk about without a keeper. . . .

There is another way of taking an objection to this concession, which I admit to be something more plausible, and worthy of a more attentive examination. It is, that this numerous class of people is mutinous, disorderly, prone to sedition, and easy to be wrought upon by the insidious arts of wicked and designing men; that, conscious of this, the sober, rational, and wealthy part of that body, who are totally of another character, do by no means desire any participation for themselves, or for any one else of their description, in the franchises of the British Constitution.

I have great doubt of the exactness of any part of this observation. But let us admit that the body of the Catholics are prone to sedition, (of which, as I have said, I entertain much doubt,) is it possible that any fair observer or fair reasoner can think of confining this description to them only? I believe it to be possible for men to be mutinous and seditious who feel no grievance, but I believe no man will assert seriously, that, when people are of a turbulent spirit, the best way to keep them in order is to furnish them with something substantial to complain of.

You separate, very properly, the sober, rational, and substantial part of their description from the rest. You give, as you ought to do, weight only to the former. What I have always thought of the matter is this—that the most poor, illiterate, and uninformed creatures upon earth are judges of a *practical* oppression. It is a matter of feeling; and as such persons generally have felt most of it, and are not of an over-lively sensibility, they are the best judges of it. But for *the real cause*, or *the appropriate remedy*, they ought never to be called into council about the one or the other. They ought to be totally shut out: because their reason is weak; because, when once roused, their passions are ungoverned; because they want information; because the smallness of the property which individually they possess renders them less attentive to the consequence of the measures they adopt in affairs of moment. . . .

The object pursued by the Catholics is, I understand, and have all along reasoned as if it were so, in some degree or measure to be again admitted to the franchises of the Constitution. Men are considered as under some derangement of their intellects, when they see good and evil in a different light from other men—when they choose nauseous and unwholesome food, and reject such as to the rest of the world seems pleasant and is known to be nutritive. I have always considered the British Constitution not to be a thing in itself so vicious as that none but men of deranged understanding and turbulent tempers could desire a share in it: on the contrary, I should think very indifferently of the understanding and temper of any body of men who did not wish to partake of this great and acknowledged benefit. . . .

As to the means which the Catholics employ to obtain this object, so worthy of sober and rational minds, I do admit that such means may be used in the pursuit of it as may make it proper for the legislature, in this case, to defer their compliance until the demandants are brought to a proper sense of their duty. A concession in which the governing power of our country loses its dignity is dearly bought even by him who obtains his object. All the people have a deep interest in the dignity of Parliament. But as the refusal of franchises which are drawn out of the first vital stamina of the British Constitution is a very serious thing, we ought to be very sure that the manner and spirit of the application is offensive and dangerous indeed, before we ultimately reject all applications of this nature. The mode of application, I hear, is by petition. It is the manner in which all the sovereign powers of the world are approached; and I never heard (except in the case of James the Second) that any prince considered this manner of supplication to be contrary to the humility of a subject or to the respect due to the person or authority of the sovereign. . . .

Since you have given to all other Dissenters these privileges without limit which are hitherto withheld without any limitation whatsoever from the Catholics—since no nation in the world has ever been known to exclude so great a body of men (not born slaves) from the civil state, and all the benefits of its Constitution—the whole question comes before Parliament as a matter for its prudence. I do not put the thing on a question of right. That discretion, which in judicature is well said by Lord Coke to be a crooked cord, in legislature is a golden rule. Supplicants ought not to appear too much in the character of litigants. If the subject thinks so highly and reverently of the sovereign authority as not to claim anything of right, so that it may seem to be independent of the power and free choice of its government—and if the sovereign, on his part, considers the advantages of the subjects as their right, and all their reasonable wishes as so many claims—in the fortunate conjunction of these mutual dispositions are laid the foundations of a happy and prosperous commonwealth. For my own part, desiring of all things that the authority of the legislature under which I was born, and which I cherish, not only with a dutiful awe, but with a partial and cordial affection, to be maintained in the utmost possible respect, I never will suffer myself to suppose that at bottom their discretion will be found to be at variance with their justice.

The whole being at discretion, I beg leave just to suggest some matters for your consideration:—Whether the government in Church or State is likely to be more secure by continuing causes of grounded discontent to a very great number (say two millions) of the subjects? or whether the Constitution, combined and balanced as it is, will be rendered more solid by depriving so large a part of the people of all concern or interest or share in its representation, actual or *virtual*? I here mean to lay an emphasis on the word *virtual*. Virtual representation is that in which there is a communion of interests and a sympathy in feelings and desires between those who act in the name of any description of people and the people in whose name they act, though the trustees are not actually chosen by them. This is virtual representation. Such a representation I think to be in many cases even better than the actual. It possesses most of its advantages, and is free from many of its inconveniences; it corrects the irregularities in the literal representation, when the shifting current of human affairs or the acting of public interests in different ways carry it obliquely from its first line of direction. The people may err in their choice; but common interest and common sentiment are rarely mistaken. But this sort of virtual representation cannot have a long or sure existence, if it has not a substratum in the actual. The member must have some relation to the constituent. As things stand, the Catholic, as a Catholic, and belonging to a description, has no *virtual* relation to the representative—but the *contrary.* There is a relation in mutual obligation. Gratitude may not always have a very lasting power; but the frequent recurrence of an application for favors will revive and refresh it, and will necessarily produce some degree of mutual attention. It will produce, at least, acquaintance. The several descriptions of people will not be kept so much apart as they now are, as if they were not only separate nations, but separate species. The stigma and reproach, the hideous mask will be taken off, and men will see each other as they are. Sure I am that there have been thousands in Ireland who have never conversed with a Roman Catholic in their whole lives, unless they happened to talk to their gardener's workmen, or to ask their way, when they had lost it in their sports—or, at best, who had known them only as footmen, or other domestics, of the second and third order: and so averse were they, some time ago, to have them near their persons, that they would not employ even those who could never find their way beyond the stable. . . .

Reduced to a question of discretion, and that discretion exercised solely upon what will appear best for the conservation of the state on its present basis, I should recommend it to your serious thoughts, whether the narrowing of the foundation is always the best way to secure the building? The body of disfranchised men will not be perfectly satisfied to remain always in that state. If they are not satisfied, you have two millions of subjects in your bosom full of uneasiness: not that they cannot overturn the Act of Settlement, and put themselves and you under an arbitrary master; or that they are not permitted to spawn a hydra of wild republics, on principles of a pretended natural equality in man; but because you will not suffer them to enjoy the ancient, fundamental, tried advantages of a British Constitution—that you will not permit them to profit of the protection of a common father or the freedom of common citizens, and that the only reason which can be assigned for this disfranchisement has a tendency more deeply to ulcerate their minds than the act of exclusion itself. What the consequence of such feelings must be it is for you to look to. To warn is not to menace.

I am far from asserting that men will not excite disturbances without just cause. I know that such an assertion is not true. But neither is it true that disturbances have never just complaints for their origin. I am sure that it is hardly prudent to furnish them with such causes of complaint as every man who thinks the British Constitution a benefit may think at least colorable and plausible. . . .

Think whether this be the way to prevent or dissolve factious combinations against the Church or the State. Reflect seriously on the possible consequences of keeping in the heart of your country a bank of discontent, every hour accumulating, upon which every description of seditious men may draw at pleasure. They whose principles of faction will dispose them to the establishment of an arbitrary monarchy will find a nation of men who have no sort or interest in freedom, but who will have an interest in that equality of justice or favor with which a wise despot must view all his subjects who do not attack the foundations of his power. Love of liberty itself may, in such men, become the means of establishing an arbitrary domination. On the other hand, they who wish for a democratic republic will find a set of men who have no choice between civil servitude and the entire ruin of a mixed Constitution. . . .

A Letter to Richard Burke, Esq., on Protestant Ascendancy in Ireland

Efforts were made in 1792 to give Catholics the vote in Ireland even though George III adamantly opposed it. Pitt, the prime minister, pleaded with the Protestant-controlled Irish Parliament to give the vote lest there be revolution in Ireland. The Irish Parliament granted Catholics the vote only in parliamentary elections, and continued to prohibit them from holding important public offices. In this published letter of 1793 to his son, who had gone to Dublin to help the Catholics obtain the vote, Burke repeats his fear that the Protestant ascendancy inadvertently plays into the devilish hands of the Jacobins.

. . . THIS SYSTEM, in its real nature, and under its proper appellations, is odious and unnatural, especially when a constitution is admitted which not only, as all constitutions do profess, has a regard to the good of the multitude, but in its theory makes profession of their power also. . . . A word has been lately struck in the mint of the Castle of Dublin; thence it was conveyed to the Tholsel, or City-Hall, where, having passed the touch of the corporation, so respectably stamped and vouched, it soon became current in Parliament, and was carried back by the Speaker of the House of Commons in great pomp, as an offering of homage from whence it came. The word is *ascendency.* . . . This Protestant ascendency means nothing less than . . . an *ascendency*, in public assemblies in England, that is, by a liberal distribution of places and pensions, and other graces of government. This last is wide indeed of the signification of the word. New *ascendency* is the old *mastership.* It is neither more nor less than the resolution of one set of people in Ireland to consider themselves as the sole citizens in the commonwealth, and to keep a dominion over the rest by reducing them to absolute slavery under a military power, and, thus fortified in their power, to divide the public estate, which is the result of general contribution, as a military booty, solely amongst themselves.

The poor word *ascendency* . . . is large enough in its comprehension. I cannot conceive what mode of oppression in civil life, or what mode of religious persecution, may not come within the methods of preserving an *ascendency.* In plain old English, as they apply it, it signifies *pride and dominion* on the one part of the relation, and on the other *subserviency and contempt*—and it signifies nothing else. . . .

This ascendency, by being a *Protestant* ascendency, does not better it from the combination of a note or two more in this anti-harmonic scale. If Protestant ascendency means the proscription from citizenship of by far the major part of the people of any country, then Protestant ascendency is a bad thing, and it ought to have no existence. But there is a deeper evil. By the use that is so frequently made of the term, and the policy which is engrafted on it, the name Protestant becomes nothing more or better than the name of a persecuting faction, with a relation of some sort of theological hostility to others, but without any sort of ascertained tenets of its own upon the ground of which it persecutes other men: for the patrons of this Protestant ascendency neither do nor can, by anything positive, define or describe what they mean by the word Protestant. It is defined, as Cowley defines wit, not by what it is, but by what it is not. It is not the Christian religion as professed in the

Churches holding communion with Rome, the majority of Christians: that is all which, in the latitude of the term, is known about its signification. This makes such persecutors ten times worse than any of that description that hitherto have been known in the world. The old persecutors, whether Arian or Orthodox, whether Catholics, Anglicans, or Calvinists, actually were, or at least had the decorum to pretend to be, strong dogmatists. They pretended that their religious maxims were clear and ascertained, and so useful that they were bound, for the eternal benefit of mankind, to defend or diffuse them, though by any sacrifices of the temporal good of those who were the objects of their system of experiment.

The bottom of this theory of persecution is false. It is not permitted to us to sacrifice the temporal good of any body of men to our own ideas of the truth and falsehood of any religious opinions. By making men miserable in this life, they counteract one of the great ends of charity, which is, in as much as in us lies, to make men happy in every period of their existence, and most in what most depends upon us. But give to these old persecutors their mistaken principle, in their reasoning they are consistent, and in their tempers they may be even kind and good-natured. But whenever a faction would render millions of mankind miserable, some millions of the race coëxistent with themselves, and many millions in their succession, without knowing or so much as pretending to ascertain the doctrines of their own school, (in which there is much of the lash and nothing of the lesson,) the errors which the persons in such a faction fall into are not those that are natural to human imbecility, nor is the least mixture of mistaken kindness to mankind an ingredient in the severities they inflict. The whole is nothing but pure and perfect malice. It is, indeed, a perfection in that kind belonging to beings of an higher order than man, and to them we ought to leave it.

This kind of persecutors without zeal, without charity, know well enough that religion, to pass by all questions of the truth or falsehood of any of its particular systems, (a matter I abandon to the theologians on all sides,) is a source of great comfort to us mortals, in this our short, but tedious journey through the world. They know, that, to enjoy this consolation, men must believe their religion upon some principle or other, whether of education, habit, theory, or authority. When men are driven from any of those principles on which they have received religion, without embracing with the same assurance and cordiality some other system, a dreadful void is left in their minds, and a terrible shock is given to their morals. They lose their guide, their comfort, their hope. None but the most cruel and hardhearted of men, who had banished all natural tenderness from their minds, such as those beings of iron, the atheists, could bring themselves to any persecution like this. . . .

The harsh methods in use with the old class of persecutors were to make converts, not apostates only. If they perversely hated other sects and factions, they loved their own inordinately. But in this Protestant persecution there is anything but benevolence at work. What do the Irish statutes? They do not make a conformity to the *established* religion, and to its doctrines and practices, the condition of getting out of servitude. No such thing. Let three millions of people but abandon all that they and their ancestors have been taught to believe sacred, and to forswear it publicly in terms the most degrading, scurrilous, and indecent for men of integrity and virtue, and to abuse the whole of their former lives, and to slander the education they have received, and nothing more is required of them. There is no system of folly, or impiety, or blasphemy, or atheism, into which they may not throw themselves, and which they may not profess openly, and as a system, consistently with the enjoyment of all the privileges of a free citizen in the happiest constitution in the world.

Some of the unhappy assertors of this strange scheme say they are not persecutors on account of religion. In the first place, they say what is not true. For what else do they disfranchise the people? If the man gets rid of a religion through which their malice operates, he gets rid of all their penalties and incapacities at once. They never afterwards inquire about him. I speak here of their pretexts, and not of the true spirit of the transaction, in which religious bigotry, I apprehend, has little share. Every man has his taste; but I think, if I were so miserable and undone as to be guilty of premeditated and continued violence towards any set of men, I had rather that my conduct was supposed to arise from wild conceits concerning their religious advantages than from low and ungenerous motives relative to my own selfish interest. I had rather be thought insane in my charity than rational in my malice. This much, my dear son, I have to say of this Protestant persecution—that is, a persecution of religion itself.

A very great part of the mischiefs that vex the world arises from words. People soon forget the meaning, but the impression and the passion remain. The word Protestant is the charm that locks up in the dungeon of servitude three millions of your people. It is not amiss to consider this spell of potency, this abracadabra, that is hung about the necks of the unhappy, not to heal, but to communicate disease. We sometimes hear of a Protestant *religion,* frequently of a Protestant *interest.* We hear of the latter the most frequently, because it has a positive meaning. The other has none. We hear of it the most frequently, because it has a word in the phrase which, well or ill understood, has animated to persecution and oppression at all times infinitely more than all the dogmas in dispute between religious factions. These are, indeed, well formed to perplex and torment the intellect, but not half so well calculated to inflame the passions and animosities of men.

I do readily admit that a great deal of the wars, seditions, and troubles of the world did formerly turn upon the contention between *interests* that went by the names of Protestant and Catholic. But I imagined that at this time no one was weak enough to believe, or impudent enough to pretend, that questions of Popish and Protestant opinions or interest are the things by which men are at present menaced with crusades by foreign invasion, or with seditions which shake the foundations of the state at home. It is long since all this combination of things has vanished from the view of intelligent observers. The existence of quite another system of opinions and interests is now plain to the grossest sense. Are these the questions that raise a flame in the minds of men at this day? If ever the Church and the Constitution of England should fall in these islands, (and they will fall together,) it is not Presbyterian discipline nor Popish hierarchy that will rise upon their ruins. It will not be the Church of Rome nor the Church of Scotland, not the Church of Luther nor the Church of Calvin. On the contrary, all these churches are menaced, and menaced alike. It is the new fanatical religion, now in the heat of its first ferment, of the Rights of Man, which rejects all establishments, all discipline, all ecclesiastical, and in truth all civil order, which will triumph, and which will lay prostrate your Church, which will destroy your distinctions, and which will put all your properties to auction, and disperse you over the earth. If the present establishment should fall, it is this religion which will triumph in Ireland and in England, as it has triumphed in France. This religion, which laughs at creeds and dogmas and confessions of faith, may be fomented equally amongst all descriptions and all sects—amongst nominal Catholics, and amongst nominal Churchmen, and amongst those Dissenters who know little and care less about a presbytery, or any of its discipline, or any of its doctrine. Against this new, this growing, this exterminatory system, all these churches have a common concern to defend themselves. How the enthusiasts of this rising sect rejoice to see you of the old churches play their game, and stir and rake the cinders of animosities sunk in their ashes, in order to keep up the execution of their plan for your common ruin! . . .

I do not pretend to take pride in an extravagant attachment to any sect. Some gentlemen in Ireland affect that sort of glory. It is to their taste. Their piety, I take it for granted, justifies the fervor of their zeal, and may palliate the excess of it. . . . Yet . . . not one of those zealots for a Protestant interest wishes more sincerely than I do, perhaps not half so sincerely, for the support of the Established Church in both these kingdoms. It is a great link towards holding fast the connection of religion with the State, and for keeping these two islands, in their present critical independence of constitution, in a close connection of *opinion and affection.* I wish it well, as the religion of the greater number of the primary land-proprietors of the kingdom, with whom all establishments of Church and State, for strong political reasons, ought in my opinion to be firmly connected. I wish it well, because it is more closely combined than any other of the church systems with the *crown*, which is the stay of the mixed Constitution—because it is, as things now stand, the sole connecting *political* principle between the constitutions of the two independent kingdoms. I have another and infinitely a stronger reason for wishing it well: it is, that in the present time I consider it as one of the main pillars of the Christian religion itself. The body and substance of every religion I regard much more than any of the forms and dogmas of the particular sects. Its fall would leave a great void, which nothing else, of which I can form any distinct idea, might fill. I respect the Catholic hierarchy and the Presbyterian republic; but I know that the hope or the fear of establishing either of them is, in these kingdoms, equally chimerical, even if I preferred one or the other of them to the Establishment, which certainly I do not. . . .

The legislature of Ireland, like all legislatures, ought to frame its laws to suit the people and the circumstances of the country, and not any longer to make it their whole business to force the nature, the temper, and the inveterate habits of a nation to a conformity to speculative systems concerning any kind of laws. Ireland has an established government, and a religion legally established, which are to be preserved. It has a people who are to be preserved too, and to be led by reason, principle, sentiment, and interest to acquiesce in that government. Ireland is a country under peculiar circumstances. The people of Ireland are a very mixed people; and the quantities of the several ingredients in the mixture are very much disproportioned to each other. Are we to govern this mixed body as if it were composed of the most simple elements, comprehending the whole in one system of benevolent legislation? or are we not rather to provide for the several parts according to the various and diversified necessities of the heterogeneous nature of the mass? Would not common reason and common honesty dictate to us the policy of regulating the people, in the several descriptions of which they are composed, according to the natural ranks and classes of an orderly civil society, under a common protecting sovereign, and under a form of constitution favorable at once to authority and to freedom—such as the British Constitution boasts to be, and such as it is to those who enjoy it?

You have an ecclesiastical establishment, which, though the religion of the prince, and of most of the first class of landed proprietors, is not the religion of the major part of the inhabitants, and which consequently does not answer to *them* any one purpose of a religious establishment. This is a state of things which no man in his senses can call perfectly happy. But it is the state of Ireland. Two hundred years of experiment show it to be unalterable. Many a fierce struggle has passed between the parties. The result is, you cannot make the people Protestants, and they cannot shake off a Protestant government. This is what experience teaches, and what all men of sense of all descriptions know. To-day the question is this: Are we to make the best of this situation, which we cannot alter? The question is: Shall the condition of the body of the people be alleviated in other things, on account of their necessary suffering from their being subject to the burdens of two religious establishments, from one of which they do not partake the least, living or dying, either of instruction or of consolation—or shall it be aggravated, by stripping the people thus loaded of everything which might support and indemnify them in this state, so as to leave them naked of every sort of right and of every name of franchise, to outlaw them from the Constitution, and to cut off (perhaps) three millions of plebeian subjects, without reference to property, or any other qualification, from all connection with the popular representation of the kingdom?

As to religion, it has nothing at all to do with the proceeding. Liberty is not sacrificed to a zeal for religion, but a zeal for religion is pretended and assumed to destroy liberty. The Catholic religion is completely free. It has no establishment—but it is recognized, permitted, and, in a degree, protected by the laws. If a man is satisfied to be a slave, he may be a Papist with perfect impunity. He may say mass, or hear it, as he pleases; but he must consider himself as an outlaw from the British Constitution. If the constitutional liberty of the subject were not the thing aimed at, the direct reverse course would be taken. The franchise would have been permitted, and the mass exterminated. But the conscience of a man left, and a tenderness for it hypocritically pretended, is to make it a trap to catch his liberty.

So much is this the design, that the violent partisans of this scheme fairly take up all the maxims and arguments, as well as the practices, by which tyranny has fortified itself at all times. Trusting wholly in their strength and power . . . they abandon all pretext of the general good of the community. . . . Therefore, they cannot so much as listen to any arguments drawn from equity or from national or constitutional policy . . .

The language of tyranny has been invariable: "The general good is inconsistent with my personal safety." Justice and liberty seem so alarming to these gentlemen, that they are not ashamed even to slander their own titles, to calumniate and call in doubt their right to their own estates, and to consider themselves as novel disseizors, usurpers, and intruders, rather than lose a pretext for becoming oppressors of their fellow-citizens, whom they (not I) choose to describe themselves as having robbed.

Instead of putting themselves in this odious point of light, one would think they would wish to let Time draw his oblivious veil over the unpleasant modes by which lordships and demesnes have been acquired in theirs, and almost in all other countries upon earth. . . .

The people desire the privileges inseparably annexed, since Magna Charta, to the freehold which they have by descent or obtain as the fruits of their industry. They call for no man's estate; they desire not to be dispossessed of their own. . . .

I shall never praise confiscations or counterconfiscations as long as I live. When they happen by necessity, I shall think the necessity lamentable and odious: I shall think that anything done under it ought not to pass into precedent, or to be adopted by choice, or to produce any of those shocking retaliations which never suffer dissensions to subside. Least of all would I fix the transitory spirit of civil fury by perpetuating and methodizing it in tyrannic government. If it were permitted to argue with power, might one not ask these gentlemen whether it would not be more natural, instead of wantonly mooting these questions concerning their property, as if it were an exercise in law, to found it on the solid rock of prescription—the soundest, the most general, and the most recognized title between man and man that is known in municipal or in public jurisprudence?—a title in which not arbitrary institutions, but the eternal order of things, gives judgment; a title which is not the creature, but the master, of positive law; a title which, though not fixed in its term, is rooted in its principle in the law of Nature itself, and is indeed the original ground of all known property: for all property in soil will always be traced back to that source, and will rest there. . . . All titles terminate in prescription. . . .

A Letter to William Smith, Esq., on the Subject of Catholic Emancipation

Burke returned, even more gloomily, to this theme in a letter to an Irish friend in 1795. Christianity and Catholicism were the principal foils to French Jacobinism as it sought to spread its ideals across Europe. Continued exclusion of Catholics from public life in Ireland ultimately served the interests of the Jacobins, who, he warned the complacent Protestants in Ireland, sought "to destroy the whole frame and fabric of the old societies of the world, and to regenerate them after their fashion."

. . . MY WHOLE POLITICS, at present, centre in one point, and to this the merit or demerit of every measure (with me) is referable—that is, what will most promote or depress the cause of Jacobinism. What is Jacobinism? It is an attempt (hitherto but too successful) to eradicate prejudice out of the minds of men, for the purpose of putting all power and authority into the hands of the persons capable of occasionally enlightening the minds of the people. For this purpose the Jacobins have resolved to destroy the whole frame and fabric of the old societies of the world, and to regenerate them after their fashion. To obtain an army for this purpose, they everywhere engage the poor by holding out to them as a bribe the spoils of the rich. This I take to be a fair description of the principles and leading maxims of the enlightened of our day who are commonly called Jacobins.

As the grand prejudice, and that which holds all the other prejudices together, the first, last, and middle object of their hostility is religion. With that they are at inexpiable war. They make no distinction of sects. A Christian, as such, is to them an enemy. What, then, is left to a real Christian, (Christian as a believer and as a statesman,) but to make a league between all the grand divisions of that name, to protect and to cherish them all, and by no means to proscribe in any manner, more or less, any member of our common party? The divisions which formerly prevailed in the Church, with all their overdone zeal, only purified and ventilated our common faith, because there was no common enemy arrayed and embattled to take advantage of their dissensions; but now nothing but inevitable ruin will be the consequence of our quarrels. I think we may dispute, rail, persecute, and provoke the Catholics out of their prejudices; but it is not in ours they will take refuge. If anything is, one more than another, out of the power of man, it is to *create* a prejudice. Somebody has said, that a king may make a nobleman, but he cannot make a gentleman.

All the principal religions in Europe stand upon one common bottom. The support that the whole or the favored parts may have in the secret dispensations of Providence it is impossible to tell; but, humanly speaking, they are all *prescriptive* religions. They have all stood long enough to make prescription and its chain of legitimate prejudices their main stay. The people who compose the four grand divisions of Christianity have now their religion as an habit, and upon authority, and not on disputation—as all men who have their religion derived from their parents and the fruits of education *must* have it, however the one more than the other may be able to reconcile his faith to his own reason or to that of other men. Depend upon it, they must all be supported, or they must all fall in the crash of a common ruin. The Catholics are the far more numerous part of the Christians in your country; and how can Christianity (that is now the point in issue) be supported under the persecution, or even under the discountenance, of the greater number of Christians? It is a great truth, and which in one of the debates I stated as strongly as I could to the House of Commons in the last session, that, if the Catholic religion is destroyed by the infidels, it is a most contemptible and absurd idea, that this, or any Protestant Church, can survive that event. Therefore my humble and decided opinion is, that all the three religions prevalent more or less in various parts of these islands ought all, in subordination to the legal establishments as they they stand in the several countries, to be all countenanced, protected, and cherished, and that in Ireland particularly the Roman Catholic religion should be upheld in high respect and veneration, and should be, in its place, provided with all the means of making it a blessing to the people who profess it—that it ought to be cherished as a good, (though not as the most preferable good, if a choice was now to be made,) and not tolerated as an inevitable evil. If this be my opinion as to the Catholic religion as a sect, you must see that I must be to the last degree averse to put a man, upon that account, upon a bad footing with relation to the privileges which the fundamental laws of this country give him as a subject. I am the more serious on the positive encouragement to be given to this religion, (always, however, as secondary,) because the serious and earnest belief and practice of it by its professors forms, as things stand, the most effectual barrier, if not the sole barrier, against Jacobinism. The Catholics form the great body of the lower ranks of your community, and no small part of those classes of the middling that come nearest to them. You know that the seduction of that part of mankind from the principles of religion, morality, subordination, and social order is the great object of the Jacobins. Let them grow lax, skeptical, careless, and indifferent with regard to religion, and, so sure as we have an existence, it is not a zealous Anglican or Scottish Church principle, but direct Jacobinism, which will enter into that breach. Two hundred years dreadfully spent in experiments to force that people to change the form of their religion have proved fruitless. You have now your choice, for full four fifths of your people, of the Catholic religion or Jacobinism. If things appear to you to stand on this alternative, I think you will not be long in making your option.

You have made, as you naturally do, a very able analysis of powers, and have separated, as the things are separable, civil from political powers. You start, too, a question, whether the civil can be secured without some share in the political. For my part, as abstract questions, I should find some difficulty in an attempt to resolve them. But as applied to the state of Ireland, to the form of our commonwealth, to the parties that divide us, and to the dispositions of the leading men in those parties, I cannot hesitate to lay before you my opinion, that, whilst any kind of discouragements and disqualifications remain on the Catholics, an handle will be made by a factious power utterly to defeat the benefits of any civil rights they may apparently possess. I need not go to very remote times for my examples. It was within the course of about a twelvemonth, that, after Parliament had been led into a step quite unparalleled in its records, after they had resisted all concession, and even hearing, with an obstinacy equal to anything that could have actuated a party domination in the second or eighth of Queen Anne, after the strange adventure of the Grand Juries, and after Parliament had listened to the sovereign pleading for the emancipation of his subjects—it was after all this, that such a grudging and discontent was expressed as must justly have alarmed, as it did extremely alarm, the whole of the Catholic body: and I remember but one period in my whole life (I mean the savage period between 1761 and 1767) in which they have been more harshly or contumeliously treated than since the last partial enlargement. And thus I am convinced it will be, by paroxysms, as long as any stigma remains on them, and whilst they are considered as no better than half citizens. If they are kept such for any length of time, they will be made whole Jacobins. Against this grand and dreadful evil of our time (I do not love to cheat myself or others) I do not know any solid security whatsoever; but I am quite certain that what will come nearest to it is to interest as many as you can in the present order of things, religiously, civilly, politically, by all the ties and principles by which mankind are held. This is like to be effectual policy: I am sure it is honorable policy: and it is better to fail, if fail we must, in the paths of direct and manly than of low and crooked wisdom. . . .

PART V

INDIA AND COLONIALISM

Speech on Mr. Fox's East India Bill

After the American Revolution and the loss of the American colonies, Burke turned his attention to the British Empire in the East, and its evolving role in India. A complicated relationship existed between the British government and the East India Company in managing the affairs of India. Burke was convinced that the Company's abuses in India were so great that only the increased sovereign role of the British government itself would bring relief to India. In this speech to the House of Commons in December 1783, which advocates the replacement of East India Company directors by a government commission to run India, Burke illustrates his detailed understanding of Indian affairs as well as his philosophical interest in preserving the ancient customs and traditions of India.

I ASKED MYSELF, and I asked myself nothing else, what part it was fit for a member of Parliament, who has supplied a mediocrity of talents by the extreme of diligence, and who has thought himself obliged by the research of years to wind himself into the in most recesses and labyrinths of the Indian detail—what part, I say, it became such a member of Parliament to take, when a minister of state, in conformity to a recommendation from the throne, has brought before us a system for the better government of the territory and commerce of the East. In this light, and in this only, I will trouble you with my sentiments.

It is not only agreed, but demanded by the right honorable gentleman, and by those who act with him, that a *whole* system ought to be produced; that it ought not to be an *half-measure*; that it ought to be no *palliative*, but a legislative provision, vigorous, substantial, and effective—I believe that no man who understands the subject can doubt for a moment that those must be the conditions of anything deserving the name of a reform in the Indian government; that anything short of them would not only be delusive, but, in this matter, which admits no medium, noxious in the extreme.

To all the conditions proposed by his adversaries the mover of the bill perfectly agrees; and on his performance of them he rests his cause. On the other hand, not the least objection has been taken with regard to the efficiency, the vigor, or the completeness of the scheme. I am therefore warranted to assume, as a thing admitted, that the bills accomplish what both sides of the House demand as essential. The end is completely answered, so far as the direct and immediate object is concerned.

But though there are no direct, yet there are various collateral objections made: objections from the effects which this plan of reform for Indian administration may have on the privileges of great public bodies in England; from its probable influence on the constitutional rights, or on the freedom and integrity, of the several branches of the legislature.

Before I answer these objections, I must beg leave to observe, that, if we are not able to contrive some method of governing India *well*, which will not of necessity become the means of governing Great Britain *ill*, a ground is laid for their eternal separation, but none for sacrificing the people of that country to our Constitution. I am, however, far from being persuaded that any such incompatibility of interest does at all exist. On the contrary, I am certain that every means effectual to preserve India from oppression is a guard to preserve the British Constitution from its worst corruption. To show this, I will consider the objections, which, I think, are four.

1st, That the bill is an attack on the chartered rights of men.

2ndly, That it increases the influence of the crown.

3rdly, That it does *not* increase, but diminishes, the influence of the crown, in order to promote the interests of certain ministers and their party.

4thly, That it deeply affects the national credit.

As to the first of these objections, I must observe that the phrase of "the chartered rights *of men*" is full of affectation, and very unusual in the discussion of privileges conferred by charters of the present description. But it is not difficult to discover what end that ambiguous mode of expression, so often reiterated, is meant to answer.

The rights of *men*—that is to say, the natural rights of mankind—are indeed sacred things; and if any public measure is proved mischievously to affect them, the objection ought to be fatal to that measure, even if no charter at all could be set up against it. If these natural rights are further affirmed and declared by express covenants, if they are clearly defined and secured against chicane, against power and authority, by written instruments and positive engagements, they are in a still better condition: they partake not only of the sanctity of the object so secured, but of that solemn public faith itself which secures an object of such importance. Indeed, this formal recognition, by the sovereign power, of an original right in the subject, can never be subverted, but by rooting up the holding radical principles of government, and even of society itself. The charters which we call by distinction *great* are public instruments of this nature: I mean the charters of King John and King Henry the Third. The things secured by these instruments may, without any deceitful ambiguity, be very fitly called *the chartered rights of men*.

These charters have made the very name of a charter dear to the heart of every Englishman. But, Sir, there may be, and there are, charters, not only different in nature, but formed on principles *the very reverse* of those of the Great Charter. Of this kind is the charter of the East India Company. *Magna Charta* is a charter to restrain power and to destroy monopoly. The East India charter is a charter to establish monopoly and to create power. Political power and commercial monopoly are *not* the rights of men; and the rights to them derived from charters it is fallacious and sophistical to call "the chartered rights of men." These chartered rights (to speak of such charters and of their effects in terms of the greatest possible moderation) do at least suspend the natural rights of mankind at large, and in their very frame and constitution are liable to fall into a direct violation of them.

It is a charter of this latter description (that is to say, a charter of power and monopoly) which is affected by the bill before you. The bill, Sir, does without question affect it: it does affect it essentially and substantially. But, having stated to you of what description the chartered rights are which this bill touches, I feel no difficulty at all in acknowledging the existence of those chartered rights in their fullest extent. They belong to the Company in the surest manner, and they are secured to that body by every sort of public sanction. They are stamped by the faith of Parliament: they have been bought for money, for money honestly and fairly paid; they have been bought for valuable consideration, over and over again.

I therefore freely admit to the East India Company their claim to exclude their fellow-subjects from the commerce of half the globe. I admit their claim to administer an annual territorial revenue of seven millions sterling, to command an army of sixty thousand men, and to dispose (under the control of a sovereign, imperial discretion, and with the due observance of the natural and local law) of the lives and fortunes of thirty millions of their fellow-creatures. All this they possess by charter, and by Acts of Parliament, (in my opinion,) without a shadow of controversy.

Those who carry the rights and claims of the Company the furthest do not contend for more than this; and all this I freely grant. But, granting all this, they must grant to me, in my turn, that all political power which is set over men, and that all privilege claimed or exercised in exclusion of them, being wholly artificial, and for so much a derogation from the natural equality of mankind at large, ought to be some way or other exercised ultimately for their benefit.

If this is true with regard to every species of political dominion and every description of commercial privilege, none of which can be original, self-derived rights, or grants for the mere private benefit of the holders, then such rights, or privileges, or whatever else you choose to call them, are all in the strictest sense *a trust*: and it is of the very essence of every trust to be rendered *accountable*—and even totally to *cease*, when it substantially varies from the purposes for which alone it could have a lawful existence.

This I conceive, Sir, to be true of trusts of power vested in the highest hands, and of such as seem to hold of no human creature. But about the application of this principle to subordinate *derivative* trusts I do not see how a controversy can be maintained. To whom, then, would I make the East India Company accountable? Why, to Parliament, to be sure—to Parliament, from whom their trust was derived—to Parliament, which alone is capable of comprehending the magnitude of its object, and its abuse, and alone capable of an effectual legislative remedy. The very charter, which is held out to exclude Parliament from correcting malversation with regard to the high trust vested in the Company, is the very thing which at once gives a title and imposes a duty on us to interfere with effect, wherever power and authority originating from ourselves are perverted from their purposes, and become instruments of wrong and violence.

If Parliament, Sir, had nothing to do with this charter, we might have some sort of Epicurean excuse to stand aloof, indifferent spectators of what passes in the Company's name in India and in London. But if we are the very cause of the evil, we are in a special manner engaged to the redress; and for us passively to bear with oppressions committed under the sanction of our own authority is in truth and reason for this House to be an active accomplice in the abuse.

That the power, notoriously grossly abused, has been bought from us is very certain. . . .

I ground myself, therefore, on this principle:—that, if the abuse is proved, the contract is broken, and we reënter into all our rights, that is, into the exercise of all our duties. Our own authority is, indeed, as much a trust originally as the Company's authority is a trust derivatively; and it is the use we make of the resumed power that must justify or condemn us in the resumption of it. When we have perfected the plan laid before us by the right honorable mover, the world will then see what it is we destroy, and what it is we create. By that test we stand or fall; and by that test I trust that it will be found, in the issue, that we are going to supersede a charter abused to the full extent of all the powers which it could abuse, and exercised in the plenitude of despotism, tyranny, and corruption—and that in one and the same plan we provide a real chartered security for *the rights of men*, cruelly violated under that charter.

This bill, and those connected with it, are intended to form the *Magna Charta* of Hindostan. Whatever the Treaty of Westphalia is to the liberty of the princes and free cities of the Empire, and to the three religions there professed—whatever the Great Charter, the Statute of Tallage, the Petition of Right, and the Declaration of Right are to Great Britain, these bills are to the people of India. Of this benefit I am certain their condition is capable: and when I know that they are capable of more, my vote shall most assuredly be for our giving to the full extent of their capacity of receiving; and no charter of dominion shall stand as a bar in my way to their charter of safety and protection.

The strong admission I have made of the Company's rights (I am conscious of it) binds me to do a great deal. I do not presume to condemn those who argue *a priori* against the propriety of leaving such extensive political powers in the hands of a company of merchants. I know much is, and much more may be, said against such a system. But, with my particular ideas and sentiments, I cannot go that way to work. I feel an insuperable reluctance in giving my hand to destroy any established institution of government, upon a theory, however plausible it may be. My experience in life teaches me nothing clear upon the subject. I have known merchants with the sentiments and the abilities of great statesmen, and I have seen persons in the rank of statesmen with the conceptions and character of peddlers. Indeed, my observation has furnished me with nothing that is to be found in any habits of life or education, which tends wholly to disqualify men for the functions of government, but that by which the power of exercising those functions is very frequently obtained: I mean a spirit and habits of low cabal and intrigue; which I have never, in one instance, seen united with a capacity for sound and manly policy.

To justify us in taking the administration of their affairs out of the hands of the East India Company, on my principles, I must see several conditions. 1st, The object affected by the abuse should be great and important. 2nd, The abuse affecting this great object ought to be a great abuse. 3rd, It ought to be habitual, and not accidental. 4th, It ought to be utterly incurable in the body as it now stands constituted. All this ought to be made as visible to me as the light of the sun, before I should strike off an atom of their charter. A right honorable gentleman has said, and said, I think, but once, and that very slightly, (whatever his original demand for a plan might seem to require,) that "there are abuses in the Company's government." If that were all, the scheme of the mover of this bill, the scheme of his learned friend, and his own scheme of reformation, (if he has any,) are all equally needless. There are, and must be, abuses in all governments. It amounts to no more than a nugatory proposition. But before I consider of what nature these abuses are, of which the gentleman speaks so very lightly, permit me to recall to your recollection the map of the country which this abused chartered right affects. This I shall do, that you may judge whether in that map I can discover anything like the first of my conditions: that is, whether the object affected by the abuse of the East India Company's power be of importance sufficient to justify the measure and means of reform applied to it in this bill.

With very few, and those inconsiderable intervals, the British dominion, either in the Company's name, or in the names of princess absolutely dependent upon the Company, extends from the mountains that separate India from Tartary to Cape Comorin, that is, one-and-twenty degrees of latitude!

In the northern parts it is a solid mass of land, about eight hundred miles in length, and four or five hundred broad. As you go southward, it becomes narrower for a space. It afterwards dilates; but, narrower or broader, you possess the whole eastern and northeastern coast of that vast country, quite from the borders of Pegu.—Bengal, Bahar, and Orissa, with Benares, (now unfortunately in our immediate possession,) measure 161,978 square English miles: a territory considerably larger than the whole kingdom of France. Oude, with its dependent provinces, is 53,286 square miles: not a great deal less than England. The Carnatic, with Tanjore and the Circars, is 65,948 square miles: very considerably larger than England. And the whole of the Company's dominions, comprehending Bombay and Salsette, amounts to 281,412 square miles: which forms a territory larger than any European dominion, Russia and Turkey excepted. Through all that vast extent of country there is not a man who eats a mouthful of rice but by permission of the East India Company.

So far with regard to the extent. The population of this great empire is not easy to be calculated. When the countries of which it is composed came into our possession, they were all eminently peopled, and eminently productive—though at that time considerably declined from their ancient prosperity. But since they are come into our hands!—!However, if we make the period of our estimate immediately before the utter desolation of the Carnatic, and if we allow for the havoc which our government had even then made in these regions, we cannot, in my opinion, rate the population at much less than thirty millions of souls: more than four times the number of persons in the island of Great Britain.

My next inquiry to that of the number is the quality and description of the inhabitants. This multitude of men does not consist of an abject and barbarous populace; much less of gangs of savages, like the Guaranies and Chiquitos, who wander on the waste borders of the River of Amazons or the Plate; but a people for ages civilized and cultivated—cultivated by all the arts of polished life, whilst we were yet in the woods. There have been (and still the skeletons remain) princes once of great dignity, authority, and opulence. There are to be found the chiefs of tribes and nations. There is to be found an ancient and venerable priesthood, the depository of their laws, learning, and history, the guides of the people whilst living and their consolation in death; a nobility of great antiquity and renown; a multitude of cities, not exceeded in population and trade by those of the first class in Europe; merchants and bankers, individual houses of whom have once vied in capital with the Bank of England, whose credit had often supported a tottering state, and preserved their governments in the midst of war and desolation; millions of ingenious manufacturers and mechanics; millions of the most diligent, and not the least intelligent, tillers of the earth. Here are to be found almost all the religions professed by men—the Braminical, the Mussulman, the Eastern and the Western Christian.

If I were to take the whole aggregate of our possessions there, I should compare it, as the nearest parallel I can find, with the Empire of Germany. Our immediate possessions I should compare with the Austrian dominions: and they would not suffer in the comparison. The Nabob of Oude might stand for the King of Prussia; the Nabob of Arcot I would compare, as superior in territory, and equal in revenue, to the Elector of Saxony. Cheit Sing, the Rajah of Benares, might well rank with the Prince of Hesse, at least; and the Rajah of Tanjore (though hardly equal in extent of dominion, superior in revenue) to the Elector of Bavaria. The Polygars and the Northern zemindars, and other great chiefs, might well class with the rest of the princes, dukes, counts, marquises, and bishops in the Empire; all of whom I mention to honor, and surely without disparagement to any or all of those most respectable princes and grandees.

All this vast mass, composed of so many orders and classes of men, is again infinitely diversified by manners, by religion, by hereditary employment, through all their possible combinations. This renders the handling of India a matter in an high degree critical and delicate. But, oh, it has been handled rudely indeed! Even some of the reformers seem to have forgot that they had anything to do but to regulate the tenants of a manor, or the shopkeepers of the next county town.

It is an empire of this extent, of this complicated nature, of this dignity and importance, that I have compared to Germany and the German government—not for an exact resemblance, but as a sort of a middle term, by which India might be approximated to our understandings, and, if possible, to our feelings, in order to awaken something of sympathy for the unfortunate natives, of which I am afraid we are not perfectly susceptible, whilst we look at this very remote object through a false and cloudy medium.

My second condition necessary to justify me in touching the charter is, whether the Company's abuse of their trust with regard to this great object be an abuse of great atrocity. I shall beg your permission to consider their conduct in two lights: first the political, and then the commercial. . . .

These are some of my reasons, grounded on the abuse of the external political trust of that body, for thinking myself not only justified, but bound, to declare against those chartered rights which produce so many wrongs. I should deem myself the wickedest of men, if any vote of mine could contribute to the continuance of so great an evil.

Now, Sir, according to the plan I proposed, I shall take notice of the Company's internal government, as it is exercised first on the dependent provinces, and then as it affects *those* under the direct and immediate authority of that body. And here, Sir, before I enter into the spirit of their interior government, permit me to observe to you upon a few of the many lines of difference which are to be found between the vices of the Company's government and those of the conquerors who preceded us in

India, that we may be enabled a little the better to see our way in an attempt to the necessary reformation.

The several irruptions of Arabs, Tartars, and Persians into India were, for the greater part, ferocious, bloody, and wasteful in the extreme: our entrance into the dominion of that country was, as generally, with small comparative effusion of blood—being introduced by various frauds and delusions, and by taking advantage of the incurable, blind, and senseless animosity which the several country powers bear towards each other, rather than by open force. But the difference in favor of the first conquerors is this. The Asiatic conquerors very soon abated of their ferocity, because they made the conquered country their own. They rose or fell with the rise or fall of the territory they lived in. Fathers there deposited the hopes of their posterity; and children there beheld the monuments of their fathers. Here their lot was finally cast; and it is the natural wish of all that their lot should not be cast in a bad land. Poverty, sterility, and desolation are not a recreating prospect to the eye of man; and there are very few who can bear to grow old among the curses of a whole people. If their passion or their avarice drove the Tartar lords to acts of rapacity or tyranny, there was time enough, even in the short life of man, to bring round the ill effects of an abuse of power upon the power itself. If hoards were made by violence and tyranny, they were still domestic hoards; and domestic profusion, or the rapine of a more powerful and prodigal hand, restored them to the people. With many disorders, and with few political checks upon power, Nature had still fair play; the sources of acquisition were not dried up; and therefore the trade, the manufactures, and the commerce of the country flourished. Even avarice and usury itself operated both for the preservation and the employment of national wealth. The husbandman and manufacturer paid heavy interest, but then they augmented the fund from whence they were again to borrow. Their resources were dearly bought, but they were sure; and the general stock of the community grew by the general effort.

But under the English government all this order is reversed. The Tartar invasion was mischievous; but it is our protection that destroys India. It was their enmity; but it is our friendship. Our conquest there, after twenty years, is as crude as it was the first day. The natives scarcely know what it is to see the gray head of an Englishman. Young men (boys almost) govern there, without society and without sympathy with the natives. They have no more social habits with the people than if they still resided in England—nor, indeed, any species of intercourse, but that which is necessary to making a sudden fortune, with a view to a remote settlement. Animated with all the avarice of age and all the impetuosity of youth, they roll in one after another, wave after wave; and there is nothing before the eyes of the natives but an endless, hopeless prospect of new flights of birds of prey and passage, with appetites continually renewing for a food that is continually wasting. Every rupee of profit made by an Englishman is lost forever to India. With us are no retributory superstitions, by which a foundation of charity compensates, through ages, to the poor, for the rapine and injustice of a day. With us no pride erects stately monuments which repair the mischiefs which pride had produced, and which adorn a country out of its own spoils. England has erected no churches, no hospitals, no palaces, no schools; England has built no bridges, made no highroads, cut no navigations, dug out no reservoirs. Every other conqueror of every other description has left some monument, either of state or beneficence, behind him. Were we to be driven out of India this day, nothing would remain to tell that it had been possessed, during the inglorious period of our dominion, by anything better than the orang-outang or the tiger.

There is nothing in the boys we send to India worse than in the boys whom we are whipping at school, or that we see trailing a pike or bending over a desk at home. But as English youth in India drink the intoxicating draught of authority and dominion before their heads are able to bear it, and as they are full grown in fortune long before they are ripe in principle, neither Nature nor reason have any opportunity to exert themselves for remedy of the excesses of their premature power. The consequences of their conduct, which in good minds (and many of theirs are probably such) might produce penitence or amendment, are unable to pursue the rapidity of their flight. Their prey is lodged in England; and the cries of India are given to seas and winds, to be blown about, in every breaking up of the monsoon, over a remote and unhearing ocean. In India all the vices operate by which sudden fortune is acquired: in England are often displayed, by the same persons, the virtues which dispense hereditary wealth. Arrived in England, the destroyers of the nobility and gentry of a whole kingdom will find the best company in this nation at a board of elegance and hospitality. Here the manufacturer and husbandman will bless the just and punctual hand that in India has torn the cloth from the loom, or wrested the scanty portion of rice and salt from the peasant of Bengal, or wrung from him the very opium in which he forgot his oppressions and his oppressor. They marry into your families; they enter into your senate; they ease your estates by loans; they raise their value by demand; they cherish and protect your relations which lie heavy on your patronage; and there is scarcely an house in the kingdom that does not feel some concern and interest that makes all reform of our Eastern government appear officious and disgusting, and, on the whole, a most discouraging attempt. In such an attempt you hurt those who are able to return kindness or to resent injury. If you succeed, you save those who cannot so much as give you thanks. All these things show the difficulty of the work we have on hand: but they show its necessity, too. Our Indian government is in its best state a grievance. It is necessary that the correctives should be uncommonly vigorous, and the work of men sanguine, warm, and even impassioned in the cause. But it is an arduous thing to plead against abuses of a power which originates from your own country, and affects those whom we are used to consider as strangers.

I shall certainly endeavor to modulate myself to this temper; though I am sensible that a cold style of describing actions, which appear to me in a very affecting light, is equally contrary to the justice due to the people and to all genuine human feelings about them. I ask pardon of truth and Nature for this compliance. But I shall be very sparing of epithets either to persons or things. It has been said, (and, with regard to one of them, with truth,) that Tacitus and Machiavel, by their cold way of relating enormous crimes, have in some sort appeared not to disapprove them; that they seem a sort of professors of the art of tyranny; and that they corrupt the minds of their readers by not expressing the detestation and horror that naturally belong to horrible and detestable proceedings. But we are in general, Sir, so little acquainted with Indian details, the instruments of oppression under which the people suffer are so hard to be understood, and even the very names of the sufferers are so uncouth and strange to our ears, that it is very difficult for our sympathy to fix upon these objects. I am sure that some of us have come down stairs from the committee-room with impressions on our minds which to us were the inevitable results of our discoveries, yet, if we should venture to express ourselves in the proper language of our sentiments to other gentlemen not at all prepared to enter into the cause of them, nothing could appear more harsh and dissonant, more violent and unaccountable, than our language and behavior. All these circumstances are not, I confess, very favorable to the idea of our attempting to govern India at all. But there we are; there we are placed by the Sovereign Disposer; and we must do the best we can in our situation. The situation of man is the preceptor of his duty. . . .

Such an universal proscription, upon any pretence, has few examples. Such a proscription, without even a pretence of delinquency, has none. It stands by itself. It stands as a monument to astonish the imagination, to confound the reason of mankind. I confess to you, when I first came to know this business in its true nature and extent, my surprise did a little suspend my indignation. I was in a manner stupefied by the desperate boldness of a few obscure young men, who, having obtained, by ways which they could not comprehend, a power of which they saw neither the purposes nor the limits, tossed about, subverted, and tore to pieces, as if it were in the gambols of a boyish unluckiness and malice, the most established rights, and the most ancient and most revered institutions, of ages and nations. Sir, I will not now trouble you with any detail with regard to what they have since done with these same lands and landholders, only to inform you that nothing has been suffered to settle for two seasons together upon any basis, and that the levity and inconstancy of these mock legislators were not the least afflicting parts of the oppressions suffered under their usurpation; nor will anything give stability to the property of the natives, but an administration in England at once protecting and stable. The country sustains, almost every year, the miseries of a revolution. . . .

In effect, Sir, every legal, regular authority, in matters of revenue, of political administration, of criminal law, of civil law, in many of the most essential parts of military discipline, is laid level with the ground; and an oppressive, irregular, capricious, unsteady, rapacious, and peculating despotism, with a direct disavowal of obedience to any authority at home, and without any fixed maxim, principle, or rule of proceeding to guide them in India, is at present the state of your charter-government over great kingdoms.

As the Company has made this use of their trust, I should ill discharge mine, if I refused to give my most cheerful vote for the redress of these abuses, by putting the affairs of so large and valuable a part of the interests of this nation and of mankind into some steady hands, possessing the confidence and assured of the support of this House, until they can be restored to regularity, order, and consistency.

I have touched the heads of some of the grievances of the people and the abuses of government. But I hope and trust you will give me credit, when I faithfully assure you that I have not mentioned one fourth part of what has come to my knowledge in your committee; and further, I have full reason to believe that not one fourth part of the abuses are come to my knowledge, by that or by any other means. Pray consider what I have said only as an index to direct you in your inquiries.

If this, then, Sir, has been the use made of the trust of political powers, internal and external, given by you in the charter, the next thing to be seen is the conduct of the Company with regard to the commercial trust. And here I will make a fair offer:—If it can be proved that they have acted wisely, prudently, and frugally, as merchants, I shall pass by the whole mass of their enormities as statesmen. That they have not done this their present condition is proof sufficient. Their distresses are said to be owing to their wars. This is not wholly true. But if it were, is not that readiness to engage in wars, which distinguishes them, and for which the Committee of Secrecy has so branded their politics, founded on the falsest principles of mercantile speculation?

The principle of buying cheap and selling dear is the first, the great foundation of mercantile dealing. Have they ever attended to this principle? Nay, for years have they not actually authorized in their servants a total indifference as to the prices they were to pay?

A great deal of strictness in driving bargains for whatever we contract is another of the principles of mercantile policy. Try the Company by that test. Look at the contracts that are made for them. Is the Company so much as a good commissary to their own armies? I engage to select for you, out of the innumerable mass of their dealings, all conducted very nearly alike, one contract only the excessive profits on which during a short term would pay the whole of their year's dividend. I shall undertake to show that upon two others the inordinate profits given, with the losses incurred in order to secure those profits, would pay a year's dividend more.

It is a third property of trading-men to see that their clerks do not divert the dealings of the master to their own benefit. It was the other day only, when their Governor and Council taxed the Company's investment with a sum of fifty thousand pounds, as an inducement to persuade only seven members of their Board of Trade to give their *honor* that they would abstain from such profits upon that investment, as they must have violated their oaths, if they had made at all.

It is a fourth quality of a merchant to be exact in his accounts. What will be thought, when you have fully before you the mode of accounting made use of in the Treasury of Bengal? I hope you will have it soon. With regard to one of their agencies, when it came to the material part, the prime cost of the goods on which a commission of fifteen per cent was allowed, to the astonishment of the factory to whom the commodities were sent, the Accountant-General reports that he did not think himself authorized to call for *vouchers* relative to this and other particulars—because the agent was upon his honor with regard to them. A new principle of account upon honor seems to be regularly established in their dealings and their treasury, which in reality amounts to an entire annihilation of the principle of all accounts.

It is a fifth property of a merchant, who does not meditate a fraudulent bankruptcy, to calculate his probable profits upon the money he takes up to vest in business. Did the Company, when they bought goods on bonds bearing eight per cent interest, at ten and even twenty per cent discount, even ask themselves a question concerning the possibility of advantage from dealing on these terms?

The last quality of a merchant I shall advert to is the taking care to be properly prepared, in cash or goods in the ordinary course of sale, for the bills which are drawn on them. Now I ask, whether they have ever calculated the clear produce of any given sales, to make them tally with the four million of bills which are come and coming upon them, so as at the proper periods to enable the one to liquidate the other. No, they have not. They are now obliged to borrow money of their own servants to purchase their investment. The servants stipulate five per cent on the capital they advance, if their bills should not be paid at the time when they become due; and the value of the rupee on which they charge this interest is taken at two shillings and a penny. Has the Company ever troubled themselves to inquire whether their sales can bear the payment of that interest, and at that rate of exchange? Have they once considered the dilemma in which they are placed—the ruin of their credit in the East Indies, if they refuse the bills—the ruin of their credit and existence in England, if they accept them?

Indeed, no trace of equitable government is found in their politics, not one trace of commercial principle in their mercantile dealing: and hence is the deepest and maturest wisdom of Parliament demanded, and the best resources of this kingdom must be strained, to restore them—that is, to restore the countries destroyed by the misconduct of the Company, and to restore the Company itself, ruined by the consequences of their plans for destroying what they were bound to preserve.

I required, if you remember, at my outset, a proof that these abuses were habitual. But surely this is not necessary for me to consider as a separate head; because I trust I have made it evident beyond a doubt, in considering the abuses themselves, that they are regular, permanent, and systematical.

I am now come to my last condition, without which, for one, I will never readily lend my hand to the destruction of any established government, which is—that, in its present state, the government of the East India Company is absolutely incorrigible.

Of this great truth I think there can be little doubt, after all that has appeared in this House. It is so very clear, that I must consider the leaving any power in their hands, and the determined resolution to continue and countenance every mode and every degree of peculation, oppression, and tyranny, to be one and the same thing. I look upon that body incorrigible, from the fullest consideration both of their uniform conduct and their present real and virtual constitution.

If they had not constantly been apprised of all the enormities committed in India under their authority, if this state of things had been as much a discovery to them as it was to many of us, we might flatter ourselves that the detection of the abuses would lead to their reformation. I will go further. If the Court of Directors had not uniformly condemned every act which this House or any of its committees had condemned, if the language in which they expressed their disapprobation against enormities and their authors had not been much more vehement and indignant than any ever used in this House, I should entertain some hopes. If they had not, on the other hand, as uniformly commended all their servants who had done their duty and obeyed their orders as they had heavily censured those who rebelled, I might say, These people have been in an error, and when they are sensible of it they will mend. But when I reflect on the uniformity of their support to the objects of their uniform censure, and the state of insignificance and disgrace to which all of those have been reduced whom they approved, and that even utter ruin and premature death have been among the fruits of their favor, I must be convinced, that in this case, as in all others, hypocrisy is the only vice that never can be cured.

Attend, I pray you, to the situation and prosperity of Benfield, Hastings, and others of that sort. The last of these has been treated by the

Company with an asperity of reprehension that has no parallel. They lament "that the power of disposing of their property for perpetuity should fall into such hands." Yet for fourteen years, with little interruption, he has governed all their affairs, of every description, with an absolute sway. He has had himself the means of heaping up immense wealth; and during that whole period, the fortunes of hundreds have depended on his smiles and frowns. He himself tells you he is incumbered with two hundred and fifty young gentlemen, some of them of the best families in England, all of whom aim at returning with vast fortunes to Europe in the prime of life. He has, then, two hundred and fifty of your children as his hostages for your good behavior; and loaded for years, as he has been, with the execrations of the natives, with the censures of the Court of Directors, and struck and blasted with resolutions of this House, he still maintains the most despotic power ever known in India. He domineers with an overbearing sway in the assemblies of his pretended masters; and it is thought in a degree rash to venture to name his offences in this House, even as grounds of a legislative remedy. . . .

Add to this, that, from the highest in place to the lowest, every British subject, who, in obedience to the Company's orders, has been active in the discovery of peculations, has been ruined. They have been driven from India. When they made their appeal at home, they were not heard; when they attempted to return, they were stopped. No artifice of fraud, no violence of power, has been omitted to destroy them in character as well as in fortune. . . .

Speech on the Nabob of Arcot's Debt

An extensive network of Englishmen benefited from the corruption and cruelty of the East India Company's administration of India. Burke singled out two groups—the directors and owners of the Company's stocks; and the officials who governed India on behalf of the Company, the "nabobs," many of whom returned to England with great wealth and became powerful figures in British politics. In this Commons speech of 1785 Burke describes the Company's avaricious and brutal pillage of India.

THAT YOU MAY JUDGE what chance any honourable and useful end of government has for a provision that comes in for the leavings of these gluttonous demands, I must take it on myself to bring before you the real condition of that abused, insulted, racked, and ruined country; though in truth my mind revolts from it; though you will hear it with horror; and I confess I tremble when I think on these awful and confounding dispensations of Providence. I shall first trouble you with a few words as to the cause.

The great fortunes made in India, in the beginnings of conquest, naturally excited an emulation in all the parts, and through the whole succession, of the Company's service. But in the Company it gave rise to other sentiments. They did not find the new channels of acquisition flow with equal riches to them. On the contrary, the high flood-tide of private emolument was generally in the lowest ebb of their affairs. They began also to fear, that the fortune of war might take away what the fortune of war had given. Wars were accordingly discouraged by repeated injunctions and menaces; and that the servants might not be bribed into them by the native princes, they were strictly forbidden to take any money whatsoever from their hands. But vehement passion is ingenious in resources. The Company's servants were not only stimulated, but better instructed by the prohibition. They soon fell upon a contrivance which answered their purposes far better than the methods which were forbidden; though in this also they violated an ancient, but they thought an abrogated, order. They reversed their proceedings. Instead of receiving presents, they made loans. Instead of carrying on wars in their own name, they contrived an authority, at once irresistible and irresponsible, in whose name they might ravage at pleasure; and being thus freed from all restraint, they indulged themselves in the most extravagant speculations of plunder. The cabal of creditors who have been the object of the late bountiful grant from his Majesty's ministers, in order to possess themselves, under the name of creditors and assignees, of every country in India, as fast as it should be conquered, inspired into the mind of the Nabob of Arcot (then a dependent on the Company of the humblest order) a scheme of the most wild and desperate ambition, that I believe ever was admitted into the thoughts of a man so situated. First, they persuaded him to consider himself as a principal member in the political system of Europe. In the next place they held out to him, and he readily imbibed, the idea of the general empire of Indostan. As a preliminary to this undertaking, they prevailed on him to propose a tripartite division of that vast country. One part to the Company; another to the Marattas; and the third to himself. To himself he reserved all the southern part of the great peninsula, comprehended under the general name of the Decan.

On this scheme of their servants, the Company was to appear in the Carnatic in no other light than as a contractor for the provision of armies, and the hire of mercenaries for his use, and under his direction. This disposition was to be secured by the Nabob's putting himself under the guarantee of France, and, by the means of that rival nation, preventing the English for ever from assuming an equality, much less a superiority, in the Carnatic. In pursuance of this treasonable project, (treasonable on the part of the English,) they extinguished the Company as a sovereign power in that part of India; they withdrew the Company's garrisons out of all the forts and strong-holds of the Carnatic; they declined to receive the ambassadors from foreign courts, and remitted them to the Nabob of Arcot; they fell upon, and totally destroyed, the oldest ally of the Company, the king of Tanjore, and plundered the country to the amount of near five millions sterling; one after another, in the Nabob's name, but with English force, they brought into a miserable servitude all the princes, and great independent nobility, of a vast country. In proportion to these treasons and violences, which ruined the people, the fund of the Nabob's debt grew and flourished.

Among the victims to this magnificent plan of universal plunder, worthy of the heroic avarice of the projectors, you have all heard (and he has made himself to be well remembered) of an Indian chief called Hyder Ali Khan. This man possessed the western, as the Company under the name of the Nabob of Arcot does the eastern, division of the Carnatic. It was among the leading measures in the design of this cabal, (according to their own emphatic language,) to *extirpate* this Hyder Ali. They declared the Nabob of Arcot to be his sovereign, and himself to be a rebel, and publicly invested their instrument with the sovereignty of the kingdom of Mysore. But their victim was not of the passive kind. They were soon obliged to conclude a treaty of peace and close alliance with this rebel, at the gates of Madras. Both before and since that treaty, every principle of policy pointed out this power as a natural alliance; and on his part, it was courted by every sort of amicable office. But the cabinet council of English creditors would not suffer their Nabob of Arcot to sign the treaty, nor even to give to a prince, at least his equal, the ordinary titles of respect and courtesy. From that time forward, a continued plot was carried on within the divan, black and white, of the Nabob of Arcot, for the destruction of Hyder Ali. As to the outward members of the double, or rather treble, government of Madras, which had signed the treaty, they were always prevented by some over-ruling influence (which they do not describe, but which cannot be misunderstood) from performing what justice and interest combined so evidently to enforce.

When at length Hyder Ali found that he had to do with men who either would sign no convention, or whom no treaty and no signature could bind, and who were the determined enemies of human intercourse itself, he decreed to make the country possessed by these incorrigible and predestinated criminals a memorable example to mankind. He resolved, in the gloomy recesses of a mind capacious of such things, to leave the whole Carnatic an everlasting monument of vengeance, and to put perpetual desolation as a barrier between him and those, against whom the faith which holds the moral elements of the world together was no protection. He became at length so confident of his force, so collected in his might, that he made no secret whatsoever of his dreadful resolution. Having terminated his disputes with every enemy, and every rival, who buried their mutual animosities in their common detestation against the creditors of the Nabob of Arcot, he drew from every quarter whatever a savage ferocity could add to his new rudiments in the arts of destruction; and compounding all the materials of fury, havoc, and desolation, into one black cloud, he hung for a while on the declivities of the mountains. Whilst the authors of all these evils were idly and stupidly gazing on this menacing meteor, which blackened all their horizon, it suddenly burst, and poured down the whole of its contents upon the plains of the Carnatic.—Then ensued a scene of woe, the like of which no eye had seen, no heart conceived, and which no tongue can adequately tell. All the horrors of war before known or heard of, were mercy to that new havoc. A storm of universal fire blasted every field, consumed every house, destroyed every temple. The miserable inhabitants flying from their flaming villages, in part were slaughtered; others, without regard to sex, to age, to the respect of rank, or sacredness of function, fathers torn from children, husbands from wives, enveloped in a whirlwind of cavalry, and amidst the goading spears of drivers, and the trampling of pursuing horses, were swept into captivity, in an unknown and hostile land. Those who were able to evade this tempest, fled to the walled cities. But escaping from fire, sword, and exile, they fell into the jaws of famine.

The alms of the settlement, in this dreadful exigency, were certainly liberal; and all was done by charity that private charity could do; but it was a people in beggary; it was a nation which stretched out its hands for food. For months together these creatures of sufferance, whose very excess and luxury in their most plenteous days had fallen short of the allowance of our austerest fasts, silent, patient, resigned, without sedition or disturbance, almost without complaint, perished by an hundred a day in the streets of Madras; every day seventy at least laid their bodies in the streets, or on the glacis of Tanjore, and expired of famine in the granary of India. I was going to awake your justice towards this unhappy part of our fellow-citizens, by bringing before you some of the circumstances of this plague of hunger. Of all the calamities which beset and waylay the life of man, this comes the nearest to our heart, and is that wherein the proudest of us all feels himself to be nothing more than he is; but I find myself unable to manage it with decorum; these details are of a species of horror so nauseous and disgusting; they are so degrading to the sufferers and to the hearers; they are so humiliating to human nature itself; that, on better thoughts, I find it more advisable to throw a pall over this hideous object, and to leave it to your general conceptions.

For eighteen months, without intermission, this destruction raged from the gates of Madras to the gates of Tanjore; and so completely did these masters in their art, Hyder Ali and his more ferocious son, absolve themselves of their impious vow, that when the British armies traversed, as they did, the Carnatic for hundreds of miles in all directions, through the whole line of their march they did not see one man, not one woman, not one child, not one four-footed beast of any description whatever. One dead, uniform silence reigned over the whole region. With the inconsiderable exceptions of the narrow vicinage of some few forts, I wish to be understood as speaking literally;—I mean to produce to you more than three witnesses, above all exception, who will support this assertion in its full extent. That hurricane of war passed through every part of the central provinces of the Carnatic. Six or seven districts to the north and to the south (and these not wholly untouched) escaped the general ravage.

The Carnatic is a country not much inferior in extent to England. Figure to yourself, Mr. Speaker, the land in whose representative chair you sit; figure to yourself the form and fashion of your sweet and cheerful country from Thames to Trent north and south, and from the Irish to the German Sea east and west, emptied and embowelled (may God avert the omen of our crimes!) by so accomplished a desolation. Extend your imagination a little farther, and then suppose your ministers taking a survey of this scene of waste and desolation; what would be your thoughts if you should be informed, that they were computing how much had been the amount of the excises, how much the customs, how much the land and malt tax, in order that they should charge (take it in the most favourable light) for public service, upon the relics of the satiated vengeance of relentless enemies, the whole of what England had yielded in the most exuberant seasons of peace and abundance? What would you call it? To call it tyranny sublimed into madness, would be too faint an image; yet this very madness is the principle upon which the ministers at your right hand have proceeded in their estimate of the revenues of the Carnatic, when they were providing, not supply for the establishments of its protection, but, rewards for the authors of its ruin. . . .

What, Sir, would a virtuous and enlightened ministry do on the view of the ruins of such works before them? On the view of such a chasm of desolation as that which yawned in the midst of those countries to the north and south, which still bore some vestiges of cultivation? They would have reduced all their most necessary establishments; they would have suspended the justest payments; they would have employed every shilling derived from the producing, to reanimate the powers of the unproductive, parts. While they were performing this fundamental duty, whilst they were celebrating these mysteries of justice and humanity, they would have told the corps of fictitious creditors, whose crimes were their claims, that they must keep an awful distance; that they must silence their inauspicious tongues; that they must hold off their profane, unhallowed paws from this holy work; they would have proclaimed with a voice that should make itself heard, that on every country the first creditor is the plough; that this original, indefeasible claim supersedes every other demand.

This is what a wise and virtuous ministry would have done and said. This, therefore, is what our minister could never think of saying or doing. A ministry of another kind would have first improved the country, and have thus laid a solid foundation for future opulence and future force. But on this grand point of the restoration of the country, there is not one syllable to be found in the correspondence of our ministers, from the first to the last; they felt nothing for a land desolated by fire, sword, and famine: their sympathies took another direction; they were touched with pity for bribery, so long tormented with a fruitless itching of its palms; their bowels yearned for usury, that had long missed the harvest of its returning months; they felt for peculation which had been for so many years raking in the dust of an empty treasury; they were melted into compassion for rapine and oppression, licking their dry, parched, unbloody jaws. These were the objects of their solicitude. These were the necessities for which they were studious to provide. . . .

But my principal objection lies a good deal deeper. That debt to the Company is the pretext under which all the other debts lurk and cover themselves. That debt forms the foul, putrid mucus, in which are engendered the whole brood of creeping ascarides, all the endless involutions, the eternal knot, added to a knot of those inexpugnable tape-worms, which devour the nutriment, and eat up the bowels of India. It is necessary, Sir, you should recollect two things: First, that the Nabob's debt to the Company carries no interest. In the next place you will observe, that whenever the Company has occasion to borrow, she has always commanded whatever she thought fit at 8 *per cent.* Carrying in your mind these two facts, attend to the process with regard to the public and private debt, and with what little appearance of decency they play into each other's hands a game of utter perdition to the unhappy natives of India. The Nabob falls into an arrear to the Company. The presidency presses for payment. The Nabob's answer is, I have no money. Good. But there are soucars who will supply you on the mortgage of your territories. Then steps forward some Paul Benfield, and, from his grateful compassion to the Nabob, and his filial regard to the Company, he unlocks the treasures of his virtuous industry; and, for a consideration of 24 or 36 *per cent.* on a mortgage of the territorial revenue, becomes security to the Company for the Nabob's arrear. . . .

In consequence of this double game, all the territorial revenues have, at one time or other, been covered by those locusts, the English soucars. Not one single foot of the Carnatic has escaped them; a territory as large as England. During these operations what a scene has that country presented! The usurious European assignee supersedes the Nabob's native farmer of the revenue; the farmer flies to the Nabob's presence to claim his bargain; whilst his servants murmur for wages, and his soldiers mutiny for pay. The mortgage to the European assignee is then resumed, and the native farmer replaced; replaced, again to be removed on the new clamour of the European assignee. Every man of rank and landed fortune being long since extinguished, the remaining miserable last cultivator, who grows to the soil, after having his back scored by the farmer, has it again flayed by the whip of the assignee, and is thus by a ravenous, because a short-lived, succession of claimants, lashed from oppressor to oppressor, whilst a single drop of blood is left as the means of extorting a single grain of corn. Do not think I paint. Far, very far, from it; I do not reach the fact, nor approach to it. Men of respectable condition, men equal to your substantial English yeomen, are daily tied up and scourged to answer the multiplied demands of various contending and contradictory titles, all issuing from one and the same source. Tyrannous exaction brings on servile concealment; and that again calls forth tyrannous coercion. They move in a circle, mutually producing and produced; till at length nothing of humanity is left in the government, no trace of integrity, spirit, or manliness in the people, who drag out a precarious and degraded existence under this system of outrage upon human nature. Such is the effect of the establishment of a debt to the Company, as it has hitherto been managed, and as it ever will remain, until ideas are adopted totally different from those which prevail at this time.

Your worthy ministers, supporting what they are obliged to condemn, have thought fit to renew the Company's old order against contracting private debts in future. They begin by rewarding the violation of the ancient law; and then they gravely re-enact provisions of which they have given bounties for the breach. This inconsistency has been well exposed. But what will you say to their having gone the length of giving positive directions for contracting the debt which they positively forbid?

I will explain myself. They order the Nabob, out of the revenues of the Carnatic, to allot four hundred and eighty thousand pounds a year, as a fund for the debts before us. For the punctual payment of this annuity, they order him to give *soucar* security. When a *soucar*, that is, a money dealer, becomes security for any native prince, the course is, for the native prince to counter-secure the money dealer, by making over to him in mortgage a portion of his territory, equal to the sum annually to be paid, with an interest of at least 24 *per cent.* The point for the House to know is, who are these soucars, to whom this security on the revenues in favour of the Nabob's creditors is to be given? The majority of the House, unaccustomed to these transactions, will hear with astonishment that these soucars are no other than the creditors themselves. The minister, not content with authorizing these transactions in a manner and to an extent unhoped for by the rapacious expectations of usury itself, loads the broken back of the Indian revenues, in favour of his worthy friends the soucars, with an additional 24 *per cent.* for being security to themselves for their own claims; for condescending to take the country in mortgage, to pay to themselves the fruits of their own extortions. . . .

But if I am to speak my private sentiments, I think that in a thousand cases for one it would be far less mischievous to the public, and full as little dishonourable to themselves, to be polluted with direct bribery, than thus to become a standing auxiliary to the oppression, usury, and peculation, of multitudes, in order to obtain a corrupt support to their power. It is by bribing, not so often by being bribed, that wicked politicians bring ruin on mankind. Avarice is a rival to the pursuits of many. It finds a multitude of checks, and many opposers, in every walk of life. But the objects of ambition are for the few; and every person who aims at indirect profit, and therefore wants other protection than innocence and law, instead of its rival becomes its instrument. There is a natural allegiance and fealty due to this domineering, paramount evil, from all the vassal vices, which acknowledge its superiority, and readily militate under its banners; and it is under that discipline alone that avarice is able to spread to any considerable extent, or to render itself a general, public mischief. It is therefore no apology for ministers, that they have not been bought by the East-India delinquents, but that they have only formed an alliance with them for screening each other from justice, according to the exigence of their several necessities. That they have done so is evident; and the junction of the power of office in England with the abuse of authority in the East, has not only prevented even the appearance of redress to the grievances of India, but I wish it may not be found to have dulled, if not extinguished, the honour, the candour, the generosity, the good nature, which used formerly to characterize the people of England. I confess, I wish that some more feeling than I have yet observed for the sufferings of our fellow-creatures and fellow-subjects in that oppressed part of the world, had manifested itself in any one quarter of the kingdom, or in any one large description of men.

That these oppressions exist, is a fact no more denied, than it is resented as it ought to be. Much evil has been done in India under the British authority. What has been done to redress it? We are no longer surprised at anything. We are above the unlearned and vulgar passion of admiration. But it will astonish posterity, when they read our opinions in our actions, that after years of inquiry, we have found out that the sole grievance of India consisted in this, that the servants of the Company there had not profited enough of their opportunities, nor drained it sufficiently of its treasures; when they shall hear that the very first and only important act of a commission specially named by act of parliament is to charge upon an undone country, in favour of a handful of men in the humblest ranks of the public service, the enormous sum of perhaps four millions of sterling money.

It is difficult for the most wise and upright government to correct the abuses of remote, delegated power, productive of unmeasured wealth, and protected by the boldness and strength of the same ill-got riches. These abuses, full of their own wild native vigour, will grow and flourish under mere neglect. But where the supreme authority, not content with winking at the rapacity of its inferior instruments, is so shameless and corrupt as openly to give bounties and premiums for disobedience to its laws, when it will not trust to the activity of avarice in the pursuit of its own gains, when it secures public robbery by all the careful jealousy and attention with which it ought to protect property from such violence, the commonwealth then is become totally perverted from its purposes; neither God nor man will long endure it; nor will it long endure itself. In that case, there is an unnatural infection, a pestilential taint fermenting in the constitution of society, which fever and convulsions of some kind or other must throw off; or in which the vital powers, worsted in an unequal struggle, are pushed back upon themselves, and, by a reversal of their whole functions, fester to gangrene, to death; and, instead of what was but just now the delight and boast of the creation, there will be cast out in the face of the sun, a bloated, putrid, noisome carcass, full of stench and poison, an offence, a horror, a lesson to the world.

In my opinion, we ought not to wait for the fruitless instruction of calamity to inquire into the abuses which bring upon us ruin in the worst of its forms, in the loss of our fame and virtue. . . .

But if the scene on the other side of the globe, which tempts, invites, almost compels, to tyranny and rapine, be not inspected with the eye of a severe and unremitting vigilance, shame and destruction must ensue. For one, the worst event of this day, though it may deject, shall not break or subdue me. The call upon us is authoritative. Let who will shrink back, I shall be found at my post. Baffled, discountenanced, subdued, discredited, as the cause of justice and humanity is, it will be only the dearer to me. Whoever therefore shall at any time bring before you anything towards the relief of our distressed fellow-citizens in India, and towards a subversion of the present most corrupt and oppressive system for its government, in me shall find a weak, I am afraid, but a steady, earnest, and faithful assistant.

Speeches on the Impeachment of Warren Hastings

Burke concluded that one person more than anyone else was responsible for the East India Company's rapacious and unjust rule in India—Warren Hastings, the Company's governor general of Bengal and India from 1772 to 1783. Convinced that the trail of systematic company abuses led to Hastings, Burke drew up formal impeachment charges against him in 1786. The impeachment trial itself, held before the House of Lords, dragged on from February 1788 to June 1794, with Hastings acquitted in 1795. The excerpts here are from trial speeches by Burke in 1788 and 1794.

WITH VERY FEW INTERMISSIONS, the affairs of India have constantly engaged the attention of the Commons for more than fourteen years. We may safely affirm we have tried every mode of legislative provision before we had recourse to anything of penal process. It was in the year 1774 we framed an act of Parliament for remedy to the then existing disorders in India. . . . Finding that the act of Parliament did not answer all the ends that were expected from it, we had, in the year 1782, recourse to a body of monitory resolutions. Neither had we the expected fruit from them. When, therefore, we found that our inquiries and our reports, our laws and our admonitions, were alike despised, that enormities increased in proportion as they were forbidden, detected, and exposed, . . . then it was time for the justice of the nation to recollect itself. To have forborne longer would not have been patience, but collusion. . . .

The crimes with which we charge the prisoner at the bar are substantial crimes, . . . they are no errors or mistakes, such as wise and good men might possibly fall into. . . . We know, as we are to be served by men, that the persons who serve us must be tried as men, and with a very large allowance indeed to human infirmity and human error. . . . But the crimes which we charge in these articles are not lapses, defects, errors of common human frailty, which, as we know and feel, we can allow for. We charge this offender with no crimes that have not arisen from passions which it is criminal to harbor—with no offences that have not their root in avarice, rapacity, pride, insolence, ferocity, treachery, cruelty, malignity of temper—in short, in [with?] nothing that does not argue a total extinction of all moral principle. . . . We urge no crimes that were not crimes of forethought. We charge him with nothing that he did not commit upon deliberation—that he did not commit against advice, supplication, and remonstrance—that he did not commit against the direct command of lawful authority. . . . The crimes of Mr. Hastings are crimes . . . not against forms, but against those eternal laws of justice which are our rule and our birthright. His offences are, not in formal, technical language, but in reality, in substance and effect, *high* crimes and high misdemeanors. . . .

My Lords, we have brought before you the first man of India, in rank, authority, and station. We have brought before you the chief of the tribe, the head of the whole body of Eastern offenders, a captain-general of iniquity, under whom all the fraud, all the peculation, all the tyranny in India are embodied, disciplined, arrayed, and paid. . . . We have brought before you such a person, that, if you strike at him with the firm and decided arm of justice, you will not have need of a great many more examples. You strike at the whole corps, if you strike at the head. . . .

When you consider the late enormous power of the prisoner—when you consider his criminal, indefatigable assiduity in the destruction of all recorded evidence—when you consider the influence he has over almost all living testimony—when you consider the distance of the scene of action—I believe your Lordships, and I believe the world, will be astonished that so much, so clear, so solid, and so conclusive evidence of all kinds has been obtained against him. I have no doubt that in nine instances in ten the evidence is such as would satisfy the narrow precision supposed to prevail, and to a degree rightly to prevail, in all subordinate power and delegated jurisdiction. But your Lordships will maintain, what we assert and claim as the right of the subjects of Great Britain, that you are not bound by any rules of evidence, or any other rules whatever, except those of natural, immutable, and substantial justice. . . .

My Lords, the powers which Mr. Hastings is charged with having abused are the powers delegated to him by the East India Company. The East India Company itself acts under two very dissimilar sorts of powers, derived from two sources very remote from each other. The first source of its power is under charters which the crown of Great Britain was authorized by act of Parliament to grant; the other is from several charters derived from the Emperor of the Moguls, the person in whose dominions they were chiefly conversant—particularly that great charter by which, in the year 1765, they acquired the high-stewardship of the kingdoms of Bengal, Bahar, and Orissa. Under those two bodies of charters, the East India Company, and all their servants, are authorized to act.

As to those of the first description, it is from the British charters that they derive the capacity by which they are considered as a public body, or at all capable of any public function. It is from thence they acquire the capacity to take from any power whatsoever any other charter, to acquire any other offices, or to hold any other possessions. This, being the root and origin of their power, renders them responsible to the party from whom all their immediate and consequential powers are derived. As they have emanated from the supreme power of this kingdom, the whole body and the whole train of their servants, the corporate body as a corporate body, individuals as individuals, are responsible to the high justice of this kingdom. In delegating great power to the East India Company, this kingdom has not released its sovereignty; on the contrary, the responsibility of the Company is increased by the greatness and sacredness of the powers that have been intrusted to it. Attempts have been made abroad to circulate a notion that the acts of the East India Company and their servants are not cognizable here. I hope on this occasion your Lordships will show that this nation never did give a power without annexing to it a proportionable degree of responsibility.

As to their other powers, the Company derives them from the Mogul empire by various charters from that crown . . . By that charter they bound themselves (and bound inclusively all their servants) to perform all the duties belonging to that new office, and to be held by all the ties belonging to that new relation. If the Mogul empire had existed in its vigor, they would have been bound, under that responsibility, to observe the laws, rights, usages, and customs of the natives, and to pursue their benefit in all things: for this duty was inherent in the nature, institution, and purpose of the office which they received. If the power of the sovereign from whom they derived these powers should by any revolution in human affairs be annihilated or suspended, their duty to the people below them, which was created under the Mogul charter, is not annihilated, is not even suspended; and for their responsibility in the performance of that duty, they are thrown back upon that country (thank God, not annihilated) from whence their original power, and all subsequent derivative powers, have flowed. When the Company acquired that high office in India, an English corporation became an integral part of the Mogul empire. When Great Britain virtually assented to that grant of office, and afterwards took advantage of it, Great Britain guarantied the performance of all its duties. Great Britain entered into a virtual act of union with that country, by which we bound ourselves as securities to preserve the people in all the rights, laws, and liberties which their natural, original sovereign was bound to support, if he had been in condition to support them. By the disposition of events, the two duties, flowing from two different sources, are now united in one. The people of India, therefore, come in the name of the Commons of Great Britain, but in their own right, to the bar of this House, before the supreme royal justice of this kingdom, from whence originally all the powers under which they have suffered were derived.

It may be a little necessary, when we are stating the powers the Company have derived from their charter, and which we state Mr. Hastings to have abused, to state in as short and as comprehensive words as I can . . . what the constitution of that Company is—I mean chiefly, what it is in reference to its Indian service, the great theatre of the abuse. . . .

The East India Company had its origin about the latter end of the reign of Elizabeth, a period of projects, when all sorts of commercial adventures, companies, and monopolies were in fashion. At that time the Company was constituted with extensive powers for increasing the commerce and the honor of this country; because increasing its commerce, without increasing its honor and reputation, would have been thought at that time, and will be thought now, a bad bargain for the country. The powers of the Company were, under that charter, merely commercial. By degrees, as the theatre of operation was distant, as its intercourse was with many great, some barbarous, and all of them armed nations, nations in which not only the sovereign, but the subjects, were armed, it was found necessary to enlarge their powers. The first power they obtained was a power of naval discipline in their ships—a power which has been since dropped; the next was a power of law martial; the next was a power of civil, and, to a degree, of criminal jurisdiction, within their own factories, upon their own people and their own servants; the next was (and here was a stride indeed) the power of peace and war. Those high and almost incommunicable prerogatives of sovereignty, which were hardly ever known before to be parted with to any subjects, and which in several states were not wholly intrusted to the prince or head of the commonwealth himself, were given to the East India Company. That Company acquired these powers about the end of the reign of Charles the Second; and they were afterwards more fully, as well as more legally, given by Parliament after the Revolution. From this time, the East India Company was no longer merely a mercantile company, formed for the extension of the British commerce: it more nearly resembled a delegation of the whole power and sovereignty of this kingdom sent into the East. From that time the Company ought to be considered as a subordinate sovereign power: that is, sovereign with regard to the objects which it touched; subordinate with regard to the power from whence its great trust was derived.

Under these successive arrangements things took a course very different from their usual order. A new disposition took place, not dreamt of in the theories of speculative politicians, and of which few examples in the least resembling it have been seen in the modern world, none at all in the ancient. In other instances, a political body that acts as a commonwealth was first settled, and trade followed as a consequence of the protection obtained by political power; but here the course of affairs was reversed. The constitution of the Company began in commerce and ended in empire. Indeed, wherever the sovereign powers of peace and war are given, there wants but time and circumstance to make these powers supersede every other. The affairs of commerce will fall at last into their proper rank and situation. However primary in their original intention, they will become secondary. The possession, therefore, and the power of assertion of these great authorities coinciding with the improved state of Europe, with the improved state of arts in Europe, with the improved state of laws, and, what is much more material, the improved state of military discipline, more and more perfected every day with us—universal improvement in Europe coinciding with the general decay of Asia, (for the proud day of Asia is passed,) this improvement coinciding with the relaxation and dissolution of the Mogul government, with the decline of its warlike spirit, with the total disuse of the ancient strictness of the military discipline established by Tamerlane, the India Company came to be what it is, a great empire, carrying on, subordinately, a great commerce; it became that thing which was supposed by the Roman law irreconcilable to reason and propriety—*eundem negotiatorem et dominum*: the same power became the general trader, the same power became the supreme lord.

In this exalted situation, the India Company, however, still preserves traces of its original mercantile character. The whole exterior order of its political service is carried on upon a mercantile plan and mercantile principles. In fact, the East India Company in Asia is a state in the disguise of a merchant. Its whole service is a system of public offices in the disguise of a counting-house. Accordingly, the whole external order and series of the service, as I observed, is commercial; the principal, the inward, the real, is almost entirely political. . . .

My Lords, we conceive, that, when a British governor is sent abroad, he is sent to pursue the good of the people as much as possible in the spirit of the laws of this country, which in all respects intend their conservation, their happiness, and their prosperity. This is the principle upon which Mr. Hastings was bound to govern, and upon which he is to account for his conduct here. His rule was, what a British governor, intrusted with the power of this country, was bound to do or to forbear. If he has performed and if he has abstained as he ought, dismiss him honorably acquitted from your bar; otherwise condemn him. He may resort to other principles and to other maxims; but this country will force him to be tried by its laws. . . .

And, first, I am to state to your Lordships . . . the principles on which Mr. Hastings declares he has conducted his government—principles which he has avowed, first in several letters written to the East India Company, next in a paper of defence delivered to the House of Commons explicitly, and more explicitly in his defence before your Lordships. Nothing in Mr. Hastings's proceedings is so curious as his several defences; and nothing in the defences is so singular as the principles upon which he proceeds. Your Lordships will have to decide not only upon a large, connected, systematic train of misdemeanors, but an equally connected system of principles and maxims of government, invented to justify those misdemeanors. He has brought them forward and avowed them in the face of day. . . .

My Lords, we contend that Mr. Hastings, as a British governor, ought to govern on British principles, not by British forms—God forbid!—for if ever there was a case in which the letter kills and the spirit gives life, it would be an attempt to introduce British forms and the substance of despotic principles together into any country. No! We call for that spirit of equity, that spirit of justice, that spirit of protection, that spirit of lenity, which ought to characterize every British subject in power. . . .

But he has told your Lordships, in his defence, that actions in Asia do not bear the same moral qualities which the same actions would bear in Europe.

My Lords, we positively deny that principle. I am authorized and called upon to deny it. And having stated at large what he means by saying that the same actions have not the same qualities in Asia and in Europe, we are to let your Lordships know that these gentlemen have formed a plan of *geographical morality*, by which the duties of men, in public and in private situations, are not to be governed by their relation to the great Governor of the Universe, or by their relation to mankind, but by climates, degrees of longitude, parallels, not of life, but of latitudes: as if, when you have crossed the equinoctial, all the virtues die. . . .

This geographical morality we do protest against; Mr. Hastings shall not screen himself under it . . . the laws of morality are the same everywhere, and . . . there is no action which would pass for an act of extortion, of peculation, or bribery, and of oppression in England, that is not an act of extortion, of peculation, of bribery, and oppression in Europe, Asia, Africa, and all the world over. . . .

Mr. Hastings comes before your Lordships not as a British governor answering to a British tribunal, but as a subahdar, as a bashaw of three tails. He says, "I had an arbitrary power to exercise: I exercised it. Slaves I found the people: slaves they are—they are so by their constitution; and if they are, I did not make it for them. I was unfortunately bound to exercise this arbitrary power, and accordingly I did exercise it. It was disagreeable to me, but I did exercise it; and no other power can be exercised in that country." This, if it be true, is a plea in bar. . . .

His plea is, that he did govern there on arbitrary and despotic, and, as he supposes, Oriental principles. And as this plea is boldly avowed and maintained, and as, no doubt, all his conduct was perfectly correspondent to these principles, the principles and the conduct must be tried together. . . .

When in this speculative way he has established, or thinks he has, the vices of the government, he conceives he has found a sufficient apology for his own crimes. . . . He lays it down as a rule, that despotism is the genuine constitution of India, that a disposition to rebellion in the subject or dependent prince is the necessary effect of this despotism, and that jealousy and its consequences naturally arise on the part of the sovereign—that the government is everything, and the subject nothing. . . .

But nothing is more false than that despotism is the constitution of any country in Asia that we are acquainted with. . . . He has declared his opinion, that he is a despotic prince, that he is to use arbitrary power; and of course all his acts are covered with that shield. *"I know,"* says he, *"the constitution of Asia only from its practice."* Will your Lordships submit to hear the corrupt practices of mankind made the principles of government? No! it will be your pride and glory to teach men intrusted with power, that, in their use of it, they are to conform to principles, and not to draw their principles from the corrupt practice of any man whatever. Was there ever heard, or could it be conceived, that a governor would dare to heap up all the evil practices, all the cruelties, oppressions, extortions, corruptions, briberies, of all the ferocious usurpers, desperate robbers, thieves, cheats, and jugglers, that ever had office, from one end of Asia to another, and, consolidating all this mass of the crimes and absurdities of barbarous domination into one code, establish it as the whole duty of an English governor? I believe that till this time so audacious a thing was never attempted by man.

He have arbitrary power! My Lords, the East India Company have not arbitrary power to give him; the king has no arbitrary power to give him; your Lordships have not; nor the Commons, nor the whole legislature. We have no arbitrary power to give, because arbitrary power is a thing which neither any man can hold nor any man can give. No man can lawfully govern himself according to his own will; much less can one person be governed by the will of another. We are all born in subjection—all born equally, high and low, governors and governed, in subjection to one great, immutable, preexistent law, prior to all our devices and prior to all our contrivances, paramount to all our ideas and all our sensations, antecedent to our very existence, by which we are knit and connected in the eternal frame of the universe, out of which we cannot stir.

This great law does not arise from our conventions or compacts; on the contrary, it gives to our conventions and compacts all the force and sanction they can have. It does not arise from our vain institutions. Every good gift is of God; all power is of God; and He who has given the power, and from whom alone it originates, will never suffer the exercise of it to be practised upon any less solid foundation than the power itself. If, then, all dominion of man over man is the effect of the Divine disposition, it is bound by the eternal laws of Him that gave it, with which no human authority can dispense—neither he that exercises it, nor even those who are subject to it; and if they were mad enough to make an express compact that should release their magistrate from his duty, and should declare their lives, liberties, and properties dependent upon, not rules and laws, but his mere capricious will, that covenant would be void. The acceptor of it has not his authority increased, but he has his crime doubled. Therefore can it be imagined, if this be true, that He will suffer this great gift of government, the greatest, the best, that was ever given by God to mankind, to be the plaything and the sport of the feeble will of a man, who, by a blasphemous, absurd, and petulant usurpation, would place his own feeble, contemptible, ridiculous will in the place of the Divine wisdom and justice?

The title of conquest makes no difference at all. No conquest can give such a right; for conquest, that is, force, cannot convert its own injustice into a just title, by which it may rule others at its pleasure. By conquest, which is a more immediate designation of the hand of God, the conqueror succeeds to all the painful duties and subordination to the power of God which belonged to the sovereign whom he has displaced, just as if he had come in by the positive law of some descent or some election. To this at least he is strictly bound: he ought to govern them as he governs his own subjects. . . .

Arbitrary power is not to be had by conquest. Nor can any sovereign have it by succession; for no man can succeed to fraud, rapine, and violence. Neither by compact, covenant, or submission—for men cannot covenant themselves out of their rights and their duties—nor by any other means, can arbitrary power be conveyed to any man. Those who give to others such rights perform acts that are void as they are given—good indeed and valid only as tending to subject themselves, and those who act with them, to the Divine displeasure; because morally there can be no such power. Those who give and those who receive arbitrary power are alike criminal; and there is no man but is bound to resist it to the best of his power, wherever it shall show its face to the world. . . .

Law and arbitrary power are in eternal enmity. Name me a magistrate, and I will name property; name me power, and I will name protection. It is a contradiction in terms, it is blasphemy in religion, it is wickedness in politics, to say that any man can have arbitrary power. In every patent of office the duty is included. For what else does a magistrate exist? To suppose for power is an absurdity in idea. Judges are guided and governed by the eternal laws of justice, to which we are all subject. We may bite our chains, if we will, but we shall be made to know ourselves, and be taught that man is born to be governed by law; and he that will substitute *will* in the place of it is an enemy to GOD.

Despotism does not in the smallest degree abrogate, alter, or lessen any one duty of any one relation of life, or weaken the force or obligation of any one engagement or contract whatsoever. Despotism, if it means anything that is at all defensible, means a mode of government bound by no written rules, and coerced by no controlling magistracies or well-settled orders in the state. But if it has no written law, it neither does nor can cancel the primeval, indefeasible, unalterable law of Nature and of nations; and if no magistracies control its exertions, those exertions must derive their limitation and direction either from the equity and moderation of the ruler, or from downright revolt on the part of the subject by rebellion, divested of all its criminal qualities. The moment a sovereign removes the idea of security and protection from his subjects, and declares that he is everything and they nothing, when he declares that no contract he makes with them can or ought to bind him, he then declares war upon them: he is no longer sovereign; they are no longer subjects.

No man, therefore, has a right to arbitrary power. . . .

Oriental governments know nothing of arbitrary power. I have taken as much pains as I could to examine into the constitutions of them. I have been endeavoring to inform myself at all times on this subject; of late my duty has led me to a more minute inspection of them; and I do challenge the whole race of man to show me any of the Oriental governors claiming to themselves a right to act by arbitrary will.

The greatest part of Asia is under Mahomedan governments. To name a Mahomedan government is to name a government by law. It is a law enforced by stronger sanctions than any law that can bind a Christian sovereign. Their law is believed to be given by God; and it has the double sanction of law and of religion, with which the prince is no more authorized to dispense than any one else. . . .

I must do justice to the East. I assert that their morality is equal to ours, in whatever regards the duties of governors, fathers, and superiors; and I challenge the world to show in any modern European book more true morality and wisdom than is to be found in the writings of Asiatic men in high trust, and who have been counsellors to princes. If this be the true morality of Asia, as I affirm and can prove that it is, the plea founded on Mr. Hastings's geographical morality is annihilated. . . .

That the people of Asia have no laws, rights, or liberty, is a doctrine that wickedly is to be disseminated through this country. But I again assert, every Mahomedan government is, by its principles, a government of law. . . .

Mr. Hastings has no refuge here. Let him run from law to law; let him fly from the common law and the sacred institutions of the country in which he was born; let him fly from acts of Parliament, from which his power originated; let him plead his ignorance of them, or fly in the face of them. Will he fly to the Mahomedan law? That condemns him. . . . Let him fly where he will, from law to law; law, I thank God, meets him everywhere. . . . I would as willingly have him tried by the law of the Koran, or the Institutes of Tamerlane, as on the common law or statute law of this kingdom. . . .

In Asia as well as in Europe the same law of nations prevails, the same principles are continually resorted to, and the same maxims sacredly held and strenuously maintained, and, however disobeyed, no man suffers from the breach of them who does not know how and where to complain of that breach. . . . Asia is enlightened in that respect as well as Europe. . . .

The principles upon which Mr. Hastings governed his conduct in India, and upon which he grounds his defence . . . may all be reduced to one short word—*arbitrary power.* . . . At the time he tells you he acted on the principles of arbitrary power, he takes care to inform you that he was not blind to the consequences. Mr. Hastings foresaw that the consequences of this system was corruption. An arbitrary system, indeed, must always be a corrupt one. My Lords, there never was a man who thought he had no law but his own will, who did not soon find that he had no end but his own profit. Corruption and arbitrary power are of natural unequivocal generation, necessarily producing one another. Mr. Hastings foresees the abusive and corrupt consequences, and then he justifies his conduct upon the necessities of that system. These are things which are new in the world; for there never was a man, I believe, who contended for arbitrary power, . . . that did not pretend, either that the system was good in itself, or that by their conduct they had mitigated or had purified it, and that the poison, by passing through their constitution, had acquired salutary properties. But if you look at his defence before the House of Commons, you will see that that very system upon which he governed, and under which he now justifies his actions, did appear to himself a system pregnant with a thousand evils and a thousand mischiefs. . . .

We say, then, not only that he governed arbitrarily, but corruptly—that is to say, that he was a giver and receiver of bribes, and formed a system for the purpose of giving and receiving them. . . .

In short, money is the beginning, the middle, and the end of every kind of act done by Mr. Hastings: pretendedly for the Company, but really for himself. . . .

It has been said of an ambassador, that he is a person employed to tell lies for the advantage of the court that sends him. His is patriotic bribery, and public-spirited corruption. He is a peculator for the good of his country. It has been said that private vices are public benefits. He goes the full length of that position, and turns his private peculation into a public good. This is what you are to thank him for. You are to consider him as a great inventor upon this occasion. Mr. Hastings improves on this principle. He is a robber in gross, and a thief in detail—he steals, he filches, he plunders, he oppresses, he extorts—all for the good of the dear East India Company—all for the advantage of his honored masters, the Proprietors. . . .

If you sanction this practice, if, after all you have exacted from the people by your taxes and public imposts, you are to let loose your servants upon them, to extort by bribery and peculation what they can from them, for the purpose of applying it to the public service only whenever they please, this shocking consequence will follow from it. If your Governor is discovered in taking a bribe, he will say, "What is that to you? mind your business; I intend it for the public service." The man who dares to accuse him loses the favor of the Governor-General and the India Company. They will say, "The Governor has been doing a meritorious action, extorting bribes for our benefit, and you have the impudence to think of prosecuting him." So that the moment the bribe is detected, it is instantly turned into a merit: and we shall prove that this is the case with Mr. Hastings, whenever a bribe has been discovered. . . .

Fatally for the natives of India, every wild project and every corrupt sale of Mr. Hastings, and those whose example he followed, is covered with a pretended increase of revenue to the Company. Mr. Hastings would not pocket his bribe of 40,000*l.* for himself without letting the Company in as a sharer and accomplice. For the province of Rungpore, the object to which I mean in this instance to confine your attention, 7,000*l.* a year was added. . . .

If Mr. Hastings can forget his covenant, you may easily believe that Debi Sing had not a more correct memory; and accordingly, as soon as he came into the province, he instantly broke every covenant which he had entered into as a restraint on his avarice, rapacity, and tyranny, which, from the highest of the nobility and gentry to the lowest husband-men, were afterwards exercised, with a stern and unrelenting impartiality, upon the whole people. . . .

It was not a rigorous collection of revenue, it was a savage war made upon the country. . . .

It is the nature of tyranny and rapacity never to learn moderation from the ill-success of first oppressions; on the contrary, all oppressors, all men thinking highly of the methods dictated by their nature, attribute the frustration of their desires to the want of sufficient rigor. Then they redouble the efforts of their impotent cruelty, which producing, as they must ever produce, new disappointments, they grow irritated against the objects of their rapacity; and then rage, fury, and malice, implacable because unprovoked, recruiting and reinforcing their avarice, their vices are no longer human. From cruel men they are transformed into savage beasts, with no other vestiges of reason left but what serves to furnish the inventions and refinements of ferocious subtlety, for purposes of which beasts are incapable and at which fiends would blush. . . .

And here, my Lords, began such a scene of cruelties and tortures as I believe no history has ever presented to the indignation of the world—such as I am sure, in the most barbarous ages, no politic tyranny, no fanatic persecution, has ever yet exceeded. . . .

This shocking series of corruption, oppression, fraud, and chicanery . . . lasted for upwards of four years. . . .

I charge all this villainy upon Warren Hastings. . . .

I impeach him in the name of the Commons of Great Britain in Parliament assembled, whose Parliamentary trust he has betrayed.

I impeach him in the name of all the Commons of Great Britain, whose national character he has dishonored.

I impeach him in the name of the people of India, whose laws, rights, and liberties he has subverted, whose properties he has destroyed, whose country he has laid waste and desolate.

I impeach him in the name and by virtue of those eternal laws of justice which he has violated.

I impeach him in the name of human nature itself, which he has cruelly outraged, injured, and oppressed, in both sexes, in every age, rank, situation, and condition of life.

. . . Our liberty is as much in danger as our honor and our national character. We, who here appear representing the Commons of England, are not wild enough not to tremble both for ourselves and for our constituents at the effect of riches. . . . We dread the operation of money. Do we not know that there are many men who wait, and who indeed hardly wait, the event of this prosecution, to let loose all the corrupt wealth of India, acquired by the oppression of that country, for the corruption of all the liberties of this, and to fill the Parliament with men who are now the object of its indignation? To-day the Commons of Great Britain prosecute the delinquents of India: to-morrow the delinquents of India may be the Commons of Great Britain. We know, I say, and feel the force of money; and we now call upon your Lordships for justice in this cause of money. We call upon you for the preservation of our manners, of our virtues. We call upon you for our national character. We call upon you for our liberties; and hope that the freedom of the Commons will be preserved by the justice of the Lords. . . .

. . . The next subject for your Lordships' consideration is the principle of the prisoner's defence. And here we must observe, that, either by confession or conviction, we are possessed of the facts, and perfectly agreed upon the matter at issue between us. In taking a view of the laws by which you are to judge, I shall beg leave to state to you upon what principles of law the House of Commons has criminated him, and upon what principles of law, or pretended law, he justifies himself: for these are the matters at issue between us; the matters of fact, as I have just said, being determined either by confession on his part or by proof on ours.

My Lords, we acknowledge that Mr. Hastings was invested with discretionary power; but we assert that he was bound to use that power according to the established rules of political morality, humanity, and equity. In all questions relating to foreign powers he was bound to act under the Law of Nature and under the Law of Nations, as it is recognized by the wisest authorities in public jurisprudence; in his relation to this country he was bound to act according to the laws and statutes of Great Britain, either in their letter or in their spirit; and we affirm, that in his relation to the people of India he was bound to act according to the largest and most liberal construction of their laws, rights, usages, institutions, and good customs; and we furthermore assert, that he was under an express obligation to yield implicit obedience to the Court of Directors. It is upon these rules and principles the Commons contend that Mr. Hastings ought to have regulated his government; and not only Mr. Hastings, but all other governors. It is upon these rules that he is responsible; and upon these rules, and these rules only, your Lordships are to judge.

My Lords, long before the Committee had resolved upon this impeachment, we had come, as I have told your Lordships, to forty-five resolutions, every one criminatory of this man, every one of them bottomed upon the principles which I have stated. We never will nor can we abandon them; and we therefore do not supplicate your Lordships upon this head, but claim and demand of right, that you will judge him upon those principles, and upon no other. If once they are evaded, you can have no rule for your judgment but your caprices and partialities. . . .

My Lords, the House of Commons has already well considered what may be our future moral and political condition, when the persons who come from that school of pride, insolence, corruption, and tyranny are more intimately mixed up with us of purer morals. Nothing but contamination can be the result, nothing but corruption can exist in this country, unless we expunge this doctrine out of the very hearts and souls of the people. It is not to the gang of plunderers and robbers of which I say this man is at the head, that we are only, or indeed principally, to look. Every man in Great Britain will be contaminated and must be corrupted, if you let loose among us whole legions of men, generation after generation, tainted with these abominable vices, and avowing these detestable principles. It is, therefore, to preserve the integrity and honor of the Commons of Great Britain that we have brought this man to your Lordships' bar. . . .

But, my Lords, we all know that there has been arbitrary power in India—that tyrants have usurped it—and that, in some instances, princes otherwise meritorious have violated the liberties of the people, and have been lawfully deposed for such violation. I do not deny that there are robberies on Hounslow Heath—that there are such things as forgeries, burglaries, and murders; but I say that these acts are against law, and that whoever commit them commit illegal acts. When a man is to defend himself against a charge of crime, it is not instances of similar violation of law that is to be the standard of his defence. A man may as well say, "I robbed upon Hounslow Heath, but hundreds robbed there before me": to which I answer, "The law has forbidden you to rob there; and I will hang you for having violated the law, notwithstanding the long list of similar violations which you have produced as precedents." No doubt princes have violated the law of this country: they have suffered for it. Nobles have violated the law: their privileges have not protected them from punishment. Common people have violated the law: they have been hanged for it. I know no human being exempt from the law. The law is the security of the people of England; it is the security of the people of India; it is the security of every person that is governed, and of every person that governs. There is but one law for all, namely, that law which governs all law, the law of our Creator, the law of humanity, justice, equity—the Law of Nature and of Nations. So far as any laws fortify this primeval law, and give it more precision, more energy, more effect by their declarations, such laws enter into the sanctuary, and participate in the sacredness of its character. But the man who quotes as precedents the abuses of tyrants and robbers pollutes the very fountain of justice, destroys the foundations of all law, and thereby removes the only safeguard against evil men, whether governors or governed—the guard which prevents governors from becoming tyrants, and the governed from becoming rebels. . . .

Wherever existing laws were applicable, the prisoner at your bar was bound by the laws and statutes of this kingdom, as a British subject; and . . . whenever he exercised authority in the name of the Company, or in the name of his Majesty, or under any other name, he was bound by the laws and statutes of this kingdom, both in letter and spirit, so far as they were applicable to him and to his case; and above all, . . . he was bound by the act to which he owed his appointment, in all transactions with foreign powers, to act according to the known recognized rules of the Law of Nations, whether these powers were really or nominally sovereign, whether they were dependent or independent. . . .

On one side, your Lordships have the prisoner declaring that the people have no laws, no rights, no usages, no distinctions of rank, no sense of honor, no property—in short, that they are nothing but a herd of slaves, to be governed by the arbitrary will of a master. On the other side, we assert that the direct contrary of this is true. And to prove our assertion we have referred you to the Institutes of Genghis Khân and of Tamerlane; we have referred you to the Mahometan law, which is binding upon all, from the crowned head to the meanest subject—a law interwoven with a system of the wisest, the most learned, and most enlightened jurisprudence that perhaps ever existed in the world. We have shown you, that, if these parties are to be compared together, it is not the rights of the people which are nothing, but rather the rights of the sovereign which are so. The rights of the people are everything, as they ought to be, in the true and natural order of things. God forbid that these maxims should trench upon sovereignty, and its true, just, and lawful prerogative!—on the contrary, they ought to support and establish them. The sovereign's rights are undoubtedly sacred rights, and ought to be so held in every country in the world, because exercised for the benefit of the people, and in subordination to that great end for which alone God has vested power in any man or any set of men. This is the law that we insist upon, and these are the principles upon which your Lordships are to try the prisoner at your bar. . . .

Your Lordships will find in the evidence before you that the inhabitants of the country were not only harassed in their fortunes, but cruelly treated in their persons. You have it upon Mr. Halhed's evidence, and it is not attempted, that I know of, to be contradicted, that the people were confined in open cages, exposed to the scorching heat of the sun, for pretended or real arrears of rent: it is indifferent which, because I consider all confinement of the person to support an arbitrary exaction to be an abomination not to be tolerated. They have endeavored, indeed, to weaken this evidence by an attempt to prove that a man day and night in confinement in an open cage suffers no inconvenience. And here I must beg your Lordships to observe the extreme unwillingness that appears in these witnesses. Their testimony is drawn from them drop by drop, their answers to our questions are never more than yes or no; but when they are examined by the counsel on the other side, it flows as freely as if drawn from a perennial spring: and such a spring we have in Indian corruption. We have, however, proved that in these cages the renters were confined till they could be lodged in the dungeons or mud forts. We have proved that some of them were obliged to sell their children, that others fled the country, and that these practices were carried to such an awful extent that Colonel Hannay was under the necessity of issuing orders against the unnatural sale and flight which his rapacity had occasioned.

The prisoner's counsel have attempted to prove that this had been a common practice in that country. And though possibly some person as wicked as Colonel Hannay might have been there before at some time or other, no man ever sold his children but under the pressure of some cruel exaction. Nature calls out against it. The love that God has implanted in the heart of parents towards their children is the first germ of that second conjunction which He has ordered to subsist between them and the rest of mankind. It is the first formation and first bond of society. It is stronger than all laws; for it is the law of Nature, which is the law of

God. Never did a man sell his children who was able to maintain them. It is, therefore, not only a proof of his exactions, but a decisive proof that these exactions were intolerable.

Next to the love of parents for their children, the strongest instinct, both natural and moral, that exists in man, is the love of his country: an instinct, indeed, which extends even to the brute creation. All creatures love their offspring; next to that they love their homes: they have a fondness for the place where they have been bred, for the habitations they have dwelt in, for the stalls in which they have been fed, the pastures they have browsed in, and the wilds in which they have roamed. We all know that the natal soil has a sweetness in it beyond the harmony of verse. This instinct, I say, that binds all creatures to their country, never becomes inert in us, nor ever suffers us to want a memory of it. Those, therefore, who seek to fly their country can only wish to fly from oppression: and what other proof can you want of this oppression, when, as a witness has told you, Colonel Hannay was obliged to put bars and guards to confine the inhabitants within the country?

We have seen, therefore, Nature violated in its strongest principles. We have seen unlimited and arbitrary exaction avowed, on no pretence of any law, rule, or any fixed mode by which these people were to be dealt with. All these facts have been proved before your Lordships by costive and unwilling witnesses. In consequence of these violent and cruel oppressions, a general rebellion breaks out in the country, as was naturally to be expected. The inhabitants rise as if by common consent; every farmer, every proprietor of land, every man who loved his family and his country, and had not fled for refuge, rose in rebellion, as they call it. My Lords, they did rebel; it was a just rebellion. Insurrection was there just and legal, inasmuch as Colonel Hannay, in defiance of the laws and rights of the people, exercised a clandestine, illegal authority, against which there can be no rebellion in its proper sense. . . .

My Lords, when we have shown plainly the utter extinction of the native Mahometan government, when we have shown the extinction of the native landed interest, what hope can there be for that afflicted country but in the servants of the Company? When we have shown the corrupt state of that service, what hope but from the Court of Directors, what hope but in the superintending control of British tribunals? I think as well of the body of my countrymen as any man can do. I do not think that any man sent out to India is sent with an ill purpose, or goes out with bad dispositions. No: I think the young men who go there are fair and faithful representatives of the people of the same age—uncorrupted, but corruptible from their age, as we all are. They are sent there young. There is but one thing held out to them—"You are going to make your fortune." The Company's service is to be the restoration of decayed noble families; it is to be the renovation of old, and the making of new ones. . . .

PART VI

THE FRENCH REVOLUTION

Speech on the Army Estimates

Burke's dramatic break with his Whig colleagues over the French Revolution occurred in February 1790 in a parliamentary debate about funding for the army. Charles James Fox announced that he "exulted" in the Revolution "from feelings and from principle." Burke, on the other hand, offered a thunderous rebuke to the revolutionaries who sought "to break all those connections, natural and civil, that regulate and hold together the community by a chain of subordination."

IN A POLITICAL VIEW, France was low indeed. She had lost everything, even to her name. . . . He was astonished at it—he was alarmed at it—he trembled at the uncertainty of all human greatness.

Since the House had been prorogued in the summer much work was done in France. The French had shown themselves the ablest architects of ruin that had hitherto existed in the world. In that very short space of time they had completely pulled down to the ground their monarchy, their church, their nobility, their law, their revenue, their army, their navy, their commerce, their arts, and their manufactures. They had done their business for us as rivals, in a way in which twenty Ramillies or Blenheims could never have done it. Were we absolute conquerors, and France to lie prostrate at our feet, we should be ashamed to send a commission to settle their affairs, which could impose so hard a law upon the French, and so destructive of all their consequence as a nation, as that they had imposed on themselves.

France, by the mere circumstance of its vicinity, had been, and in degree always must be, an object of our vigilance, either with regard to her actual power, or to her influence and example. As to the former, he had spoken; as to the latter, (her example,) he should say a few words: for by this example our friendship and our intercourse with that nation had once been, and might again become, more dangerous to us than their worst hostility.

In the last century, Louis the Fourteenth had established a greater and better disciplined military force than ever had been before seen in Europe, and with it a perfect despotism. Though that despotism was proudly arrayed in manners, gallantry, splendour, magnificence, and even covered over with the imposing robes of science, literature, and arts, it was, in government, nothing better than a painted and gilded tyranny; in religion, a hard, stern intolerance, the fit companion and auxiliary to the despotic tyranny which prevailed in its government. The same character of despotism insinuated itself into every court of Europe—the same spirit of disproportioned magnificence—the same love of standing armies, above the ability of the people. In particular, our then sovereigns, King Charles and King James, fell in love with the government of their neighbour, so flattering to the pride of kings. A similarity of sentiments brought on connexions equally dangerous to the interests and liberties of their country. It were well that the infection had gone no further than the throne. The admiration of a government flourishing and successful, unchecked in its operations, and seeming therefore to compass its objects more speedily and effectually, gained something upon all ranks of people. The good patriots of that day, however, struggled against it. They sought nothing more anxiously than to break off all communication with France, and to beget a total alienation from its councils and its example; which, by the animosity prevalent between the abettors of their religious system and the assertors of ours, was in some degree effected.

This day the evil is totally changed in France: but there is an evil there. The disease is altered; but the vicinity of the two countries remains, and must remain; and the natural mental habits of mankind are such, that the present distemper of France is far more likely to be contagious than the old one; for it is not quite easy to spread a passion for servitude among the people; but in all evils of the opposite kind our natural inclinations are flattered. In the case of despotism there is the *fœdum crimen servitutis*; in the last the *falsa* species *libertatis*; and accordingly, as the historian says, *pronis auribus accipitur.*

In the last age we were in danger of being entangled by the example of France in the net of a relentless despotism. It is not necessary to say anything upon that example. It exists no longer. Our present danger from the example of a people, whose character knows no medium, is, with regard to government, a danger from anarchy; a danger of being led, through an admiration of successful fraud and violence, to an imitation of the excesses of an irrational, unprincipled, proscribing, confiscating, plundering, ferocious, bloody, and tyrannical democracy. On the side of religion, the danger of their example is no longer from intolerance, but from atheism; a foul, unnatural vice, foe to all the dignity and consolation of mankind; which seems in France, for a long time, to have been embodied into a faction, accredited, and almost avowed.

These are our present dangers from France; but, in his opinion, the very worst part of the example set, is in the late assumption of citizenship by the army, and the whole of the arrangement, or rather disarrangement, of their military.

He was sorry that his right honourable friend (Mr. Fox) had dropped even a word expressive of exultation on that circumstance; or that he seemed of opinion that the objection from standing armies was at all lessened by it. He attributed this opinion of Mr. Fox entirely to his known zeal for the best of all causes, Liberty. That it was with a pain inexpressible he was obliged to have even the shadow of a difference with his friend, whose authority would always be great with him, and with all thinking people—*Quæ maxima semper censetur nobis, et* erit *quæ maxima semper.*—His confidence in Mr. Fox was such, and so ample, as to be almost implicit. That he was not ashamed to avow that degree of docility. That when the choice is well made, it strengthens instead of oppressing our intellect. That he who calls in the aid of an equal understanding doubles his own. He who profits of a superior understanding raises his powers to a level with the height of the superior understanding he unites with. He had found the benefit of such a junction, and would not lightly depart from it. He wished almost, on all occasions, that his sentiments were understood to be conveyed in Mr. Fox's words; and he wished, as amongst the greatest benefits he could wish the country, an eminent share of power to that right honourable gentleman; because he knew, that, to his great and masterly understanding, he had joined the greatest possible degree of that natural moderation, which is the best corrective of power; that he was of the most artless, candid, open, and benevolent disposition; disinterested in the extreme; of a temper mild and placable even to a fault; without one drop of gall in his whole constitution.

That the House must perceive, from his coming forward to mark an expression or two of his best friend, how anxious he was to keep the distemper of France from the least countenance in England, where he was sure some wicked persons had shown a strong disposition to recommend an imitation of the French spirit of reform. He was so strongly opposed to any the least tendency towards the *means* of introducing a democracy like theirs, as well as to the *end* itself, that much as it would afflict him, if such thing could be attempted, and that any friend of his could concur in such measures, (he was far, very far, from believing they could,) he would abandon his best friends, and join with his worst enemies to oppose either the means or the end; and to resist all violent exertions of the spirit of innovation, so distant from all principles of true and safe reformation;

a spirit well calculated to overturn states, but perfectly unfit to amend them.

That he was no enemy to reformation. Almost every business in which he was much concerned, from the first day he sat in that House to that hour, was a business of reformation; and when he had not been employed in correcting, he had been employed in resisting, abuses. Some traces of this spirit in him now stand on their statute book. In his opinion, anything which unnecessarily tore to pieces the contexture of the state, not only prevented all real reformation, but introduced evils which would call, but perhaps call in vain, for new reformation.

That he thought the French nation very unwise. What they valued themselves on, was a disgrace to them. They had gloried (and some people in England had thought fit to take share in that glory) in making a revolution; as if revolutions were good things in themselves. All the horrors, and all the crimes, of the anarchy which led to their revolution, which attend its progress, and which may virtually attend it in its establishment, pass for nothing with the lovers of revolutions. The French have made their way, through the destruction of their country, to a bad constitution, when they were absolutely in possession of a good one. They were in possession of it the day the states met in separate orders. Their business, had they been either virtuous or wise, or had they been left to their own judgment, was to secure the stability and independence of the states, according to those orders, under the monarch on the throne. It was then their duty to redress grievances.

Instead of redressing grievances, and improving the fabric of their state, to which they were called by their monarch, and sent by their country, they were made to take a very different course. They first destroyed all the balances and counterpoises which serve to fix the state, and to give it a steady direction; and which furnish sure correctives to any violent spirit which may prevail in any of the orders. These balances existed in their oldest constitution; and in the constitution of this country; and in the constitution of all the countries in Europe. These they rashly destroyed, and then they melted down the whole into one incongruous, ill-connected mass.

When they had done this, they instantly, and with the most atrocious perfidy and breach of all faith among men laid the axe to the root of all property, and consequently of all national prosperity, by the principles they established, and the example they set, in confiscating all the possessions of the church. They made and recorded a sort of *institute* and *digest* of anarchy, called the rights of man, in such a pedantic abuse of elementary principles as would have disgraced boys at school; but this declaration of rights was worse than trifling and pedantic in them; as by their name and authority they systematically destroyed every hold of authority by opinion, religious or civil, on the minds of the people. By this mad declaration they subverted the state; and brought on such calamities as no country, without a long war, has ever been known to suffer; and which may in the end produce such a war, and perhaps, many such.

With them the question was not between despotism and liberty. The sacrifice they made of the peace and power of their country was not made on the altar of freedom. Freedom, and a better security for freedom than that they have taken, they might have had without any sacrifice at all. They brought themselves into all the calamities they suffer, not that through them they might obtain a British constitution; they plunged themselves headlong into those calamities, to prevent themselves from settling into that constitution, or into anything resembling it.

That if they should perfectly succeed in what they propose, as they are likely enough to do, and establish a democracy, or a mob of democracies, in a country circumstanced like France, they will establish a very bad government—a very bad species of tyranny.

That the worst effect of all their proceeding was on their military, which was rendered an army for every purpose but that of defence. That if the question was, whether soldiers were to forget they were citizens, as an abstract proposition, he could have no difference about it; though, as it is usual when abstract principles are to be applied, much was to be thought on the manner of uniting the character of citizen and soldier. But as applied to the events which had happened in France, where the abstract principle was clothed with its circumstances, he thought that his friend would agree with him, that what was done there furnished no matter of exultation, either in the act or the example. These soldiers were not citizens; but base hireling mutineers, and mercenary sordid deserters, wholly destitute of any honourable principle. Their conduct was one of the fruits of that anarchic spirit, from the evils of which a democracy itself was to be resorted to, by those who were the least disposed to that form, as a sort of refuge. It was not an army in corps and with discipline, and embodied under the respectable patriot citizens of the state in resisting tyranny. Nothing like it. It was the case of common soldiers deserting from their officers, to join a furious, licentious populace. It was a desertion to a cause, the real object of which was to level all those institutions, and to break all those connexions, natural and civil, that regulate and hold together the community by a chain of subordination; to raise soldiers against their officers; servants against their masters; tradesmen against their customers; artificers against their employers; tenants against their landlords; curates against their bishops; and children against their parents. That this cause of theirs was not an enemy to servitude, but to society.

He wished the House to consider, how the members would like to have their mansions pulled down and pillaged, their persons abused, insulted, and destroyed; their title deeds brought out and burned before their faces, and themselves and their families driven to seek refuge in every nation throughout Europe, for no other reason than this, that, without any fault of theirs, they were born gentlemen and men of property, and were suspected of a desire to preserve their consideration and their estates. The desertion in France was to aid an abominable sedition, the very professed principle of which was an implacable hostility to nobility and gentry, and whose savage war-whoop was "*à l'Aristocrate*," by which senseless, bloody cry, they animated one another to rapine and murder; whilst abetted by ambitious men of another class, they were crushing everything respectable and virtuous in their nation, and to their power disgracing almost every name, by which we formerly knew there was such a country in the world as France. . . .

He felt some concern that this strange thing, called a Revolution in France, should be compared with the glorious event commonly called the Revolution in England; and the conduct of the soldiery, on that occasion, compared with the behaviour of some of the troops of France in the present instance. At that period the Prince of Orange, a prince of the blood-royal in England, was called in by the flower of the English aristocracy to defend its ancient constitution, and not to level all distinctions. To this prince, so invited, the aristocratic leaders who commanded the troops went over with their several corps, in bodies, to the deliverer of their country. Aristocratic leaders brought up the corps of citizens who newly enlisted in this cause. Military obedience changed its object; but military discipline was not for a moment interrupted in its principle. The troops were ready for war, but indisposed to mutiny.

But as the conduct of the English armies was different, so was that of the whole English nation at that time. In truth, the circumstances of our revolution (as it is called) and that of France are just the reverse of each other in almost every particular, and in the whole spirit of the transaction. With us it was the case of a legal monarch attempting arbitrary power—in France it is the case of an arbitrary monarch, beginning, from whatever cause, to legalize his authority. The one was to be resisted, the other was to be managed and directed; but in neither case was the order of the state to be changed, lest government might be ruined, which ought only to be corrected and legalized. With us we got rid of the man, and preserved the constituent parts of the state. There they get rid of the constituent parts of the state, and keep the man. What we did was in truth and substance, and in a constitutional light, a revolution, not made, but prevented. We took solid securities; we settled doubtful questions; we corrected anomalies in our law. In the stable, fundamental parts of our constitution we made no revolution; no, nor any alteration at all. We did not impair the monarchy. Perhaps it might be shown that we strengthened it very considerably. The nation kept the same ranks, the same orders, the same privileges, the same franchises, the same rules for property, the same subordinations, the same order in the law, in the revenue, and in the magistracy; the same Lords, the same Commons, the same corporations, the same electors.

The church was not impaired. Her estates, her majesty, her splendour, her orders and gradations, continued the same. She was preserved in her full efficiency, and cleared only of a certain intolerance, which was her weakness and disgrace. The church and the state were the same after the Revolution that they were before, but better secured in every part.

Was little done because a revolution was not made in the constitution? No! Everything was done; because we commenced with reparation, not with ruin. Accordingly the state flourished. Instead of lying as dead, in a sort of trance, or exposed, as some others, in an epileptic fit, to the pity or derision of the world, for her wild, ridiculous, convulsive movements, impotent to every purpose but that of dashing out her brains against the pavement, Great Britain rose above the standard even of her former self. An æra of a more improved domestic prosperity then commenced, and still continues not only unimpaired, but growing, under the wasting hand of time. All the energies of the country were awakened. England never presented a firmer countenance, nor a more vigorous arm, to all her enemies and to all her rivals. Europe under her respired and revived. Everywhere she appeared as the protector, assertor, or avenger, of liberty. A war was made and supported against fortune itself.

The treaty of Ryswick, which first limited the power of France, was soon after made: the grand alliance very shortly followed, which shook to the foundations the dreadful power which menaced the independence of mankind. The states of Europe lay happy under the shade of a great and free monarchy, which knew how to be great without endangering its own peace at home, or the internal or external peace of any of its neighbours.

Mr. Burke said he should have felt very unpleasantly if he had not delivered these sentiments. He was near the end of his natural, probably still nearer the end of his political, career; that he was weak and weary; and wished for rest. That he was little disposed to controversies, or what is called a detailed opposition. That at his time of life, if he could not do something by some sort of weight of opinion, natural or acquired, it was useless and indecorous to attempt anything by mere struggle. *Turpe senex miles.* That he had for that reason little attended the army business, or that of the revenue, or almost any other matter of detail, for some years past. That he had, however, his task. He was far from condemning such opposition; on the contrary, he mostly highly applauded it, where a just occasion existed for it, and gentlemen had vigour and capacity to pursue it. Where a great occasion occurred, he was, and, while he continued in parliament, would be, amongst the most active and the most earnest: as he hoped he had shown on a late event. With respect to the constitution itself, he wished few alterations in it. Happy if he left it not the worse for any share he had taken in its service.

Reflections on the Revolution in France

Burke's most important work, and the sacred text for his conservative disciples, was published in November 1790. It began as a rebuttal to the praise heaped on the French Revolution by the dissenting minister Richard Price. In a sermon given in November 1789, Price had argued that the French Revolution further developed the principles of the English Revolution of 1688. Not so for Burke, for whom the French Revolution was a uniquely malevolent event which signaled that "the age of chivalry is gone, that of sophisters, economists, and calculators has succeeded, and the glory of Europe is extinguished forever."

YOU IMAGINED, when you wrote last, that I might possibly be reckoned among the approvers of certain proceedings in France, from the solemn public seal of sanction they have received from two clubs of gentlemen in London, called the Constitutional Society, and the Revolution Society.

I certainly have the honor to belong to more clubs than one in which the Constitution of this kingdom and the principles of the glorious Revolution are held in high reverence; and I reckon myself among the most forward in my zeal for maintaining that Constitution and those principles in their utmost purity and vigor. It is because I do so that I think it necessary for me that there should be no mistake. Those who cultivate the memory of our Revolution, and those who are attached to the Constitution of this kingdom, will take good care how they are involved with persons who, under the pretext of zeal towards the Revolution and Constitution, too frequently wander from their true principles, and are ready on every occasion to depart from the firm, but cautious and deliberate, spirit which produced the one and which presides in the other. . . .

I flatter myself that I love a manly, moral, regulated liberty as well as any gentlemen. . . . But I cannot stand forward, and give praise or blame to anything which relates to human actions and human concerns on a simple view of the object, as it stands stripped of every relation, in all the nakedness and solitude of metaphysical abstraction. Circumstances (which with some gentlemen pass for nothing) give in reality to every political principle its distinguishing color and discriminating effect. The circumstances are what render every civil and political scheme beneficial or noxious to mankind. Abstractedly speaking, government, as well as liberty, is good; yet could I, in common sense, ten years ago, have felicitated France on her enjoyment of a government, (for she then had a government,) without inquiry what the nature of that government was, or how it was administered? Can I now congratulate the same nation upon its freedom? Is it because liberty in the abstract may be classed amongst the blessings of mankind, that I am seriously to felicitate a madman who has escaped from the protecting restraint and wholesome darkness of his cell on his restoration to the enjoyment of light and liberty? Am I to congratulate a highwayman and murderer who has broke prison upon the recovery of his natural rights? . . .

When I see the spirit of liberty in action, I see a strong principle at work; and this, for a while, is all I can possibly know of it. The wild gas, the fixed air, is plainly broke loose: but we ought to suspend our judgment until the first effervescence is a little subsided, till the liquor is cleared, and until we see something deeper than the agitation of a troubled and frothy surface. I must be tolerably sure, before I venture publicly to congratulate men upon a blessing, that they have really received one. Flattery corrupts both the receiver and the giver; and adulation is not of more service to the people than to kings. I should therefore suspend my congratulations on the new liberty of France, until I was informed how it had been combined with government, with public force, with the discipline and obedience of armies, with the collection of an effective and well-distributed revenue, with morality and religion, with solidity and property, with peace and order, with civil and social manners. All these (in their way) are good things, too; and without them, liberty is not a benefit whilst it lasts, and is not likely to continue long. The effect of liberty to individuals is, that they may do what they please: we ought to see what it will please them to do, before we risk congratulations, which may be soon turned into complaints. Prudence would dictate this in the case of separate, insulated, private men. But liberty, when men act in bodies, is *power.* Considerate people, before they declare themselves, will observe the use which is made of *power*—and particularly of so trying a thing as *new* power in *new* persons, of whose principles, tempers, and dispositions they have little or no experience, and in situations where those who appear the most stirring in the scene may possibly not be the real movers. . . .

All circumstances taken together, the French Revolution is the most astonishing that has hitherto happened in the world. The most wonderful things are brought about in many instances by means the most absurd and ridiculous, in the most ridiculous modes, and apparently by the most contemptible instruments. Everything seems out of nature in this strange chaos of levity and ferocity, and of all sorts of crimes jumbled together with all sorts of follies. In viewing this monstrous tragi-comic scene, the most opposite passions necessarily succeed and sometimes mix with each other in the mind: alternate contempt and indignation, alternate laughter and tears, alternate scorn and horror.

It cannot, however, be denied that to some this strange scene appeared in quite another point of view. Into them it inspired no other sentiments than those of exultation and rapture. They saw nothing in what has been done in France but a firm and temperate exertion of freedom—so consistent, on the whole, with morals and with piety as to make it deserving not only of the secular applause of dashing Machiavelian politicians, but to render it a fit theme for all the devout effusions of sacred eloquence.

On the forenoon of the fourth of November last, Doctor Richard Price, a Non-Conforming minister of eminence, preached at the Dissenting meeting-house of the Old Jewry, to his club or society, a very extraordinary miscellaneous sermon, in which there are some good moral and religious sentiments, and not ill expressed, mixed up with a sort of porridge of various political opinions and reflections: but the Revolution in France is the grand ingredient in the caldron. . . .

I looked on that sermon as the public declaration of a man much connected with literary caballers and intriguing philosophers, with political theologians and theological politicians, both at home and abroad. I know they set him up as a sort of oracle; because, with the best intentions in the world, he naturally *philippizes*, and chants his prophetic song in exact unison with their designs.

That sermon is in a strain which I believe has not been heard in this kingdom, in any of the pulpits which are tolerated or encouraged in it, since the year 1648—when a predecessor of Dr. Price, the Reverend Hugh Peters, made the vault of the king's own chapel at St. James's ring with the honor and privilege of the saints, who, with the "high praises of God in their mouths, and a *two*-edged sword in their hands, were to execute judgment on the heathen, and punishments upon the *people*; to bind their *kings* with chains, and their *nobles* with fetters of iron." Few harangues from the pulpit, except in the days of your League in France, or in the days of our Solemn League and Covenant in England, have ever breathed less of the spirit of moderation than this lecture in the Old Jewry. . . .

This pulpit style, revived after so long a discontinuance, had to me the air of novelty, and of a novelty not wholly without danger. . . . If the noble *Seekers* should find nothing to satisfy their pious fancies in the old staple of the national Church, or in all the rich variety to be found in the well-assorted warehouses of the Dissenting congregations, Dr. Price advises them to improve upon Non-Conformity, and to set up, each of them, a separate meeting-house upon his own particular principles. It is somewhat remarkable that this reverend divine should be so earnest for setting up new churches, and so perfectly indifferent concerning the doctrine which may be taught in them. His zeal is of a curious character. It is not for the propagation of his own opinions, but of any opinions. It is not for the diffusion of truth, but for the spreading of contradiction. Let the noble teachers but dissent, it is no matter from whom or from what. This great point once secured, it is taken for granted their religion will be rational and manly. . . .

His doctrines affect our Constitution in its vital parts. He tells the Revolution Society, in this political sermon, that his Majesty "is almost the *only* lawful king in the world, because the *only* one who owes his crown to *the choice of his people*." As to the kings of *the world*, all of whom (except one) this arch-pontiff of the *rights of men*, with all the plenitude and with more than the boldness of the Papal deposing power in its meridian fervor of the twelfth century, puts into one sweeping clause of ban and anathema, and proclaims usurpers by circles of longitude and latitude over the whole globe, it behooves them to consider how they admit into their territories these apostolic missionaries, who are to tell their subjects they are not lawful kings. That is their concern. It is ours, as a domestic interest of some moment, seriously to consider the solidity of the *only* principle upon which these gentlemen acknowledge a king of Great Britain to be entitled to their allegiance.

This doctrine, as applied to the prince now on the British throne, either is nonsense, and therefore neither true nor false, or it affirms a most unfounded, dangerous, illegal, and unconstitutional position. According to this spiritual doctor of politics, if his Majesty does not owe his crown to the choice of his people, he is no *lawful* king. Now nothing can be more untrue than that the crown of this kingdom is so held by his Majesty. Therefore, if you follow their rule, the king of Great Britain, who most certainly does not owe his high office to any form of popular election, is in no respect better than the rest of the gang of usurpers, who reign, or rather rob, all over the face of this our miserable world, without any sort of right or title to the allegiance of their people. The policy of this general doctrine, so qualified, is evident enough. The propagators of this political gospel are in hopes their abstract principle (their principle that a popular choice is necessary to the legal existence of the sovereign magistracy) would be overlooked, whilst the king of Great Britain was not affected by it. In the mean time the ears of their congregations would be gradually habituated to it, as if it were a first principle admitted without dispute. For the present it would only operate as a theory, pickled in the preserving juices of pulpit eloquence, and laid by for future use. . . . By this policy, whilst our government is soothed with a reservation in its favor, to which it has no claim, the security which it has in common with all governments, so far as opinion is security, is taken away. . . .

At some time or other, to be sure, all the beginners of dynasties were chosen by those who called them to govern. There is ground enough for the opinion that all the kingdoms of Europe were at a remote period elective, with more or fewer limitations in the objects of choice. But whatever kings might have been here or elsewhere a thousand years ago, or in whatever manner the ruling dynasties of England or France may have begun, the king of Great Britain is at this day king by a fixed rule of succession, according to the laws of his country; and whilst the legal conditions of the compact of sovereignty are performed by him, (as they are performed,) he holds his crown in contempt of the choice of the Revolution Society, who have not a single vote for a king amongst them, either individually or collectively. . . .

These gentlemen of the Old Jewry, in all their reasonings on the Revolution of 1688, have a revolution which happened in England about forty years before, and the late French Revolution, so much before their eyes and in their hearts, that they are constantly confounding all the three together. It is necessary that we should separate what they confound. We must recall their erring fancies to the *acts* of the Revolution which we revere, for the discovery of its true *principles.* If the *principles* of the Revolution of 1688 are anywhere to be found, it is in the statute called the *Declaration of Right.* . . .

This Declaration of Right . . . is the corner-stone of our Constitution, as reinforced, explained, improved, and in its fundamental principles forever settled. It is called "An act for declaring the rights and liberties of the subject, and for *settling* the *succession* of the crown." You will observe that these rights and this succession are declared in one body, and bound indissolubly together.

A few years after this period, a second opportunity offered for asserting a right of election to the crown. On the prospect of a total failure of issue from King William, and from the princess, afterwards Queen Anne, the consideration of the settlement of the crown, and of a further security for the liberties of the people, again came before the legislature. Did they this second time make any provision for legalizing the crown on the spurious Revolution principles of the Old Jewry? No. They followed the principles which prevailed in the Declaration of Right. . . .

Unquestionably there was at the Revolution, in the person of King William, a small and a temporary deviation from the strict order of a regular hereditary succession; but it is against all genuine principles of jurisprudence to draw a principle from a law made in a special case and regarding an individual person. . . . If ever there was a time favorable for establishing the principle that a king of popular choice was the only legal king, without all doubt it was at the Revolution. Its not being done at that time is a proof that the nation was of opinion it ought not to be done at any time. . . .

In the very act in which, for a time, and in a single case, Parliament departed from the strict order of inheritance, in favor of a prince who, though not next, was, however, very near in the line of succession, it is curious to observe how Lord Somers, who drew the bill called the Declaration of Right, has comported himself on that delicate occasion. It is curious to observe with what address this temporary solution of continuity is kept from the eye; whilst all that could be found in this act of necessity to countenance the idea of an hereditary succession is brought forward, and fostered, and made the most of, by this great man, and by the legislature who followed him. Quitting the dry, imperative style of an act of Parliament, he makes the Lords and Commons fall to a pious legislative ejaculation, and declare that they consider it "as a marvellous providence, and merciful goodness of God to this nation, to preserve their said Majesties' *royal* persons most happily to reign over us *on the throne of their ancestors*, for which, from the bottom of their hearts, they return their humblest thanks and praises." . . .

The two Houses, in the act of King William, did not thank God that they had found a fair opportunity to assert a right to choose their own governors, much less to make an election the *only lawful* title to the crown. Their having been in a condition to avoid the very appearance of it, as much as possible, was by them considered as a providential escape. They threw a politic, well-wrought veil over every circumstance tending to weaken the rights which in the meliorated order of succession they meant to perpetuate, or which might furnish a precedent for any future departure from what they had then settled forever. . . .

They knew that a doubtful title of succession would but too much resemble an election, and that an election would be utterly destructive of the "unity, peace, and tranquillity of this nation," which they thought to be considerations of some moment. . . .

So far is it from being true that we acquired a right by the Revolution to elect our kings, that, if we had possessed it before, the English nation did at that time most solemnly renounce and abdicate it, for themselves, and for all their posterity forever. . . .

It is true, that, aided with the powers derived from force and opportunity, the nation was at that time, in some sense, free to take what course it pleased for filling the throne—but only free to do so upon the same grounds on which they might have wholly abolished their monarchy, and every other part of their Constitution. However, they did not think such bold changes within their commission. It is, indeed, difficult, perhaps impossible, to give limits to the mere *abstract* competence of the supreme power, such as was exercised by Parliament at that time; but the limits of a *moral* competence, subjecting, even in powers more indisputably sovereign, occasional will to permanent reason, and to the steady maxims of faith, justice, and fixed fundamental policy, are perfectly intelligible, and perfectly binding upon those who exercise any authority, under any name, or under any title, in the state. The House of Lords, for instance, is not morally competent to dissolve the House of Commons—no, nor even to dissolve itself, nor to abdicate, if it would, its portion in the legislature of the kingdom. Though a king may abdicate for his own person, he cannot abdicate for the monarchy. By as strong, or by a stronger reason, the House of Commons cannot renounce its share of authority. The engagement and pact of society, which generally goes by the name of the Constitution, forbids such invasion and such surrender. The constituent parts of a state are obliged to hold their public faith with each other, and with all those who derive any serious interest under their engagements, as much as the whole state is bound to keep its faith with separate communities: otherwise, competence and power would soon be confounded, and no law be left but the will of a prevailing force. On this principle, the succession of the crown has always been what it now is, an hereditary succession by law: in the old line it was a succession by the Common Law; in the new by the statute law, operating on the principles of the Common Law, not changing the substance, but regulating the mode and describing the persons. Both these descriptions of law are of the same force, and are derived from an equal authority, emanating from the common agreement and original compact of the state, . . and as such are equally binding on king, and people too, as long as the terms are observed, and they continue the same body politic.

It is far from impossible to reconcile, if we do not suffer ourselves to be entangled in the mazes of metaphysic sophistry, the use both of a fixed rule and an occasional deviation the sacredness of an hereditary principle of succession in our government with a power of change in its application in cases of extreme emergency. . . .

A state without the means of some change is without the means of its conservation. Without such means it might even risk the loss of that part of the Constitution which it wished the most religiously to preserve. The two principles of conservation and correction operated strongly at the two critical periods of the Restoration and Revolution, when England found itself without a king. At both those periods the nation had lost the bond of union in their ancient edifice: they did not, however, dissolve the whole fabric. On the contrary, in both cases they regenerated the deficient part of the old Constitution through the parts which were not impaired. . . .

On this principle, the law of inheritance had admitted some amendment in the old time, and long before the era of the Revolution. . . . This is the spirit of our Constitution, not only in its settled course, but in all its revolutions. Whoever came in, or however he came in, whether he obtained the crown by law or by force, the hereditary succession was either continued or adopted. . . .

Do these new doctors of the rights of men presume to assert that King James the Second, who came to the crown as next of blood, according to the rules of a then unqualified succession, was not to all intents and purposes a lawful king of England, before he had done any of those acts which were justly construed into an abdication of his crown? If he was not, much trouble in Parliament might have been saved at the period these gentlemen commemorate. But King James was a bad king with a good title, and not an usurper. . . .

No experience has taught us that in any other course or method than that of an *hereditary crown* our liberties can be regularly perpetuated and preserved sacred as our *hereditary right*. An irregular, convulsive movement may be necessary to throw off an irregular, convulsive disease. But the course of succession is the healthy habit of the British Constitution. . .

A few years ago I should be ashamed to overload a matter so capable of supporting itself by the then unnecessary support of any argument; but this seditious, unconstitutional doctrine is now publicly taught, avowed, and printed. The dislike I feel to revolutions, the signals for which have so often been given from pulpits—the spirit of change that is gone abroad—the total contempt which prevails with you, and may come to prevail with us, of all ancient institutions, when set in opposition to a present sense of convenience, or to the bent of a present inclination—all these considerations make it not unadvisable, in my opinion, to call back our attention to the true principles of our own domestic laws, that you, my French friend, should begin to know, and that we should continue to cherish them. We ought not, on either side of the water, to suffer ourselves to be imposed upon by the counterfeit wares which some persons, by a double fraud, export to you in illicit bottoms, as raw commodities of British growth, though wholly alien to our soil, in order afterwards to smuggle them back again into this country, manufactured after the newest Paris fashion of an improved liberty.

The people of England will not ape the fashions they have never tried, nor go back to those which they have found mischievous on trial. They look upon the legal hereditary succession of their crown as among their rights, not as among their wrongs—as a benefit, not as a grievance—as a security for their liberty, not as a badge of servitude. They look on the frame of their commonwealth, *such as it stands*, to be of inestimable value; and they conceive the undisturbed succession of the crown to be a pledge of the stability and perpetuity of all the other members of our Constitution.

I shall beg leave, before I go any further, to take notice of some paltry artifices which the abettors of election as the only lawful title to the crown are ready to employ, in order to render the support of the just principles of our Constitution a task somewhat invidious. These sophisters substitute a fictitious cause, and feigned personages, in whose favor they suppose you engaged, whenever you defend the inheritable nature of the crown. It is common with them to dispute as if they were in a conflict with some of those exploded fanatics of slavery who formerly maintained, what I believe no creature now maintains, "that the crown is held by divine, hereditary, and indefeasible right." These old fanatics of single arbitrary power dogmatized as if hereditary royalty was the only lawful government in the world—just as our new fanatics of popular arbitrary power maintain that a popular election is the sole lawful source of authority. The old prerogative enthusiasts, it is true, did speculate foolishly, and perhaps impiously too, as if monarchy had more of a divine sanction than any other mode of government—and as if a right to govern by inheritance were in strictness *indefeasible* in every person who should be found in the succession to a throne, and under every circumstance, which no civil or political right can be. But an absurd opinion concerning the king's hereditary right to the crown does not prejudice one that is rational, and bottomed upon solid principles of law and policy. If all the absurd theories of lawyers and divines were to vitiate the objects in which they are conversant, we should have no law and no religion left in the world. But an absurd theory on one side of a question forms no justification for alleging a false fact or promulgating mischievous maxims on the other.

The second claim of the Revolution Society is "a right of cashiering their governors for *misconduct*." . . .

No government could stand a moment, if it could be blown down with anything so loose and indefinite as an opinion of *"misconduct."* They who led at the Revolution grounded their virtual abdication of King James upon no such light and uncertain principle. They charged him with nothing less than a design, confirmed by a multitude of illegal overt acts, to *subvert the Protestant Church and State*, and their *fundamental*, unquestionable laws and liberties: they charged him with having broken the *original contract* between king and people. This was more than *misconduct*. A grave and overruling necessity obliged them to take the step they took, and took with infinite reluctance, as under that most rigorous of all laws. Their trust for the future preservation of the Constitution was not in future revolutions. The grand policy of all their regulations was to render it almost impracticable for any future sovereign to compel the states of the kingdom to have again recourse to those violent remedies. . . .

Dr. Price, in this sermon, condemns, very properly, the practice of gross adulatory addresses to kings. Instead of this fulsome style, he proposes that his Majesty should be told, on occasions of congratulation, that "he is to consider himself as more properly the servant than the sovereign of his people." . . .

Kings, in one sense, are undoubtedly the servants of the people, because their power has no other rational end than that of the general advantage; but it is not true that they are, in the ordinary sense, (by our Constitution, at least,) anything like servants—the essence of whose situation is to obey the commands of some other, and to be removable at pleasure. But the king of Great Britain obeys no other person; all other persons are individually, and collectively too, under him, and owe to him a legal obedience. The law, which knows neither to flatter nor to insult, calls this high magistrate, not our servant, as this humble divine calls him, but *"our sovereign lord the king"*; and we, on our parts, have learned to speak only the primitive language of the law, and not the confused jargon of their Babylonian pulpits.

As he is not to obey us, but we are to obey the law in him, our Constitution has made no sort of provision towards rendering him, as a servant, in any degree responsible. Our Constitution knows nothing of . . . any court legally appointed, nor of any process legally settled, for submitting the king to the responsibility belonging to all servants. In this he is not distinguished from the commons and the lords, who, in their several public capacities, can never be called to an account for their conduct; although the Revolution Society chooses to assert, in direct opposition to one of the wisest and most beautiful parts of our Constitution, that "a king is no more than the first servant of the public, created by it, *and responsible to it.*" . . .

The ceremony of cashiering kings, of which these gentlemen talk so much at their ease, can rarely, if ever, be performed without force. It then becomes a case of war, and not of constitution. . . . The question of dethroning, or, if these gentlemen like the phrase better, "cashiering kings," will always be, as it has always been, an extraordinary question of state, and wholly out of the law: a question (like all other questions of state) of dispositions, and of means, and of probable consequences, rather than of positive rights. As it was not made for common abuses, so it is not to be agitated by common minds. The speculative line of demarcation, where obedience ought to end and resistance must begin, is faint, obscure, and not easily definable. It is not a single act or a single event which determines it. Governments must be abused and deranged indeed, before it can be thought of; and the prospect of the future must be as bad as the experience of the past. When things are in that lamentable condition, the nature of the disease is to indicate the remedy to those whom Nature has qualified to administer in extremities this critical, ambiguous, bitter potion to a distempered state. Times and occasions and provocations will teach their own lessons. The wise will determine from the gravity of the case; the irritable, from sensibility to oppression; the high-minded, from disdain and indignation at abusive power in unworthy hands; the brave and bold, from the love of honorable danger in a generous cause: but, with or without right, a revolution will be the very last resource of the thinking and the good.

The third head of right asserted by the pulpit of the Old Jewry, namely, the "right to form a government for ourselves," has, at least, as little countenance from anything done at the Revolution, either in precedent or principle, as the two first of their claims. The Revolution was made to preserve our *ancient* indisputable laws and liberties, and that *ancient* constitution of government which is our only security for law and liberty. If you are desirous of knowing the spirit of our Constitution, and the policy which predominated in that great period which has secured it to this hour, pray look for both in our histories, in our records, in our acts of Parliament and journals of Parliament, and not in the sermons of the Old Jewry, and the after-dinner toasts of the Revolution Society. . . . The very idea of the fabrication of a new government is enough to fill us with disgust and horror. We wished at the period of the Revolution, and do now wish, to derive all we possess as *an inheritance from our forefathers.* Upon that body and stock of inheritance we have taken care not to inoculate any scion alien to the nature of the original plant. All the reformations we have hitherto made have proceeded upon the principle of reference to antiquity. . . .

Our oldest reformation is that of Magna Charta. . . .

You will observe, that, from Magna Charta to the Declaration of Right, it has been the uniform policy of our Constitution to claim and assert our liberties as an *entailed inheritance* derived to us from our forefathers, and to be transmitted to our posterity—as an estate specially belonging to the people of this kingdom, without any reference whatever to any other more general or prior right. By this means our Constitution preserves an unity in so great a diversity of its parts. We have an inheritable crown, an inheritable peerage, and a House of Commons and a people inheriting privileges, franchises, and liberties from a long line of ancestors.

This policy appears to me to be the result of profound reflection—or rather the happy effect of following Nature, which is wisdom without reflection, and above it. A spirit of innovation is generally the result of a selfish temper and confined views. People will not look forward to posterity, who never look backward to their ancestors. Besides, the people of England well know that the idea of inheritance furnishes a sure principle of conservation, and a sure principle of transmission, without at all excluding a principle of improvement. It leaves acquisition free; but it secures what it acquires. Whatever advantages are obtained by a state proceeding on these maxims are locked fast as in a sort of family settlement, grasped as in a kind of mortmain forever. By a constitutional policy working after the pattern of Nature, we receive, we hold, we transmit our government and our privileges, in the same manner in which we enjoy and transmit our property and our lives. The institutions of policy, the goods of fortune, the gifts of Providence, are handed down to us, and from us, in the same course and order. Our political system is placed in a just correspondence and symmetry with the order of the world, and with the mode of existence decreed to a permanent body composed of transitory parts—wherein, by the disposition of a stupendous wisdom, moulding together the great mysterious incorporation of the human race, the whole, at one time, is never old or middle-aged or young, but, in a condition of unchangeable constancy, moves on through the varied tenor of perpetual decay, fall, renovation, and progression. Thus, by preserving the method of Nature in the conduct of the state, in what we improve we are never wholly new, in what we retain we are never wholly obsolete. By adhering in this manner and on those principles to our forefathers, we are guided, not by the superstition of antiquarians, but by the spirit of philosophic analogy. In this choice of inheritance we have given to our frame of polity the image of a relation in blood: binding up the Constitution of our country with our dearest domestic ties; adopting our fundamental laws into the bosom of our family affections; keeping inseparable, and cherishing with the warmth of all their combined and mutually reflected charities, our state, our hearths, our sepulchres, and our altars.

Through the same plan of a conformity to Nature in our artificial institutions, and by calling in the aid of her unerring and powerful instincts to fortify the fallible and feeble contrivances of our reason, we have derived several other, and those no small benefits, from considering our liberties in the light of an inheritance. Always acting as if in the presence of canonized forefathers, the spirit of freedom, leading in itself to misrule and excess, is tempered with an awful gravity. This idea of a liberal descent inspires us with a sense of habitual native dignity, which prevents that upstart insolence almost inevitably adhering to and disgracing those who are the first acquirers of any distinction. By this means our liberty becomes a noble freedom. It carries an imposing and majestic aspect. It has a pedigree and illustrating ancestors. It has its bearings and its ensigns armorial. It has its gallery of portraits, its monumental inscriptions, its records, evidences, and titles. We procure reverence to our civil institutions on the principle upon which Nature teaches us to revere individual men: on account of their age, and on account of those from whom they are descended. All your sophisters cannot produce anything better adapted to preserve a rational and manly freedom than the course that we have pursued, who have chosen our nature rather than our speculations, our breasts rather than our inventions, for the great conservatories and magazines of our rights and privileges.

You might, if you pleased, have profited of our example, and have given to your recovered freedom a correspondent dignity. Your privileges, though discontinued, were not lost to memory. Your Constitution, it is true, whilst you were out of possession, suffered waste and dilapidation; but you possessed in some parts the walls, and in all the foundations, of a noble and venerable castle. You might have repaired those walls; you might have built on those old foundations. Your Constitution was suspended before it was perfected; but you had the elements of a Constitution very nearly as good as could be wished. In your old states you possessed that variety of parts corresponding with the various descriptions of which your community was happily composed; you had all that combination and all that opposition of interests, you had that action and counteraction, which, in the natural and in the political world, from the reciprocal struggle of discordant powers draws out the harmony of the universe. These opposed and conflicting interests, which you considered as so great a blemish in your old and in our present Constitution, interpose a salutary check to all precipitate resolutions. They render deliberation a matter, not of choice, but of necessity; they make all change a subject of *compromise*, which naturally begets moderation; they produce *temperaments*, preventing the sore evil of harsh, crude, unqualified reformations, and rendering all the headlong exertions of arbitrary power, in the few or in the many, forever impracticable. Through that diversity of members and interests, general liberty had as many securities as there were separate views in the several orders; whilst by pressing down the whole by the weight of a real monarchy, the separate parts would have been prevented from warping and starting from their allotted places.

You had all these advantages in your ancient states; but you chose to act as if you had never been moulded into civil society, and had everything to begin anew. You began ill, because you began by despising everything that belonged to you. . . . Respecting your forefathers, you would have been taught to respect yourselves. You would not have chosen to consider the French as a people of yesterday, as a nation of lowborn, servile wretches until the emancipating year of 1789. . . . Or if, diffident of yourselves, and not clearly discerning the almost obliterated Constitution of your ancestors, you had looked to your neighbors in this land, who had kept alive the ancient principles and models of the old common law of Europe, meliorated and adapted to its present state—by following wise examples you would have given new examples of wisdom to the world. You would have rendered the cause of liberty venerable in the eyes of every worthy mind in every nation. You would have shamed despotism from the earth, by showing that freedom was not only reconcilable, but, as, when well disciplined, it is, auxiliary to law. You would have had an unoppressive, but a productive revenue. You would have had a flourishing commerce to feed it. You would have had a free Constitution, a potent monarchy, a disciplined army, a reformed and venerated clergy—a mitigated, but spirited nobility, to lead your virtue, not to overlay it; you would have had a liberal order of commons, to emulate and to recruit that nobility; you would have had a protected, satisfied, laborious, and obedient people, taught to seek and to recognize the happiness that is to be found by virtue in all conditions. . . .

Compute your gains; see what is got by those extravagant and presumptuous speculations which have taught your leaders to despise all their predecessors, and all their contemporaries, and even to despise themselves, until the moment in which they became truly despicable. By following those false lights, France has bought undisguised calamities at a higher price than any nation has purchased the most unequivocal blessings. France has bought poverty by crime. France has not sacrificed her virtue to her interest; but she has abandoned her interest, that she might prostitute her virtue. All other nations have begun the fabric of a new government, or the reformation of an old, by establishing originally, or by enforcing with greater exactness, some rites or other of religion. All other people have laid the foundations of civil freedom in severer manners, and a system of a more austere and masculine morality. France, when she let loose the reins of regal authority, doubled the license of a ferocious dissoluteness in manners, and of an insolent irreligion in opinions and practices—and has extended through all ranks of life, as if she were communicating some privilege, or laying open some secluded benefit, all the unhappy corruptions that usually were the disease of wealth and power. This is one of the new principles of equality in France.

France, by the perfidy of her leaders, has utterly disgraced the tone of lenient council in the cabinets of princes, and disarmed it of its most potent topics. She has sanctified the dark, suspicious maxims of tyrannous distrust, and taught kings to tremble at (what will hereafter be called) the delusive plausibilities of moral politicians. Sovereigns will consider those who advise them to place an unlimited confidence in their people as subverters of their thrones—as traitors who aim at their destruction, by leading their easy good-nature, under specious pretences, to admit combinations of bold and faithless men into a participation of their power. This alone (if there were nothing else) is an irreparable calamity to you and to mankind. Remember that your Parliament of Paris told your king, that, in calling the states together, he had nothing to fear but the prodigal excess of their zeal in providing for the support of the throne. It is right that these men should hide their heads. It is right that they should bear their part in the ruin which their counsel has brought on their sovereign and their country. Such sanguine declarations tend to lull authority asleep—to encourage it rashly to engage in perilous adventures of untried policy—to neglect those provisions, preparations, and precautions which distinguish benevolence from imbecility, and without which no man can answer for the salutary effect of any abstract plan of government or of freedom. For want of these, they have seen the medicine of the state corrupted into its poison. They have seen the French rebel against a mild and lawful monarch, with more fury, outrage, and insult than ever any people has been known to rise against the most illegal usurper or the most sanguinary tyrant. Their resistance was made to concession; their revolt was from protection; their blow was aimed at a hand holding out graces, favors, and immunities.

This was unnatural. The rest is in order. They have found their punishment in their success. Laws overturned; tribunals subverted; industry without vigor; commerce expiring; the revenue unpaid, yet the people impoverished; a church pillaged, and a state not relieved; civil and military anarchy made the constitution of the kingdom; everything human and divine sacrificed to the idol of public credit, and national bankruptcy the consequence; and, to crown all, the paper securities of new, precarious, tottering power, the discredited paper securities of impoverished fraud and beggared rapine, held out as a currency for the support of an empire, in lieu of the two great recognized species that represent the lasting, conventional credit of mankind, which disappeared and hid themselves in the earth from whence they came, when the principle of property, whose creatures and representatives they are, was systematically subverted.

Were all these dreadful things necessary? Were they the inevitable results of the desperate struggle of determined patriots, compelled to wade through blood and tumult to the quiet shore of a tranquil and prosperous liberty? No! nothing like it. The fresh ruins of France, which shock our feelings wherever we can turn our eyes, are not the devastation of civil war: they are the sad, but instructive monuments of rash and ignorant counsel in time of profound peace. They are the display of inconsiderate and presumptuous, because unresisted and irresistible authority. . . .

This unforced choice, this fond election of evil, would appear perfectly unaccountable, if we did not consider the composition of the National Assembly: I do not mean its formal constitution, which, as it now stands, is exceptionable enough, but the materials of which in a great measure it is composed, which is of ten thousand times greater consequence than all the formalities in the world. If we were to know nothing of this assembly but by its title and function, no colors could paint to the imagination anything more venerable. . . . But no name, no power, no function, no artificial institution whatsoever, can make the men, of whom any system of authority is composed, any other than God, and Nature, and education, and their habits of life have made them. Capacities beyond these the people have not to give. . . .

After I had read over the list of the persons and descriptions elected into the *Tiers État*, nothing which they afterwards did could appear astonishing. Among them, indeed, I saw some of known rank, some of shining talents; but of any practical experience in the state not one man was to be found. The best were only men of theory. But whatever the distinguished few may have been, it is the substance and mass of the body which constitutes its character, and must finally determine its direction. . . .

Nothing can secure a steady and moderate conduct in such assemblies, but that the body of them should be respectably composed, in point of condition in life, of permanent property, of education, and of such habits as enlarge and liberalize the understanding.

In the calling of the States-General of France, the first thing that struck me was a great departure from the ancient course. I found the representation for the third estate composed of six hundred persons. They were equal in number to the representatives of both the other orders. If the orders were to act separately, the number would not, beyond the consideration of the expense, be of much moment. But when it became apparent that the three orders were to be melted down into one, the policy and necessary effect of this numerous representation became obvious. A very small desertion from either of the other two orders must throw the power of both into the hands of the third. In fact, the whole power of the state was soon resolved into that body. Its due composition became, therefore, of infinitely the greater importance.

Judge, Sir, of my surprise, when I found that a very great proportion of the Assembly (a majority, I believe, of the members who attended) was composed of practitioners in the law. It was composed, not of distinguished magistrates, who had given pledges to their country of their science, prudence, and integrity—not of leading advocates, the glory of the bar—not of renowned professors in universities—but for the far greater part, as it must in such a number, of the inferior, unlearned, mechanical, merely instrumental members of the profession. There were distinguished exceptions; but the general composition was of obscure provincial advocates, of stewards of petty local jurisdictions, country attorneys, notaries, and the whole train of the ministers of municipal litigation, the fomenters and conductors of the petty war of village vexation. From the moment I read the list, I saw distinctly, and very nearly as it has happened, all that was to follow. . . .

Whenever the supreme authority is vested in a body so composed, it must evidently produce the consequences of supreme authority placed in the hands of men not taught habitually to respect themselves—who had no previous fortune in character at stake—who could not be expected to bear with moderation or to conduct with discretion a power which they themselves, more than any others, must be surprised to find in their hands. Who could flatter himself that these men, suddenly, and as it were by enchantment, snatched from the humblest rank of subordination, would not be intoxicated with their unprepared greatness? Who could conceive that men who are habitually meddling, daring, subtle, active, of litigious dispositions and unquiet minds, would easily fall back into their old condition of obscure contention, and laborious, low, and unprofitable chicane? . . . It was inevitable; it was necessary; it was planted in the nature of things. They must *join* (if their capacity did not permit them to *lead*) in any project which could procure to them a *litigious constitution*—which could lay open to them those innumerable lucrative jobs which follow in the train of all great convulsions and revolutions in the state, and particularly in all great and violent permutations of property. Was it to be expected that they would attend to the stability of property, whose existence had always depended upon whatever rendered property questionable, ambiguous, and insecure? . . .

Well! but these men were to be tempered and restrained by other descriptions, of more sober minds and more enlarged understandings. Were they, then, to be awed by the supereminent authority and awful dignity of a handful of country clowns, who have seats in that assembly, some of whom are said not to be able to read and write—and by not a greater number of traders, who, though somewhat more instructed, and more conspicuous in the order of society, had never known anything beyond their counting-house? No! both these descriptions were more formed to be overborne and swayed by the intrigues and artifices of lawyers than to become their counterpoise. . . .

To the faculty of law was joined a pretty considerable proportion of the faculty of medicine. This faculty had not, any more than that of the law, possessed in France its just estimation. Its professors, therefore, must have the qualities of men not habituated to sentiments of dignity. But supposing they had ranked as they ought to do, and as with us they do actually, the sides of sick-beds are not the academies for forming statesmen and legislators. Then came the dealers in stocks and funds, who must be eager, at any expense, to change their ideal paper wealth for the more solid substance of land. To these were joined men of other descriptions, from whom as little knowledge of or attention to the interests of a great state was to be expected, and as little regard to the stability of any institution—men formed to be instruments, not controls.—Such, in general, was the composition of the *Tiers État* in the National Assembly; in which was scarcely to be perceived the slightest traces of what we call the natural landed interest of the country.

We know that the British House of Commons, without shutting its doors to any merit in any class, is, by the sure operation of adequate causes, filled with everything illustrious in rank, in descent, in hereditary and in acquired opulence, in cultivated talents, in military, civil, naval, and politic distinction, that the country can afford. But supposing, what hardly can be supposed as a case, that the House of Commons should be composed in the same manner with the *Tiers État* in France—would this dominion of chicane be borne with patience, or even conceived without horror? . . .

After all, if the House of Commons were to have an wholly professional and faculty composition, what is the power of the House of Commons, circumscribed and shut in by the immovable barriers of laws, usages, positive rules of doctrine and practice, counterpoised by the House of Lords, and every moment of its existence at the discretion of the crown to continue, prorogue, or dissolve us? The power of the House of Commons, direct or indirect, is, indeed, great. . . . The power, however, of the House of Commons, when least diminished, is as a drop of water in the ocean, compared to that residing in a settled majority of your National Assembly. That assembly, since the destruction of the orders, has no fundamental law, no strict convention, no respected usage to restrain it. Instead of finding themselves obliged to conform to a fixed constitution, they have a power to make a constitution what shall conform to their designs. Nothing in heaven or upon earth can serve as a control on them. What ought to be the heads, the hearts, the dispositions, that are qualified, or that dare, not only to make laws under a fixed constitution, but at one heat to strike out a totally new constitution for a great kingdom, and in every part of it, from the monarch on the throne to the vestry of a parish? But

> *"Fools rush in where angels fear to tread."*

In such a state of unbounded power, for undefined and undefinable purposes, the evil of a moral and almost physical inaptitude of the man to the function must be the greatest we can conceive to happen in the management of human affairs.

Having considered the composition of the third estate, as it stood in its original frame, I took a view of the representatives of the clergy. There, too, it appeared that full as little regard was had to the general security of property, or to the aptitude of the deputies for their public purposes, in the principles of their election. That election was so contrived as to send a very large proportion of mere country curates to the great and arduous work of new-modelling a state: men who never had seen the state so much as in a picture; men who knew nothing of the world beyond the bounds of an obscure village; who, immersed in hopeless poverty, could regard all property, whether secular or ecclesiastical, with no other eye than that of envy; among whom must be many who, for the smallest hope of the meanest dividend in plunder, would readily join in any attempts upon a body of wealth in which they could hardly look to have any share, except in a general scramble. Instead of balancing the power of the active chicaners in the other assembly, these curates must necessarily become the active coadjutors, or at best the passive instruments, of those by whom they had been habitually guided in their petty village concerns. . . .

To observing men it must have appeared from the beginning, that the majority of the third estate, in conjunction with such a deputation from the clergy as I have described, whilst it pursued the destruction of the nobility, would inevitably become subservient to the worst designs of individuals in that class. In the spoil and humiliation of their own order these individuals would possess a sure fund for the pay of their new followers. To squander away the objects which made the happiness of their fellows would be to them no sacrifice at all. Turbulent, discontented men of quality, in proportion as they are puffed up with personal pride and arrogance, generally despise their own order. One of the first symptoms they discover of a selfish and mischievous ambition is a profligate disregard of a dignity which they partake with others. To be attached to the subdivision, to love the little platoon we belong to in society, is the first principle (the germ, as it were) of public affections. It is the first link in the series by which we proceed towards a love to our country and to mankind. The interest of that portion of social arrangement is a trust in the hands of all those who compose it; and as none but bad men would justify it in abuse, none but traitors would barter it away for their own personal advantage. . . .

When men of rank sacrifice all ideas of dignity to an ambition without a distinct object, and work with low instruments and for low ends, the whole composition becomes low and base. Does not something like this now appear in France? Does it not produce something ignoble and inglorious: a kind of meanness in all the prevalent policy; a tendency in all that is done to lower along with individuals all the dignity and importance of the state? Other revolutions have been conducted by persons who, whilst they attempted or affected changes in the commonwealth, sanctified their ambition by advancing the dignity of the people whose peace they troubled. . . .

These disturbers were not so much like men usurping power as asserting their natural place in society. Their rising was to illuminate and  beautify the world. Their conquest over their competitors was by outshining them. . . . I do not say that the virtues of such men were to be taken as a balance to their crimes; but they were some corrective to their effects. Such was . . . our Cromwell. Such were your whole race of Guises, Condés, and Colignys. Such the Richelieus, who in more quiet times acted in the spirit of a civil war. Such, as better men, and in a less dubious cause, were your Henry the Fourth, and your Sully, though nursed in civil confusions, and not wholly without some of their taint. It is a thing to be wondered at, to see how very soon France, when she had a moment to respire, recovered and emerged from the longest and most dreadful civil war that ever was known in any nation. Why? Because, among all their massacres, they had not slain the *mind* in their country. A conscious dignity, a noble pride, a generous sense of glory and emulation, was not extinguished. On the contrary, it was kindled and inflamed. The organs also of the state, however shattered, existed. All the prizes of honor and virtue, all the rewards, all the distinctions, remained. But your present confusion, like a palsy, has attacked the fountain of life itself. Every person in your country, in a situation to be actuated by a principle of honor, is disgraced and degraded, and can entertain no sensation of life, except in a mortified and humiliated indignation. . . . Believe me, Sir, those who attempt to level never equalize. In all societies consisting of various descriptions of citizens, some description must be uppermost. The levellers, therefore, only change and pervert the natural order of things: they load the edifice of society by setting up in the air what the solidity of the structure requires to be on the ground. . . .

There is no qualification for government but virtue and wisdom, actual or presumptive. Wherever they are actually found, they have, in whatever state, condition, profession, or trade, the passport of Heaven to human place and honor. Woe to the country which would madly and impiously reject the service of the talents and virtues, civil, military, or religious, that are given to grace and to serve it; and would condemn to obscurity everything formed to diffuse lustre and glory around a state! Woe to that country, too, that, passing into the opposite extreme, considers a low education, a mean, contracted view of things, a sordid, mercenary occupation, as a preferable title to command! . . . I do not hesitate to say that the road to eminence and power, from obscure condition, ought not to be made too easy, nor a thing too much of course. If rare merit be the rarest of all rare things, it ought to pass through some sort of probation. The temple of honor ought to be seated on an eminence. If it be opened through virtue, let it be remembered, too, that virtue is never tried but by some difficulty and some struggle.

Nothing is a due and adequate representation of a state, that does not represent its ability, as well as its property. But as ability is a vigorous and active principle, and as property is sluggish, inert, and timid, it never can be safe from the invasions of ability, unless it be, out of all proportion, predominant in the representation. It must be represented, too, in great masses of accumulation, or it is not rightly protected. The characteristic essence of property, formed out of the combined principles of its acquisition and conservation, is to be *unequal.* The great masses, therefore, which excite envy, and tempt rapacity, must be put out of the possibility of danger. Then they form a natural rampart about the lesser properties in all their gradations. The same quantity of property which is by the natural course of things divided among many has not the same operation. Its defensive power is weakened as it is diffused. In this diffusion each man's portion is less than what, in the eagerness of his desires, he may flatter himself to obtain by dissipating the accumulations of others. The plunder of the few would, indeed, give but a share inconceivably small in the distribution to the many. But the many are not capable of making this calculation; and those who lead them to rapine never intend this distribution.

The power of perpetuating our property in our families is one of the most valuable and interesting circumstances belonging to it, and that which tends the most to the perpetuation of society itself. It makes our weakness subservient to our virtue; it grafts benevolence even upon avarice. The possessors of family wealth, and of the distinction which attends hereditary possession, (as most concerned in it,) are the natural securities for this transmission. With us the House of Peers is formed upon this principle. It is wholly composed of hereditary property and hereditary distinction, and made, therefore, the third of the legislature, and, in the last event, the sole judge of all property in all its subdivisions. The House of Commons, too, though not necessarily, yet in fact, is always so composed, in the far greater part. Let those large proprietors be what they will, (and they have their chance of being amongst the best,) they are, at the very worst, the ballast in the vessel of the commonwealth. For though hereditary wealth, and the rank which goes with it, are too much idolized by creeping sycophants, and the blind, abject admirers of power, they are too rashly slighted in shallow speculations of the petulant, assuming, shortsighted coxcombs of philosophy. . . .

Your leaders in France began by affecting to admire, almost to adore, the British Constitution; but as they advanced, they came to look upon it with a sovereign contempt. The friends of your National Assembly amongst us have full as mean an opinion of what was formerly thought the glory of their country. The Revolution Society has discovered that the English nation is not free. . . .

These gentlemen value themselves on being systematic, and not without reason. They must therefore look on this gross and palpable defect of representation, this fundamental grievance, (so they call it,) as a thing not only vicious in itself, but as rendering our whole government absolutely *illegitimate*, and not at all better than a downright *usurpation*. Another revolution, to get rid of this illegitimate and usurped government, would of course be perfectly justifiable, if not absolutely necessary. . . .

Something they must destroy, or they seem to themselves to exist for no purpose. One set is for destroying the civil power through the ecclesiastical; another for demolishing the ecclesiastic through the civil. They are aware that the worst consequences might happen to the public in accomplishing this double ruin of Church and State; but they are so heated with their theories, that they give more than hints that this ruin, with all the mischiefs that must lead to it and attend it, and which to themselves appear quite certain, would not be unacceptable to them, or very remote from their wishes. . . .

It is no wonder, therefore, that, with these ideas of everything in their Constitution and government at home, either in Church or State, as illegitimate and usurped, or at best as a vain mockery, they look abroad with an eager and passionate enthusiasm. Whilst they are possessed by these notions, it is vain to talk to them of the practice of their ancestors, the fundamental laws of their country, the fixed form of a Constitution whose merits are confirmed by the solid test of long experience and an increasing public strength and national prosperity. They despise experience as the wisdom of unlettered men; and as for the rest, they have wrought under ground a mine that will blow up, at one grand explosion, all examples of antiquity, all precedents, charters, and acts of Parliament. They have "the rights of men." Against these there can be no prescription; against these no argument is binding: these admit no temperament and no compromise: anything withheld from their full demand is so much of fraud and injustice. Against these their rights of men let no government look for security in the length of its continuance, or in the justice and lenity of its administration. The objections of these speculatists, if its forms do not quadrate with their theories, are as valid against such an old and beneficent government as against the most violent tyranny or the greenest usurpation. They are always at issue with governments, not on a question of abuse, but a question of competency and a question of title. . . .

Far am I from denying in theory, full as far is my heart from withholding in practice, (if I were of power to give or to withhold,) the *real* rights of men. In denying their false claims of right, I do not mean to injure those which are real, and are such as their pretended rights would totally destroy. If civil society be made for the advantage of man, all the advantages for which it is made become his right. It is an institution of beneficence; and law itself is only beneficence acting by a rule. Men have a right to live by that rule; they have a right to justice, as between their fellows, whether their fellows are in politic function or in ordinary occupation. They have a right to the fruits of their industry, and to the means of making their industry fruitful. They have a right to the acquisitions of their parents, to the nourishment and improvement of their offspring, to instruction in life and to consolation in death. Whatever each man can separately do, without trespassing upon others, he has a right to do for himself; and he has a right to a fair portion of all which society, with all its combinations of skill and force, can do in his favor. In this partnership all men have equal rights; but not to equal things. He that has but five shillings in the partnership has as good a right to it as he that has five hundred pounds has to his larger proportion; but he has not a right to an equal dividend in the product of the joint stock. And as to the share of power, authority, and direction which each individual ought to have in the management of the state, that I must deny to be amongst the direct original rights of man in civil society; for I have in my contemplation the civil social man, and no other. It is a thing to be settled by convention.

If civil society be the offspring of convention, that convention must be its law. That convention must limit and modify all the descriptions of constitution which are formed under it. Every sort of legislative, judicial, or executory power are its creatures. They can have no being in any other state of things; and how can any man claim, under the conventions of civil society, rights which do not so much as suppose its existence—rights which are absolutely repugnant to it? One of the first motives to civil society, and which becomes one of its fundamental rules, is, *that no man should be judge in his own cause.* By this each person has at once divested himself of the first fundamental right of uncovenanted man, that is, to judge for himself, and to assert his own cause. He abdicates all right to be his own governor. He inclusively, in a great measure, abandons the right of self-defence, the first law of Nature. Men cannot enjoy the rights of an uncivil and of a civil state together. That he may obtain justice, he gives up his right of determining what it is in points the most essential to him. That he may secure some liberty, he makes a surrender in trust of the whole of it.

Government is not made in virtue of natural rights, which may and do exist in total independence of it—and exist in much greater clearness, and in a much greater degree of abstract perfection: but their abstract perfection is their practical defect. By having a right to everything they want everything. Government is a contrivance of human wisdom to provide for human *wants.* Men have a right that these wants should be provided for by this wisdom. Among these wants is to be reckoned the want, out of civil society, of a sufficient restraint upon their passions. Society requires not only that the passions of individuals should be subjected, but that even in the mass and body, as well as in the individuals, the inclinations of men should frequently be thwarted, their will controlled, and their passions brought into subjection. This can only be done *by a power out of themselves*, and not, in the exercise of its function, subject to that will and to those passions which it is its office to bridle and subdue. In this sense the restraints on men, as well as their liberties, are to be reckoned among their rights. But as the liberties and the restrictions vary with times and circumstances, and admit of infinite modifications, they cannot be settled upon any abstract rule; and nothing is so foolish as to discuss them upon that principle.

The moment you abate anything from the full rights of men each to govern himself, and suffer any artificial, positive limitation upon those rights, from that moment the whole organization of government becomes a consideration of convenience. This it is which makes the constitution of a state, and the due distribution of its powers, a matter of the most delicate and complicated skill. It requires a deep knowledge of human nature and human necessities, and of the things which facilitate or obstruct the various ends which are to be pursued by the mechanism of civil institutions. The state is to have recruits to its strength and remedies to its distempers. What is the use of discussing a man's abstract right to food or medicine? The question is upon the method of procuring and administering them. In that deliberation I shall always advise to call in the aid of the farmer and the physician, rather than the professor of metaphysics.

The science of constructing a commonwealth, or renovating it, or reforming it, is, like every other experimental science, not to be taught *a priori*. Nor is it a short experience that can instruct us in that practical science; because the real effects of moral causes are not always immediate, but that which in the first instance is prejudicial may be excellent in its remoter operation, and its excellence may arise even from the ill effects it produces in the beginning. The reverse also happens; and very plausible schemes, with very pleasing commencements, have often shameful and lamentable conclusions. In states there are often some obscure and almost latent causes, things which appear at first view of little moment, on which a very great part of its prosperity or adversity may most essentially depend. The science of government being, therefore, so practical in itself, and intended for such practical purposes, a matter which requires experience, and even more experience than any person can gain in his whole life, however sagacious and observing he may be, it is with infinite caution that any man ought to venture upon pulling down an edifice which has answered in any tolerable degree for ages the common purposes of society, or on building it up again without having models and patterns of approved utility before his eyes.

These metaphysic rights entering into common life, like rays of light which pierce into a dense medium, are, by the laws of Nature, refracted from their straight line. Indeed, in the gross and complicated mass of human passions and concerns, the primitive rights of men undergo such a variety of refractions and reflections that it becomes absurd to talk of them as if they continued in the simplicity of their original direction. The nature of man is intricate; the objects of society are of the greatest possible complexity: and therefore no simple disposition or direction of power can be suitable either to man's nature or to the quality of his affairs. When I hear the simplicity of contrivance aimed at and boasted of in any new political constitutions, I am at no loss to decide that the artificers are grossly ignorant of their trade or totally negligent of their duty. The simple governments are fundamentally defective, to say no worse of them. If you were to contemplate society in but one point of view, all these simple modes of polity are infinitely captivating. In effect each would answer its single end much more perfectly than the more complex is able to attain all its complex purposes. But it is better that the whole should be imperfectly and anomalously answered than that while some parts are provided for with great exactness, others might be totally neglected, or perhaps materially injured, by the over-care of a favorite member.

The pretended rights of these theorists are all extremes; and in proportion as they are metaphysically true, they are morally and politically false. The rights of men are in a sort of *middle*, incapable of definition, but not impossible to be discerned. The rights of men in governments are their advantages; and these are often in balances between differences of good—in compromises sometimes between good and evil, and sometimes between evil and evil. Political reason is a computing principle: adding, subtracting, multiplying, and dividing, morally, and not metaphysically or mathematically, true moral denominations.

By these theorists the right of the people is almost always sophistically confounded with their power. The body of the community, whenever it can come to act, can meet with no effectual resistance; but till power and right are the same, the whole body of them has no right inconsistent with virtue, and the first of all virtues, prudence. Men have no right to what is not reasonable, and to what is not for their benefit . . .

I never liked this continual talk of resistance and revolution, or the practice of making the extreme medicine of the Constitution its daily bread. It renders the habit of society dangerously valetudinary; it is taking periodical doses of mercury sublimate, and swallowing down repeated provocatives of cantharides to our love of liberty. . . .

Hypocrisy, of course, delights in the most sublime speculations; for, never intending to go beyond speculation, it costs nothing to have it magnificent. But even in cases where rather levity than fraud was to be suspected in these ranting speculations, the issue has been much the same. These professors, finding their extreme principles not applicable to cases which call only for a qualified, or, as I may say, civil and legal resistance, in such cases employ no resistance at all. It is with them a war or a revolution, or it is nothing. Finding their schemes of politics not adapted to the state of the world in which they live, they often come to think lightly of all public principle, and are ready, on their part, to abandon for a very trivial interest what they find of very trivial value. . . . They have some change in the Church or State, or both, constantly in their view. When that is the case, they are always bad citizens, and perfectly unsure connections. For, considering their speculative designs as of infinite value, and the actual arrangement of the state as of no estimation, they are, at best, indifferent about it. They see no merit in the good, and no fault in the vicious management of public affairs; they rather rejoice in the latter, as more propitious to revolution. They see no merit or demerit in any man, or any action, or any political principle, any further than as they may forward or retard their design of change; they therefore take up, one day, the most violent and stretched prerogative, and another time the wildest democratic ideas of freedom, and pass from the one to the other without any sort of regard to cause, to person, or to party. . . .

The worst of these politics of revolution is this: they temper and harden the breast, in order to prepare it for the desperate strokes which are sometimes used in extreme occasions. But as these occasions may never arrive, the mind receives a gratuitous taint; and the moral sentiments suffer not a little, when no political purpose is served by the depravation. This sort of people are so taken up with their theories about the rights of man, that they have totally forgot his nature. Without opening one new avenue to the understanding, they have succeeded in stopping up those that lead to the heart. They have perverted in themselves, and in those that attend to them, all the well-placed sympathies of the human breast.

This famous sermon of the Old Jewry breathes nothing but this spirit through all the political part. Plots, massacres, assassinations, seem to some people a trivial price for obtaining a revolution. A cheap, bloodless reformation, a guiltless liberty, appear flat and vapid to their taste. There must be a great change of scene; there must be a magnificent stage effect; there must be a grand spectacle to rouse the imagination, grown torpid with the lazy enjoyment of sixty years' security, and the still unanimating repose of public prosperity. The preacher found them all in the French Revolution. This inspires a juvenile warmth through his whole frame. His enthusiasm kindles as he advances; and when he arrives at his peroration, it is in a full blaze. . . .

Among the revolutions in France must be reckoned a considerable revolution in their ideas of politeness. In England we are said to learn manners at second-hand from your side of the water, and that we dress our behavior in the frippery of France. If so, we are still in the old cut, and have not so far conformed to the new Parisian mode of good breeding as to think it quite in the most refined strain of delicate compliment (whether in condolence or congratulation) to say, to the most humiliated creature that crawls upon the earth, that great public benefits are derived from the murder of his servants, the attempted assassination of himself and of his wife, and the mortification, disgrace, and degradation that he has personally suffered. . . .

History will record, that, on the morning of the sixth of October, 1789, the king and queen of France, after a day of confusion, alarm, dismay, and slaughter, lay down, under the pledged security of public faith, to indulge nature in a few hours of respite, and troubled, melancholy repose. From this sleep the queen was first startled by the voice of the sentinel at her door, who cried out to her to save herself by flight—that this was the last proof of fidelity he could give—that they were upon him, and he was dead. Instantly he was cut down. A band of cruel ruffians and assassins, reeking with his blood, rushed into the chamber of the queen, and pierced with a hundred strokes of bayonets and poniards the bed, from whence this persecuted woman had but just time to fly almost naked, and, through ways unknown to the murderers, had escaped to seek refuge at the feet of a king and husband not secure of his own life for a moment.

This king, to say no more of him, and this queen, and their infant children, (who once would have been the pride and hope of a great and generous people,) were then forced to abandon the sanctuary of the most splendid palace in the world, which they left swimming in blood, polluted by massacre, and strewed with scattered limbs and mutilated carcasses. Thence they were conducted into the capital of their kingdom. . . .

It is now sixteen or seventeen years since I saw the queen of France, then the Dauphiness, at Versailles; and surely never lighted on this orb, which she hardly seemed to touch, a more delightful vision. I saw her just above the horizon, decorating and cheering the elevated sphere she just began to move in—glittering like the morning-star, full of life and splendor and joy. Oh! what a revolution! and what an heart must I have, to contemplate without emotion that elevation and that fall! Little did I dream, when she added titles of veneration to those of enthusiastic, distant, respectful love, that she should ever be obliged to carry the sharp antidote against disgrace concealed in that bosom! little did I dream that I should have lived to see such disasters fallen upon her in a nation of gallant men, in a nation of men of honor, and of cavaliers! I thought ten thousand swords must have leaped from their scabbards to avenge even a look that threatened her with insult. But the age of chivalry is gone. That of sophisters, economists, and calculators has succeeded; and the glory of Europe is extinguished forever. Never, never more, shall we behold that generous loyalty to rank and sex, that proud submission, that dignified obedience, that subordination of the heart, which kept alive, even in servitude itself, the spirit of an exalted freedom! The unbought grace of life, the cheap defence of nations, the nurse of manly sentiment and heroic enterprise, is gone! It is gone, that sensibility of principle, that chastity of honor, which felt a stain like a wound, which inspired courage whilst it mitigated ferocity, which ennobled whatever it touched, and under which vice itself lost half its evil by losing all its grossness!

This mixed system of opinion and sentiment had its origin in the ancient chivalry; and the principle, though varied in its appearance by the varying state of human affairs, subsisted and influenced through a long succession of generations, even to the time we live in. If it should ever be totally extinguished, the loss, I fear, will be great. It is this which has given its character to modern Europe. It is this which has distinguished it under all its forms of government, and distinguished it to its advantage, from the states of Asia, and possibly from those states which flourished in the most brilliant periods of the antique world. It was this, which, without confounding ranks, had produced a noble equality, and handed it down through all the gradations of social life. It was this opinion which mitigated kings into companions, and raised private men to be fellows with kings. Without force or opposition, it subdued the fierceness of pride and power; it obliged sovereigns to submit to the soft collar of social esteem, compelled stern authority to submit to elegance, and gave a domination, vanquisher of laws, to be subdued by manners.

But now all is to be changed. All the pleasing illusions which made power gentle and obedience liberal, which harmonized the different shades of life, and which by a bland assimilation incorporated into politics the sentiments which beautify and soften private society, are to be dissolved by this new conquering empire of light and reason. All the decent drapery of life is to be rudely torn off. All the superadded ideas, furnished from the wardrobe of a moral imagination, which the heart owns and the understanding ratifies, as necessary to cover the defects of our naked, shivering nature, and to raise it to dignity in our own estimation, are to be exploded, as a ridiculous, absurd, and antiquated fashion.

On this scheme of things, a king is but a man, a queen is but a woman, a woman is but an animal—and an animal not of the highest order. All homage paid to the sex in general as such, and without distinct views, is to be regarded as romance and folly. Regicide, and parricide, and sacrilege, are but fictions of superstition, corrupting jurisprudence by destroying its simplicity. The murder of a king, or a queen, or a bishop, or a father, are only common homicide—and if the people are by any chance or in any way gainers by it, a sort of homicide much the most pardonable, and into which we ought not to make too severe a scrutiny.

On the scheme of this barbarous philosophy, which is the offspring of cold hearts and muddy understandings, and which is as void of solid wisdom as it is destitute of all taste and elegance, laws are to be supported only by their own terrors, and by the concern which each individual may find in them from his own private speculations, or can spare to them from his own private interests. In the groves of *their* academy, at the end of every vista, you see nothing but the gallows. Nothing is left which engages the affections on the part of the commonwealth. On the principles of this mechanic philosophy, our institutions can never be embodied, if I may use the expression, in persons—so as to create in us love, veneration, admiration, or attachment. But that sort of reason which banishes the affections is incapable of filling their place. These public affections, combined with manners, are required sometimes as supplements, sometimes as correctives, always as aids to law. . . . There ought to be a system of manners in every nation which a well-formed mind would be disposed to relish. To make us love our country, our country ought to be lovely.

But power, of some kind or other, will survive the shock in which manners and opinions perish; and it will find other and worse means for its support. The usurpation, which, in order to subvert ancient institutions, has destroyed ancient principles, will hold power by arts similar to those by which it has acquired it. When the old feudal and chivalrous spirit of *fealty*, which, by freeing kings from fear, freed both kings and subjects from the precautions of tyranny, shall be extinct in the minds of men, plots and assassinations will be anticipated by preventive murder and preventive confiscation, and that long roll of grim and bloody maxims which form the political code of all power not standing on its own honor and the honor of those who are to obey it. Kings will be tyrants from policy, when subjects are rebels from principle.

When ancient opinions and rules of life are taken away, the loss cannot possibly be estimated. From that moment we have no compass to govern us, nor can we know distinctly to what port we steer. Europe, undoubtedly, taken in a mass, was in a flourishing condition the day on which your Revolution was completed. How much of that prosperous state was owing to the spirit of our old manners and opinions is not easy to say; but as such causes cannot be indifferent in their operation, we must presume, that, on the whole, their operation was beneficial.

We are but too apt to consider things in the state in which we find them, without sufficiently adverting to the causes by which they have been produced, and possibly may be upheld. Nothing is more certain than that our manners, our civilization, and all the good things which are connected with manners and with civilization, have, in this European world of ours, depended for ages upon two principles, and were, indeed, the result of both combined: I mean the spirit of a gentleman, and the spirit of religion. The nobility and the clergy, the one by profession, and the other by patronage, kept learning in existence, even in the midst of arms and confusions, and whilst governments were rather in their causes than formed. Learning paid back what it received to nobility and to priesthood, and paid it with usury, by enlarging their ideas, and by furnishing their minds. Happy, if they had all continued to know their indissoluble union, and their proper place! Happy, if learning, not debauched by ambition, had been satisfied to continue the instructor, and not aspired to be the master! Along with its natural protectors and guardians, learning will be cast into the mire and trodden down under the hoofs of a swinish multitude.

If, as I suspect, modern letters owe more than they are always willing to own to ancient manners, so do other interests which we value full as much as they are worth. Even commerce, and trade, and manufacture, the gods of our economical politicians, are themselves perhaps but creatures, are themselves but effects, which, as first causes, we choose to worship. They certainly grew under the same shade in which learning flourished. They, too, may decay with their natural protecting principles. With you, for the present at least, they all threaten to disappear together. Where trade and manufactures are wanting to a people, and the spirit of nobility and religion remains, sentiment supplies, and not always ill supplies, their place; but if commerce and the arts should be lost in an experiment to try how well a state may stand without these old fundamental principles, what sort of a thing must be a nation of gross, stupid, ferocious, and at the same time poor and sordid barbarians, destitute of religion, honor, or manly pride, possessing nothing at present, and hoping for nothing hereafter?

I wish you may not be going fast, and by the shortest cut, to that horrible and disgustful situation. Already there appears a poverty of conception, a coarseness and vulgarity, in all the proceedings of the Assembly and of all their instructors. Their liberty is not liberal. Their science is presumptuous ignorance. Their humanity is savage and brutal.

It is not clear whether in England we learned those grand and decorous principles and manners, of which considerable traces yet remain, from you, or whether you took them from us. But to you, I think, we trace them best. . . . France has always more or less influenced manners in England; and when your fountain is choked up and polluted, the stream will not run long or not run clear with us, or perhaps with any nation. This gives all Europe, in my opinion, but too close and connected a concern in what is done in France. Excuse me, therefore, if I have dwelt too long on the atrocious spectacle of the sixth of October, 1789, or have given too much scope to the reflections which have arisen in my mind on occasion of the most important of all revolutions, which may be dated from that day: I mean a revolution in sentiments, manners, and moral opinions. As things now stand, with everything respectable destroyed without us, and an attempt to destroy within us every principle of respect, one is almost forced to apologize for harboring the common feelings of men. . . .

If it could have been made clear to me that the king and queen of France (those, I mean, who were such before the triumph) were inexorable and cruel tyrants, that they had formed a deliberate scheme for massacring the National Assembly, (I think I have seen something like the latter insinuated in certain publications,) I should think their captivity just. If this be true, much more ought to have been done, but done, in my opinion, in another manner. The punishment of real tyrants is a noble and awful act of justice; and it has with truth been said to be consolatory to the human mind. But if I were to punish a wicked king, I should regard the dignity in avenging the crime. Justice is grave and decorous, and in its punishments rather seems to submit to a necessity than to make a choice. . . .

I have often been astonished, considering that we are divided from you but by a slender dike of about twenty-four miles, and that the mutual intercourse between the two countries has lately been very great, to find how little you seem to know of us. I suspect that this is owing to your forming a judgment of this nation from certain publications, which do, very erroneously, if they do at all, represent the opinions and dispositions generally prevalent in England. The vanity, restlessness, petulance, and spirit of intrigue of several petty cabals, who attempt to hide their total want of consequence in bustle and noise, and puffing and mutual quotation of each other, makes you imagine that our contemptuous neglect of their abilities is a general mark of acquiescence in their opinions. No such thing, I assure you. Because half a dozen grasshoppers under a fern make the field ring with their importunate chink, whilst thousands of great cattle reposed beneath the shadow of the British oak chew the cud and are silent, pray do not imagine that those who make the noise are the only inhabitants of the field—that, of course, they are many in number—or that, after all, they are other than the little, shrivelled, meagre, hopping, though loud and troublesome insects of the hour. . . .

Thanks to our sullen resistance to innovation, thanks to the cold sluggishness of our national character, we still bear the stamp of our forefathers. We have not . . . lost the generosity and dignity of thinking of the fourteenth century; nor as yet have we subtilized ourselves into savages. We are not the converts of Rousseau; we are not the disciples of Voltaire; Helvétius has made no progress amongst us. Atheists are not our preachers; madmen are not our lawgivers. We know that *we* have made no discoveries, and we think that no discoveries are to be made, in morality—nor many in the great principles of government, nor in the ideas of liberty, which were understood long before we were born altogether as well as they will be after the grave has heaped its mould upon our presumption, and the silent tomb shall have imposed its law on our pert loquacity. In England we have not yet been completely embowelled of our natural entrails: we still feel within us, and we cherish and cultivate, those inbred sentiments which are the faithful guardians, the active monitors of our duty, the true supporters of all liberal and manly morals. We have not been drawn and trussed, in order that we may be filled, like stuffed birds in a museum, with chaff and rags, and paltry, blurred shreds of paper about the rights of man. We preserve the whole of our feelings still native and entire, unsophisticated by pedantry and infidelity. We have real hearts of flesh and blood beating in our bosoms. We fear God; we look up with awe to kings, with affection to Parliaments, with duty to magistrates, with reverence to priests, and with respect to nobility. Why? Because, when such ideas are brought before our minds, it is *natural* to be so affected; because all other feelings are false and spurious, and tend to corrupt our minds, to vitiate our primary morals, to render us unfit for rational liberty, and, by teaching us a servile, licentious, and abandoned insolence, to be our low sport for a few holidays, to make us perfectly fit for and justly deserving of slavery through the whole course of our lives.

You see, Sir, that in this enlightened age I am bold enough to confess that we are generally men of untaught feelings: that, instead of casting away all our old prejudices, we cherish them to a very considerable degree; and, to take more shame to ourselves, we cherish them because they are prejudices; and the longer they have lasted, and the more generally they have prevailed, the more we cherish them. We are afraid to put men to live and trade each on his own private stock of reason; because we suspect that the stock in each man is small, and that the individuals would do better to avail themselves of the general bank and capital of nations and of ages. Many of our men of speculation, instead of exploding general prejudices, employ their sagacity to discover the latent wisdom which prevails in them. If they find what they seek, (and they seldom fail,) they think it more wise to continue the prejudice, with the reason involved, than to cast away the coat of prejudice, and to leave nothing but the naked reason; because prejudice, with its reason, has a motive to give action to that reason, and an affection which will give it permanence. Prejudice is of ready application in the emergency; it previously engages the mind in a steady course of wisdom and virtue, and does not leave the man hesitating in the moment of decision, skeptical, puzzled, and unresolved. Prejudice renders a man's virtue his habit, and not a series of unconnected acts. Through just prejudice, his duty becomes a part of his nature.

Your literary men, and your politicians, and so do the whole clan of the enlightened among us, essentially differ in these points. They have no respect for the wisdom of others; but they pay it off by a very full measure of confidence in their own. With them it is a sufficient motive to destroy an old scheme of things, because it is an old one. As to the new, they are in no sort of fear with regard to the duration of a building run up in haste; because duration is no object to those who think little or nothing has been done before their time, and who place all their hopes in discovery. They conceive, very systematically, that all things which give perpetuity are mischievous, and therefore they are at inexpiable war with all establishments. They think that government may vary like modes of dress, and with as little ill effect; that there needs no principle of attachment, except a sense of present conveniency, to any constitution of the state. They always speak as if they were of opinion that there is a singular species of compact between them and their magistrates, which binds the magistrate, but which has nothing reciprocal in it, but that the majesty of the people has a right to dissolve it without any reason but its will. Their attachment to their country itself is only so far as it agrees with some of their fleeting projects: it begins and ends with that scheme of polity which falls in with their momentary opinion.

These doctrines, or rather sentiments, seem prevalent with your new statesmen. But they are wholly different from those on which we have always acted in this country. . . .

Formerly your affairs were your own concern only. We felt for them as men; but we kept aloof from them, because we were not citizens of France. But when we see the model held up to ourselves, we must feel as Englishmen, and, feeling, we must provide as Englishmen. . . .

We know, and, what is better, we feel inwardly, that religion is the basis of civil society, and the source of all good, and of all comfort. In

England we are so convinced of this, that there is no rust of superstition, with which the accumulated absurdity of the human mind might have crusted it over in the course of ages, that ninety-nine in a hundred of the people of England would not prefer to impiety. We shall never be such fools as to call in an enemy to the substance of any system to remove its corruptions, to supply its defects, or to perfect its construction. If our religious tenets should ever want a further elucidation, we shall not call on Atheism to explain them. . . .

We know, and it is our pride to know, that man is by his constitution a religious animal; that atheism is against, not only our reason, but our instincts; and that it cannot prevail long. But if, in the moment of riot, and in a drunken delirium from the hot spirit drawn out of the alembic of hell, which in France is now so furiously boiling, we should uncover our nakedness, by throwing off that Christian religion which has hitherto been our boast and comfort, and one great source of civilization amongst us, and among many other nations, we are apprehensive (being well aware that the mind will not endure a void) that some uncouth, pernicious, and degrading superstition might take the place of it.

For that reason, before we take from our establishment the natural, human means of estimation, and give it up to contempt, as you have done, and in doing it have incurred the penalties you well deserve to suffer, we desire that some other may be presented to us in the place of it. We shall then form our judgment.

On these ideas, instead of quarrelling with establishments, as some do, who have made a philosophy and a religion of their hostility to such institutions, we cleave closely to them. We are resolved to keep an established church, an established monarchy, an established aristocracy, and an established democracy, each in the degree it exists, and in no greater. I shall show you presently how much of each of these we possess.

It has been the misfortune (not, as these gentlemen think it, the glory) of this age, that everything is to be discussed, as if the Constitution of our country were to be always a subject rather of altercation than enjoyment. For this reason, as well as for the satisfaction of those among you (if any such you have among you) who may wish to profit of examples, I venture to trouble you with a few thoughts upon each of these establishments. . . .

First I beg leave to speak of our Church Establishment, which is the first of our prejudices—not a prejudice destitute of reason, but involving in it profound and extensive wisdom. I speak of it first. It is first, and last, and midst in our minds. For, taking ground on that religious system of which we are now in possession, we continue to act on the early received and uniformly continued sense of mankind. That sense not only, like a wise architect, hath built up the august fabric of states, but, like a provident proprietor, to preserve the structure from profanation and ruin, as a sacred temple, purged from all the impurities of fraud and violence and injustice and tyranny, hath solemnly and forever consecrated the commonwealth, and all that officiate in it. This consecration is made, that all who administer in the government of men, in which they stand in the person of God Himself, should have high and worthy notions of their function and destination; that their hope should be full of immortality; that they should not look to the paltry pelf of the moment, nor to the temporary and transient praise of the vulgar, but to a solid, permanent existence, in the permanent part of their nature, and to a permanent fame and glory, in the example they leave as a rich inheritance to the world.

Such sublime principles ought to be infused into persons of exalted situations, and religious establishments provided that may continually revive and enforce them. Every sort of moral, every sort of civil, every sort of politic institution, aiding the rational and natural ties that connect the human understanding and affections to the divine, are not more than necessary, in order to build up that wonderful structure, Man—whose prerogative it is, to be in a great degree a creature of his own making, and who, when made as he ought to be made, is destined to hold no trivial place in the creation. But whenever man is put over men, as the better nature ought ever to preside, in that case more particularly he should as nearly as possible be approximated to his perfection.

The consecration of the state by a state religious establishment is necessary also to operate with a wholesome awe upon free citizens; because, in order to secure their freedom, they must enjoy some determinate portion of power. To them, therefore, a religion connected with the state, and with their duty towards it, becomes even more necessary than in such societies where the people, by the terms of their subjection, are confined to private sentiments, and the management of their own family concerns. All persons possessing any portion of power ought to be strongly and awfully impressed with an idea that they act in trust, and that they are to account for their conduct in that trust to the one great Master, Author, and Founder of society.

This principle ought even to be more strongly impressed upon the minds of those who compose the collective sovereignty than upon those of single princes. Without instruments, these princes can do nothing. Whoever uses instruments, in finding helps, finds also impediments. Their power is therefore by no means complete; nor are they safe in extreme abuse. Such persons, however elevated by flattery, arrogance, and self-opinion, must be sensible, that, whether covered or not by positive law, in some way or other they are accountable even here for the abuse of their trust. If they are not cut off by a rebellion of their people, they may be strangled by the very janissaries kept for their security against all other rebellion. Thus we have seen the king of France sold by his soldiers for an increase of pay. But where popular authority is absolute and unrestrained, the people have an infinitely greater, because a far better founded, confidence in their own power. They are themselves in a great measure their own instruments. They are nearer to their objects. Besides, they are less under responsibility to one of the greatest controlling powers on earth, the sense of fame and estimation. The share of infamy that is likely to fall to the lot of each individual in public acts is small indeed: the operation of opinion being in the inverse ratio to the number of those who abuse power. Their own approbation of their own acts has to them the appearance of a public judgment in their favor. A perfect democracy is therefore the most shameless thing in the world. As it is the most shameless, it is also the most fearless. No man apprehends in his person that he can be made subject to punishment. Certainly the people at large never ought: for, as all punishments are for example towards the conservation of the people at large, the people at large can never become the subject of punishment by any human hand. It is therefore of infinite importance that they should not be suffered to imagine that their will, any more than that of kings, is the standard of right and wrong. They ought to be persuaded that they are full as little entitled, and far less qualified, with safety to themselves, to use any arbitrary power whatsoever; that therefore they are not, under a false show of liberty, but in truth to exercise an unnatural, inverted domination, tyrannically to exact from those who officiate in the state, not an entire devotion to their interest, which is their right, but an abject submission to their occasional will: extinguishing thereby, in all those who serve them, all moral principle, all sense of dignity, all use of judgment, and all consistency of character; whilst by the very same process they give themselves up a proper, a suitable, but a most contemptible prey to the servile ambition of popular sycophants or courtly flatterers.

When the people have emptied themselves of all the lust of selfish will, which without religion it is utterly impossible they ever should—when they are conscious that they exercise, and exercise perhaps in a higher link of the order of delegation, the power which to be legitimate must be according to that eternal, immutable law in which will and reason are the same—they will be more careful how they place power in base and incapable hands. In their nomination to office, they will not appoint to the exercise of authority as to a pitiful job, but as to a holy function; not according to their sordid, selfish interest, nor to their wanton caprice, nor to their arbitrary will; but they will confer that power (which any man may well tremble to give or to receive) on those only in whom they may discern that predominant proportion of active virtue and wisdom, taken together and fitted to the charge, such as in the great and inevitable mixed mass of human imperfections and infirmities is to be found.

When they are habitually convinced that no evil can be acceptable, either in the act or the permission, to Him whose essence is good, they will be better able to extirpate out of the minds of all magistrates, civil, ecclesiastical, or military, anything that bears the least resemblance to a proud and lawless domination.

But one of the first and most leading principles on which the commonwealth and the laws are consecrated is lest the temporary possessors and life-renters in it, unmindful of what they have received from their ancestors, or of what is due to their posterity, should act as if they were the entire masters; that they should not think it amongst their rights to cut off the entail or commit waste on the inheritance, by destroying at their pleasure the whole original fabric of their society: hazarding to leave to those who come after them a ruin instead of an habitation—and teaching these successors as little to respect their contrivances as they had themselves respected the institutions of their forefathers. By this unprincipled facility of changing the state as often and as much and in as many ways as there are floating fancies or fashions, the whole chain and continuity of the commonwealth would be broken; no one generation could link with the other; men would become little better than the flies of a summer.

And first of all, the science of jurisprudence, the pride of the human intellect, which, with all its defects, redundancies, and errors, is the collected reason of ages, combining the principles of original justice with the infinite variety of human concerns, as a heap of old exploded errors, would be no longer studied. Personal self-sufficiency and arrogance (the certain attendants upon all those who have never experienced a wisdom greater than their own) would usurp the tribunal. Of course no certain laws, establishing invariable grounds of hope and fear, would keep the actions of men in a certain course, or direct them to a certain end. Nothing stable in the modes of holding property or exercising function could form a solid ground on which any parent could speculate in the education of his offspring, or in a choice for their future establishment in the world. No principles would be early worked into the habits. As soon as the most able instructor had completed his laborious course of institution, instead of sending forth his pupil accomplished in a virtuous discipline fitted to procure him attention and respect in his place in society, he would find everything altered, and that he had turned out a poor creature to the contempt and derision of the world, ignorant of the true grounds of estimation. Who would insure a tender and delicate sense of honor to beat almost with the first pulses of the heart, when no man could know what would be the test of honor in a nation continually varying the standard of its coin? No part of life would retain its acquisitions. Barbarism with regard to science and literature, unskilfulness with regard to arts and manufactures, would infallibly succeed to the want of a steady education and settled principle; and thus the commonwealth itself would in a few generations crumble away, be disconnected into the dust and powder of individuality, and at length dispersed to all the winds of heaven.

To avoid, therefore, the evils of inconstancy and versatility, ten thousand times worse than those of obstinacy and the blindest prejudice, we have consecrated the state, that no man should approach to look into its defects or corruptions but with due caution; that he should never dream of beginning its reformation by its subversion; that he should approach to the faults of the state as to the wounds of a father, with pious awe and trembling solicitude. By this wise prejudice we are taught to look with horror on those children of their country who are prompt rashly to hack that aged parent in pieces and put him into the kettle of magicians, in hopes that by their poisonous weeds and wild incantations they may regenerate the paternal constitution and renovate their father's life.

Society is, indeed, a contract. Subordinate contracts for objects of mere occasional interest may be dissolved at pleasure; but the state ought not to be considered as nothing better than a partnership agreement in a trade of pepper and coffee, calico or tobacco, or some other such low concern, to be taken up for a little temporary interest, and to be dissolved by the fancy of the parties. It is to be looked on with other reverence; because it is not a partnership in things subservient only to the gross animal existence of a temporary and perishable nature. It is a partnership in all science, a partnership in all art, a partnership in every virtue and in all perfection. As the ends of such a partnership cannot be obtained in many generations, it becomes a partnership not only between those who are living, but between those who are living, those who are dead, and those who are to be born. Each contract of each particular state is but a clause in the great primeval contract of eternal society, linking the lower with the higher natures, connecting the visible and invisible world, according to a fixed compact sanctioned by the inviolable oath which holds all physical and all moral natures each in their appointed place. This law is not subject to the will of those who, by an obligation above them, and infinitely superior, are bound to submit their will to that law. The municipal corporations of that universal kingdom are not morally at liberty, at their pleasure, and on their speculations of a contingent improvement, wholly to separate and tear asunder the bands of their subordinate community, and to dissolve it into an unsocial, uncivil, unconnected chaos of elementary principles. It is the first and supreme necessity only, a necessity that is not chosen, but chooses, a necessity paramount to deliberation, that admits no discussion and demands no evidence, which alone can justify a resort to anarchy. This necessity is no exception to the rule; because this necessity itself is a part, too, of that moral and physical disposition of things to which man must be obedient by consent or force: but if that which is only submission to necessity should be made the object of choice, the law is broken, Nature is disobeyed, and the rebellious are outlawed, cast forth, and exiled, from this world of reason, and order, and peace, and virtue, and fruitful penitence, into the antagonist world of madness, discord, vice, confusion, and unavailing sorrow. . . .

Persuaded that all things ought to be done with reference, and referring all to the point of reference to which all should be directed, they think themselves bound, not only as individuals in the sanctuary of the heart, or as congregated in that personal capacity, to renew the memory of their high origin and cast, but also in their corporate character to perform their national homage to the Institutor and Author and Protector of civil society, without which civil society man could not by any possibility arrive at the perfection of which his nature is capable, nor even make a remote and faint approach to it. They conceive that He who gave our nature to be perfected by our virtue willed also the necessary means of its perfection: He willed, therefore, the state: He willed its connection with the source and original archetype of all perfection. They who are convinced of this His will, which is the law of laws and the sovereign of sovereigns, cannot think it reprehensible that this our corporate fealty and homage, that this our recognition of a signiory paramount, I had almost said this oblation of the state itself, as a worthy offering on the high altar of universal praise, should be performed, as all public, solemn acts are performed, in buildings, in music, in decoration, in speech, in the dignity of persons, according to the customs of mankind, taught by their nature—that is, with modest splendor, with unassuming state, with mild majesty and sober pomp. For those purposes they think some part of the wealth of the country is as usefully employed as it can be in fomenting the luxury of individuals. It is the public ornament. It is the public consolation. It nourishes the public hope. The poorest man finds his own importance and dignity in it, whilst the wealth and pride of individuals at every moment makes the man of humble rank and fortune sensible of his inferiority, and degrades and vilifies his condition. It is for the man in humble life, and to raise his nature, and to put him in mind of a state in which the privileges of opulence will cease, when he will be equal by nature, and may be more than equal by virtue, that this portion of the general wealth of his country is employed and sanctified. . . .

It is on some such principles that the majority of the people of England, far from thinking a religious national establishment unlawful, hardly think it lawful to be without one. . . .

This principle runs through the whole system of their polity. They do not consider their Church establishment as convenient, but as essential to their state: not as a thing heterogeneous and separable—something added for accommodation—what they may either keep up or lay aside, according to their temporary ideas of convenience. They consider it as the foundation of their whole Constitution, with which, and with every part of which, it holds an indissoluble union. Church and State are ideas inseparable in their minds, and scarcely is the one ever mentioned without mentioning the other.

Our education is so formed as to confirm and fix this impression. Our education is in a manner wholly in the hands of ecclesiastics, and in all stages from infancy to manhood. Even when our youth, leaving schools and universities, enter that most important period of life which begins to link experience and study together, and when with that view they visit other countries, instead of old domestics whom we have seen as governors to principal men from other parts, three fourths of those who go abroad with our young nobility and gentlemen are ecclesiastics: not as austere masters, not as mere followers; but as friends and companions of a graver character, and not seldom persons as well born as themselves. With them, as relations, they most commonly keep up a close connection through life. By this connection we conceive that we attach our gentlemen to the Church; and we liberalize the Church by an intercourse with the leading characters of the country.

So tenacious are we of the old ecclesiastical modes and fashions of institution, that very little alteration has been made in them since the fourteenth or fifteenth century: adhering in this particular, as in all things else, to our old settled maxim, never entirely nor at once to depart from antiquity. We found these old institutions, on the whole, favorable to morality and discipline; and we thought they were susceptible of amendment, without altering the ground. We thought that they were capable of receiving and meliorating, and above all of preserving, the accessions of science and literature, as the order of Providence should successively produce them. And after all, with this Gothic and monkish education, (for such it is in the groundwork,) we may put in our claim to as ample and as early a share in all the improvements in science, in arts, and in literature, which have illuminated and adorned the modern world, as any other nation in Europe: we think one main cause of this improvement was our not despising the patrimony of knowledge which was left us by our forefathers.

It is from our attachment to a Church establishment, that the English nation did not think it wise to intrust that great fundamental interest of the whole to what they trust no part of their civil or military public service—that is, to the unsteady and precarious contribution of individuals. They go further. They certainly never have suffered, and never will suffer, the fixed estate of the Church to be converted into a pension, to depend on the Treasury, and to be delayed, withheld, or perhaps to be extinguished by fiscal difficulties: which difficulties may sometimes be pretended for political purposes, and are in fact often brought on by the extravagance, negligence, and rapacity of politicians. The people of England think that they have constitutional motives, as well as religious, against any project of turning their independent clergy into ecclesiastical pensioners of state. They tremble for their liberty, from the influence of a clergy dependent on the crown; they tremble for the public tranquility, from the disorders of a factious clergy, if it were made to depend upon any other than the crown. They therefore made their Church, like their king and their nobility, independent.

From the united considerations of religion and constitutional policy, from their opinion of a duty to make a sure provision for the consolation of the feeble and the instruction of the ignorant, they have incorporated and identified the estate of the Church with the mass of *private property*, of which the state is not the proprietor, either for use or dominion, but the guardian only and the regulator. . . .

The Christian statesmen of this land would, indeed, first provide for the *multitude*, because it is the *multitude*, and is therefore, as such, the first object in the ecclesiastical institution, and in all institutions. They have been taught that the circumstances of the Gospel's being preached to the poor was one of the great tests of its true mission. They think, therefore, that those do not believe it who do not take care it should be preached to the poor. But as they know that charity is not confined to any one description, but ought to apply itself to all men who have wants, they are not deprived of a due and anxious sensation of pity to the distresses of the miserable great. . . .

The English people are satisfied, that to the great the consolations of religion are as necessary as its instructions. They, too, are among the unhappy. They feel personal pain and domestic sorrow. . . .

The people of England know how little influence the teachers of religion are likely to have with the wealthy and powerful of long standing, and how much less with the newly fortunate, if they appear in a manner no way assorted to those with whom they must associate, and over whom they must even exercise, in some cases, something like an authority. What must they think of that body of teachers, if they see it in no part above the establishment of their domestic servants? If the poverty were voluntary, there might be some difference. Strong instances of self-denial operate powerfully on our minds; and a man who has no wants has obtained great freedom and firmness, and even dignity. But as the mass of any description of men are but men, and their poverty cannot be voluntary, that disrespect which attends upon all lay poverty will not depart from the ecclesiastical. Our provident Constitution has therefore taken care that those who are to instruct presumptuous ignorance, those who are to be censors over insolent vice, should neither incur their contempt nor live upon their alms; nor will it tempt the rich to a neglect of the true medicine of their minds. For these reasons, whilst we provide first for the poor, and with a parental solicitude, we have not relegated religion (like something we were ashamed to show) to obscure municipalities or rustic villages. No! we will have her to exalt her mitred front in courts and parliaments. We will have her mixed throughout the whole mass of life, and blended with all the classes of society. The people of England will show to the haughty potentates of the world, and to their talking sophisters, that a free, a generous, an informed nation honors the high magistrates of its Church; that it will not suffer the insolence of wealth and titles, or any other species of proud pretension, to look down with scorn upon what they look up to with reverence, nor presume to trample on that acquired personal nobility which they intend always to be, and which often is, the fruit, not the reward, (for what can be the reward?) of learning, piety, and virtue. They can see, without pain or grudging, an archbishop precede a duke. They can see a bishop of Durham or a bishop of Winchester in possession of ten thousand pounds a year, and cannot conceive why it is in worse hands than estates to the like amount in the hands of this earl or that squire; although it may be true that so many dogs and horses are not kept by the former, and fed with the victuals which ought to nourish the children of the people. It is true, the whole Church revenue is not always employed, and to every shilling, in charity; nor perhaps ought it; but something is generally so employed. It is better to cherish virtue and humanity, by leaving much to free will, even with some loss to the object, than to attempt to make men mere machines and instruments of a political benevolence. The world on the whole will gain by a liberty without which virtue cannot exist. . . .

In this state of real, though not always perceived, warfare between the noble ancient landed interest and the new moneyed interest, the greatest, because the most applicable, strength was in the hands of the latter. The moneyed interest is in its nature more ready for any adventure, and its possessors more disposed to new enterprises of any kind. Being of a recent acquisition, it falls in more naturally with any novelties. It is therefore the kind of wealth which will be resorted to by all who wish for change.

Along with the moneyed interest, a new description of men had grown up, with whom that interest soon formed a close and marked union: I mean the political men of letters. Men of letters, fond of distinguishing themselves, are rarely averse to innovation. Since the decline of the life and greatness of Louis the Fourteenth, they were not so much cultivated either by him, or by the Regent, or the successors to the crown; nor were they engaged to the court by favors and emoluments so systematically as during the splendid period of that ostentatious and not impolitic reign. What they lost in the old court protection they endeavored to make up by joining in a sort of incorporation of their own; to which the two academies of France, and afterwards the vast undertaking of the Encyclopædia, carried on by a society of these gentlemen, did not a little contribute.

The literary cabal had some years ago formed something like a regular plan for the destruction of the Christian religion. This object they pursued with a degree of zeal which hitherto had been discovered only in the propagators of some system of piety. They were possessed with a spirit of proselytism in the most fanatical degree—and from thence, by an easy progress, with the spirit of persecution according to their means. What was not to be done towards their great end by any direct or immediate act might be wrought by a longer process through the medium of opinion. To command that opinion, the first step is to establish a dominion over those who direct it. They contrived to possess themselves, with great method and perseverance, of all the avenues to literary fame. Many of them, indeed, stood high in the ranks of literature and science. The world had done them justice, and in favor of general talents forgave the evil tendency of their peculiar principles. This was true liberality; which they returned by endeavoring to confine the reputation of sense, learning, and taste to themselves or their followers. I will venture to say that this narrow, exclusive spirit has not been less prejudicial to literature and to taste than to morals and true philosophy. These atheistical fathers have a bigotry of their own; and they have learnt to talk against monks with the spirit of a monk. But in some things they are men of the world. The resources of intrigue are called in to supply the defects of argument and wit. To this system of literary monopoly was joined an unremitting industry to blacken and discredit in every way, and by every means, all those who did not hold to their faction. To those who have observed the spirit of their conduct it has long been clear that nothing was wanted but the power of carrying the intolerance of the tongue and of the pen into a persecution which would strike at property, liberty, and life.

The desultory and faint persecution carried on against them, more from compliance with form and decency than with serious resentment, neither weakened their strength nor relaxed their efforts. The issue of the whole was, that, what with opposition, and what with success, a violent and malignant zeal, of a kind hitherto unknown in the world, had taken an entire possession of their minds, and rendered their whole conversation, which otherwise would have been pleasing and instructive, perfectly disgusting. A spirit of cabal, intrigue, and proselytism pervaded all their thoughts, words, and actions. And as controversial zeal soon turns its thoughts on force, they began to insinuate themselves into a correspondence with foreign princes—in hopes, through their authority, which at first they flattered, they might bring about the changes they had in view. To them it was indifferent whether these changes were to be accomplished by the thunderbolt of despotism or by the earthquake of popular commotion. The correspondence between this cabal and the late king of Prussia will throw no small light upon the spirit of all their proceedings. For the same purpose for which they intrigued with princes, they cultivated, in a distinguished manner, the moneyed interest of France; and partly through the means furnished by those whose peculiar offices gave them the most extensive and certain means of communication, they carefully occupied all the avenues to opinion.

Writers, especially when they act in a body and with one direction, have great influence on the public mind; the alliance, therefore, of these writers with the moneyed interest had no small effect in removing the popular odium and envy which attended that species of wealth. These writers, like the propagators of all novelties, pretended to a great zeal for the poor and the lower orders, whilst in their satires they rendered hateful, by every exaggeration, the faults of courts, of nobility, and of priesthood. They became a sort of demagogues. They served as a link to unite, in favor of one object, obnoxious wealth to restless and desperate poverty.

As these two kinds of men appear principal leaders in all the late transactions, their junction and politics will serve to account, not upon any principles of law or of policy, but as a *cause*, for the general fury with which all the landed property of ecclesiastical corporations has been attacked, and the great care which, contrary to their pretended principles, has been taken of a moneyed interest originating from the authority of the crown. All the envy against wealth and power was artificially directed against other descriptions of riches. On what other principle than that which I have stated can we account for an appearance so extraordinary and unnatural as that of the ecclesiastical possessions, which had stood so many successions of ages and shocks of civil violences, and were guarded at once by justice and by prejudice, being applied to the payment of debts comparatively recent, invidious, and contracted by a decried and subverted government. . . .

When all the frauds, impostures, violences, rapines, burnings, murders, confiscations, compulsory paper currencies, and every description of tyranny and cruelty employed to bring about and to uphold this Revolution have their natural effect, that is, to shock the moral sentiments of all virtuous and sober minds, the abettors of this philosophic system immediately strain their throats in a declamation against the old monarchical government of France. When they have rendered that deposed power sufficiently black, they then proceed in argument, as if all those who disapprove of their new abuses must of course be partisans of the old—that those who reprobate their crude and violent schemes of liberty ought to be treated as advocates for servitude. I admit that their necessities do compel them to this base and contemptible fraud. Nothing can reconcile men to their proceedings and projects but the supposition that there is no third option between them and some tyranny as odious as can be furnished by the records of history or by the invention of poets. This prattling of theirs hardly deserves the name of sophistry. It is nothing but plain impudence. Have these gentlemen never heard, in the whole circle of the worlds of theory and practice, of anything between the despotism of the monarch and the despotism of the multitude? Have they never heard of a monarchy directed by laws, controlled and balanced by the great hereditary wealth and hereditary dignity of a nation, and both again controlled by a judicious check from the reason and feeling of the people at large, acting by a suitable and permanent organ? Is it, then, impossible that a man may be found who, without criminal ill intention or pitiable absurdity, shall prefer such a mixed and tempered government to either of the extremes—and who may repute that nation to be destitute of all wisdom and of all virtue, which, having in its choice to obtain such a government with ease, *or rather to confirm it when actually possessed,* thought proper to commit a thousand crimes, and to subject their country to a thousand evils, in order to avoid it? Is it, then, a truth so universally acknowledged, that a pure democracy is the only tolerable form into which human society can be thrown, that a man is not permitted to hesitate about its merits, without the suspicion of being a friend to tyranny, that is, of being a foe to mankind?

I do not know under what description to class the present ruling authority in France. It affects to be a pure democracy, though I think it in a direct train of becoming shortly a mischievous and ignoble oligarchy. But for the present I admit it to be a contrivance of the nature and effect of what it pretends to. I reprobate no form of government merely upon abstract principles. There may be situations in which the purely democratic form will become necessary. There may be some (very few, and very particularly circumstanced) where it would be clearly desirable. This I do not take to be the case of France, or of any other great country. Until now, we have seen no examples of considerable democracies. The ancients were better acquainted with them. Not being wholly unread in the authors who had seen the most of those constitutions, and who best understood them, I cannot help concurring with their opinion, that an absolute democracy no more than absolute monarchy is to be reckoned among the legitimate forms of government. They think it rather the corruption and degeneracy than the sound constitution of a republic. If I recollect rightly, Aristotle observes, that a democracy has many striking points of resemblance with a tyranny. Of this I am certain, that in a democracy the majority of the citizens is capable of exercising the most cruel oppressions upon the majority, whenever strong divisions prevail in that kind of polity, as they often must—and that oppression of the minority will extend to far greater numbers, and will be carried on with much greater fury, than can almost ever be apprehended from the dominion of a single sceptre. In such a popular persecution, individual sufferers are in a much more deplorable condition than in any other. Under a cruel prince they have the balmy compassion of mankind to assuage the smart of their wounds, they have the plaudits of the people to animate their generous constancy under their sufferings: but those who are subjected to wrong under multitudes are deprived of all external consolation; they seem deserted by mankind, overpowered by a conspiracy of their whole species. . . .

Your government in France, though usually, and I think justly, reputed the best of the unqualified or ill-qualified monarchies, was still full of abuses. These abuses accumulated in a length of time, as they must accumulate in every monarchy not under the constant inspection of a popular representative. I am no stranger to the faults and defects of the subverted government of France; and I think I am not inclined by nature or policy to make a panegyric upon anything which is a just and natural object of censure. But the question is not now of the vices of that monarchy, but of its existence. Is it, then, true, that the French government was such as to be incapable or undeserving of reform, so that it was of absolute necessity the whole fabric should be at once pulled down, and the area cleared for the erection of a theoretic, experimental edifice in its place? All France was of a different opinion in the beginning of the year 1789. The instructions to the representatives to the States-General, from every district in that kingdom, were filled with projects for the reformation of that government, without the remotest suggestion of a design to destroy it. Had such a design been then even insinuated, I believe there would have been but one voice, and that voice for rejecting it with scorn and horror. Men have been sometimes led by degrees, sometimes hurried, into things of which, if they could have seen the whole together, they never would have permitted the most remote approach. When those instructions were given, there was no question but that abuses existed, and that they demanded a reform: nor is there now. In the interval between the instructions and the Revolution things changed their shape; and in consequence of that change, the true question at present is, whether those who would have reformed or those who have destroyed are in the right.

To hear some men speak of the late monarchy of France, you would imagine that they were talking of Persia bleeding under the ferocious sword of Thamas Kouli Khân—or at least describing the barbarous anarchic despotism of Turkey, where the finest countries in the most genial climates in the world are wasted by peace more than any countries have been worried by war, where arts are unknown, where manufactures languish, where science is extinguished, where agriculture decays, where the human race itself melts away and perishes under the eye of the observer. Was this the case of France? I have no way of determining the question but by a reference to facts. Facts do not support this resemblance. Along with much evil, there is some good in monarchy itself; and some corrective to its evil from religion, from laws, from manners, from opinions, the French monarchy must have received, which rendered it (though by no means a free, and therefore by no means a good constitution) a despotism rather in appearance than in reality. . . .

Indeed, when I consider the face of the kingdom of France, the multitude and opulence of her cities, the useful magnificence of her spacious high-roads and bridges, the opportunity of her artificial canals and navigations opening the conveniences of maritime communication through a solid continent of so immense an extent—when I turn my eyes to the stupendous works of her ports and harbors, and to her whole naval apparatus, whether for war or trade—when I bring before my view the number of her fortifications, constructed with so bold and masterly a skill, and made and maintained at so prodigious a charge, presenting an armed front and impenetrable barrier to her enemies upon every side—when I recollect how very small a part of that extensive region is without cultivation, and to what complete perfection the culture of many of the best productions of the earth have been brought in France—when I reflect on the excellence of her manufactures and fabrics, second to none but ours, and in some particulars not second—when I contemplate the grand foundations of charity, public and private—when I survey the state of all the arts that beautify and polish life—when I reckon the men she has bred for extending her fame in war, her able statesmen, the multitude of her profound lawyers and theologians, her philosophers, her critics, her historians and antiquaries, her poets and her orators, sacred and profane—I behold in all this something which awes and commands the imagination, which checks the mind on the brink of precipitate and indiscriminate censure, and which demands that we should very seriously examine what and how great are the latent vices that could authorize us at once to level so spacious a fabric with the ground. I do not recognize in this view of things the despotism of Turkey. Nor do I discern the character of a government that has been on the whole so oppressive, or so corrupt, or so negligent, as to be utterly unfit *for all reformation*. I must think such a government well deserved to have its excellences heightened, its faults corrected, and its capacities improved into a British Constitution. . . .

The advocates for this Revolution, not satisfied with exaggerating the vices of their ancient government, strike at the fame of their country itself, by painting almost all that could have attracted the attention of strangers, I mean their nobility and their clergy, as objects of horror. If this were only a libel, there had not been much in it. But it has practical consequences. Had your nobility and gentry, who formed the great body of your landed men and the whole of your military officers, resembled those of Germany, at the period when the Hanse towns were necessitated to confederate against the nobles in defence of their property—had they been like the Orsini and Vitelli in Italy, who used to sally from their fortified dens to rob the trader and traveller—had they been such as the Mamelukes in Egypt, or the Nayres on the coast of Malabar—I do admit that too critical an inquiry might not be advisable into the means of freeing the world from such a nuisance. The statues of Equity and Mercy might be veiled for a moment. The tenderest minds, confounded with the dreadful exigence in which morality submits to the suspension of its own rules in favor of its own principles, might turn aside whilst fraud and violence were accomplishing the destruction of a pretended nobility, which disgraced, whilst it persecuted, human nature. The persons most abhorrent from blood and treason and arbitrary confiscation might remain silent spectators of this civil war between the vices.

But did the privileged nobility who met under the king's precept at Versailles in 1789, or their constituents, deserve to be looked on as the Nayres or Mamelukes of this age, or as the Orsini and Vitelli of ancient times? If I had then asked the question, I should have passed for a madman. What have they since done, that they were to be driven into exile, that their persons should be hunted about, mangled, and tortured, their families dispersed, their houses laid in ashes, and that their order should be abolished, and the memory of it, if possible, extinguished, by ordaining them to change the very names by which they were usually known? Read their instructions to their representatives. They breathe the spirit of liberty as warmly, and they recommend reformation as strongly, as any other order. Their privileges relative to contribution were voluntarily surrendered; as the king, from the beginning, surrendered all pretence to a right of taxation. Upon a free constitution there was but one opinion in France. The absolute monarchy was at an end. It breathed its last without a groan, without struggle, without convulsion. All the struggle, all the dissension, arose afterwards, upon the preference of a despotic democracy to a government of reciprocal control. The triumph of the victorious party was over the principles of a British Constitution. . . .

I do not pretend to know France as correctly as some others; but I have endeavored through my whole life to make myself acquainted with human nature—otherwise I should be unfit to take even my humble part in the service of mankind. In that study I could not pass by a vast portion of our nature as it appeared modified in a country but twenty-four miles from the shore of this island. On my best observation, compared with my best inquiries, I found your nobility for the greater part composed of men of a high spirit, and of a delicate sense of honor, both with regard to themselves individually, and with regard to their whole corps, over whom they kept, beyond what is common in other countries, a censorial eye. They were tolerably well bred; very officious, humane, and hospitable; in their conversation frank and open; with a good military tone; and reasonably tinctured with literature, particularly of the authors in their own language. Many had pretensions far above this description. . . .

As to their behavior to the inferior classes, they appeared to me to comport themselves towards them with good-nature, and with something more nearly approaching to familiarity than is generally practised with us in the intercourse between the higher and lower ranks of life. To strike any person, even in the most abject condition, was a thing in a manner unknown, and would be highly disgraceful. Instances of other ill-treatment of the humble part of the community were rare; and as to attacks made upon the property or the personal liberty of the commons, I never heard of any whatsoever from *them*—nor, whilst the laws were in vigor under the ancient government, would such tyranny in subjects have been permitted. As men of landed estates, I had no fault to find with their conduct, though much to reprehend, and much to wish changed, in many of the old tenures. Where the letting of their land was by rent, I could not discover that their agreements with their farmers were oppressive; nor when they were in partnership with the farmer, as often was the case, have I heard that they had taken the lion's share. The proportions seemed not inequitable. There might be exceptions, but certainly they were exceptions only. I have no reason to believe that in these respects the landed noblesse of France were worse than the landed gentry of this country—certainly in no respect more vexatious than the landholders, not noble, of their own nation. In cities the nobility had no manner of power; in the country very little. You know, Sir, that much of the civil government, and the police in the most essential parts, was not in the hands of that nobility which presents itself first to our consideration. The revenue, the system and collection of which were the most grievous parts of the French government, was not administered by the men of the sword; nor were they answerable for the vices of its principle, or the vexations, where any such existed, in its management.

Denying, as I am well warranted to do, that the nobility had any considerable share in the oppression of the people, in cases in which real oppression existed, I am ready to admit that they were not without considerable faults and errors. A foolish imitation of the worst part of the manners of England, which impaired their natural character, without substituting in its place what perhaps they meant to copy, has certainly rendered them worse than formerly they were. Habitual dissoluteness of manners, continued beyond the pardonable period of life, was more common amongst them than it is with us; and it reigned with the less hope of remedy, though possibly with something of less mischief, by being covered with more exterior decorum. They countenanced too much that licentious philosophy which has helped to bring on their ruin. There was another error amongst them more fatal. Those of the commons who approached to or exceeded many of the nobility in point of wealth were not fully admitted to the rank and estimation which wealth, in reason and good policy, ought to bestow in every country—though I think not equally with that of other nobility. The two kinds of aristocracy were too punctiliously kept asunder: less so, however, than in Germany and some other nations.

This separation, as I have already taken the liberty of suggesting to you, I conceive to be one principal cause of the destruction of the old nobility. The military, particularly, was too exclusively reserved for men of family. But, after all, this was an error of opinion, which a conflicting opinion would have rectified. A permanent Assembly, in which the commons had their share of power, would soon abolish whatever was too invidious and insulting in these distinctions; and even the faults in the morals of the nobility would have been probably corrected, by the greater varieties of occupation and pursuit to which a constitution by orders would have given rise.

All this violent cry against the nobility I take to be a mere work of art. To be honored and even privileged by the laws, opinions, and inveterate usages of our country, growing out of the prejudice of ages, has nothing to provoke horror and indignation in any man. Even to be too tenacious of those privileges is not absolutely a crime. The strong struggle in every individual to preserve possession of what he has found to belong to him, and to distinguish him, is one of the securities against injustice and despotism implanted in our nature. It operates as an instinct to secure property, and to preserve communities in a settled state. What is there to shock in this? Nobility is a graceful ornament to the civil order. It is the Corinthian capital of polished society. . . . It is, indeed, one sign of a liberal and benevolent mind to incline to it with some sort of partial propensity. He feels no ennobling principle in his own heart, who wishes to level all the artificial institutions which have been adopted for giving a body to opinion and permanence to fugitive esteem. It is a sour, malignant, envious disposition, without taste for the reality, or for any image or representation of virtue, that sees with joy the unmerited fall of what had long flourished in splendor and in honor. I do not like to see anything destroyed, any void produced in society, any ruin on the face of the land. It was therefore with no disappointment or dissatisfaction that my inquiries and observations did not present to me any incorrigible vices in the noblesse of France, or any abuse which could not be removed by a reform very short of abolition. Your noblesse did not deserve punishment; but to degrade is to punish.

It was with the same satisfaction I found that the result of my inquiry concerning your clergy was not dissimilar. It is no soothing news to my ears, that great bodies of men are incurably corrupt. It is not with much credulity I listen to any, when they speak evil of those whom they are going to plunder. I rather suspect that vices are feigned or exaggerated, when profit is looked for in their punishment. An enemy is a bad witness; a robber is a worse. Vices and abuses there were undoubtedly in that order, and must be. It was an old establishment, and not frequently revised. But I saw no crimes in the individuals that merited confiscation of their substance, nor those cruel insults and degradations, and that unnatural persecution, which have been substituted in the place of meliorating regulation. . . .

But the present ruling power has shown a disposition only to plunder the Church. It has punished *all* prelates: which is to favor the vicious, at least in point of reputation. It has made a degrading pensionary establishment, to which no man of liberal ideas or liberal condition will destine his children. It must settle into the lowest classes of the people. As with you the inferior clergy are not numerous enough for their duties, as these duties are beyond measure minute and toilsome, as you have left no middle classes of clergy at their ease, in future nothing of science or erudition can exist in the Gallican Church. To complete the project, without the least attention to the rights of patrons, the Assembly has provided in future an elective clergy: an arrangement which will drive out of the clerical profession all men of sobriety, all who can pretend to independence in their function or their conduct—and which will throw the whole direction of the public mind into the hands of a set of licentious, bold, crafty, factious, flattering wretches, of such condition and such habits of life as will make their contemptible pensions (in comparison of which the stipend of an exciseman is lucrative and honorable) an object of low and illiberal intrigue. Those officers whom they still call bishops are to be elected to a provision comparatively mean, through the same arts, (that is, electioneering arts,) by men of all religious tenets that are known or can be invented. The new lawgivers have not ascertained anything whatsoever concerning their qualifications, relative either to doctrine or to morals, no more than they have done with regard to the subordinate clergy; nor does it appear but that both the higher and the lower may, at their discretion, practise or preach any mode of religion or irreligion that they please. I do not yet see what the jurisdiction of bishops over their subordinates is to be, or whether they are to have any jurisdiction at all.

In short, Sir, it seems to me that this new ecclesiastical establishment is intended only to be temporary, and preparatory to the utter abolition, under any of its forms, of the Christian religion, whenever the minds of men are prepared for this last stroke against it by the accomplishment of the plan for bringing its ministers into universal contempt. They who will not believe that the philosophical fanatics who guide in these matters have long entertained such a design are utterly ignorant of their character and proceedings. These enthusiasts do not scruple to avow their opinion, that a state can subsist without any religion better than with one, and that they are able to supply the place of any good which may be in it by a project of their own—namely, by a sort of education they have imagined, founded in a knowledge of the physical wants of men, progressively carried to an enlightened self-interest, which, when well understood, they tell us, will identify with an interest more enlarged and public. . . .

Those of you who have robbed the clergy think that they shall easily reconcile their conduct to all Protestant nations, because the clergy whom they have thus plundered, degraded, and given over to mockery and scorn, are of the Roman Catholic, that is, of *their own* pretended persuasion. I have no doubt that some miserable bigots will be found here as well as elsewhere, who hate sects and parties different from their own more than they love the substance of religion, and who are more angry with those who differ from them in their particular plans and systems than displeased with those who attack the foundation of our common hope. These men will write and speak on the subject in the manner that is to be expected from their temper and character. . . .

The teachers who reformed our religion in England bore no sort of resemblance to your present reforming doctors in Paris. Perhaps they were (like those whom they opposed) rather more than could be wished under the influence of a party spirit; but they were most sincere believers; men of the most fervent and exalted piety; ready to die (as some of them did die) like true heroes in defence of their particular ideas of Christianity—as they would with equal fortitude, and more cheerfully, for that stock of general truth for the branches of which they contended with their blood. These men would have disavowed with horror those wretches who claimed a fellowship with them upon no other titles than those of their having pillaged the persons with whom they maintained controversies, and their having despised the common religion, for the purity of which they exerted themselves with a zeal which unequivocally bespoke their highest reverence for the substance of that system which they wished to reform. Many of their descendants have retained the same zeal, but (as less engaged in conflict) with more moderation. They do not forget that justice and mercy are substantial parts of religion. Impious men do not recommend themselves to their communion by iniquity and cruelty towards any description of their fellow-creatures. . . .

An Appeal from the New to the Old Whigs

In the several years before the execution of Louis XVI in January 1793 and before the Reign of Terror and the revolutionary mob violence of 1793 and 1794, Burke stood virtually alone in his indictment of the Jacobins as evil incarnate. As Fox described the new French Constitution as "the most stupendous and glorious edifice of liberty which had been erected on the foundation of human integrity in any time or country," Burke insisted that he alone stood for the "old Whig" principles of the 1688 Glorious Revolution, while Fox and others were seduced by the "New Whig" ideals of popular sovereignty. Burke made this case in this pamphlet, published in August 1791, which contains some of his most important philosophical speculations about the nature of society.

IT IS CERTAINLY WELL for Mr. Burke that there are impartial men in the world. To them I address myself, pending the appeal which on his part is made from the living to the dead, from the modern Whigs to the ancient. . . .

If the party had denied his doctrines to be the current opinions of the majority in the nation, they would have put the question on its true issue. . . . His censurers will find, on the trial, that the author is as faithful a representative of the general sentiment of the people of England, as any person amongst them can be of the ideas of his own party.

The French Revolution can have no connection with the objects of any parties in England formed before the period of that event, unless they choose to imitate any of its acts, or to consolidate any principles of that Revolution with their own opinions. The French Revolution is no part of their original contract. . . . But if any considerable number of British subjects, taking a factious interest in the proceedings of France, begin publicly to incorporate themselves for the subversion of nothing short of the *whole* Constitution of this kingdom—to incorporate themselves for the utter overthrow of the body of its laws, civil and ecclesiastical, and with them of the whole system of its manners, in favor of the new Constitution and of the modern usages of the French nation—I think no party principle could bind the author not to express his sentiments strongly against such a faction. . . .

He had undertaken to demonstrate, by arguments which he thought could not be refuted, and by documents which he was sure could not be denied, that no comparison was to be made between the British government and the French usurpation.—That they who endeavored madly to compare them were by no means making the comparison of one good system with another good system, which varied only in local and circumstantial differences; much less that they were holding out to us a superior pattern of legal liberty, which we might substitute in the place of our old, and, as they describe it, superannuated Constitution. He meant to demonstrate that the French scheme was not a comparative good, but a positive evil.—That the question did not at all turn, as it had been stated, on a parallel between a monarchy and a republic. He denied that the present scheme of things in France did at all deserve the respectable name of a republic: he had therefore no comparison between monarchies and republics to make.—That what was done in France was a wild attempt to methodize anarchy, to perpetuate and fix disorder. . . .

The excellencies of the British Constitution had already exercised and exhausted the talents of the best thinkers and the most eloquent writers and speakers that the world ever saw. But in the present case a system declared to be far better, and which certainly is much newer, (to restless and unstable minds no small recommendation,) was held out to the admiration of the good people of England. In that case it was surely thought proper for those who had far other thoughts of the French

Constitution to scrutinize that plan which has been recommended to our imitation by active and zealous factions at home and abroad. . . .

When we praise our Revolution of 1688, though the nation in that act was on the defensive, and was justified in incurring all the evils of a defensive war, we do not rest there. We always combine with the subversion of the old government the happy settlement which followed. When we estimate that Revolution, we mean to comprehend in our calculation both the value of the thing parted with and the value of the thing received in exchange.

The burden of proof lies heavily on those who tear to pieces the whole frame and contexture of their country, that they, could find no other way of settling a government fit to obtain its rational ends, except that which they have pursued by means unfavorable to all the present happiness of millions of people, and to the utter ruin of several hundreds of thousands. In their political arrangements, men have no right to put the well-being of the present generation wholly out of the question. Perhaps the only moral trust with any certainty in our hands is the care of our own time. With regard to futurity, we are to treat it like a ward. We are not so to attempt an improvement of his fortune as to put the capital of his estate to any hazard.

It is not worth our while to discuss, like sophisters, whether in no case some evil for the sake of some benefit is to be tolerated. Nothing universal can be rationally affirmed on any moral or any political subject. Pure metaphysical abstraction does not belong to these matters. The lines of morality are not like the ideal lines of mathematics. They are broad and deep as well as long. They admit of exceptions; they demand modifications. These exceptions and modifications are not made by the process of logic, but by the rules of prudence. Prudence is not only the first in rank of the virtues political and moral, but she is the director, the regulator, the standard of them all. Metaphysics cannot live without definition; but Prudence is cautious how she defines. Our courts cannot be more fearful in suffering fictitious cases to be brought before them for eliciting their determination on a point of law than prudent moralists are in putting extreme and hazardous cases of conscience upon emergencies not existing. Without attempting, therefore, to define, what never can be defined, the case of a revolution in government, this, I think, may be safely affirmed—that a sore and pressing evil is to be removed, and that a good, great in its amount and unequivocal in its nature, must be probable almost to certainty, before the inestimable price of our own morals and the well-being of a number of our fellow-citizens is paid for a revolution. If ever we ought to be economists even to parsimony, it is in the voluntary production of evil. Every revolution contains in it something of evil.

It must always be, to those who are the greatest amateurs, or even professors, of revolutions, a matter very hard to prove, that the late French government was so bad that nothing worse in the infinite devices of men could come in its place. They who have brought France to its present condition ought to prove also, by something better than prattling about the Bastile, that their subverted government was as incapable as the present certainly is of all improvement and correction. How dare they to say so who have never made that experiment? They are experimenters by their trade. They have made an hundred others, infinitely more hazardous.

The English admirers of the forty-eight thousand republics which form the French federation praise them not for what they are, but for what they are to become. They do not talk as politicians, but as prophets. But in whatever character they choose to found panegyric on prediction, it will be thought a little singular to praise any work, not for its own merits, but for the merits of something else which may succeed to it. When any political institution is praised, in spite of great and prominent faults of every kind, and in all its parts, it must be supposed to have something excellent in its fundamental principles. . . .

The gentlemen of the party . . . have . . . publicly represented him as . . . disgracing his whole public life by a scandalous contradiction of every one of his own acts, writings, and declarations. . . .

On their ideas, the new Whig party have . . . acted as became them. The author of the Reflections, however, on his part, cannot, without great shame to himself, . . . admit the truth or justice of the charges which have been made upon him. . . . He must believe, if he does not mean wilfully to abandon his cause and his reputation, that principles fundamentally at variance with those of his book are fundamentally false. . . . He is very unwilling to suppose that the doctrines of some books lately circulated are the principles of the party; though, from the vehement declarations against his opinions, he is at some loss how to judge otherwise. . . .

I pass to the next head of charge—Mr. Burke's inconsistency. . . .

This is the great gist of the charge against him. It is not so much that he is wrong in his book (that, however, is alleged also) as that he has therein belied his whole life. I believe, if he could venture to value himself upon anything, it is on the virtue of consistency that he would value himself the most. Strip him of this, and you leave him naked indeed. . . . .

He who thinks that the British Constitution ought to consist of the three members, of three very different natures, of which it does actually consist, and thinks it his duty to preserve each of those members in its proper place and with its proper proportion of power, must (as each shall happen to be attacked) vindicate the three several parts on the several principles peculiarly belonging to them. He cannot assert the democratic part on the principles on which monarchy is supported, nor can he support monarchy on the principles of democracy, nor can he maintain aristocracy on the grounds of the one or of the other or of both. All these he must support on grounds that are totally different, though practically they may be, and happily with us they are, brought into one harmonious body. A man could not be consistent in defending such various, and, at first view, discordant, parts of a mixed Constitution, without that sort of inconsistency with which Mr. Burke stands charged.

As any one of the great members of this Constitution happens to be endangered, he that is a friend to all of them chooses and presses the topics necessary for the support of the part attacked, with all the strength, the earnestness, the vehemence, with all the power of stating, of argument, and of coloring, which he happens to possess, and which the case demands. He is not to embarrass the minds of his hearers, or to incumber or overlay his speech, by bringing into view at once (as if he were reading an academic lecture) all that may and ought, when a just occasion presents itself, to be said in favor of the other members. At that time they are out of the court; there is no question concerning them. Whilst he opposes his defence on the part where the attack is made, he presumes that for his regard to the just rights of all the rest he has credit in every candid mind. He ought not to apprehend that his raising fences about popular privileges this day will infer that he ought on the next to concur with those who would pull down the throne; because on the next he defends the throne, it ought not to be supposed that he has abandoned the rights of the people. . . .

If the principles of a mixed Constitution be admitted, he wants no more to justify to consistency everything he has said and done during the course of a political life just touching to its close. I believe that gentleman has kept himself more clear of running into the fashion of wild, visionary theories, or of seeking popularity through every means, than any man perhaps ever did in the same situation.

He was the first man who, on the hustings, at a popular election, rejected the authority of instructions from constituents—or who, in any place, has argued so fully against it. Perhaps the discredit into which that doctrine of compulsive instructions under our Constitution is since fallen may be due in a great degree to his opposing himself to it in that manner and on that occasion.

The reforms in representation, and the bills for shortening the duration of Parliaments, he uniformly and steadily opposed for many years together, in contradiction to many of his best friends. These friends, however, in his better days, when they had more to hope from his service and more to fear from his loss than now they have, never chose to find any inconsistency between his acts and expressions in favor of liberty and his votes on those questions. But there is a time for all things.

Against the opinion of many friends, even against the solicitation of some of them, he opposed those of the Church clergy who had petitioned the House of Commons to be discharged from the subscriptions. Although he supported the Dissenters in their petition for the indulgence which he had refused to the clergy of the Established Church, in this, as he was not guilty of it, so he was not reproached with inconsistency. At the same time he promoted, and against the wish of several, the clause that give the Dissenting teachers another subscription in the place of that which was then taken away. Neither at that time was the reproach of inconsistency brought against him. People could then distinguish between a difference in conduct under a variation of circumstances and an inconsistency in principle. It was not then thought necessary to be freed of him as of an incumbrance.

These instances, a few among many, are produced as an answer to the insinuation of his having pursued high popular courses which in his late book he has abandoned. Perhaps in his whole life he has never omitted a fair occasion, with whatever risk to him of obloquy as an individual, with whatever detriment to his interest as a member of opposition, to assert the very same doctrines which appear in that book. . . .

At his first offering himself to Bristol, where he was almost sure he should not obtain, on that or any occasion, a single Tory vote, (in fact, he did obtain but one,) and rested wholly on the Whig interest, he thought himself bound to tell to the electors, both before and after his election, exactly what a representative they had to expect in him.

"The *distinguishing* part of our Constitution," he said, "is its liberty. To preserve that liberty inviolate is the *peculiar* duty and *proper* trust of a member of the House of Commons. But the liberty, the *only* liberty, I mean is a liberty connected with *order*, and that not only exists *with* order and virtue, but cannot exist at all *without* them. It inheres in good and steady government, as in *its substance and vital principle*."

The liberty to which Mr. Burke declared himself attached is not French liberty. That liberty is nothing but the rein given to vice and confusion. Mr. Burke was then, as he was at the writing of his Reflections, awfully impressed with the difficulties arising from the complex state of our Constitution and our empire, and that it might require in different emergencies different sorts of exertions, and the successive call upon all the various principles which uphold and justify it. . . .

Seventeen years ago, he spoke, not like a partisan of one particular member of our Constitution, but as a person strongly, and on principle, attached to them all. He thought these great and essential members ought to be preserved, and preserved each in its place—and that the monarchy ought not only to be secured in its peculiar existence, but in its preeminence too, as the presiding and connecting principle of the whole. Let it be considered whether the language of his book, printed in 1790, differs from his speech at Bristol in 1774.

With equal justice his opinions on the American war are introduced, as if in his late work he had belied his conduct and opinions in the debates which arose upon that great event. On the American war he never had any opinions which he has seen occasion to retract, or which he has ever retracted. He, indeed, differs essentially from Mr. Fox as to the cause of that war. Mr. Fox has been pleased to say that the Americans rebelled "because they thought they had not enjoyed liberty enough." This cause of the war, *from him*, I have heard of for the first time. It is true that those who stimulated the nation to that measure did frequently urge this topic. They contended that the Americans had from the beginning aimed at independence—that from the beginning they meant wholly to throw off the authority of the crown, and to break their connection with the parent country. This Mr. Burke never believed. When he moved his second conciliatory proposition, in the year 1776, he entered into the discussion of this point at very great length, and, from nine several heads of presumption, endeavored to prove the charge upon that people not to be true.

If the principles of all he has said and wrote on the occasion be viewed with common temper, the gentlemen of the party will perceive, that, on a supposition that the Americans had rebelled merely in order to enlarge their liberty, Mr. Burke would have thought very differently of the American cause.. What might have been in the secret thoughts of some of their leaders it is impossible to say. As far as a man so locked up as Dr. Franklin could be expected to communicate his ideas, I believe he opened them to Mr. Burke. It was, I think, the very day before he set out for America that a very long conversation passed between them, and with a greater air of openness on the Doctor's side than Mr. Burke had observed in him before. In this discourse Dr. Franklin lamented, and with apparent sincerity, the separation which he feared was inevitable between Great Britain and her colonies. He certainly spoke of it as an event which gave him the greatest concern. America, he said, would never again see such happy days as she had passed under the protection of England. He observed, that ours was the only instance of a great empire in which the most distant parts and members had been as well governed as the metropolis and its vicinage, but that the Americans were going to lose the means which secured to them this rare and precious advantage. The question with them was not, whether they were to remain as they had been before the troubles—for better, he allowed, they could not hope to be—but whether they were to give up so happy a situation without a struggle. Mr. Burke had several other conversations with him about that time, in none of which, soured and exasperated as his mind certainly was, did he discover any other wish in favor of America than for a security to its *ancient* condition. Mr. Burke's conversation with other Americans was large, indeed, and his inquiries extensive and diligent. Trusting to the result of all these means of information, but trusting much more in the public presumptive indications I have just referred to, and to the reiterated solemn declarations of their Assemblies, he always firmly believed that they were purely on the defensive in that rebellion. He considered the Americans as standing at that time, and in that controversy, in the same relation to England as England did to King James the Second in 1688. He believed that they had taken up arms from one motive only: that is, our attempting to tax them without their consent—to tax them for the purposes of maintaining civil and military establishments. If this attempt of ours could have been practically established, he thought, with them, that their Assemblies would become totally useless—that, under the system of policy which was then pursued, the Americans could have no sort of security for their laws or liberties, or for any part of them—and that the very circumstance of *our* freedom would have augmented the weight of *their* slavery.

Considering the Americans on that defensive footing, he thought Great Britain ought instantly to have closed with them by the repeal of the taxing act. He was of opinion that our general rights over that country would have been preserved by this timely concession. When, instead of this, a Boston Port Bill, a Massachusetts Charter Bill, a Fishery Bill, an Intercourse Bill, I know not how many hostile bills, rushed out like so many tempests from all points of the compass, and were accompanied first with great fleets and armies of English, and followed afterwards with great bodies of foreign troops, he thought that their cause grew daily better, because daily more defensive—and that ours, because daily more offensive, grew daily worse. He therefore, in two motions, in two successive years, proposed in Parliament many concessions beyond what he had reason to think in the beginning of the troubles would ever be seriously demanded.

So circumstanced, he certainly never could and never did wish the colonists to be subdued by arms. He was fully persuaded, that, if such should be the event, they must be held in that subdued state by a great body of standing forces, and perhaps of foreign forces. He was strongly of opinion that such armies, first victorious over Englishmen, in a conflict for English constitutional rights and privileges, and afterwards habituated (though in America) to keep an English people in a state of abject subjection, would prove fatal in the end to the liberties of England itself; that in the mean time this military system would lie as an oppressive burden upon the national finances; that it would constantly breed and feed new discussions, full of heat and acrimony, leading possibly to a new series of wars; and that foreign powers, whilst we continued in a state at once burdened and distracted, must at length obtain a decided superiority over us. On what part of his late publication, or on what expression that might have escaped him in that work, is any man authorized to charge Mr. Burke with a contradiction to the line of his conduct and to the current of his doctrines on the American war? The pamphlet is in the hands of his accusers: let them point out the passage, if they can. . . .

Is it because he did not wish the Americans to be subdued by arms, that he must be inconsistent with himself, if he reprobates the conduct of those societies in England, who, alleging no one act of tyranny or oppression, and complaining of no hostile attempt against our ancient laws, rights, and usages, are now endeavoring to work the destruction of the crown of this kingdom, and the whole of its Constitution? Is he obliged, from the concessions he wished to be made to the colonies, to keep any terms with those clubs and federations who hold out to us, as a pattern for imitation, the proceedings in France, in which a king, who had voluntarily and formally divested himself of the right of taxation, and of all other species of arbitrary power, has been dethroned? Is it because Mr. Burke wishes to have America rather conciliated than vanquished, that he must wish well to the army of republics which are set up in France—a country wherein not the people, but the monarch, was wholly on the defensive, (a poor, indeed, and feeble defensive,) to preserve *some fragments* of the royal authority against a determined and desperate body of conspirators, whose object it was, with whatever certainty of crimes, with whatever hazard of war, and every other species of calamity, to annihilate the *whole* of that authority, to level all ranks, orders, and distinctions in the state, and utterly to destroy property, not more by their acts than in their principles?

Mr. Burke has been also reproached with an inconsistency between his late writings and his former conduct, because he had proposed in Parliament several economical, leading to several constitutional reforms. Mr. Burke thought, with a majority of the House of Commons, that the influence of the crown at one time was too great; but after his Majesty had, by a gracious message, and several subsequent acts of Parliament, reduced it to a standard which satisfied Mr. Fox himself, and, apparently at least, contented whoever wished to go farthest in that reduction, is Mr. Burke to allow that it would be right for us to proceed to indefinite lengths upon that subject? that it would therefore be justifiable in a people owing allegiance to a monarchy, and professing to maintain it, not to *reduce*, but wholly to *take away all* prerogative and *all* influence whatsoever? Must his having made, in virtue of a plan of economical regulation, a reduction of the influence of the crown compel him to allow that it would be right in the French or in us to bring a king to so abject a state as in function not to be so respectable as an undersheriff, but in person not to differ from the condition of a mere prisoner? One would think that such a thing as a medium had never been heard of in the moral world.

This mode of arguing from your having done *any* thing in a certain line to the necessity of doing *every* thing has political consequences of other moment than those of a logical fallacy. If no man can propose any diminution or modification of an invidious or dangerous power or influence in government, without entitling friends turned into adversaries to argue him into the destruction of all prerogative, and to a spoliation of the whole patronage of royalty, I do not know what can more effectually deter persons of sober minds from engaging in any reform, nor how the worst enemies to the liberty of the subject could contrive any method more fit to bring all correctives on the power of the crown into suspicion and disrepute.

If, say his accusers, the dread of too great influence in the crown of Great Britain could justify the degree of reform which he adopted, the dread of a return under the despotism of a monarchy might justify the people of France in going much further, and reducing monarchy to its present nothing.—Mr. Burke does not allow that a sufficient argument *ad hominem* is inferable from these premises. If the horror of the excesses of an absolute monarchy furnishes a reason for abolishing it, no monarchy once absolute (all have been so at one period or other) could ever be limited. It must be destroyed; otherwise no way could be found to quiet the fears of those who were formerly subjected to that sway. But the principle of Mr. Burke's proceeding ought to lead him to a very different conclusion—to this conclusion—that a monarchy is a thing perfectly susceptible of reform, perfectly susceptible of a balance of power, and that, when reformed and balanced, for a great country it is the best of all governments. The example of our country might have led France, as it has led him, to perceive that monarchy is not only reconcilable to liberty, but that it may be rendered a great and stable security to its perpetual enjoyment. No correctives which he proposed to the power of the crown could lead him to approve of a plan of a republic (if so it may be reputed) which has no correctives, and which he believes to be incapable of admitting any. No principle of Mr. Burke's conduct or writings obliged him from consistency to become an advocate for an exchange of mischiefs; no principle of his could compel him to justify the setting up in the place of a mitigated monarchy a new and far more despotic power, under which there is no trace of liberty, except what appears in confusion and in crime. . . .

So far as to the attack on Mr. Burke in consequence of his reforms.

To show that he has in his last publication abandoned those principles of liberty which have given energy to his youth, and in spite of his censors will afford repose and consolation to his declining age, those who have thought proper in Parliament to declare against his book ought to have produced something in it which directly or indirectly militates with any rational plan of free government. It is something extraordinary, that they whose memories have so well served them with regard to light and ludicrous expressions, which years had consigned to oblivion, should not have been able to quote a single passage in a piece so lately published, which contradicts anything he has formerly ever said in a style either ludicrous or serious. They quote his former speeches and his former votes, but not one syllable from the book. It is only by a collation of the one with the other that the alleged inconsistency can be established. But as they are unable to cite any such contradictory passage, so neither can they show anything in the general tendency and spirit of the whole work unfavorable to a rational and generous spirit of liberty; unless a warm opposition to the spirit of levelling, to the spirit of impiety, to the spirit of proscription, plunder, murder, and cannibalism, be adverse to the true principles of freedom.

The author of that book is supposed to have passed from extreme to extreme; but he has always kept himself in a medium. This charge is not so wonderful. It is in the nature of things, that they who are in the centre of a circle should appear directly opposed to those who view them from any part of the circumference. In that middle point, however, he will still remain, though he may hear people who themselves run beyond Aurora and the Ganges cry out that he is at the extremity of the West.

In the same debate Mr. Burke was represented by Mr. Fox as arguing in a manner which implied that the British Constitution could not be defended, but by abusing all republics ancient and modern. He said nothing to give the least ground for such a censure. He never abused all republics. He has never professed himself a friend or an enemy to republics or to monarchies in the abstract. He thought that the circumstances and habits of every country, which it is always perilous and productive of the greatest calamities to force, are to decide upon the form of its government. There is nothing in his nature, his temper, or his faculties which should make him an enemy to any republic, modern or ancient. Far from it. He has studied the form and spirit of republics very early in life; he has studied them with great attention, and with a mind undisturbed by affection or prejudice. He is, indeed, convinced that the science of government would be poorly cultivated without that study. But the result in his mind from that investigation has been and is, that neither England nor France, without infinite detriment to them, as well in the event as in the experiment, could be brought into a republican form; but that everything republican which can be introduced with safety into either of them must be built upon a monarchy—built upon a real, not a nominal monarchy, *as its essential basis*; that all such institutions, whether aristocratic or democratic, must originate from their crown, and in all their proceedings must refer to it; that by the energy of that main-spring alone those republican parts must be set in action, and from thence must derive their whole legal effect, (as amongst us they actually do,) or the whole will fall into confusion. These republican members have no other point but the crown in which they can possibly unite.

This is the opinion expressed in Mr. Burke's book. He has never varied in that opinion since he came to years of discretion. . . .

To fortify the imputation of a desertion from his principles, his constant attempts to reform abuses have been brought forward. It is true, it has been the business of his strength to reform abuses in government, and his last feeble efforts are employed in a struggle against them. Politically he has lived in that element; politically he will die in it. Before he departs, I will admit for him that he deserves to have all his titles of merit brought forth, as they have been, for grounds of condemnation, if one word justifying or supporting abuses of any sort is to be found in that book which has kindled so much indignation in the mind of a great man. On the contrary, it spares no existing abuse. Its very purpose is to make war with abuses—not, indeed, to make war with the dead, but with those which live, and flourish, and reign.

The *purpose* for which the abuses of government are brought into view forms a very material consideration in the mode of treating them. The complaints of a friend are things very different from the invectives of an enemy. The charge of abuses on the late monarchy of France was not intended to lead to its reformation, but to justify its destruction. They who have raked into all history for the faults of kings, and who have aggravated every fault they have found, have acted consistently, because they acted as enemies. No man can be a friend to a tempered monarchy who bears a decided hatred to monarchy itself. He, who, at the present time, is favorable or even fair to that system, must act towards it as towards a friend with frailties who is under the prosecution of implacable foes. I think it a duty, in that case, not to inflame the public mind against the obnoxious person by any exaggeration of his faults. It is our duty rather to palliate his errors and defects, or to cast them into the shade, and industriously to bring forward any good qualities that he may happen to possess. But when the man is to be amended, and by amendment to be preserved, then the line of duty takes another direction. When his safety is effectually provided for, it then becomes the office of a friend to urge his faults and vices with all the energy of enlightened affection, to paint them in their most vivid colors, and to bring the moral patient to a better habit. Thus I think with regard to individuals; thus I think with regard to ancient and respected governments and orders of men. A spirit of reformation is never more consistent with itself than when it refuses to be rendered the means of destruction. . . . These revolutionists, indeed, may be well thought to vary in their conduct. He is, however, far from accusing them, in this variation, of the smallest degree of inconsistency. He is persuaded that they are totally indifferent at which end they begin the demolition of the Constitution. Some are for commencing their operations with the destruction of the civil powers, in order the better to pull down the ecclesiastical—some wish to begin with the ecclesiastical, in order to facilitate the ruin of the civil; some would destroy the House of Commons through the crown, some the crown through the House of Commons, and some would overturn both the one and the other through what they call the people. But I believe that this injured writer will think it not at all inconsistent with his present duty or with his former life strenuously to oppose all the various partisans of destruction, let them begin where or when or how they will. No man would set his face more determinedly against those who should attempt to deprive them, or any description of men, of the rights they possess. No man would be more steady in preventing them from abusing those rights to the destruction of that happy order under which they enjoy them. As to their title to anything further, it ought to be grounded on the proof they give of the safety with which power may be trusted in their hands. When they attempt without disguise, not to win it from our affections, but to force it from our fears, they show, in the character of their means of obtaining it, the use they would make of their dominion. That writer is too well read in men not to know how often the desire and design of a tyrannic domination lurks in the claim of an extravagant liberty. . . .

The attacks on the author's consistency relative to France are (however grievous they may be to his feelings) in a great degree external to him and to us, and comparatively of little moment to the people of England.

The substantial charge upon him is concerning his doctrines relative to the Revolution of 1688. Here it is that they who speak in the name of the party have thought proper to censure him the most loudly and with the greatest asperity. Here they fasten, and, if they are right in their fact, with sufficient judgment in their selection. If he be guilty in this point, he is equally blamable, whether he is consistent or not. If he endeavors to delude his countrymen by a false representation of the spirit of that leading event, and of the true nature and tenure of the government formed in consequence of it, he is deeply responsible, he is an enemy to the free Constitution of the kingdom. But he is not guilty in any sense. I maintain that in his Reflections he has stated the Revolution and the Settlement upon their true principles of legal reason and constitutional policy. . . .

His construction is in perfect harmony with that of the ancient Whigs, to whom, against the sentence of the modern, on his part, I here appeal. . . .

These new Whigs hold that the sovereignty, whether exercised by one or many, did not only originate *from* the people, (a position not denied nor worth denying or assenting to,) but that in the people the same sovereignty constantly and unalienably resides; that the people may lawfully depose kings, not only for misconduct, but without any misconduct at all; that they may set up any new fashion of government for themselves, or continue without any government, at their pleasure; that the people are essentially their own rule, and their will the measure of their conduct; that the tenure of magistracy is not a proper subject of contract, because magistrates have duties, but no rights; and that, if a contract *de facto* is made with them in one age, allowing that it binds at all, it only binds those who are immediately concerned in it, but does not pass to posterity. These doctrines concerning *the people* (a term which they are far from accurately defining, but by which, from many circumstances, it is plain enough they mean their own faction, if they should grow, by early arming, by treachery, or violence, into the prevailing force) tend, in my opinion, to the utter subversion, not only of all government, in all modes, and to all stable securities to rational freedom, but to all the rules and principles of morality itself.

I assert that the ancient Whigs held doctrines totally different from those I have last mentioned. I assert, that the foundations laid down by the Commons, on the trial of Dr. Sacheverell, for justifying the Revolution of 1688, are the very same laid down in Mr. Burke's Reflections—

that is to say, a breach of the *original contract*, implied and expressed in the Constitution of this country, as a scheme of government fundamentally and inviolably fixed in King, Lords, and Commons;—that the fundamental subversion of this ancient Constitution, by one of its parts, having been attempted, and in effect accomplished, justified the Revolution;—that it was justified *only* upon the *necessity* of the case, as the *only* means left for the recovery of that *ancient* Constitution formed by the *original contract* of the British state, as well as for the future preservation of the *same* government. . . .

The factions now so busy amongst us, in order to divest men of all love for their country, and to remove from their minds all duty with regard to the state, endeavor to propagate an opinion, that the *people*, in forming their commonwealth, have by no means parted with their power over it. This is an impregnable citadel, to which these gentlemen retreat, whenever they are pushed by the battery of laws and usages and positive conventions. Indeed, it is such, and of so great force, that all they have done in defending their outworks is so much time and labor thrown away. Discuss any of their schemes, their answer is, It is the act of the *people*, and that is sufficient. Are we to deny to a *majority* of the people the right of altering even the whole frame of their society, if such should be their pleasure? They may change it, say they, from a monarchy to a republic to-day, and to-morrow back again from a republic to a monarchy; and so backward and forward as often as they like. They are masters of the commonwealth, because in substance they are themselves the commonwealth. The French Revolution, say they, was the act of the majority of the people; and if the majority of any other people, the people of England, for instance, wish to make the same change, they have the same right.

Just the same, undoubtedly. That is, none at all. Neither the few nor the many have a right to act merely by their will, in any matter connected with duty, trust, engagement, or obligation. The Constitution of a country being once settled upon some compact, tacit or expressed, there is no power existing of force to alter it, without the breach of the covenant, or the consent of all the parties. Such is the nature of a contract. And the votes of a majority of the people, whatever their infamous flatterers may teach in order to corrupt their minds, cannot alter the moral any more than they can alter the physical essence of things. The people are not to be taught to think lightly of their engagements to their governors; else they teach governors to think lightly of their engagements towards them. In that kind of game, in the end, the people are sure to be losers. To flatter them into a contempt of faith, truth, and justice is to ruin them; for in these virtues consists their whole safety. To flatter any man, or any part of mankind, in any description, by asserting that in engagements he or they are free, whilst any other human creature is bound, is ultimately to vest the rule of morality in the pleasure of those who ought to be rigidly submitted to it—to subject the sovereign reason of the world to the caprices of weak and giddy men.

But, as no one of us men can dispense with public or private faith, or with any other tie of moral obligation, so neither can any number of us. The number engaged in crimes, instead of turning them into laudable acts, only augments the quantity and intensity of the guilt. I am well aware that men love to hear of their power, but have an extreme disrelish to be told of their duty. This is of course; because every duty is a limitation of some power. Indeed, arbitrary power is so much to the depraved taste of the vulgar, of the vulgar of every description, that almost all the dissensions which lacerate the commonwealth are not concerning the manner in which it is to be exercised, but concerning the hands in which it is to be placed. Somewhere they are resolved to have it. Whether they desire it to be vested in the many or the few depends with most men upon the chance which they imagine they themselves may have of partaking in the exercise of that arbitrary sway, in the one mode or in the other.

It is not necessary to teach men to thirst after power. But it is very expedient that by moral instruction they should be taught, and by their civil constitutions they should be compelled, to put many restrictions upon the immoderate exercise of it, and the inordinate desire. The best method of obtaining these two great points forms the important, but at the same time the difficult problem to the true statesman. He thinks of the place in which political power is to be lodged with no other attention than as it may render the more or the less practicable its salutary restraint and its prudent direction. For this reason, no legislator, at any period of the world, has willingly placed the seat of active power in the hands of the multitude; because there it admits of no control, no regulation, no steady direction whatsoever. The people are the natural control on authority; but to exercise and to control together is contradictory and impossible.

As the exorbitant exercise of power cannot, under popular sway, be effectually restrained, the other great object of political arrangement, the means of abating an excessive desire of it, is in such a state still worse provided for. The democratic commonwealth is the foodful nurse of ambition. Under the other forms it meets with many restraints. Whenever, in states which have had a democratic basis, the legislators have endeavored to put restraints upon ambition, their methods were as violent as in the end they were ineffectual—as violent, indeed, as any the most jealous despotism could invent. . . .

I cannot too often recommend it to the serious consideration of all men who think civil society to be within the province of moral jurisdiction, that, if we owe to it any duty, it is not subject to our will. Duties are not voluntary. Duty and will are even contradictory terms. Now, though civil society might be at first a voluntary act, (which in many cases it undoubtedly was,) its continuance is under a permanent standing covenant, coexisting with the society; and it attaches upon every individual of that society, without any formal act of his own. This is warranted by the general practice, arising out of the general sense of manking. Men without their choice derive benefits from that association; without their choice they are subjected to duties in consequence of these benefits; and without their choice they enter into a virtual obligation as binding as any that is actual. Look through the whole of life and the whole system of duties. Much the strongest moral obligations are such as were never the results of our option. I allow, that, if no Supreme Ruler exists, wise to form, and potent to enforce, the moral law, there is no sanction to any contract, virtual or even actual, against the will of prevalent power. On that hypothesis, let any set of men be strong enough to set their duties at defiance, and they cease to be duties any longer. . . . Taking it for granted that I do not write to the disciples of the Parisian philosophy, I may assume that the awful Author of our being is the Author of our place in the order of existence—and that, having disposed and marshalled us by a divine tactic, not according to our will, but according to His, He has in and by that disposition virtually subjected us to act the part which belongs to the place assigned us. We have obligations to mankind at large, which are not in consequence of any special voluntary pact. They arise from the relation of man to man, and the relation of man to God, which relations are not matters of choice. On the contrary, the force of all the pacts which we enter into with any particular person or number of persons amongst mankind depends upon those prior obligations. In some cases the subordinate relations are voluntary, in others they are necessary—but the duties are all compulsive. When we marry, the choice is voluntary, but the duties are not matter of choice: they are dictated by the nature of the situation. Dark and inscrutable are the ways by which we come into the world. The instincts which give rise to this mysterious process of Nature are not of our making. But out of physical causes, unknown to us, perhaps unknowable, arise moral duties, which, as we are able perfectly to comprehend, we are bound indispensably to perform. Parents may not be consenting to their moral relation; but, consenting or not, they are bound to a long train of burdensome duties towards those with whom they have never made a convention of any sort. Children are not consenting to their relation; but their relation, without their actual consent, binds them to its duties—or rather it implies their consent, because the presumed consent of every rational creature is in unison with the predisposed order of things. Men come in that manner into a community with the social state of their parents, endowed with all the benefits, loaded with all the duties of their situation. If the social ties and ligaments, spun out of those physical relations which are the elements of the commonwealth, in most cases begin, and always continue, independently of our will, so, without any stipulation on our own part, are we bound by that relation called our country, which comprehends (as it has been well said) "all the charities of all." Nor are we left without powerful instincts to make this duty as dear and grateful to us as it is awful and coercive. Our country is not a thing of mere physical locality. It consists, in a great measure, in the ancient order into which we are born. We may have the same geographical situation, but another country; as we may have the same country in another soil. The place that determines our duty to our country is a social, civil relation. . . .

I admit, indeed, that in morals, as in all things else, difficulties will sometimes occur. Duties will sometimes cross one another. Then questions will arise, which of them is to be placed in subordination? which of them may be entirely superseded? . . . Duties, at their extreme bounds, are drawn very fine, so as to become almost evanescent. In that state some shade of doubt will always rest on these questions, when they are pursued with great subtilty. But the very habit of stating these extreme cases is not very laudable or safe; because, in general, it is not right to turn our duties into doubts. They are imposed to govern our conduct, not to exercise our ingenuity; and therefore our opinions about them ought not to be in a state of fluctuation, but steady, sure, and resolved.

Amongst these nice, and therefore dangerous points of casuistry, may be reckoned the question so much agitated in the present hour—

Whether, after the people have discharged themselves of their original power by an habitual delegation, no occasion can possibly occur which may justify the resumption of it? This question, in this latitude, is very hard to affirm or deny: but I am satisfied that no occasion can justify such a resumption, which would not equally authorize a dispensation with any other moral duty, perhaps with all of them together. However, if in general it be not easy to determine concerning the lawfulness of such devious proceedings, which must be ever on the edge of crimes, it is far from difficult to foresee the perilous consequences of the resuscitation of such a power in the people. The practical consequences of any political tenet go a great way in deciding upon its value. Political problems do not primarily concern truth or falsehood. They relate to good or evil. What in the result is likely to produce evil is politically false; that which is productive of good, politically true.

Believing it, therefore, a question at least arduous in the theory, and in the practice very critical, it would become us to ascertain as well as we can what form it is that our incantations are about to call up from darkness and the sleep of ages. When the supreme authority of the people is in question, before we attempt to extend or to confine it, we ought to fix in our minds, with some degree of distinctness, an idea of what it is we mean, when we say, the PEOPLE.

In a state of *rude* Nature there is no such thing as a people. A number of men in themselves have no collective capacity. The idea of a people is the idea of a corporation. It is wholly artificial, and made, like all other legal fictions, by common agreement. What the particular nature of that agreement was is collected from the form into which the particular society has been cast. Any other is not *their* covenant. When men, therefore, break up the original compact or agreement which gives its corporate form and capacity to a state, they are no longer a people—they have no longer a corporate existence—they have no longer a legal coactive force to bind within, nor a claim to be recognized abroad. They are a number of vague, loose individuals, and nothing more. With them all is to begin again. Alas! they little know how many a weary step is to be taken before they can form themselves into a mass which has a true politic personality.

We hear much, from men who have not acquired their hardiness of assertion from the profundity of their thinking, about the omnipotence of a *majority*, in such a dissolution of an ancient society as hath taken place in France. But amongst men so disbanded there can be no such thing as majority or minority, or power in any one person to bind another. The power of acting by a majority, which the gentlemen theorists seem to assume so readily, after they have violated the contract out of which it has arisen, (if at all it existed,) must be grounded on two assumptions: first, that of an incorporation produced by unanimity; and secondly, an unanimous agreement that the act of a mere majority (say of one) shall pass with them and with others as the act of the whole.

We are so little affected by things which are habitual, that we consider this idea of the decision of a *majority* as if it were a law of our original nature. But such constructive whole, residing in a part only, is one of the most violent fictions of positive law that ever has been or can be made on the principles of artificial incorporation. Out of civil society Nature knows nothing of it; nor are men, even when arranged according to civil order, otherwise than by very long training, brought at all to submit to it. The mind is brought far more easily to acquiesce in the proceedings of one man, or a few, who act under a general procuration for the state, than in the vote of a victorious majority in councils in which every man has his share in the deliberation. For there the beaten party are exasperated and soured by the previous contention, and mortified by the conclusive defeat. This mode of decision, where wills may be so nearly equal, where, according to circumstances, the smaller number may be the stronger force, and where apparent reason may be all upon one side, and on the other little else than impetuous appetite—all this must be the result of a very particular and special convention, confirmed afterwards by long habits of obedience, by a sort of discipline in society, and by a strong hand, vested with stationary, permanent power to enforce this sort of constructive general will. . . .

If men dissolve their ancient incorporation in order to regenerate their community, in that state of things each man has a right, if he pleases, to remain an individual. Any number of individuals, who can agree upon it, have an undoubted right to form themselves into a state apart and wholly independent. If any of these is forced into the fellowship of another, this is conquest and not compact. On every principle which supposes society to be in virtue of a free covenant, this compulsive incorporation must be null and void. . . .

As in the abstract it is perfectly clear, that, out of a state of civil society, majority and minority are relations which can have no existence, and that, in civil society, its own specific conventions in each corporation determine what it is that constitutes the people, so as to make their act the signification of the general will—to come to particulars, it is equally clear that neither in France nor in England has the original or any subsequent compact of the state, expressed or implied, constituted *a majority of men, told by the head*, to be the acting people of their several communities. And I see as little of policy or utility as there is of right, in laying down a principle that a majority of men told by the head are to be considered as the people, and that as such their will is to be law. What policy can there be found in arrangements made in defiance of every political principle? To enable men to act with the weight and character of a people, and to answer the ends for which they are incorporated into that capacity, we must suppose them (by means immediate or consequential) to be in that state of habitual social discipline in which the wiser, the more expert, and the more opulent conduct, and by conducting enlighten and protect, the weaker, the less knowing, and the less provided with the goods of fortune. When the multitude are not under this discipline, they can scarcely be said to be in civil society. . . .

A true natural aristocracy is not a separate interest in the state, or separable from it. It is an essential integrant part of any large body rightly constituted. It is formed out of a class of legitimate presumptions, which, taken as generalities, must be admitted for actual truths. To be bred in a place of estimation; to see nothing low and sordid from one's infancy; to be taught to respect one's self; to be habituated to the censorial inspection of the public eye; to look early to public opinion; to stand upon such elevated ground as to be enabled to take a large view of the wide-spread and infinitely diversified combinations of men and affairs in a large society; to have leisure to read, to reflect, to converse; to be enabled to draw the court and attention of the wise and learned, wherever they are to be found; to be habituated in armies to command and to obey; to be taught to despise danger in the pursuit of honor and duty; to be formed to the greatest degree of vigilance, foresight, and circumspection, in a state of things in which no fault is committed with impunity and the slightest mistakes draw on the most ruinous consequences; to be led to a guarded and regulated conduct, from a sense that you are considered as an instructor of your fellow-citizens in their highest concerns, and that you act as a reconciler between God and man; to be employed as an administrator of law and justice, and to be thereby amongst the first benefactors of mankind; to be a professor of high science, or of liberal and ingenuous art; to be amongst rich traders, who from their success are presumed to have sharp and vigorous understandings, and to possess the virtues of diligence, order, constancy, and regularity, and to have cultivated an habitual regard to commutative justice: these are the circumstances of men that form what I should call a *natural* aristocracy, without which there is no nation.

The state of civil society which necessarily generates this aristocracy is a state of Nature—and much more truly so than a savage and incoherent mode of life. For man is by nature reasonable; and he is never perfectly in his natural state, but when he is placed where reason may be best cultivated and most predominates. Art is man's nature. We are as much, at least, in a state of Nature in formed manhood as in immature and helpless infancy. Men, qualified in the manner I have just described, form in Nature, as she operates in the common modification of society, the leading, guiding, and governing part. It is the soul to the body, without which the man does not exist. . . .

When great multitudes act together, under that discipline of Nature, I recognize the PEOPLE. I acknowledge something that perhaps equals, and ought always to guide, the sovereignty of convention. In all things the voice of this grand chorus of national harmony ought to have a mighty and decisive influence. But when you disturb this harmony—when you break up this beautiful order, this array of truth and Nature, as well as of habit and prejudice—when you separate the common sort of men from their proper chieftains, so as to form them into an adverse army—I no longer know that venerable object called the people in such a disbanded race of deserters and vagabonds. . . .

To apply this to our present subject. When the several orders, in their several bailliages, had met in the year 1789, (such of them, I mean, as had met peaceably and constitutionally,) to choose and to instruct their representatives, so organized and so acting, (because they were organized and were acting according to the conventions which made them a people,) they were the *people* of France. They had a legal and á natural capacity to be considered as that people. But observe, whilst they were in this state, that is, whilst they were a people, in no one of their instructions did they charge or even hint at any of those things which have drawn upon the usurping Assembly and their adherents the detestation of the rational and thinking part of mankind. . . . Their instructions purported the direct contrary to all those famous proceedings which are defended as the acts of the people. Had such proceedings been expected, the great probability is, that the people would then have risen, as to a man, to prevent them. The whole organization of the Assembly was altered, the whole frame of the kingdom was changed, before these things could be done. . . .

After the weighty and respectable part of the people had been murdered, or driven by the menaces of murder from their houses, or were dispersed in exile into every country in Europe—after the soldiery had been debauched from their officers—after property had lost its weight and consideration, along with its security—after voluntary clubs and associations of factious and unprincipled men were substituted in the place of all the legal corporations of the kingdom arbitrarily dissolved—after freedom had been banished from those popular meetings whose sole recommendation is freedom—after it had come to that pass that no dissent dared to appear in any of them, but at the certain price of life—after even dissent had been anticipated, and assassination became as quick as suspicion—such pretended ratification by addresses could be no act of what any lover of the people would choose to call by their name. It is that voice which every successful usurpation, as well as this before us, may easily procure, even without making (as these tyrants have made) donatives from the spoil of one part of the citizens to corrupt the other.

The pretended *rights of man*, which have made this havoc, cannot be the rights of the people. For to be a people, and to have these rights, are things incompatible. The one supposes the presence, the other the absence, of a state of civil society. The very foundation of the French commonwealth is false and self-destructive; nor can its principles be adopted in any country, without the certainty of bringing it to the very same condition in which France is found. . . .

The whole scheme of our mixed Constitution is to prevent any one of its principles from being carried as far as, taken by itself, and theoretically, it would go. Allow that to be the true policy of the British system, then most of the faults with which that system stands charged will appear to be, not imperfections into which it has inadvertently fallen, but excellencies which it has studiously sought. To avoid the perfections of extreme, all its several parts are so constituted as not alone to answer their own several ends, but also each to limit and control the others; insomuch that, take which of the principles you please, you will find its operation checked and stopped at a certain point. The whole movement stands still rather than that any part should proceed beyond its boundary. From thence it results that in the British Constitution there is a perpetual treaty and compromise going on, sometimes openly, sometimes with less observation. To him who contemplates the British Constitution, as to him who contemplates the subordinate material world, it will always be a matter of his most curious investigation to discover the secret of this mutual limitation. . . .

They who have acted, as in France they have done, upon a scheme wholly different, and who aim at the abstract and unlimited perfection of power in the popular part, can be of no service to us in any of our political arrangements. . . . Our fabric is so constituted, one part of it bears so much on the other, the parts are so made for one another, and for nothing else, that to introduce any foreign matter into it is to destroy it. . . .

The British Constitution has not been struck out at an heat by a set of presumptuous men, like the Assembly of pettifoggers run mad in Paris.

> *" 'T is not the hasty product of a day,*
> *But the well-ripened fruit of wise delay."*

It is the result of the thoughts of many minds in many ages. It is no simple, no superficial thing, nor to be estimated by superficial understandings. An ignorant man, who is not fool enough to meddle with his clock, is, however, sufficiently confident to think he can safely take to pieces and put together, at his pleasure, a moral machine of another guise, importance, and complexity, composed of far other wheels and springs and balances and counteracting and coöperating powers. Men little think how immorally they act in rashly meddling with what they do not understand. Their delusive good intention is no sort of excuse for their presumption. They who truly mean well must be fearful of acting ill. The British Constitution may have its advantages pointed out to wise and reflecting minds, but it is of too high an order of excellence to be adapted to those which are common. It takes in too many views, it makes too many combinations, to be so much as comprehended by shallow and superficial understandings. Profound thinkers will know it in its reason and spirit. The less inquiring will recognize it in their feelings and their experience. They will thank God they have a standard, which, in the most essential point of this great concern, will put them on a par with the most wise and knowing. . . .

Rational and experienced men tolerably well know, and have always known, how to distinguish between true and false liberty, and between the genuine adherence and the false pretence to what is true. But none, except those who are profoundly studied, can comprehend the elaborate contrivance of a fabric fitted to unite private and public liberty with public force, with order, with peace, with justice, and, above all, with the institutions formed for bestowing permanence and stability, through ages, upon this invaluable whole.

Place, for instance, before your eyes such a man as Montesquieu. Think of a genius not born in every country or every time: a man gifted by Nature with a penetrating, aquiline eye—with a judgment prepared with the most extensive erudition—with an Herculean robustness of mind, and nerves not to be broken with labor—a man who could spend twenty years in one pursuit. Think of a man like the universal patriarch in Milton (who had drawn up before him in his prophetic vision the whole series of the generations which were to issue from his loins): a man capable of placing in review, after having brought together from the East, the West, the North, and the South, from the coarseness of the rudest barbarism to the most refined and subtle civilization, all the schemes of government which had ever prevailed amongst mankind, weighing, measuring, collating, and comparing them all, joining fact with theory, and calling into council, upon all this infinite assemblage of things, all the speculations which have fatigued the understandings of profound reasoners in all times. Let us then consider, that all these were but so many preparatory steps to qualify a man, and such a man, tinctured with no national prejudice, with no domestic affection, to admire, and to hold out to the admiration of mankind, the Constitution of England. . . .

Thoughts on French Affairs

Several months later, in December 1791, Burke made the case for England and other European powers' launching a military attack on the revolutionary regime in France. The events there were not traditional self-contained political rearrangements but something utterly new and menacing, "a revolution of doctrine and theoretic dogma." The Protestant Reformation was the only analogy; like it, Jacobinism's reach knew no national boundaries and had to be met with force.

IN THIS STATE OF THINGS, (that is, in the case of a *divided* kingdom,) by the law of nations, Great Britain, like every other power, is free to take any part she pleases. She may decline, with more or less formality, according to her discretion, to acknowledge this new system; or she may recognize it as a government *de facto*, setting aside all discussion of its original legality, and considering the ancient monarchy as at an end. The law of nations leaves our court open to its choice. We have no direction but what is found in the well-understood policy of the king and kingdom.

This declaration of a *new species* of government, on new principles, (such it professes itself to be,) is a real crisis in the politics of Europe. The conduct which prudence ought to dictate to Great Britain will not depend (as hitherto our connection or quarrel with other states has for some time depended) upon merely *external* relations, but in a great measure also upon the system which we may think it right to adopt for the internal government of our own country.

If it be our policy to assimilate our government to that of France, we ought to prepare for this change by encouraging the schemes of authority established there. We ought to wink at the captivity and deposition of a prince with whom, if not in close alliance, we were in friendship. We ought to fall in with the ideas of Monsieur Montmorin's circular manifesto, and to do business of course with the functionaries who act under the new power by which that king to whom his Majesty's minister has been sent to reside has been deposed and imprisoned. On that idea we ought also to withhold all sorts of direct or indirect countenance from those who are treating in Germany for the reëstablishment of the French monarchy and the ancient orders of that state. This conduct is suitable to this policy.

The question is, whether this policy be suitable to the interests of the crown and subjects of Great Britain. Let us, therefore, a little consider the true nature and probable effects of the Revolution which, in such a very unusual manner, has been twice diplomatically announced to his Majesty.

There have been many internal revolutions in the government of countries, both as to persons and forms, in which the neighboring states have had little or no concern. Whatever the government might be with respect to those persons and those forms, the stationary interests of the nation concerned have most commonly influenced the new governments in the same manner in which they influenced the old; and the revolution, turning on matter of local grievance or of local accommodation, did not extend beyond its territory.

The present Revolution in France seems to me to be quite of another character and description, and to bear little resemblance or analogy to any of those which have been brought about in Europe, upon principles merely political. *It is a Revolution of doctrine and theoretic dogma.* It has a much greater resemblance to those changes which have been made upon religious grounds, in which a spirit of proselytism makes an essential part.

The last revolution of doctrine and theory which has happened in Europe is the Reformation. It is not for my purpose to take any notice here of the merits of that revolution, but to state one only of its effects.

That effect was, *to introduce other interests into all countries than those which arose from their locality and natural circumstances.* The principle of the Reformation was such as, by its essence, could not be local or confined to the country in which it had its origin. For instance, the doctrine of "Justification by Faith or by Works," which was the original basis of the Reformation, could not have one of its alternatives true as to Germany and false as to every other country. Neither are questions of theoretic truth and falsehood governed by circumstances any more than by places. On that occasion, therefore, the spirit of proselytism expanded itself with great elasticity upon all sides: and great divisions were everywhere the result.

These divisions, however in appearance merely dogmatic, soon became mixed with the political; and their effects were rendered much more intense from this combination. Europe was for a long time divided into two great factions, under the name of Catholic and Protestant, which not only often alienated state from state, but also divided every state within itself. The warm parties in each state were more affectionately attached to those of their own doctrinal interest in some other country than to their fellow-citizens or to their natural government, when they or either of them happened to be of a different persuasion. These factions, wherever they prevailed, if they did not absolutely destroy, at least weakened and distracted the locality of patriotism. The public affections came to have other motives and other ties.

It would be to repeat the history of the two last centuries to exemplify the effects of this revolution.

Although the principles to which it gave rise did not operate with a perfect regularity and constancy, they never wholly ceased to operate.

Few wars were made, and few treaties were entered into, in which they did not come in for some part. They gave a color, a character, and direction to all the politics of Europe.

These principles of internal as well as external division and coalition are but just now extinguished. But they who will examine into the true character and genius of some late events must be satisfied that other sources of faction, combining parties among the inhabitants of different countries into one connection, are opened, and that from these sources are likely to arise effects full as important as those which had formerly arisen from the jarring interests of the religious sects. The intention of the several actors in the change in France is not a matter of doubt. It is very openly professed. . . .

The political dogma, which, upon the new French system, is to unite the factions of different nations, is this: "That the majority, told by the head, of the taxable people in every country, is the perpetual, natural, unceasing, indefeasible sovereign; that this majority is perfectly master of the form as well as the administration of the state, and that the magistrates, under whatever names they are called, are only functionaries to obey the orders (general as laws or particular as decrees) which that majority may make; that this is the only natural government; that all others are tyranny and usurpation."

In order to reduce this dogma into practice, the republicans in France, and their associates in other countries, make it always their business, and often their public profession, to destroy all traces of ancient establishments, and to form a new commonwealth in each country, upon the basis of the French *Rights of Men*. On the principle of these rights, they mean to institute in every country, and as it were the germ of the whole, parochial governments, for the purpose of what they call equal representation. From them is to grow, by some media, a general council and representative of all the parochial governments. In that representative is to be vested the whole national power,—totally abolishing hereditary name and office, levelling all conditions of men, (except where money *must* make a difference,) breaking all connection between territory and dignity, and abolishing every species of nobility, gentry, and Church establishments: all their priests and all their magistrates being only creatures of election and pensioners at will.

Knowing how opposite a permanent landed interest is to that scheme, they have resolved, and it is the great drift of all their regulations, to reduce that description of men to a mere peasantry for the sustenance of the towns, and to place the true effective government in cities, among the tradesmen, bankers, and voluntary clubs of bold, presuming young persons,—advocates, attorneys, notaries, managers of newspapers, and those cabals of literary men called academies. Their republic is to have a first functionary, (as they call him,) under the name of King, or not, as they think fit. This officer, when such an officer is permitted, is, however, neither in fact nor name to be considered as sovereign, nor the people as his subjects. The very use of these appellations is offensive to their ears.

This system, as it has first been realized, dogmatically as well as practically, in France, makes France the natural head of all factions formed on a similar principle, wherever they may prevail, as much as Athens was the head and settled ally of all democratic factions, wherever they existed. The other system has no head.

This system has very many partisans in every country in Europe, but particularly in England, where they are already formed into a body, comprehending most of the Dissenters of the three leading denominations. To these are readily aggregated all who are Dissenters in character, temper, and disposition, though not belonging to any of their congregations: that is, all the restless people who resemble them, of all ranks and all parties,—Whigs, and even Tories; the whole race of half-bred speculators; all the Atheists, Deists, and Socinians; all those who hate the clergy and envy the nobility; a good many among the moneyed people; the East Indians almost to a man, who cannot bear to find that their present importance does not bear a proportion to their wealth. These latter have united themselves into one great, and, in my opinion, formidable club, which, though now quiet, may be brought into action with considerable unanimity and force.

Formerly, few, except the ambitious great or the desperate and indigent, were to be feared as instruments in revolutions. What has happened in France teaches us, with many other things, that there are more causes than have commonly been taken into our consideration, by which government may be subverted. The moneyed men, merchants, principal tradesmen, and men of letters (hitherto generally thought the peaceable and even timid part of society) are the chief actors in the French Revolution. But the fact is, that, as money increases and circulates, and as the circulation of news in politics and letters becomes more and more diffused, the persons who diffuse this money and this intelligence become more and more important. This was not long undiscovered. Views of ambition were in France, for the first time, presented to these classes of men: objects in the state, in the army, in the system of civil offices of every kind. Their eyes were dazzled with this new prospect. They were, as it were, electrified, and made to lose the natural spirit of their situation. A bribe, great without example in the history of the world, was held out to them,—the whole government of a very large kingdom.

There are several who are persuaded that the same thing cannot happen in England, because here (they say) the occupations of merchants, tradesmen, and manufacturers are not held as degrading situations. I once thought that the low estimation in which commerce was held in France might be reckoned among the causes of the late Revolution; and I am still of opinion that the exclusive spirit of the French nobility did irritate the wealthy of other classes. But I found long since, that persons in trade and business were by no means despised in France in the manner I had been taught to believe. As to men of letters, they were so far from being despised or neglected, that there was no country, perhaps, in the universe, in which they were so highly esteemed, courted, caressed, and even feared: tradesmen naturally were not so much sought in society, (as not furnishing so largely to the fund of conversation as they do to the revenues of the state,) but the latter description got forward every day. M. Bailly, who made himself the popular mayor on the rebellion of the Bastile, and is a principal actor in the revolt, before the change possessed a pension or office under the crown of six hundred pound English a year,—for that country, no contemptible provision; and this he obtained solely as a man of letters, and on no other title. As to the moneyed men, whilst the monarchy continued, there is no doubt, that, merely as such, they did not enjoy the *privileges* of nobility; but nobility was of so easy an acquisition, that it was the fault or neglect of all of that description who did not obtain its privileges, for their lives at least, in virtue of office. It attached under the royal government to an innumerable multitude of places, real and nominal, that were vendible; and such nobility were as capable of everything as their degree of influence or interest could make them,—that is, as nobility of no considerable rank or consequence. M. Necker, so far from being a French gentleman, was not so much as a Frenchman born, and yet we all know the rank in which he stood on the day of the meeting of the States.

As to the mere matter of estimation of the mercantile or any other class, this is regulated by opinion and prejudice. In England, a security against the envy of men in these classes is not so very complete as we may imagine. We must not impose upon ourselves. What institutions and manners together had done in France manners alone do here. It is the natural operation of things, where there exists a crown, a court, splendid orders of knighthood, and an hereditary nobility,—where there exists a fixed, permanent, landed gentry, continued in greatness and opulence by the law of primogeniture, and by a protection given to family settlements,—where there exists a standing army and navy,—where there exists a Church establishment, which bestows on learning and parts an interest combined with that of religion and the state;—in a country where such things exist, wealth, new in its acquisition, and precarious in its duration, can never rank first, or even near the first: though wealth has its natural weight further than as it is balanced and even preponderated amongst us, as amongst other nations, by artificial institutions and opinions growing out of them. At no period in the history of England have so few peers been taken out of trade or from families newly created by commerce. In no period has so small a number of noble families entered into the counting-house. I can call to mind but one in all England, and his is of near fifty years' standing. Be that as it may, it appears plain to me, from my best observation, that envy and ambition may, by art, management, and disposition, be as much excited amongst these descriptions of men in England as in any other country, and that they are just as capable of acting a part in any great change.

What direction the French spirit of proselytism is likely to take, and in what order it is likely to prevail in the several parts of Europe, it is not easy to determine. The seeds are sown almost everywhere, chiefly by newspaper circulations, infinitely more efficacious and extensive than ever they were. And they are a more important instrument than generally is imagined. They are a part of the reading of all; they are the whole of the reading of the far greater number. There are thirty of them in Paris alone. The language diffuses them more widely than the English,—though the English, too, are much read. The writers of these papers, indeed, for the greater part, are either unknown or in contempt, but they are like a battery, in which the stroke of any one ball produces no great effect, but the amount of continual repetition is decisive. Let us only suffer any person to tell us his story, morning and evening, but for one twelve-month, and he will become our master.

All those countries in which several states are comprehended under some general geographical description, and loosely united by some federal constitution,—countries of which the members are small, and greatly diversified in their forms of government, and in the titles by which they are held,—these countries, as it might be well expected, are the principal objects of their hopes and machinations. Of these, the chief are Germany and Switzerland; after them, Italy has its place, as in circumstances somewhat similar. . . .

It is not to be imagined, because a political system is, under certain aspects, very unwise in its contrivance, and very mischievous in its effects, that it therefore can have no long duration. Its very defects may tend to its stability, because they are agreeable to its nature. The very faults in the Constitution of Poland made it last; the *veto* which destroyed all its energy preserved its life. What can be conceived so monstrous as the republic of Algiers, and that no less strange republic of the Mamelukes in Egypt? They are of the worst form imaginable, and exercised in the worst manner, yet they have existed as a nuisance on the earth for several hundred years.

From all these considerations, and many more that crowd upon me, three conclusions have long since arisen in my mind.

First, that no counter revolution is to be expected in France from internal causes solely.

Secondly, that, the longer the present system exists, the greater will be its strength, the greater its power to destroy discontents at home, and to resist all foreign attempts in favor of these discontents.

Thirdly, that, as long as it exists in France, it will be the interest of the managers there, and it is in the very essence of their plan, to disturb and distract all other governments, and their endless succession of restless politicians will continually stimulate them to new attempts.

Princes are generally sensible that this is their common cause; and two of them have made a public declaration of their opinion to this effect. Against this common danger, some of them, such as the king of Spain, the king of Sardinia, and the republic of Bern, are very diligent in using defensive measures.

If they were to guard against an invasion from France, the merits of this plan of a merely defensive resistance might be supported by plausible topics; but as the attack does not operate against these countries externally, but by an internal corruption, (a sort of dry rot,) they who pursue this merely defensive plan against a danger which the plan itself supposes to be serious cannot possibly escape it. For it is in the nature of all defensive measures to be sharp and vigorous under the impressions of the first alarm, and to relax by degrees, until at length the danger, by not operating instantly, comes to appear as a false alarm,—so much so, that the next menacing appearance will look less formidable, and will be less provided against. But to those who are on the offensive it is not necessary to be always alert. Possibly it is more their interest not to be so. For their unforeseen attacks contribute to their success.

In the mean time a system of French conspiracy is gaining ground in every country. This system, happening to be founded on principles the most delusive indeed, but the most flattering to the natural propensities of the unthinking multitude, and to the speculations of all those who think, without thinking very profoundly, must daily extend its influence. A predominant inclination towards it appears in all those who have no religion, when otherwise their disposition leads them to be advocates even for despotism. Hence Hume, though I cannot say that he does not throw out some expressions of disapprobation on the proceedings of the levellers in the reign of Richard the Second, yet affirms that the doctrines of John Ball were "conformable to the ideas of primitive equality *which are engraven in the hearts of all men.*"

Boldness formerly was not the character of atheists as such. They were even of a character nearly the reverse; they were formerly like the old Epicureans, rather an unenterprising race. But of late they are grown active, designing, turbulent, and seditious. They are sworn enemies to kings, nobility, and priesthood. We have seen all the Academicians at Paris, with Condorcet, the friend and correspondent of Priestley, at their head, the most furious of the extravagant republicans. . . .

Letter to a Member of the National Assembly

Just as Warren Hastings personified British misrule in India, so Jean-Jacques Rousseau, who had died in 1778, embodied for Burke the villainy of the revolutionaries in France. It was the ideas of Rousseau, the "philosopher of vanity," that inspired them. "Him they study; him they meditate. . . . Rousseau is their canon of holy writ," Burke wrote in this published letter-pamphlet of 1791 to M. de Memonville, a member of the French National Assembly.

SIR—I HAD THE HONOR to receive your letter of the 17th of November last, in which, with some exceptions, you are pleased to consider favorably the letter I have written on the affairs of France. . . .

As to the cavils which may be made on some part of my remarks with regard to the *gradations* in your new Constitution, you observe justly that they do not affect the substance of my objections. . . .

I published my thoughts on that Constitution, that my countrymen might be enabled to estimate the wisdom of the plans which were held out to their imitation. . . .

I am unalterably persuaded that the attempt to oppress, degrade, impoverish, confiscate, and extinguish the original gentlemen and landed property of a whole nation cannot be justified under any form it may assume. . . .

The indulgence of a sort of undefined hope, an obscure confidence, that some lurking remains of virtue, some degree of shame, might exist in the breasts of the oppressors of France, has been among the causes which have helped to bring on the common ruin of king and people. There is no safety for honest men, but by believing all possible evil of evil men, and by acting with promptitude, decision, and steadiness on that belief. I well remember, at every epocha of this wonderful history, in every scene of this tragic business, that, when your sophistic usurpers were laying down mischievous principles, and even applying them in direct resolutions, it was the fashion to say that they never intended to execute those declarations in their rigor. This made men careless in their opposition, and remiss in early precaution. By holding out this fallacious hope, the imposters deluded sometimes one description of men, and sometimes another, so that no means of resistance were provided against them, when they came to execute in cruelty what they had planned in fraud.

There are cases in which a man would be ashamed not to have been imposed on. There is a confidence necessary to human intercourse, and without which men are often more injured by their own suspicions than they would be by the perfidy of others. But when men whom we *know* to be wicked impose upon us, we are something worse than dupes.

When we know them, their fair pretences become new motives for distrust. There is one case, indeed, in which it would be madness not to give the fullest credit to the most deceitful of men—that is, when they make declarations of hostility against us.

I find that some persons entertain other hopes, which I confess appear more specious than those by which at first so many were deluded and disarmed. They flatter themselves that the extreme misery brought upon the people by their folly will at last open the eyes of the multitude, if not of their leaders. Much the contrary, I fear. As to the leaders in this system of imposture—you know that cheats and deceivers never can repent. The fraudulent have no resource but in fraud. They have no other goods in their magazine. They have no virtue or wisdom in their minds, to which, in a disappointment concerning the profitable effects of fraud and cunning, they can retreat. The wearing out of an old serves only to put them upon the invention of a new delusion. Unluckily, too, the credulity of dupes is as inexhaustible as the invention of knaves. They never give people possession; but they always keep them in hope. Your state doctors do not so much as pretend that any good whatsoever has hitherto been derived from their operations, or that the public has prospered in any one instance under their management. The nation is sick, very sick, by their medicines. But the charlatan tells them that what is past cannot be helped;—they have taken the draught, and they must wait its operation with patience;—that the first effects, indeed, are unpleasant, but that the very sickness is a proof that the dose is of no sluggish operation;—that sickness is inevitable in all constitutional revolutions;—that the body must pass through pain to ease;—that the prescriber is not an empiric who proceeds by vulgar experience, but one who grounds his practice on the sure rules of art, which cannot possibly fail. . . .

The people of France, almost generally, have been taught to look for other resources than those which can be derived from order, frugality, and industry. They are generally armed; and they are made to expect much from the use of arms. . . . Besides this, the retrograde order of society has something flattering to the dispositions of mankind. The life of adventurers, gamesters, gypsies, beggars, and robbers is not unpleasant. It requires restraint to keep men from falling into that habit. The shifting tides of fear and hope, the flight and pursuit, the peril and escape, the alternate famine and feast of the savage and the thief, after a time, render all course of slow, steady, progressive, unvaried occupation, and the prospect only of a limited mediocrity at the end of long labor, to the last degree tame, languid, and insipid. Those who have been once intoxicated with power, and have derived any kind of emolument from it, even though but for one year, never can willingly abandon it. They may be distressed in the midst of all their power; but they will never look to anything but power for their relief. . . .

The more active and stirring part of the lower orders having got government and the distribution of plunder into their hands, they will use its resources in each municipality to form a body of adherents. These rulers and their adherents will be strong enough to overpower the discontents of those who have not been able to assert their share of the spoil. The unfortunate adventurers in the cheating lottery of plunder will probably be the least sagacious or the most inactive and irresolute of the gang. If, on disappointment, they should dare to stir, they will soon be suppressed as rebels and mutineers by their brother rebels. . . .

From the forced repentance of invalid mutineers and disbanded thieves you can hope for no resource. Government itself, which ought to constrain the more bold and dexterous of these robbers, is their accomplice. . . .

Till the justice of the world is awakened, such as these will go on, without admonition, and without provocation, to every extremity. . . . They do not commit crimes for their designs; but they form designs that they may commit crimes. It is not their necessity, but their nature, that impels them. They are modern philosophers, which when you say of them, you express everything that is ignoble, savage, and hard-hearted.

Besides the sure tokens which are given by the spirit of their particular arrangements, there are some characteristic lineaments in the general policy of your tumultuous despotism, which, in my opinion, indicate, beyond a doubt, that no revolution whatsoever *in their disposition* is to be expected: I mean their scheme of educating the rising generation, the principles which they intend to instil and the sympathies which they wish to form in the mind at the season in which it is the most susceptible. Instead of forming their young minds to that docility, to that modesty, which are the grace and charm of youth, to an admiration of famous examples, and to an averseness to anything which approaches to pride, petulance, and self-conceit, (distempers to which that time of life is of itself sufficiently liable,) they artificially foment these evil dispositions, and even form them into springs of action. Nothing ought to be more weighed than the nature of books recommended by public authority. So recommended, they soon form the character of the age. Uncertain indeed is the efficacy, limited indeed is the extent, of a virtuous institution. But if education takes in *vice* as any part of its system, there is no doubt but that it will operate with abundant energy, and to an extent indefinite. The magistrate, who in favor of freedom thinks himself obliged to suffer all sorts of publications, is under a stricter duty than any other well to consider what sort of writers he shall authorize, and shall recommend by the strongest of all sanctions, that is, by public honors and rewards. He ought to be cautious how he recommends authors of mixed or ambiguous morality. He ought to be fearful of putting into the hands of youth writers indulgent to the peculiarities of their own complexion, lest they should teach the humors of the professor, rather than the principles of the science. He ought, above all, to be cautious in recommending any writer who has carried marks of a deranged understanding: for where there is no sound reason, there can be no real virtue; and madness is ever vicious and malignant.

The Assembly proceeds on maxims the very reverse of these. The Assembly recommends to its youth a study of the bold experiments in morality. Everybody knows that there is a great dispute amongst their leaders, which of them is the best resemblance of Rousseau. In truth, they all resemble him. His blood they transfuse into their minds and into their manners. Him they study; him they meditate; him they turn over in all the time they can spare from the laborious mischief of the day or the debauches of the night. Rousseau is their canon of holy writ; in his life he is their canon of Polycletus; he is their standard figure of perfection. To this man and this writer, as a pattern to authors and to Frenchmen, the foundries of Paris are now running for statues, with the kettles of their poor and the bells of their churches. If an author had written like a great genius on geometry, though his practical and speculative morals were vicious in the extreme, it might appear that in voting the statue they honored only the geometrician. But Rousseau is a moralist or he is nothing. It is impossible, therefore, putting the circumstances together, to mistake their design in choosing the author with whom they have begun to recommend a course of studies.

Their great problem is, to find a substitute for all the principles which hitherto have been employed to regulate the human will and action. They find dispositions in the mind of such force and quality as may fit men, far better than the old morality, for the purposes of such a state as theirs, and may go much further in supporting their power and destroying their enemies. They have therefore chosen a selfish, flattering, seductive, ostentatious vice, in the place of plain duty. True humility, the basis of the Christian system, is the low, but deep and firm foundation of all real virtue. But this, as very painful in the practice, and little imposing in the appearance, they have totally discarded. Their object is to merge all natural and all social sentiment in inordinate vanity. In a small degree, and conversant in little things, vanity is of little moment. When full-grown, it is the worst of vices, and the occasional mimic of them all. It makes the whole man false. It leaves nothing sincere or trustworthy about him. His best qualities are poisoned and perverted by it, and operate exactly as the worst. When your lords had many writers as immoral as the object of their statue (such as Voltaire and others) they chose Rousseau, because in him that peculiar vice which they wished to erect into ruling virtue was by far the most conspicuous.

We have had the great professor and founder of *the philosophy of vanity* in England. As I had good opportunities of knowing his proceedings almost from day to day, he left no doubt on my mind that he entertained no principle, either to influence his heart or to guide his understanding, but *vanity.* With this vice he was possessed to a degree little short of madness. It is from the same deranged, eccentric vanity, that this, the insane Socrates of the National Assembly, was impelled to publish a mad confession of his mad faults, and to attempt a new sort of glory from bringing hardily to light the obscure and vulgar vices which we know may sometimes be blended with eminent talents. He has not observed on the nature of vanity who does not know that it is omnivorous—that it has no choice in its food—that it is fond to talk even of its own faults and vices, and what will excite surprise and draw attention, and what will pass at worst for openness and candor.

It was this abuse and perversion, which vanity makes even of hypocrisy, which has driven Rousseau to record a life not so much as checkered or spotted here and there with virtues, or even distinguished by a single good action. It is such a life he chooses to offer to the attention of mankind. It is such a life that, with a wild defiance, he flings in the face of his Creator, whom he acknowledges only to brave. Your Assembly, knowing how much more powerful example is found than precept, has chosen this man (by his own account without a single virtue) for a model. To him they erect their first statue. From him they commence their series of honors and distinctions.

It is that new-invented virtue which your masters canonize that led their moral hero constantly to exhaust the stores of his powerful rhetoric in the expression of universal benevolence, whilst his heart was incapable of harboring one spark of common parental affection. Benevolence to the whole species, and want of feeling for every individual with whom the professors come in contact, form the character of the new philosophy. Setting up for an unsocial independence, this their hero of vanity refuses the just price of common labor, as well as the tribute which opulence owes to genius, and which, when paid, honors the giver and the receiver; and then he pleads his beggary as an excuse for his crimes. He melts with tenderness for those only who touch him by the remotest relation, and then, without one natural pang, casts away, as a sort of offal and excrement, the spawn of his disgustful amours, and sends his children to the hospital of foundlings. The bear loves, licks, and forms her young: but bears are not philosophers. Vanity, however, finds its account in reversing the train of our natural feelings. Thousands admire the sentimental writer; the affectionate father is hardly known in his parish.

Under this philosophic instructor in *the ethics of vanity*, they have attempted in France a regeneration of the moral constitution of man. Statesmen like your present rulers exist by everything which is spurious, fictitious, and false—by everything which takes the man from his house, and sets him on a stage—which makes him up an artificial creature, with painted, theatric sentiments, fit to be seen by the glare of candle-light, and formed to be contemplated at a due distance. Vanity is too apt to prevail in all of us, and in all countries. To the improvement of Frenchmen, it seems not absolutely necessary that it should be taught upon system. But it is plain that the present rebellion was its legitimate offspring, and it is piously fed by that rebellion with a daily dole.

If the system of institution recommended by the Assembly is false and theatric, it is because their system of government is of the same character. To that, and to that alone, it is strictly conformable. To understand either, we must connect the morals with the politics of the legislators. Your practical philosophers, systematic in everything, have wisely began at the source. As the relation between parents and children is the first among the elements of vulgar, natural morality, they erect statues to a wild, ferocious, low-minded, hard-hearted father, of fine general feelings—a lover of his kind, but a hater of his kindred. Your masters reject the duties of this vulgar relation, as contrary to liberty, as not founded in the social compact, and not binding according to the rights of men; because the relation is not, of course, the result of *free election*—never so on the side of the children, not always on the part of the parents.

The next relation which they regenerate by their statues to Rousseau is that which is next in sanctity to that of a father. They differ from those old-fashioned thinkers who considered pedagogues as sober and venerable characters, and allied to the parental. . . . In this age of light they teach the people that preceptors ought to be in the place of gallants. They systematically corrupt a very corruptible race, (for some time a growing nuisance amongst you,)—a set of pert, petulant literators, to whom, instead of their proper, but severe, unostentatious duties, they assign the brilliant part of men of wit and pleasure, of gay, young, military sparks, and danglers at toilets. They call on the rising generation in France to take a sympathy in the adventures and fortunes, and they endeavor to engage their sensibility on the side, of pedagogues who betray the most awful family trusts and vitiate their female pupils. They teach the people that the debauchers of virgins, almost in the arms of their parents, may be safe inmates in their house, and even fit guardians of the honor of those husbands who succeed legally to the office which the young literators had preoccupied without asking leave of law or conscience.

Thus they dispose of all the family relations of parents and children, husbands and wives. Through this same instructor, by whom they corrupt the morals, they corrupt the taste. Taste and elegance, though they are reckoned only among the smaller and secondary morals, yet are of no mean importance in the regulation of life. A moral taste is not of force to turn vice into virtue; but it recommends virtue with something like the blandishments of pleasure, and it infinitely abates the evils of vice. Rousseau, a writer of great force and vivacity, is totally destitute of taste in any sense of the word. Your masters, who are his scholars, conceive that all refinement has an aristocratic character. The last age had exhausted all its powers in giving a grace and nobleness to our natural appetites, and in raising them into a higher class and order than seemed justly to belong to them. Through Rousseau, your masters are resolved to destroy these aristocratic prejudices. The passion called love has so general and powerful an influence, it makes so much of the entertainment, and indeed so much the occupation, of that part of life which decides the character forever, that the mode and the principles on which it engages the sympathy and strikes the imagination become of the utmost importance to the morals and manners of every society. Your rulers were well aware of this; and in their system of changing your manners to accommodate them to their politics, they found nothing so convenient as

Rousseau. Through him they teach men to love after the fashion of philosophers: that is, they teach to men, to Frenchmen, a love without gallantry—a love without anything of that fine flower of youthfulness and gentility which places it, if not among the virtues, among the ornaments of life. Instead of this passion, naturally allied to grace and manners, they infuse into their youth an unfashioned, indelicate, sour, gloomy, ferocious medley of pedantry and lewdness—of metaphysical speculations blended with the coarsest sensuality. Such is the general morality of the passions to be found in their famous philosopher, in his famous work of philosophic gallantry, the *Nouvelle Éloise.*

When the fence from the gallantry of preceptors is broken down, and your families are no longer protected by decent pride and salutary domestic prejudice, there is but one step to a frightful corruption. The rulers in the National Assembly are in good hopes that the females of the first families in France may become an easy prey to dancing-masters, fiddlers, pattern-drawers, friseurs, and valets-de-chambre, and other active citizens of that description, who, having the entry into your houses, and being half domesticated by their situation, may be blended with you by regular and irregular relations. By a law they have made these people their equals. By adopting the sentiments of Rousseau they have made them your rivals. In this manner these great legislators complete their plan of levelling, and establish their rights of men on a sure foundation.

I am certain that the writings of Rousseau lead directly to this kind of shameful evil. I have often wondered how he comes to be so much more admired and followed on the Continent than he is here. Perhaps a secret charm in the language may have its share in this extraordinary difference. We certainly perceive, and to a degree we feel, in this writer, a style glowing, animated, enthusiastic, at the same time that we find it lax, diffuse, and not in the best taste of composition—all the members of the piece being pretty equally labored and expanded, without any due selection or subordination of parts. He is generally too much on the stretch, and his manner has little variety. We cannot rest upon any of his works, though they contain observations which occasionally discover a considerable insight into human nature. But his doctrines, on the whole, are so inapplicable to real life and manners, that we never dream of drawing from them any rule for laws or conduct, or for fortifying or illustrating anything by a reference to his opinions. . . .

Perhaps bold speculations are more acceptable because more new to you than to us, who have been long since satiated with them. We continue, as in the two last ages, to read, more generally than I believe is now done on the Continent, the authors of sound antiquity. These occupy our minds; they give us another taste and turn; and will not suffer us to be more than transiently amused with paradoxical morality. It is not that I consider this writer as wholly destitute of just notions. Amongst his irregularities, it must be reckoned that he is sometimes moral, and moral in a very sublime strain. But the *general spirit and tendency* of his works is mischievous—and the more mischievous for this mixture: for perfect depravity of sentiment is not reconcilable with eloquence; and the mind (though corruptible, not complexionally vicious) would reject and throw off with disgust a lesson of pure and unmixed evil. These writers make even virtue a pander to vice.

However, I less consider the author than the system of the Assembly in perverting morality through his means. This I confess makes me nearly despair of any attempt upon the minds of their followers, through reason, honor, or conscience. The great object of your tyrants is to destroy the gentlemen of France; and for that purpose they destroy, to the best of their power, all the effect of those relations which may render considerable men powerful or even safe. To destroy that order, they vitiate the whole community. That no means may exist of confederating against their tyranny, by the false sympathies of this *Nouvelle Éloise* they endeavor to subvert those principles of domestic trust and fidelity which form the discipline of social life. They propagate principles by which every servant may think it, if not his duty, at least his privilege, to betray his master. By these principles, every considerable father of a family loses the sanctuary of his house. . . . They destroy all the tranquillity and security of domestic life: turning the asylum of the house into a gloomy prison, where the father of the family must drag out a miserable existence, endangered in proportion to the apparent means of his safety—where he is worse than solitary in a crowd of domestics, and more apprehensive from his servants and inmates than from the hired, bloodthirsty mob without doors who are ready to pull him to the *lanterne.*

It is thus, and for the same end, that they endeavor to destroy that tribunal of conscience which exists independently of edicts and decrees. Your despots govern by terror. They know that he who fears God fears nothing else; and therefore they eradicate from the mind, through their Voltaire, their Helvétius, and the rest of that infamous gang, that only sort of fear which generates true courage. . . .

Letters on a Regicide Peace

Britain had joined the coalition against the French Republic in 1793. By late 1795 and throughout 1796, however, Pitt's administration sought a peace treaty with France. Burke wrote four letters in this period denouncing the peace overtures, claiming that the very future of Christian Europe was at stake. In these letters Burke's rage at what he depicts as the pestilential, even cannibalistic Jacobins reaches its greatest emotional intensity.

IN THE WAR of the grand alliance, most of these considerations voluntarily and naturally had their part. Some were pressed into the service. The political interest easily went in the track of the natural sentiment. In the reverse course the carriage does not follow freely. I am sure the natural feeling, as I have just said, is a far more predominant ingredient in this war, than in that of any other that ever was waged by this kingdom.

If the war made to prevent the union of two crowns upon one head was a just war; this, which is made to prevent the tearing of all crowns from all heads which ought to wear them, and with the crowns to smite off the sacred heads themselves, this is a just war.

If a war to prevent Louis XIV. from imposing his religion was just, a war to prevent the murderers of Lous XVI. from imposing their irreligion upon us is just; a war to prevent the operation of a system, which makes life without dignity, and death without hope, is a just war.

If to preserve political independence and civil freedom to nations was a just ground of war; a war to preserve national independence, property, liberty, life, and honour, from certain, universal havoc, is a war just, necessary, manly, pious: and we are bound to persevere in it by every principle, Divine and human, as long as the system which menaces them all, and all equally, has an existence in the world.

You, who have looked at this matter with as fair and impartial an eye as can be united with a feeling heart, you will not think it a hardy assertion, when I affirm, that it were far better to be conquered by any other nation, than to have this faction for a neighbour. Before I felt myself authorized to say this, I considered the state of all the countries in Europe for these last three hundred years, which have been obliged to submit to a foreign law. In most of those I found the condition of the annexed countries even better, certainly not worse, than the lot of those which were the patrimony of the conqueror. They wanted some blessings—but they were free from many great evils. They were rich and tranquil. Such was Artois, Flanders, Lorrain, Alsatia, under the old government of France. Such was Silesia under the king of Prussia. They, who are to live in the vicinity of this new fabric, are to prepare to live in perpetual conspiracies and seditions; and to end at last, in being conquered, if not to her dominion, to her resemblance. But when we talk of conquest by other nations, it is only to put a case. This is the only power in Europe by which it is *possible* we should be conquered. To live under the continual dread of such immeasurable evils is itself a grievous calamity. To live without the dread of them is to turn the danger into the disaster. The influence of such a France is equal to a war, its example was more wasting than a hostile irruption. The hostility with any other power is separable and accidental; this power, by the very condition of its existence, by its very essential constitution, is in a state of hostility with us, and with all civilized people.

A government of the nature of that set up at our very door has never been hitherto seen, or even imagined, in Europe. What our relation to it will be cannot be judged by other relations. It is a serious thing to have connexion with a people, who live only under positive, arbitrary, and changeable institutions; and those not perfected, nor supplied, nor explained, by any common acknowledged rule of moral science. I remember that in one of my last conversations with the late Lord Camden, we were struck much in the same manner with the abolition in France of the law, as a science of methodized and artificial equity. France, since her revolution, is under the sway of a sect, whose leaders have deliberately, at one stroke, demolished the whole body of that jurisprudence which France had pretty nearly in common with other civilized countries. In that jurisprudence were contained the elements and principles of the law of nations, the great ligament of mankind. With the law they have of course destroyed all seminaries in which jurisprudence was taught, as well as all the corporations established for its conservation. I have not heard of any country, whether in Europe or Asia, or even in Africa on this side of Mount Atlas, which is wholly without some such colleges and such corporations, except France. No man in a public or private concern, can divine by what rule or principle her judgments are to be directed; nor is there to be found a professor in any university, or a practitioner in any court, who will hazard an opinion of what is or is not law in France, in any case whatever. They have not only annulled all their old treaties, but they have renounced the law of nations, from whence treaties have their force. With a fixed design they have outlawed themselves, and to their power outlawed all other nations.

Instead of the religion and the law by which they were in a great politic communion with the Christian world, they have constructed their republic on three bases, all fundamentally opposite to those on which the communities of Europe are built. Its foundation is laid in regicide, in Jacobinism, and in atheism; and it has joined to those principles a body of systematic manners, which secures their operation.

If I am asked, how I would be understood in the use of these terms, regicide, Jacobinism, atheism, and a system of corresponding manners, and their establishment? I will tell you:

I call a commonwealth *regicide*, which lays it down as a fixed law of nature, and a fundamental right of man, that all government, not being a democracy, is an usurpation. That all kings, as such, are usurpers; and for being kings may and ought to be put to death, with their wives, families, and adherents. The commonwealth which acts uniformly upon those principles, and which, after abolishing every festival of religion, chooses the most flagrant act of a murderous regicide treason for a feast of eternal commemoration, and which forces all her people to observe it—this I call *regicide by establishment.*

Jacobinism is the revolt of the enterprising talents of a country against its property. When private men form themselves into associations for the purpose of destroying the pre-existing laws and institutions of their country; when they secure to themselves an army, by dividing amongst the people of no property the estates of the ancient and lawful proprietors; when a state recognises those acts; when it does not make confiscations for crimes, but makes crimes for confiscations; when it has its principal strength, and all its resources, in such a violation of property; when it stands chiefly upon such a violation; massacring by judgments, or otherwise, those who make any struggle for their old legal government, and their legal, hereditary, or acquired possessions—I call this *Jacobinism by establishment.*

I call it *atheism by establishment*, when any state, as such, shall not acknowledge the existence of God as a moral governor of the world; when it shall offer to him no religious or moral worship;—when it shall abolish the Christian religion by a regular decree;—when it shall persecute with a cold, unrelenting, steady cruelty, by every mode of confiscation, imprisonment, exile, and death, all its ministers;—when it shall generally shut up or pull down churches; when the few buildings which remain of this kind shall be opened only for the purpose of making a profane apotheosis of monsters, whose vices and crimes have no parallel amongst men, and whom all other men consider as objects of general detestation, and the severest animadversion of law. When, in the place of that religion of social benevolence, and of individual self-denial, in mockery of all religion, they institute impious, blasphemous, indecent theatric rites, in honour of their vitiated, perverted reason, and erect altars to the personification of their own corrupted and bloody republic;—when schools and seminaries are founded at the public expense to poison mankind, from generation to generation, with the horrible maxims of this impiety;—when wearied out with incessant martyrdom, and the cries of a people hungering and thirsting for religion, they permit it, only as a tolerated evil—I call this *atheism by establishment*.

When to these establishments of regicide, of Jacobinism, and of atheism, you add the *correspondent system of manners*, no doubt can be left on the mind of a thinking man concerning their determined hostility to the human race. Manners are of more importance than laws. Upon them, in a great measure, the laws depend. The law touches us but here and there, and now and then. Manners are what vex or soothe, corrupt or purify, exalt or debase, barbarize or refine us, by a constant, steady, uniform, insensible operation, like that of the air we breathe in. They give their whole form and colour to our lives. According to their quality, they aid morals, they supply them, or they totally destroy them. Of this the new French legislators were aware; therefore, with the same method, and under the same authority, they settled a system of manners, the most licentious, prostitute, and abandoned, that ever has been known, and at the same time the most coarse, rude, savage, and ferocious. Nothing in the Revolution, no, not to a phrase or a gesture, not to the fashion of a hat or a shoe, was left to accident. All has been the result of design; all has been matter of institution. No mechanical means could be devised in favour of this incredible system of wickedness and vice, that has not been employed. The noblest passions, the love of glory, the love of country, have been debauched into means of its preservation and its propagation. All sorts of shows and exhibitions, calculated to inflame and vitiate the imagination, and pervert the moral sense, have been contrived. They have sometimes brought forth five or six hundred drunken women, calling at the bar of the Assembly for the blood of their own children, as being royalists or constitutionalists. Sometimes they have got a body of wretches, calling themselves fathers, to demand the murder of their sons, boasting that Rome had but one Brutus, but that they could show five hundred. There were instances, in which they inverted, and retaliated the impiety, and produced sons, who called for the execution of their parents. The foundation of their republic is laid in moral paradoxes. Their patriotism is always prodigy. All those instances to be found in history, whether real or fabulous, of a doubtful public spirit at which morality is perplexed, reason is staggered, and from which affrighted nature recoils, are their chosen, and almost sole, examples for the instruction of their youth.

The whole drift of their institution is contrary to that of the wise legislators of all countries, who aimed at improving instincts into morals, and at grafting the virtues on the stock of the natural affections. They, on the contrary, have omitted no pains to eradicate every benevolent and noble propensity in the mind of men. In their culture it is a rule always to graft virtues on vices. They think everything unworthy of the name of public virtue, unless it indicates violence on the private. All their new institutions (and with them everything is new) strike at the root of our social nature. Other legislators, knowing that marriage is the origin of all relations, and consequently the first element of all duties, have endeavoured, by every art, to make it sacred. The Christian religion, by confining it to the pairs, and by rendering that relation indissoluble, has by these two things done more towards the peace, happiness, settlement, and civilization of the world, than by any other part in this whole scheme of Divine Wisdom. The direct contrary course has been taken in the synagogue of antichrist, I mean in that forge and manufactory of all evil, the sect which predominated in the Constituent Assembly of 1789. Those monsters employed the same, or greater industry, to desecrate and degrade that state, which other legislators have used to render it holy and honourable. By a strange, uncalled-for declaration, they pronounced, that marriage was no better than a common, civil contract. It was one of their ordinary tricks, to put their sentiments into the mouths of certain personated characters, which they theatrically exhibited at the bar of what ought to be a serious assembly. One of these was brought out in the figure of a prostitute, whom they called by the affected name of "a mother without being a wife." This creature they made to call for a repeal of the incapacities, which in civilized states are put upon bastards. The prostitutes of the Assembly gave to this their puppet the sanction of their greater impudence. In consequence of the principles laid down, and the manners authorized, bastards were not long after put on the footing of the issue of lawful unions. Proceeding in the spirit of the first authors of their constitution, succeeding assemblies went the full length of the principle, and gave a licence to divorce at the mere pleasure of either party, and at a month's notice. With them the matrimonial connexion is brought into so degraded a state of concubinage, that I believe, none of the wretches in London who keep warehouses of infamy, would give out one of their victims to private custody on so short and insolent a tenure. There was indeed a kind of profligate equity in giving to women the same licentious power. The reason they assigned was as infamous as the act; declaring that women had been too long under the tyranny of parents and of husbands. It is not necessary to observe upon the horrible consequences of taking one half of the species wholly out of the guardianship and protection of the other.

The practice of divorce, though in some countries permitted, has been discouraged in all. In the East, polygamy and divorce are in discredit; and the manners correct the laws. In Rome, whilst Rome was in its integrity, the few causes allowed for divorce amounted in effect to a prohibition. They were only three. The arbitrary was totally excluded, and accordingly some hundreds of years passed, without a single example of that kind. When manners were corrupted, the laws were relaxed; as the latter always follow the former, when they are not able to regulate them, or to vanquish them. Of this circumstance the legislators of vice and crime were pleased to take notice, as an inducement to adopt their regulation; holding out a hope, that the permission would as rarely be made use of. They knew the contrary to be true; and they had taken good care, that the laws should be well seconded by the manners. Their law of divorce, like all their laws, had not for its object the relief of domestic uneasiness, but the total corruption of all morals, the total disconnexion of social life.

It is a matter of curiosity to observe the operation of this encouragement to disorder. I have before me the Paris paper, correspondent to the usual register of births, marriages, and deaths. Divorce, happily, is no regular head of registry amongst civilized nations. With the Jacobins it is remarkable, that divorce is not only a regular head, but it has the post of honour. It occupies the first place in the list. In the three first months of the year 1793, the number of divorces in that city amounted to 562. The marriages were 1785; so that the proportion of divorces to marriages was not much less than one to three; a thing unexampled, I believe, among mankind. I caused an inquiry to be made at Doctors' Commons, concerning the number of divorces; and found, that all the divorces (which, except by special act of parliament, are separations, and not proper divorces) did not amount in all those courts, and in a hundred years, to much more than one-fifth of those that passed, in the single city of Paris, in three months. I followed up the inquiry relative to that city through several of the subsequent months until I was tired, and found the proportions still the same. Since then I have heard that they have declared for a revisal of these laws; but I know of nothing done. It appears as if the contract that renovates the world was under no law at all. From this we may take our estimate of the havoc that has been made through all the relations of life. With the Jacobins of France, vague intercourse is without reproach; marriage is reduced to the vilest concubinage; children are encouraged to cut the throats of their parents; mothers are taught that tenderness is no part of their character, and, to demonstrate their attachment to their party, that they ought to make no scruple to rake with their bloody hands in the bowels of those who came from their own.

To all this let us join the practice of *cannibalism*, with which, in the proper terms, and with the greatest truth, their several factions accuse each other. By cannibalism, I mean their devouring as a nutriment of their ferocity, some part of the bodies of those they have murdered; their drinking the blood of their victims, and forcing the victims themselves to drink the blood of their kindred slaughtered before their faces. By cannibalism, I mean also to signify all their nameless, unmanly, and abominable insults on the bodies of those they slaughter.

As to those whom they suffer to die a natural death, they do not permit them to enjoy the last consolations of mankind, or those rights of sepulture, which indicate hope, and which mere nature has taught to mankind, in all countries, to soothe the afflictions, and to cover the infirmity, of mortal condition. They disgrace men in the entry into life, they vitiate and enslave them through the whole course of it, and they deprive them of all comfort at the conclusion of their dishonoured and depraved existence. Endeavouring to persuade the people that they are no better than beasts, the whole body of their institution tends to make them beasts of prey, furious and savage. For this purpose the active part of them is disciplined into a ferocity which has no parallel. To this ferocity there is joined not one of the rude, unfashioned virtues, which accompany the vices, where the whole are left to grow up together in the rankness of uncultivated nature. But nothing is left to nature in their systems.

The same discipline which hardens their hearts relaxes their morals. Whilst courts of justice were thrust out by revolutionary tribunals, and silent churches were only the funeral monuments of departed religion, there were no fewer than nineteen or twenty theatres, great and small, most of them kept open at the public expense, and all of them crowded every night. Among the gaunt, haggard forms of famine and nakedness, amidst the yells of murder, the tears of affliction, and the cries of despair, the song, the dance, the mimic scene, the buffoon laughter, went on as regularly as in the gay hour of festive peace. I have it from good authority, that under the scaffold of judicial murder, and the gaping planks that poured down blood on the spectators, the space was hired out for a show of dancing dogs. I think, without concert, we have made the very same remark on reading some of their pieces, which being written for other purposes, let us into a view of their social life. It struck us that the habits of Paris had no resemblance to the finished virtues, or to the polished vice, and elegant, though not blameless, luxury, of the capital of a great empire. Their society was more like that of a den of outlaws upon a doubtful frontier; of a lewd tavern for the revels and debauches of banditti, assassins, bravos, smugglers, and their more desperate paramours, mixed with bombastic players, the refuse and rejected offal of strolling theatres, puffing out ill-sorted verses about virtue, mixed with the licentious and blasphemous songs, proper to the brutal and hardened course of life belonging to that sort of wretches. This system of manners in itself is at war with all orderly and moral society, and is in its neighbourhood unsafe. If great bodies of that kind were anywhere established in a bordering territory, we should have a right to demand of their governments the suppression of such a nuisance. What are we to do if the government and the whole community is of the same description? Yet that government has thought proper to invite ours to lay by its unjust hatred, and to listen to the voice of humanity as taught by their example.

The operation of dangerous and delusive first principles obliges us to have recourse to the true ones. In the intercourse between nations, we are apt to rely too much on the instrumental part. We lay too much weight upon the formality of treaties and compacts. We do not act much more wisely when we trust to the interests of men as guarantees of their engagements. The interests frequently tear to pieces the engagements; and the passions trample upon both. Entirely to trust to either, is to disregard our own safety, or not to know mankind. Men are not tied to one another by papers and seals. They are led to associate by resemblances, by conformities, by sympathies. It is with nations as with individuals. Nothing is so strong a tie of amity between nation and nation as correspondence in laws, customs, manners, and habits of life. They have more than the force of treaties in themselves. They are obligations written in the heart. They approximate men to men, without their knowledge, and sometimes against their intentions. The secret, unseen, but irrefragable bond of habitual intercourse holds them together, even when their perverse and litigious nature sets them to equivocate, scuffle, and fight, about the terms of their written obligations.

As to war, if it be the means of wrong and violence, it is the sole means of justice amongst nations. Nothing can banish it from the world. They who say otherwise, intending to impose upon us, do not impose upon themselves. But it is one of the greatest objects of human wisdom to mitigate those evils which we are unable to remove. The conformity and analogy of which I speak, incapable, like everything else, of preserving perfect trust and tranquility among men, has a strong tendency to facilitate accommodation, and to produce a generous oblivion of the rancour of their quarrels. With this similitude, peace is more of peace, and war is less of war. I will go further. There have been periods of time in which communities, apparently in peace with each other, have been more perfectly separated than, in latter times, many nations in Europe have been in the course of long and bloody wars. The cause must be sought in the similitude throughout Europe of religion, laws, and manners. At bottom, these are all the same. The writers on public law have often called this *aggregate* of nations a commonwealth. They had reason. It is virtually one great state having the same basis of general law, with some diversity of provincial customs and local establishments. The nations of Europe have had the very same Christian religion, agreeing in the fundamental parts, varying a little in the ceremonies and in the subordinate doctrines. The whole of the polity and economy of every country in Europe has been derived from the same sources. It was drawn from the old Germanic or Gothic custumary, from the feudal institutions which must be considered as an emanation from that custumary; and the whole has been improved and digested into system and discipline by the Roman law. From hence arose the several orders, with or without a monarch, (which are called states,) in every European country; the strong traces of which, where monarchy predominated, were never wholly extinguished or merged in despotism. In the few places where monarchy was cast off, the spirit of European monarchy was still left. Those countries still continued countries of states; that is, of classes, orders, and distinctions such as had before subsisted, or nearly so. Indeed the force and form of the institution called states continued in greater perfection in those republican communities than under monarchies. From all those sources arose a system of manners and of education which was nearly similar in all this quarter of the globe; and which softened, blended, and harmonized the colours of the whole. There was little difference in the form of the universities for the education of their youth, whether with regard to faculties, to sciences, or to the more liberal and elegant kinds of erudition. From this resemblance in the modes of intercourse, and in the whole form and fashion of life, no citizen of Europe could be altogether an exile in any part of it. There was nothing more than a pleasing variety to recreate and instruct the mind, to enrich the imagination, and to meliorate the heart. When a man travelled or resided for health, pleasure, business, or necessity from his own country, he never felt himself quite abroad.

The whole body of this new scheme of manners, in support of the new scheme of politics, I consider as a strong and decisive proof of determined ambition and systematic hostility. I defy the most refining ingenuity to invent any other cause for the total departure of the Jacobin republic from every one of the ideas and usages, religious, legal, moral, or social, of this civilized world, and for her tearing herself from its communion with such studied violence, but from a formed resolution of keeping no terms with that world. It has not been, as has been falsely and insidiously represented, that these miscreants had only broke with their old government. They made a schism with the whole universe, and that schism extended to almost everything great and small. For one, I wish, since it is gone thus far, that the breach had been so complete, as to make all intercourse impracticable: but partly by accident, partly by design, partly from the resistance of the matter, enough is left to preserve intercourse, whilst amity is destroyed or corrupted in its principle.

This violent breach of the community of Europe we must conclude to have been made (even if they had not expressly declared it over and over again) either to force mankind into an adoption of their system, or to live in perpetual enmity with a community the most potent we have ever known. Can any person imagine, that, in offering to mankind this desperate alternative, there is no indication of a hostile mind, because men in possession of the ruling authority are supposed to have a right to act without coercion in their own territories? As to the right of men to act anywhere according to their pleasure, without any moral tie, no such right exists. Men are never in a state of *total* independence of each other. It is not the condition of our nature: nor is it conceivable how any man can pursue a considerable course of action without its having some effect upon others; or, of course, without producing some degree of responsibility for his conduct. The *situations* in which men relatively stand produce the rules and principles of that responsibility, and afford directions to prudence in exacting it.

Distance of place does not extinguish the duties or the rights of men: but it often renders their exercise impracticable. The same circumstance of distance renders the noxious effects of an evil system in any community less pernicious. But there are situations where this difficulty does not occur; and in which, therefore, these duties are obligatory, and these rights are to be asserted. It has ever been the method of public jurists to draw a great part of the analogies, on which they form the law of nations, from the principles of law which prevail in civil community. Civil laws are not all of them merely positive. Those, which are rather conclusions of legal reason than matters of statutable provision, belong to universal equity, and are universally applicable. Almost the whole prætorian law is such. There is a *Law of Neighbourhood* which does not leave a man perfectly master on his own ground. When a neighbour sees a *new erection*, in the nature of a nuisance, set up at his door, he has a right to represent it to the judge; who, on his part, has a right to order the work to be stayed; or, if established, to be removed. On this head the parent law is express and clear, and has made many wise provisions, which, without destroying, regulate and restrain the right of *ownership*, by the right of *vicinage*. No *innovation* is permitted that may redound, even secondarily, to the prejudice of a neighbour. The whole doctrine of that important head of prætorian law, "*De novi operis nunciatione*," is founded on the principle, that no *new* use should be made of a man's private liberty of operating upon his private property, from whence a detriment may be justly apprehended by his neighbour. This law of denunciation is prospective. It is to anticipate what is called *damnum infectum*, or *damnum nondum factum*, that is, a damage justly apprehended, but not actually done. Even before it is clearly known, whether the innovation be damageable or not, the judge is competent to issue a prohibition to innovate, until the point can be determined. This prompt interference is grounded on principles favourable to both parties. It is preventive of mischief difficult to be repaired, and of ill blood difficult to be softened. The rule of law, therefore, which comes before the evil, is amongst the very best parts of equity, and justifies the promptness of the remedy; because, as it is well observed, *Res damni infecti celeritatem desiderat, et periculosa est dilatio.* This right of denunciation does not hold, when things continue, however inconveniently to the neighbourhood, according to the *ancient* mode. For there is a sort of presumption against novelty, drawn out of a deep consideration of human nature and human affairs; and the maxim of jurisprudence is well laid down, *Vetustas pro lege semper habetur.*

Such is the law of civil vicinity. Now, where there is no constituted judge, as between independent states there is not, the vicinage itself is the natural judge. It is, preventively, the assessor of its own rights, or remedially, their avenger. Neighbours are presumed to take cognizance of each other's acts. "*Vicini vicinorum facta presumuntur scire.*" This principle, which, like the rest, is as true of nations as of individual men, has bestowed on the grand vicinage of Europe a duty to know, and a right to prevent, any capital innovation which may amount to the erection of a dangerous nuisance. Of the importance of that innovation, and the mischief of that nuisance, they are, to be sure, bound to judge, not litigiously; but it is in their competence to judge. They have uniformly acted on this right. What in civil society is a ground of action, in politic society is a ground of war. But the exercise of that competent jurisdiction is a matter of moral prudence. As suits in civil society, so war in the political, must ever be a matter of great deliberation. It is not this or that particular proceeding, picked out here and there, as a subject of quarrel, that will do. There must be an aggregate of mischief. There must be marks of deliberation, there must be traces of design, there must be indications of malice, there must be tokens of ambition. There must be force in the body where they exist, there must be energy in the mind. When all these circumstances are combined, or the important parts of them, the duty of the vicinity calls for the exercise of its competence; and the rules of prudence do not restrain, but demand it.

In describing the nuisance erected by so pestilential a manufactory, by the construction of so infamous a brothel, by digging a night-cellar for such thieves, murderers, and house-breakers, as never infested the world, I am so far from aggravating, that I have fallen infinitely short of the evil. No man who has attended to the particulars of what has been done in France, and combined them with the principles there asserted, can possibly doubt it. When I compare with this great cause of nations, the trifling points of honour, the still more contemptible points of interest, the light ceremonies and undefinable punctilios, the disputes about precedency, the lowering or the hoisting of a sail, the dealing in a hundred or two of wild cat-skins on the other side of the globe, which have often kindled up the flames of war between nations, I stand astonished at those persons, who do not feel a resentment, not more natural than politic, at the atrocious insults that this monstrous compound offers to the dignity of every nation, and who are not alarmed with what it threatens to their safety.

I have therefore been decidedly of opinion, with our declaration at Whitehall, in the beginning of this war, that the vicinage of Europe had not only a right, but an indispensable duty, and an exigent interest, to denunciate this new work before it had produced the danger we have so sorely felt, and which we shall long feel. The example of what is done by France is too important not to have a vast and extensive influence; and that example, backed with its power, must bear with great force on those who are near it; especially on those who shall recognise the pretended republic on the principle upon which it now stands. It is not an old structure which you have found as it is, and are not to dispute of the original end and design with which it had been so fashioned. It is a recent wrong, and can plead no prescription. It violates the rights upon which not only the community of France, but those on which all communities are founded. The principles on which they proceed are *general* principles, and are as true in England as in any other country. They, who (though with the purest intentions) recognise the authority of these regicides and robbers upon principle, justify their acts and establish them as precedents. It is a question not between France and England. It is a question between property and force. The property claims; and its claim has been allowed. The property of the nation is the nation. They, who massacre, plunder, and expel the body of the proprietary, are murderers and robbers. The state, in its essence, must be moral and just: and it may be so, though a tyrant or usurper should be accidentally at the head of it. This is a thing to be lamented: but this notwithstanding, the body of the commonwealth may remain in all its integrity and be perfectly sound in its composition. The present case is different. It is not a revolution in government. It is not the victory of party over party. It is a destruction and decomposition of the whole society; which never can be made of right by any faction, however powerful, nor without terrible consequences to all about it, both in the act and in the example. This pretended republic is founded in crimes, and exists by wrong and robbery; and wrong and robbery, far from a title to anything, is war with mankind. To be at peace with robbery is to be an accomplice with it. . . .

PART VII

SELECTED LETTERS

To the Duke of Richmond

In this letter of November 17, 1772, to Charles Lennox, third duke of Richmond, a member of the Rockingham party, Burke offers his memorable characterization of the aristocracy as "the great oaks that shade a country." It is interesting to compare the tone of this letter with Burke's bitter criticism of the Russells in his "Letter to a Noble Lord."

. . . DECORUM, FIRMNESS, consistency, courage, patient, manly perseverance,—these are the virtues of despair. They are worth something, surely; and none has profited so much of that situation as your grace, nor could you have shown of what materials you are made in any other. Persons in your station of life ought to have long views. You people of great families and hereditary trusts and fortunes, are not like such as I am, who, whatever we may be, by the rapidity of our growth, and even by the fruit we bear, and flatter ourselves that, while we creep on the ground, we belly into melons that are exquisite for size and flavour, yet still are but annual plants, that perish with our season, and leave no sort of traces behind us. You, if you are what you ought to be, are in my eye the great oaks that shade a country, and perpetuate your benefits from generation to generation. The immediate power of a Duke of Richmond, or a Marquis of Rockingham, is not so much of moment; but if their conduct and example hand down their principles to their successors, then their houses become the public repositories and offices of record for the constitution; not like the Tower, or Rolls-chapel, where it is searched for and sometimes in vain, in rotten parchments under dripping and perishing walls, but in full vigour, and acting with vital energy and power, in the character of the leading men and natural interests of the country. It has been remarked that there were two eminent families at Rome, that for several ages were distinguished uniformly by opposite characters and principles, the Claudian and Valerian. The former were high and haughty, but public-spirited, firm, and active, and attached to the aristocracy. The latter were popular in their tempers, manners, and principles. So far the remark:—but I add that any one, who looks attentively to their history, will see that the balance of that famous constitution was kept up for some ages, by the personal characters, dispositions, and traditionary politics of certain families, as much as by any thing in the laws and orders of the state; so that I do not look upon your time or lives lost, if, in this sliding away from the genuine spirit of the country, certain parties, if possible, if not the heads of certain families, should make it their business, by the whole course of their lives, principally by their example, to mould into the very vital stamina of their descendants, those principles which ought to be transmitted pure and unmixed to posterity. Neither Lord Rockingham nor your grace have children: however, you do not want successors of your blood; nor, I trust, heirs of your qualities and your virtues, and of the power which sooner or later will be derived from them. This I say to comfort myself, and possibly your grace, in the present melancholy view of our affairs. "Although the field is lost all is not lost," to give you a line of your Milton, who has somewhat reconciled you to poetry,—and he is an able advocate.

To William Burgh, Esq.

Burke wrote on February 9, 1775, to the Oxford religious writer Dr. William Burgh. He makes very clear that he would prefer official toleration of all religious groups—"Jews, Mahometans, and even Pagans."

Dear Sir,

I beg you will not think that my delay in returning you the proof sheet of your most ingenious and most obliging dedication, could proceed from a want of the liveliest sensibility to the great honour you have done me. I now return the proof with my sincerest and most grateful acknowledgments.

Some topics are touched in that dedication, on which I could wish to explain myself to you. I should have been glad to do it through Mr. Mason; but to my great loss, on this and many other accounts, he left town suddenly. Indeed, at that time and ever since, the pressure of American business on one hand, and a petition against my election on the other, left me not a single minute at my disposal, and I have now little leisure enough to explain myself clearly on some points in that dedication, which I either misunderstand, or they go upon a misapprehension of some part of my public conduct; for which reason, I wish, if I might presume to interfere, that they may be a little altered.

It is certain that I have, to the best of my power, supported the establishment of the church, upon grounds and principles which I am happy to find countenanced by your approbation. This you have been told; but you have not heard that I supported also the petition of the dissenters, for a larger toleration than they enjoy at present under the letter of the act of King William. In fact, my opinion in favour of toleration goes far beyond the limits of that act, which was no more than a provision for certain sets of men, under certain circumstances, and by no means what is commonly called "an act of toleration." I am greatly deceived, if my opinions on this subject are not consistent with the strictest and the best supported church establishment. I cannot consider our dissenters, of almost any kind, as schismatics; whatever some of their leaders might originally have been in the eye of Him, who alone knows whether they acted under the direction of such a conscience as they had, or at the instigation of pride and passion. There are many things amongst most of them, which I rather *dislike* than dare to *condemn*. My ideas of toleration go far beyond even theirs. I would give a full civil protection, in which I include an immunity from all disturbance of their public religious worship, and a power of teaching in schools as well as temples, to Jews, Mahometans, and even Pagans; especially if they are already possessed of those advantages by long and prescriptive usage, which is as sacred in this exercise of rights, as in any other. Much more am I inclined to tolerate those whom I look upon as our brethren. I mean all those who profess our common hope, extending to all the reformed and unreformed churches, both at home and abroad; in none of whom I find any thing capitally amiss, but their mutual hatred of each other. I can never think any man a heretic, or schismatic, by *education*. It must be, as I conceive, by an act, in which his *own choice* (influenced by blamable passions) is more concerned than it can be by his early prejudices, and his being aggregated to bodies, for whom men naturally form a great degree of reverence and affection. This is my opinion, and my conduct has been conformable to it. Another age will see it more general; and I think that this general affection to religion will never introduce indifference, but will rather increase real zeal, Christian fervour, and pious emulation; that it will make a common cause against Epicurism, and every thing that corrupts the mind and renders it unworthy of its family. But toleration does not exclude national preference, either as to mode or opinions, and all the lawful and honest means which may be used for the support of that preference.

I should be happy to converse with you, and such as you, on these subjects, and to unlearn my mistaken opinions, if such they should be; for, however, erroneous, I believe there is no evil ingredient in them. In looking over that dedication, if you should agree with me, that there are some expressions that carry with them an idea of my pushing my ideas of church establishment further than I do, you will naturally soften or change them accordingly. I do not know very well how to excuse the great liberty I take, in troubling you with observations, where I ought to speak only my obligations. Be assured, that I feel myself extremely honoured by your good opinion, and shall be made very happy by your friendship.

I AM, WITH THE GREATEST ESTEEM, & C.

To the Marquis of Rockingham

In this letter to his parliamentary patron, written on August 23, 1775, Burke reveals his sadness at the outbreak of hostilities in America as a result of Britain's repressive response to events in Boston. Rockingham had "saved" America ten years earlier, Burke notes; would that he could do it again.

. . . WE ARE, AT LENGTH, actually involved in that war which your lordship, to your infinite honour, has made so many efforts to keep at a distance. It has come upon us in a manner more disagreeable and unpromising, than the most gloomy prognostic had ever foretold it. Your lordship's observation on the general temper of the nation at this crisis, is certainly just. If any indication is to be taken from external appearances, the king is entirely satisfied with the present state of his government. His spirits at his levees, at the play, every where, seem to be remarkably good. His ministers, too, are perfectly at their ease. Most of them are amusing themselves in the country, while England is disfurnished of its forces in the face of armed Europe, and Gibraltar and Minorca are delivered over to the custody of foreigners. They are at their ease relative to the only point which could give them anxiety,—they are assured of their places.

As to the good people of England, they seem to partake every day, more and more, of the character of that administration which they have been induced to tolerate. I am satisfied, that within a few years, there has been a great change in the national character. We seem no longer that eager, inquisitive, jealous, fiery people, which we have been formerly, and which we have been a very short time ago. The people look back, without pleasure or indignation; and forward, without hope or fear. No man commends the measures which have been pursued, or expects any good from those which are in preparation; but it is a cold, languid opinion, like what men discover in affairs that do not concern them. It excites to no passion; it prompts to no action.

In all this state of things I find my observation and intelligence perfectly agree with your lordship's. In one point, indeed, I have the misfortune to differ. I do not think that weeks, or even months, or years, will bring the monarch, the ministers, or the people, to feeling. To bring the people to a feeling, such a feeling, I mean, as tends to amendment, or alteration of system, there must be a plan and management. All direction of public humour and opinion must originate in a few. Perhaps a good deal of that humour and opinion must be owing to such direction. Events supply materials; times furnish dispositions; but conduct alone can bring them to bear to any useful purpose. I never yet knew an instance of any general temper in the nation, that might not have been tolerably well traced to some particular persons. If things are left to themselves, it is my clear opinion that a nation may slide down fair and softly from the highest point of grandeur and prosperity to the lowest state of imbecility and meanness, without any one's marking a particular period in this declension, without asking a question about it, or in the least speculating on any of the innumerable acts which have stolen in this silent and insensible revolution. Every event so prepares the subsequent, that, when it arrives, it produces no surprise, nor any extraordinary alarm. I am certain that if pains, great and immediate pains, are not taken to prevent it, such must be the fate of this country. We look to the merchants in vain—they are gone from us, and from themselves. They consider America as lost, and they look to administration for an indemnity. Hopes are accordingly held out to them, that some equivalent for their debts will be provided.

In the mean time, the leading men among them are kept full fed with contracts, and remittances, and jobs of all descriptions; and they are indefatigable in their endeavours to keep the others quiet, with the prospect of their share in those emoluments, of which they see their advisers already so amply in possession. They all, or the greatest number of them, begin to snuff the cadaverous *haut gout* of lucrative war. War, indeed, is become a sort of substitute for commerce. The freighting business never was so lively, on account of the prodigious taking up for transport service. Great orders for provisions and stores of all kinds, new clothing for the troops, and the intended six thousand Canadians, puts life into the woollen manufacture; and a number of men of war, ordered to be equipped, has given a pretence for such a quantity of nails and other iron work, as to keep the midland parts tolerably quiet. All this, with the incredible increase of the northern market since the peace between Russia and the Porte, keeps up the spirits of the mercantile world, and induces them to consider the American war, not so much their calamity, as their resource in an inevitable distress. This is the state of *most*, not of *all* the merchants.

All this, however, would not be of so much consequence. The great evil and danger will be, the full and decided engagement of parliament in this war. Then we shall be thoroughly dipped, and then there will be no way of getting out, but by disgracing England, or enslaving America. In that state, ministry has a lease of power, as long as the war continues. The hinge between war and peace is, indeed, a dangerous juncture to ministers; but a determined state of the one or the other, is a pretty safe position. When their cause, however absurdly, is made the cause of the nation, the popular cry will be with them. The style will be, that their hands must be strengthened by an unreserved confidence. When that cry is once raised, and raised it infallibly will be, if not prevented, the puny voice of reason will not be heard. As sure as we have now an existence, if the meeting of parliament should catch your lordship and your friends in an unprepared state, nothing but disgrace and ruin can attend the cause you are at the head of. Parliament will plunge over head and ears. They will vote the war with every supply of domestic and foreign force. They will pass an act of attainder;—they will lay their hands upon the press. The ministers will even procure addresses from those very merchants, who, last session, harassed them with petitions; and then,—what is left for us, but to spin out of our bowels, under the frowns of the court and the hisses of the people, the little slender thread of a peevish and captious opposition, unworthy of our cause and ourselves, and without credit, concurrence, or popularity in the nation!

I hope I am as little awed out of my senses by the fear of vulgar opinion, as most of my acquaintance. I think, on a fair occasion, I could look it in the face; but speaking of the prudential consideration, we know that all opposition is absolutely crippled, if it can obtain no kind of support without doors. If this should be found impracticable, I must revert to my old opinion, that much the most effectual, and much the most honourable course is, without the obligation of a formal secession, to absent ourselves from parliament. My experience is worth nothing, if it has not made it as clear to me as the sun, that, in affairs like these, a feeble opposition is the greatest service which can be done to ministry; and surely, if there be a state of decided disgrace, it is to add to the power of your enemies by every step you take to distress them.

I am confident that your lordship considers my importunity with your usual goodness. You will not attribute my earnestness to any improper cause. I shall, therefore, make no apology for urging, again and again, how necessary it is for your lordship and your great friends, most seriously to take under immediate deliberation, what you are to do in this crisis. Nothing like it has happened in your political life. I protest to God, I think that your reputation, your duty, and the duty and honour of us all, who profess your sentiments, from the highest to the lowest of us, demand at this time one honest, hearty effort, in order to avert the heavy calamities that are impending; to keep our hands from blood, and, if possible, to keep the poor, giddy, thoughtless people of our country from plunging headlong into this impious war. If the attempt is necessary, it is honourable. You will, at least, have the comfort that nothing has been left undone, on your part, to prevent the worst mischief that can befal the public. Then, and not before, you may shake the dust from your feet, and leave the people and their leaders to their own conduct and fortune.

I see, indeed, many, many difficulties in the way; but we have known as great, or greater, give way to a regular series of judicious and active exertions. This is no time for taking public business in their course and order, and only as a part in the scheme of life, which comes and goes at its proper periods, and is mixed in with occupations and amusements. It calls for the whole of the best of us; and every thing else, however just or even laudable at another time, ought to give way to this great, urgent, instant concern. Indeed, my dear lord, you are called upon in a very peculiar manner. America is yours. You have saved it once, and you may very possibly save it again. The people of that country are worth preserving; and preserving, if possible, to England. I believe your lordship remembers that last year or the year before, I am not sure which, you fixed your quarters for awhile in London, and sent circular letters to your friends, who were concerned in the business on which you came to town. It was on occasion of the Irish absentee-tax. Your friends met, and the attempt was defeated. It may be worth your lordship's consideration, whether you ought not, as soon as possible, to draw your principal friends together. It may be then examined, whether a larger meeting might not be expedient, to see whether some plan could not be thought of for doing something in the countries and towns. The October meeting at Newmarket will be too late in the year, and then the business of the meeting would take up too much time from the other.

It might be objected to doing any thing in this immature condition of the public temper, that the interests of your lordship's friends might suffer in making an attempt, which might be vigorously and rather generally opposed and counterworked. On ordinary occasions this might be a matter of very serious consideration. The risk ought to be proportioned to the object; but this is no ordinary occasion. In the first place, I lay it down that the present state of opposition is so bad, that the worst judged and most untimely exertions would only vary the mode of its utter dissolution. Such a state of things justifies every hazard. But, supposing our condition better, what is an interest cultivated for, but its aptness for public purposes? And for what public purpose do gentlemen wait, that will be more worthy of the use of all the interests they have? I should certainly consider the affair as desperate, if your success in such an effort depended on any thing like an unanimous concurrence in the nation. But in times of trouble, this is impossible. In such times, it is not necessary. A minority cannot make or carry on a war; but a minority, well composed and acting steadily, may clog a war in such a manner, as to make it not very easy to proceed. When you once begin to show yourselves, many will be animated to join you, who are now faint and uncertain. Your adversaries will raise the spirit of your friends; and the very contest will excite that concern and curiosity in the nation, the want of which is now the worst part of the public distemper. . . .

To Mons. Dupont

In this letter of October 1789 to a French acquaintance can be found Burke's first response to "the astonishing scene now displayed in France." The tripartite States General had been transformed into the unicameral National Assembly in June, the Bastille had been liberated in July, the Declaration of the Rights of Man and of the Citizen adopted in August, and in October the Parisian mob had forced the royal family to return to Paris from Versailles. Burke offers his "reflections" and "emotions" on "what has been done and is doing in France."

YOU MAY EASILY BELIEVE, that I have had my eyes turned, with great curiosity, to the astonishing scene now displayed in France. It has certainly given rise in my mind to many reflections, and to some emotions. These are natural and unavoidable; but it would ill become me to be too ready in forming a positive opinion upon matters transacted in a country, with the correct political map of which I must be very imperfectly acquainted. Things, indeed, have already happened so much beyond the scope of all speculation, that persons of infinitely more sagacity than I am, ought to be ashamed of any thing like confidence, in their reasoning upon the operation of any principle, or the effect of any measure. It would become me, least of all, to be so confident, who ought, at my time of life, to have well learned the important lesson of self-distrust,—a lesson of no small value in company with the best information, but which alone can make any sort of amends for our not having learned other lessons so well as it was our business to learn them. I beg you, once for all, to apply this corrective of the diffidence I have, on my own judgment, to whatever I may happen to say with more positiveness than suits my knowledge and situation. If I should seem any where to express myself in the language of disapprobation, be so good as to consider it as no more than the expression of doubt.

You hope, sir, that I think the French deserving of liberty. I certainly do. I certainly think that all men who desire it, deserve it. It is not the reward of our merit, or the acquisition of our industry. It is our inheritance. It is the birthright of our species. We cannot forfeit our right to it, but by what forfeits our title to the privileges of our kind. I mean the abuse, or oblivion, of our rational faculties, and a ferocious indocility which makes us prompt to wrong and violence, destroys our social nature, and transforms us into something little better than the description of wild beasts. To men so degraded, a state of strong constraint is a sort of necessary substitute for freedom; since, bad as it is, it may deliver them in some measure from the worst of all slavery,—that is, the despotism of their own blind and brutal passions.

You have kindly said, that you began to love freedom from your intercourse with me. Permit me then to continue our conversation, and to tell you what the freedom is that I love, and that to which I think all men entitled. This is the more necessary, because, of all the loose terms in the world, liberty is the most indefinite. It is not solitary, unconnected, individual, selfish liberty, as if every man was to regulate the whole of his conduct by his own will. The liberty I mean is *social* freedom. It is that state of things in which liberty is secured by the equality of restraint. A constitution of things in which the liberty of no one man, and no body of men, and no number of men, can find means to trespass on the liberty of any person, or any description of persons, in the society. This kind of liberty is, indeed, but another name for justice; ascertained by wise laws, and secured by well-constructed institutions. I am sure that liberty, so incorporated, and in a manner identified with justice, must be infinitely dear to every one who is capable of conceiving what it is. But whenever a separation is made between liberty and justice, neither is, in my opinion, safe. I do not believe that men ever did submit, certain I am that they never ought to have submitted, to the arbitrary pleasure of one man; but, under circumstances in which the arbitrary pleasure of many persons in the community pressed with an intolerable hardship upon the just and equal rights of their fellows, such a choice might be made, as among evils. The moment *will* is set above reason and justice, in any community, a great question may arise in sober minds, in what part or portion of the community that dangerous dominion of *will* may be the least mischievously placed.

If I think all men who cultivate justice entitled to liberty, and, when joined in states, entitled to a constitution framed to perpetuate and secure it, you may be assured, sir, that I think your countrymen eminently worthy of a blessing which is peculiarly adapted to noble, generous, and humane natures. Such I found the French, when, more than fifteen years ago, I had the happiness, though but for too short a time, of visiting your country; and I trust their character is not altered since that period.

I have nothing to check my wishes towards the establishment of a solid and rational scheme of liberty in France. On the subject of the relative power of nations, I may have my prejudices; but I envy internal freedom, security, and good order, to none. When, therefore, I shall learn that, in France, the citizen, by whatever description he is qualified, is in a perfect state of legal security, with regard to his life,—to his property,—to the uncontrolled disposal of his person,—to the free use of his industry and his faculties:—When I hear that he is protected in the beneficial enjoyment of the estates to which, by the course of settled law, he was born, or is provided with a fair compensation for them;—that he is maintained in the full fruition of the advantages belonging to the state and condition of life in which he had lawfully engaged himself, or is supplied with a substantial, equitable equivalent:—When I am assured that a simple citizen may decently express his sentiments upon public affairs, without hazard to his life or safety, even though against a predominant and fashionable opinion:—When I know all this of France, I shall be as well pleased as every one must be, who has not forgot the general communion of mankind, nor lost his natural sympathy, in local and accidental connexions.

If a constitution is settled in France upon those principles, and calculated for those ends, I believe there is no man in this country whose heart and voice would not go along with you. I am sure it will give me, for one, a heartfelt pleasure when I hear that, in France, the great public assemblies, the natural securities for individual freedom, are perfectly free themselves; when there can be no suspicion that they are under the coercion of a military power of any description;—when it may be truly said, that no armed force can be seen, which is not called into existence by their creative voice, and which must not instantly disappear at their dissolving word; when such assemblies, after being freely chosen, shall proceed with the weight of magistracy, and not with the arts of candidates;—when they do not find themselves under the necessity of feeding one part of the community at the grievous charge of other parts, as necessitous as those who are so fed;—when they are not obliged (in order to flatter those who have their lives in their disposal) to tolerate acts of doubtful influence on commerce and on agriculture; and for the sake of a precarious relief, under temporary scarcity, to sow (if I may be allowed the expression) the seeds of lasting want;—when they are not compelled daily to stimulate an irregular and juvenile imagination for supplies, which they are not in a condition firmly to demand;—when they are not obliged to diet the state from hand to mouth, upon the casual alms of choice, fancy, vanity, or caprice, on which plan the value of the object to the public which receives, often bears no sort of proportion to the loss of the individual who gives;—when they are not necessitated to call for contributions to be estimated on the conscience of the contributor, by which the most pernicious sorts of exemptions and immunities may be established,—by which virtue is taxed and vice privileged, and honour and public spirit are obliged to bear the burdens of craft, selfishness, and avarice;—when they shall not be driven to be the instruments of the violence of others from a sense of their own weakness, and from a want of authority to assess equal and proportioned charges upon all, they are not compelled to lay a strong hand upon the possessions of a part;—when, under the exigencies of the state, (aggravated, if not caused, by the imbecility of their own government, and of all government,) they are not obliged to resort to *confiscation* to supply the defect of *taxation*, and thereby to hold out a pernicious example, to teach the different descriptions of the community to prey upon one another;—when they abstain religiously from all general and extra-judicial declarations concerning the property of the subject;—when they look with horror upon all arbitrary decisions in their legislative capacity, striking at prescriptive right, long undisturbed possession, opposing an uninterrupted stream of regular judicial determinations, by which sort of decisions they are conscious no man's possession could be safe, and individual property, to the very idea, would be extinguished;—when I see your great sovereign bodies, your now supreme power, in this condition of deliberative freedom, and guided by these or similar principles in acting and forbearing, I shall be happy to behold in assemblies whose name is venerable to my understanding and dear to my heart, an authority, a dignity, a moderation, which, in all countries and governments, ought ever to accompany the collected reason and representative majesty of the commonwealth.

I shall rejoice no less in seeing a judicial power established in France, correspondent to such a legislature as I have presumed to hint at, and worthy to second it in its endeavours to secure the freedom and property of the subject. When your courts of justice shall obtain an ascertained condition, before they are made to decide on the condition of other men;—when they shall not be called upon to take cognizance of public offences, whilst they themselves are considered only to exist as a tolerated abuse;—when, under doubts of the legality of their rules of decision, their forms and modes of proceeding, and even of the validity of that system of authority to which they owe their existence;—when, amidst circumstances of suspense, fear, and humiliation, they shall not be put to judge on the lives, liberties, properties, or estimation of their fellow-citizens;—when they are not called upon to put any man to his trial upon undefined crimes of state, not ascertained by any previous rule, statute, or course of precedent;—when victims shall not be snatched from the fury of the people, to be brought before a tribunal, itself subject to the effects of the same fury, and where the acquittal of the parties accused might only place the judge in the situation of the criminal;—when I see tribunals placed in this state of independence of every thing but law, and with a clear law for their direction,—as a true lover of equal justice, (under the shadow of which alone true liberty can live,) I shall rejoice in seeing such a happy order established in France, as much as I do in my consciousness that an order of the same kind, or one not very remote from it, has been long settled, and I hope on a firm foundation, in England. I am not so narrowminded as to be unable to conceive that the same object may be attained in many ways, and perhaps in ways very different from those which we have followed in this country. If this real *practical* liberty, with a government powerful to protect, impotent to evade it, be established, or is in a fair train of being established in the democracy, or rather collection of democracies, which seem to be chosen for the future frame of society in France, it is not my having long enjoyed a sober share of freedom, under a qualified monarchy, that shall render me incapable of admiring and praising your system of republics. I should rejoice, even though England should hereafter be reckoned only as one among the happy nations, and should no longer retain her proud distinction, her monopoly of fame for a practical constitution, in which the grand secret had been found, of reconciling a government of real energy for all foreign and all domestic purposes, with the most perfect security to the liberty and safety of individuals. The government, whatever its name or form may be, that shall be found substantially and practically to unite these advantages, will most merit the applause of all discerning men.

But if (for in my present want of information I must only speak hypothetically,) neither your great assemblies, nor your judicatures, nor your municipalities, act, and forbear to act, in the particulars, upon the principles, and in the spirit that I have stated, I must delay my congratulations on your acquisition of liberty. You may have made a revolution, but not a reformation. You may have subverted monarchy, but not recovered freedom.

You see, sir, that I have merely confined myself in my few observations on what has been done and is doing in France, to the topics of the liberty, property, and safety of the subjects. I have not said much on the influence of the present measures upon your country, as a state. It is not my business, as a citizen of the world; and it is unnecessary to take up much time about it, as it is sufficiently visible.

You are now to live in a new order of things, under a plan of government of which no man can speak from experience. Your talents, your public spirit, and your fortune, give you fair pretensions to a considerable share in it. Your settlement may be at hand; but that it is still at some distance, is more likely. The French may be yet to go through more transmigrations. They may pass, as one of our poets says, "through many varieties of untried being," before their state obtains its final form. In that progress through chaos and darkness, you will find it necessary (at all times it is more or less so) to fix rules to keep your life and conduct in some steady course. You have theories enough concerning the rights of men;—it may not be amiss to add a small degree of attention to their nature and disposition. It is with man in the concrete;—it is with common human life, and human actions, you are to be concerned. I have taken so many liberties with you, that I am almost got the length of venturing to suggest something which may appear in the assuming tone of advice. You will, however, be so good as to receive my very few hints with your usual indulgence, though some of them, I confess, are not in the taste of this enlightened age; and, indeed, are no better than the late ripe fruit of mere experience. Never wholly separate in your mind the merits of any political question from the men who are concerned in it. You will be told, that if a measure is good, what have you to do with the character and views of those who bring it forward. But designing men never separate their plans from their interests; and, if you assist them in their schemes, you will find the pretended good, in the end, thrown aside or perverted, and the interested object alone compassed, and that, perhaps, through your means. The power of bad men is no indifferent thing.

At this moment you may not perceive the full sense of this rule; but you will recollect it when the cases are before you;—you will then see and find its use. It will often keep your virtue from becoming a tool of the ambition and ill designs of others. Let me add what I think has some connexion with the rule I mentioned,—that you ought not to be so fond of any political object, as not to think the means of compassing it a serious consideration. No man is less disposed than I am to put you under the tuition of a petty pedantic scruple, in the management of arduous affairs. All I recommend is, that whenever the sacrifice of any subordinate point of morality, or of honour, or even of common liberal sentiment and feeling is called for, one ought to be tolerably sure that the object is worth it. Nothing is good, but in proportion and with reference. There are several who give an air of consequence to very petty designs and actions, by the crimes through which they make their way to their objects. Whatever is obtained smoothly and by easy means, appears of no value in their eyes. But when violent measures are in agitation, one ought to be pretty clear that there are no others to which we can resort, and that a predilection from character to such methods is not the true cause of their being proposed. The state was reformed by Sylla and by Cæsar; but the Cornelian law and the Julian law were not worth the proscription. The pride of the Roman nobility deserved a check; but I cannot, for that reason, admire the conduct of Cinna, and Marius, and Saturninus.

I admit that evils may be so very great and urgent, that other evils are to be submitted to for the mere hope of their removal. A war, for instance, may be necessary, and we know what are the rights of war; but before we use those rights, we ought to be clearly in the state which alone can justify them; and not, in the very fold of peace and security, by a bloody sophistry, to act towards any persons at once as citizens and as enemies, and, without the necessary formalities and evident distinctive lines of war, to exercise upon our countrymen the most dreadful of all hostilities. Strong party contentions, and a very violent opposition to our desires and opinions, are not war, nor can justify any one of its operations.

One form of government may be better than another, and this difference may be worth a struggle. I think so. I do not mean to treat any of those forms which are often the contrivances of deep human wisdom (not the rights of men, as some people, in my opinion, not very wisely, talk of them) with slight or disrespect; nor do I mean to level them.

A positively vicious and abusive government ought to be changed, —and, if necessary, by violence,—if it cannot be (as sometimes it is the case) reformed. But when the question is concerning the more or the less *perfection* in the organization of a government, the allowance to *means* is not of so much latitude. There is, by the essential fundamental constitution of things, a radical infirmity in all human contrivances; and the weakness is often so attached to the very perfection of our political mechanism, that some defect in it,—something that stops short of its principle,—something that controls, that mitigates, that moderates it,—becomes a necessary corrective to the evils that the theoretic perfection would produce. I am pretty sure it often is so; and this truth may be exemplified abundantly.

It is true that every defect is not of course such a corrective as I state; but supposing it is not, an imperfect good is still a good. The defect may be tolerable, and may be removed at some future time. In that case, prudence (in all things a virtue, in politics, the first of virtues,) will lead us rather to acquiesce in some qualified plan, that does not come up to the full perfection of the abstract idea, than to push for the more perfect, which cannot be attained without tearing to pieces the whole contexture of the commonwealth, and creating a heart-ache in a thousand worthy bosoms. In that case, combining the means and end, the less perfect is the more desirable. The *means* to any end being first in order, are *immediate* in their good or their evil;—they are always, in a manner, *certainties.* The *end* is doubly problematical; first, whether it is to be attained; then, whether, supposing it attained, we obtain the true object we sought for.

But allow it in any degree probable, that theoretic and practical perfection may differ,—that an object pure and absolute may not be so good as one lowered, mixed, and qualified; then, what we abate in our demand, in favour of moderation and justice, and tenderness to individuals, would be neither more nor less than a real improvement which a wise legislator would make, if he had no collateral motive whatsoever, and only looked, in the formation of his scheme, to his own independent ends and purposes. Would it then be right to make way, through temerity and crime, to a form of things which, when obtained, evident reason, perhaps imperious necessity, would compel us to alter, with the disgrace of inconsistency in our conduct, and of want of foresight in our designs?

Believe me, sir, in all changes in the state, moderation is a virtue, not only amiable but powerful. It is a disposing, arranging, conciliating, cementing virtue. In the formation of new constitutions, it is in its province. Great powers reside in those who can make great changes. Their own moderation is their only check; and if this virtue is not paramount in their minds, their acts will taste more of their power than of their wisdom, or their benevolence. Whatever they do will be in extremes; it will be crude, harsh, precipitate. It will be submitted to with grudging and reluctance. Revenge will be smothered and hoarded, and the duration of schemes marked in that temper, will be as precarious as their establishment was odious. This virtue of moderation (which times and situations will clearly distinguish from the counterfeits of pusillanimity and indecision) is the virtue only of superior minds. It requires a deep courage, and full of reflection, to be temperate when the voice of multitudes (the specious mimic of fame and reputation) passes judgment against you. The impetuous desire of an unthinking public will endure no course, but what conducts to splendid and perilous extremes. Then, to dare to be fearful, when all about you are full of presumption and confidence, and when those who are bold at the hazard of others would punish your caution and disaffection, is to show a mind prepared for its trial; it discovers, in the midst of general levity, a self-possessing and collected character, which, sooner or later, bids fair to attract every thing to it, as to a centre. If, however, the tempest should prove to be so very violent, that it would make public prudence itself unseasonable, and, therefore, little less than madness for the individual and the public too; perhaps a young man could not do better than to retreat for a while into study,—to leave the field to those whose duty or inclination, or the necessities of their condition, have put them in possession of it, and wait for the settlement of such a commonwealth as an honest man may act in with satisfaction and credit. This he can never do when those who counsel the public, or the prince, are under terror, let the authority under which they are made to speak other than the dictates of their conscience, be never so imposing in its name and attributes.

This moderation is no enemy to zeal and enthusiasm. There is room enough for them; for the restraint is no more than the restraint of principle, and the restraint of reason.

I have been led further than I intended; but every day's account shows more and more, in my opinion, the ill consequence of keeping good principles, and good general views, within no bounds. Pardon the liberty I have taken; though it seems somewhat singular that I, whose opinions have so little weight in my own country, where I have some share in a public trust, should write as if it were possible they should affect one man with regard to affairs in which I have no concern. But, for the present, my time is my own, and to tire your patience is the only injury I can do you.

I AM, & C.
EDM. BURKE.

To Philip Francis, Esq.

Burke confides to his close friend in this letter, written on February 20, 1790, that as he wrote the moving passage about the assault on the room of Marie Antoinette in his Reflections on the Revolution in France *tears came to his eyes "and wetted my paper."*

. . . YOUR MAIN OBJECTIONS ARE, however, of a much deeper nature, and go to the political opinions and moral sentiments of the piece; in which I find, though with no sort of surprise, having often talked with you on the subject,—that we differ only in every thing. You say, "the mischief you are going to do yourself, is to my apprehension palpable; I snuff it in the wind, and my taste sickens at it." This anticipated stench, that turns your stomach at such a distance, must be nauseous indeed. You seem to think I shall incur great (and not wholly undeserved) infamy, by this publication. This makes it a matter of some delicacy to me, to suppress what I have written; for I must admit in my own feelings, and in that of those who have seen the piece, that my sentiments and opinions deserved the infamy with which they are threatened. If they do not, I know nothing more than that I oppose the prejudices and inclinations of many people. This I was well aware of from the beginning; and it was in order to oppose those inclinations and prejudices, that I proposed to publish my letter. I really am perfectly astonished how you could dream, with my paper in your hand, that I found no other cause than the beauty of the queen of France (now, I suppose, pretty much faded) for disapproving the conduct which has been held towards her, and for expressing my own particular feelings. I am not to order the natural sympathies of my own heart, and of every honest breast, to wait until all the jokes of all the anecdotes of the coffee-houses of Paris, and of the dissenting meeting-houses of London, are scoured of all the slander of those who calumniate persons, that, afterwards, they may murder them with impunity. I know nothing of your story of Messalina. Am I obliged to prove juridically the virtues of all those I shall see suffering every kind of wrong, and contumely, and risk of life, before I endeavour to interest others in their sufferings,—and before I endeavour to excite horror against midnight assassins at back-stairs, and their more wicked abettors in pulpits?—What!—Are not high rank, great splendour of descent, great personal elegance and outward accomplishments, ingredients of moment in forming the interest we take in the misfortunes of men? The minds of those who do not feel thus, are not even systematically right. "What's Hecuba to him, or he to Hecuba, that he should weep for her?"—Why,—because she was Hecuba, the queen of Troy,—the wife of Priam,—and suffered, in the close of life, a thousand calamities? I felt too for Hecuba, when I read the fine tragedy of Euripides upon her story; and I never inquired into the anecdotes of the court or city of Troy, before I gave way to the sentiments which the author wished to inspire;—nor do I remember that he ever said one word of her virtue. It is for those who applaud or palliate assassination, regicide, and base insult to women of illustrious place, to prove the crimes (in sufferings) which they allege, to justify their own. But if they have proved fornication on any such woman,—taking the manners of the world, and the manners of France,—I shall never put it in a parallel with assassination!—No: I have no such inverted scale of faults, in my heart or my head.

You find it perfectly ridiculous, and unfit for me in particular, to take these things as my ingredients of commiseration. Pray why is it absurd in me to think, that the chivalrous spirit which dictated a veneration for women of condition and of beauty, without any consideration whatever of enjoying them, was the great source of those manners which have been the pride and ornament of Europe for so many ages? And am I not to lament that I have lived to see those manners extinguished in so shocking a manner, by means of speculations of finance, and the false science of a sordid and degenerate philosophy? I tell you again,—that the recollection of the manner in which I saw the queen of France, in the year 1774, and the contrast between that brilliancy, splendour, and beauty, with the prostrate homage of a nation to her, and the abominable scene of 1789, which I was describing,—*did* draw tears from me and wetted my paper. These tears came again into my eyes, almost as often as I looked at the description;—they may again. You do not believe this fact, nor that these are my real feelings; but that the whole is affected, or, as you express it, downright foppery. My friend,—I tell you it is truth; and that it is true, and will be truth, when you and I are no more; and will exist as long as men with their natural feelings shall exist. I shall say no more on this foppery of mine. Oh! by the way, you ask me how long I have been an admirer of German ladies? Always the same. Present me the idea of such massacres about any German lady here, and such attempts to assassinate her, and such a triumphant procession from Windsor to the Old Jewry, and I assure you, I shall be quite as full of natural concern and just indignation.

As to the other points, they deserve serious consideration, and they shall have it. I certainly cannot profit quite so much by your assistance, as if we agreed. In that case, every correction would be forwarding the design. We should work with one common view. But it is impossible that any man can correct a work according to its true spirit, who is opposed to its object, or can help the expression of what he thinks should not be expressed at all.

I should agree with you about the vileness of the controversy with such miscreants as the "Revolution Society," and the "National Assembly;" and I know very well that they, as well as their allies, the Indian delinquents, will darken the air with their arrows. But I do not yet think they have the advowson of reputation. I shall try that point. My dear sir, you think of nothing but controversies; "I challenge into the field of battle, and retire defeated, &c." If their having the last word be a defeat, they most assuredly will defeat me. But I intend no controversy with Dr. Price, or Lord Shelburne, or any other of their set. I mean to set in full view the danger from their wicked principles and their black hearts. I intend to state the true principles of our constitution in church and state, upon grounds opposite to theirs. If any one be the better for the example made of them, and for this exposition, well and good. I mean to do my best to expose them to the hatred, ridicule, and contempt of the whole world; as I always shall expose such calumniators, hypocrites, sowers of sedition, and approvers of murder and all its triumphs. When I have done that, they may have the field to themselves; and I care very little how they triumph over me, since I hope they will not be able to draw me at their heels, and carry my head in triumph on their poles.

I have been interrupted, and have said enough. Adieu! believe me always sensible of your friendship; though it is impossible that a greater difference can exist on earth, than, unfortunately for me, there is on those subjects, between your sentiments and mine.

EDM. BURKE.

To Captain Mercer

Written in February 1790 as well, this is an example of Burke's response to one of the many who found his opposition to the French Revolution surprising. Mercer, an Irishman who had made a large fortune in India, simply does not understand the "injustice and tyranny . . . practised in a few months by . . . French democracy."

. . . I NEVER WILL SUFFER YOU, if I can help it, to be deprived of the well-earned fruits of your industry, because others may want your fortune more than you do, and may have laboured, and do now labour, in vain to acquire even a subsistence. Neither, on the contrary, if success had less smiled upon your endeavours, and you had come home insolvent, would I take from any "pampered and luxurious lord" in your neighbourhood, one acre of his land, or one spoon from his sideboard, to compensate your losses; though incurred, as they would have been incurred, in the course of a well-spent, virtuous, and industrious life. God is the distributor of his own blessings. I will not impiously attempt to usurp his throne, but will keep, according to the subordinate place and trust in which he has stationed me, the order of property which I find established in my country. No guiltless man has ever been, nor, I trust, ever will be, able to say with truth, that he has been obliged to retrench a dish at his table, for any reformations of mine.

You pay me the compliment to suppose me a foe to tyranny and oppression; and you are, therefore, surprised at the sentiments I have lately delivered in parliament. I *am* that determined foe to tyranny, or I greatly deceive myself in my character, and am an idiot in my conduct. It is because I am such a foe, and mean to continue so, that I abominate the example of France for this country. I know that tyranny seldom attacks the poor,—never in the first instance. They are not its proper prey. It falls upon the wealthy and the great, whom, by rendering them objects of envy, and otherwise obnoxious to the multitude, they the more easily destroy; and when they are destroyed, that multitude which was led to that ill work by the arts of bad men, is itself undone for ever. I hate tyranny, at least I think so; but I hate it most of all where most are concerned in it. The tyranny of a multitude is but a multiplied tyranny. If, as society is constituted in these large countries of France and England,—full of unequal property, I must make my choice (which God avert) between the despotism of a single person, or of the many, my election is made:—For, in the forty years of my observation, as much injustice and tyranny has been practised in a few months by a French democracy, as by all the arbitrary monarchs in Europe. I speak of public, glaring acts of tyranny. I say nothing of the common effects of old abusive governments, because I do not know that as bad may not be found from the new. This democracy begins very ill; and I feel no security that what has been rapacious and bloody in its commencement, in its final settlement will be mild and protecting. They cannot, indeed, in future rob so much, because they have left little that can be taken. I go to the full length of my principle. I should think the government of the deposed King of France, or of the late King of Prussia, or the present Emperor, or the present Czarina, none of them, perhaps, perfectly good,—to be far better than the government of twenty-four millions of men *all as good as you*, (and I do not know any body better,)—supposing that those twenty-four millions would be subject, as infallibly they would, to the same unrestrained, though virtuous impulses; because, it is plain, you would think every thing justified by your warm good intentions; you would heat one another by your common zeal; counsel and advice would be lost on you; you would not listen to temperate individuals; and you would be infinitely less capable of moderation than the most heady of those princes.

What have I to do with France, but as the common interest of humanity, and its example to this country engages me? I know France, by observation and inquiry, pretty tolerably for a stranger; and I am not a man to fall in love with the faults or follies of the old or new government. You reason as if I were running a parallel between its former abusive government and the present tyranny. What had all this to do with the opinions I delivered in parliament, which run a parallel between the liberty they might have had, and this frantic delusion? This is the way by which you blind and deceive yourself, and beat the air in your argument with me. Why do you instruct me on a state of case which has no existence? You know how to reason very well. What most of the newspapers make me say, I know not, nor do I much care. I don't, however, think they have thus stated me. There is a very fair abstract of my speech printed in a little pamphlet, which I would send you if it were worth putting you to the expense.

To discuss the affairs of France and its revolution, would require a volume,—perhaps many volumes. Your general reflections about revolutions may be right or wrong; they conclude nothing. I don't find myself disposed to controvert them, for I do not think they apply to the present affairs; nay, I am sure they do not. I conceive you have got very imperfect accounts of these transactions. I believe I am much more exactly informed concerning them.

I am sorry, indeed, to find that our opinions do differ essentially,—fundamentally, and are at the utmost possible distance from each other, if I understand you or myself clearly on this subject. Your freedom is far from displeasing to me,—I love it; for I always wish to know the full of what is in the mind of the friend I converse with. I give you mine as freely, and I hope I shall offend you as little as you do me.

I shall have no objection to your showing my letter to as many as you please. I have no secrets with regard to the public. I have never shrunk from obloquy, and I have never courted popular applause. If I have ever met with any share of it—*non rapui sed recepi*. No difference of opinion, however, shall hinder me from cultivating your friendship, whilst you permit me to do so. I have not wrote this to discuss these matters in a prolonged controversy. I wish we may never say more of them; but to comply with your commands, which ever shall have due weight with me.

I AM,
MOST RESPECTFULLY AND AFFECTIONATELY YOURS,
EDM. BURKE.

To Chevalier de la Bintinnaye

In this interesting letter of March 1791 to an acquaintance in France, who ultimately emigrated to England, Burke is clearly critical of Louis XVI. He bears some responsibility for the "astonishing scene" that is France, but surely his "safe and languid domination" was no justification for the excesses of the revolutionaries.

. . . THE REST was to show, from the actual state of France, (as well as I was able to enter into its condition,) the utter impossibility of a counter-revolution from any internal cause. You know, sir, that no party can act without a resolute, vigorous, zealous, and enterprising chief. The chief of every monarchical party must be the monarch himself;—at least, he must lend himself readily to the spirit and energy of others. You have a well-intentioned and virtuous prince; but minds like his, bred with no other view than to a safe and languid domination, are not made for breaking their prisons, terrifying their enemies, and animating their friends. Besides, in a wife and children, he has given hostages to his enemies. If the king can do nothing in his situation, the wonder is not great. It is much greater, on all appearance, that not one man is to be found in the numerous nobility of France, who to great military talents adds any sort of lead, consideration, or following, in the country or in the army. To strengthen itself, the monarchy had weakened every other force. To unite the nation to itself, it had dissolved all other ties. When the chain which held the people to the prince was once broken, the whole frame of the commonwealth was found in a state of disconnexion. There was neither force nor union any where, to sustain the monarchy, or the nobility, or the church. As to great and commanding talents, they are the gift of Providence in some way unknown to us. They rise where they are least expected. They fail when every thing seems disposed to produce them, or at least to call them forth. Your sole hope seems to me to rest in the disposition of the neighbouring powers, and in their ability to yield you assistance. I can conjecture nothing with certainty of this, in either of the points. But at present I see nothing that in the smallest degree looks that way. In the mean time the usurpation gathers strength by continuance, and credit by success. People will look to power, and join, or, at least, accommodate themselves to it. I confess I am astonished at the blindness of the states of Europe, who are contending with each other about points of trivial importance, and on old worn-out principles and topics of policy, when the very existence of all of them is menaced by a new evil, which none of the ancient maxims are of the least importance in dissipating. But in all these things, we must acknowledge and revere, in silence, a superior hand. In the spirit of this submission I, however, am so far from blaming every sort of endeavour, that I much lament the remissness of the gentlemen of France. Their adversaries have seized upon all the newspapers which circulate within this kingdom, and which from hence are dispersed all over Europe. That they are masters of the presses of Paris, is a thing of course. But surely, the oppressed party might amongst them maintain a person here, to whom they might transmit a true state of affairs. The emissaries of the usurpation here, are exceedingly active in propagating stories which tend to alienate the minds of people of this country from the suffering cause. Not one French refugee has intelligence or spirit enough to contradict them. I have done all which the common duties of humanity can claim from one who has not the honour of being a subject of France. I have duties and occupations at home, public and private, which will not suffer me to continue longer with my thoughts abroad. But if any gentleman from France would undertake such a task, with proper materials for it, he should have my best advice. The expense of such a person stationed here would not be great; and surely, reduced as the *noblesse* of France not expatriated are, enough remains to them to do this and more. If their avarice, or their dissipation, will afford nothing to their honour or their safety, their case is additionally deplorable. . . .

To William Weddell, Esq.

Burke wrote to his fellow member of Parliament on January 31, 1792, reviewing the reasons for deserting his Whig friends in Parliament. It boiled down to "this French dirt-pie." His "old Whig" principles lead him "to detest the French Revolution."

. . . NOW LET me say a word to you, on what would not have been so proper to say to the public, as it regards the particular interests of the party, and my conduct towards them and their leader, Mr. Fox.

As to the party which has thought proper to proscribe me on account of a book which I published on the idea, that the principles of a new, republican, frenchified Whiggism, were gaining ground in this country, I cannot say it was written *solely* with a view to the service of that party. I hope its views were more general. But I am perfectly sure this was *one* of the objects in my contemplation; and I am hardly less sure, that (bating the insufficiency of the execution) it was well calculated for that purpose; and that it had actually produced that effect upon the minds of all those at whose sentiments it is not disrespectful to guess. Possibly it produced that effect without that exception. Mr. Montagu knows, many know, what a softening towards our party it produced in the thoughts and opinions of many men in many places. It presented to them sentiments of liberty which were not at war with order, virtue, religion, and good government; and though, for reasons which I have cause to rejoice that I listened to, I disclaimed myself as the organ of any party, it was the general opinion that I had not wandered very widely from the sentiments of those with whom I was known to be so closely connected. It was indeed then, and it is much more so now, absolutely necessary to separate those who cultivate a rational and sober liberty upon the plan of our existing constitution, from those who think they have no liberty, if it does not comprehend a right in them of making to themselves new constitutions at their pleasure.

The party with which I acted had, by the malevolent and unthinking, been reproached, and by the wise and good always esteemed and confided in, as an aristocratic party. Such I always understood it to be, in the true sense of the word. I understood it to be a party, in its composition, and in its principles, connected with the solid, permanent, long-possessed property of the country; a party which, by a temper derived from that species of property, and affording a security to it, was attached to the ancient tried usages of the kingdom; a party, therefore, essentially constructed upon a ground-plot of stability and independence; a party, therefore, equally removed from servile court compliances, and from popular levity, presumption, and precipitation.

Such was the general opinion of the substance and original stamina of that party. For one, I was fully persuaded that the spirit, genius, and character of that party *ought* to be adopted, and, for a long time, I thought *was* adopted, by all the *new* men who in the course of time should be aggregated to that body; whether any of these *new* men should be a person possessed of a large fortune of his own creating; or whether the *new* man should be (though of a family long decorated with the honours and distinctions of the state,) only a younger brother, who had an importance to acquire by his industry and his talents;—or whether the *new* man should be (as was my case) *wholly* new in the country, and aimed to illustrate himself and his family by the services he might have the fortune to render to the public. All these descriptions of new men, and more, if more there are, I conceived, without any formal engagement, by the very constitution of the party, to be bound with all the activity and energy of minds animated and awakened by great hopes and views, to support those aristocratic principles, and the aristocratic interests connected with them, as essential to the real benefit of the body of the people, to which all names of party, all ranks and orders in the state, and even government itself, ought to be entirely subordinate. These principles and interests, I conceived, were to give the bias to all their proceedings. Adhering to these principles, the aspiring minds that exalt and vivify a party, could not be held in too much honour and consideration:—departing from them, they lose more than they can gain. They lose the advantages which they might derive from *such* a party, and they cannot make it for the purposes for which they desire to employ it. Such a party, pushed forward by a blind impulse, may for some time proceed without an exact knowledge of the point to which it is going. It may be deluded; and, by being deluded, it may be discredited and hurt; but it is too unwieldy, both from its numbers and from its property, to perform the services expected from a corps of light horse.

Against the existence of any such description of men as our party is in a great measure composed of,—against the existence of any mode of government on such a basis, we have seen a serious and systematic attack attended with the most complete success, in another country, but in a country at our very door. It is an attack made against the thing and against the name. If I were to produce an example of something diametrically opposite to the composition, to the spirit, to the temper, to the character, and to all the maxims of our old and unregenerated party, something fitted to illustrate it by the strongest opposition, I would produce—what has been done in France. I would except nothing. I would bring forward the principles; I would bring forward the means; I would bring forward the ultimate object. They who cry up the French revolution, cry down the party which you and I had so long the honour and satisfaction to belong to. "But that party was formed on a system of liberty." Without question it was; and God forbid that you and I should ever belong to any party that was not built upon that foundation. But this French dirt-pie,—this its hateful contrast, is founded upon *slavery*; and a slavery which is not the less slavery, because it operates in an inverted order. It is a slavery the more shameful, the more humiliating, the more galling, upon that account, to every liberal and ingenuous mind. It is, on that account, ten thousand times the more destructive to the peace, the prosperity, and the welfare, in every instance, of that undone and degraded country in which it prevails.

My party principles, as well as my general politics and my natural sentiments, must lead me to detest the French revolution, in the act, in the spirit, in the consequences, and most of all, in the example. I saw the sycophants of a court, who had, by engrossing to themselves the favours of the sovereign, added to his distress and to the odium of his government, take advantage of that distress and odium to subvert his authority and imprison his person; and passing, by a natural progression, from flatterers to traitors, convert their ingratitude into a claim to patriotism, and become active agents in the ruin of that order, from their belonging to which they had derived all the opulence and power of their families. Under the auspices of these base wretches, I had seen a senseless populace employed totally to annihilate the ancient government of their country, under which it had grown, in extent, compactness, population, and riches, to a greatness even formidable; a government which discovered the vigour of its principle, even in the many vices and errors, both of its own and its people's, which were not of force enough to hinder it from producing those effects. They began its destruction by subverting, under pretexts of rights of man, the foundations of civil society itself. They trampled upon the religion of their country, and upon all religion;—they systematically gave the rein to every crime and every vice. They destroyed the trade and manufacturers of their country. They rooted up its finances. They caused the greatest accumulation of coin, probably ever collected amongst any people, totally to disappear as by magic; and they filled up the void by a fraudulent, compulsory paper-currency, and a coinage of the bells from their churches. They possessed the fairest and the most flourishing colonies which any nation had perhaps ever planted. These they rendered a scene of carnage and desolation, that would excite compassion and remorse in any hearts but theirs. They possessed a vast body of nobility and gentry, *amongst* the first in the world for splendour, and the *very* first for disinterested services to their country: in which I include the most disinterested and incorrupt judicature (even by the confession of its enemies) that ever was. These they persecuted, they hunted down like wild beasts; they expelled them from their families and their houses, and dispersed them into every country in Europe; obliging them either to pine in fear and misery at home, or to escape into want and exile in foreign lands; nay, (they went so far in the wantonness of their insolence,) abrogated their very name and their titular descriptions, as something horrible and offensive to the ears of mankind.

The means by which all this was done leaves an example in Europe never to be effaced, and which no thinking man, I imagine, can present to his mind without consternation;—that is, the bribing of an immense body of soldiers, taken from the lowest of the people, to an universal revolt against their officers, who were the whole body of the country gentlemen, and the landed interest of the nation, to set themselves up as a kind of democratic military, governed and directed by their own clubs and committees!

When I saw all this mingled scene of crime, of vice, of disorder, of folly, and of madness, received by very many here, not with the horror and disgust which it ought to have produced, but with rapture and exultation, as some almost supernatural benefit showered down upon the race of mankind; and when I saw that arrangements were publicly made for communicating to these islands their full share of these blessings, I thought myself bound to stand out, and by every means in my power to distinguish the ideas of a sober and virtuous liberty, (such as I thought our party had ever cultivated,) from that profligate, immoral, impious, and rebellious licence, which, through the medium of every sort of disorder and calamity, conducts to some kind or other of tyrannic domination.

At first I had no idea that this base contagion had gained any considerable ground in the party. Those who were the first and most active in spreading it, were their mortal and declared enemies; I mean the leading dissenters. They had long shown themselves wholly adverse to, and unalliable with, the party. They had shown it, as you know, signally, in 1784. At the time of the regency, (which, when Price's sermon appeared, was still green and raw,) they had seized the opportunity of divisions amongst the great, to bring forward their democratic notions; and the object against which they chiefly directed their seditious doctrines, and the passions of the vulgar, was your party; and I confess they were in the right in their choice; for they knew very well, that, as long as you were true to your principles, no considerable innovations could be made in the country; and that this independent embodied aristocracy would form an impenetrable fence against all their attempts to break into the constitution. When I came to town, though I had heard of Dr. Price's sermon, I had not read it. I dined the day of my arrival with our friend Dr. Walker King; and there, in a large and mixed company, partly composed of dissenters, one of that description, a most worthy man, of learning, sense, and ingenuity, one of the oldest and best friends I had in the world, and no way indisposed to us, lamented that the dissenters never could be reconciled to us, or confide in us, or hear of our being possessed of the government of the country, as long as we were led by Fox;—this was far from his own opinion; but he declared that it was very general in that body, who regarded him, and spoke of him on all occasions, in a manner that one would not speak of some better sort of highwaymen. Of the rest of the party they had a good opinion; but thought them weak men, and dupes, and the mere instruments of the person of whom they had conceived such unfounded ideas. I was warmed; and continued, with vehemence, in a conversation which lasted some hours, to do justice to Mr. Fox; and in as ample and strenuous a manner as I thought the duties of friendship, and a matter that touched the public interest, required. It is unnecessary to enter into further details on the subject. I went home, and, late as it was, before I went to bed, I read Dr. Price's sermon; and *in that very sermon* (in which were all the shocking sentiments and seditious principles which I have endeavoured to expose) the leading feature was a personal invective against Mr. Fox,—very much in the style and manner (a trifle, indeed, less coarse,) in which my worthy friend had represented the general conversation of the dissenters, when Mr. Fox was the subject.

It was, I think, but a day or two after that conversation and reading, that I met Mr. Sheridan at Lord North's. He was just come to town; and, of himself, he spoke with great resentment of the dissenters for their treatment of Mr. Fox in other parts of the kingdom; which from him I learned was as bad, particularly at Birmingham, as in London. Concerning the French revolution not a word passed between us. I felt as Mr. Sheridan did, and it does not rest on my single assertion. It is known to others, that some part of the asperity with which I expressed myself against these gentlemen, arose from my resentment for their incurable, and, as I thought, treacherous animosity to Mr. Fox; particularly when I knew that, during the whole of the preceding summer, they were soliciting his friendship and connexion. However, they knew Mr. Fox better than I did. The several shots they fired to bring him to, produced their effect. I take it for granted that public principles, connected with magnanimity of sentiment, made him equally regardless of their enmity and of my friendship;—regardless of my friendship, who was weak enough to adopt his cause with a warmth which his wisdom and temper condemned.

What I had thrown down on the first reading of Price's Declaration and Correspondence with France, was only in a few notes, (though intended for publication,) when Mr. Fox, to my great astonishment and sorrow, chose for his theme of panegyric on the French revolution, the behaviour of the French Guards. I said what occurred to me on that occasion. The day ended with sentiments not very widely divided, and with unbroken friendship. I do not think that at any period of my life I have given stronger proofs of my attachment to that gentleman and to his party, than I had done after that explanation, during the whole of that session and the next both within and without doors.

In the mean time the opinions, principles, and practices, which I thought so very mischievous, were gaining ground, particularly in our party. The festival of the fourteenth of July was celebrated with great splendour for the first time. There Mr. Sheridan made a strong declaration of his sentiments, which was printed. All that could be got together of the party were convened at the Shakespeare the night before; that, as the expression was, they might go in force to that anniversary. Applications were made to some of the Prince of Wales's people, that it might appear to have his royal highness's countenance. These things, and many more, convinced me, that the best service which could be done to the party, and to the prince, was to strike a strong blow at those opinions and practices which were carrying on for their common destruction.

As to the prince, I thought him deeply concerned that the ideas of an elective crown should not prevail. He had experienced, and you had all of you fully experienced, the peril of these doctrines on the question of the Regency. You know that I endeavoured, as well as I could, to supply the absence of Mr. Fox during that great controversy. You cannot forget that I supported the prince's title to the *regency* upon the principle of his hereditary right to the crown; and I endeavoured to explode the false notions, drawn from what had been stated as the revolution maxims, by much the same arguments which I afterwards used in my printed reflections. I endeavoured to show, that the hereditary succession could not be supported, whilst a person who had the chief interest in it was, during a virtual interregnum, excluded from the government; and that the direct tendency of the measure, as well as the grounds upon which it was argued, went to make the crown itself elective, contrary (as I contended) to the fundamental settlement made after the revolution. I meant to do service to the prince when I took this ground on the regency; I meant to do him service when I took the same ground in my publication.

Here the conduct of the party towards themselves, towards the prince, and (if with these names I could mix myself,) towards me, has been such as to have no parallel. The prince has been persuaded not only to look with all possible coldness on myself, but to lose no opportunity of publicly declaring his disapprobation of a book written to prove that the crown, to which (I hope) he is to succeed, is not elective. For this I am in disgrace at Carlton House. The prince, I am told, has expressed his displeasure that I have not mentioned in that book his right to the regency; I never was so astonished as when I heard this. In the first place, the persons against whom I maintained that controversy had said nothing at all upon the subject of the regency. They went much deeper. I was weak enough to think that the succession to the *crown* was a matter of other importance to his royal highness than his right to the *regency*. At a time when the king was in perfect health, and no question existing of arrangements to be made, on a supposition of his falling into his former, or any other grievous malady, it would have been an imprudence of the first magnitude, and such as would have hurt the prince most essentially, if it were to be supposed he had given me the smallest encouragement to have wantonly brought on that most critical discussion. Not one of the friends whom his royal highness "delighteth to honour," have thought proper to say one word upon the subject, in parliament or out of parliament. But the silence which in them is respectful and prudent, in me is disaffection. I shall say no more on this matter. The prince must have been strangely deceived. He is much more personally concerned, in all questions of *succession*, than the king, who is in possession. Yet his majesty has received, with every mark of a gracious protection, my intended service to his family. The prince has been made to believe it to be some sort of injury to himself. Those, the most in his favour and confidence, are avowed admirers of the French democracy. Even his attorney and his solicitor-general, who, by their legal knowledge and their eloquence as advocates, ought to be the pillars of his succession, are enthusiasts, public and declared, for the French revolution and its principles. These, my dear sir, are strange symptoms about a future court; and they make no small part of that fear of impending mischief to this constitution, which grows upon me every hour. A Prince of Wales with democratic law-servants, with democratic political friends, with democratic personal favourites! If this be not ominous to the crown, I know not what is.

As to the party and its interests, in endeavouring to support the legal hereditary succession of the Prince of Wales, I consider their power as included in the assertion of his right. I could not say positively how soon the ideas they entertained might have recommended them to the favour of the reigning king. I did not, however, conceive that, whatever their notions might be, the probability of their being called to the helm was quite so great under his present majesty as under a successor; and that, therefore, the maintenance of the right of that successor, against those who at once attacked the settlement of the crown, and were the known, declared enemies of the party, was, in a *political light*, the greatest service I could do to that party, and more particularly to Mr. Fox; infinitely more so than to the Duke of Portland, or Lord Fitzwilliam; because, for many reasons, I am satisfied that these two noble persons are not so ill at St. James's as he is; and that they (or one of them at least) are not near so well at Carlton House as Mr. Fox and Mr. Sheridan.

According to the common principles of vulgar politics, this would be thought a service, not ill intended, and aimed at its mark with tolerable discretion and judgment. For this, the gentlemen have thought proper to render me obnoxious to the party, odious to the prince, (from whose future prerogative alone my family can hope for any thing,) and at least suspected by the body of my country. That is, they have endeavoured completely and fundamentally to ruin me and mine, in all the ways in which it is in the power of man to destroy the interests and objects of man, whether in his friendship, his fortunes, or his reputation.

But I thought there was another, and a more important point in view, in which what I had done for the public might eminently serve the party, and in concerns of infinitely more importance to those who compose the major part of the body, than any share of power they might obtain. I considered the party as the particular mark of that anarchical faction; and that the principle of the French revolution which they preached up, would have *them* for its first and most grateful victims. It is against them, as a part of an aristocracy, that the nefarious principles of that grovelling rebellion and tyranny strike; and not at monarchy, further than as it is supposed to be built upon an aristocratic basis. They, who would cheat the nobility and gentry of this nation to their ruin, talk of that monster of turpitude as nothing but the subversion of monarchy. Far from it. The French pride themselves on the idea, however absurd, that theirs is a *démocracie royale.* The name of the monarchy, and of the hereditary monarchy too, they preserve in France; and they feed the person whom they call "king," with such a revenue, given to mere luxury and extravagance totally separated from all provision for the state, as I believe no people ever before dreamed of granting for such purposes. But against the nobility and gentry they have waged inexpiable war. There are, at this day, no fewer than ten thousand heads of respectable families driven out of France; and those who remain at home, remain in depression, penury, and continued alarm for their lives. You and I know that (in order, as I conceive, still to blind and delude the gentlemen of England,) the French faction here pretended that the persecution of the gentlemen of France could not last;—that at the next election they would recover the consideration which belonged to them, and that we should see that country represented by its best blood, and by all its considerable property. They knew at the time that they were setting forward an imposture. The present assembly, the first born, the child of the strength of their constitution, demonstrates the value of their prediction. At the very instant in which they were making it, they knew, or they knew nothing, that the two hundred and fifty clubs which govern that country had settled their lists. They must have known that the gentlemen of France were not degraded and branded in order to exalt them to greater consequence than ever they possessed. Such they would have had, if they were to compose the whole, or even the major part, of an assembly which rules, in every thing legislative and executive, without any sort of balance or control. No such thing:—the assembly has not fifty men in it (I believe I am at the outside of the number) who are possessed of a hundred pounds a year, in any description of property whatsoever. About six individuals of enormous wealth, and thereby sworn enemies to the prejudice which affixes a dignity to virtuous well-born poverty, are in the number of the fifty. The rest are, what might be supposed, men whose names never were before heard of beyond their market-town. About four hundred of the seven are country practitioners of the law; several of them the stewards and men of business who managed the affairs of gentlemen, bishops, or convents; who, for their merits towards their former employers, are now made the disposers of their lives and fortunes. The rest no one can give an account of, except of those who have passed to this temple of honour, through the temple of virtue called the house of correction. When the king asked the president who the gentlemen were who attended him with a message, the president answered, that he did not know one of them even by name. The gentlemen of this faction here, I am well aware, attribute this to the perverseness of the gentlemen themselves, who would not offer themselves as candidates. That they did not offer themselves is very true; because they knew that they could appear at the primary assemblies only to be insulted, at best; perhaps even murdered, as some of them have been; and many more have been threatened with assassination. What are we to think of a constitution, as a pattern, from which the whole gentry of a country, instead of courting a share in it with eagerness and assiduity, fly as from a place of infection? But the gentlemen of France are all base, vicious, servile, &c. &c. &c. Pray, let not the gentlemen of England be flattered to their destruction, by railing at their neighbours. They are as good as we are, to the full. If they were thus base and corrupt in their sentiments, there is nothing they would not submit to in order to have their share in this scramble for wealth and power. But they have declined it, from sentiments of honour and virtue, and the purest patriotism. One turns with pity and indignation from the view of what they suffer for those sentiments; and, I must confess, my animosity is doubled against those amongst us, who, in that situation, can rail at persons who bear such things with fortitude, even supposing that they suffered for principles in which they were mistaken. But neither you, nor I, nor any fair man, can believe, that a whole nation is free from honour and real principle; or that if these things exist in it, they are not to be found in the men the best born, and the best bred, and in those possessed of rank which raises them in their own esteem, and in the esteem of others, and possessed of hereditary settlement in the same place, which secures, with an hereditary wealth, an hereditary inspection. That these should be all scoundrels, and that the virtue, honour, and public spirit of a nation should be only found in its attorneys, pettifoggers, stewards of manors, discarded officers of police, shop-boys, clerks of counting-houses, and rustics from the plough, is a paradox, not of false ingenuity, but of envy and malignity. It is an error, not of the head, but of the heart. The whole man is turned upside down before such an inversion of all natural sentiment and all natural reason can take place. I do not wish to you, no, nor to those who applaud such scenes, angry as I am with them, masters of that description.

Visible as it was to the world, that not the despotism of a prince, but the condition of a gentleman, was the grand object of attack; I thought I should do service to a party of gentlemen, to caution the public against giving countenance to a project calculated for the ruin of such a party.

When such an attempt was not excused, even as well-intended, there was but one way of accounting for the conduct of gentlemen towards me; it is, that from my hands they are resolved not to accept any service. Be it so. They are rid of an incumbrance; and I retire to repose of body and mind, with a repose of conscience too; perfect, with regard to the party and the public, however I may feel myself, as I do, faulty and deficient in other respects. The only concern I feel is, that I am obliged to continue an hour longer in parliament. Whilst I am there, except in some deep constitutional question, I shall take no part. Lord Fitzwilliam and the Duke of Portland shall not be seen voting one way in the House of Lords whilst I vote another in the House of Commons; and any vote of mine, by which I may add even my mite of contribution towards supporting the system or advancing the power of the new French whigs, I never will give. That corruption has cast deep roots in that party, and they vegetate in it (however discredited amongst the people in general) every day with greater and greater force. The particular gentlemen who are seized with that malady (such I must consider it), have, to my thinking, so completely changed their minds, that one knows no longer what to depend upon, or upon what ground we stand. Some of them (besides the two leaders) are, indeed, so high in character, and of such great abilities, that their mistake, if such it be, must make a most mischievous impression. I know they say, that they do not want to introduce these things here, &c. &c.,—but this is a poor business, while they propagate all the abstract principles, and exalt to the stars the realization of them at our door. They are sublime metaphysicians; and the horrible consequences produced by their speculations affect them not at all. They only ask whether the proposition be true?—Whether it produces good or evil, is no part of their concern. This long letter, my dear friend, is for you; but so for you, as that you may show it to such of our friends who, though they cannot in prudence support, will not in justice condemn me.

My dear sir,

Most faithfully, your most obliged and obedient humble servant,

EDM. BURKE.

To William Elliot

Writing to a friend on May 26, 1795, Burke captures his historical role as patron theorist of conservatism. What he had sought to do since 1790 was "warn the people against the greatest of all evils—a blind and furious spirit of innovation, under the name of reform."

. . . I HAVE BEEN stimulated, I know not how, to give you this trouble by what very few, except myself, would think worth any trouble at all. In a speech in the House of Lords, I have been attacked for the defence of a scheme of government, in which that body inheres, and in which alone it can exist. Peers of Great Britain may become as penitent as the sovereign of Prussia. They may repent of what they have done in assertion of the honour of their king and in favour of their own safety. But never the gloom that lowers over the fortune of the cause, nor anything which the great may do towards hastening their own fall, can make me repent of what I have done by pen or voice (the only arms I possess) in favour of the order of things into which I was born, and in which I fondly hope to die.

In the long series of ages which have furnished the matter of history, never was so beautiful and so august a spectacle presented to the moral eye, as Europe afforded the day before the Revolution in France. I knew indeed that this prosperity contained in itself the seeds of its own danger. In one part of the society it caused laxity and debility; in the other it produced bold spirits and dark designs. A false philosophy passed from academies into courts; and the great themselves were infected with the theories which conducted to their ruin. Knowledge, which in the two last centuries either did not exist at all, or existed solidly on right principles and in chosen hands, was now diffused, weakened, and perverted. General wealth loosened morals, relaxed vigilance, and increased presumption. Men of talent began to compare, in the partition of the common stock of public prosperity, the proportions of the dividends with the merits of the claimants. As usual, they found their portion not equal to their estimate (or perhaps to the public estimate) of their own worth. When it was once discovered by the Revolution in France, that a struggle between establishment and rapacity could be maintained, though but for one year, and in one place, I was sure that a practicable breach was made in the whole order of things and in every country. Religion, that held the materials of the fabric together, was first systematically loosened. All other opinions, under the name of prejudices, must fall along with it; and property, left undefended by principles, became a repository of spoils to tempt cupidity, and not a magazine to furnish arms for defence. I knew, that, attacked on all sides by the infernal energies of talents set in action by vice and disorder, authority could not stand upon authority alone. It wanted some other support than the poise of its own gravity. Situations formerly supported persons. It now became necessary that personal qualities should support situations. Formerly, where authority was found, wisdom and virtue were presumed. But now the veil was torn, and, to keep off sacrilegious intrusion, it was necessary that in the sanctuary of government something should be disclosed not only venerable but dreadful. Government was at once to show itself full of virtue and full of force. It was to invite partisans, by making it appear to the world that a generous cause was to be asserted; one fit for a generous people to engage in. From passive submission was it to expect resolute defence? No! It must have warm advocates and passionate defenders, which a heavy, discontented acquiescence never could produce. What a base and foolish thing is it for any consolidated body of authority to say, or to act as if it said, "I will put my trust not in my own virtue, but in your patience; I will indulge in effeminacy, in indolence, in corruption; I will give way to all my perverse and vicious humours, because you cannot punish me without the hazard of ruining yourselves!"

I wished to warn the people against the greatest of all evils,—a blind and furious spirit of innovation, under the name of reform. I was indeed well aware that power rarely reforms itself. So it is undoubtedly when all is quiet about it. But I was in hopes that provident fear might prevent fruitless penitence. I trusted that danger might produce at least circumspection; I flattered myself, in a moment like this, that nothing would be added to make authority top-heavy; that the very moment of an earthquake would not be the time chosen for adding a story to our houses. I hoped to see the surest of all reforms, perhaps the only sure reform, the ceasing to do ill. In the mean time I wished to the people, the wisdom of knowing how to tolerate a condition which none of their efforts can render much more than tolerable. It was a condition, however, in which everything was to be found that could enable them to live to nature, and, if so they pleased, to live to virtue and to honour.

I do not repent that I thought better of those to whom I wished well, than they will suffer me long to think that they deserved. Far from repenting, I would to God that new faculties had been called up in me, in favour not of this or that man, or this or that system, but of the general, vital principle, that whilst it was in its vigour produced the state of things transmitted to us from our fathers; but which, through the joint operation of the abuses of authority and liberty, may perish in our hands. I am not of opinion that the race of men, and the commonwealths they create, like the bodies of individuals, grow effete and languid and bloodless, and ossify by the necessities of their own conformation, and the fatal operation of longevity and time. These analogies between bodies natural and politic, though they may sometimes illustrate arguments, furnish no argument of themselves. They are but too often used under the colour of a specious philosophy, to find apologies for the despair of laziness and pusillanimity, and to excuse the want of all manly efforts, when the exigencies of our country call for them the more loudly.

How often has public calamity been arrested on the very brink of ruin by the seasonable energy of a single man! Have we no such man amongst us? I am as sure as I am of my being, that one vigorous mind without office, without situation, without public functions of any kind, (at a time when the want of such a thing is felt, as I am sure it is,) I say, one such man, confiding in the aid of God, and full of just reliance in his own fortitude, vigour, enterprise, and perseverance, would first draw to him some few like himself, and then that multitudes, hardly thought to be in existence, would appear, and troop about him.

If I saw this auspicious beginning, baffled and frustrated as I am, yet on the very verge of a timely grave, abandoned abroad and desolate at home, stripped of my boast, my hope, my consolation, my helper, my counsellor, and my guide, (you know in part what I have lost, and would to God I could clear myself of all neglect and fault in that loss,) yet thus, even thus, I would rake up the fire under all the ashes that oppress it. I am no longer patient of the public eye; nor am I of force to win my way, and to justle and elbow in a crowd. But, even in solitude, something may be done for society. The meditations of the closet have infected senates with a subtle phrensy, and inflamed armies with the brands of the furies. The cure might come from the same source with the distemper. I would add my part to those who would animate the people (whose hearts are yet right) to new exertions in the old cause.

Novelty is not the only source of zeal. Why should not a Maccabeus and his brethren arise to assert the honour of the ancient law, and to defend the temple of their forefathers, with as ardent a spirit, as can inspire any innovator to destroy the monuments of the piety and the glory of ancient ages? It is not a hazarded assertion, it is a great truth, that when once things are gone out of their ordinary course, it is by acts out of the ordinary course they can alone be reestablished. Republican spirit can only be combated by a spirit of the same nature; of the same nature, but informed with another principle, and pointing to another end. I would persuade a resistance both to the corruption and to the reformation that prevails. It will not be the weaker, but much the stronger, for combating both together. A victory over real corruptions would enable us to baffle the spurious and pretended reformations. I would not wish to excite, or even to tolerate, that kind of evil spirit which invokes the powers of hell to rectify the disorders of the earth. No! I would add my voice with better, and I trust, more potent charms, to draw down justice, and wisdom, and fortitude from heaven, for the correction of human vice, and the recalling of human error from the devious ways into which it has been betrayed. I would wish to call the impulses of individuals at once to the aid and to the control of authority. By this which I call the true republican spirit, paradoxical as it may appear, monarchies alone can be rescued from the imbecility of courts and the madness of the crowd. This republican spirit would not suffer men in high place to bring ruin on their country and on themselves. It would reform, not by destroying, but by saving, the great, the rich, and the powerful. Such a republican spirit, we perhaps fondly conceive to have animated the distinguished heroes and patriots of old, who knew no mode of policy but religion and virtue. These they would have paramount to all constitutions; they would not suffer monarchs, or senates, or popular assemblies, under pretences of dignity, or authority, or freedom, to shake off those moral riders which reason has appointed to govern every sort of rude power. These, in appearance loading them by their weight, do by that pressure augment their essential force. The momentum is increased by the extraneous weight. It is true in moral, as it is in mechanical science. It is true, not only in the draught, but in the race. These riders of the great, in effect, hold the reins which guide them in their course, and wear the spur that stimulates them to the goals of honour and of safety. The great must submit to the dominion of prudence and of virtue; or none will long submit to the dominion of the great. . . .